Auto Mechanics Fundamentals

HOW and WHY of the Design, Construction, and Operation of Automotive Units

by

MARTIN W. STOCKEL

and

MARTIN T. STOCKEL

South Holland, Illinois

THE GOODHEART-WILLCOX COMPANY, INC.

Publishers

IMPORTANT SAFETY NOTICE

Proper service and repair is important to the safe, reliable operation of motor vehicles. Procedures recommended and described in this book are effective methods of performing service operations. Some require the use of tools specially designed for the purpose and should be used as recommended. Note that this book also contains various safety procedures and cautions which should be carefully followed to minimize the risk of personal injury or the possibility that improper service methods may damage parts or render the vehicle unsafe. It is also important to understand that these notices and cautions are not exhaustive. Those performing a given service procedure or using a particular tool must first satisfy themselves that neither their safety nor vehicle safety will be jeopardized by the service method selected.

This book contains the most complete and accurate information that could be obtained from various authoritative sources at the time of publication. The Goodheart-Willcox Company, Inc. cannot assume responsibility for any changes, errors, or omissions.

Library of Congress Cataloging in Publication Data

Stockel, Martin W.
   Auto mechanics fundamentals.

   Includes index.
   1. Automobiles—Design and construction.
   2. Automobile engineering.
   I. Stockel, Martin T.   II. Title.
   TL240.S84   1985   629.2'3   84-27978
   ISBN 0-87006-516-5   AACR2

INTRODUCTION

AUTO MECHANICS FUNDAMENTALS provides you with a thorough understanding of the Design, Construction, and Operation of Automotive Systems.

This text has many unusual features.

Each system is approached by starting with basic theory, then parts are added until the system is complete. By following this procedure, the function of each system is explained, and its relationship to the complete car is made clear. Objectives at the beginning of each chapter briefly detail the content and scope of the chapter.

A build-it-yourself approach is used in a number of areas. You will "build" on paper the systems being described. This stimulates interest and provides a thorough understanding of the basic principles that are so essential in learning the HOW and WHY of auto mechanics. Math, physics, chemistry, electricity, magnetism, and hydraulics are covered right in the text where they apply.

Hundreds of illustrations were drawn especially for AUTO MECHANICS FUNDAMENTALS. Important areas are featured in these drawings, and many are exaggerated to place emphasis on parts being discussed. Nonrelated, unimportant features are minimized or completely removed. Color is used generously and is carefully coordinated with the specific needs of each illustration. This adds a positive visual impact that enhances both reader interest and learning.

Unfamiliar or new words that may baffle the reader are defined immediately following the terms. In addition, the Dictionary of Terms in the back of the book defines more than 1,500 terms with which you should be familiar. Every effort has been made to develop and retain the reader's keen interest.

Safety Precautions and Safe Working Practices are stressed in red where jobs discussed involve the possibility of serious accident. In this way, safety instruction becomes meaningful. You will better understand and appreciate the need and value of Safety.

Important words and terms are highlighted in a special Know These Terms section in each chapter. A clear and concise summary is provided. Each chapter also contains thought-provoking questions that test both comprehension and retention, and determine your grasp of the overall picture presented.

Most chapters include a brief "shop talk" aimed at pointing up the value of proper attitudes, good work and study habits, and the relationship between these traits and job success.

An entire chapter is devoted to exploring Career Opportunities and the ways and means of obtaining additional training in auto mechanics. An attempt is made to develop pride in the trade and an awareness of the importance of the professional auto mechanic.

An AUTO MECHANICS FUNDAMENTALS WORKBOOK is also available. It is a convenient study guide directly related to the text copy and illustrations.

Martin W. Stockel
Martin T. Stockel

CONTENTS

1 BUILDING AN ENGINE. 7

2 DESIGN, CONSTRUCTION, APPLICATION OF

   ENGINE COMPONENTS. 23

3 IGNITION SYSTEMS. 53

4 COOLING SYSTEMS. 81

5 LUBRICATION SYSTEMS. 99

6 FUEL SYSTEMS—CARBURETION. 119

7 FUEL SYSTEMS—FUEL INJECTION. 163

8 EXHAUST SYSTEMS AND EMISSION CONTROLS. 185

9 ENGINE CLASSIFICATION, PARTS IDENTIFICATION. 211

10 ENGINE TESTS, MEASUREMENTS. 249

11 ENGINE CLUTCHES. 257

12 MANUAL TRANSMISSIONS AND TRANSFER CASES. 269

13 TRANSMISSION OVERDRIVES. 293

14 AUTOMATIC TRANSMISSIONS. 307

15 DRIVE LINES. 339

16 DRIVE AXLE ASSEMBLIES. 349

17 FRAMES, BODIES, SPRINGS, SUSPENSION SYSTEMS. 369

18 WHEELS, HUBS, TIRES. 393

19 FRONT WHEEL ALIGNMENT AND STEERING SYSTEMS. . . . 405

20 AUTOMOBILE BRAKES. 431

21 ELECTRICAL SYSTEM FUNDAMENTALS. 465

22 AUTOMOBILE AIR CONDITIONING. 515

23 TOOL IDENTIFICATION, TOOL USE **537**

24 CAREER OPPORTUNITIES IN THE AUTOMOTIVE FIELD **561**

METRIC TABLES **570**

DICTIONARY OF AUTOMOTIVE TERMS **577**

INDEX **599**

Chapter 1

BUILDING AN ENGINE

After studying this chapter, you will be able to:
- Identify the basic parts of an engine.
- Explain engine operating principles.
- Describe the function of the major parts of an engine.
- Recall the four-stroke cycle sequence.

WHAT IS AN ENGINE?

An engine is a related group of parts assembled in a specific order. In operation, it is designed to convert the energy given off by burning fuel into a useful form.

There are many parts in a modern engine, each one being essential to the engine operation. For the time being, however, we may think of an engine as a device that allows us to pour fuel into one end and get power from the other. Fig. 1-1.

INTERNAL COMBUSTION GASOLINE ENGINE

Internal combustion means burning within. Gasoline indicates what is being burned. Engine refers to the device in which the gasoline is burned.

BUILDING A PAPER ENGINE

An excellent way to learn about engines is to build one—on paper. Make believe that the engine has not yet been invented. YOU will be the inventor. YOU will solve the problems involved, step by step.

WHAT TO USE FOR FUEL

If you are going to convert fuel into useful energy, you will need something that will ignite (burn) easily. It should burn cleanly, be reasonably inexpensive, and should produce sufficient power with good burning characteristics. It must be available in quantity, should be safe to use and easy to transport.

How about dynamite? NO, it is expensive and burns violently. In short, it would blow up the engine. Fig. 1-2.

Kerosene? NO, it is too hard to ignite and does not burn cleanly.

Gasoline? Now you have found a fuel which will serve your purpose.

Fig. 1-1. Converting fuel into energy.

Fig. 1-2. It will explode.

7

WHAT IS GASOLINE?

Gasoline is a product obtained by refining crude oil. Figs. 1-3 and 1-4. Basically, the crude oil (obtained from oil wells in the earth) is treated in various ways to produce gasoline. Gasoline is only one of the many items produced from crude oil (petroleum).

Gasoline used in engines is a complex mixture of basic fuels and special additives. Since gasoline is a mixture of carbon and hydrogen atoms, it is termed a HYDROCARBON. Fig. 1-3.

Gasoline is available in various grades such as REGULAR (contains some lead), UNLEADED (used in late model cars with catalytic converters) and PREMIUM (for use in high compression engines). All grades are assigned an OCTANE rating. The octane rating indicates how well the gasoline will resist detonation (too rapid burning) in the cylinders. The use of leaded gas will quickly destroy the catalytic converter on cars so equipped.

Many factors enter into the quality of any gasoline. It must past exhaustive tests, both in the laboratory and in actual use. Basically, gasoline must burn cleanly, ignite readily and resist vapor lock (turning too quickly from a liquid to a vapor from exposure to excessive heat). It should contain a minimum amount of harmful ingredients and be free from detonation.

Fig. 1-3. Gasoline is a complex mixture.

PREPARING THE FUEL

As you know, gasoline burns readily. However, to get the most power from this fuel and, in fact, to get it to run an engine, special treatment is required.

If you were to place a small amount of gasoline in a jar and drop a match in it, it would burn. Fig. 1-5.

Fig. 1-5. Gasoline burns.

Such burning is fine to produce heat, but it will not give us an explosive burning effect which we need to run an engine. How can we get the gas to burn fast enough to produce an explosive force?

If you will examine Fig. 1-5, you will notice that the gasoline is burning on the top side. Why is it not burning along the sides and bottom of the container? In order to burn, gasoline must combine with oxygen in the air. The sides and bottom are not exposed to air so they do not burn.

BREAKING UP GASOLINE

For purposes of illustration, imagine having gasoline in the same amount and shape, but with no container, left, Fig. 1-6. It will then burn on all sides. This will increase the burning speed. However, it still will not burn quickly enough for use in an engine.

Fig. 1-4. Before reaching your auto, crude oil requires much handling.

What to do? The answer: break the gasoline into smaller particles. Notice that as you divide it into smaller particles, right, Fig. 1-6, you expose more and more edges to the air. If you ignite it now, it will burn considerably faster.

If you break up gasoline into very tiny particles, burning is fierce. Rapid burning produces a tremendous amount of heat which, in turn, causes a rapid and powerful expansion. The burning gasoline is now giving off ENERGY in the form of HEAT. Fig. 1-7.

You now have the necessary basic force with which to do work. How do you harness it and make it work for you?

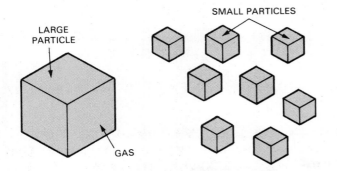

Fig. 1-6. Breaking gasoline into smaller particles exposes more surface to the air, increasing the burning rate.

TRAPPING THE EXPLOSION

If you were to take a sturdy metal container, spray a gasoline and air mixture into it, place a lid over the top and then light it, the resulting explosion would blow the lid high into the air. Fig. 1-8.

This is an example of using gasoline to do work. In this case the work is blowing the lid into the air. It is obvious that a flying lid will not push a car but, think a minute, and see if the flying lid does not suggest some way of converting the power into useful motion.

A SIMPLE ENGINE

Make the same setup, only this time hook the lid to a simple crankshaft by means of a connecting rod.

Then place a wheel on the other end of the crankshaft. Fig. 1-9.

Now if you explode the mixture, the lid, as it blows up, will give the crankshaft a sharp upward push and cause the wheel to spin. You have built a very simple engine, not practical, but it is pointing the way!

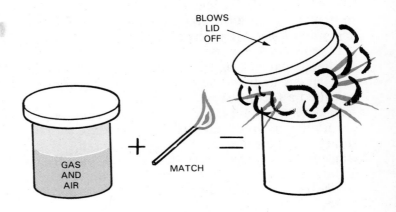

Fig. 1-8. Blowing the lid off.

Fig. 1-9. A simple engine.

Fig. 1-7., When gas particles are small enough they will explode.

WHAT IS WRONG WITH IT?

Many things. Let us discuss them one at a time. The lid would fly up; as the wheel spun, it would be forced down. It can come down in any position, but to work, it must be over the container.

Instead of putting the lid over the container, cut it so that it just slips inside. Make the container longer so the lid can push the crank to the top of its travel, and still not get out of the container. Fig. 1-10.

If you were to bolt the container and shaft bearing so they could not change position, you would then have an engine that would spin the wheel every time you fired a fuel mixture.

In order to cause the wheel to spin in the proper direction, you would have to fire the mixture with the crank in a position similar to A, Fig. 1-10. If the crank is in the B position, the lid could not fly up without pushing the crank bearing up or the container down. If it were fired with the crank in C position, the wheel would spin backwards.

It is important that the mixture be fired when the crank is in the proper position. By studying Fig. 1-10, you can see that the crankshaft changes the RECIPROCATING (up and down) motion of the lid into ROTARY (round and round) motion.

NAME THE PARTS

At this time, it is well to name the parts you have developed. By doing so, you will learn what to call parts in a gasoline engine that serve the same general purpose.

The container would be called the BLOCK. The hole in the container, or block, would be called the CYLINDER. The lid would be termed the PISTON. The shaft, with a section bent in the shape of a crank, would be called the CRANKSHAFT. The rod that connects the crankshaft to the piston, is called the CONNECTING ROD. The bearings that support the

Fig. 1-10. Lid placed inside container forms a simple engine.

crankshaft are called MAIN BEARINGS. The connecting rod has an upper and lower bearing. The lower bearing (the one on the crankshaft) is called a CONNECTING ROD BEARING. The wheel is called the FLYWHEEL.

Refer back to Fig. 1-9, and see if you can substitute the correct names for those listed.

FASTENING THE PARTS

Since you are going to fasten the parts so the main bearing and cylinder cannot move, it would be wise to invert your engine and place the cylinder on top. Just why, will soon be obvious.

Make the block heavy to give it strength to withstand the fuel explosions. Bring it down to support the main bearing. Fig. 1-11.

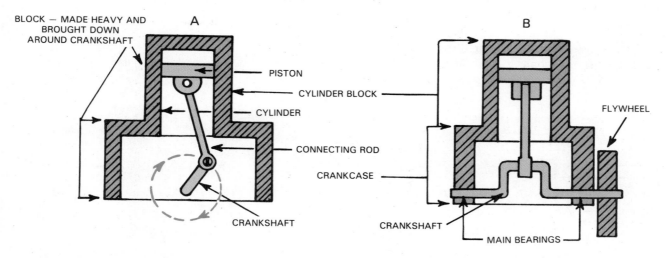

Fig. 1-11. Front, side views showing how engine is inverted, block strengthened and brought down and around crankshaft. This forms the crankcase.

By bringing the block out and down around main bearing, you now have a strong unit. Note in B, Fig. 1-11, that lower block end forms a case around the crank. It allows you to have two main bearings. This lower block end is called a CRANKCASE.

LENGTHEN THE PISTON

Now make the piston longer. This stops it from tipping sideways in the cylinder. In order to avoid a piston that is too heavy, it can be made hollow as shown in Fig. 1-12.

Tipping is illustrated in Fig. 1-13.

If the piston is to travel straight up and down, and the connecting rod is to swing back and forth in order to follow the crank, it is obvious that the connecting rod must be able to move where it is fastened to the piston. Fig. 1-14.

Now, drill a hole through the upper end of the connecting rod; also drill a hole through the piston. Line up the two and pass a pin through them. This pin is called a PISTON PIN or WRIST PIN. It is secured in various ways (more on this later). Fig. 1-15.

GETTING FUEL INTO THE ENGINE

You have probably noticed no way has been provided to get fuel into the upper cylinder area of your assembled engine. Your next problem is to develop a system to admit fuel, and to exhaust (blow out) the fuel after it is burned.

One opening in the upper cylinder area (called the COMBUSTION CHAMBER) will not be adequate. You cannot very well admit fuel and exhaust the burned gas out the same opening. You need TWO openings.

REMOVABLE CYLINDER HEAD

Redesign your cylinder block and make the top removable. You will call this removable head a CYLINDER HEAD. It will be fastened in place with bolts or studs and nuts, Fig. 1-16.

Fig. 1-14. Connecting rod must swing. Note position in A compared to C.

Fig. 1-15. Pin secures rod to piston.

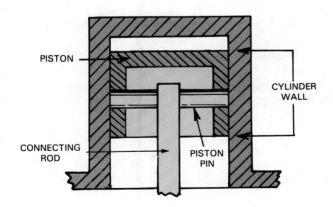

Fig. 1-12. Piston is lengthened to avoid tipping.

Fig. 1-13. Effect of short piston.

Fig. 1-16. Cylinder head. Top of cylinder has been removed.

11

FUEL INTAKE AND EXHAUST PASSAGES

Making your cylinder head removable has not yet solved all of the problems. You cannot take it off, and put it on, each time the engine fires.

Now make a block of much thicker metal and make two holes or passages like those shown in Fig. 1-17. This will give you a passage to take in fuel mixture, and one to exhaust it. These passages are called VALVE PORTS.

You will notice at A, Fig. 1-17, that the ports do not connect to the cylinder. To make a connection, you must make the cylinder head thicker and cut an opening in it that will straddle the intake and exhaust ports, plus the cylinder. Fig. 1-18.

VALVES

The next logical step is to provide a device to open and close the ports. If the ports are left open, and fuel explodes in the combustion chamber, it will blow out the openings and fail to push the piston down.

This port control device (valve) will have to be arranged so that it can be opened and closed when desired. Now arrange a valve in each opening. This may be done as shown in Fig. 1-19.

The valves may be held in a straight up and down position by a hole bored in the block metal at A, Fig. 1-19. This hole is called a VALVE GUIDE because it guides the valve up and down in a straight line.

Note that another opening, B, beneath each valve guide, is cut into the block. You will use this opening to install a spring, spring washer and keeper. The spring is necessary to keep the valve tightly closed against its seat. When the valve is opened, the spring will close it again. Arrange your spring, spring washer, and keepers, as shown in Fig. 1-20.

The valves provide a satisfactory method of opening and closing the passages.

FOUR-STROKE CYCLE

At this point you have an intake valve to allow fuel to enter the cylinder and an exhaust valve to let the burned fuel out. The next problem is how to get fuel into the cylinder and out when burned.

A VACUUM IS THE CLUE

You understand that the air in which we live presses on all things. Fig. 1-21. This pressure is approximately 15 lbs. per square inch (103 kPa) at sea level.

Were we to draw all of the air out of a container, we would form a vacuum. A vacuum is unnatural and atmospheric pressure will do all it can to get into the low pressure area. If there is the slightest leak in the container, air will seep in until the pressure is the same on the inside as it is on the outside.

A vacuum, then, is any area in which the air pressure is lower than that of the prevailing or outside atmospheric pressure.

Fig. 1-17. Valve ports.

Fig. 1-18. Note opening in head allowing fuel mixture to enter and leave cylinder. This opening is called combustion chamber.

Fig. 1-19. Valves installed in ports.

YOU ALREADY HAVE A VACUUM PUMP

Fig. 1-22 illustrates a simple vacuum pump, or a cylinder into which a snug fitting piston is placed. You will see in A, Fig. 1-22, that the piston is against the end of the cylinder. Obviously there is no air between these two surfaces.

When you pull the piston through the cylinder, as in B, Fig. 1-22, you will have a large area between the

Fig. 1-20. Installation of valve, spring, washer, etc.

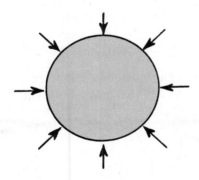

Fig. 1-21. Air presses on all things with a pressure of 15 lbs. per square inch.

Fig. 1-22. Simple vacuum pump.

face of the piston, and the end of the cylinder. If there was no air between them before, and if the piston fits snugly against the cylinder, there still could be no air between them. This gives you a large area in which there is no air, or in other words, a vacuum.

If you were to drill a hole into the closed end of the cylinder, C, Fig. 1-22, air would immediately rush in and fill the cylinder. Any material, such as a fuel mixture, that happened to be in the surrounding air would be drawn into the cylinder.

WHERE IS YOUR VACUUM PUMP?

If the cylinder and piston, in Fig. 1-22, forms a vacuum, the cylinder and piston in your engine will do the same. If the piston is at the top of the cylinder (with both valves closed) and you turned the crankshaft, the piston will be drawn down into the cylinder. This forms a strong vacuum in the cylinder. If you now open the intake valve, the air will rush into the cylinder. This is called the INTAKE STROKE.

STROKE NO. 1 — THE INTAKE STROKE

The first stroke in your engine is the intake. Instead of opening the intake valve after you have drawn the piston down, you will find it better to open the intake valve as the piston starts down. This allows the air to draw fuel in all the time the piston is moving down. If you wait until the piston is down before opening the valve, the piston will be starting up before the cylinder can be filled with air. Fig. 1-23.

Fig. 1-23. Intake stroke.

Remember: The intake stroke starts with the piston at the top of the cylinder, intake valve open and exhaust valve closed, and it stops with the piston at the bottom of its travel. This requires one-half turn of the crankshaft.

STROKE NO. 2—THE COMPRESSION STROKE

You have discovered that the smaller the particles of gasoline, mixed in air, the more powerful the explosion.

As the crankshaft continues to move, the piston is forced up through the cylinder. If you keep both valves closed, the fuel mixture will be squeezed, or compressed, as the piston reaches the top. This is called the compression stroke. Fig. 1-24. It, too, requires one-half turn of the crankshaft.

Fig. 1-24. Compression stroke.

INTAKE VALVE CLOSED

EXHAUST VALVE CLOSED

PISTON TRAVELING UP, COMPRESSES FUEL MIXTURE

The compression stroke serves several purposes. First, it tends to break up the fuel into even smaller particles. This happens due to the sudden swirling and churning of the mixture as it is compressed.

When engine fuel mixture is subjected to a sudden sharp compression force, its temperature rises. This increase in temperature makes the mixture easier to ignite, and causes it to explode with greater force.

As the piston reaches the top of its travel on the compression stroke, it has returned to the proper position to be pushed back down by the explosion.

Remember: The compression stroke starts with the piston at the bottom of the cylinder while both valves are closed, and it stops with the piston at the top of the cylinder. This requires an additonal one-half turn of the crankshaft.

COMPRESSION RATIO

The amount your engine will compress the fuel mixture depends on how small a space the mixture is squeezed into. Notice in Fig. 1-25, the piston in A has traveled down 6 in. from the top of the cylinder. This is the intake stroke. In B the piston, on the compression stroke, has traveled up to within 1 in. of the cylinder top. It is obvious that 6 in. of cylinder volume has been squeezed into 1 in. of cylinder volume. This gives you a ratio of 6 to 1. This is termed the COMPRESSION RATIO.

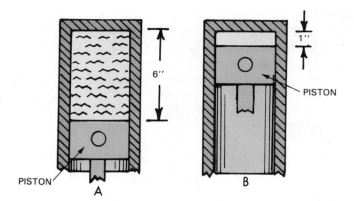

Fig. 1-25. Compression ratio.

PISTON

PISTON

STROKE NO. 3—FIRING OR POWER STROKE

As the piston reaches the top of the compression stroke, the mixture is broken into tiny particles, and heated up. When ignited, it will explode with great force.

This is the right time to explode the mixture. A spark is provided inside the combustion chamber by means of a spark plug. The spark produced at the plug is formed by the ignition system. This will be discussed later.

Just imagine that a hot spark has been provided in the fuel mixture. The mixture will explode and, in turn, force the piston down through the cylinder. This gives the crankshaft a quick and forceful push.

Both valves must be kept closed during the firing stroke or the pressure of the burning fuel will squirt out the valve ports. Fig. 1-26.

Remember: The firing stroke starts with the piston at the top of the cylinder while both valves are closed, and it stops with the piston at the bottom of the cylinder. This requires another one-half turn of the crankshaft.

STROKE NO. 4—THE EXHAUST STROKE

When the piston reaches the bottom of the firing stroke the exhaust valve opens. The spinning crank-

Fig. 1-26. Firing stroke.

INTAKE VALVE CLOSED

EXHAUST VALVE CLOSED

PISTON TRAVELING DOWN FORCED DOWN BY EXPLODING GAS

shaft forces the piston up through the cylinder blowing burned gases out of the cylinder. Fig. 1-27.

Remember: The exhaust stroke starts with the piston at the bottom of the cylinder while the exhaust valve is open and intake valve is closed. It stops with the piston at the top of the cylinder. This requires one more one-half turn of the crankshaft.

COMPLETED CYCLE

If you will count the number of one-half turns in the intake, compression, firing and exhaust strokes, you will find you have four one-half turns. This gives you two complete turns (called revolutions) of the crankshaft. Fig. 1-28.

While the crankshaft is turning around twice, it is receiving power only during one-half turn, or one-fourth of the time.

CYCLE REPEATED

As soon as the piston reaches the top of the exhaust stroke, it starts down on another intake, compression, firing and exhaust cycle. This is repeated time after time. Each complete cycle consists of four strokes of the piston, hence the name FOUR-STROKE CYCLE engine. There is another type, called a two-stroke cycle, that will be covered later.

WHAT OPENS AND CLOSES THE VALVES?

You have seen that the intake valve must be opened for the intake stroke. Both valves remain closed during the compression and firing strokes. The exhaust valve opens during the exhaust stroke. You must now design a device to open and close the valves.

Start by machining a round shaft that will lie beneath the valve stem, at some distance. This shaft is supported in bearings placed in the front and the rear of the crankcase. See Fig. 1-29.

CAMSHAFT OPENS VALVES

Each shaft will have a bump, called a cam lobe, machined as a part of the shaft. This shaft, with the cam lobes, is called a CAMSHAFT. Fig. 1-30.

The distance the valve will be raised, how long it will stay open, how fast it opens and closes, can all be controlled by the height and shape of the lobe. The lobe must, of course, be located directly beneath the valve stem. Fig. 1-31.

As you will see later, it is impractical to have the cam lobe contact the end of the valve stem itself. You have placed the camshaft some distance below the end of the valve stem. When you turn the camshaft, the lobes will not even touch the valve stem.

VALVE LIFTER

Your next step is to construct a round, bar-like unit called a cam follower or VALVE LIFTER. This valve

INTAKE VALVE CLOSED

EXHAUST VALVE OPEN

PISTON TRAVELING UP FORCES BURNED GASES OUT THROUGH EXHAUST PORT

Fig. 1-27. Exhaust stroke.

CRANKSHAFT TURNS ONE-HALF REVOLUTION FOR THE:

INTAKE STROKE
COMPRESSION STROKE
FIRING STROKE
EXHAUST STROKE

Fig. 1-28. Four strokes make two revolutions of the crankshaft.

lifter will have an adjusting bolt screwed into the top so the distance between the valve stem and lifter may be adjusted. Fig. 1-32.

The lifter is installed between the cam lobe and the valve stem. The lower end rides on the lobe and the upper end almost touches the valve stem. The lifter slides up and down in a hole bored in the crankcase metal that separates the valve stem from the camshaft. Fig. 1-33.

THE VALVE TRAIN

You have now built the essential parts of the valve system. The parts, in their proper positions, are referred to as the VALVE TRAIN. Fig. 1-34.

CAMSHAFT SPEED

You have developed a method of opening and closing the valves. The next problem is how to turn the camshafts, and at WHAT SPEED.

Fig. 1-29. Engine section showing how camshaft is positioned.

Fig. 1-30. Section of camshaft showing cam lobe. Study names of various parts of lobe.

Fig. 1-31. How valve is opened.

Now stop a minute and think—each valve must be open for one stroke only. The intake is open during the intake, and remains closed during the compression, firing and exhaust strokes. This would indicate that the cam lobe must turn fast enough to raise the valve every fourth stroke. Fig. 1-35.

You can see, from Fig. 1-35, that it takes one complete revolution of the cam lobe for every four strokes. Remembering back, four strokes of the

Fig. 1-32. Valve lifter.

Fig. 1-33. Valve lifter installation.

VALVE STEM

VALVE STEM TO ADJUSTING SCREW CLEARANCE (CALLED TAPPET CLEARANCE)

ADJUSTING SCREW OR BOLT

BLOCK METAL ACTS AS LIFTER GUIDE. SEE "X" IN FIG. 1-29

VALVE LIFTER

CAMSHAFT

CAM LOBE

Fig. 1-34. Valve train. Note that the cam lobe has forced the valve open against the pressure of the valve spring.

VALVE HEAD

MARGIN

VALVE FACE

CYLINDER

VALVE STEM

VALVE PORT

PISTON

VALVE GUIDE

VALVE SPRING

SPRING WASHER

VALVE LOCK OR KEEPER ADJUSTING SCREW

VALVE LIFTER

CAM LOBE

CAMSHAFT

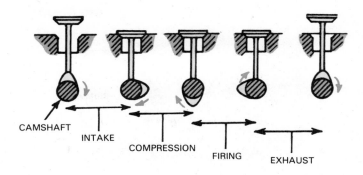

Fig. 1-35. Intake valve is opened once every fourth stroke. Each stroke turns camshaft one-quarter turn.

CAMSHAFT   INTAKE   COMPRESSION   FIRING   EXHAUST

piston required two revolutions of the crankshaft. You can say then, that for every two revolutions of the crankshaft, the camshaft must turn once. If you are speaking of the speed of the camshaft, you can say that the camshaft must turn at one-half the crankshaft speed.

TURNING THE CAMSHAFT

If the crankshaft is turning, and the camshaft must turn at one-half crankshaft speed, it seems logical to use the spinning crankshaft to turn the camshaft.

One very simple way to drive the camshaft would be by means of gears, one fastened on the end of the crankshaft and the other on the end of the camshaft. If you put a small gear on the crankshaft and a larger gear with twice as many teeth on the camshaft, the crankshaft will turn the camshaft. It will also turn it at exactly one-half crankshaft speed. Fig. 1-36.

Fig. 1-37 shows a front view of the crankshaft gear and both camshaft gears as they would appear on the engine. In your engine, the crankshaft gear will turn clockwise (to the right). The timing or camshaft gears will then be driven counterclockwise (to the left).

TIMING THE VALVES

You have now developed a method of not only turning the camshaft, but also at the correct speed. The

Fig. 1-36. Crankshaft turns camshaft at one-half crankshaft speed. Drive is through gears.

CAMSHAFT GEAR   CAM LOBE   CAMSHAFT   TIMING MARKS   CRANKSHAFT GEAR   CRANKSHAFT

Fig. 1-37. Front view. Crankshaft gear driving both camshaft gears.

next question to be answered is how will you get the valves to open at the proper time. This is called VALVE TIMING.

Start with intake stroke. As you have discovered, the intake valve must open as the piston starts down in the cylinder. Place your piston at top dead center (TDC—topmost point of piston travel), Fig. 1-38.

Insert the intake camshaft, then turn it in a counterclockwise direction until the flank of the cam lobe contacts the lifter. The timing gear should be meshed with the crankshaft gear. Fig. 1-39.

Fig. 1-38. Piston at top dead center (TDC).

Fig. 1-39. Position of cam lobe at the start of the intake stroke.

MARK THE GEARS

You should punch a mark on the crankshaft gear, and a mark on the camshaft gear. These are called TIMING MARKS. See Fig. 1-40.

If the camshafts are removed, they may be reinstalled by merely lining up the timing marks.

Were you to crank the engine, the crankshaft would pull the piston down on the intake stroke. The camshaft would also rotate, causing the cam lobe to turn and raise and lower the valve. The crankshaft would make one-half turn; camshaft one-quarter turn during this stroke. Fig. 1-41.

Fig. 1-40. Timing gears meshed and marked.

Fig. 1-41. Camshaft makes one-quarter turn during each stroke.

INTAKE REMAINS CLOSED

As the crank continues to turn, it will push the piston up on compression, down on firing, and up on exhaust. During these three strokes, the intake cam lobe continues to turn. When the piston reaches top dead center (TDC) on the exhaust stroke, the flank of the cam lobe will again be touching the intake lifter.

As your next stroke will be the intake, the piston is ready to start down and the cam lobe is ready to raise the lifter to provide proper timing. Fig. 1-42.

INTAKE   COMPRESSION   FIRING   EXHAUST

Fig. 1-42. Position of lobe at start of each stroke.

EXHAUST TIMED THE SAME WAY

The only difference between the intake and exhaust timing is that you place the piston on bottom dead center (BDC). Turn the exhaust camshaft until the lobe contacts the lifter, then mesh and mark the gears. Use two marks on the crankshaft gear and two on the camshaft gear for the exhaust camshaft. This prevents aligning with the wrong marks.

THE FLYWHEEL

When you crank an engine, it turns through all the necessary strokes. The only time the crankshaft receives power is during the firing stroke. After the firing stroke is completed, the crankshaft must continue to turn to exhaust the burned gases, take in fresh fuel and then compress it. One power stroke is not enough to keep the crankshaft turning during the four required strokes. Fig. 1-43.

Fig. 1-43. After the firing stroke, the crankshaft must coast through the next three strokes.

You will recall that one end of the crankshaft has a timing gear attached. If you will fasten a fairly large, heavy wheel, called a FLYWHEEL, to the other end, the engine will run successfully.

The flywheel, which is caused to spin by the firing stroke, will continue to spin because it is heavy. In other words, the inertia built up within the flywheel will cause it to keep turning. As it is attached to the crankshaft, it will cause the shaft to continue to turn. The shaft will now spin long enough to reach the next firing stroke. Fig. 1-44.

ENGINE WILL RUN MORE SMOOTHLY

You can see that every time the engine fires, the crank receives a hard push. This will speed it up. As the power stroke is finished, the shaft coasts. This slows it down. The alternating fast and slow speed would make for a very rough running engine.

With the heavy flywheel in place, the firing stroke cannot increase the crankshaft speed so quickly since it must also speed up the flywheel. When the crankshaft is coasting, it cannot slow down so fast because the flywheel wants to keep spinning. This will cause the crankshaft speed to become more constant and will, in turn, give a smooth running engine.

BASIC ENGINE COMPLETED

You have now completed a basic engine. Fig. 1-45. With the addition of fuel, spark and oil, it will run. This is a one cylinder engine, and its uses would be confined to such small tasks as powering lawnmowers, scooters, generators, carts, etc.

There are many modifications and improvements that can be made to your simple engine. These will be discussed in following chapters.

SUMMARY

How an engine works; Fig. 1-46:

As the piston is pulled down by the crankshaft, the camshaft opens the intake valve and the air-fuel mixture is drawn into the cylinder. View A.

When the piston reaches the bottom of its stroke, the intake valve closes, and the crankshaft forces the piston up through the cylinder. This compresses the air-fuel mixture in the combustion chamber. View B.

As the piston nears the top of the compression stroke, the air-fuel mixture is ignited by a spark from the spark plug. This explodes the mixture, and the pressure of the rapidly expanding gas drives the piston down through the cylinder. Both valves are closed during this firing stroke. View C.

After reaching the bottom of the firing stroke, the exhaust valve opens, and the spinning crankshaft forces the piston up through the cylinder. This time all the burned gases are driven (exhausted) from the cylinder and combustion chamber. View D.

When the piston reaches the top of the exhaust stroke, the exhaust valve closes and the intake opens.

Fig. 1-44. Flywheel inertia helps engine to run.

Fig. 1-45. The various parts of the basic engine you have developed.

The piston is drawn down on another intake stroke.

Once the cylinder has fired, the heavy flywheel will keep the crankshaft spinning long enough to go through the exhaust, intake and compression strokes. It will then receive power from another firing stroke. This cycle is repeated over and over, and thus the engine will run on its own power.

DO NOT BE CONFUSED

Regardless of the size, number of cylinders, and horsepower a four-stroke cycle engine may have, it will contain the same basic parts that do the same job, in the same way, as the small engine you have just built. The parts may be arranged in different ways and their shape changed, but you will not find ANY different BASIC parts, just more of them.

A MOST IMPORTANT CHAPTER

The chapter you have just completed is most important. To properly understand the theory and operation of the internal combustion engine, it is essential that you COMPLETELY UNDERSTAND

Building an Engine

A INTAKE STROKE

B COMPRESSION STROKE

C FIRING OR POWER STROKE

D EXHAUST STROKE

CYLINDER HEAD

VALVE HEAD

COMBUSTION CHAMBER

INTAKE PORT

EXHAUST PORT

CYLINDER

VALVE GUIDE

VALVE STEM

PISTON

ADJUSTING SCREW

VALVE LIFTER

VALVE LIFTER

INTAKE CAM LOBE

EXHAUST CAM LOBE

CAMSHAFT GEAR

CRANKSHAFT GEAR

E

Fig. 1-46. Four-stroke cycle engine operation. Study relationship between piston and valve operation for each of the separate strokes. Note valve train layout in basic engine in view E.

ALL THE MATERIAL PRESENTED IN THIS CHAPTER.

To help you check your grasp of the chapter, answer the following questions. When you CAN answer all of the questions correctly, you are on your way.

KNOW THESE TERMS

Internal combustion, Gasoline, Cylinder, Piston, Crankshaft, Connecting rod, Cylinder head, Valve ports, Valves, Vacuum, Four-stroke cycle, Camshaft, Valve train, Flywheel.

REVIEW QUESTIONS—CHAPTER 1

Write on separate sheet of paper. DO NOT write in this book.

1. What is an engine?
2. Gasoline is obtained from _____ _____.
3. Gasoline is a mixture of _____ and _____ atoms.
4. List four features of a good gasoline.
5. In order to burn, gasoline must have _____.
6. What must be done to gasoline to speed up the burning rate?
7. Gasoline, when it reaches the cylinder, must be _____ into tiny _____, and mixed with _____.
8. When the gasoline explodes in the cylinder, what movable part of the engine first receives the force?
9. The connecting rod must have a bearing at _____.
10. What is a vacuum?
11. How is a vacuum developed in an engine?
12. What do you need a vacuum for?
13. What is the purpose of valve ports?
14. What is placed in each port to open and close the port?
15. List the strokes, in order, in a four-stroke cycle engine.
16. The position of each valve during the various strokes is important. Give the position of each valve for each of the strokes in question 15.
17. What opens and closes the valves?
18. The camshaft is turned by the _____ through means of _____.
19. What is the speed of the camshaft in relation to that of the crankshaft?
20. Give two uses for the flywheel.
21. Fig. 1-45 shows all of the parts of your engine. Examine each part. List the part names and use of each of the parts.

STORY:

Do not be like the eager bear hunter who grabbed a gun and went charging through the woods. Upon encountering a bear, the hunter discovered that the gun was unloaded!

MORAL:

There are many BEARS in this book. This chapter contains a lot of ammunition—LOAD UP!

Four-wheel drive vehicles are becoming increasingly popular. This one is a Jeep "Cherokee" two-door wagon. (American Motors "Jeep")

Chapter 2

DESIGN, CONSTRUCTION, APPLICATION OF ENGINE COMPONENTS

By studying this chapter, you will learn to:
■ Describe engine part design.
■ Explain the construction of engine components.
■ Define the purpose of each engine part.
■ Identify engine part variations.

You have already designed and built an engine, on paper. To give you a clear idea of how the engine works, it was necessary to move from step to step without studying the finer points of engine construction.

Now that you are familiar with the general theory involved in engine design, it is desirable for you to study the parts of the basic engine in greater detail.

It is important for you to understand HOW the parts are built, of WHAT material, WHY they are built the way they are, and the PURPOSE each part serves.

THE ENGINE BLOCK

The BLOCK, Fig. 2-1, serves as a rigid metal foundation for all parts of an engine. It contains the cylinders and supports the crankshaft and camshaft. In older engines, the valve seats, ports, and guides are built into the block. Accessory units and clutch housing are bolted to it. Note in Fig. 2-1 that the crankcase is formed with the block.

Blocks are made of either cast iron or aluminum. In some of the small, one cylinder engines, the material is die cast metal. Die cast metal is a relatively light, soft metal especially suited to the die casting process.

Blocks are commonly formed in two ways. One method is to pour molten cast iron, or aluminum, into a mold made of sand. A core is placed within the mold to form the cavities and passageways within the block. See Fig. 2-2. After the casting has cooled, it is removed from the mold, and the sand core is dissolved and washed out.

The second method is to use a mold of metal and force molten aluminum, or die-cast metal, into the mold under pressure. The pressure casting process has several advantages. It produces a block free of air

Fig. 2-1. Typical block construction for a four cylinder valve-in-head engine. (Nissan)

Fig. 2-2. Simple mold for casting.

23

bubbles (called voids), gives sharp corners, and a high degree of accuracy can be maintained. This reduces machining operations to a minimum. The same mold can be used over and over.

All parts of the aluminum or die cast block that are subjected to wear will have metal inserts either pressed in place or actually cast into the block.

The lighter the block (providing it has sufficient strength) the better. A more modern process, called PRECISION THIN WALL CASTING, controls core size and placement much more accurately than the older casting process. This permits casting the block walls much thinner, thereby effectively reducing the weight. Since wall thicknesses are more uniform, block distortion during service is less severe.

CYLINDERS

The cylinder is a round hole formed in the block. See Figs. 2-1 and 2-3. It is first cast into the block, then bored on a special machine and honed to a smooth finish. The cylinder dimensions must be kept extremely accurate. A good cylinder will not vary in diameter more than .0005 in. (0.013 mm). The paper on which this is printed is around .004 in. (0.102 mm) in thickness.

The cylinder forms a guide for the piston and acts as a container for taking in, compressing, firing, and exhausting the fuel charge. See Fig. 1-46.

Cylinders have been made of both steel and cast iron. Cast iron is by far the most popular. When steel cylinders are desired, they are in the form of cylinder sleeves (round, pipe-like liners). These sleeves may be either cast or pressed into the block.

Another manufacturing process die casts the block of aluminum that contains particles of silicon. After the cylinder is formed, an electro-chemical process is used to etch (eat) away the aluminum cylinder surface. This leaves the silicon exposed. The pistons are iron-plated aluminum and operate directly on the silicon surface of the aluminum cylinders.

CYLINDER SLEEVES

Some engines use removable cylinder sleeves. When the cylinder has become worn, the old sleeves may be pulled out and new ones pressed in. Fig. 2-4. The sleeves are pressed into oversize cylinder holes.

Cylinder sleeves are widely used in heavy-duty truck and industrial engines. If a cylinder wall is badly damaged, the old sleeve may be removed and a new one installed.

WET AND DRY SLEEVES

Cylinder sleeves are either wet type or dry type. The DRY SLEEVE, Fig. 2-5, is pressed into a hole in the block and is supported, and surrounded, over its full length. This type sleeve can be quite thin as it utilizes

the block metal to give it full length support.

The WET SLEEVE, Fig. 2-6, is also pressed into a hole in the block. It is supported at the top and bottom only. The cooling water in the engine is allowed to directly contact the sleeve. The wet sleeve must be of heavier construction because it receives no central support from the block.

Fig. 2-3. Section of an engine showing cylinder location.

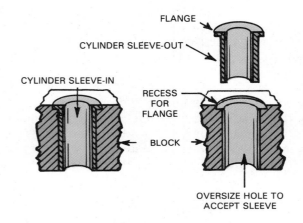

Fig. 2-4. Section of a block showing typical cylinder sleeve.

Fig. 2-5. ''Dry'' sleeve in place in cylinder hole.

SLEEVE IS THICK - FOR STRENGTH

SLEEVE

WATER SURROUNDS LARGE AREA OF SLEEVE

SLEEVE SUPPORTED AT TOP AND BOTTOM

Fig. 2-6. "Wet" sleeve in place in cylinder hole.

SECURING THE SLEEVE

Sleeves can be secured in the block in several ways. Where a cast iron or steel sleeve is placed in an aluminum block to provide a wearing surface, it can be cast into place. See Fig. 2-7.

The removable sleeve may be held in place by friction alone, Fig. 2-8. However, this requires a very

SLEEVE

BLOCK

BLOCK METAL IS CAST AROUND SLEEVE

Fig. 2-7. Sleeve held by casting in block. Grooved sleeves prevent movement.

SLEEVE

BLOCK

Fig. 2-8. Sleeve held in place by friction between sleeve and block.

tight fit and is not altogether dependable.

A better method is to have a flange on the top edge of the cylinder sleeve that drops into a corresponding groove in the block. See Fig. 2-9. When the cylinder head is bolted on, it presses on the flange and holds it in place. This type of sleeve can be fitted with a greater degree of freedom. However, any sleeve must be a fairly snug fit so heat that is built up in the sleeve is conducted away by the surrounding block material.

PISTONS

The piston is literally a sliding plunger that rides up and down in the cylinder. It has several jobs to do in proper sequence. See Fig. 1-46.

The piston must move down through the cylinder to produce a vacuum to draw a fuel charge into the cylinder. It then travels up in the cylinder and compresses the mixture. When the mixture is fired, the pressure of the expanding gas is transmitted to the top of the piston. This drives the piston back down through the cylinder with great force, transmitting the energy of this firing stroke to the crankshaft. The piston then travels up through the cylinder, and exhausts the burned fuel charge.

Study the cross-sectional drawing of a piston in Fig. 2-10. Learn the names of all the parts of the piston.

The overall job the piston performs is a difficult one indeed. A piston is subjected to intense heat from the burning air-fuel mixture. It must change directions at "blurring speeds." It is "hounded" by friction against the cylinder walls. In addition to all this, the piston receives the tremendous thrust of power on the firing stroke. That a piston not only survives these forces, but will do so for many thousands of miles of driving, is a tribute to the engineering skill of engine manufacturers.

PISTON MATERIALS

Pistons are usually made of aluminum. Often, aluminum pistons are tin-plated to allow a good

CYLINDER HEAD

SLEEVE HELD IN PLACE BY HEAD PRESSING ON FLANGE

Fig. 2-9. Flange on sleeve fits groove in block.

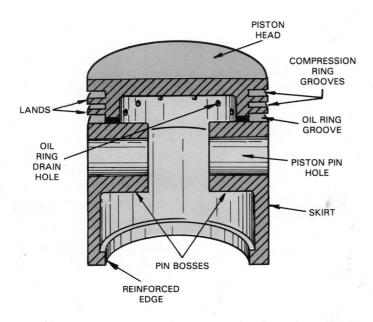

Fig. 2-10. Sectional view of a typical piston.

COLD PISTON   HOT PISTON

Fig. 2-11. Exaggerated view shows effect of heat on piston expansion.

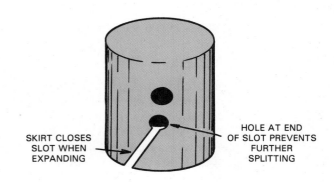

SKIRT CLOSES SLOT WHEN EXPANDING

HOLE AT END OF SLOT PREVENTS FURTHER SPLITTING

Fig. 2-12. Split skirt piston is designed to solve expansion problem.

breaking-in job when the engine is started. Aluminum pistons can be forged, but are more commonly cast.

The aluminum piston is light and, for most purposes, this gives it an advantage over the cast iron type. A piston must change its direction of travel at the end of every stroke. At engine speeds sometimes in excess of 5000 revolutions per minute (rpm), it is obvious that the lighter the piston is, the more efficient it will be.

Cast iron is a good material for pistons used in a slow speed engine. It has excellent wear characteristics and will perform admirably in an engine suited to its needs. Pistons which are designed to operate in silicon aluminum cylinders are iron-plated aluminum.

EXPANSION PROBLEMS

Pistons must be carefully "fitted" into engine cylinders to prevent them from tipping from side to side ("slapping"). They must hold the burning fuel charges above the piston heads and be tight enough to form a vacuum and compress and exhaust burned gases.

A piston will expand when it gets hot, so enough clearance must be left between the piston skirt and cylinder wall to allow for this. Aluminum pistons expand more than cast iron, Fig. 2-11.

The problem of fitting the aluminum piston close enough to prevent "slapping," and still leave clearance enough for an oil film to separate the piston and the cylinder, has been solved in several ways.

SPLIT SKIRT

In a SPLIT SKIRT PISTON, Fig. 2-12, the skirt is either partially or, in some cases, completely split.

When the piston warms and begins to expand, it cannot bind in the cylinder since the skirt merely closes the split.

T-SLOT

The T-SLOT PISTON, Fig. 2-13, is another variation of the split skirt. The top of the T tends to retard the transfer of heat from the head to the skirt of the piston. The vertical slot allows the skirt of the piston to close in when heated.

STEEL STRUT

Steel braces and in some cases, steel rings are cast into aluminum pistons. See Fig. 2-14. Steel expands less than aluminum and as a result, the steel struts tend to control or minimize piston expansion.

CAM GROUND

The CAM GROUND PISTON, Fig. 2-15, is a popular type. The piston, instead of being made round, is ground so that it is elliptical or egg shaped. Note in Fig. 2-15 that diameter A is larger than diameter B.

Diameter A is established so that the piston has a minimum amount of clearance in the cylinder. This clearance, around .001 in. (0.025 mm), is necessary to allow oil to form a lubrication film between the piston and cylinder wall. The larger diameter, at A, Fig. 2-15, is always at right angles to the block (in relation to the crankshaft center line).

As the piston heats up, it will not expand much in diameter A, but will tend to expand in diameter B. This will cause the piston to become round when fully heated. See Fig. 2-16.

Fig. 2-13. T-slot piston is another means of controlling expansion.

Fig. 2-14. Steel rings control or minimize piston expansion.

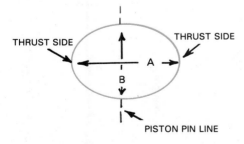

Fig. 2-15. Exaggerated top view of a cam ground piston, which is designed to be wider across the thrust surfaces.

Fig. 2-16. Cam ground piston becomes round when hot. Diameter A remains constant; diameter B expands.

Cam grinding, then, will give a minimum clearance at the thrust surfaces. These are the two sides of the piston that contact the cylinder walls at right angles to the crankshaft. The thrust surfaces support the piston and prevent tipping. The thrust surfaces are also at right angles to the piston pin, Figs. 2-15 and 2-17.

PARTIAL SKIRT

In manufacturing PARTIAL SKIRT PISTONS, (also called slipper skirt), cam grinding is used but a large area of the skirt is removed. This reduces piston weight and allows the piston to approach the crankshaft more closely. Since the non-thrust sides of the skirts are removed, the counterbalances on the crankshaft, Fig. 2-18, will not strike the piston. Since

Fig. 2-17. Exaggerated view shows how a loose piston is pushed from one side of cylinder to other. Sides that rub cylinder wall are called thrust surfaces.

Fig. 2-18. Non-thrust sides of skirt are removed from partial skirt pistons. This allows piston to approach crankshaft more closely without striking.

the non-thrust sides of a piston do not carry much of a load, their removal is not detrimental.

PISTON TEMPERATURE

The piston head is subjected to the direct heat of the exploding fuel. This heat can raise the temperature of the piston crown (very top) somewhat above 600°F (316°C). The temperature will lower as you go down the piston. The bottom of the skirt will be about 300°F (149°C), Fig. 2-19.

The temperatures will vary according to engine design and work application. As the bottom of the skirt is the coolest, some pistons have the skirt slightly wider at the bottom. The top area of the skirt would be a trifle smaller in diameter.

HEAD CONSTRUCTION

It is obvious that the piston head is by far the hottest part of the piston. As a result, it expands more. In order to avoid having the head grow tight in the cylinder, the piston head is turned to a smaller diameter than the skirt of the piston (not cam ground). The head will generally be .030 to .040 in. (0.76 to 1.02 mm) smaller than the skirt. Fig. 2-20.

HEAD SHAPE

Some pistons have flat-topped heads. Others are dome shaped. Still others have irregular shapes designed to help in exhausting burned gases, and also to assist in creating a rapid swirling to help break up gasoline particles on the compression stroke. One type forms the shape of the combustion chamber in the head of the pistons, thus allowing the use of a flat surfaced cylinder head. Fig. 2-21.

PISTON PIN BOSS

The section of the piston that supports the piston pin must be thicker and stronger. This area is called the PIN BOSS, as shown in Fig. 2-22.

THE PISTON CANNOT SEAL THE CYLINDER

The piston must have some clearance in the cylinder. If the skirt has .001 to .002 in. (0.025 to 0.05 mm) clearance and the head .030 to .040 in. (0.76 to 1.02 mm), it is obvious that the piston cannot seal the cylinder effectively. Fig. 2-23.

SKIRT DIAMETER LARGER
HEAD DIAMETER SMALLER

Fig. 2-20. As piston head is hottest part of piston, it must be ground approximately .030—.040 in. (0.76 to 1.02 mm) smaller than skirt.

PISTON TOP
600—700 DEG. F.

450—550 DEG. F.
TOP RING AREA

300—450 DEG. F.
PIN BOSS AREA

300—350 DEG. F.
BOTTOM OF
SKIRT

Fig. 2-19. Approximate temperature range is noted from piston head to skirt. Temperature can vary considerably depending on engine type, design, use, etc.

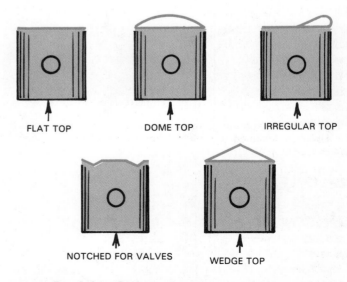

FLAT TOP   DOME TOP   IRREGULAR TOP

NOTCHED FOR VALVES   WEDGE TOP

Fig. 2-21. Several types of piston heads.

Fig. 2-22. Pin boss must be strong to withstand directional changes during each stroke of the piston.

Fig. 2-23. Piston cannot seal by itself because clearance with cylinder wall must be maintained.

Fig. 2-24. Piston rings seal gap between piston and cylinder wall.

PISTON RINGS

The solution to the leakage problem is the use of PISTON RINGS. A properly constructed and fitted ring will rub against the cylinder wall with good contact all around the cylinder. The ring will ride in grooves that are cut into the piston head. The sides of the ring will fit the edges of the grooves quite closely. This side clearance can be around .002 in. (0.05 mm).

The rings will not contact the bottom of the ring grooves. Actually then, the ring will rub the cylinder wall at all times but will not be solidly fastened to the piston at any point. See Fig. 2-24.

RING GAP

The ring is built so it must be squeezed together to place it in the cylinder. This will cause the ring to exert an outward pressure, thus keeping it tightly against the cylinder wall. See Fig. 2-25.

The ring is not solid all the way around but is cut through in one spot. This cut spot forms what is

Fig. 2-25. Top view of cylinder shows sealing action of piston ring.

called the RING GAP. Fig. 2-26.

When the ring is in the cylinder, the cut ends must not touch. When the ring heats up, it will lengthen. Since it cannot expand outwardly, it will close the gap. If there is not enough gap clearance, the ends will soon touch and as the ring continues to lengthen, it will break up into several pieces. This can ruin a good engine.

A general rule for ring gap clearance is to allow .003 to .004 in. per inch (0.07 to 0.10 mm per 25.4 mm) of cylinder diameter. For example, a four inch cylinder would require from .012 to .016 in. clearance in the gap. Fig. 2-27.

Many different types of joints have been used in an endeavor to stop leakage through the ring gap. THIS LEAKAGE IS COMMONLY REFERRED TO AS BLOW-BY. It has been found that the common butt joint is about as effective as any and is much simpler to adjust. Fig. 2-28 illustrates a few of the types of joints that have been used.

The ring is placed in the groove by expanding it out until it will slip over the piston head and slide down and into the ring groove.

Fig. 2-29 illustrates how a compression type ring fits piston groove. Note that there is side as well as back clearance.

TYPES OF RINGS

There are two distinct types of rings. One is called a COMPRESSION RING and the other an OIL CONTROL RING.

Fig. 2-26. Simplified piston ring showing ring gap.

Fig. 2-27. Rings close gap when hot.

Fig. 2-28. Types of piston ring gap joints.

Most engines use three rings on each piston, two compression rings and one oil control ring. Others use two compression rings and two oil rings. Some diesel engines use five or more rings.

All rings may be above the piston pin; or a second oil control ring may be set into a groove near the bottom of the skirt. The compression rings are always used in the top grooves and the oil control rings in the lower grooves. Fig. 2-30.

Fig. 2-29. Compression ring-to-groove fit. Note that ring has both side and back clearance. Side clearance is actually quite small, running around .0015 to .002 in. (0.04 to 0.05 mm).

Fig. 2-30. Location of compression and oil control rings.

COMPRESSION RINGS

Compression rings are designed to prevent leakage between the piston and the cylinder. Fig. 2-31.

Various shapes are used to achieve this goal. Fig. 2-31. The idea behind the various grooves, bevels and chamfers is to create an internal stress within the ring. This stress will tend to force the ring to twist in such a fashion as to press the lower edge to the cylinder wall on the intake stroke. This will cause the ring to act as

Fig. 2-31. Typical compression ring shapes, as they would look in a cylinder.

Fig. 2-33. On compression and exhaust strokes rings tip and slide easily on a film of oil.

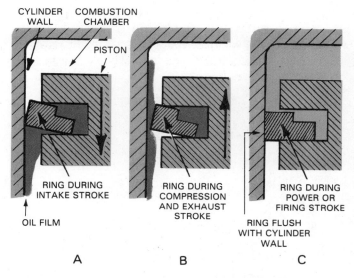

Fig. 2-34. Pressure of burning gases during firing stroke force ring down and out so that it is flush with wall.

a mild scraper. The scraping effect will tend to assist in the removal of any surplus oil that may have escaped the oil control rings. Fig. 2-32.

On compression and exhaust strokes, the rings will tend to slip lightly over the oil film. This will prolong the life of the ring. Fig. 2-33.

On the firing stroke, pressure of the burning gases will force the top edges of the ring downward. This causes the ring to rub the wall with full face contact and to provide a good seal for the enormous pressure generated by the firing stroke. See Fig. 2-34.

HEAT DAM

The compression rings, especially the top ring, are subjected to intense heat. In an endeavor to minimize

the transfer of heat from the head of the piston to the top ring, a HEAT DAM is sometimes used. This is actually a thin groove cut into the head of the piston between the top ring groove and the top of the piston. The heat, instead of passing through the aluminum of the piston to the ring, encounters the heat dam. This helps to minimize heat transfer. Fig. 2-35.

Fig. 2-32. Internal stress causes rings to tip and act as mild scrapers.

Fig. 2-35. Heat dam keeps top ring cooler.

TOP RING GROOVE INSERT

Some aluminum pistons have nickel-iron or comparable metal inserts cast into the piston heads. The top ring groove is cut in this metal. As top ring grooves in aluminum pistons pound out of shape, this insert groove will prolong the useful life of the piston and ring. Fig. 2-36.

OIL CONTROL RINGS

The oil control ring is used to scrape the surplus oil from the cylinder walls. This is not an easy task, and much time and money have gone into the design and construction of oil rings. Fig. 2-37.

All oil rings are slotted and have scraping edges designed to scrape the surplus oil from the cylinder walls. The oil between scrapers passes through slots in the ring on through slots or drilled holes in the bottom of the ring groove. From there the oil drips down into the crankcase area. Fig. 2-38.

EXPANDER DEVICES

Some ring sets, especially those designed for worn cylinders, utilize expanding springs between the bottom of the ring groove and the ring. This will force the ring outward against the cylinder wall.

If a cylinder is worn, the top is invariably wider than the bottom. When the head of the piston is on the bottom of its stroke, the rings will be squeezed in the smaller section of the cylinder. Fig. 2-39.

When the piston travels up the cylinder, the rings must expand outward to follow the ever-widening cylinder diameter. Fig. 2-40.

Fig. 2-36. Top ring insert groove, cast into piston.

Fig. 2-37. Common types of oil control rings.

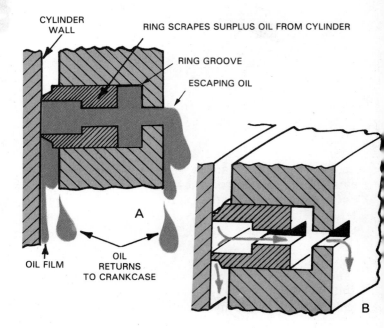

Fig. 2-38. A shows action of oil ring as it travels down cylinder. Note path oil takes in B.

This makes it necessary for the rings to expand, then contract, for every stroke. If engine speed is high enough, the piston will travel up the cylinder and will be snapped back down before the rings have time to expand. This leaves the piston at the top of the stroke with the rings not touching the cylinder walls.

Expander devices used for rings designed for worn cylinders are stronger than those used for a new or rebored cylinder. Fig. 2-41 illustrates a common type of ring expander.

Expanders are generally used under the oil ring, or rings, and the lower compression ring. The upper ring does not use one as the heat in this area would eventually destroy the temper in the expander spring.

Some expanders do not touch the bottom of the grooves. In this type, the ends butt together and when

Fig. 2-39. Rings are compressed in bottom of cylinder.

Fig. 2-40. Rings expand at top of cylinder.
Note large end gaps.

closing up the ring to get it into the cylinder, the expander is compressed within itself. This type is illustrated in D, Fig. 2-37. Notice in E, Fig. 2-37, that the expander has been developed into a complete ring.

Another type of expander is a round wire spring type. The ends butt together, and even though the spring does not touch the bottom of the groove, it still pushes out on the ring, as shown in Fig. 2-42.

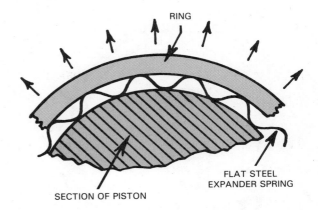

Fig. 2-41. Spring expander rests on bottom of ring groove and forces ring outward. This pressure will keep ring in constant contact with cylinder wall.

Fig. 2-42. Round wire spring expander does not touch bottom of ring groove. When ring is compressed to enter cylinder, spring is compressed within itself to keep constant tension on ring.

RINGS MUST FIT CYLINDER

In addition to following the cylinder walls, rings must make perfect contact all the way around. Fig. 2-43 illustrates a poorly fitted ring that would do a poor job of sealing.

Even with accurately bored cylinders, and new rings, it is impossible to secure a perfect fit when the rings are first installed. After the engine has operated for several hundred miles, the rings will wear into perfect contact with the cylinder walls.

WEAR-IN

To facilitate a fast job of wearing-in, the ring outer face is left rough. This surface feels smooth to the touch but a close inspection will show that fine grooves are left in the ring surface.

The cylinders may look smooth but final honing with fine stones leaves tiny surface scratches in the walls.

When the engine is started, the rings will be drawn up and down the cylinder. Since both the ring faces and the walls have fine scratches, this will cause some

Fig. 2-43. Poor ring contact with cylinder wall is shown. Arrows indicate high spots that touch; area between does not touch.

wear. Any high spots on the ring faces will soon be worn off and the ring will fit properly. Fig. 2-44.

The ring and wall surfaces must be designed with a degree of roughness that will cause the rings to wear-in. As soon as a near perfect fit is achieved, the initial roughness will be gone and excessive wear will cease.

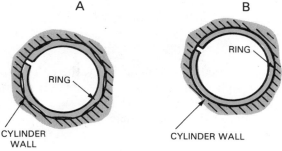

Fig. 2-44. Fine scratches in cylinder wall and grooves in ring face rub against each other to assist prompt wear-in. In detail A, ring touches cylinder only on high spots. Detail B shows ring contact after wear-in.

SPECIAL COATINGS

To assist with a fast wearing-in period, ring faces are often coated with a soft, porous material. Materials such as graphite, phosphate, and molybdenum are used for this purpose. See Fig. 2-45.

This soft, porous material also absorbs some oil and allows a gentle wear-in. Rings can also be tin coated.

All the expanding pressure of new rings is applied to the walls at the ring high spots. This can cause overheating and scuffing at these points. (Scuffing is a roughening of the cylinder wall. It is caused when there is no oil film separating the moving parts, and a hard metal-to-metal contact is made.) The porous coating wears quickly and, since it holds oil, the danger of scuffing is lessened.

Some rings have the outer edge chrome plated. This chrome surface will produce a ring that wears very well and stands up under severe operating conditions.

Chrome plated rings are generally finished somewhat smoother and to a higher degree of accuracy, giving less high points to retard wear-in. See Fig. 2-46.

RING MATERIAL

Piston rings are made from high quality cast iron having excellent wear properties. It also possesses a springy quality that will hold it out against the walls. The springiness of cast iron makes installation and handling a chore that must be done carefully to avoid breaking brittle rings.

Thin oil ring rails are made of steel. Some special expanding oil rings also utilize steel in their construction. Fig. 2-47. Some rings are made of stainless steel. Often, a molybdenum-filled cast iron ring is used in the top ring groove.

RING TYPES ARE NUMEROUS

Ring design is steadily improving. Many new designs are constantly appearing. All rings are designed to provide good sealing, long wear, quick

Fig. 2-45. Porous coating on ring face assures rapid and scuff-free break-in.

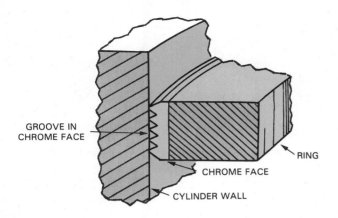

Fig. 2-46. Chrome face of chrome plated ring is grooved to aid break-in.

Fig. 2-47. Three-piece oil ring. Top and bottom rails are made of steel.

break-in, excellent oil control, and freedom from breakage.

PISTON PINS

Pistons are fastened to connecting rods by means of steel pins. These pins, called PISTON PINS, pass through one side of the piston, through the rod upper end, then on through the outer side of the piston. Look at Fig. 2-48.

The piston pin is usually hollow, to reduce weight. It is also casehardened to provide a long wearing surface. Casehardening is a process that hardens the surface of the steel but leaves the inner part fairly soft and tough to prevent brittleness. This hardness penetrates from .004 in. (0.10 mm) up to any depth desired. However, there would be little advantage in making the hard shell any deeper than a few thousandths of an inch. Fig. 2-49. Piston pins are ground to a very accurate size and are highly polished.

PIN INSTALLATION

Piston pins are installed and secured to provide a bearing action in three separate ways.

One way is to have the piston pin fastened to the rod and use the piston bosses for bearings. At times, bronze bushings are pressed into the bosses to provide bearing surfaces. Current practice favors a press fit (friction holds the two pieces together) between the piston pin and the connecting rod, with the pin oscillating in the aluminum pin bosses. See the illustration at right in Fig. 2-50.

Another method is to fasten the pin to one boss and let the rod oscillate on the pin. In this method, the upper connecting rod end must have a bronze bushing for a bearing surface. See Fig. 2-51.

The third method is to have the pin held in place at each end by a SNAP RING that rides in a shallow groove cut in the end of each pin boss. The pin is free to turn in the bosses or in the rod. This is called a free floating pin. Fig. 2-52.

Fig. 2-48. Piston is fastened to the connecting rod with a piston pin.

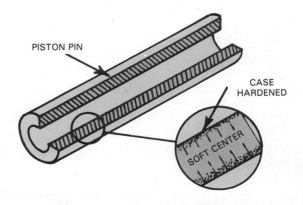

Fig. 2-49. Sectioned piston pin shows thin skin of casehardening.

35

Fig. 2-50. Piston pin locked to rod turns in bronze bushings.

Fig. 2-52. Piston pin is free to turn in rod and in pin bosses. See Fig. 2-48 for full view.

Fig. 2-51. Piston pin locked to one pin boss allows rod to oscillate on pin.

Fig. 2-53. Typical connecting rod; forged steel rod used in conjunction with aluminum piston.   (Jaguar)

CONNECTING RODS

As the name implies, connecting rods are used to connect pistons to the crankshaft. Fig. 2-53.

The upper end of a rod oscillates (swings back and forth), while the lower or big end bearing rotates (turns).

As there is very little bearing movement in the upper end, the bearing area can be reasonably small. The lower (big) end rotates very fast, and the crankshaft journal turns inside the connecting rod. This rotational speed tends to produce heat and wear. To make the rod wear well, a larger bearing area is required.

The upper end of the rod has a hole through it for the piston pin. The lower end must be split so the rod can be installed on the crankshaft journal.

The upper and lower halves of the lower end of the rod are bolted together. The upper and lower halves should be numbered and when installed, the numbers should be on the same side. This prevents turning the cap around when installing the rod.

Turning the connecting rod cap around would make the rod bearing hole out-of-round. In making rods, the upper and lower halves are bolted together and the holes are bored to an accurate size. The hole may be slightly off-center. If the caps are crossed, the upper hole half may not line up with the lower hole. Fig. 2-54.

CONNECTING ROD CONSTRUCTION

Connecting rods are normally made of alloy steel. They are drop-forged to shape, then machined. The customary shape uses I-beam construction. Fig. 2-53.

Some rods are built of aluminum. Generally these are for small engines designed for light duty. Small engines often utilize the rod material for both upper and lower bearing surfaces. Special aluminum rods

Fig. 2-54. Numbers on rod and cap must be kept together.

for high speed, high performance engines can be purchased from specialty machine shops.

CONNECTING ROD BEARINGS

As mentioned, the upper end of the connecting rod may use a bronze bushing for a bearing surface. If the rod is bolted, or pressed to the piston pin, it will not use any special bearing. The bearings in this case would be in the piston boss holes.

The lower end uses what is termed a precision insert bearing. The rod bearing hole is bored larger than the crank journal and an INSERT BEARING is placed between the rod and journal. Fig. 2-55.

Fig. 2-55. Connecting rod precision insert bearing is properly fitted when bearing parting surfaces (ends) will touch before the rod halves meet. This provides crush.   (Sunnen)

A bearing insert usually does not turn in the rod. It is held in place by a locating tab (locking lip) on the insert that is placed in a corresponding notch in the rod. Look at Figs. 2-53, 2-56, 2-57.

The insert must fit the rod snugly in order to transfer heat to connecting rod. To insure a proper fit, the insert will protrude a small amount above the rod bore parting surface. This distance (from less than .001 in. to .002 in. or less than 0.025 to 0.050 mm) is called CRUSH HEIGHT. When the rod halves

are drawn together, the inserts touch before the halves, forcing the insert tightly into place. Fig. 2-55.

INSERT CONSTRUCTION

An insert is started as a steel shell. This gives it shape and rigidity. The inner part of the shell that contacts the journal, is then coated to form a lining.

Some bearings have steel shells with a thin (.002 – .005 in. or 0.05 – 0.13 mm) babbitt lining. Others use steel shells, then coat them with a copper-lead-tin matrix followed by a very thin (.001 in. or 0.025 mm) coating of pure tin. Others use aluminum coating. Fig. 2-57 illustrates a typical bearing insert.

BEARING CHARACTERISTICS

The ideal bearing is not easy to construct. For every advantage, there seems to be a disadvantage that goes with it. A good bearing must have many characteristics.

LOAD STRENGTH

The bearing is subjected to tremendous stress from the firing stroke. There is pounding as the crank first pushes up, then pulls down. The bearing must not become fatigued and crack, nor must it spread out from the pounding force.

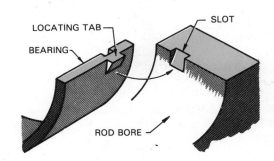

Fig. 2-56. Connecting rod precision insert is aligned and held in place by bearing locating tab engaging a slot in rod bore. (Clevite)

Fig. 2-57. Makeup of precision insert bearing is shown.

ANTISCUFFING

The material in the bearing should be such that in the event the oil surface skin is destroyed, the shaft journal will not be damaged by scuffing and scratching.

CORROSION

The bearing material must resist any tendency to corrode when exposed to vapors and acids in the crankcase.

CONFORMATION

No surface is perfectly true. Even with a highly accurate shaft, new rod, and insert, we cannot expect the bearing to fit the journal without some minute imperfection. A good bearing is soft and ductile enough to shape to the journal after it has been used for some time.

EMBEDABILITY

If a small abrasive particle enters the bearing area, the bearing should allow the particle to embed itself in the bearing material so it will not scratch the journal.

CONDUCTIVITY

All bearings produce heat. It is essential that the bearing material be of a type that will conduct heat to the rod. This is one reason why insert bearings must be a near-perfect fit.

TEMPERATURE CHANGE

The bearing strength must not be lessened when it reaches its operating temperature. It must have reasonable strength when both cold and hot. Fig. 2-58 illustrates various forces that work to destroy bearings.

Each insert must have a small hole to allow oil to enter for lubrication. Some inserts have shallow grooves in the surface to allow oil to spread out across the bearing. See Fig. 2-57.

CRANKSHAFT

The engine crankshaft provides a constant turning force to the wheels. It has throws to which connecting rods are attached, and its function is to change reciprocating motion of the piston to a rotary motion to drive the wheels. Crankshafts are made of alloy steel or cast iron. Fig. 2-59.

MAIN BEARINGS

The crankshaft is held in position by a series of main bearings. The maximum number of main bearings for a crankshaft is one more than the number of cylinders. It may have less main bearings than the number of cylinders.

Fig. 2-58. Bearing inserts must resist many destructive forces.

Fig. 2-59. Typical four cylinder engine crankshaft. A—Main bearing journals. B—Rod bearing journals. (Peugeot)

Most engines use precision insert bearings that are constructed like the connecting rod bearings, but somewhat larger. See Fig. 2-60.

In addition to supporting the crankshaft, one of the main bearings must control the forward and backward movement (end play) of the shaft. This bearing has flanges on the edges that rub against a ground surface on the edge of the crankshaft main journal. This bearing is referred to as a THRUST BEARING. Fig. 2-60.

CRANKSHAFT THROWS

The crankshaft throws (part of the shaft the connecting rod fastens to) must be arranged in such a way as to bring the piston to top dead center at the proper time for the firing stroke. As the pistons in a

Engine Components

Cutaway view of an overhead camshaft, 6-cylinder gasoline engine. Study various parts and their locations. (Mercedes-Benz)

Fig. 2-60. Set of main bearings, some with an aluminum coating, others employ babbitt. Note thrust flanges on thrust bearing. (Cadillac)

multicylinder (more than one) engine do not fire one after the other, but fire in a staggered sequence, the throw position is very important. Fig. 2-61 illustrates an end view of four, six, and eight cylinder crankshafts. Illustrations A, C, D, and E are for in-line engines. An in-line engine is one in which all the cylinders are arranged one after the other in a straight row.

An eight cylinder in-line engine, Fig. 2-61D, requires eight connecting rod throws. A V-8 engine, B and F, has only four throws. Each throw services two connecting rods.

CRANK VIBRATION

To offset the unbalanced condition caused by off-center throws, many crankshafts use counterbalances to stop vibration. They may be forged as part of the crankshaft, or they may be bolted. Fig. 2-62.

VIBRATION DAMPER

When the front cylinders fire, power is transmitted through the rather long, crooked crankshaft. The pressure the piston applies can exceed 3,000 lbs. (1350 kg). The front of the crankshaft receiving this power tends to move before the rear, causing a twisting motion. When the torque is removed from the front, the

Fig. 2-61A. A four cylinder crankshaft will normally have throws spaced 180 deg. apart with cylinders 1 and 4 on the same side.

Fig. 2-61D. A straight eight crankshaft of 4-4 type resembles two four cylinder crankshafts connected end to end.

Fig. 2-61B. A V-8 engine may have the crankshaft throws arranged the same as a four cylinder engine, or method shown here which is widely used.

Fig. 2-61E. A left-hand crankshaft for a six cylinder engine will have No. 3 and 4 throws to the left of No. 1 and 6.

Fig. 2-61C. A right-hand crankshaft for a six cylinder engine will have throws arranged like this.

Fig. 2-61F. A typical V-8 engine crankshaft has same arrangement of connecting rod throws as shown in Fig. 2-61B. (Ford)

partially twisted shaft will unwind and snap back in the other direction. This unwinding, although minute, causes what is known as torsional vibration.

To stop the winding motion, a vibration damper, sometimes called a HARMONIC BALANCER, is attached to the front of the crankshaft. Basically the damper is built in two pieces. These pieces may be connected by rubber plugs, or spring loaded friction discs, or a combination of the two. Fig. 2-63.

When a front cylinder fires and the shaft tries to speed up, it tries to spin the heavy section of the damper. In doing this, the rubber connecting the two parts of the damper is twisted. The shaft does not speed up as much with the damper attached.

The force necessary to twist the rubber and to speed up the heavy damper wheel, tends to smooth out the crankshaft operation.

When the firing pressure is removed from the shaft, the shaft cannot spring back quickly because the twisted rubber attempts to keep the damper wheel turning. The unwinding force of the crankshaft cancels out the twist in the opposite direction.

DRILLED, GROUND AND POLISHED

The crankshaft is drilled so oil being fed to the main bearings will pass through the shaft to the connecting rod throws.

Fig. 2-62. Crankshaft needs counterweights to bring shaft into proper balance.

All bearing surfaces are precision ground and are highly polished. Fig. 2-64.

TIMING GEAR OR SPROCKET

A timing gear or a chain sprocket is installed on the front end of the crankshaft. A chain sprocket is usually made of steel. In the case of the timing gear, the teeth are helical in shape.

Fig. 2-63. Vibration damper utilizes small flywheel which moves a limited amount, bending rubber plugs. See A and B.

A timing gear is used to turn a camshaft timing gear. Where a sprocket is used, the sprocket will drive a timing chain that operates the camshaft by means of a larger sprocket. Fig. 2-65.

A timing gear or sprocket is secured to the crankshaft by means of a metal key that rides in a slot

Fig. 2-64. Crankshaft partially cut away shows how oil is pumped into center main bearing. From there it enters an oil gallery drilled through the crankshaft to each rod journal.

Fig. 2-65. Timing gear drive gear on crankshaft; also timing chain (or belt) drive sprocket on crankshaft.

cut in the crankshaft. The gear or sprocket also has a slot or groove in it. Fig. 2-66.

FLYWHEEL

A heavy flywheel is attached to the rear end of the crankshaft by means of bolts. The function of the flywheel is to smooth out engine speed and keep the crankshaft spinning between power strokes.

In some engines the flywheel also serves as a mounting surface for the clutch. See Fig. 2-67.

The outer rim of the flywheel has a large ring attached with gear teeth cut into it. The teeth of the starter motor engage this gear and spin the flywheel to crank the engine. When an automatic transmission is used, the torque converter assembly acts as a flywheel.

CAMSHAFT

An engine camshaft is used to open and close the valves. There is one cam on the camshaft for each valve in the engine. Generally only one camshaft is used in each engine. (On the elementary engine you designed in Chapter 1, you used two camshafts and

Fig. 2-66. A steel key, sliding in a slot in the crankshaft, passes through a similar slot in the gear to secure the gear to the shaft.

Fig. 2-67. Heavy flywheel is bolted to the crankshaft flange.

the valves were arranged in a T-fashion to better illustrate the action in relation to an end view of the crankshaft.) A camshaft has a series of support bearings along its length.

Camshafts turn at one-half crankshaft speed.

The cam lobes are usually not flat across the top as they might appear. The bottom of the valve lifter may be slightly crowned and the cam lobe tapered. This places the lobe-to-lifter contact to one side of center. Fig. 2-68.

Fig. 2-68. A—Section of camshaft showing one method of tapering cam lobes. Lifter bottom is crowned. B—Typical camshaft design.

A gear cut into the camshaft is used to drive the distributor and oil pump.

The camshaft is kept in place by using a thrust washer behind the timing gear bolted to the block. Or, a spring loaded plunger is used to push on the end of the camshaft. An additional cam may be ground on the shaft to drive the fuel pump.

The typical camshaft is made of cast, or forged, steel. The cam surfaces are hardened for long life. Fig. 2-69 illustrates a typical camshaft with gear and thrust washer. The camshaft may be turned by a gear, timing chain, or a toothed timing belt. Figs. 2-70, 2-71, 2-72.

The camshaft gear can be made of cast steel, aluminum or a special pressed fiber. Chain sprockets are made of cast steel.

VALVES

Each engine cylinder ordinarily has two valves. However, some special racing engines use four valves per cylinder.

Exhaust valves are made of heat resistant metal, because the head of a valve operates at temperatures up to 1300°F (704°C). It is obvious that the steel used in valve construction must be of high quality.

In order to prevent burning, the valve must give off heat to the valve guide and to the valve seat. The valve must make good contact with the seat, and must run with minimum clearance in the guide.

Fig. 2-69. Typical camshaft. A—Main camshaft bearings. B—Cam lobes. C—Eccentric to drive fuel pump. D—Gear to drive distributor. E—Camshaft sprocket. F—Thrust washer. G—Key. H—Retaining capscrew. I—Timing chain. J—Rubbing block. (Renault)

Fig. 2-70. Front view of typical timing chain drive. Shows alignment of valve timing marks. (Cadillac)

Fig. 2-72. Overhead camshaft driven by a toothed drive belt. (Ford)

Fig. 2-71. Timing gear drive for camshaft also requires alignment of timing marks. (Pontiac)

Some valves have special hardfacing on the face areas to increase their useful life. Others use hollow stems filled with metallic sodium. Fig. 2-73. At operating temperature, the sodium becomes a liquid and splashes up into the head. This draws the heat into the stem where it transfers to the valve guide.

VALVE SEATS

Two angles commonly used for valve seats are 30 and 45 deg. Some makers grind a one degree difference between the valve face and seat to permit fast seating. Fig. 2-74. The seat may be ground to 45 deg. and the valve, 44 deg., or vice versa (the other way around).

Valve seats can be cut in the cylinder head, or special, hard steel inserts may be pressed into the

Fig. 2-73. A—Valve with special hard facing to lengthen useful life. B—Special heat resistant valve utilizing a hollow stem partially filled with metallic sodium.
DANGER—The sodium inside the valve is dangerous! Never drill, cut, etc., into such a valve. If worn out, dispose of carefully as recommended by manufacturer!

Fig. 2-74. Common valve seat angles.

head. Fig. 2-75. Seats can also be induction hardened.

The valve face and seat must make perfect contact to insure efficient operation.

VALVE GUIDES

The valve guide can be an integral part of the cylinder head; or it may be made as a separate unit, pressed into a hole in the head or block, depending on which unit contains the valves.

The pressed-in type of valve guide is made of cast iron. The valve stem must fit this guide with about .002 — .003 in. (0.05 — 0.08 mm) clearance. Fig. 2-76.

VALVE SPRINGS

Springs push the valves closed when the cams lower. Since the springs are compressed and expanded

over 70,000 times per hour at 50 mph (80.5 km/h), they must be made of high quality spring wire.

You have already learned how the spring is fastened to the valve by means of a spring washer and split keepers.

Some springs have the coils closer together at one end than at the other. In an installation of this kind, the end with the more closely spaced coils must be placed against the head, or block, whichever the case may be. Some engines use two springs per valve, one spring inside of another.

VALVE LIFTERS
(Mechanical Type)

Mechanical lifters are usually made of cast iron. The bottom part that contacts the camshaft is hardened. Some lifters are hollow to reduce weight. A screw is placed in the top to adjust clearance between end of valve stem and lifter. Fig. 2-77.

VALVE LIFTERS
(Hydraulic Type)

The hydraulic valve lifter performs the same job as the mechanical lifter. The major difference is that the

Fig. 2-75. Valve insert is often frozen to shrink diameter, then pressed into warm head to secure insert. Head metal, A, can be peened over edge of insert to aid in securing.

Fig. 2-76. Examples of valve guides. A—Integral (not removable). B—Pressed-in (removable).

hydraulic lifter is self-adjusting, operates with no lifter-to-rocker arm clearance, Fig. 2-78, and uses engine oil under pressure to operate. Hydraulic lifters are quiet in operation.

To operate, engine oil under pressure enters the hydraulic lifter body. The oil passes through a small opening in the bottom of an inner piston, into a cavity beneath the piston. The oil raises the piston up until it contacts the push rod (the oil pressure is not high enough to open the valve).

When the cam raises the lifter, pressure is applied to the inner piston. The piston tries to squirt the oil back through the small opening but cannot do so as a small check ball seals the opening.

As the cam raises, the lifter becomes solid and lifts the valve. When the cam lowers, the lifter will be pushed down by the push rod. The lifter will then

automatically adjust to remove clearances. Fig. 2-78 shows one type of hydraulic valve lifter. See Fig. 2-79 for complete lifter action.

Fig. 2-78. Typical hydraulic valve lifter. Oil enters channel 3 in block, passes through hole 4 in lifter body 5, then enters hole 12 in inner piston. It fills inner piston cavity and passes through hole 13. This pressure will push check ball 6 off its seat. It now flows through hole 14 in the lifter cage 7. It fills the cavity under inner piston 11. The pressure raises inner piston up until it contacts valve push rod, or stem, whichever is used. Other parts are: 1—Push rod seat. 2—Inner piston cap. 15—Block. 8—Inner piston spring. 10—Ball check spring. 9—Camshaft. 16—Lobe.

Fig. 2-77. Mechanical valve lifters usually are solid. Hollow lifters reduce weight.

Fig. 2-79. Hydraulic valve lifter operation during two stages. A—Valve closed. B—Valve open.   (Cadillac)

TURNING HELPS

If the valve goes up and comes down in the same place time after time, carbon buildup between valve face and seat may cause the valve to remain partially open. This will cause valve burning. If the valve turns even a few degrees on each opening, a wiping action between face and seat will be developed. This keeps carbon from building up.

Turning also helps to prevent localized hot spots since the valve will keep moving away from the hottest areas.

RELEASE TYPE ROTATOR

There are several methods of causing valves to rotate as they open and close. One is through the use of a release type mechanism. This removes the spring tension from the valve, while open, and induces rotation from engine vibration. See Fig. 2-80.

POSITIVE TYPE ROTATOR

An example of the positive type rotator is shown in Figs. 2-81 and 2-82. In this mechanism, when the lifter applies pressure to the valve stem or push rod, the valve spring pressure on the seating collar causes the collar to press down on the flexible washer.

The washer then presses down on the balls, causing them to roll downward in their inclined races (small grooves guide ball). This rolling action causes the retainer and the valve to turn a few degrees.

When the valve closes, lifter pressure is removed and the ball springs cause the balls to move back up the inclined races. The unit is then ready to function again.

Fig. 2-81. Thompson Rotocap—positive type.

Fig. 2-82. Thompson Rotocoil—positive type.

ROLLER LIFTERS

Some heavy-duty engines, as well as those having a special camshaft, use valve lifters with rollers that contact the camshaft. The roller reduces wear on both the lifter and the cam. Fig. 2-83.

VALVE TIMING

Both the intake and exhaust valves are open longer than it takes the piston to make a stroke. The exact number of degrees that a valve will open or close before top or bottom dead center varies widely, depending on engine design. The degrees shown in Fig. 2-84 are for one specific engine. You will note that the intake valve opens about 20 deg. before the piston starts down on the intake stroke. It closes about 67 deg. after the piston reaches the bottom of its stroke.

The exhaust valve opens about 69 deg. before the piston reaches bottom dead center (BDC) on the power stroke. It does not close until about 27 deg. after top dead center (TDC) on the intake stroke.

Fig. 2-80. Thompson Rotovalve—release type.
(Thompson Products)

The early opening and late closing of both valves greatly improves the intake of fresh fuel mixture and the thorough exhausting of burned gases.

The intake and exhaust valves, Fig. 2-84, are partially open at the same time. For example, the intake valve opens 20 deg. before TDC and the exhaust valve closes 27 deg. after TDC, on the same intake stroke. This situation is termed VALVE OVERLAP. It does not impair engine performance.

When a valve closes or opens, how fast it will rise, how long it will stay open, and how fast it will close depends on the shape of cam lobe and the position of the camshaft in relation to the crankshaft.

The two timing chain sprockets are generally marked to insure correct valve timing. When a line drawn through the center of both shafts bisects the timing marks, timing is correct.

Fig. 2-83. Roller lifter is used in some heavy-duty applications.

Fig. 2-84. Valve timing diagram. The angles will vary widely depending upon engine design. The length of time, in degrees, that a valve is held open is referred to as valve duration.

The camshaft is mounted to one side of the crankshaft on most in-line engines (except engines using overhead camshafts). Fig. 2-85.

On V-type engines, the camshaft is generally mounted above the crankshaft in the center region of the block. See Fig. 2-86.

Engine valves are not always operated directly from a camshaft. The valve-in-head engine utilizes additional linkage to operate the valves. This will be discussed in the chapter on engine types.

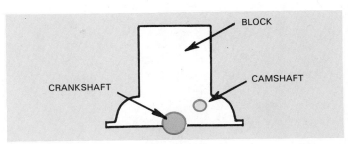

Fig. 2-85. One location for camshaft in an in-line engine. See Fig. 2-72 for cam location in an overhead camshaft, in-line engine.

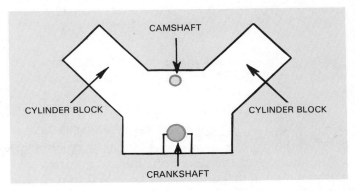

Fig. 2-86. Camshaft location in a cam-in-block or valve-in-head (OHV) V-type engine.

CYLINDER HEAD

The cylinder head serves as a cover for the cylinders and forms the top of the combustion chamber. It may contain one or both valves. The head also holds the spark plugs.

If the cylinder head contains the valves, it is called a VALVE-IN-HEAD engine.

Cylinder heads are usually made of cast iron or aluminum. They must be strong and rigid. They are bolted to the block with HEAD BOLTS. Fig. 2-92.

The surfaces of the head and block that make contact must be absolutely flat. Figs. 2-87, 2-93.

OIL PAN

The oil pan acts as a reservoir for oil, and it also serves as a dust shield for the bottom of the engine. It is attached to the bottom of the block with cap screws.

Fig. 2-87. A typical overhead camshaft cylinder head arrangement. 1—Cylinder head cover. 2—Camshaft sprocket. 3—Camshaft. 4—Rocker arm assembly. 5—Semi-circular seal. 6—Cylinder head. 7—Spark plug. 8—Valve keeper. 9—Upper spring seat. 10—Spring. 11—Lower spring seat. 12—Valve seal. 13—Valve. (Mazda)

The pan is generally made of thin steel stamped to shape, Fig. 2-88. Plastic may also be used.

TIMING GEAR COVER

The timing gears must be covered to prevent the entrance of dirt and dust and to eliminate the loss of oil.

In addition to this function, the cover often contains an oil seal that allows the crankshaft to protrude through the cover and yet not leak oil.

Timing gear covers may be made of thin steel, plastic, aluminum, or cast iron. Figs. 2-89, 2-93.

GASKETS AND SEALS

In an engine where machined parts fit together, gaskets are used to make the joints tight and to prevent leakage of oil, water, and/or gasoline.

The cylinder heads must seal in the water of the cooling system and must also contain the pressure of the exploding fuel. Thin steel, copper, and asbestos gaskets are used between the head and engine block.

It is very difficult to machine metal parts to the degree of accuracy necessary for leakproof joints. As the engine expands and contracts during warmup and cooling periods, there are minute shifts in the fastened parts. This, coupled with vibration, will loosen many parts to the point of leakage.

Gasket material is somewhat resilient (soft and springy) and will adapt itself to expansion and contraction. It will also conform to irregularities in the surfaces of the mating parts. Fig. 2-90.

Fig. 2-88. Engine oil pan size and shape will vary widely. (Nissan)

Fig. 2-91 illustrates some of the common gaskets found in a car engine.

OTHER PARTS

Other engine parts that are required by the various systems—carburetion, ignition, lubrication, and cooling will be discussed in other sections, Fig. 2-92.

In this chapter you have studied about many engine parts. A thorough understanding of design, construction and application is an absolute essential for every good auto mechanic. Go through the questions on pages 48, 49, and 50 carefully, and do not be satisfied until you can answer each and every one.

KNOW THESE TERMS

Engine block, Sleeves, Piston expansion, Piston skirt, Piston rings, Ring gap, Blow-by, Compression rings, Oil ring, Ring expander, Piston pin, Connecting rod cap, Connecting rod bearing, Main bearing, Crankshaft throw, Vibration damper, Timing sprocket, Camshaft, Valves, Valve seats, Valve springs, Valve guides, Valve lifters, Valve timing, Oil pan, Timing gear cover, Gaskets and seals.

REVIEW QUESTIONS—CHAPTER 2

Think of these questions as a special sort of scale to weigh your progress. STEP ON AND SEE HOW HEAVY YOU ARE!

1. The unit that forms a basic foundation upon which the whole engine is built is called the _____.
2. What are cylinder sleeves?
3. The cylinders in a new engine should be glassy smooth. True or False?
4. A cylinder that is round to within .100 in. (2.54 mm) is accurate enough. True or False?
5. The main advantage of using aluminum in engine construction is that it is rustproof. True or False?
6. A piston must be _____ and yet _____.

FRONT OF CRANKSHAFT PROTRUDES THROUGH HOLE. OIL SEAL IS PLACED IN HOLE

GASKET

FLANGE WITH BOLT HOLES FOR MOUNTING

Fig. 2-89. One type of stamped steel timing gear cover. (British-Leyland)

CONFINED OIL

A

OIL LEAK

CONFINED OIL

B

GASKET

GASKET FILLS LOW SPOT AND STOPS OIL LEAK

Fig. 2-90. Gaskets are designed to compress and seal irregular surfaces. Note in A how oil is leaking out through two areas while in B a gasket has sealed off leaks.

PAN GASKET

HEAD

MANIFOLD

FUEL PUMP

PAN

BREATHER

HEAD

ROCKER ARM GASKET

EXHAUST

WATER OUTLET

MANIFOLD

PAN GASKET

MANIFOLD

HEAD GASKET

Fig. 2-91. A few of the typical gaskets used in an engine.

7. What are three common ways of controlling piston expansion?
8. Cast iron pistons work best in a _____ speed engine.
9. Piston heads are of different shapes. What are some of the reasons for these shapes?
10. What is a partial or slipper skirt piston?
11. Temperature of piston heads often runs up to about _____ degrees.
12. What is placed on the piston to help it seal the cylinder?
13. What is a heat dam?
14. There are two types of piston rings. What are they?
15. Some rings are made of _____, while others are made of _____ _____.
16. What are ring expanders?
17. Some rings have special grooves cut into the inner circumference. What are these grooves supposed to accomplish?
18. What are the approximate number of rings usually found on pistons used in auto engines?

19. What is a break-in period?
20. What is the advantage of chrome plated rings?
21. How can wear in top ring groove be lessened?
22. Are plain butt joints alright for piston rings?
23. One kind of ring is always used at the top of the piston. What type is it?
24. The bottom rings are always _____ rings.
25. Piston pins fasten the _____ to the _____ _____.
26. What is casehardening?
27. Connecting rods are used to connect the _____ to the _____.
28. The smaller connecting rod upper end bearing is _____, but the big end bearing is _____ to facilitate installation.
29. Connecting rods use precision _____ for the big end bearings.
30. Name five characteristics of a good bearing material.
31. Crankshafts are usually cast of aluminum. True or False?
32. Crankshafts are subject to vibration from being off balance and also from twisting. How are the vibrations controlled?
33. The flow of power is smoother in an eight cylinder engine than in a four. True or False?
34. Crankshafts have drilled passageways. What are these for?
35. Camshafts are driven in two ways. Name them.
36. Name three basic purposes of the flywheel.
37. Exhaust valves are made of cast iron. True or False?

38. A valve sheds its heat in two manners. What are they?
39. Two valve seat angles are _____ degrees and _____ degrees.
40. Explain how a hydraulic valve lifter works.
41. What are the advantages of the hydraulic lifter?
42. The oil pan holds _____ and provides _____ against dust, dirt, etc.
43. Gaskets are used to prevent the loss of oil, gasoline, water, etc. Why are they needed?

Fig. 2-92. This is a typical four cylinder, overhead valve engine. Although a different design than basic engine that you have "built on paper," see if you can find and identify the following parts: Piston, Crankshaft, Valve guide, Camshaft, Cylinder head, Valve spring, Crankshaft, Connecting rod, Cylinder, Cam lobe, Piston pin, Crankshaft main bearing journals, Camshaft timing belt and sprockets, and Valve. (Mazda)

Fig. 2-93. Exploded view shows major components of Cadillac's HT 4100 digital fuel injection engine. This lightweight V-8 has an 8.5 to 1 compression ratio and is rated at 124 hp. Reduced displacement from 368 cu. in. (6.0 L) to 252 cu. in. (4.1 L) and efficient use of aluminum cut engine weight by over 200 lb.

Buick V-6 computer controlled coil ignition system. This system does not use a distributor. Three coils, in conjunction with an ignition module, a ECM (Electronic Control Module), a crankshaft sensor, a camshaft sensor, and necessary wiring, make up the basic parts. Crank sensor (Hall effect type) triggers proper ignition coil while camshaft position sensor (also Hall effect) emits a signal to ECM whenever number one piston is on compression stroke. This along with other input signals such as engine air flow volume through intake, engine temperature, etc., allows ECM to adjust both spark and fuel injection timing. As each coil is triggered, it will fire a pair of opposite cylinders (1-4, 5-2, 3-6). One of the cylinders will be on compression while other is on exhaust. Discharge into exhaust is referred to as a "waste spark." This coil hookup technique allows three coils to service six cylinders. (Buick)

Fig. 3-1. Ignition system schematics. A—Breaker point controlled ignition system. No transistor used. B—Transistor ignition system. Note sensor used to trigger transistor. C—Typical ignition coil. D—Ignition system wiring setup on breaker point system. E—Ignition system primary circuit action. Points closed, current through primary builds magnetic field in coil. F—Ignition system secondary action. Points open, breaking primary circuit. Coil field collapses inducing high voltage in secondary. Plug fires.   (Ford, Deere & Co.)

Chapter 3

IGNITION SYSTEMS

After studying this chapter, you will be able to:
- Explain the primary and secondary circuits of an ignition system.
- Describe the construction of major ignition system components.
- Summarize the basic function and operating principles of ignition system parts.
- List the differences between a breaker point and an electronic type ignition system.
- Explain the action of spark advance mechanisms.

Chapters 1 and 2 made frequent reference to the use of a spark to ignite the fuel mixture. This chapter will provide you with a clear and concise description of the various units in the ignition system. The theory, design, and construction of the parts will be discussed. You will also learn how they are combined to produce, control, and distribute the spark.

READ FIRST PART OF CHAPTER ON ELECTRICAL SYSTEM

At this time it is recommended that you read the first eight pages of the chapter on Electrical Systems. This will provide you with a basic introduction to the field of electricity. Common electrical terms and theory will be discussed. SUCH KNOWLEDGE IS ESSENTIAL TO UNDERSTAND THIS SECTION ON IGNITION SYSTEMS.

HIGH VOLTAGE IS NECESSARY

For many years batteries were of 6 volt design. Increasing engine size and the addition of numerous electrical accessories, however, made it necessary to change to the 12V battery that is in common use today.

Voltage of 6 or 12V will not produce a spark that will jump across the electrodes of a spark plug in the combustion chamber.

In modern cars, the voltage available at the spark plug usually exceeds 30,000V. The ignition system must produce such voltage in a completely reliable manner. This means that the battery voltage of 12V must be increased many times.

PRIMARY AND SECONDARY CIRCUITS

The ignition system is divided into two separate circuits.

The PRIMARY circuit voltage is low, operating on the battery voltage of 12 volts. The wiring in this circuit is covered with a thin layer of rubber, or plastic, to insulate the wire and to prevent short circuits.

CAUTION: The spark delivered to the plugs may exceed 30,000V. If you touch a plug and are shocked, there is little real danger involved. The reason for this is that there is very little amperage. DO NOT CONFUSE THIS WITH VOLTAGE IN YOUR HOME ELECTRICAL SYSTEM. IN THE HOME UNDER CERTAIN CONDITIONS A CURRENT OF 120V CAN, AND OFTEN DOES, ELECTROCUTE PEOPLE. ALWAYS TREAT ELECTRICITY WITH GREAT CAUTION AND RESPECT.

Study Fig. 3-1. Notice the two circuits. Learn the names of the various units and remember where they are inserted in the circuit.

SYSTEM COMPONENTS—BATTERY

To fully comprehend the functions of the parts or components of an ignition system, we will start at the battery and trace the flow of electricity through the system.

The battery, Fig. 3-2, is the source of electrical energy needed to operate the ignition system. The battery does not "store" electricity. When "charging," it converts electricity into chemical energy. When "discharging" (producing current), the battery converts chemical energy into electricity. See Chapter 21, Electrical System Fundamentals.

To function properly, the battery must be close to fully charged. (Fully charged means that the battery is in the proper condition to produce the highest output of electricity.)

The battery is generally located as close to the

Fig. 3-2. Typical maintenance-free battery construction. Note charge indicator. (Delco)

engine as feasible. This reduces the length of wiring necessary to connect the battery to the component parts. The close location will cut costs of excessive lengths of wire, and will reduce voltage drop. An under-the-hood location also makes the battery readily accessible for repair and maintenance.

A battery has two heavy lead terminals. One is positive and one is negative. Common practice in this country is to ground the negative terminal. The ground wire may be uninsulated. The ground is fastened to the engine or to some other suitable metal location.

IGNITION SWITCH

The primary circuit starts at the battery and flows through an insulated wire to the ignition switch. The usual ignition switch utilizes a key to operate it. It connects or disconnects the flow of electricity across the terminals. The ignition switch may have additional terminals that supply electricity to other units on the car when the key is turned on. Fig. 3-3.

RESISTOR

Electricity flows from the ignition switch to the resistor. From the resistor, the current travels to the coil.

The resistor controls the amount of current reaching the coil. The resistor may be either the simple or the ballast type.

There are resistors designed for specific jobs. One type, used on Ford V-8 engines for many years, was a simple unit used to reduce battery voltage reaching the coil. The primary circuit passed through the resistor, cutting down the voltage to a predetermined level. The type of coil utilized in these installations

would overheat if the battery voltage reached the coil without being reduced.

This type of simple resistor was not temperature sensitive. It would deliver about the same voltage to the coil regardless of whether or not the coil had reached operating temperature. Fig. 3-4.

Another adaptation of the resistor is used in high-compression, high horsepower engines. This type is known as the BALLAST resistor. It is a temperature sensitive, variable resistance unit.

A ballast resistor is designed to reduce the voltage available to the coil at low engine speeds, and to increase the voltage at the higher rpm range when it is needed. Without the resistor, the coil would require enough voltage to function efficiently at high speeds. Such voltage would cause excessive heating at low speeds. It would also cause oxidation of the contact points (a blue scale-like deposit).

The ballast type resistor tends to heat up at low engine speeds as the duration of flow in the primary circuit is longer, and with less interruption by the contact point opening. As it heats up, its resistance value goes up, causing lower voltage to pass into the coil.

As engine speed increases, the points open and close more rapidly and the duration of current flow lessens. This causes a lowering of temperature. As the

Fig. 3-3. Typical ignition switch. Note various connections. (Ford)

Fig. 3-4. Simple resistor in primary circuit of ignition system.

temperature drops, the resistor allows the voltage to the coil to increase. At high speeds, the coil received most all the battery voltage.

High engine speeds shorten the coil saturation period. (The saturation period is the length of time the points are closed and current is flowing through the primary windings of the coil.) It is obvious that this condition would require full voltage.

The ballast resistor is constructed of a special type wire, the properties of which tend to increase or decrease the voltage in direct proportion to the heat of the wire. Fig. 3-5.

Fig. 3-5. Ballast resistor principle. A illustrates long pulsations of current passing through special ballast resistor wire at slow engine speeds. This heats special wire and lowers amount of current reaching coil. B shows short pulsations at high speed. This allows wire to cool, allowing a heavier current to flow to coil.

Current practice employs a simple calibrated resistance wire that lowers battery voltage to around 9 — 10 1/2 volts during normal engine operation. A bypass wire runs from the ignition switch or starter solenoid to the coil. While the engine is cranking, the coil will receive full battery voltage. When the key is released, the circuit is through the resistance wire. Some systems, such as the transistor ignition system, use two ballast resistors to control coil voltage.

COIL

The primary circuit leads from the resistor to the coil.

An ignition coil is actually a pulse-type transformer that steps up battery voltage to, and exceeding, 30,000 volts.

COIL CONSTRUCTION

The coil is constructed with a special laminated iron core.

Around this central core, many thousands of turns of very fine copper wire are wound. This fine wire is insulated by a thin coating of special insulation material. Fig. 3-6. One end of the fine wire is connected to the high tension terminal, and the other is connected to the primary circuit wire within the coil. All these turns of fine wire form what is called the SECONDARY circuit coil windings.

Fig. 3-6. Ignition coil. One end of secondary circuit wire is attached to high voltage terminal; other end is connected to primary circuit wire within coil.   (Chevrolet)

Several hundred turns of heavier copper wire are wrapped around the secondary coil windings. Each end is connected to a primary circuit terminal on the coil. These windings are also insulated. The turns of heavier wire form the PRIMARY CIRCUIT COIL WINDINGS. Check winding connections in Fig. 3-1.

The core, with both the SECONDARY and PRIMARY windings attached, is placed inside a laminated iron shell. The job of the shell is to help concentrate the magnetic lines of force that will be developed by the windings.

This entire unit is then placed inside a steel, aluminum, or Bakelite case. In some coil designs, the case is filled with a special oil. It is then hermetically sealed to prevent the entrance of dirt or moisture. Electrical outlets, such as the primary terminals, are generally contained in the coil cap. They are carefully sealed because the coil must withstand vibration, heat, moisture, and the stresses of high induced voltages.

Coils vary in size and shape to meet the varying demands of different types of installations. Fig. 3-6.

HOW A COIL WORKS

When the ignition switch is turned on, the current flows through the primary windings of the coil, to the ground, and back to the battery via the frame. See Fig. 3-7.

A MAGNETIC FIELD IS DEVELOPED

As you know, when a current flows through a wire, a magnetic force field is built up around the conductor. As there are several hundred turns of wire in the primary windings, a rather strong magnetic field is produced. This magnetic field surrounds the secondary as well as the primary windings. See Fig. 3-8.

Fig. 3-7. Primary current flows through primary coil winding when points are closed.

Fig. 3-8. Magnetic field is built up around coil primary when current is flowing.

COLLAPSE OF THE FIELD

If there is a quick and clean interruption of current flow on its way to the ground after passing through the coil, the magnetic field will collapse and pass quickly to the laminated iron core.

As you have learned, whenever a wire is passed through a magnetic force field, a current will be induced (set up) in the wire. By the same token, if the wire is held still and the magnetic field is passed around it, a current will still be induced in the wire. This is what happens when the magnetic field collapses and passes through the secondary windings on

the way to the core. Fig. 3-9.

The magnetic field that passes through the secondary windings produces a tiny current in each turn. The windings possess thousands of turns, however, and as they are in series (connected together, positive to negative), the voltage of each turn of wire is multiplied by the number of turns. In the average coil, this will produce a voltage exceeding 30,000V.

As the field also passes through the primary turns, a voltage will be induced in the primary circuit also. As the turns are far less numerous, the voltage multiplication will be considerably less, somewhat over 200V.

The high voltage produced by the secondary windings is made available to the plugs at the high tension coil terminal.

Fig. 3-9. Collapse of primary field. When primary circuit is broken, magnetic field will collapse through secondary winding to core. See arrows.

POLARITY IS IMPORTANT

Most coils have primary terminals marked with (+) or (−). The plus sign indicates positive, and the minus indicates negative. The coil must be installed in the primary circuit according to the way the battery is grounded. If the battery has the negative terminal grounded, the negative terminal of the coil must be connected to the ground, or distributor side. If the battery positive terminal is grounded, the positive side of the coil must be connected to the distributor lead.

This is done to insure the correct polarity at the spark plug. The flow of electrons (current) is made easier if they flow from a hot surface to a cooler one. As the center electrode of the plug is always the hotter of the two, a negative polarity at the plug inner electrode will insure a flow of current from the center electrode. This will require less voltage and will lighten the load of the coil. Current practice grounds the NEGATIVE battery terminal.

The coil will build up enough voltage to cause a flow of current across the electrode gap. Even though a coil voltage can exceed 30,000V, it will only build up voltage high enough to produce an adequate spark. This will generally run between 2,000 and 10,000V, Fig. 3-10.

PRIMARY CURRENT FLOW MUST BE INTERRUPTED!

For efficient coil operation, the current flow through the primary windings must be interrupted (broken) instantly and cleanly with NO flashover (current jumps or arcs across space) at the point of disconnection.

METHODS OF CURRENT INTERRUPTION

Primary current flow can be interrupted in one of three basic ways: 1. By using a set of BREAKER POINTS to break current flow thus collapsing the coil primary field. 2. By using a set of breaker points in conjunction with a transistor switch. 3. By using a FULLY TRANSISTORIZED SWITCHING UNIT in which the mechanical breaker points are completely eliminated.

Current practice, in most all instances, favors the use of the transistorized method of primary circuit control. This method will be covered after discussing the breaker point technique. Millions upon millions of cars still on the road employ breaker points.

Remember, the only basic difference between the old, conventional breaker point ignition and the newer transistorized systems is the method employed to interrupt the coil primary circuit.

BREAKER POINT PRIMARY CIRCUIT CONTROL

Generally, breaker points are constructed as two separate pieces. Fig. 3-11. The stationary piece is fastened directly to the ground through the distributor breaker plate. This section does not move other than for an initial point adjustment.

The second piece is the movable breaker point. It is pivoted on a steel post. A fiber bushing is used as a bearing on the pivot post. A thin steel spring (flat type) is used to press the movable breaker arm against the stationary unit, thereby causing the two contact points to bear firmly together.

The movable arm is pushed outward by a cam lobe. The cam lobe is turned at one-half engine rpm by the distributor shaft. The distributor shaft is turned by means of a gear that is meshed with an integral gear cut on the camshaft.

The breaker arm contacts the cam by means of a fiber rubbing block. This block is fastened to the breaker arm and rubs against the cam. A special high temperature lubricant is used on the block to prevent undue wear.

The movable breaker arm is insulated so that when

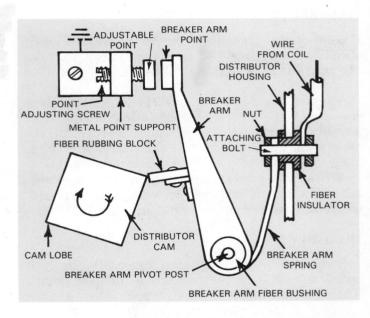

Fig. 3-10. Correct polarity is important. When NEGATIVE POLARITY is used, voltage necessary to fire plug diminishes. This makes task of coil easier.

Fig. 3-11. Typical breaker point construction. Most, however, incorporate the adjustable point into an adjustable support base. Average point gap specifications run around .018 to .022 in. (0.457 to 0.559 mm).

the primary lead from the coil is attached to it, the primary circuit will not be grounded unless the contact points are touching. Fig. 3-11.

CONTACT POINTS MUST FIT

The breaker contact points must be carefully aligned so that the two points make perfect contact. They must be clean and free of oil, and open an exact amount. Each system, as developed by the manufacturer, must be held to specifications. If the point opening (gap) is specified as .020 in. (0.508 mm) it must be set to that amount. A variation in gap will upset the cam angle and ignition timing.

SPECIAL METAL

Contact points are made of tungsten steel. Tungsten is resistant to burning and will give good service.

The movable breaker arm must be rigid enough to hold the contact point in line. At the same time, it must be light enough to function at high speeds without undue spring pressure that would cause premature wear of the rubbing block. Too light a spring pressure, or too heavy a breaker arm, would cause the arm to float at high speeds. (Float is when the breaker arm is pushed out as the cam strikes the rubbing block; and before the arm can return after the cam has passed, the next cam strikes the block and reopens it. In other words, the breaker arm never has time to fully close before being opened again.)

Fig. 3-12 illustrates a typical breaker arm, or as it is sometimes called, a breaker lever.

CAM ANGLE

Cam angle, sometimes referred to as degrees of dwell, is the number of degrees the cam rotates from the time the points close until they open again. See Fig. 3-13.

The cam angle is important. The longer the points are closed, the greater the magnetic buildup of the primary windings. If the cam angle is too small, the points will open and collapse the field before it has built up enough to produce a satisfactory spark.

When setting breaker point gaps, remember that when the gap is lessened, cam angle is increased. When the gap is enlarged, cam angle is decreased.

DUAL POINTS

Some distributors, designed especially for high speed operation, utilize two sets of breaker points. The points are mounted opposite each other, and are designed so that when one contact set is snapped open, the other closes. Fig. 3-14.

In the single point setup, the points are held open as the rubbing block passes up on the toe of the cam, across the top and down the heel of the cam. This represents a considerable number of degrees of cam rotation. The longer the points are open, the less the cam angle can be.

The dual point set cuts down the open time to which the circuit is exposed. As the cam angle is increased, the engine can operate at much higher speeds and still produce a satisfactory spark.

POINTS WILL BURN

If you were to set up the ignition system as discussed so far, you would find that each time the points opened, there would be a heavy electrical arc across the points. Unless the points break the primary circuit quickly and cleanly, the magnetic collapse of

Fig. 3-12. One type of breaker arm design. Another design uses a flexible arm that does not pivot on a post.   (Toyota)

Fig. 3-13. Cam angle. Points close at 1 and remain closed as cam rotates to 2. The number of degrees formed by this angle determines cam angle.

Fig. 3-14. Dual points. Rubbing block 3 is being contacted by cam lobe to open points at 2. Points 1 have just closed as rubbing block 4 comes off cam lobe.

the primary windings will be poor and a satisfactory voltage will not be produced in the secondary windings.

In addition to insufficient voltage, the points would soon burn beyond use. There is a tendency for a moving stream of electrons (current) to keep moving when the circuit is broken. When the contact points start to open, the magnetic field starts to collapse. This will induce extra voltage into the primary circuit.

Between the reluctance of the moving current to stop, and the added surge of induced voltage in the primary circuit, the circuit will not be broken cleanly, and a heavy spark will leap across the point opening. As mentioned, this will prevent the ignition system from functioning properly. Fig. 3-15.

Fig. 3-15. Arcing at points. Notice how current leaps gap and burns contact face.

CONDENSER

When a condenser of proper size is inserted into the primary circuit, heavy arcing at the points will stop, and secondary voltage will reach satisfactory limits. This is accomplished by breaking the primary circuit cleanly. The condenser provides a place into which the primary current may flow when the points are opened.

CONDENSER CONSTRUCTION

Most condensers are constructed of two sheets of very thin foil separated by two or three layers of insulation. The foil may be lead or aluminum. The long narrow sheets of foil, separated by the insulation, are wound together into a cylindrical shape.

The cylinder is then placed in a small metal can or case. The cap, with condenser lead attached, is put on and the edges of the case pulled down, forcing the cap and seal into tight contact with the case. A spring is sometimes used at the bottom of the case to constantly push the condenser foil cylinder against the cap. This increases the seal pressure, eliminates vibration and series resistance caused by corrosion or vibration. The condenser is hermetically sealed to prevent the entrance of moisture.

Condensers will vary in size according to the rated capacities and if standard or heavy duty. An average capacity is around .20 microfarads (capacity measurement). Fig. 3-16 illustrates the construction of the typical condenser.

HOW A CONDENSER WORKS

A, Fig. 3-17, shows how a condenser is installed in the circuit. The primary circuit flows through the points to the ground and back to the battery. The primary field (magnetic force field) is strong.

In B, Fig. 3-17, the points have started to open.

Fig. 3-16. Condenser construction. Unit is hermatically sealed in a metal case. Note how condenser is attached in distributor. (Delco, Deere & Co.)

The primary field has started to collapse, but no current flows across the points. It has flowed into the condenser. The condenser cannot hold much of a charge but, by the time it has become fully charged, the points have opened too far for the current to jump. The primary field collapse will be strong and quick.

Latest theory is that at the instant the spark at the plug is formed, the condenser (because of its charge) will discharge back into the primary. It does this because its charge, due to the high induced voltage in the primary, is higher than the primary after field collapse is complete. See C, Fig. 3-17.

Each time the condenser discharges back into the primary windings, it produces another field in the opposite direction and collapses the one just built by its first discharge. The bouncing back and forth is termed oscillatory discharge. It will continue, weaker each time, until completely worn out, or stopped by the closing of the contact points. See D, Fig. 3-17.

PRIMARY CIRCUIT COMPLETE

You have now traced the flow of current through the primary system. After going on to the ground, it returns to the battery through the metal parts of the car to which the battery is grounded.

Be sure you understand how each unit works and its relationship to the other parts.

TRANSISTOR PRIMARY CIRCUIT CONTROL

As you learned, in the ignition system PRIMARY circuit the flow of current was controlled by breaker points. The development of the TRANSISTOR has made it possible to make or break the primary circuit WITHOUT using any type of mechanical points. The

Fig. 3-17. Oscillatory discharge. A—Steady straight current flow through coil primary, points closed. B—As points open, induced voltage causes current in primary to flow into condenser, creating a voltage difference between insulated foil sheets. C—High charge on insulated foil sheet forces current back through coil primary, sustaining ignition spark. Drained insulated foil sheets then have lower voltage charge than adjacent grounded sheets, current flow again reverses until all coil energy is used up. D—Oscillatory discharge.   (Delco-Remy)

TRANSISTOR ignition system thus offers several distinct advantages. Transistor systems will be covered thoroughly very shortly but first, the ignition system SECONDARY CIRCUIT will be discussed. This will provide a clear picture of the overall system and will aid in your understanding of the transistor.

SECONDARY CIRCUIT

You have seen how the coil produces a high voltage in the secondary circuit. The current flows from the coil to the spark plug. (How it is timed and distributed will be covered shortly.) The current jumps from the center electrode of the plug to the side, or ground, electrode. When it jumps across, it produces a hot spark that ignites the air-fuel mixture.

SPARK PLUG

A spark plug is made up of three major parts: the electrodes, insulator and shell. Fig. 3-18.

Electrodes of a spark plug must be constructed of material that will be resistant to heat, oxidization, and burning. A typical material is nickel alloy. Platinum, although expensive, is sometimes used. It makes top quality electrode material.

In an ordinary spark plug there are two electrodes, the center electrode and the side electrode. The space between the two is called the plug GAP. The gap varies from .030 to .060 in. (0.762 to 1.524 mm) for most cars.

The center electrode is usually negative to assist the flow of electrons. The electrons will then leave the hotter center electrode and pass to the side electrode. Air is more easily ionized (broken down from a nonconductor to a conductor) near the hotter center electrode.

The center electrode is insulated from the rest of the plug by a ceramic insulator. The top terminates in a snap-on terminal to which the plug wire may be attached. Fig. 3-18.

Fig. 3-18. Typical spark plug.
(Prestolite Co.)

SPARK PLUG INSULATORS

Insulators must have special properties. They must resist heat, cold, and sudden temperature changes. Vibration and physical shock must leave them undamaged, and they must resist chemical corrosion.

A common material used for making spark plug insulators is aluminum oxide, fired at high temperature. This produces a glassy smooth, dense, and very hard insulator. The length, diameter, and location of the insulator has a direct bearing on the heat range of the particular plug. This is covered under Plug Heat Range characteristics.

The top end of the insulator is often ribbed, or grooved, to prevent shorting. (Termed flashover.) Fig. 3-18.

SPARK PLUG SHELLS

The center electrode, surrounded by the insulator, is placed in a steel shell. The steel shell top is generally crimped over to bear against a seal. The crimping process grips the insulator tightly and also forms a seal pressure at both top and bottom insulator seals. This prevents combustion leaks.

The side electrode is welded to the steel shell.

The shell is threaded so it will screw into a threaded hole in the cylinder head. The shell threaded area will vary in length according to hole depths and ignition recommendations.

The shell forms a seal with the head by means of

a copper gasket or a beveled edge that wedges against a similar bevel in the cylinder head. Fig. 3-19.

The thread seal is important since this is an area through which a great deal of the plug heat is transferred to the head metal. The insulator is subjected to tremendous temperatures. In order to prevent burning, it must get rid of surplus heat.

Fig. 3-19. Thread seals.

SPARK PLUG HEAT RANGE

Spark plugs are designed for various types of engines. It is important that the plug extend into the combustion chamber just the right amount.

The heat range is determined by the diameter and length of the insulator as measured from the sealing ring down to the tip. Fig. 3-20.

Notice, in Fig. 3-20, that the heat generated in the insulator must travel up the insulator until it can escape through the seal, to the shell, and then to the head. The longer and thinner the insulator tip, the less efficiently it can transfer heat. As a result it will run hotter (hot plug). The short, heavy insulator carries heat well and will operate much cooler (cold plug).

SHORT, HEAVY INSULATOR TIP CONDUCTS HEAT UP TIP, THROUGH SEAL, INTO SHELL, THROUGH GASKET INTO HEAD AND WATER JACKET. PLUG RUNS COLD.

LONG, THIN INSULATOR TIP IS A POOR CONDUCTOR. HEAT MUST TRAVEL FURTHER TO ESCAPE. PLUG RUNS HOT.

Fig. 3-20. Spark plug heat range.   (Ignition Mfgs. Institute)

All engine manufacturers specify heat ranges for the plugs to be used in their engines.

PROJECTED CORE NOSE

One spark plug design extends the insulator beyond the end of the shell, thus placing the electrode tip and insulator, further down into the combustion chamber. This lengthening, termed Projected Core Nose, places the insulator more directly in the path of the incoming fuel charge. As the intake stroke draws in fresh fuel, it passes over and around the plug insulator. This will cool it down. Its shape is not usually adaptable to L-head engines since there is insufficient room for piston clearance.

The projected core nose, due to its long tip, tends to run hot at low engine speeds because the tip cannot transfer the heat fast enough. The incoming fuel charge is moving slowly and provides little cooling effect. This prevents slow speed fouling and assists in producing a spark without excessive voltage from the coil.

At high engine speeds, the insulator temperature is kept from exceeding acceptable limits by the rapid flow of the incoming fuel charges. The washing effect of the hot escaping exhaust tends to keep the plug clean. Fig. 3-21.

Fig. 3-21. Projected core nose plug.

PREIGNITION

If a plug runs too cold, it will foul. If it runs too hot (much above 1,700°F or 967°C), it will cause PRE-IGNITION (igniting the fuel charge from red-hot deposits before the plug fires). The projected core nose will perform satisfactorily within acceptable temperature limits over a wider car speed range. See Fig. 3-22.

RESISTOR SPARK PLUG

The spark at the plug electrodes is delivered in two stages. The first part is called the CAPACITIVE por-

tion; the second, the longest portion, the INDUCTIVE.

The voltage at the plug center electrode will rise rapidly until the voltage is sufficient to ionize the gap and cause the plug to fire. The first firing is the capacitive part. The voltage at the plug produces the capacitive portion.

The inductive portion is longer and follows the capacitive. It is produced by the remaining voltage in the system (coil residual and oscillatory action of the condenser).

The combustion process takes place during the capacitive section. The inductive portion causes radio interference and is hard on electrodes. The inductive part, therefore, is undesirable and attempts have been made to shorten it.

By placing a resistor (around 10,000 ohms) in the ceramic insulator, it is possible to shorten both the capacitive and inductive phases. It does not require any higher voltage and will lengthen electrode life as well as suppress radio interference. A resistor plug is shown in Fig. 3-23.

Fig. 3-24 illustrates the difference between the spark produced by a standard plug and a resistor type plug. Notice that no more voltage is required for the resistor plug. Late model cars use special resistance spark plug wires to cut down radio interference.

AUXILIARY GAP

Another feature of some spark plugs is the use of a small gap between the center electrode top and its terminal. This is designed to build up higher voltage and to reduce misfiring of dirty plugs. The terminal post is ventilated to allow ozone (produced by sparking at auxiliary gap) to escape. Fig. 3-25.

You have seen how the necessary voltage is produced. How this voltage is delivered to each plug at the proper time will now be covered.

DISTRIBUTOR CAP

High voltage from the coil is carried by an insulated wire, or brush, to the center terminal of the distributor

Fig. 3-22. Speed range performance graph.

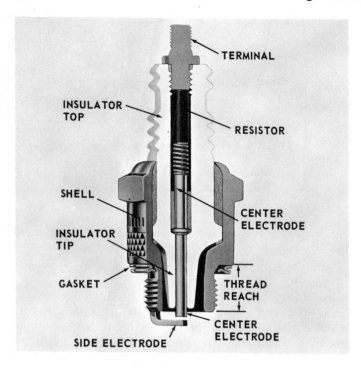

Fig. 3-23. A resistor spark plug. (Champion)

Fig. 3-24. Spark discharge graph. Notice how resistor plug reduces undesirable inductive portion of spark.

Fig. 3-25. Spark plug with an auxiliary gap.

Fig. 3-26. A distributor cap for a six cylinder engine. (G.M.C.)

cap. Additional terminals, one per cylinder, will be arranged in a circle around the center terminal. Each one of these will have a heavily insulated wire connecting it with a spark plug.

The distributor cap is made of a plastic material, sometimes mica filled to reduce flashover tendency. Material used must provide excellent insulation. See Fig. 3-26.

On the inside of the cup-like cap, the plug terminals have brass lugs extending down past the cap material. The center, or coil terminal, has a round ball, Fig. 3-28, or a carbon rod extending down. Note the fixed carbon rod used in Fig. 3-27.

ROTOR

To carry the secondary voltage from the center terminal to any one side terminal requires what is known as a ROTOR. This rotor is attached to the top of the distributor shaft. Its outer edge has a brass terminal that passes, as it turns, very close to the side terminals. This outer edge terminal is connected to a spring that rubs against the center coil terminal carbon post. When the current from the coil arrives at the center terminal, it travels down the carbon rod, through the spring, and out to the rotor outer edge terminal. From this point, it jumps the small gap between the rotor and side terminal and goes on to the plug. Fig. 3-28. Rotor is made of non-conductive material.

The cap, and whirling rotor, distributes the spark to each plug at the proper time. It is essential that the plug wires be arranged in the proper sequence. The firing order (order in which pistons reach TDC on the compression stroke) in a typical six cylinder engine is 1, 5, 3, 6, 2, 4.

Fig. 3-27. Distributor cap—section view.

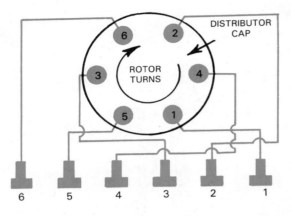

Fig. 3-29. Firing order—six cylinder engine: 1, 5, 3, 6, 2, 4. Notice how plug wires are arranged in distributor cap to produce this firing order.

The plug wires are arranged in distributor cap in that order. Direction of rotation of the rotor dictates whether a clockwise or counterclockwise order is required. Fig. 3-29.

TIMING

For correct ignition timing, each cylinder should receive a spark at the plug electrodes as the piston nears the top (few degrees before TDC) of its compression stroke. This is made possible by the proper hookup of the distributor shaft to the camshaft, which turns at one-half crankshaft speed.

The distributor shaft gear is meshed with the camshaft gear so that the breaker points are just opening when number one cylinder is ready to fire. The rotor will then point toward the number one cap plug terminal. Number one cylinder plug wire is attached to this terminal. Following the firing order, and with due regard to shaft rotation, the remaining wires are

attached to the cap.

As the engine turns, the distributor shaft will revolve and cause the distributor cam lobes to open the points and collapse the primary field. The lobes are spaced equidistantly. Each time the distributor shaft has turned enough to cause the rotor to point to the next plug terminal, the cam lobe will once again break the points. This causes a secondary voltage surge from the coil to the cap center terminal, into the rotor and to the cap plug terminal. This cycle is repeated over and over.

The engine manufacturer specifies specific timing in regard to the number of degrees before TDC number one cylinder should fire. All other cylinders will fire at the same number of degrees before TDC.

SETTING BASIC TIMING

Most engines have the timing location, in the form of a line, dent, etc., marked on the rim of the vibration damper. A pointer is attached to the timing

1. CURRENT FROM COIL ENTERS CENTER TERMINAL

2. PASSES TO SPRING

3. TRAVELS THROUGH SPRING TO ROTOR TERMINAL

6. PASSES INTO PLUG WIRE AND TRAVELS TO SPARK PLUG

CAP

5. LEAPS GAP FROM ROTOR TERMINAL TO SIDE TERMINAL

ROTOR

4. PASSES THROUGH FLAT ROTOR TERMINAL

DISTRIBUTOR CAP

DISTRIBUTOR SHAFT

Fig. 3-28. Distributor cap and rotor. Rotor transfers current from center terminal to outer terminal. (Oldsmobile) cover. When the mark is exactly under the pointer, the engine is ready to fire number one cylinder. The points should just break with the rotor pointing to the number one cap terminal. Fig. 3-30. Some engines have the timing mark on the flywheel.

The timing is generally set by using a strobe lamp (a light that is operated by high voltage surges from the spark plug wire). Fig. 3-31.

After the contact point gap is accurately set, the strobe lamp is connected to the number one (or other as may be specified) plug wire. The engine is started and idled quite slowly. Usually, the vacuum line to the distributor is removed.

The strobe lamp is set to illuminate the pointer over the vibration damper. Every time number one plug fires, the strobe lamp lights. Each time it fires with the damper in the same position in relation to the pointer, the damper timing mark looks as though it were standing still.

To adjust the timing, the distributor hold-down clamp is loosened and the distributor is turned, by hand, one way or the other. As it is turned, the timing mark will move. When turned in the proper direction, the mark will line up with the pointer. When the two are aligned, the distributor hold-down is tightened and the engine is properly timed.

TIMING NEEDS VARY

As engine speed increases, it is necessary to fire the mixture somewhat sooner. If this is not done, the piston would reach TDC and start down before the air-fuel mixture can be properly ignited.

Fig. 3-31. Using a strobe light to time ignition. Every time No. 1 plug fires, strobe light will illuminate timing marks. (Sun Electric)

The pressure of the burning fuel charge should reach its peak with the piston somewhere between 15 and 25 deg. past TDC. With the engine at slow idle, very little advance is necessary. At the higher engine speeds, it is necessary to fire the mixture somewhat sooner. Notice in A, Fig. 3-32, that the combustion cycle must start at 18 deg. before TDC in order to be complete by 23 deg. after TDC. In B, Fig. 3-32, engine speed has tripled. It is now necessary to ignite the charge 40 deg. before TDC in order to complete combustion by 23 deg. after TDC.

From this you can see that it is necessary to have some way of advancing (firing more degrees before TDC) the timing as the engine speed increases. It is also necessary to retard the timing at certain times in order to help control exhaust emissions.

Fig. 3-30. Ignition timing marks. Note degrees are marked before and after top dead center. This setup also incorporates a magnetic timing probe receptacle. (Chrysler)

Fig. 3-32. When engine speed increases, spark must be timed sooner. Notice in A that only 41 deg. of crankshaft travel is required while in B, at 3,600 rpm, 63 deg. are necessary. (Ford)

CENTRIFUGAL ADVANCE

One method of advancing the timing is through the use of a centrifugal advance mechanism which is assembled in the distributor housing. Figs. 3-33 and 3-34. When the distributor shaft turns, it turns the centrifugal unit and the centrifugal unit turns the cam.

When the engine is idling, spring pressure keeps the two weights drawn together and the shaft and cam assume the position for low speed timing.

As the engine speeds up, the weights are drawn out by centrifugal force. As the weights move apart, they force the cam to move, in an advance direction, in relation to the shaft. As the cam is advanced, the lobes strike the rubbing block sooner, causing the plugs to fire more degrees before TDC. The faster the engine turns, the farther apart the weights move, until they finally reach the limit of their travel.

As speed is decreased, the centrifugal pull on the weights is lessened and the springs pull the weights together, retarding the timing. By calculating the pull of the springs and the size of the weights, it is possible to properly advance the timing over a long rpm range. Fig. 3-34 illustrates how the weights control advance.

VACUUM ADVANCE

It has been found that at part throttle position, additional advance over and above that provided by a centrifugal mechanism, is desirable.

This is due to the fact that during part throttle (carburetor throttle valve part way open) operation, there is high vacuum in the intake manifold (pipes connecting the carburetor to the valve port openings in the head, or block). This high vacuum draws in a lesser amount of air-fuel mixture. The smaller amount will be compressed less and will burn slower.

To get the utmost economy from this part of the fuel charge, it is necessary to advance the timing beyond that provided by centrifugal weights. Any benefit from additional advance applies only to the part throttle position. During acceleration or full

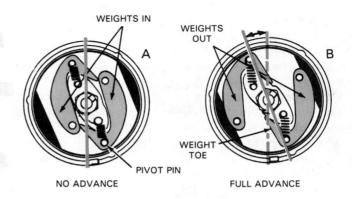

Fig. 3-34. Centrifugal advance unit action. In A, the engine is idling. Springs draw weights in. Timing has no advance. In B, engine is running at high speed. Centrifugal force has drawn weights outward. As they pivot, the weight toe ends force the cam plate to turn thus advancing the timing.

throttle operation, no vacuum advance is provided. Fig. 3-35.

HOW VACUUM ADVANCE MECHANISM WORKS

Vacuum advance may be accomplished in two ways. One method is to rotate the entire distributor housing against the direction of rotation of the distributor shaft. The breaker point rubbing block will then strike the oncoming cam sooner, advancing the spark timing.

Current practice mounts the breaker points on a movable breaker plate. This plate can revolve either on a center bushing, or on ball bearings on its outer edge. The hardened steel balls roll in a groove cut into the distributor housing.

With either type of plate, an advance in timing may be obtained by turning the plate against distributor shaft rotation. Fig. 3-36.

VACUUM ADVANCE DIAPHRAGM

The breaker plate is rotated by means of a vacuum advance diaphragm. This is a stamped steel container with a neoprene-coated cloth diaphragm stretched across the center. One end, airtight, is connected to the carburetor slightly above the closed position of the throttle valve. The other end is open to the at-

Fig. 3-33. Two different types of centrifugal advance mechanism. (Automotive Electric Association)

Fig. 3-35. Vacuum advance chart. Notice that part throttle vacuum advance is in addition to regular centrifugal advance.

mosphere. The diaphragm has a lever rod attached to its center. The lever rod is connected to either the distributor housing, or to the breaker plate, depending on which type is used. See Figs. 3-37, 3-38, 3-39, and 3-40.

When throttle valve is in part throttle position, as shown in A, Fig. 3-37, there is high vacuum in the intake manifold. The vacuum pulls the diaphragm back toward the vacuum side. This in turn pulls the breaker plate around and advances the timing.

When the throttle is opened, the vacuum drops and the breaker spring draws the diaphragm back toward the distributor. This rotates the breaker plate in the retard direction. When the engine is idling, the throttle valve closes below the vacuum advance opening.

Fig. 3-36. Breaker plate action. In A, points are closed. When breaker plate is turned, as in B, the rubbing block will strike cam sooner and open the points, causing spark to be advanced. Notice that cam is in the same position in both A and B.

Fig. 3-38. Distributor with cap and rotor removed. (GMC)

Fig. 3-37. Vacuum advance mechanism. In A, the carburetor throttle valve is in part throttle position, thus drawing a heavy vacuum. With a vacuum on the left side, atmospheric pressure forces the diaphragm to the left. Diaphragm link will pull cam breaker plate around and advance timing. When throttle is opened and vacuum is lowered, B, the breaker plate primary spring will pull the breaker plate back and retard the timing. The vacuum spring also controls the limits of advance. (Ford)

Fig. 3-39 Cutaway showing distributor head and vacuum advance construction.

Fig. 3-40. Distributor vacuum advance unit utilizes engine vacuum to move distributor breaker plate. (Buick)

This removes vacuum pull, and the spark will be retarded for idling. The vacuum advance mechanism is constantly working as the throttle valve position is changed.

A dual vacuum advance mechanism is pictured in Fig. 3-41. It utilizes two different vacuum sources (carburetor venturi and intake manifold) to provide a greater range of advance-retard control.

ELECTRONIC (TRANSISTOR) IGNITION SYSTEM

A very important development in ignition systems makes use of a solid state electronic switching device called a TRANSISTOR. A transistor is a low voltage unit with a current carrying capacity superior to conventional ignition breaker points and is in almost universal use today.

By making and breaking the PRIMARY circuit with a transistor instead of distributor breaker points, it is possible to increase primary current flow and thus produce higher available voltage at the coil.

Changes in DWELL, TIMING, POINT GAP, and CURRENT FLOW that took place as breaker points wore and oxidized, are eliminated by the fully transistorized system. This makes possible a hotter spark, wider plug electrode gaps, stable ignition timing, etc., that help to increase fuel efficiency, emission control, and operating dependability.

Fig. 3-41. Dual vacuum advance unit. A—Full advance. B—Full retard. C—Unit at rest. (Ford)

TRANSISTOR CONSTRUCTION

The transistor, Fig. 3-42, actually is of fairly thin, wafer design. The thickness of the parts shown is exaggerated for clarity. The transistor is made up of two outer layers of POSITIVE (P) materials with a center section of NEGATIVE (N) material. The three are fused together. Think of the transistor as two DIODES sandwiched around a common base material.

The method of combining the two materials determines the polarity of the transistor. The one shown in 1, Fig. 3-42, would be a PNP type. Detail 3 shows the conventional wiring symbol and detail 2 illustrates how the transistor connections are made.

TRANSISTOR OPERATION

By connecting wires to the transistor, as shown in Fig. 3-43, we find that when a battery is placed in the circuit, current will flow through the transistor in TWO ways. A small BASE current (.5 amp.) will pass through BASE CIRCUIT E-B.

When the base current is flowing, the transistor will pass a much heavier COLLECTOR CURRENT (5 amps.) through the COLLECTOR CIRCUIT C-E. When the base circuit E-B is broken, collector current instantly stops. This makes the transistor an excellent switch for making and breaking the ignition system primary circuit. Study Fig. 3-43.

In the conventional breaker point ignition system, the breaker contact points must carry current that has passed through the ignition coil. In order for the coil to function properly, it must carry a fairly heavy current (4 to 5 amps., based on engine RPM). This places a comparable load on the points. When they open and break the coil circuit, there is some arcing despite the condenser. Eventually this causes the points to erode, pit and burn, which gives them a limited service life.

The transistor on the other hand, offers a method

of making and breaking the full current—with only a light load on the points. This lowers point current load and gives them an extended life.

BREAKER CONTROLLED TRANSISTOR IGNITION

When the transistor was first utilized in the ignition system it was triggered (operated) by conventional breaker points much as shown in Fig. 3-43.

The system, shown in Fig. 3-43, is incomplete and will not function properly. Through the addition of HEAT SINK (AMPLIFIER HOUSING), RESISTORS, ZENER DIODE, CONDENSER, etc., a workable system is produced.

A wiring diagram of an early CONTACT CONTROLLED TRANSISTOR IGNITION SYSTEM IS SHOWN IN Fig. 3-44. Note the addition of the parts just named. The term CONTACT CONTROLLED means that the conventional type breaker points are used to make and break the BASE circuit to trigger the transistor COLLECTOR circuit.

STILL SOME PROBLEMS

While a big improvement over the conventional system, the breaker contact controlled transistor system still left room for improvement. Even though much less current flow through the points prolonged their life, they were highly susceptible to the slightest film of oil or dampness. The low current reduced the burning but at the same time lost some of the ability to flow across dirty contact points. The breaker point rubbing block would still wear down thus altering both DWELL and TIMING. This problem was solved

Fig. 3-43. Transistor as a switch. Just before points opened, a .5 amp. current was passing from bat. neg. terminal through points to transistor B connection. From there it passed to E connection and on to bat. pos. terminal. This caused a heavier 5 amp. current to flow from bat. neg. post through switch, through coil on to transistor C connection.

Flow continued from C through transistor to E connection to bat. pos. terminal, energizing the coil. When points opened and broke B—E circuit, C—E flow also stopped, collapsing coil magnet field. High voltage was induced in coil secondary windings to fire the plug.

Fig. 3-42. 1—PNP transistor. 2—Transistor connections. 3—Wiring symbol for a transistor. B—Base. E—Emitter. C—Collector. (Delco-Remy)

Fig. 3-44. Ford contact controlled transistor ignition system. Point circuit (double-head arrows) join coil circuit (single-head arrows) at E.   (Ford)

by completely eliminating the breaker points and by triggering the transistor with a magnetic impulse sensor, (also termed magnetic pickup, signal generator, pickup, etc.) located in the distributor. These sensing units can be of two basic designs; the permanent magnet-magnetic pickup (sensor) or the oscillator excited sensor.

PICKUP COIL

The schematic in Fig. 3-45 depicts a typical pickup coil (oscillator excited sensor). Note the sensor or pickup coil inside the distributor. When the ignition circuit is ON, an oscillator circuit (electronic circuit that causes the current to periodically reverse or

Fig. 3-45. Transistor ignition system using an oscillator excited sensor. Study circuit connections. Note that no rotor or reluctor teeth are aligned with sensor. Current is now flowing through system primary circuit.
(Deere & Co.)

oscillate) in the control unit excites (sends current through) the sensor wire coil thus developing an electromagnetic field around the sensor.

A reluctor (also called "trigger wheel") is attached (much like the breaker cam on a regular distributor) to the distributor shaft. The reluctor has one "tooth" for each cylinder. Each tooth is designed to pass very close to the sensor as the reluctor rotates. This distance between the tooth end and the sensor is termed "air gap." Study Fig. 3-45. Note that the sensor has been excited and a magnetic field is built up around it. Current is also flowing through the ignition coil. Follow the complete circuit.

As the distributor shaft turns, it revolves the metal reluctor. When the reluctor tooth approaches the sensor magnetic field, the strength of the field is altered. This triggers a demodulator circuit that in turn triggers a control unit power switch transistor thus breaking the coil primary circuit. Study Fig. 3-46. Note that the reluctor tooth has entered the sensor field. Ignition coil primary current is broken causing the coil primary magnetic field to collapse and induce a high voltage surge in the secondary system, Fig. 3-46.

PERMANENT MAGNET SENSOR

A permanent magnet sensor, one of the most common types used in modern ignition systems, utilizes a permanent magnet, a metal sensor rotor (armature, reluctor, etc.), and a pickup coil of very fine wire. These parts are all placed inside the distributor hous-

ing. Fig. 3-47 illustrates a setup as used by one maker.

An exploded view of a similar permanent magnet sensor is shown in Fig. 3-48.

The sensor and its relationship to the basic ignition circuit is pictured in Fig. 3-49. Note how sensor rotor tooth passes across face of the pickup coil.

Fig. 3-47. Transistor ignition system distributor utilizing a permanent magnet type sensor.   (Plymouth)

Fig. 3-46. Transistor ignition system using an oscillator excited sensor. Note that a reluctor tooth has aligned with sensor thus altering field strength. This causes transistor (in control unit) to break primary circuit collapsing coil magnetic field and inducing high voltage in secondary to fire plug.   (Deere & Co.)

71

Fig. 3-48. Exploded view of a distributor employing a permanent magnet sensor to activate or ''trigger'' switching transistor. (Toyota)

SENSOR OPERATION

The permanent magnet sets up a magnetic field around the pickup coil. This magnetic field is sensitive to and increased by the ferrous metal (iron) sensor rotor teeth as they rotate past the pickup coil. When the rotor tooth is exactly in line with the pickup coil (as shown in Fig. 3-49) the magentic field will be at its strongest. As the tooth rotates past the coil, the magnetic field suffers a sharp reduction in strength. This increase followed by the sharp reduction, induces an alternating current into the pickup coil windings. This alternating current triggers the control unit causing the transistor to switch the primary current ON and OFF in a direct relationship to the position of the rotor teeth to the pickup coil. Each tooth not only triggers the transistor but also "times" the occurrence of the spark. System operation is the same as that depicted in Figs. 3-45 and 3-46.

In that the rotor teeth never actually touch anything, there is no wear as with regular breaker points. Dwell (electronically controlled in transistor ignition) and timing remain constant.

''DWELL'' IN THE TRANSISTOR IGNITION SYSTEM

Dwell angle (degrees of distributor shaft rotation from the time the primary circuit is closed until it is opened) is electronically controlled in the transistor ignition system. A control unit electronic timer is actuated when the transistor is triggered to OPEN (break) the circuit. The timer is designed to provide only a sufficient length of time for the coil primary field to fully collapse. The timer then CLOSES (reconnects) the primary circuit. Dwell, in this case, can be measured in TIME—from the instant the circuit was closed to the instant of opening.

TYPICAL TRANSISTOR IGNITION SYSTEMS

We will very briefly examine several transistor ignition systems as employed by various auto makers.

Fig. 3-49. Schematic of transistor ignition system. Study the circuits. Note use of a permanent magnet sensor. (Toyota)

Study illustrations shown. Note that in principle, they are all quite similar and vary mostly in layout and sensor design. The system as developed by one maker is fully integrated. It combines basic system into one compact distributor setup. It is called H.E.I. system.

GENERAL MOTORS H.E.I. SYSTEM

The HIGH ENERGY IGNITION (H.E.I.) system combines the coil, sensor, control unit (module), rotor, cap, vacuum and centrifugal advance, etc., all into the distributor. Fig. 3-50 shows an exploded view of a typical H.E.I. system. Can you find all the parts?

The H.E.I. system magnetic impulse pickup sensor contains a pickup coil, permanent magnet, and a pole piece with internal teeth. The timer core (trigger wheel), Fig. 3-50, is mounted on the distributor shaft and rotates inside the pole piece. Whenever the external teeth of the timer core line up with the teeth of the pole piece, a voltage is induced in the pickup coil. This voltage triggers the control unit (module) and the transistor opens the primary circuit causing a voltage surge in the ignition coil secondary system. Study the sensor parts shown in Fig. 3-51. The capacitor (condenser) is for radio noise suppression only and plays no part in the ignition system development.

The H.E.I. control module contains a very complex electronic circuit. Many parts are so tiny that they must be viewed with a magnifying glass. The module also provides an automatic dwell period that is increased as engine rpm climbs.

Fig. 3-51. H.E.I. system magnetic impulse sensor parts. Note that control module (small but highly complex) is also contained in distributor. (General Motors)

H.E.I. SYSTEM ELECTRONIC SPARK TIMING (EST) CONTROL

One version of the H.E.I. system incorporates a module that in conjunction with a digital computer also controls spark timing and dwell.

This distributor setup does NOT employ the conventional centrifugal and vacuum timing mechanisms. The electronic system, receiving signals from various engine sensors such as coolant temperature, barometric pressure, throttle position, engine rpm, intake manifold pressure, etc., determines and instantly adjusts both timing and dwell for best control of emissions and maximum fuel economy. Fig. 3-52 is a schematic showing the Electronic Spark Timing (EST) circuit. Note sensors used to determine timing and dwell.

FORD DURA SPARK II SYSTEM

The Dura Spark II system employs a permanent magnet sensor. As with other systems of this type, the sensor rotor (armature, reluctor, etc.) teeth produce a fluctuating voltage in the pickup coil when they move across the face of the coil. Fig. 3-53 shows the Dura Spark II sensor setup in the distributor.

An exploded view of the same type distributor is il-

Fig. 3-50. Exploded view of fully integrated H.E.I. system. (General Motors)

Fig. 3-52. Schematic of GM Electronic Spark Timing (EST) circuit. Note various sensors that constantly feed information to computer. (General Motors)

Fig. 3-53. Ford ''Dura Spark II'' distributor. Note use of permanent magnet sensor.

Fig. 3-54. Exploded view of Ford ''Dura Spark II'' distributor permanent magnet type sensor. (Ford)

lustrated in Fig. 3-54. Note the relationship of the various parts of the sensor assembly.

The voltage pulses in the pickup coil cause the control unit (amplifier or control module) switching tran-

sistor to make and break the coil primary circuit. Study the ignition circuit schematic in Fig. 3-55.

FORD DURA SPARK III DISTRIBUTOR

The Dura Spark III system (not Dura Spark II) distributor offers a very wide range of distributor ADVANCE—up to 50 degrees. In order to accommodate this wide range, a special bi-level rotor (distributor cap rotor—not ignition sensor rotor) and distributor cap were designed. Both cap and rotor have two electrode (terminal) levels—upper and lower.

In the regular distributor cap setup, the rotor, as it revolves, fires each cap terminal in turn—one after the other. In this bi-level cap, however, the upper and lower terminals not only fire alternately but in a pattern that fires on one side of the cap and then on the other. The plug wires have to be arranged in the cap following this pattern to secure the proper firing order. Fig. 3-56 shows both cap rotor A and cap B.

CHRYSLER IGNITION SYSTEM

The Chrysler system uses a permanent magnet sensor setup as shown in Fig. 3-47. An exploded view of the same type distributor is pictured in Fig. 3-57.

AMERICAN MOTORS "BID" IGNITION

One setup used by American Motors is termed the BREAKERLESS INDUCTIVE DISCHARGE (BID) system. It employs an oscillator excited pickup sensor. System operation is similar to that described earlier and pictured in Figs. 3-45 and 3-46. An exploded view of the BID system distributor is illustrated in Fig. 3-58.

ELECTRONIC (COMPUTER) SPARK CONTROL IGNITION SYSTEM

In addition to the H.E.I. spark control, Fig. 3-52, several other makers offer ignition systems designed to provide electronic control of the spark timing. These systems do not use the conventional mechanical and vacuum advance units. In their place, a number of sensors are utilized.

The basic timing is provided by the magnetic pickup coil sensor in the distributor. Other sensors can determine engine manifold vacuum, engine temperature, carburetor throttle position, etc. This

Fig. 3-55. Schematic of Ford "Dura Spark II" ignition system circuit. (Ford)

Fig. 3-56. Ford "Bi-Level" rotor and distributor cap as used on their "Dura Spark III" transistor ignition system. This cap design permits a wide advance—retard range. (Ford)

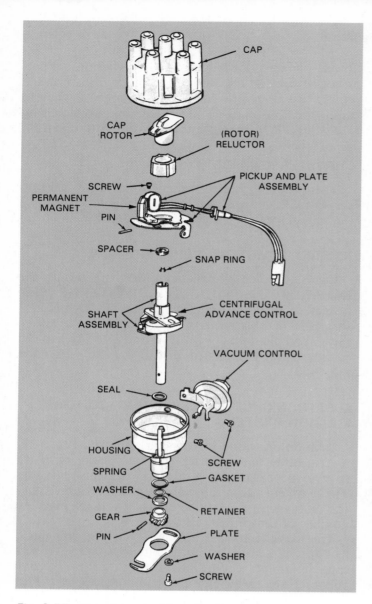

Fig. 3-57. Transistor ignition distributor as employed by some Chrysler systems. Note use of permanent magnet sensor. (Chrysler)

Fig. 3-58. Distributor using oscillator excited sensor. This one is used in American Motors Corporation "Breakerless Induction Discharge" (BID) ignition system. (AMC)

information is fed into a solid state computer which in turn determines and provides, within milliseconds, (one-thousandth of a second), optimum (best) spark advance.

Fig. 3-59 pictures a schematic of the Chrysler computer controlled ignition system. Study the circuit. This type of system offers infinite and variable spark advance curves that will time the spark so that it will occur at precisely the best possible time for any given condition or engine loading. The system actually uses TWO pickup coil setups in the distributor. One is used for the START mode, the other for the RUN mode. Fig. 3-59 shows the RUN pickup only. They never function together. In the event the RUN mode becomes inoperative, the START mode will take over and keep the engine running although not up to full efficiency.

If the computer fails, a "limp-in" mode takes over

that will allow the engine to run well enough to get to a repair facility. Another system, the Computer Controlled Coil Ignition by Buick, is fully electronic and does NOT use a conventional distributor. See page 51.

USE CARE

Transistor ignition system service requires proper tools and know-how. DO NOT ATTEMPT TO CHECK, ADJUST, OR REPAIR SUCH A SYSTEM WITHOUT THE PROPER INSTRUMENTS—AND INSTRUCTIONS.

IGNITION SYSTEM AFFECTS EMISSION CONTROL

The modern transistorized ignition system provides very accurate control of spark timing. The system can be fully integrated with the overall emission control

Fig. 3-59. Schematic of Chrysler transistor ignition system utilizing numerous sensors to feed information to a computer so as to provide constant and instant spark timing control. No regular vacuum and centrifugal devices are needed. (Chrysler)

system so as to provide the best possible timing in light of fuel efficiency, performance, and exhaust emission requirements. Great care must be exercised in servicing either the ignition or emission systems as even small adjustments or changes in one can have a profound effect on the other.

MAGNETO IGNITION

A magneto is an electrical device which generates and distributes electricity to ignite the combustible mixture in the combustion chamber. A magneto does not require a battery to operate.

The lawn mower, garden tractor, and outboard

boat engine are just a few of the many engines that use the magneto ignition system.

The magneto system is also practical for a variety of industrial and aircraft piston engines. It is compact and dependable.

PRINCIPLE OF MAGNETO OPERATION

Other than the lack of a battery to furnish current for the primary system, the magneto system is quite similar to the battery system. With no battery, a way must be found to impart voltage in the primary windings, Fig. 3-60.

The magnetic lines of force that travel from the

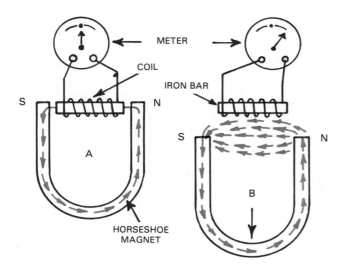

Fig. 3-60. Using a magnet and coil to produce induced voltage. In A, magnetic lines of force are channeled through laminated iron bar. A coil of wire is wound around bar. Ends of coil are hooked to meter. No voltage is produced. In B, magnet has been jerked down away from coil. As lines of force cut across coil, voltage is induced in coil. Notice meter. You can also see lines of force when iron bar is removed from magnet. They are no longer channeled and spread out.

Fig. 3-61. Action of rotating magnet. Force field traveling through coil core. Field is carried up pole shoe, through core, and down other pole shoe. Just as rotor (rotating magnet) arrived at this point, lines of force cut across coils. We now have an induced voltage.

Fig. 3-62. Action of rotating magnet. Magnet is in neutral position. Lines of force travel through pole shoes and not through core. Field will now collapse. Field built up by primary will continue to flow as points are still closed.

north to the south pole of the permanent magnet provide the answer. If a coil is placed within these lines, and if these lines are suddenly collapsed, a current will be induced in the coil.

Notice in Figs. 3-61, 3-62, and 3-63, that as the rotating magnet is turned between the laminated coil pole shoes, the magnetic field is built up, collapsed, and then built up again in the opposite direction. This gives the effect of moving a magnetic field through a coil of wire and induces voltage in the coil.

If we connect the primary wires through a set of breaker points, voltage will be built up when the field is established. When the magnet is turned and the field collapses, the field that has been built up by the primary itself will be retained through electromagnetic action (tendency of current to keep flowing).

As the magnet turns, an attempt is made to reestablish lines of force in the opposite direction. However, the magnetic field built up around the primary by the current flowing in it will resist field reversal. At this time, tremendous stress is set up in the field. If the points are opened, the field will collapse the lines of force in one direction, and instantly reestablish them in the opposite direction. This gives two fast flux, or force field, line changes and is sufficient to induce a high voltage in the secondary circuit. Figs. 3-61, 3-62, and 3-63.

FLYWHEEL MAGNETO

Examine the simple type of FLYWHEEL MAGNETO shown in Fig. 3-64. This is commonly used on small one and two cylinder engines.

Notice that the flywheel Q has a ring magnet A fastened to it. This will cause magnet A to spin around with the flywheel. As it spins, it passes close to the laminated core and pole shoe assembly B. As you know, the magnetic lines of force flow from the north pole to the south pole of the magnet. Since they will bend to flow through an iron conductor, if it is nearby, see how they flow through laminated assembly B when the flywheel brings the poles in line. These lines surround both primary and secondary windings. As the primary breaker points are closed, the magnetic lines passing through the primary will build up a voltage in the primary circuit (voltage induced when lines first whip across coil-windings).

As the flywheel continues to spin, it brings the magnetic south pole in line with the coil core. The north pole moves in line with the laminated pole shoe R.

Once the points close, the original field set up in the primary will remain (through electromagnetic action). As the magnet poles move to the second position, and the field flow attempts to reverse itself, great stress is set up in the field.

At this time of maximum current flow in the primary (also time when cylinder is ready to fire), cam lobe J will strike rubbing block K and open the points. As in a battery system, when the current flow

Fig. 3-63. Action of rotating magnet. As magnet has now turned to this position, force field attempts to reverse itself. Old field in primary resists this and, as a result, tremendous stress is set up in field. When points are snapped open, old field will collapse and force lines will instantly reestablish themselves in opposite direction. This double flux field change will produce a high voltage in secondary and plug will fire.

Fig. 3-64. Flywheel magneto.

through the primary is broken, the magnetic field around the primary and secondary windings will collapse and induce a high voltage in the secondary circuit sufficient to fire the plug.

This particular setup requires no distributor as it is timed to fire when the piston is ready. To provide for advanced timing for higher speeds, a centrifugal advance will move the rubbing block ahead against cam rotation to provide for increased degrees of timing.

Notice that the coil in this system has the primary windings on the inside of the secondary windings. Also notice that this system will produce one spark for every turn of the crankshaft. We thus have a spark on the firing stroke and another, called a "maverick spark," at the end of the exhaust stroke. The maverick spark can be eliminated by opening and closing the points with a gear driven cam to cut cam speed in half.

The flywheel, when in place, covers the entire assembly in most engines. Some have small openings cut into the flywheel to adjust the points. Some engines mount the breaker points and condenser outside to make servicing easier, Fig. 3-64.

SUMMARY

Current from the battery flows to the key switch. When the switch is turned on, current flows through a resistor to the primary windings in the coil. From the primary coil windings, the current travels to the breaker points, and on to ground where it returns to the battery via the metal parts of the car.

Current flow through the primary windings builds up a magnetic field that surrounds the secondary windings. When the points are opened by the distributor cam, current in the primary is stopped. A clean stoppage is made possible by use of a condenser. When the primary flow is broken, the magnetic field around the secondary windings collapses and induces a high voltage in the secondary circuit.

Trace the flow of current in both primary and secondary circuits in A, D, E, and F, Fig. 3-1.

The vast majority of cars now use a transistor ignition system. The transistor system makes and breaks the primary circuit with a transistor. The transistor can be controlled (triggered) by using breaker points or as is the current practice, by using a sensor. This eliminates points and their problems.

Sensors are of two basic types—the oscillator excited sensor or the permanent magnet—magnetic pickup type. Both types are designed to trigger the transistor, thus causing it to break the primary circuit.

Transistor ignition systems often use the conventional centrifugal and vacuum spark advance mechanism. Some systems provide complete electronic control of spark timing. Dwell can also be electronically controlled.

The modern transistor ignition system is a very important part of the overall exhaust emission control system.

Use proper tools and procedures when checking transistor systems. Many of the electronic parts are easily ruined by improper methods.

Magneto ignition systems require no external source of electricity.

KNOW THESE TERMS

Primary and secondary circuits, Battery, Ignition switch, Ignition coil, Breaker points, Condenser, Spark plug, Preignition, Distributor cap, Rotor, Centrifugal advance, Vacuum advance, Transistor ignition system, Pickup coil, Dwell, Computer controlled ignition, Magneto.

REVIEW QUESTIONS—CHAPTER 3

1. An ignition system in good condition will produce over _____ volts.
2. Normal voltage requirements for successful plug firing are around _____ volts.
3. Name the two circuits in the conventional breaker point ignition system.
4. What part does a ballast resistor play in the ignition system?
5. What is the procedure involved in determining how to hook up a coil?
6. Major duty of a coil is to reduce the primary voltage. True or False?
7. What happens when the primary field in the coil collapses?
8. Breaker points are placed in combustion chamber to fire fuel charge. True or False?
9. Breaker points commonly utilize _____ to provide a long service life.
10. What opens and closes the breaker points?
11. An average breaker point gap would run from _____ to _____.
12. What is cam angle?
13. What is the condenser for in a conventional breaker point system?
14. Would an engine run without a condenser with conventional breaker points?
15. What are the three major parts of the spark plug?
16. What is meant by plug heat range?
17. What advantages are found in the projected nose core plug?
18. Spark plug gaps will vary from about _____ to _____.
19. What causes preignition?
20. The spark at the plug is divided into two stages. Name them.
21. What effect does the resistor plug have on the

two stages?
22. Sometimes a plug will utilize an auxiliary gap to increase its efficiency. Just how does this work?
23. What function does the distributor cap serve?
24. When the high voltage reaches the distributor center terminal, how does it reach any given plug?
25. What is meant by timing an engine?
26. There are two common methods of advancing the timing in a breaker point system while the engine is operating. Name them.
27. How do the mechanisms that advance and retard the timing function?
28. The transistor ignition system, regardless of type, is quite similar to the conventional system with the exception of the transistor and related parts. True or False?
29. Describe the operation of a transistor.
30. The transistor can be triggered (operated) by using conventional _____ _____ or by using a _____.
31. Transistor ignition systems will, through a normal service life, provide accurate dwell and proper spark _____.
32. All transistor ignition systems use mechanical vacuum and centrifugal advance units. True or False?
33. "Dwell" is controlled by the:
    a. Vacuum advance.
    b. Centrifugal advance.
    c. Distributor cap.
    d. None of the above.
34. Describe the action of an oscillator excited sensor.
35. Name another sensor type other than the oscillator excited.
36. Proper tools and service techniques are an absolute MUST for transistor ignition systems. True or False?
37. Ignition systems can affect emission levels. True or False?
38. The major difference between a battery system and a magneto system is: (Explain).
39. What happens when a magnetic field is passed over and around a coil or wire?
40. For what purpose is the coil core and shoe assembly used?
41. A magneto can be used only on one cylinder engines. True or False?
42. Take a blank piece of paper and sketch an entire battery ignition (conventional breaker point) system on it.
43. Similar to that in question 42, sketch a sensor controlled transistor type ignition system.

Chapter 4

COOLING SYSTEMS

After studying this chapter, you will be able to:
- List the functions of an engine cooling system.
- Define the major parts of a cooling system.
- Trace the flow of coolant through the cooling system.
- Identify the basic parts of a cooling system.

When fuel is burned in an engine, a great deal of heat is produced. In fact, temperatures in excess of 4,000°F (2 204°C) attained by the burning air-fuel mixture. Normal operating flame temperature is around 2,000°F (1 094°C).

A considerable amount of this heat is carried off by the exhaust system, but the pistons, cylinder head, valves, cylinder walls, etc., will still absorb an excessive amount of heat.

As the temperature of the engine parts increases, a point is reached where the vital oil film will break down. When this happens, lubrication is no longer possible, and the engine will be ruined.

SOME HEAT IS ESSENTIAL

At the same time, an engine that is cold is very inefficient, runs poorly, contaminates the oil, forms deposits, increases wear, cuts down horsepower, and will not achieve good fuel mileage. Study A and B, Fig. 4-1.

THREE JOBS FOR COOLING SYSTEM

The cooling system must remove surplus or unwanted heat. It must maintain an efficient

Fig. 4-1. The relationship between engine temperature and performance, life and economy. (Continental Motors)

81

temperature under all operating conditions. It must also bring an engine, when starting, up to operating temperature as soon as possible.

TWO METHODS

As we often do with something that is too hot, we either blow on it or pour water on it. These same two methods, highly refined, are utilized in cooling an internal combustion engine.

Most automobile engines use a water-cooling system. A few compact car engines, as well as a host of small one and two cylinder engines, use air-cooling systems. This chapter will deal with both.

WATER-COOLED ENGINES

The water-cooled engine must have water passages through the cylinder block and head. Indirectly, the water must contact the cylinder walls, valve seats, valve guides, combustion chamber, etc. This is accomplished by literally taking the basic engine and building a container around it. In actual practice, the engine block is made in one piece, with water passages cast into the block and cylinder head. When water is placed in these passages, the engine is surrounded by a jacket of water. Hence the term, WATER JACKET. Fig. 4-2.

TRANSFER OF HEAT

Engine parts absorb the heat of the burning fuel. This heat is conducted through the part to the other side, which is surrounded with water.

The water then absorbs the heat from the part. In turn, the water transfers some of its heat to the outside of the engine. Fig. 4-3.

WATER MUST CIRCULATE

You will notice from Fig. 4-3, that the water will absorb just so much heat, then it will boil away. If the water stands still, it is of no value for cooling purposes. In order to function as a cooling agent, the water must circulate.

As the water is heated, it must move out of the engine and be replaced with cooler water. There must be no dead spots (areas in which there is little or no circulation). Fig. 4-4.

A PUMP IS NEEDED

To circulate water (commonly referred to as coolant, which usually is a mixture of 50 percent water and 50 percent ethylene glycol) through the engine, a water pump is needed. A common type water pump is the centrifugal pump utilizing an impeller. Fig. 4-5.

The impeller consists of a round plate fastened to a rotating shaft to which a series of flat or curved vanes are attached.

When the impeller whirls, the water is thrown outward by centrifugal force.

By placing the impeller in a closed housing and providing an inlet to allow water to contact the front face of the vanes, and an outlet to carry away water thrown outward, such a pump will move water efficiently. Fig. 4-6.

Fig. 4-2. Water jacket. 1, water enters block here, circulates around cylinder to 2, then flows up into the head 3, where it leaves at 4. Notice how water surrounds cylinder, valve seats, guides, head, plug and top of combustion chamber.

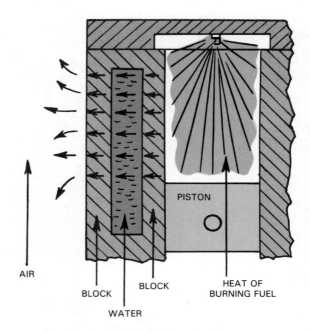

Fig. 4-3. Transfer of heat—water not circulating.

Fig. 4-4. Circulation is vital. Notice in A, that heat from torch has heated water and entire bar. The gauge reads hot. In B, water is circulating through water jacket and carries heat away from bar. Gauge now reads cold.

Fig. 4-6. Impeller housing. Water directed to center of impeller is thrown outward into housing. An outlet directs flow upon leaving.

Fig. 4-5. Action of water pump impeller.

Fig. 4-7. Water pump in which impeller operates in a special shaped opening in the timing chain cover. Some applications place a pump similar to this in a properly designed hole in the front face of the engine block. The opening must be designed to produce the proper pumping action.   (Pontiac)

PUMP CONSTRUCTION

The pump housing is cast either of iron or aluminum. The impeller shaft is supported on double row ball bearings, usually of the sealed type. A special seal is used to prevent water leakage. A hub is fastened to the front of the impeller shaft. A pulley and a fan are bolted to this hub. See Figs. 4-7 and 4-8 following.

Some pumps place the impeller in the water jacket of the engine, Fig. 4-7, while others keep the impeller enclosed in the pump housing. Fig. 4-8 illustrates a typical water pump. The water pump is usually secured to the front of the engine by bolts.

BELT DRIVE

Figs. 4-8, 4-18, 4-46 show a V-belt being used to drive a water pump. The belt is driven by a pulley on the front of the crankshaft. This same belt may be used to drive other accessories such as the alternator, etc. Typical V-belt construction is shown in Fig. 4-9. A modification of the V-belt, the RIBBED BELT, is

Fig. 4-8. Typical water pump. 1—Bolts-pump to block. 2—Bolts-fan and pulley. 3—Pump shaft. 4—Hub. 5—Water outlet. 6—Bypass. 7—Pump housing. 8—Seal. 9—Ball bearings. 10—Pulley. 11—V-belt. 12—Dust seal. 13—Seal spring. 14—Fan. 15—Water inlet. 16—Hose. 17—Block. 18—Bearing race. 19—Impeller.

Fig. 4-9. V-belt construction. This particular belt uses steel wires and is designed to drive the air conditioning compressor. (Gates)

CONTROLLED CIRCULATION

It is not enough to pump water into the bottom of an engine and let it flow out the top. If this were done, some areas would receive rapid circulation, while others would contain "dead" water with resultant localized overheating.

The coolant may be channeled into an engine block by means of distribution tubes. This assures an even flow throughout the engine. Fig. 4-11 illustrates a typical distribution tube.

The tube is placed in the water jacket. The outlet holes line up with selected areas. This will give certain hard-to-cool areas the type of circulation they need.

If distribution tubes are not used, great care must be used in designing the water jacket and its passages.

WATER NOZZLE

In addition to distribution tubes, some engines employ water nozzles in the cooling system. Such

Fig. 4-10. This engine uses a ribbed belt to drive water pump. Note difference between this belt and regular V-belt. (Ford)

Fig. 4-11. Distribution tube. This may be in the block, head or both.

pictured in Fig. 4-10. It is a wide belt with several ribs that act as several small V-belts.

Belts must be in good condition and properly adjusted. Excessive tightness will place a heavy load on pump bearings, alternator bearings, etc., causing premature wear. Belt looseness will permit slippage and "whip" or "flap." The slippage will reduce pump and fan speed thus causing overheating. Belt "flap" causes intermittent heavy loading of the bearings and possible bearing failure.

nozzles speed up water circulation around the valve seats. Fig. 4-12.

COOLANT FLOW

The coolant must flow around the cylinders and pass up through the cylinder head on its way out. It must reach every part of the system and must keep moving with no "dead" spots. Figs. 4-13, 4-14, 4-15, and 4-46 illustrate the path the water takes on its way through the engine.

THE RADIATOR

When the coolant leaves the engine, it is quite hot—often well over 200°F (93.3°C). If it were to be immediately pumped back into the engine, it would start to boil and would be ineffective as a coolant.

Therefore, before the water can be reused, it must be cooled by circulation of water and air. Fig. 4-16.

Cooling is accomplished by passing the water, as it leaves the engine, into the top or side tank of a radiator.

From the top tank, it flows down through tiny copper tubes. The tubes have thin copper fins soldered over their entire length. As the water makes its way down through the tubes, it gives off heat to the tubes. Since copper is an excellent conductor, the tubes give off their heat, via the fins, to the air passing around the tubes.

By the time the water reaches the bottom tank, it is cool enough to reuse. Fig. 4-16 shows a typical radiator.

Fig. 4-14. Coolant flow through an engine and radiator. Note use of expansion tank. (Nissan)

Fig. 4-12. Action of a water nozzle. Notice how water is pumped into nozzle tube. As it leaves small hole in top, it squirts out and causes a strong circulation around valve seat area.

Fig. 4-13. Coolant flow path in a system employing a cross-flow radiator. This is a closed system. Note use of overflow tank. (Cadillac)

Fig. 4-15. Coolant flow path in a system using a down-flow radiator.

Fig. 4-16. Typical radiator. Water enters the top hose connection 4, then passes into top tank. 3. From there it flows down through core tubes 5. When it reaches bottom tank 6, it has cooled. 1—Filler neck. 2—Overflow tube. 7—Lower hose connections. 8—Drain petcock. Not shown are thin fins soldered to core tubes.

Fig. 4-17. Radiator construction. A—Round tube and flat fin. B—Flat tube and corrugated fin. C—Flat tube and flat fin. (Harrison)

Many cars use the cross-flow radiator, Fig. 4-13. The coolant enters one side tank and then passes through the horizontal tubes to the opposite tank.

Expansion tanks, Fig. 4-14, were sometimes used to provide additional coolant storage and space for coolant expansion. Late practice employs an OVERFLOW tank (often called coolant reservoir), Fig. 4-13.

The radiator may also contain a heat exchanger to provide cooling for the automatic transmission fluid.

A radiator is made of brass and copper to facilitate cooling, and to protect it from rust and corrosion. All joints are soldered. Aluminum and plastic are also being used in radiator construction to reduce the weight of the unit.

The radiator is so placed that it can avail itself of the air that rushes through the grille of the car when it is in motion.

The radiator tubes, or core section, use various designs, all designed to cool the water quickly. Fig. 4-17 illustrates several different types.

FORCED AIR

To speed up cooling action of a radiator, an engine or electrically driven fan or fans are used to draw air through the radiator core. Look at Fig. 4-18.

If a fan is set back from the core, it will recirculate the same air, Fig. 4-19. To avoid the loss of fan efficiency, some fans require a radiator shroud. This

Fig. 4-18. Fan, six blade type. Some fans have two blades, others four, etc. 1—Pulley. 2—Lock washer. 3—Locknut. 4—Bolt. 5—Fan blade. 6—V-belt. (M.G. Car Co.)

prevents recirculation of air. Fig. 4-20.

The flow of the air over the outside of an engine will help, in a small way, to remove engine heat.

As the car gains speed on the road, a natural ram

effect will force air through the radiator core. As a result, the need of a fan is not as great. Since a fan requires engine power to spin, some fans have a thermostatic control that will allow the fan to slow up when not needed. See Fig. 4-46.

Another type uses a centrifugal unit that cuts fan speed when engine rpm is high. These units are designed to save horsepower and to cut down on objectionable fan noise.

Some fans use two blades; others use three, four, and occasionally more, depending on specific requirements. Blades are sometimes arranged in an uneven manner in an attempt to lessen noise.

One type of fan employs flexible blades that reduce the pitch (angle at which blade is mounted) at higher speeds, permitting the fan to turn more easily.

The fan is often mounted as an integral part of the water pump, or it can be mounted as an independent unit. Some fans are electric. Fig. 4-50.

BEWARE!

A FAN CAN INFLICT SERIOUS INJURY. KEEP HANDS, TOOLS, CORDS, ETC., AWAY FROM THE FAN. DO NOT STAND IN LINE WITH A REVOLVING FAN—A BLADE CAN FLY OUT WITH LETHAL FORCE. ELECTRIC FANS COME ON AUTOMATICALLY!

HOSES

The radiator is connected to the engine and pump by means of rubber hoses. These hoses are of different diameters, depending upon the particular engine. There are three common types of hoses, Fig. 4-21.

HOSE CLAMPS

Hoses are secured to their fittings by clamps. There are two popular types. One is the adjustable, screw

Fig. 4-20. Fan shroud stops recirculation. Thin sheet metal or plastic shroud is attached to radiator. Airflow is improved.

Fig. 4-21. Radiator hose types. A—Common hose. Straight. Made of rubber with one or two layers of fabric for strength. Will not stand much bending without collapsing. B—Molded or shaped. Same construction as A. Since all necessary bends are molded in, this hose will not collapse. C—Accordian type. Will stand severe bending without collapse. Reduces transfer of vibration from engine to radiator. D—Top hose has collapsed when bent. Middle hose has bent with no sign of collapse. Middle hose has a spiral spring-like wire inserted into it before bending. Wire is shown beneath middle hose. All three types of hose may use the spiral wire in their construction. It can be molded in or placed in.

Fig. 4-19. Fan too far from radiator—allows recirculation. Some air is being pulled through radiator, but a great deal is moving through the fan, back around and through again.

tightened type, and the other is the snap type.

The screw type has many adaptations. Two common screw types, as well as the snap type, are illustrated in Fig. 4-22.

FIRST JOB COMPLETE

As mentioned earlier, the cooling system has three jobs. The first job is to remove surplus heat from the engine. With a water jacket, pump, radiator, hoses, and fan, this job is complete. Fig. 4-23.

The second job is to maintain an even, efficient heat level. The third job is to bring a cold engine up to this temperature as soon as possible after starting. As yet, the system we have discussed will not perform the last two functions.

SNAP TYPE

SCREW TYPE

Fig. 4-22. Three types of hose clamps.

HOSE

FAN
V-BELT

PUMP

WATER JACKET

RADIATOR   HOSE

Fig. 4-23. Basic cooling system.

THE THERMOSTAT

The system, as studied so far, would cool at a constant rate. If the capacity is sufficient to cool the engine in hot areas under heavy loads, it would obviously overcool in cold weather.

Some type of temperature control is necessary.

To provide constant temperature control, a THERMOSTAT is installed in the cooling system. It is often placed directly beneath the top water outlet. The water outlet may have a bowl-shaped bottom to house the thermostat.

WHAT DOES A THERMOSTAT DO?

When the engine is cold, the thermostat shuts off the flow of water from the engine to the radiator. As the water is confined to the engine, it heats quickly. When it reaches a predetermined temperature, the thermostat opens and allows free circulation of coolant.

If it is quite cold, the thermostat may not open all the way. Water can circulate, but slowly, and the engine temperature can be kept to the proper level. The thermostat constantly changes the size of its opening depending on heat conditions.

This action will bring a cold engine up to proper heat in a minimum amount of time. It will also maintain an even, efficient temperature level under all conditions. See Figs. 4-24 and 4-25.

Note in Fig. 4-47, how the water is heated in three stages. A shows the thermostat closed, no flow to radiator and with the top area of engine (cylinder heads) heating. B illustrates stage 2, with the entire block heating up. C pictures the cooling system with the thermostat open and the coolant circulating throughout the system.

THERMOSTAT VALVE
IS CLOSED

WATER IS COLD.
THERMOSTAT IS
CLOSED. WATER
CANNOT LEAVE
ENGINE. WILL NOW
HEAT QUICKLY.

Fig. 4-24. Cold engine.

THERMOSTAT VALVE
IS OPEN

WATER IS HOT.
THERMOSTAT HAS OPENED.
WATER WILL NOW CIRCULATE.

Fig. 4-25. Hot engine.

HOW IT WORKS—PELLET TYPE

The PELLET thermostat (named after the pellet of wax that operates it) is in common use today. It has superseded the older BELLOWS type whose operating action was upset by the modern pressurized cooling systems.

A small cylindrical case containing a pellet of copper impregnated (filled) wax operates the thermostat. The thermostat is placed in the water outlet, Fig. 4-26, so that the pellet case rests in the engine block coolant.

When the engine is cold, there is no pellet action and the spring holds the thermostat valve closed. See A, Fig. 4-26.

As the engine coolant warms, the wax pellet is heated. This causes the wax to expand and force the rubber tightly against the steel piston or pin. When the coolant temperature reaches a predetermined level, the wax will have expanded to the point that the pressure on the rubber is so great that it will force the case downward against spring pressure, thus pulling the valve open and allowing coolant to flow through the thermostat on into the radiator. B, Fig. 4-26.

Fig. 4-26. Pellet type thermostat action. Pellet end rests in block coolant. A—Engine coolant cold, coolant cannot pass by closed thermostat valve. B—Coolant has reached operating temperature. Wax pellet expands, squeezing rubber against piston hard enough to force pellet case downward to open valve. (Toyota)

There are numerous pellet thermostat designs. Many have a pull-push valve similar to that shown while others operate a flap type or a butterfly type valve.

The pellet thermostat is not pressure sensitive and works well in a fully pressurized system.

A small pinhole may be located in the thermostat valve. This acts as an aid when refilling the system as it permits the air trapped in the block to escape as the coolant flows upward in the block.

DIFFERENT HEAT RANGES

Thermostats are available in different heat ranges. Common heat ranges are the 180 and 195°F (82.2—90.6°C) thermostats. The 180°F thermostat opens near this temperature and is fully opened around 200°F (93.3°C). The 195°F type starts opening near 195°F and is fully open around 218°F (103.3°C). Some thermostats range above 200°F.

These higher range thermostats raise the engine operating temperature and, in so doing, aid in emission (exhaust pollution) control.

The exact thermostat temperature range used will depend on the engine, load requirements, weather, etc.

If alcohol (methanol) antifreeze is used in the cooling system (ITS USE IS NOT RECOMMENDED!), a 160°F (71.1°C) thermostat should be used. If a 180°F thermostat is used, boilover and coolant loss will result. The 180°F and higher thermostats work well with permanent (ethylene-glycol) base antifreeze.

WHEN THERMOSTAT IS CLOSED

A thermostat will remain closed until the water in the engine reaches a specific temperature. Fig. 4-26.

Until this temperature is reached, the water in the engine still circulates, but only in the engine.

Two methods are used to allow the pump to circulate water through the engine and not through the thermostat.

One method uses a spring loaded bypass valve that opens and allows the water to reenter the pump. The bypass valve spring is weaker than that of the thermostat and will be forced open whenever the thermostat is closed. Fig. 4-27. Another version provides a similar setup but eliminates the bypass valve and

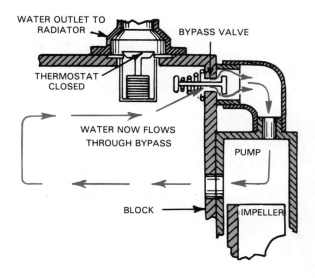

Fig. 4-27. One form of bypass construction. Water flows into block from pump. As thermostat is closed, water forces bypass valve open and water reenters the pump. When thermostat opens, bypass will close.

provides a constant, metered flow of coolant.

Coolant flow action through another bypass setup is pictured in A, B, Fig. 4-28. In A, thermostat is closed, bypass cover finger is raised and coolant moves from the pump, through the distribution tube, back out, down through the open bypass pipe on into the pump. Coolant continues to recirculate until the thermostat is fully open. In B, pellet thermostat case has moved down pulling valve open and at the same time, forcing finger to close off bypass pipe. Coolant now moves through thermostat to radiator. Fig. 4-28.

The other method uses a special bypass opening from the cylinder head, through the block, to the pump. This may contain a fixed type bypass that allows continuous recirculation of a small portion of the coolant.

PRESSURIZED COOLING SYSTEM

The modern, high speed, high horsepower engine produces terrific heat. It has been found that if the cooling system is pressurized, the boiling point of the water is raised. For this reason a pressurized cooling system provides a greater difference between the boiling point of water and the desirable engine operating temperature. By permitting high coolant temperatures, the engine tends to produce less exhaust pollutants.

When operating a car at high altitudes, especially during the hot weather with heavy loads, the water in the cooling system will boil quickly. As the car gains altitude, atmospheric pressure goes down.

The less the atmospheric pressure on the water, the sooner the water will boil. By adding pressurization to the system, it is possible to operate an engine at temperatures exceeding 250 °F (121°C) without boiling.

Pressurization also increases water pump efficiency by reducing cavitation (water in the low pressure area near pump blades turning to steam, allowing the pump impeller blades to spin in the air bubbles).

Each pound of pressure on the water in the cooling system will raise the boiling point around 3°F. Study the chart in Fig. 4-29. Notice the difference between the boiling point of water, ethylene glycol, and methyl alcohol. Also notice that as you go up, the boiling point goes down.

HOW SYSTEM IS PRESSURIZED

Pressurizing a cooling system is done by placing a special pressure cap on the radiator filler neck. The system must, of course, be designed for this purpose.

The pressure cap presses firmly against a seat in the filler neck. As the water in the cooling system heats, it also expands. As it continues heating, and expanding, it squeezes the air on the top of the water.

Fig. 4-28. Thermostat and bypass action. A—Coolant still cold, thermostat closed. Bypass pipe cover finger is UP exposing bypass pipe opening. Coolant circulates from pump, through distribution tube, down through bypass pipe to pump. B—Coolant has heated causing pellet thermostat to open. This closes bypass pipe and coolant flows through thermostat valve to radiator. (Volvo)

Fig. 4-29. Effect of altitude on boiling point of coolant. If you were driving a car with plain water in the cooling system, how high a mountain could you climb if your engine was running at 200 °F? You can go up till it boils. How high?
(Continental Motor)

The air cannot escape, as the pressure cap has sealed the opening. When the pressure is too great, the spring holding the pressure cap seal valve will no longer hold and allows the seal valve to rise. As soon as pressure (over what cap is built for) escapes, the spring closes the seal and keeps the predetermined pressure constant. The escaping air passes out through the radiator overflow pipe.

When the engine is shut off and cools down, another small valve in the cap opens. As the water cools, it contracts and tries to form a vacuum in the tank. This draws the vacuum valve open and allows air from the overflow pipe to enter the tank. Without a vacuum valve, the hose and the tank could collapse.

HOW CAP WORKS

The radiator filler neck has a flange near the bottom. When the pressure cap is put on, it has a spring loaded valve that seats against the flange.

The spring loaded valve has a valve in the center that pulls open when a vacuum is formed in the tank. This vacuum valve can also be spring loaded. The large pressure release control spring is calibrated to open at a specific pressure (15–16 psi or 103.4–110.3 kPa average). Fig. 4-30 shows the construction of a pressure cap.

CLOSED SYSTEM

The CLOSED cooling system, now in widespread use, is actually a standard pressurized cooling system with the addition of an overflow tank (also called coolant reservoir) and a somewhat different pressure cap design. Figs. 4-13, 4-35.

The closed system pressure cap seals not only the

Fig. 4-30. Construction details of pressure cap, shown in place on radiator filler neck.

radiator filler neck lower flange, as pictured in Figs. 4-31 and 4-32, but the top flange of the neck as well. Fig. 4-33 shows the typical non-closed system cap. Note that the upper flange is sealed only by a thin metal seal. This will prevent boilover leakage but does not form a positive airtight seal. Fig. 4-33.

The closed system cap, illustrated in Fig. 4-34, provides an additional seal ring for the filler neck upper flange. This cap provides sealing at both upper and lower neck flanges. Note the nonloaded (no spring pressure) center vent valve.

The overflow pipe is located between the two sealed areas and is connected to the overflow tank via a rubber hose. The hose (or a rigid pipe) passes through the cover of the overflow tank and extends nearly to the bottom. The tank is filled about one-quarter full of coolant. The radiator, unlike the older open system, is filled to the top. Fig. 4-35.

When the coolant heats, it expands and flows up through the non-loaded center vent valve. This displaced coolant flows through the overflow pipe and on into the overflow tank. Any air that is in the

Fig. 4-31. Pressure cap in action. Water has expanded until pressure cap limit has been reached. Cap has opened and excess pressure is being released out the overflow.

Fig. 4-32. Pressure cap in action. Water has cooled and contracted. This forms vacuum in radiator. Vacuum valve is drawn open and air passes into tank through overflow pipe. In closed cooling system, coolant from overflow tank would flow back into tank, instead of air.

Fig. 4-33. Note typical pressure cap used on many open cooling systems. Upper flange seal does not use soft seal insert common on both lower flange seal and vacuum valve seal. (American Motors)

Fig. 4-34. Typical closed cooling system pressure cap. Note that unlike upper seal in Fig. 4-33, this cap uses an additional soft seal to provide an airtight seal at top flange. (British-Leyland)

system rises to the top of the coolant in the overflow tank and escapes out the overflow tank vent hose. At this point, the entire cooling system is completely filled with coolant and all air has been displaced.

As the coolant temperature nears the boiling point, the vent will be forced closed to create pressure on the system. At extremely high temperatures, the system may exceed the maximum cap pressure. When this happens, system pressure forces the bottom cap seal valve to raise off its seat and dissipate the pressure in the form of coolant flow into the overflow tank.

When the engine cools, the coolant contracts forming a mild vacuum. This draws the cap center vent valve open (as in Fig. 4-32) and coolant (not air) is drawn into the system from the overflow tank.

Fig. 4-35. One closed cooling system setup. Excess coolant moves through overflow hose 5 into downpipe 8 and into overflow tank 9. When system cools, coolant will be drawn back into the system from the tank supply 10. Other components: 1—Top hose. 2—Radiator top tank filler neck. 3—Pressure cap. 4—Radiator top tank. 6—Tank cover cap. 7—Overflow tank vent hose.

The closed system, in eliminating air, operates more efficiently, helps to reduce corrosion and allows a visual inspection of the system coolant level without removing the radiator cap. To replace any coolant lost to leakage, do not remove the pressure cap, merely bring the coolant in the overflow tank up to the indicated level. Study Fig. 4-35.

SYSTEM MUST BE IN GOOD REPAIR

Whenever a cooling system is pressurized, an additional strain is placed on all the system. Hoses must be in good condition, clamps tight and no coolant leaks anywhere.

DANGER!

BE VERY CAREFUL WHEN REMOVING THE CAP FROM THE RADIATOR OF A PRESSURIZED SYSTEM. OPEN THE CAP TO THE FIRST STOP—WAIT A FEW SECONDS AND THEN REMOVE. COVER CAP WITH A RAG DURING THIS OPERATION AND KEEP FACE AWAY. WHEN THE PRESSURE IS SUDDENLY REMOVED FROM THE SYSTEM, IT CAN CAUSE SUPERHOT STEAM TO ESCAPE IN A VIOLENT FASHION. BE CAREFUL!

TEMPERATURE GAUGE

The temperature of the coolant can be determined by observing the temperature gauge or indicator on the dash.

Two types of gauges are used. See Figs. 4-36 and 4-37. One uses an electric sender receiver; the other uses a gas-filled capillary tube, bulb, and Bourdon tube instrument. Both instruments are quite effective and will give good service. The electric gauge has one advantage. It can span greater distances from engine to instrument panel by merely adding enough wire to reach.

CARE OF COOLING SYSTEM

It is essential that the cooling system receive proper care. Good care will insure long and trouble free operation, and will add greatly to the efficiency and life of the engine.

To protect against engine and radiator freeze-up in the winter, as well as to protect the system from rust and corrosion, manufacturers install a permanent type of antifreeze (about 50 percent water and 50 percent ethylene glycol plus corrosion and rust inhibitor chemicals) in the cooling system. Most recommend one or two year drain, flush and refill cycles. Always refill with recommended coolant.

Keep fan and pump belt, or belts, properly adjusted and also check their condition. Make certain hoses are in good condition. Watch for irregular operation that might indicate a faulty thermostat.

Fig. 4-36. Bourdon Tube Temperature Gauge. Bourdon tube is made of thin brass. One end is fixed to gauge fitting and free end is fastened to indicator needle.

When liquid in bulb is heated, it will vaporize and create pressure. This pressure is transmitted to the hollow Bourdon tube through capillary tube.

When Bourdon tube receives pressure, it will spring apart—the free end swings away from fixed end; see B. This movement causes needle to swing across face of gauge.

The bulb is placed in water jacket of engine.

Capillary tubing is strengthened by wire wrapped around it for its entire length.

When water cools, pressure is removed from tube and needle moves back to cold.

Fig. 4-37. Electric Temperature Gauge. Current from battery flows through wire coil that surrounds bimetal (two different metals fastened together) hairpin. It then passes on to the terminal of the sender unit, traveling from the terminal through the spring to the temperature sensitive disc.

As water heats disc, the disc will carry more electricity to ground. Resistance coil on the hairpin will start to heat up. This will transfer heat to hairpin.

Expansion of two dissimilar metals in hairpin causes it to bend as it heats. This bending actuates needle and causes it to move to hot. See B.

When water cools, disc will slow down flow of electricity and hairpin will cool, bending back to its original shape. See A.

Keep all connections tight. Keep radiator core clean and free of bugs, dirt, etc. Check the level of the coolant often. Check when cold. Check pressure cap for proper operation. Remember that system coolant is made up of water and ethylene glycol in about a 50/50 mix. Never refill with plain water.

AIR-COOLED ENGINES

The air cooling of engines has found a wide application in the field of small engines. It is also applicable to large engines. Several small, early model autos have used air cooling to remove excess heat from the engine.

Air cooling for engines is efficient and dependable. Generally an air-cooled engine warms up more quickly and operates at a somewhat higher temperature than the water-cooled engine.

Basically an air cooling system consists of fins on the engine head and block, a fan to force air, a shroud to direct the air over the fins, and in some cases a thermostatically adjusted air control.

Air cooling is most efficient when applied to engines that are constructed of aluminum. Aluminum is a better conductor of heat than cast iron. In fact, aluminum will conduct heat about three times better than cast iron. However, air cooling is successfully used on cast iron engines.

It is essential that the engine block and head have a number of rather deep cooling fins. The fins are cast right into the engine parts. The theory behind the use of fins is simple. Heat generated inside a metal container must pass through the walls of the container and be carried away by flow of the air.

Let us assume that we have a square cylinder block of aluminum 6 in. wide and 6 in. high. Inside the block is our engine combustion chamber.

As heat is generated by the burning fuel mixture, it will be conducted through the walls of our block and will be carried away by the air. If we produce enough heat in the combustion chamber, it is obvious that the block will not be able to dissipate the heat into the air fast enough and will, in time, melt. Fig. 4-38.

Fig. 4-38. Heat is conducted through walls of block and is carried away by surrounding air.

The rate at which the aluminum block will be able to cool itself will, to a considerable degree, be determined by the amount of block surface that is exposed to the air.

Computing the number of lineal inches on the top and two sides of the block, we find three sides (6 in. per side) equals 18 lineal in. In other words, the air moving around the block can draw heat only from these 18 in. of exposed surface.

By adding fins to the sides and top, see how much more surface the air can strike. Fig. 4-39.

Fig. 4-39 shows that by adding 2 in. fins to the top and sides, the air can now circulate over 162 lineal in. of block surface. The block now has nine times the cooling surface.

Fig. 4-39. Fins added to block increase contact surface for air.

So far we have considered lineal inches as viewed on three sides. If we consider our cylinder block to be square, this would give us five sides upon which to calculate the number of SQUARE INCHES of contact area. We will ignore the bottom side, as this would be fastened to the crankcase and would not be finned. Fig. 4-40.

FINS ARE NECESSARY

By adding fins as shown in Fig. 4-40, we would now have a total of about 1,800 sq. in. of contact area. This would be compared to five sides of the unfinned block at 180 sq. in. This represents a sizeable increase in cooling efficiency.

THE AIR MUST BE MOVED

In addition to adding fins, it is essential that we provide a fan or blower to produce a moving stream of air. The air, if not moved, will soon heat up and be unsuitable for further cooling of the finned surfaces.

Moving of the air may be done in several ways. One way is to have a separate fan or blower. Another method is to cast fan fins on the flywheel. Some engines, such as aircraft, depend on the forward speed of the engine through the air to provide sufficient airflow for proper cooling. Automobile engines use a separate fan, while most small engines use the flywheel fan, Figs. 4-41 and 4-42.

From the drawing, you can see that the flywheel fan throws air in a fashion similar to the way a water pump impeller throws water. Fig. 4-42 demonstrates

Fig. 4-40. Block with fins on five sides.

Fig. 4-41. Separate blower for cooling.

Fig. 4-42. Flywheel fan. Such a fan is very inefficient without a shroud.

that even though the fan is throwing air, it is not directed onto the fins.

The separate fan in Fig. 4-41 does a better job, but it is not always possible to line up the fan with the fins. The fan is also losing efficiency by recirculating some of the air near the outer edges of the blades.

These problems are overcome by the use of a sheet metal air shroud. The shroud prevents recirculation and also guides the air into the fins. Figs. 4-43 and 4-44 illustrate the use of shrouds. Some shrouds are

Fig. 4-43. Separate fan with sheet metal shroud. Notice that shroud prevents recirculation and also guides air to the fins.

Fig. 4-44. Flywheel fan with sheet metal shroud. Shroud collects air thrown off by fan and guides it to fins. Fan acts as a centrifugal blower.

designed to form a plenum chamber (an enclosed area in which the air pressure is higher than that of the surrounding atmospheric pressure).

A THERMOSTAT IS SOMETIMES USED

It is possible to have an air-cooled engine run too cool. To prevent this, a thermostatically controlled shutter, or valve, to limit airflow, is sometimes used. The thermostat is located in a spot that will allow it to accurately measure engine temperature. The bellows thermostat is the type commonly used.

The bellows is filled with butyl alcohol, under a vacuum. If the bellows leaks, or in any other way becomes inoperative, the shutter will then return to the full open position. This eliminates the possibility of the shutter remaining in the closed position with resultant engine failure. Fig. 4-45 demonstrates the use of such a bellows.

Fig. 4-45. Schematic of temperature control for an air-cooled engine. When engine is cold, thermostat contracts and will close shutter. As engine heats up, air passing engine will warm thermostat, causing it to expand and open shutter.

SOME ENGINES NEED NO FAN

Engines designed to move rapidly through the air, such as motorcycles and aircraft, often use no fan, depending entirely upon forward momentum to provide a cooling stream of air. Such equipment should not be operated for prolonged periods while standing still.

ALL UNITS MUST FUNCTION

In the air-cooled engine, it is essential that the fan turn at the proper speed. Also, metal shrouds must be in place, cooling fins clean, drive belt properly adjusted and, if a thermostat is used, it must operate properly.

SUMMARY

All internal combustion gasoline engines must be cooled, either with air or a liquid; the liquid commonly used being a 50/50 mix of water and ethylene-glycol.

In the case of the liquid-cooled engine, the coolant must surround all the areas that are subjected to heat from the burning fuel charge. The coolant is contained in an area referred to as the water jacket.

When the engine is first started, the thermostat is closed and the coolant in the jacket cannot circulate. Pressure from the water pump then forces water

through the bypass. This allows coolant to circulate from the pump into the block, then back into the pump.

As soon as the coolant in the engine reaches a high enough temperature, the thermostat will open and allow the coolant to be forced from the engine into the top, or the side, radiator tank, depending on radiator type used. From this tank, the coolant flows through the radiator core to the other radiator tank. The coolant is then pumped back into the engine. The coolant repeats this circulation pattern over and over.

COOLING SYSTEM UNITS

The main units in the system are:
1. Radiator for cooling.
2. Water pump for circulation.
3. Thermostat for temperature control.
4. Pressure cap for pressurization of the entire system.
5. Bypass valve to allow recirculation while heating up.
6. Fan to provide a moving stream of air through the radiator.

Study Figs. 4-46 through 4-49. Learn the names of all the parts. If in doubt as to the function of any part, refer to that specific item in this chapter.

SUMMARY — AIR-COOLED

When the engine is started, the block heats quickly. The heat is transferred by conduction to the fins. Air, moved by a fan, passes through a shroud surrounding the fins. Moving air removes the heat from the cooling fins. The amount of air can be controlled by a thermostatic shutter.

KNOW THESE TERMS

Water cooling system, Air cooling system, Water pump, V-belt, Radiator, Engine fan, Shroud, Hoses, Hose clamps, Thermostat, Radiator cap, Closed cooling system, Temperature gauge.

REVIEW QUESTIONS — CHAPTER 4

If you sweat trying to answer these questions, YOU need cooling — Cooling System review.
1. Give six reasons why an engine must not run too cool.
2. What are the three jobs that the cooling system must perform?
3. There are two popular methods of cooling the engine. Name them.
4. Water pumps are generally of the gear type. True or False?
5. Water pumps are usually chain driven. True or False?
6. To prevent dead spots and to produce a better

Fig. 4-46. Cutaway view of complete system. Notice how water moves to rear of block, passes through water passage to head, then moves forward. Since thermostat is open, it does not enter bypass, but passes into top tank. Radiator pressure cap is not shown.

Fig. 4-47. A, B, and C illustrate how cooling system comes up to operating temperature in three stages. D—Cutaway of a typical water pump. E—One form of pellet thermostat. F—Cutaway of a radiator pressure cap. G—Pellet type thermostat in closed position. H—When pellet heats, thermostat opens. I—Open form of hose clamp. J—Pellet is hot. Note how special wax has expanded, squeezing rubber together and forcing piston away from cylinder. K—When pellet cylinder cools, wax contracts and rubber returns to its normal position, drawing piston with it.

Fig. 4-48. Cross-sectional view of a water pump assembly using a thermostatically controlled variable speed fan hub unit. (Toyota)

Fig. 4-49. Cross-sectional view of a water pump assembly employing a fixed fan hub unit. Fan speed is always the same as that of pump. 1—Fan. 2—Attaching capscrew. 3—Pulley (note double V grooves). 4—Ball bearings. 5—Bearing retaining screw. 6—Seal. 7—Impeller blade. 8—Impeller. 9—Pump shaft. 10—Water slinger. 11—Drain hole. 12—Bearing outer race. 13—Pulley hub. 14—Pulley hub adapter. 15—V-belt (double groove type). (British-Leyland)

than normal circulation in some vital areas, cooling systems use _____.

7. A radiator is generally made of copper and brass to aid in cooling. True or False?
8. Name two common core types.
9. How many blades are there on the ordinary auto engine fan?
10. A fan will inflict a serious injury if you come in contact with it. True or False?
11. List three types of water hose.
12. What is the purpose of the thermostat?
13. Name two types of thermostats.
14. How do thermostats work?
15. What is meant by the heat range of a thermostat?
16. What is the function of a bypass valve?
17. Why are cooling systems pressurized?
18. How does a pressure cap work?
19. List the general points to be considered in the proper care of the cooling system.
20. Of what value are fins on an air-cooled engine?
21. What two types of units are used to produce a stream of moving air?
22. What method is used to control the temperature of the air-cooled engine?
23. Name principal units in an engine cooling system.
24. The pressure cap for a CLOSED system is different from that used on an OPEN SYSTEM. True or False?
25. The CLOSED system has:
   a. Around 1 in. of space between the top of the coolant and the bottom of the filler neck.
   b. No space between coolant and filler neck.
   c. About 3 in. of space between coolant and filler neck.

Fig. 4-50. One particular electric fan setup. Fan can be controlled by radiator coolant temperature, engine coolant temperature, etc. (Plymouth)

Chapter 5

LUBRICATION SYSTEMS

After studying this chapter, you will be able to:
■ Define the major parts of a lubrication system.
■ Explain engine oil classifications.
■ Summarize the operation of an engine lubrication system.
■ Identify the components of an engine lubrication system.
■ List the different types of oil pumps.

If you were to start and run an engine without oil, it would last only a short time. The bearing surfaces in the engine would heat up and scuff, and finally the engine would freeze. (Freezing occurs when lack of lubrication causes two parts in moving contact to overheat, expand, tear bits of metal from each other, then stick and refuse to move.) Fig. 5-1.

The force that causes wear and heat, and robs the engine of a portion of its potential power, is called FRICTION.

FRICTION DEFINED

Friction may be defined as the resistance to movement between any two objects when placed in contact with each other. The amount of friction depends on the type of material, surface finish, amount of pressure holding the two objects together, and relative amount of movement between the objects.

You can see in Fig. 5-2, that it takes a force to pull block A over block B.

Fig. 5-2. Friction. It takes force to pull block A along the surface of block B.

If you were to examine the contact surfaces of the two blocks under a microscope, regardless of how smooth they were polished, you would find a series of sharp points, grooves, etc. When the two objects contact each other, these jagged surfaces touch each other. Fig. 5-3.

FRICTION CAUSES WEAR

As soon as block A starts to move, the edges bump into each other and impede the movement. If there is considerable pressure holding the two blocks together

Fig. 5-1. Ruined journal and bearing. Oil would have prevented this. Size exaggerated.

BEARING RUINED FROM LACK OF LUBRICATION

SURFACE FINISH MAGNIFIED MANY TIMES (NOTE JAGGED EDGES)

Fig. 5-3. Microscopic view (exaggerated) of block contact surfaces.

(and in the engine, bearing pressures can soar to over 1,000 lbs. or 450 kg) and the movement is continued, two things happen.

Each block will literally tear pieces from both itself and the other block. These tiny particles roll and bang along under block A until they work out the back edge. Removal of these pieces is continual and will result in wear.

FRICTION GENERATES HEAT

A fire may be started by rubbing sticks together. Dragging brakes heat up and smoke. These are examples of heat produced by friction.

In an engine, the rubbing speeds and pressures are tremendous. This will build up enough heat to melt bearings.

FRICTION CANNOT BE ELIMINATED

It is impossible to completely eliminate friction between moving parts. If this were possible, perpetual motion machines could be easily constructed.

All that can be done is to reduce friction to an absolute minimum.

HOW FRICTION IS REDUCED

Friction is of two kinds, DRY friction and WET friction. So far we have dealt with DRY friction.

Dry friction is when both rubbing parts are clean and free of other materials.

Wet friction is when rubbing parts have other material or materials placed between them.

Have you ever tried playing a fast game of basketball on a well-waxed dance floor? This is a good example of DRY friction being changed into WET friction by placing something between your shoes and the floor—in this case, wax. It is obvious that the engine must operate under conditions of WET friction.

BEARING CONSTRUCTION

Bearing construction also plays a part in determining the amount of friction involved. There are two principal types of bearings used in engines. One is called a FRICTION bearing. The friction bearing is literally two smooth surfaces sliding against each other. The only motion involved is a sliding effect. The babbitt insert and the crankshaft journal are examples of this type.

The other type is called ANTIFRICTION bearing. This bearing utilizes balls or rollers between the moving parts.

Both types of bearings must be used wet.

The FRICTION type, as it is less expensive and cheaper to service, in addition to being satisfactory, is generally used in all major auto engine bearings. Ball and roller bearings are used in many small, high speed engines, especially the two-cycle types. Fig. 5-4 illustrates both bearing types.

OIL REDUCES FRICTION

It has been found that high quality lubricating oil successfully reduces friction to an acceptable level.

Engine oils are derived from crude oil or petroleum that is removed from the earth by means of wells.

PETROLEUM MAKES MANY THINGS

Crude oil is heated and is then pumped into a tall distillation tower. As the crude is heated, the lighter or more volatile (easily evaporated) components turn to a vapor and "flash" or travel to the top of the tank. As heat is increased, the heavier or less volatile parts will vaporize.

As all these component parts have a different specific gravity, and evaporate at different heats, it is possible to connect a series of pipes entering the distillation tower at different heights. If the pipes are arranged correctly, and other operating conditions are correct, a different vapor will travel out of each pipe.

The pipes enter a cooling tank and the vapors within condense and run down into storage tanks.

Liquefied petroleum gas (LP-Gas) is the most volatile part and leaves first. In fact, it is so volatile it will remain in the form of a gas until pressurized, at which time it will become a liquid.

DISTILLATION PROCESS

The production of lubricating oil is quite complicated. After distillation, it must have the impurities removed. This process takes several steps. Various additives such as oxidation inhibitors, detergents, defoamers, corrosion inhibitors, pour point depressants, viscosity index (VI) improvers, etc., may be added to produce oil for specific requirements. Study the schematic diagram, Fig. 5-5, showing how lubricating oil is refined.

ENGINE OIL SERVICE CLASSIFICATION

Currently, there are six basic oils adapted for use in gasoline engines. The API (American Petroleum Institute) has classified these oils as SA, SB, SC, SD,

Fig. 5-4. Friction and antifriction bearings.

Fig. 5-5. Refining of lubricating oil is a somewhat complicated task. Study the various steps involved. (John Deere)

SE, and SF. These replace the OLD designations of ML, MM, and MS.

The letter "S" indicates the oil is basically for Service Station (gasoline engine) use. Commercial and fleet (diesel engines) oils use the letter "C" and are classified as CA, CB, CC, and CD.

SA (Utility Gasoline and Diesel Engine Service). This oil is for use in utility engine operation under highly favorable conditions (light loads, moderate speeds, and clean conditions). It generally contains no additives.

SB (Minimum Duty Gasoline Engine Service). This oil is for gasoline engines operating under mild conditions where little oil compounding (addition of other materials to the oil) is required. They will provide resistance to oil oxidation (gum formation), bearing corrosion, and scuffing (parts scratching each other).

SC (1964 Gasoline Engine Warranty Maintenance Service). Oil similar to that used for service in auto engines manufactured from 1964 through 1967. These oils have additives which offer control of wear, rust, corrosion, and high or low temperature deposits.

SD (1968 Gasoline Engine Warranty Maintenance Service). An oil for service typical of that required for 1968 through 1970 auto and light truck engines. The oil is also applicable to some 1971 and later auto engines when so stated by the auto maker. This oil provides additional protection (as compared with SC) against wear, rust, corrosion, and high or low temperature deposits.

SE (1972 Gasoline Engine Warranty Maintenance Service). This is specified for 1972 through 1979 car and light truck engines. It provides excellent protection against rust, corrosion, wear, oil oxidation, and high temperature deposits that can cause oil thickening. Obviously, this oil can be used in all engines in which SD or SC is normally recommended.

SF (1980 Gasoline Engine Warranty Service). This is currently the top ranked oil and is generally specified for 1980 and later car and light truck engines. This oil provides improved anti-wear qualities along with increased oxidation stability and protection against corrosion, rust, engine deposits, etc. SF oils can be used in all engines where SE, SD, or SC are recommended.

Study the chart in Fig. 5-6. Note the relationship between the new oil classification numbers and that previously used.

In addition to classifying oil acccording to the severity of service, (SA, SB, SC, etc.), oil for SF service may also be required to pass certain actual use tests to determine how well the oil prevents engine rusting, oxidation, corrosion, scuffing, wear, thickening, and the formation of sludge and varnish. These laboratory engine tests are called ENGINE SEQUENCE TESTS. They are also sometimes referred to as "ASTM Sequence Tests" or "Car Manufacturers Sequence Tests."

Oils may also be classified according to MILITARY SPECIFICATIONS (specifications set up for oils to be used by the Military). MANUFACTURER'S SPECIFICATIONS (developed by some engine makers) can also be used.

OIL HAS SEVERAL JOBS

In addition to lubricating the engine, the oil must also assist in COOLING. The steady flow of oil through the bearings carries away a great deal of the heat that is generated. Oil strikes the piston head and carries heat with it. As the oil is returned to the sump before being recirculated, it is much cooler by the time it reaches the bearings again.

Some high speed and heavy-duty engines, plus many air-cooled engines, run the oil through a cooler (similar to the regular radiator only smaller). Others use fins on the oil pan to aid in the cooling.

Oil must SEAL. Piston rings would not be too effective without oil as a final sealing agent. It also assists in sealing around valve stems.

A good oil will CLEAN. The detergents in the oil assist in removing sludge, gum, some carbon, etc.

OIL CLEANS, COOLS, SEALS AND LUBRICATES

SF oils have many extra additives (compounds designed to improve the oil) added to them. These additives fight bearing corrosion; help to keep small foreign particles in suspension; reduce oxidization; minimize carbon, lacquer and gum formation; and reduce engine wear.

SF oils have a high detergent quality that tend to keep the engine clean by preventing the formation of sludge and gum. Sludge is produced by engine oil combining with water and dust. When these three ingredients get together and are thoroughly mixed, they

REFERENCE CHART

	NEW API ENGINE SERVICE CLASSIFICATIONS	**PREVIOUS API ENGINE SERVICE CLASSIFICATIONS**	**RELATED DESIGNATIONS MILITARY AND INDUSTRY**
GASOLINE ENGINES	SERVICE STATION ENGINE SERVICES		
	SA	ML	Straight Mineral Oil
	SB	MM	Inhibited Oil
	SC	MS (1964)	1964 MS Warranty Approved, M2C101-A
	SD	MS (1968)	1968 MS Warranty Approved, M2C101-B, 6041 (Prior to July, 1970)
	SE	None	1972 Warranty Approved, M2C101-C, 6041-M (July 1970)
	SF	None	1980 Warranty Approved
DIESEL ENGINES	COMMERCIAL AND FLEET ENGINE SERVICES		
	CA	DG	MIL-L-2104A
	CB	DM	Supp. 1
	CC	DM	MIL-L-2104B
	CD	DS	MIL-L-45199B, Series 3

Fig. 5-6. Chart shows the relationship between the old and the new API Service Classifications.

produce the thick, black, greasy substance known as sludge.

OIL VISCOSITY

Oil viscosity refers to the thickness or fluidity of the oil. In other words, it is a measure of an oil's ability to resist flowing.

The Society of Automotive Engineers (SAE) have set low (0°F or −18°C) and high (210°F or 99°C) temperature requirements for oil.

Oils that meet special SAE low temperature requirements have the letter W following the viscosity rating, i.e., (SAE 10W). Oils that meet the high temperature requirements have no such letter, but are merely designated as (SAE 30), etc.

Viscosity is determined by taking any measured sample of oil and heating it to a certain point. The heated oil is then allowed to flow out of a very precise hole. The length of time it takes to flow determines its viscosity rating. The faster is flows, the lower the rating. This testing device is referred to as a VISCO-SIMETER . Fig. 5-7.

VISCOSITY INDEX

Oils thin out when heated and thicken when cooled. As a good engine oil must be reasonably thin for cold starts, as well as thick enough at high temperatures, the Viscosity Index (VI) is important.

When oils are heated, they tend to lose their body (resistance to oil film failure). If a given oil is thin at

Fig. 5-7. Principle of the viscosimeter.

cold temperatures and when heated, does not thin out much more, it is said to have a high VI. If the heating produces a great change in viscosity, it will have a low VI. The VI, then, is a measure of the ability of an oil to resist changes in viscosity when heated.

MULTI-GRADE OILS (MULTI-VISCOSITY)

Multi-grade oils meet SAE specifications for both the low temperature requirements of a light oil and the high temperature requirements of a heavy oil. They meet the viscosity and performance requirements of two or more SAE grades and are marked SAE 5W-20, SAE 5W-30, SAE 10W-20W-30, SAE 10W-30, SAE 10W-40, SAE 10W-20W-40, etc. They are often referred to as multi-viscosity, all-season, and all-weather.

CHOOSING OIL VISCOSITY

Always follow the manufacturer's recommendation for viscosity rating. The most commonly used oils are SAE 10W, SAE 20W, SAE 20, SAE 30, SAE 10W-30, and SAE 10W-20W-40. These recommendations are based on engine design and the lowest anticipated temperatures. See Fig. 5-8.

Fig. 5-8. Symbol or "logo" is designed to be used on cans of engine oil to assist purchaser in selecting proper lubricant. The oil's quality and service recommendation is given by API (American Petroleum Institute) numbers. In this example, Service SF/CC (an oil for diesel engines), the viscosity is indicated by the SAE (Society of Automotive Engineers) number —10W-30. The term "energy conserving" indicates oil has special properties that provide additional friction reduction which improves fuel mileage. (Chevrolet)

WHEN SHOULD OIL BE CHANGED?

The answer to this popular problem depends on so many variables that a general recommendation is very difficult to make.

Many manufacturers suggest from 1,000 to 7,500 miles (1 600 to 12 000 km) or 3 to 12 months between oil changes.

Any quality of oil will retain proper lubricating properties longer if:
1. The engine is operated for reasonably long periods each time it is started.
2. The engine is in good mechanical condition.
3. The engine operates at a temperature between 180 and 200°F (82.2 – 93.3°C) or higher.
4. The engine has a good oil filter.
5. The crankcase ventilation system is open and the PCV valve is functioning properly.
6. The engine is operated at moderate to fairly high speeds.
7. The engine is provided with an efficient air cleaner.
8. The carburetion system is properly adjusted.

9. The engine is operated under clean conditions. There are other considerations but these are the most important.

The conditions given are ideal. If your engine operates under them, you can use the oil for the maximum recommended time.

Engines that are started and stopped frequently, that are driven short distances, that never warm up, that are operated under dusty conditions, that are in poor mechanical condition, that have no filter system, should have the oil changed at least every 500 miles (805 km).

Very few engines are operated at either extreme. Knowing the conditions surrounding the operation of any particular engine will allow you to determine, in an intelligent manner, when to change the oil.

When you do change it, drain only when the engine is hot. Do not use kerosene as a flushing agent.

Do not be confused by the color of the oil. Oils containing detergents will keep small particles in suspension and will LOOK dirty but in reality will still be usable. Base your oil change on mileage—after considering all the factors involved.

HOW OIL WORKS

When oil is injected into a bearing, Fig. 5-9, it is drawn between the two bearing surfaces. The oil then separates the parts, and they revolve without actually touching each other. When the shaft stops revolving, and oil is no longer supplied, the shaft will settle down and squeeze the oil film apart and will rest on the bearing. Some residual oil (oil that clings to the parts) will be retained. When the engine is started, the shaft will have only residual oil for the first few seconds of

RESIDUAL OIL ONLY. SHAFT RESTS ON BEARING

OIL ENTERING JOURNAL. SHAFT ROTATING

OIL HAS WEDGED SHAFT UP. BEARING AND JOURNAL WILL NOT TOUCH

1. SHAFT RESTING ON BEARING.
2. OIL ENTERING BEARING.
3. OIL IS PULLED THROUGH BY SHAFT. SHAFT IS NOW FREE OF BEARING.

Fig. 5-9. How oil enters a bearing.

103

operation. This is why engines should run slowly, in neutral, for a minute when first started.

OIL SLIPS

The top of the film that contacts the shaft journal, and the bottom of the film that contacts the bearing, resist movement to some extent. The sliding effect of the oil is achieved nearer the center of the film. See Fig. 5-10.

This slipping action allows the journal to spin easily and still not contact the bearing surface.

OIL TENDS TO RESIST SLIPPING ON BEARING AND JOURNAL SURFACES

MOST OF SLIPPING OCCURS NEAR CENTER OF OIL FILM

Fig. 5-10. Action of oil in bearing.

BEARING CLEARANCE

It is important that all bearings have the proper clearances. The ideal being loose enough for oil to enter, but tight enough to resist pounding. Oil clearances will average around .002 in. (0.05 mm).

HOW OIL GETS TO THE BEARINGS

Engines are lubricated in three ways:
1. Full pressure oiling.
2. Splash oiling.
3. Combination splash and pressure.
The full pressure system will be discussed first.

FULL PRESSURE SYSTEM

The pressure system draws oil from the pan sump by means of an oil pump. The pump then forces oil, through special passages, to the crankshaft and camshaft journals. The crankshaft is drilled to permit oil to flow to the connecting rod journals. In some engines the rods are drilled their full length to allow oil to pass up to the wrist pin bushings. Bearing throw-off may be helped, by spurt holes in the rod, to lubricate the cylinder walls. Timing gears, lifters, and rocker arms, where used, are also oiled. In the pressure system, all bearings are oiled by either pumping oil into the bearings, or squirting or dripping it on. Fig. 5-11.

SPLASH SYSTEM

The splash system supplies oil to moving parts by attaching dippers to the bottom of the connecting

Fig. 5-11. Schematic of pressure system. Notice how oil travels to all major bearings. When it passes through bearing, it is thrown around creating an oil spray and mist. Oil then returns to sump in pan.

rods. These dippers can either dip into the sump itself, or they can dip into shallow trays. The whirling dippers splash oil over the inside of the engine. The dipper is usually drilled so that oil is forced into the connecting rod bearings.

An oil pump may be used to keep oil trays full at all times. The splash system is used primarily on small one cylinder engines. Fig. 5-12.

COMBINATION SPLASH AND PRESSURE

This system uses dippers and trays. An oil pump supplies oil to the camshaft and crankshaft bearings. On overhead engines, oil is pumped to the rocker arms and valves.

Small pipes are sometimes used to squirt oil over the trays. The whirling dipper is drilled to permit oil

ROD DIPPER SPLASHES OIL OVER ENGINE INTERIOR

Fig. 5-12. Simple splash oiling system.

to enter the connecting rod bearing. When the dipper strikes the stream of oil, it throws oil over the interior of the engine. At the same time, oil is driven up the dipper hole into the rod bearing. When idling, the oil stream may not quite reach the dippers but will keep the trays full. Fig. 5-13.

Fig. 5-13. Combination splash and pressure oiling system. Oil pump 6 draws oil up pipe 5 from sump 9. It then pumps oil to main bearings 1 through discharge pipe 7. Oil is also pumped down discharge to nozzle 8 where oil sprays out and strikes dipper 3. This rams oil into rod bearing 2. Tray 4 also holds oil for dipper to strike.

FOURTH METHOD OF OILING

Most two-cycle engines (discussed later) draw gas and air into the crankcase. In the case of these engines, lubricating oil is mixed with the gasoline and upon entry into the crankcase, provides ample lubrication for the bearings.

PRESSURE SYSTEM WIDELY USED

The pressure system best meets the needs of the modern car engine and is therefore in almost universal use. This chapter will deal primarily with the pressure system.

SUMP

Oil is poured into the engine and flows down into the pan. One end of the pan is lower and forms a reservoir called a SUMP. Baffle plates are sometimes used to prevent the oil from sloshing around. The drain plug is placed in the bottom of the sump. See Fig. 5-14.

OIL PICKUP

Some engines have a rigid pipe leading down into the oil in the sump. It does not come too close to the bottom to avoid picking up sediment. Some engines use a floating pickup. This actually floats on top of

the oil and therefore draws only from the top of the sump. As the oil level drops, the pickup will also drop, to maintain a constant supply of oil.

Both types of oil pickup use screens to exclude the larger particles that may be drawn into the system. In the event the screen becomes clogged, there may be a small valve that will be drawn open, thus allowing the pump to bypass the screen and obtain oil. Fig. 5-15.

OIL PUMPS

There are four principal types of oil pumps that have been used on engines. They are the GEAR,

Fig. 5-14. Oil pan with sump and baffle. There are many designs for sumps and baffles.

Fig. 5-15. Rigid type oil pickup. Note screen 7 over pump inlet. Study oil flow: 1—Pump gear shaft. 2—Pump housing. 3—Bushings. 4—Driving gear. 5—Cover. 6—Retainer. 7—Screen. 8—Driven gear. 9—Relief valve spring. 10—Relief valve ball. (Volvo)

ROTARY, VANE, and PLUNGER pumps. The two most widely used are the GEAR and the ROTARY types.

GEAR PUMP

The gear pump uses a driving and a driven spur gear as the moving force to pump oil. These gears are placed in a compact housing. The driven gear revolves on a short shaft, while the driving gear is fastened to a longer shaft that is turned by a spiral gear meshed with a similar gear on the camshaft.

The teeth of the two gears must mesh with a minimum amount of clearance. The housing just clears the top, bottom, and sides of both gears.

An inlet pipe allows oil to be drawn in by the whirling gear teeth. Each tooth catches what is will hold and carries it around. When the oil reaches the opposite side, it cannot come back through the center of the gears as they are closely meshed.

As each tooth carries a load of oil around and deposits it on the outlet sides, the oil has nowhere to go but through the outlet to the oil channels. The gear pump is efficient and produces oil pressure needed. Figs. 5-15, 5-16, 5-17.

Fig. 5-17. Exploded view of a gear type oil pump. (Datsun)

Fig. 5-16. Gear oil pump. Notice how oil is caught in teeth and carried around. As pump whirls rapidly, it will produce a steady stream of oil.

A somewhat different adaptation of the gear pump is pictured in Fig. 5-18. The driving gear (center) and driven gear (outer) teeth carry oil around to the outlet area. As the teeth mesh, the oil is compressed and forced through the outlet. An exploded view of a similar pump is shown in Fig. 5-19.

Fig. 5-18. Gear oil pump using one gear with internal teeth and another with external teeth. As gears rotate, oil is carried past filler block in teeth of each gear. This oil is deposited in outlet area. Since gears mesh, oil has no place to escape and pressure is built up forcing oil through outlet. (Deere & Co.)

Fig. 5-19. One form of gear oil pump. Principle of operation is same as that in Fig. 5-18. (Toyota)

ROTARY PUMP

A rotary pump uses a housing, an inner rotor, and an outer rotor. The outer rotor is cut away in the form of a star with rounded points.

The inner rotor is shaped in the form of a cross with rounded points that fit in the outer rotor star. The inner rotor is much smaller. It is driven by a shaft turned by the camshaft.

The inner rotor is mounted off center so that when it turns, the rounded points "walk" around in the star-shaped outer rotor. This causes the outer rotor to revolve also. As the inner rotor "walks" the outer rotor around, the outer rotor openings pick up oil at the inlet pipe and pull it around until it lines up with outlet. It is then forced out as the inner and outer rotor points close together. The oil cannot make a circuit around, as the inner rotor fits snugly against the outer rotor at one spot. Figs. 5-20 and 5-21 illustrate the rotor pump.

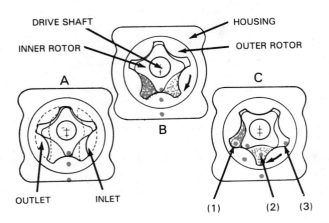

Fig. 5-20. Rotor oil pump action. A—Pump inlet and outlet areas. B—Drive shaft turns inner rotor causing it to walk around in outer rotor. Outer rotor will also turn. C—Rotor pulls around a charge of oil and forces it through the outlet (1). While this is happening, another charge is moving around (2) and another is being picked up at the inlet (3). (Jaguar)

Fig. 5-21. Exploded view of a rotor type oil pump. Note gear on drive shaft. This gear will mesh with another gear on the camshaft.

VANE PUMP

This pump uses a round housing with a round rotor placed off center. This rotor contains two or more VANES, or rotor blades, that fit into slots in the rotor. The vanes are held out against the round housing by springs between the vanes. Some designs feed oil, under pressure, to the inner vane ends. This pressure along with centrifugal force, helps hold the vanes in firm contact with the housing wall.

As the shaft turns, the vanes are forced in and out to keep contact with the housing. As they swing out, they pick up a charge of oil and carry it around. As the vane is forced in, this places a squeeze on the oil and it is pushed out of the pump. As a steady stream of charges are picked up, carried around, and squeezed out, the pump produces a good stream of oil. Figs. 5-22 and 5-23.

PLUNGER PUMP

The plunger type pump is used in many small one cylinder engines to maintain the oil level in the dipper trays.

It utilizes a cylinder, plunger, and check valves. It is usually driven by a cam on the camshaft.

As the cam releases the plunger, it is pushed upward by a strong spiral spring. The inlet check valve opens and oil is drawn in. As the cam continues to rotate, it will press the plunger down. This closes the inlet valve and opens the outlet. The process is repeated over and over, producing a steady stream of oil. Fig. 5-24 illustrates one type of plunger pump.

Fig. 5-22. Vane oil pump. Vane 1 has just passed inlet hole. As it continues by, it will form a vacuum that will continue to draw oil in until vane 2 passes inlet. As vane 2 passes inlet it will push oil around and at the same time, draw a vacuum behind to pull oil in for vane 1.

As each vane, pushing a charge of oil, arrives near outlet, spaces grow small and the oil is squeezed out of pump.

Fig. 5-23. Exploded view of vane type oil pump. (Allis Chalmers)

PRESSURE RELIEF VALVE

An oil pump will produce pressures far beyond those necessary. The pumps are designed to carry a large flow of oil but when the usable pressure limits are reached, a pressure relief valve opens and allows oil to return to the sump.

The relief valve will allow the pressure reaching the bearings to remain at any predetermined level. By varying spring tension, the pressure can be raised or lowered.

The relief valve can be located right at the pump, Fig. 5-17, or at any spot between the pump and the bearings. Figs. 5-25 and 5-26 illustrate a relief valve located in the side of the block.

OIL GALLERIES AND LINES

Oil that is allowed to pass the pressure relief valve is carried to the bearing through tubes and oil galleries (passageways cast in the block or made up of large

Fig. 5-24. Plunger oil pump. When plunger travels up it forms vacuum within pump. This opens inlet check and closes outlet. Cam pushes plunger down to create pressure. This shuts intake check and forces oil through outlet check valve.

Fig. 5-25. Oil pressure relief valve. Oil in main oil gallery is under pressure from oil pump. When pressure exceeds setting for relief valve, it will push plunger check valve back against plunger spring pressure. When valve is forced back enough to expose oil outlet channel, oil will pass from main oil gallery past valve, through oil outlet and back into pan sump.

tubing). The main oil gallery runs lengthwise in the block and most other lines connect with it. Most engines have a plug at each end of the main gallery. When overhauling the engine, the plugs may be removed and the gallery cleaned.

Lines from the main gallery are drilled to the main bearings. The crankshaft is drilled to carry oil from the main journals to the rod journals. See Figs. 5-27 and 5-28.

Some rods are drilled full length to carry oil to the

Fig. 5-26. Exploded view of an oil pressure relief valve. Valve is located in side of block. 1—Valve. 2—Spring. 3—Gasket. 4—Locking bolt.   (Austin)

wrist pins. Others have tiny holes that line up with the crank journal once every revolution. When the two holes align, oil is squirted through the "spit" hole and onto the cylinder wall. Spit holes are also used to lubricate the camshaft lobes in some engines.

The timing chain is oiled either by spray or by oil discharged from the No. 1 camshaft bearing.

The valve train is lubricated by oil spray and in the case of overhead valve engines, by oil pumped into the rocker arm shaft, through rockers, to valves, Fig. 5-28. Oil can also reach the rocker arms via hollow push rods. Some engines, such as shown in Fig. 5-27, do not employ rocker arms but operate the valves directly from the camshaft lobes.

Camshafts receive oil under pressure to their journals. The lobes are lubed by oil spray.

Fig. 5-27. Full pressure engine oiling system. 1—Oil filler cap. 2—Camshaft and tappet oil squirt hole. 3—Exhaust valve camshaft. 4—Intake camshaft. 5—Oil drain. 6—Connecting rod squirt holes for cylinder lubrication. 7—Oil pressure gauge sending unit. 8—Low oil pressure warning switch. 9—Oil entrance from filter. 10—Oil filter (pleated paper surface type). 11—Relief valve. 12—Dipstick. 13—Oil drain plug. 14—Oil pump pickup. 15—Oil pressure relief valve. 16—Oil pump (gear type). 17—Oil pump drive gear lubrication squirt hole.   (Fiat)

Fig. 5-28. Cutaway showing oil flow through a V-8 engine. Follow path of oil from pickup through galleries to various components.   (Jeep)

VALVE CLOSED

VALVE OPEN

PUSH ROD PRESSES
AGAINST CUP

PLUNGER EXTENDED
MAINTAINING ZERO
CLEARANCE

OIL UNDER
PRESSURE

BALL CHECK
VALVE OPEN

OIL FORCED UPWARD
CLOSES CHECK VALVE

SLIGHT LEAKAGE
BETWEEN PLUNGER
AND BODY

Fig. 5-29. Hydraulic valve lifter, showing tappet action—cutaway views.

OIL ENTERS BEARING

The bearing receives oil from a hole drilled through the bearing support. The insert has a hole that aligns with the one in the bearing support. The oil passes through and engages the turning journal and is pulled around between the insert and journal.

Some inserts have shallow grooves cut in them to assist in spreading the oil.

Oil is constantly forced through the bearings. Oil leaving a bearing is thrown violently outward. This helps to produce the fine oil mist inside the engine that is useful in lubricating hard-to-reach spots. All oil eventually flows back into the sump. Figs. 5-30 and 5-31.

HYDRAULIC VALVE LIFTERS

Hydraulic type valve lifters are used on many engines. One type of hydraulic lifter is shown in Fig. 5-29. In this lifter, oil under pressure is forced into the tappet when the valve is closed. This extends the

110

FULL FLOW FILTER

ROCKER ARM LUBRICATION

WATER JACKET

SPIT HOLE

DIP STICK

CAMSHAFT

PRESSURE GAUGE SENDER

MAIN BEARING

OIL PUMP

SUMP

OIL PICKUP

DRAIN PLUG

ROCKER ARM SHAFT GALLERY

WATER JACKET

LINE TO ROCKER ARM GALLERY

MAIN OIL GALLERY

PAN

SUMP

BAFFLE

OIL PUMP

Fig. 5-30. Above. Front section of a four cylinder engine. Solid brown shows areas receiving oil under pressure (except sump). Fig. 5-31. Below. Longitudinal section. Brown dots indicate areas lubricated by splash, spray or oil mist.

plunger in the tappet so valve clearance is eliminated.

When the camshaft lobe moves around and starts to raise the tappet, oil is forced upward in the lower chamber of the tappet. This closes the ball check valve and oil cannot escape. Since oil does not compress, the valve is actually lifted on the column of oil and is supported by the oil while the valve is open.

When the cam lobe moves from under the tappet and the spring causes the valve to close, pressure in the lower chamber of the tappet is relieved. Oil loss from the lower chamber is replaced by oil pressure from the lubricating system of the engine.

STUDY THE COLORED CROSS SECTION VIEWS

Study Figs. 5-30 and 5-31. They show a typical four cylinder, valve-in-head engine. The solid brown lines indicate lubrication by direct pressure. The dotted brown areas are lubricated by splash, dripping, spray, or oil mist.

OIL NEEDS CLEANING

Engine oil soon becomes contaminated with dust, bits of carbon, metal dust, and sludge. If these impurities are allowed to remain in the oil, it will hasten engine wear. Most modern engines are equipped with an oil filtering system to remove these harmful impurities.

FILTERS

Many materials have been tried in an effort to find a satisfactory filtering medium. Cotton waste, special fibers, metal, clay and paper have all been used.

For auto engines, cotton waste provides DEPTH filtration and paper provides SURFACE filtration. Both are in general use. Heavy-duty engines sometimes employ a metal filter that is very good where contaminants build up quickly.

All filters eventually clog up and must be replaced. Replacement varies but will average 4,000 to 6,000 miles (6 437 to 9 656 km) per filter. A, B, and C, Fig. 5-32, illustrates the filtering principle used in metal, cotton, and paper filters.

FILTER OPERATION

Some oil filters use a permanent metal container that holds the filtering element. Others use a disposable type in which the entire filter, container and all, are thrown away.

Oil is pumped into the container and surrounds the filter. The oil passes through the filtering element to the center outlet pipe. It is then returned to the sump, or to the bearings, depending on the type of system.

Most bypass filters (only part of oil supplied by pump goes through the filter) use either flexible hose or tubing to connect them to the engine. The full-flow type (entire output of pump goes through filter) gen-

Fig. 5-32. Oil filter materials. A—Cotton waste between thin perforated metal sheets. B—Paper, treated with resins. C—Cuno type. Thin layers of metal sheet held apart by bumps or bars.

erally fastens directly to the engine. See Figs. 5-33 and 5-34.

FULL-FLOW FILTER SYSTEM

In the widely used full-flow filter system, the oil is pumped directly to the filter from the pump. After passing through the filter, the oil then goes to the oil galleries. In this way, all oil is filtered before reaching the bearings.

In the event the filter becomes clogged, a small relief valve opens and allows the oil to flow directly to the bearings. This avoids the possibility of starving the bearings when the filter becomes unusable. See Fig. 5-35.

Fig. 5-33. Full-flow type of oil filter. When a change is required, the entire filter is replaced. 1—Relief valve. 2—Filter element (folded paper). 3—Body. 4—Connecting pipe. 5—Gasket. 6—Engine block. This pleated paper filter provides surface filtration in that all particles are trapped on the outer surface. (Volvo)

Fig. 5-34. Depth type filtration oil filter. 1—Housing. 2—Seal. 3—Oil inlet. 4—Oil outlet. 5—Check valve to prevent oil drainback when filter is mounted in either a horizontal or inverted (upside down) position. 6—Filter material. 7—Relief valve opens if filter clogs. (Volvo)

Fig. 5-35. Full-flow oil filter system. Note built-in relief valve to allow oil to flow even if filter becomes clogged. This system filters all oil before it reaches the bearings. (John Deere)

BYPASS FILTER SYSTEM

The bypass system differs from the full-flow in that it does not filter the oil before it reaches the bearings. It is constantly filtering some of the oil from the system and then returning it to the sump. Fig. 5-36.

CRANKCASE MUST BE VENTILATED

Even in new engines there is a certain amount of hot gas spurting by the piston rings and on into the crankcase. This causes pressure in the crankcase and unless it is vented, will force oil to escape by the oil seals.

It is also important to eliminate these gases, as they form moisture and deposit sulphuric acid in the oil.

A certain amount of raw gasoline will also pass the pistons and enter the oil. As the oil becomes hot, the

moisture and gasoline will evaporate and the ventilation system will remove them.

An entrance, called a BREATHER, was provided on older engines at the top or side. A cover cap, usually filled with oil soaked metal wool, was furnished to prevent the entrance of dust and dirt.

The whirling engine parts create an air disturbance within the engine. An outlet pipe at the opposite end runs down below the engine. When the car is in motion, a partial vacuum is formed at the end of the pipe. This draws air through the engine. A baffle is provided to prevent oil vapor from being drawn through the road draft tube. Fig. 5-37 illustrates a basic crankcase ventilation system as was used on engines for many years.

Fig. 5-36. Bypass filter system. This setup filters some of the oil all of the time, but does not filter oil before it reaches the bearings. (John Deere)

Fig. 5-37. Airflow in a road draft crankcase ventilation system. Notice filter material in both inlet and outlet. Good ventilation is important.

POSITIVE (FORCED) CRANKCASE VENTILATION

The road draft ventilation system, shown in Fig. 5-37, allowed air pollutants to enter the atmosphere. To prevent this, all car engines NOW employ a POSITIVE CRANKCASE VENTILATION SYSTEM.

This system uses engine vacuum to draw a stream of fresh air through the engine. Clean air is taken from either the breather cap (open system) or the air cleaner (closed system). All engines now use the CLOSED SYSTEM to prevent fumes backfeeding (traveling backward) out of the breather cap during periods of high crankcase pressure (rapid acceleration for example).

The air is then pulled through the engine where it mixes with gases in the crankcase. The mixture of air and gases is then drawn into the intake manifold where it is burned in the cylinders. Fig. 5-38 shows a cross-sectional view of the current CLOSED positive crankcase ventilation system.

Fig. 5-39 illustrates the difference between the OPEN and CLOSED ventilation systems.

The complete operation of the positive crankcase ventilation system will be covered in the chapter on EMISSION CONTROL.

Fig. 5-39. Two types of positive crankcase ventilation systems. A—Closed type that draws air in through air cleaner. B—Airflow control valve. C—Open type that draws air in through breather cap. (Plymouth)

OIL SEALS

Oil is retained in the engine by gaskets and oil seals. The seals are placed at the front and the rear of the crankshaft. Figs. 5-40, 5-41, and 5-42 illustrate a gasket, seals, and an oil slinger. The slinger catches

Fig. 5-40. A neoprene gasket is used to prevent oil leakage between the timing gear cover and engine pan. (Chevrolet)

Fig. 5-38. Positive Crankcase Ventilation (PCV) system. Vacuum in intake manifold draws air (from air cleaner) through engine interior. (Nissan)

Fig. 5-41. Front crankshaft oil seal. Seal is pressed into timing chain cover. Open end of seal faces inward so oil pressure tends to squeeze seal against shaft. Spring pulls seal against shaft. Seal will be neoprene or leather.

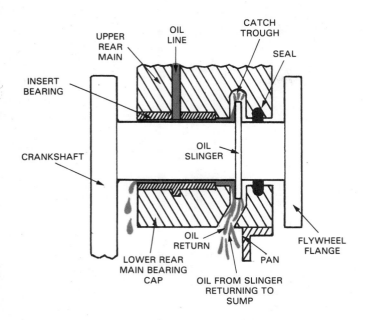

Fig. 5-42. Rear crankshaft oil seals. Oil that escapes past bearing is stopped by slinger and seal. Oil on slinger is thrown out into the catch trough and returned to sump. Some engines use a seal only. One seal is made of asbestos rope, oil impregnated and covered with graphite. Others are made of synthetic rubber.

what oil may escape past the bearing and, as it is whirling, the slinger throws the oil outward into a catch trough that returns the oil to the sump. Many engines do not use slingers.

OIL PRESSURE GAUGES

One type of oil pressure gauge utilizes the Bourdon tube gauge connected to the oil gallery via a tube. This type of gauge was covered in the COOLING section.

An electric oil pressure gauge uses a different sender unit than that used by an electric water temperature gauge. Fig. 5-43 shows a typical electric oil pressure gauge setup using the balancing magnetic coil principle.

Fig. 5-44 shows a heating coil electric pressure gauge setup. Note the difference between this unit and the one in Fig. 5-43.

Some cars use a warning light to indicate when the pressure drops below a certain point. The light warns of system failure but does not indicate actual pressure, Fig. 5-45.

DIPSTICK

A long metal rod, commonly referred to as a "dipstick," is used to check the amount of oil in the crankcase sump. The rod is held in a tube, the end of which protrudes into the sump. It may be withdrawn and the level of the oil in the sump checked by examining the rod to see where the oil reached. Fig. 5-46 shows a dipstick and its markings.

Fig. 5-43. Schematic diagram of electric oil gauge. Electricity travels from battery, through key switch to coil 2, then across wire 4 to coil 1 and on to ground. Both coils are connected by wire 4 to resistance type unit 8, mounted on engine.

Oil entering 5 will raise diaphragm 6 causing sliding contact 7 to slide further out on resistance unit. This will increase resistance.

When resistance is increased, coil 1 will strengthen magnetic pull on armature 3. This will pull armature and indicating needle over to read more pressure.

When pressure drops, sliding contact will come back and decrease resistance. This strengthens coil 2 and weakens coil 1. Coil 2 will now pull armature and needle down to read less pressure.

COOLING THE OIL

Oil removes much heat from the pistons, cylinder walls, etc., and becomes quite hot. It is important that the oil have some way to rid itself of excess heat. In the average engine this is accomplished by the airstream passing over the thin oil pan thus drawing much heat from the oil. The cooling system keeps the cylinder block and head area within an acceptable temperature range thus limiting oil heat exposure. Oil moving through the filter gives off some heat to the airstream and the entire engine surface gives off heat. All these sources of heat removal will normally prevent excess heating of the oil.

Many high speed and heavy duty engines as well as some normal duty engines that may occasionally be exposed to heavy operating loads (trailer towing, steep roads, etc.), are equipped with an oil cooler. Numerous designs have been used. One type of auto engine oil cooler is shown in Fig. 5-47.

This particular cooler fits between the oil filter and the engine block. Engine coolant circulates around the thin discs making up the oil compartment. As the oil passes through the cooler on its way to the filter it is forced through the thin disc compartments where it gives off heat to the passing coolant.

SUMMARY

Friction, the enemy of all engines, is controlled through the use of lubricating oil.

OPERATION WITH LOW OIL PRESSURE

OPERATION WITH HIGH OIL PRESSURE

Fig. 5-44. Heating coil type oil pressure gauge. Current flows through gauge heating coil and then on through sender heating coil. Both coils heat up and cause bimetal strips to bend. Gauge bimetal will move pointer when it bends. How far pointer moves depends on how hot bimetal gets. Gauge bimetal temperature is controlled by sender bimetal strip. As sender heats up, bimetal bends away from ground contact breaking circuit. When circuit is broken, sender coil cools and bimetal makes contact again, reestablishing current flow. Bimetal heats, bends, makes circuit, etc., over and over.

In A, sender diaphragm is not pushing insulated contact up. Bimetal breaks current easily so coils heat for short period. In B, oil pressure is high forcing diaphragm up which bends grounded contact up. Sender coil will now have to stay on much longer to heat bimetal enough to break contact. This keeps gauge coil heating longer thus imparting a greater bend to its bimetal strip. Pointer now moves further across gauge indicating more oil pressure.   (Deere & Co.)

Lubricating oil must cool, clean, seal, and lubricate. The VISCOSITY (SAE 20W, 30, 40, etc.) and the SERVICE RATING (SA, SB, SC, SD, SE, and SF) are important factors in choosing the proper oil for a specific engine.

Engine oil is drawn from a crankcase sump, through a strainer, by the oil pump. It is then pumped to all the major bearings through a network of oil galleries and tubes.

Maximum oil pressure is controlled by a pressure relief valve. The most commonly used oil pumps are

Fig. 5-45. Schematic diagram of oil pressure indicator light. Oil enters 6 and raises diaphragm 5. This separates points 4, breaking circuit through indicator light 3. When pressure drops, spring 1 will close points and light will burn. Insulation 2 prevents circuit from grounding out. Indicator will light when engine stops or when pressure drops to around 7 lbs.

the GEAR and the ROTOR types. Two others are the VANE and the PLUNGER pumps. Most are either turned or actuated by the camshaft.

Upon entering the bearings, the engine oil separates the moving parts with a fine film. As it passes through the bearings, it is thrown outward in every direction. Oil drops down on some parts and is sprayed against others. The whirling parts create an oily mist that lubricates the other areas. It is then returned to the sump for recirculation. The system is ventilated to remove moisture, hot gases and excessive pressure.

Oil can be filtered by a FULL-FLOW or a BYPASS system. Even with filtering, oil must be changed periodically. The length of time between changes depends on driving conditions and the number of miles driven.

Oil pressure is measured by means of an electric or a Bourdon tube gauge. The amount of oil in the sump can be checked by using the dipstick.

Some engines are equipped with oil coolers.

KNOW THESE TERMS

Friction, Dry friction, Wet friction, Crude oil, Distillation, Viscosity, Multi-grade oil, Bearing clearance, Full pressure system, Sump, Oil pickup, Oil pump, Pressure relief valve, Oil galleries, Oil filter.

REVIEW QUESTIONS—CHAPTER 5

1. What is meant by the term FRICTION?
2. For purposes of illustration, friction was defined or divided into two kinds. Name them.
3. What is a FROZEN bearing?
4. Name two kinds of bearings that can be used in an engine.

Fig. 5-46. Dipstick. Keep oil level above low or add oil level. Do not fill above full mark.

Fig. 5-47. Engine oil cooling. This unit mounts between oil filter and engine. Engine coolant flowing around oil compartments cools oil. 1—Coolant inlet. 2—Discs. 3—Coolant outlet. 4—Rubber seal. 5—Coolant drain plug. (Volvo)

5. Explain how oil reduces friction.
6. Oil for an engine is produced from crude oil by a process known as _____.
7. The American Petroleum Institute has classified oil for auto engines into six types. Name them.
8. What is a detergent oil?
9. Sludge is made up of _____, _____ and _____.
10. A good engine oil has four tasks. What are they?
11. Define the word VISCOSITY.
12. If an oil has this marking on the can, SAE 20W, what would it mean?
13. What would SAE 10W–30 mean?
14. If an oil is very thick when cold, and very thin when hot, this oil would have a _____ VI.
15. List some of the factors to be considered in determining when an oil should be changed.
16. What would an average bearing oil clearance be?
17. Name the major ways of lubricating an engine.
18. How are two-stroke cycle engines lubricated?
19. The most popular type of lubrication system is the _____ system.
20. Name four types of oil pumps and explain how each one works.
21. The two most widely used types of oil pumps are the _____ and the _____.
22. The oil pressure in a system cannot exceed a predetermined pressure. How is this pressure controlled?
23. What is an oil gallery?
24. What is the difference between the full-flow filter system and the bypass filter system?
25. Two popular filter elements would be the _____ and the _____ elements.
26. What happens, in the full-flow system, when the filter becomes clogged?
27. Why is it important to provide adequate ventilation for the engine?
28. How does the engine crankcase ventilation system (PCV) work?
29. In addition to gaskets, oil _____ are placed on the front and rear of the crankshaft.
30. What does the oil pressure gauge tell you?
31. How do you determine how much oil there is in the oil sump?
32. Name the major bearings in the engine, and tell how each is lubricated, i.e., spray, drip, mist, or direct pressure.

Typical fuel system layout designed for use in certain late model Dodge and Plymouth cars.

Dual venturi, electronic feedback carburetor used in fuel system shown above.   (Chrysler)

Chapter 6

FUEL SYSTEMS—CARBURETION

After studying this chapter, you will be able to:
- Explain the basic function of a carburetor type fuel system.
- Describe the major parts of a carburetor type fuel system.
- Identify the basic parts of a carburetor.
- Summarize carburetor operating principles.
- List the seven carburetor circuits.

As you have learned in a preceding chapter, an engine uses a mixture of gasoline and air for its fuel. This mixture is drawn into the engine by the vacuum formed during the intake stroke. It is then compressed, fired and exhausted. This cycle is repeated over and over in each cylinder or combustion chamber.

You will recall that gasoline is derived from crude oil or petroleum, and that it is made up of hydrocarbons (hydrogen and carbon). Gasoline also has various additives designed to prevent rust, resist freezing, control vapor lock, and resist detonation.

MIXTURE PROPORTIONS

The proportion of gasoline and air necessary to secure proper combustion will vary according to engine speed, load, temperature, and design of the engine. An average mixture for a moderate cruising speed could be 15 to 17 parts of air to one part of gasoline. These proportions are based on weight. For a mixture that produces more power, 12 to 13 parts of air to one of gasoline would be average.

If you were to consider VOLUME instead of WEIGHT, you will find that one gallon of gasoline would require around 9,000 gallons (34 065 L) of air (for part throttle operation). Fig. 6-1.

CHEMICAL CHANGES

Oxygen in the air is what is used for combustion. Nitrogen is not used. Air is about 21 percent oxygen and 79 percent nitrogen. Other elements are present but in small amounts.

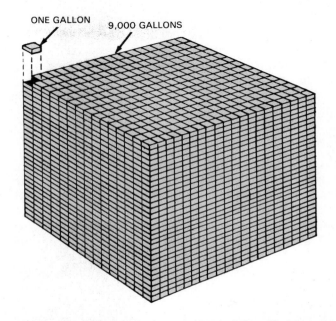

Fig. 6-1. Ratio of gasoline to air, by volume. If this were 9,000 one gallon cans, 8,999 would be filled with air and 1 with gasoline. This is an average fuel mixture ratio.

The engine draws in air (nitrogen and oxygen) and gasoline (hydrogen and carbon). When this mixture is ignited and burned, it produces several things. For each gallon of gasoline that is burned, about one gallon of water (steam) is produced. Other products include carbon dioxide, hydrogen, nitrogen, carbon monoxide (deadly gas), hydrocarbons (unburned gasoline), oxides of nitrogen, hydrochloric acid, lead oxides, and sulfurous acid. Fig. 6-2.

The exhaust stroke rids the engine of most of the combustion products. As you learned, some slip by the rings and enter the crankcase. Unless disposed of, these can raise havoc with the engine.

A DIFFICULT TASK

It is the job of the fuel system to constantly deliver the proper air-fuel mixture to the engine. The mixture

Fig. 6-2. Combustion brings about chemical changes.

Fig. 6-3. Construction of a typical gasoline tank.

and amount must be variable to meet the ever changing needs of the engine.

The basic key to an adequate fuel system is the carburetor itself. Here, the actual mixing of the fuel and air takes place. There are other parts, too, and all play an important role. For a complete understanding of the system and the role of each part, it is perhaps best to start with the source of supply—the gasoline tank.

GASOLINE TANK

Gasoline tanks are located in just about every conceivable spot—in the rear, under the seat, in the front, etc. An ideal location is a spot where the tank is protected from flying stones, where it will not bottom on the road and where, in event of an accident, it will not burst. The overall design features of a car often dictate the location of the tank.

The tank is usually constructed of thin sheet steel, coated with a lead-tin alloy to protect against rusting. Capacity generally is around 18-26 U.S. gallons (68–98L). Internal baffles are arranged to prevent sloshing. A filler neck, reaching to a convenient spot, is attached either directly or by a neoprene hose. The filler cap normally seals the tank but does have a vacuum and pressure relief valve to allow air to either enter or leave the tank in the event the emission control vent lines were to become inoperative. The tank is vented to a charcoal canister (see section on emission controls—Chapter 8) that in turn is vented to the carburetor. The tank must be vented to allow fuel to be drawn out. The tank is securely strapped into place. It is often protected on the outside by an application of undercoating material. A drain plug may be provided at the bottom. Fig. 6-3. Tanks can also be made of aluminum or plastics such as polyethylene.

CAUTION:

A GASOLINE TANK, EVEN WHEN APPARENTLY EMPTY, IS AS DANGEROUS AS A BOMB! NEVER WELD, CUT, SOLDER OR BRAZE A GASOLINE TANK UNTIL YOU HAVE BEEN THOROUGHLY TRAINED IN THE SAFE-TY PRECAUTIONS NECESSARY. IN FACT, KEEP ALL SPARKS, HEAT AND OPEN FLAMES AWAY FROM THE TANK. REMEMBER—IT CAN KILL YOU!

GASOLINE PICKUP PIPE

A tube enters the tank to draw off fuel for the engine. This tube can enter from the top, side or bottom. The tube end is generally located about one-half inch from the tank bottom. This allows considerable water and sediment to form before being drawn into the pickup tube.

Several types of filters are used on the ends of gasoline pickup tubes, including plastic, screen and sintered bronze (small particles of bronze pressed together, leaving the mass porous). An effort is made to design screens that will not clog and yet filter out sediment and most water, Fig. 6-4.

Fig. 6-4. Gasoline pickup pipe. Notice that screen is above bottom of tank. Pickup tube is fastened to bottom of tank.

WATER FORMS IN TANK

When a gasoline tank is only partially full, water tends to form within the tank. The moisture in the air within the tank condenses on the tank wall, then runs under the gasoline. Since water is heavier than gasoline, it will remain at the bottom where it will fail to evaporate as it is not exposed to the air. This contamination of the gasoline through condensation is a slow process but can cause trouble. Fig. 6-5.

Fig. 6-5. Gasoline tank showing condensation when tank fuel level is low.

TANK GAUGE UNIT

The gasoline tank contains a float that is attached to a resistance device quite similar to that used in an electric oil pressure sender. In this case, the travel of the float, up and down, causes the resistance to vary, depending on the depth to which the tank is filled.

The gauge on the instrument panel may be a double coil and armature type (described in the Lubrication chapter), or it can use a bimetal receiver.

Most gauges are designed to read empty when one or two gallons of gasoline are left in the tank. This is a concession to human nature as people are inclined to drive until the tank does read empty. Figs. 6-6 and 6-7 illustrate a typical tank sender and bimetal receiver. When the float drops, current flow to ground through the bimetal wire coil will be less, because it must travel through more resistance wire. This cools the bimetal hairpin and pulls it together. When the tank is filled, the contact slides up, cutting out resistance and current flow increases. This heats the

hairpin and the ends separate, causing the needle to move toward the full mark.

HOW GASOLINE LEAVES THE TANK

Fuel tanks usually are lower than the carburetor, so the gasoline will not flow under its own power. Some method of drawing it from the tank to the carburetor must be used. Two types of pumps are commonly used. One is mechanically operated, the other electrically.

MECHANICAL FUEL PUMP

A mechanical pump is mounted on the engine and is operated by the camshaft. Basically, it consists of an air chamber divided in the center by a flexible diaphragm. The diaphragm is made of several layers of cloth, impregnated (filled) with a special compound that makes it airtight and resistant to petroleum products. The diaphragm is pinched between the halves by a series of machine screws that hold the pump halves together, Fig. 6-8. Most pumps are nonserviceable and the halves are crimped together, Fig. 6-22.

Fig. 6-7. Fuel gauge operation with tank full.

Fig. 6-6. Fuel gauge operation with tank empty.   (Plymouth)

Fig. 6-8. Air chamber and diaphragm.

CHECK VALVES

Two check valves, one inlet and one outlet, are now added to the top chamber. The inlet is connected to the fuel tank and the outlet to the carburetor via copper, steel or plastic tubing. These checks use flat washer type valves held with a fine spring. The valve and the spring are contained in a perforated (full of holes) housing. Fig. 6-9.

PULL ROD AND RETURN SPRING

A pull rod is now fastened to the diaphragm. A large, cupped edge washer is placed on the top and bottom of the diaphragm, and the pull rod is riveted to the center. A fairly stiff return spring pushes upward, thus flexing the diaphragm in an upward direction. Fig. 6-10.

HOW DOES IT WORK?

If you were to connect the inlet of a fuel pump to a container of gasoline, then run the outlet to another container, the pump could be worked by pulling down on the pull rod with your fingers. Figs. 6-11 and 6-12.

ROCKER ARM AND LINK

In order to pull the diaphragm down, it is necessary to install a link and rocker arm. The link hooks in the slotted end of the pull rod and the rocker arm extends out where it rides on a cam on the camshaft. The link and rocker arm are pivoted together so when the cam lobe pushes up on the rocker arm, it pulls the link and pull rod down. When the cam turns, the rocker fol-

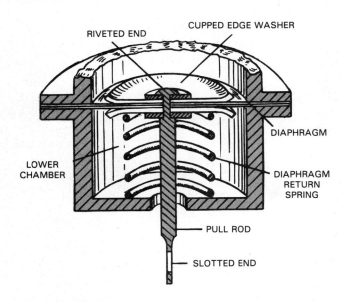

Fig. 6-10. Pull rod and return spring added to diaphragm.

Fig. 6-11. Intake stroke. When pull rod is drawn down, diaphragm is flexed downward. This forms vacuum in air chamber. Intake check will open and gasoline will be drawn into pump.

lows the lobe down. The link and pull rod are raised by the spring—not the rocker arm. A small spring keeps the rocker firmly against the cam lobe.

It is necessary to extend metal from the lower chamber to form a housing for the rocker and link, and also to prevent engine oil from running out where the rocker enters the engine. The fuel pump mounting flange is part of this housing. Fig. 6-13.

You will notice in Fig. 6-13 that a seal has been placed around the pull rod. This keeps hot engine oil and fumes from entering the lower chamber. A vent is provided in the lower chamber so the diaphragm can be pulled down without compressing the air in the chamber. Current practice is toward the use of a solid rocker arm as shown in Fig. 6-14, instead of an ar-

Fig. 6-9. Check valves added to top chamber. Small spring holds valve shut until vacuum or pressure overcomes spring tension.

Fig. 6-12. Outlet stroke. When pull rod is released, diaphragm is pushed up by return spring. This creates pressure, forcing inlet valve shut and opening outlet. Gasoline will be forced from outlet.

ticulated link. Note that when the diaphragm is held down by fuel pressure in the carburetor, the rocker arm can slide up and down on the diaphragm pull rod.

Fig. 6-13. Lower housing, rocker and link added. Notice that cam lobe has raised rocker arm, pulling diaphragm 4 down. This opens inlet pulling in fuel. When cam lobe turns, spring 3 will force rocker to follow. Diaphragm spring will push diaphragm up, close inlet, and expel gasoline through outlet. Vent 2 is provided so diaphragm can flex without compressing air in lower chamber. Seal keeps engine oil from entering lower chamber. All link and rocker rubbing surfaces are hardened to retard wear.

COMPLETE BASIC FUEL PUMP

Fig. 6-13 shows the entire basic fuel pump. Study the parts; learn their names and functions. As illustrated, this fuel pump will move gasoline efficiently but will not filter nor dampen the pulsating movement of gasoline leaving the outlet.

FUEL PUMP EFFICIENCY MEASUREMENTS

The amount of pressure the fuel pump exerts on the fuel line to the carburetor depends on the strength of the diaphragm spring. Pump pressures can be de-

Fig. 6-14. Cutaway of a typical fuel pump. Note valve action, paper filter, and vapor return or discharge valve. (Ford)

signed into the pump by the manufacturer according to need. An average would be around 4 to 6 psi (28 to 41 kPa). The normal pump will discharge over a quart per minute.

FILTERS ARE ESSENTIAL

The tank pickup screen will not filter out the very fine particles. It is necessary to have an additional filter either between the tank and the pump or between the pump and the carburetor.

Some pumps have a filter built as an integral part of the assembly. The fuel pump illustrated in Fig. 6-14 uses a screw-in, nonserviceable pleated paper fuel filter. Fig. 6-15 shows an exploded view of the same pump. Note the solid rocker arm. Note also the vapor return valve that allows a certain amount of vapor and gasoline to return to the tank through a separate line. This prevents vapor lock during periods of high underhood temperature.

Fig. 6-15. Exploded view of fuel pump pictured in Fig. 6-14. Study relationship of various parts. (Ford)

TYPES OF FUEL FILTERS

Many materials have been used in an attempt to find an ideal fuel filter. Fine screen, metal plate, ceramic, treated paper, and sintered bronze elements have been installed. All filters need periodic cleaning or replacement. Fig. 6-16 illustrates an in-line (placed in the fuel line) filter. This particular type of fuel filter uses a glass settling bowl (to hold dirt, water, etc.) along with a replaceable cleaning element. All fuel moving to the carburetor must pass through the

Fig. 6-16. Cutaway of a fuel filter. This filter uses a glass sediment or settling bowl and a paper filtering element. (Toyota)

cleaning element. A special pleated paper is widely used for cleaning elements. See Fig. 6-16.

FUEL PULSATION

A fuel pump delivers fuel to the carburetor in little spurts. Even though it forms a solid stream, the pressure pulsates (rises and falls) as the pump operates. This moving column of gasoline can create a slamming effect against the float needle valve, causing it to come off its seat and flood the carburetor. Fig. 6-17 illustrates this effect.

Fig. 6-17. Pulsation effect. Notice how float pressure controls flow of gasoline in A. In B, fuel is being delivered in a jerky manner, called pulsation. See how it slams against the scale and upsets needle pressure.

PULSATION DAMPER

To smooth out the flow of gasoline, many systems are equipped with pulsation dampers. Such a damper can be built into the pump or mounted in the line as a separate unit.

A pulsation damper consists of a flexible diaphragm stretched across an air compartment. The trapped air acts as a spring against which the diaphragm can flex. Some pulsation devices use a spring.

When the pump ejects fuel into the line, instead of ramming the fuel column, the ejected gasoline bulges the diaphragm outward, absorbing the blow. While the pump is getting ready to eject another stream, the diaphragm will return to its normal position to continue the pressure. In this manner, the fuel flow is smoothed out. Fig. 6-18.

Fig. 6-19 shows a fuel pump with an integral pulsation damper. A filter is also attached. Notice the use of a magnet in the filter to trap any metallic particles. Figs. 6-14, 6-15, and 6-23 also show a pulsation damper setup.

ELECTRIC FUEL PUMP

An electric fuel pump is quite efficient. It has a couple of advantages not offered by the mechanical type pump.

The electric pump will fill the carburetor merely by turning on the key. Another feature is the electric pump's adaptability to most any location. This allows the pump to be mounted away from the heat of the engine to reduce the chance of vapor lock. Some electric pumps are run submerged inside the fuel tank.

The basic difference between the electric and the mechanical pump is that the electric pump uses an electromagnet (a magnet produced by electricity flowing through a coil) to operate a metal bellows that alternately forms a vacuum and then pressure. Some electric pumps use an electromagnet to work a regular diaphragm. Other models drive either a vane or impeller type pump with a small electric motor.

When the key is turned on, the electromagnet is energized (filled with electricity by passing an electric current through it) and attracts a metal armature that is attached to the bellows, or to a diaphragm. This stretches the bellows and forms a vacuum. Gasoline is drawn in through the inlet check valve.

Fig. 6-18. Pulsation damper principle. A—Pump ejects fuel. Diaphragm pushes up against trapped air in air chamber. This absorbs slamming effect. B—No fuel from pump. Trapped air pushes diaphragm down, continuing some pressure during lull. C—Pump ejects another spurt. Again it is absorbed by diaphragm.

Fig. 6-19. Pump with pulsation damper. Notice magnet, in addition to ceramic filter, to trap any metal particles. (Lincoln)

As the armature continues downward, it strikes a pair of contact points and opens them. This breaks the circuit to the electromagnet and it releases its pull on the bellows. A return spring shoves the armature and bellows up. As the bellows close, gasoline is forced out the outlet check. When the armature has traveled up far enough to expel the gasoline, the points close and it is drawn down again. This process is repeated over and over.

As in the case of the mechanical fuel pump, when the carburetor float bowl is full, the return spring cannot collapse the bellows and the pump will be inoperative until some of the gasoline has been drawn from the bowl.

An electric fuel pump, using a bellows to produce the pumping action, is shown in Fig. 6-20. The diaphragm type (diaphragm instead of bellows) operates much as the bellows type except that a diaphragm is employed. Centrifugal and rotor type electric pumps are also used. Fig. 6-21 shows a cutaway of the rotor type.

SERVICEABLE AND NONSERVICEABLE FUEL PUMPS

Many makers are using a nonserviceable fuel pump. Note in Fig. 6-22, that the pump body and cover are crimped together. If the pump is defective, it is discarded.

A serviceable (may be taken apart and repaired) fuel pump is shown in Fig. 6-15. Note the various parts making up the pump. Fig. 6-19 shows a serviceable pump in cutaway form. Study fuel flow. Fig. 6-23 illustrates a similar pump. Note pulsator diaphragm.

Fig. 6-21. Rotor type electric fuel pump can produce reasonably high pressure. This type pump is often needed on fuel injection systems. (Volvo)

Fig. 6-22. Cutaway of a nonserviceable fuel pump. Note how lower housing is crimped over upper section. (Plymouth)

COMBINATION FUEL AND VACUUM PUMP

For a number of years, many cars used vacuum-operated windshield wipers. When the engine was pulling hard, such as in passing, the vacuum dropped and the wipers would almost stop.

To overcome this problem, a combination fuel and vacuum pump was used. It is similar to the regular mechanical fuel pump and the two are placed back to back in one main assembly. A single rocker arm operates both diaphragm pull rods. One diaphragm pumps fuel, the other air, forming a vacuum to keep the wipers running when engine vacuum is low.

VAPOR LOCK

It is important to shield fuel lines, pump, and carburetor from excessive heat. When gasoline reaches a certain temperature, it will turn to a vapor. Depending on the amount and location of the vaporization, the fuel flow can either be reduced or completely

Fig. 6-20. Electric fuel pump utilizing a bellows to produce the pumping action. (John Deere)

Fig. 6-23. Typical serviceable fuel pump construction. Learn part names. Study fuel flow in B.   (Nissan)

stopped. Upon cooling, fuel flow will resume at the normal rate.

Baffles or shields in the form of metal plates, asbestos gaskets and covering for lines made of asbestos tubing are used to prevent vapor lock. Gasoline itself is controlled to eliminate this tendency as much as possible. A fuel pump vapor discharge (return) valve, Fig. 6-14, can be incorporated to prevent vapor lock when underhood temperatures are high. The vapors return, via a separate line, to the gasoline tank where they condense and rejoin the liquid fuel. Cars equipped with air conditioning often utilize vapor return devices to offset the danger of vapor lock due to increased underhood temperatures.

FUEL LINES

Gasoline is carried from the tank to the carburetor in plated steel, copper or, in some cases, plastic lines. When plastic is used, it is often from the pump to the carburetor. All joints must be tight. Secure all lines to prevent destructive vibration and rubbing.

FIRE! FIRE! FIRE!

BE THOROUGH IN YOUR WORK. A LOOSE CONNECTION OR UNSECURED GASOLINE LINE CAN COME LOOSE, BREAK OR LEAK. IF THIS HAPPENS, A GREAT DEAL OF GASOLINE CAN BE SPRAYED OVER THE ENGINE. IF IGNITED, THIS GAS WILL CAUSE A DANGEROUS FIRE.

ALWAYS HAVE A FIRE EXTINGUISHER HANDY IN THE SHOP AND CARRY ONE IN YOUR VEHICLE!

SUPPLY SYSTEM IS COMPLETE

At this point you are able to supply a steady, smooth flow of clean gasoline to the carburetor. How this gasoline is mixed with air, in the correct proportions, and delivered to the cylinders, will be covered next.

THE CARBURETOR

In the early days of automobiles, the carburetor was called a mixing valve. This was a rather appropriate name in that its main function was plain mixing of gasoline and air.

The modern carburetor, although it still mixes gasoline and air, has become a highly developed and complex unit. There are many types and sizes; however, they all share the same basic concepts.

BUILD A CARBURETOR

As you have done with an engine, you will now "build" a basic carburetor on paper. You have already learned that the gasoline must be mixed with air. The proportion should be anywhere from 9 to 1 up to 16 to 1 by weight, depending on engine temperature, speed, load, and design.

A rapidly moving stream of air enters each cylinder on the intake stroke. You will use this airstream to make your carburetor work.

Each intake port feeds into the intake manifold. The intake manifold runs from the ports to the carburetor. More on the manifold later.

AIR HORN

You will start with a plain round metal tube. This tube is called the air horn. The tube will have a flange that bolts to the intake manifold. Fig. 6-24.

FUEL BOWL

A fuel bowl is attached to the air horn to hold a supply of gasoline. Inside of the bowl, a float will be hinged. This float will control a tapered pin (needle valve) that will open and close to admit gasoline. When the bowl fills, the float will rise and shove the needle valve against its seat to stop the flow of gasoline. When the fuel level drops, the float releases its pressure, the needle valve lifts from the seat and more gasoline enters. The float and needle valve will keep the fuel level constant. The bowl must have a hole (vent) to allow air to enter or leave as the fuel level changes. The bowl may be vented to the air horn, Fig. 6-25, to the atmosphere, or to both.

If the air cleaner becomes clogged, a stronger vacuum will result in the air horn. This tends to suck in more fuel unless the bowl is vented into the air horn. If it is vented, the pressure on the fuel in the bowl will decrease in the same proportion and fuel intake will tend to remain constant. This type is called a balanced carburetor. A common setup employs the internal bowl vent plus an external vent that opens during periods of engine idle. This type of external

Fig. 6-24. Air horn. Arrows indicate flow of air through horn, into manifold and on into cylinders.

Fig. 6-25. Float bowl, float, needle valve and bowl vent added to carburetor air horn. Notice how float has pushed needle valve into its seat to shut off flow of gasoline 1—Air horn. 2—Bowl vent or balance tube. 3—Fuel inlet. 4—Needle valve. 5—Hinge. 6—Float bowl. 7—Gasoline. 8—Flange.

vent helps prevent hot (engine overheated) starting problems by venting fuel vapors, to the atmosphere, that would otherwise be forced into the carburetor air horn. The external vents are now channeled to the emission control charcoal canister. The canister absorbs the vapor. The action of the canister will be covered in Chapter 8.

MAIN DISCHARGE TUBE

In order to allow the gasoline to be drawn into the air horn, it is necessary to connect the fuel bowl and horn with a small tube. This tube is called the main discharge tube. Fig. 6-26.

A VACUUM IS NEEDED

Notice in Fig. 6-26, that the gasoline level in the discharge tube is slightly below the nozzle. In order to

Fig. 6-27. Venturi increases vacuum. A—Air rushing into air horn near top produces some vacuum. B—As it travels down into venturi throat it speeds up. This causes an increase in vacuum. C—After leaving venturi throat, air expands and slows down somewhat. This reduces vacuum.

NOZZLE

MAIN DISCHARGE TUBE

Fig. 6-26. Main discharge tube. Note fuel level in discharge tube.

get the gasoline to flow out the nozzle and mix with the airstream, a vacuum is necessary. Some vacuum is created by the moving air, but it is not strong enough.

VENTURI

By building a restriction (venturi) in the air horn, the air will be forced to speed up where it strikes the venturi. As the air suddenly speeds up, it tends to be "stretched." In other words, a vacuum is created. The more the air speeds up, the stronger the vacuum. This vacuum will be strongest in the throat of the venturi but will still exist for a short distance below it.

Fig. 6-27 illustrates an air horn with a venturi. Three tubes containing mercury enter through the horn at different points. Notice the variations in vacuum at different spots in the horn. The higher the air velocity, the more vacuum formed. This is evident by examining the distance the atmospheric pressure has pushed the mercury up the tube. Fig. 6-27.

SECONDARY VENTURI

The vacuum can be increased still more by constructing a smaller venturi in the center of the air horn and positioned so that its outlet end is even with the throat of the main (primary) venturi. The primary venturi forms a vacuum at the outlet of the secondary venturi, causing the air to really whip through the secondary venturi. This produces a sizable increase in vacuum. The secondary venturi is sometimes called a "booster" venturi. Some carburetors use a third booster venturi just above the secondary. A recent carburetor features a vacuum controlled, variable sized venturi.

The main discharge tube nozzle enters the secondary venturi. When the engine starts, rushing air draws off drops of gasoline that join the passing air. See Fig. 6-28.

AIR BLEED

The setup so far would administer gasoline to the air, but the drops would be rather large and would tend to stick to the nozzle. By adding a tiny stream of air to the fuel as it travels through the nozzle, the drops will leave readily and will be quite small. This added air is termed "air bleeding." The tube through which the air travels is called an air bleed passage. See Fig. 6-29.

JETS

There are numerous jets used in a modern carburetor. Their job is to control the passage of gasoline and air through a very carefully calculated size hole. The jets are constructed of brass and screw into the ends of the various passageways in the carburetor. Some of the permanent types are pressed in-

Fig. 6-28. Secondary venturi. This increases vacuum. Note large drops of fuel being drawn from nozzle. An air bleed is needed to break up drops.

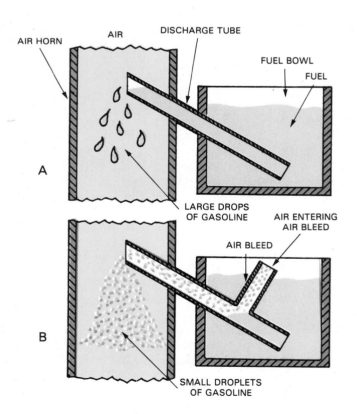

Fig. 6-29. Air bleed function. A—No air bleed. Large fuel drops. B—Air bleed mixes air in fuel breaking gasoline into small droplets.

to place and are not removed for routine maintenance. A jet is placed at the lower end of the main discharge tube to control the amount of gasoline that can pass through the tube. See Fig. 6-30.

ENGINE WILL NOT START

If you were to try to start an engine when cold, the carburetor as built so far would not work. A cold engine needs a mixture rich with gasoline (8 or 9 to 1). Our main discharge jet will furnish a mixture suitable for running. For starting only, the mixture must be much richer.

Fig. 6-30. Main discharge jet. This jet controls amount of fuel entering discharge tube.

CHOKE IS NEEDED

If a choke valve (sometimes called a "butterfly" valve) is placed near the top of the air horn, it will be possible to close it and shut off the air supply. As the intake stroke forms a vacuum that cannot be relieved through the air horn, the vacuum will pull on the main discharge nozzle and draw out a large quantity of gasoline. This provides the proper starting mixture. The choke valve can be opened or closed either manually or automatically. More on this later. See Fig. 6-31.

ENGINE STARTS BUT RUNS WILD

The engine will now start by closing the choke. As soon as it starts, the choke will have to be partially opened. When the engine is hot, the choke should be fully opened.

There is one trouble yet, and that is the engine will run "wild" or wide open. We have not provided a way to control the speed. A throttle valve is needed.

THROTTLE VALVE

A throttle valve is similar to a choke valve but is placed between the bottom of the primary venturi and

Fig. 6-31. Choke valve. A—Choke valve open. Air passing through air horn. B—Choke valve closed. Vacuum from intake drawing on discharge nozzle. Note heavy amount of fuel being delivered.

Fig. 6-32. Throttle valve. Throttle valve controls flow of fuel mixture. Shown in wide open, half open, and closed positions.

the mounting flange. This will give us control of the amount of air-fuel mixture reaching the cylinders. It is controlled by linkage connected to the accelerator pedal. Fig. 6-32 illustrates a throttle valve, and Fig. 6-33 shows the necessary linkage.

BASIC CARBURETOR IS COMPLETE

Study the basic carburetor in Fig. 6-34. Notice the position of the choke and throttle valves. Study the venturi design and notice the relationship of the secondary to the primary venturi.

A basic carburetor as shown could be used to operate an engine. The choke is open (engine hot), the throttle at about one-half speed, and the main discharge nozzle is metering fuel into the airstream. If the main discharge jet was of the correct size, the

engine would run efficiently as long as this certain engine speed was maintained.

MANY FAULTS

The basic carburetor, however, has many faults. The engine will not idle without stalling. The engine will have little power at speeds just above an idle. Whenever the throttle valve is quickly opened to full throttle, the engine will have a flat spot (engine seems to die, power fades and for a brief second there is no response). The engine will then catch and pull smoothly. The engine will not get sufficient gasoline to operate at top speed with full power. The choke must be operated by the driver instead of automatically. The carburetor would be subject to vapor lock. There is no air bleed to the main discharge tube.

This basic carburetor would look rather hopeless. As it stands, it is; but it is the foundation upon which

Fig. 6-33. One type of carburetor throttle control linkage. Linkage arrangements vary widely.   (Chevrolet)

BASIC CARBURETOR

CHOKE (OPEN)

BALANCE TUBE VENT

FUEL IS BEING DRAWN
FROM DISCHARGE
NOZZLE

FUEL INLET

SECONDARY VENTURI

NEEDLE VALVE

PRIMARY VENTURI

FLOAT HINGE

FLOAT

FLOAT BOWL

MAIN
DISCHARGE TUBE   FUEL

MAIN DISCHARGE JET

TO CYLINDERS   THROTTLE VALVE PARTIALLY OPEN

AIR

FUEL

AUTOMOBILE FUEL SYSTEM

NOZZLE

FUEL TANK

FUEL
INTAKE
VALVE

FUEL LINE

THROTTLE

AIR   FUEL

AIR AND FUEL
MIXTURE

FUEL PUMP

Fig. 6-34. Above. Basic carburetor. Below. Automobile fuel supply system.

all carburetors are built. With further developments, it will operate quite satisfactorily.

WHAT ARE THE DEVELOPMENTS?

To function at all speeds under varying conditions of heat, load, etc., the carburetor must have a number of basic CIRCUITS, or SYSTEMS. The circuits actually are passageways in the carburetor designed to perform certain functions. Some mechanical parts in addition to the passageways are used. When all the necessary circuits are incorporated, the carburetor becomes efficient.

CARBURETOR CIRCUITS—WHAT THEY DO

The job of the various carburetor circuits is to produce the proper air-fuel ratio to meet all possible needs of the engine. For example: when starting, ratios can be 8–1; when idling 12–1; part throttle (30 to 55 mph or 48 to 89 km/h) 16–1; full throttle 13–1; and upon full acceleration 12–1. These ratios are merely averages and will vary from engine to engine.

Circuits (often called "systems") can be listed as:
1. Idle circuit.
2. Low speed circuit.

3. High speed circuit.
4. High speed full power circuit.
5. Acceleration circuit.
6. Choke circuit.
7. Float circuit.

There are other devices that are used in the construction of carburetors, but they are not classified as circuits. These will be discussed in succeeding pages.

HOW CIRCUITS WORK

Thinking back to the faults of the basic carburetor, let us see how each circuit ovecomes a specific problem or fault. The problem will be given first, followed by the manner in which a particular circuit functions.

PROBLEM—ENGINE WILL NOT IDLE

When the throttle valve is closed to slow the engine to idle speed, the main discharge nozzle stops supplying fuel, and the engine will stall. The nozzle fails to feed gasoline because, when the throttle is closed, the rush of air through the air horn is cut off.

SOLUTION—IDLE CIRCUIT

Notice in Fig. 6-35, that an additional passage branches off the main discharge tube. It runs up through the low speed jet, across, down through the economizer jet and on to the idle port. From the idle port it runs down to the idle screw port, where it enters the air horn slightly beneath the throttle valve.

Since there is no vacuum above the throttle but a strong vacuum below, the vacuum will pull at the idle screw port.

This vacuum will draw fuel from the bowl up through the low speed jet, which calibrates or con-

trols the amount that passes. As the fuel is being pulled toward the economizer, the vacuum is also drawing air in at the bypass and air bleed openings. The fuel is thoroughly mixed with this air and travels down through the economizer, which further meters the flow and tends to mix it better. The fuel and air proportions are controlled by the size of the air bleed, bypass and low speed jet openings.

Moving down through the passage and the idle port, the mixture arrives at the idle screw port. The amount that can be drawn into the engine is determined by the position of the idle adjustment screw. When screwed in, it reduces the amount and when backed out, it admits larger quantities. To adjust, the idle screw is turned in until the engine misses and then turned out until the engine "rolls." The screw is then set halfway between these two positions. The engine will now idle smoothly. This is the IDLE CIRCUIT. Another idle circuit is illustrated in Fig. 6-36. Note that the idle adjustment screw is set at the factory and unlike the screw shown in Fig. 6-35, has a tamper proof plug to prevent anyone from easily changing the setting.

PROBLEM—ENGINE WILL NOT OPERATE AT PART THROTTLE

As soon as the throttle valve is opened past the idle position, more fuel mixture is necessary. The idle screw port will not furnish enough and airflow through the venturi is not strong enough to cause the fuel to be drawn from the main discharge nozzle. The engine will not operate properly in this range.

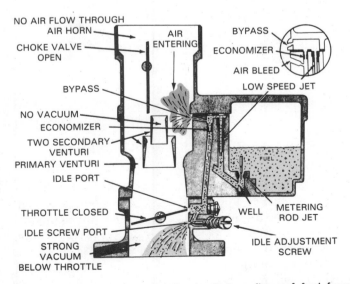

Fig. 6-35. Carburetor idle circuit. Follow flow of fuel from metering rod jet to idle screw port. Study position of choke and throttle and note that there is no vacuum above throttle. (Carter Carburetor)

Fig. 6-36. Idle circuit using a factory set idle adjustment needle. Access hole to needle is plugged. (Ford)

SOLUTION—LOW SPEED CIRCUIT

Going back to Fig. 6-35, you will see a slot-shaped opening just above the throttle. This is called the idle port. It opens into the idle fuel passage.

When the throttle valve starts to open, this port is uncovered and it will begin to supply fuel mixture to the engine. This is in addition to what is already supplied through the idle screw port.

This additional mixture will furnish enough extra fuel to allow the engine speed to increase to the point where the main discharge nozzle will function. Instead of the slot-shaped opening, some carburetors use a series of small round holes. As the throttle opening grows wider, it keeps uncovering extra holes. This type is illustrated in Fig. 6-37. The individual holes perform the same function as the slot-shaped idle port. This is the LOW SPEED CIRCUIT. Fig. 6-37 illustrates the low speed circuit in action.

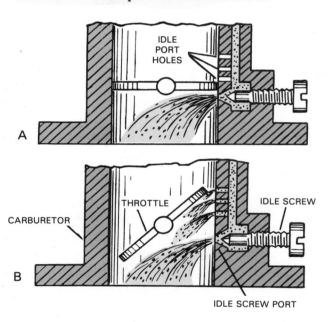

Fig. 6-37. Low speed circuit—part throttle. A—Throttle is closed. Idle screw port feeding fuel. Idle port holes inoperative B—Throttle part way open. Idle port holes uncovered and feeding fuel mixture. Idle screw port also feeding mixture.

PROBLEM—MORE FUEL NEEDED FOR HIGH SPEED CRUISING

As the throttle continues to open, the idle and low speed circuits will not furnish enough fuel. Unless another source begins feeding additional fuel, the engine will not gain speed.

SOLUTION—HIGH SPEED CRUISING CIRCUIT

This problem is solved with your basic carburetor as it feeds the engine through the main discharge jet.

When the throttle valve is opened past the idle and low speed ports, it allows air to start flowing through the air horn. This will build a vacuum in the venturi, and the main discharge nozzle will begin to feed fuel. At this time, the idle and low speed ports are still feeding fuel.

As the throttle valve opens further, venturi vacuum becomes quite strong, and the main nozzle supplies ample fuel. With the throttle in this position, vacuum is lowered at the idle screw port, and both it and the idle port will stop supplying fuel until the throttle is closed again. Fig. 6-38.

Notice that the throttle is well open, and there is a strong vacuum in the venturi. See how the fuel is being drawn from the bowl through the main discharge tube metering rod jet (which controls fuel flow). Fuel is then pulled up the discharge tube and out the nozzle where it is thoroughly mixed with the passing air. This is the HIGH SPEED CRUISING CIRCUIT.

ANTIPERCOLATOR

The antipercolator plug is shown just above and to the right of the main discharge nozzle. Fig. 6-38. When gasoline becomes heated, it will form bubbles of vapor which expand and shove on the surrounding gasoline. If vapor were to form in the discharge tube, or in the well, the vapor would push gasoline out the discharge nozzle, causing an overly rich mixture.

The antipercolator plug hole will allow these vapors to escape before they form sufficient pressure to force the fuel out. The circled cut to the left of the air horn in Fig. 6-38, shows an enlargement of the antipercolator plug. Notice the vapors leaving the fuel.

The antipercolator plug is especially useful in hot weather when the engine temperature climbs and heats the carburetor.

Some carburetors use a very thick composition spacer block between the carburetor flange and the intake manifold to prevent carburetor overheating.

PROBLEM—NOT ENOUGH FUEL FOR HIGH SPEED—FULL POWER

When the throttle reaches the wide open position, venturi vacuum peaks off (reaches its highest point). Under this condition, engine top speed will not be sufficient since not enough fuel can pass the metering rod jet.

SOLUTION—HIGH SPEED— FULL POWER CIRCUIT

You will see in Fig. 6-38, that a stepped rod, called the metering rod, is placed in the center of the metering rod jet. This metering rod partially plugs the opening, thereby limiting the fuel flow. Fig. 6-39.

To obtain more fuel for our high speed—full power range, it will be necessary to lift the metering rod up far enough so the larger step is removed from the jet. This leaves the small step in the jet, and it will allow more gas to flow. Fig. 6-40.

AIR NOW FLOWING
THROUGH AIR HORN

PUMP LIFTER LINK

METERING ROD ARM

UPPER PUMP SPRINGS

ANTI-PERCOLATOR PLUG

DIAPHRAGM
PULL ROD

STRONG VACUUM

VAPOR ESCAPING

LOWER
PUMP DIAPHRAGM
SPRING

METERING ROD

NOZZLE

EXTRA INTAKE
PASSAGE
VERY SMALL

VACUUM AIR BLEED

DIAPHRAGM

VACUUM RESTRICTION

METERING ROD JET

MOUNTING FLANGE

VACUUM ALMOST
GONE BELOW
THROTTLE

VACUUM PASSAGE TO INTAKE MANIFOLD

Fig. 6-38. High speed cruising circuit. Choke open and throttle is almost wide open. Main discharge nozzle is feeding fuel mixture into venturi and idle circuit is inoperative.   (Carter Carburetor)

METERING
ROD DOWN

ROD BLOCKING
JET

JET

MAIN
DISCHARGE TUBE

Fig. 6-39. Metering rod controls size of jet opening. Large step of metering rod now in jet. When rod is raised, small step will block jet.

METERING
ROD UP

JET

Fig. 6-40. Metering rod in raised position. Small step allows more fuel to pass.

HOW METERING ROD IS CONTROLLED

The metering rod may be lifted in three ways. One method hooks the top of the rod to linkage (actuating rods hooked together to work something) connecting the rod to the throttle lever. When the throttle valve is moved to the wide open position, it will lift the metering rod up. This mechanical control must be designed to raise metering rod at exactly the right spot. Fig. 6-41.

A mechanically controlled metering rod is fine for wide open throttle operation. If an engine is laboring under a hard pull, it needs a richer mixture. The throttle valve may not be open far enough to raise the metering rod, however, and the fuel mixture will not be rich enough. To overcome this fault, the metering rod is often lifted by a vacuum controlled piston.

VACUUM CONTROLLED METERING ROD

The metering rod is hooked to a vacuum piston or, in some cases, to a diaphragm. The piston is spring loaded (pushed by a spring) to keep it in a certain

Fig. 6-41. Mechanical control of metering rod. A—Throttle closed. B—Throttle fully opened.

position, in this case UP. When vacuum is applied to the piston, it overcomes the spring pressure and pulls the metering rod down, partially closing the jet.

This vacuum passage reaches from the piston, or diaphragm, down through the carburetor, through the mounting flange and into the intake manifold.

As the car moves along with the throttle in high speed cruising range, there is a fairly strong vacuum in the intake manifold. This vacuum keeps the metering rod piston in the down position. When the engine begins to labor and the throttle valve is opened a little more, vacuum in the manifold will drop. This will reduce the pull on the piston, so the spring will shove it up, thereby lifting the metering rod. Fig. 6-42.

DUAL METERING ROD CONTROL

Some carburetors control the metering rod mechanically, some by vacuum only; others use both. The carburetor in Fig. 6-38 uses both means. Notice

that the metering rod is hooked to the diaphragm pull rod. This pull rod is being held down by vacuum from the manifold acting on the diaphragm. The pump lifter also passes under the metering rod arm. Either loss of vacuum or full opening of the throttle valve will cause the metering rod to be lifted.

FEEDBACK SOLENOID CONTROLLED METERING ROD

An electrically controlled metering rod can also be used. In this type of setup, a solenoid (coil of wire through which an electrical current is passed) is used to move the rod. Rod position is determined by engine fuel needs. An oxygen sensor in the exhaust stream and a control circuit energize (pass current through) or deenergize the rod solenoid as needed. This setup is called a CLOSED LOOP system. Figs. 6-43 and 6-44 illustrate one type of solenoid operated rod.

HIGH SPEED— FULL POWER BYPASS JET

Some carburetors do not use a metering rod. The main discharge jet remains a fixed size. Another jet, called a power jet, will open and allow additional fuel to pass through the main discharge tube. This additional fuel enters the discharge tube via a bypass opening. The power jet can be controlled mechanically, by vacuum, or both. Figs. 6-45 and 6-46 illustrate the power jet in closed and open positions. The power jet or a metering rod makes up the HIGH SPEED— FULL POWER CIRCUIT or SYSTEM.

PROBLEM—A FLAT SPOT UPON ACCELERATION

The carburetor, as discussed so far, would still allow a "flat spot" when sudden acceleration is attempted. This is especially true at speeds below 30

Fig. 6-42. Vacuum control of metering rod. A—No load on engine, intake vacuum high. Piston is held down against spring. B—Vacuum gone, spring raises piston and raises rod.

Fig. 6-43. Solenoid operated metering rod provides the control needed by the "closed loop" system employing an exhaust sensor. (Chevrolet)

Fig. 6-44. Close-up and detailed look at a solenoid controlled metering rod such as that in Fig. 6-43.

Fig. 6-46. Power jet operation. Vacuum is low, actuating rod is pushed down by vacuum piston spring and power bypass jet is opened.   (Dodge)

Fig. 6-45. Power jet operation. Vacuum is strong (part throttle) and holds actuating rod up. This leaves power bypass jet closed.

mph (48 km/h). When the throttle valve is thrown open, the engine will hesitate, seem to die, may even pop, then catch and accelerate. The momentary flat spot is the problem.

SOLUTION—ACCELERATION PUMP CIRCUIT

An accelerator pump using either a piston or a diaphragm is incorporated in the carburetor. In the case of the diaphragm type, Fig. 6-47, the diaphragm is connected to a pull rod which, in turn, is fastened to a lifter link.

A spring is placed on the pull rod, both below the link and above. The lower spring is the strongest and is designed to keep the diaphragm up against the pull of the vacuum chamber below the diaphragm. Normal vacuum, however, will overcome the spring tension and hold down the diaphragm.

As in the case of the metering rod, the moment in-

take manifold vacuum drops, the pull rod spring will draw the diaphragm up. This up action reduces the size of the pump gasoline reservoir, the intake check will be forced shut, the outlet pushed open and fuel will be sprayed into the air horn.

When vacuum increases, the diaphragm will be drawn down. This shuts the discharge check and draws gasoline through the intake check, filling the pump reservoir.

The very same action takes place when the throttle valve is opened. This raises the pump link mechanically and forces the diaphragm up.

The pump can discharge fuel into the air horn either through the main fuel nozzle or through one or more special pump discharge jets. Some carburetors control the pump diaphragm or piston with linkage only, others use linkage and vacuum. The pump illustrated in Fig. 6-47 is controlled by both.

Notice in Fig. 6-47 that in addition to an intake check, there is also a tiny intake passage. This passage will let a measured quantity of fuel return to the bowl during the pump stroke. Some carburetors do not have this feature.

The springs on the pull rod play an important role. If the pump lifter link is suddenly raised by slapping the accelerator to the floor, this will not smash the diaphragm against the fuel in the reservoir. On the contrary, it allows the link to raise and compress the top spring. The tension of this spring will then quickly and smoothly, draw the diaphragm up. Instead of a short, heavy burst of fuel, a long, smooth stream will be discharged.

When the link is suddenly dropped by releasing the accelerator, the diaphragm will not be squashed down, since the link will slide down the pull rod and the diaphragm will be pulled down by vacuum. The top spring acts as a bumper during this down movement.

The amount of fuel discharged by the accelerator pump depends on the size of the piston and length of the piston stroke. In some carburetors, a ther-

Fig. 6-47. Accelerator pump circuit. Pump lifter link compressing pump upper spring will raise diaphragm pull rod, compressing fuel above diaphragm. This fuel will be forced out of pump jet. Study names of various parts.   (Carter)

mostatically controlled bypass permits part of the pump discharge to flow back into the bowl when engine temperatures are such that a full discharge is not needed.

MECHANICALLY OPERATED PISTON PUMP

Fig. 6-48 shows a mechanically operated piston type accelerator pump. It uses one spring that is placed above the piston and attempts to shove it down. It cannot go down as the pump lever is held in the up position by the pump rod which is connected to a throttle lever.

The reservoir below the piston is filled with fuel through the inlet check. It is ready to spray gasoline into the air horn as soon as the throttle valve is opened.

As the throttle valve opens, the throttle connector rod releases the upward pressure on the accelerator pump rod, allowing the pump piston spring to force the piston down. This closes the inlet check ball and forces gasoline past the discharge check, through the pump jet and into the air horn. When the throttle is closed, the connector rod will raise the piston and refill the reservoir through the inlet check.

PROBLEM—TO SECURE A RICH MIXTURE FOR COLD STARTING

As mentioned, when an engine is cold it must have a rich mixture to start. As it warms up, the mixture

must lean out and, when hot, the mixture must be even leaner.

SOLUTION—AUTOMATIC CHOKE CIRCUIT

The basic carburetor had a choke valve, but it was necessary to operate it by hand. Although some cars

Fig. 6-48. Mechanically operated accelerator pump piston. When piston is forced down, it will compress gasoline in pump reservoir, closing inlet check and forcing gasoline by discharge check needle. Pullover passage vents discharge area to prevent vacuum from drawing gasoline from accelerator discharge jet during normal operation.   (Ford)

use the manually (by hand) operated choke, most modern carburetors are equipped with an automatic choke control.

CHOKE THERMOSTATIC COIL

The choke valve shaft extends through the carburetor into a round housing. Inside the housing, there is a thermostatic coil spring (a bimetallic spring formed of two dissimilar metals that cause spring to wind, or unwind, depending on temperature change). One end of the spring is attached to the housing cover and the other end is attached to a lever on the choke shaft. When it is cold, the coil will hold the choke valve in the closed position. When the coil is hot, it will tend to lose its tension and allow the choke valve to open. Fig. 6-49.

CHOKE VACUUM PISTON

A small vacuum-operated piston is connected, by means of a link, to the choke shaft. As soon as the engine starts, the vacuum will pull on this piston and cause it to attempt to open the choke valve against the pull of the thermostatic coil. Fig. 6-50. Fig. 6-57 shows a vacuum break diaphragm that is used to open the choke.

OFFSET CHOKE VALVE

The choke shaft does not grasp the choke valve in the center, but is positioned so that it is slightly off center. When the engine starts, the velocity of air trying to enter the carburetor will push more on the long side and partially open the valve. Fig. 6-51. A small inlet valve is sometimes placed in the choke valve to admit extra air.

A BALANCED CONDITION

The cold thermostatic coil closes the offset choke valve. When the engine starts, air entering the carburetor will open the valve slightly. The vacuum piston will also pull to open the choke valve a little more. Between the two, they will be able to offset the pull of the coil and open the valve enough to permit the engine to run. See choke action in Fig. 6-52. A cutaway of the choke assembly is pictured in Fig. 6-55. Study the relationship of the parts.

If the engine is accelerated, the vacuum pull on the piston will diminish and allow the choke valve to close more tightly and enrich the mixture.

CHOKE STOVE

When the engine starts, tiny slots or grooves in the walls of the choke piston cylinder are uncovered. The slots open up inside the choke housing. A tube, or heating pipe, runs from the housing, down to the exhaust manifold where it enters a heating compartment

Fig. 6-49. Thermostatic coil and cover. When cold, spring pulls down in direction of arrow. Cover can be turned to increase or decrease spring tension.

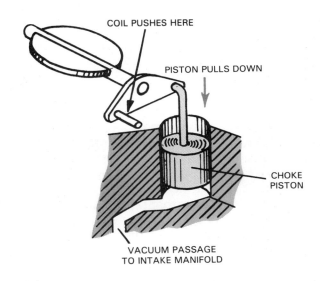

Fig. 6-50. Choke vacuum piston. Vacuum in manifold draws on bottom of piston, causing it to pull down against force of coil and partially open choke valve.

Fig. 6-51. Choke shaft is offset on valve. Less air pushes on side A and, as a result, side B is pushed down and partially opened against pull of thermostatic coil. Sometimes a small auxiliary air valve is set in choke valve C.

Fig. 6-52. Thermostatically controlled choke action. A—Choke closed, engine stopped. B—Engine started, vacuum piston and offset choke valve force choke open a small amount. C—Engine at operating temperature, thermostatic spring allows choke to fully open. (Toyota)

(choke stove). Fig. 6-53.

With the engine running, the vacuum will draw air through the tube from the stove up and around the thermostatic coil. As the engine heat up, the air passing the tube becomes hotter and heats the coil. The coil will release tension on the choke valve, allowing it to start to open. When the engine is fully heated up, the coil tension is so weak that the piston and passing air keep the valve fully open.

When the engine is stopped, the coil cools off and closes the choke for another start. Fig. 6-53.

FLOODING

In case the carburetor "floods the engine" (puts too rich a mixture in cylinders), use is made of a choke

Fig. 6-53. Choke stove. Notice how exhaust gases warm choke stove. Clean, heated air is then drawn up through tube, across thermostatic coil and down through vacuum passage. This soon heats coil causing it to unwind.

"unloader," an additional lever attached to the choke shaft. In the event of flooding, the throttle valve is opened all the way, causing linkage from the throttle lever to strike the unloader trip lever and open the choke to allow air to enter the cylinders.

FAST IDLE

When the engine is warming up, it is necessary to idle the engine somewhat faster to prevent stalling. This is accomplished by connecting the choke shaft to a fast idle cam.

When the choke is on, the fast idle cam swings out in front of the throttle idle speed adjustment screw. This holds the throttle partially open to speed up the engine. As the choke opens, the fast idle cam swings down and the throttle returns to its regular hot idle position. The fast idle cam is sometimes curved or notched. Fig. 6-54.

Fig. 6-54. Action of fast idle cam during engine warmup. As choke opens, fast idle rod will lower fast idle cam. As cam lowers, it will allow idle throttle stop screw to close throttle more and more. This will reduce engine speed. When choke is fully opened, engine will idle at normal rpm. (Bendix)

A complete carburetor, with the automatic choke attached, is shown in Fig. 6-55. Study the complete choke circuit to determine exactly how it works. Also note the normal three sections of a carburetor:
1. Air horn assembly.
2. Main body.
3. Throttle body.

OTHER TYPES OF CHOKES

There are other automatic choke arrangements. One type uses an electrically heated coil to speed up the opening of the choke thermostatic spring, Fig. 6-56. Another employs an electromagnet that is energized when the engine is cranked. The electromagnet helps hold the choke CLOSED. When the starter is released, the thermostatic spring takes over. Another passes engine coolant around the choke housing.

Another type places the thermostatic coil in a well in either the exhaust manifold or in the exhaust crossover (V-type engine) section of the intake manifold. Linkage connects from the well control to the choke lever. Note that the choke circuit shown in Fig. 6-57, utilizes a vacuum break diaphragm unit to provide initial opening of the choke.

Fig. 6-56. An electric assist choke. Note rivets used to retain choke cover. This prevents tampering with choke setting. (Ford)

Fig. 6-57. Automatic choke, well type. Thermostatic coil may be placed in exhaust crossover (hot) area of intake manifold. This setup uses a diaphragm unit instead of a piston to partially open choke when engine starts. (Chevrolet)

MANUAL CONTROL

The choke can be controlled by hand instead of automatically. This is done by using a flexible cable control. One end of the control is attached to the choke valve shaft lever and the other ending in a knob on the dash, Fig. 6-58.

WATCH OUT!

CARBURETORS ARE OCCASIONALLY PRIMED, WHEN DRY, BY POURING A SMALL AMOUNT OF GASOLINE DOWN THE AIR HORN. NEVER DO THIS WITH THE ENGINE

Fig. 6-55. Cutaway of complete carburetor with automatic choke. Note relationship of choke control parts. (AMC)

BEING CRANKED. DO NOT SPILL GASOLINE ON THE ENGINE. BEFORE TRYING TO START, PUT AWAY THE PRIMING GASOLINE CAN AND STAND WELL BACK.

NEVER PLACE YOUR HAND OVER THE AIR HORN TO CHOKE THE ENGINE. A BACKFIRE THROUGH THE CARBURETOR COULD TURN YOUR HAND INTO A MOST UNSAVORY HAMBURGER—WELL DONE!

Fig. 6-58. One type of manual choke control arrangement. (British-Leyland)

Fig. 6-59. Float circuit. Study all parts and learn their names. Trace flow of fuel from inlet into bowl. Note use of internal vent. (Buick)

FLOAT CIRCUIT

The basic carburetor used a typical float circuit. Fig. 6-59 shows the float, float bowl, bowl vent, needle and needle seat. Correct float settings are very important. If the fuel level in the bowl is too high, it will cause excessive amounts of gasoline to be delivered to the engine (rich mixture). If the setting is too low, not enough gasoline will be administered (lean mixture). The float may be constructed of thin brass or of closed-cell plastic. As mentioned earlier, the bowl must be vented. To prevent fuel vapors from escaping to atmosphere, all carburetors can either vent the bowl to the air horn, Fig. 6-25, and/or to the charcoal canister. From there, they will be fed back to the engine for burning. Fig. 6-60 shows one setup for venting to the canister.

OTHER CARBURETION FEATURES— IDLE COMPENSATOR

To prevent stalling when idling in very hot weather, some carburetors utilize a thermostatically controlled air valve. Fig. 6-61. When the carburetor becomes hot, the bimetallic strip will curl upward and open the hot idle air valve. This feeds extra air to the manifold below the throttle valve. The extra air compensates for an overly rich idle mixture, due to heat-produced vapors entering the carburetor.

Fig. 6-60. Setup designed to vent float bowl to charcoal canister. (Ford)

THROTTLE RETURN DASHPOT

On cars equipped with automatic transmissions, the drag placed on the engine when the throttle is suddenly returned to idle will result in engine stalling. The dashpot is arranged so the throttle lever will strike the dashpot just before reaching idling range. The dashpot diaphragm rod will slowly collapse and allow the throttle to slowly return to the idling position. This stalling occurs when the car is stopped. Fig. 6-62. Some dashpots are built as an integral part

Fig. 6-61. Hot idle compensator. Note how heat has caused bimetallic strip to open air valve. (Pontiac)

Fig. 6-62. Throttle return dashpot. When throttle lever strikes dashpot rod, rod must push diaphragm back. Before it can move back, air must be forced out vent. This causes diaphragm to move slowly. When throttle lever is moved away, spring will force diaphragm out. Air will be drawn in vent and dashpot is ready to work again.

of the carburetor. Some engines, using air injection systems for smog control, do not need throttle return dashpots.

IDLE SPEEDUP CONTROL FOR AIR CONDITIONING

To compensate for the increased load on the engine when the air conditioning compressor clutch is en-gaged, an idle speed control is often used. The speed-up during idle also provides increased airflow for better cooling.

Such units used to control idle speed for various reasons are often termed THROTTLE POSITIONERS. See Fig. 6-63.

When the compressor clutch is energized, electricity is fed to a small solenoid on the side of the carburetor. The solenoid then opens an air valve, thus permitting increased airflow below the throttle plates.

Fig. 6-63. Various styles of vacuum and electric throttle positioners.

Fig. 6-64 illustrates the idle speedup control as well as the hot idle compensator valve.

Another type setup uses a vacuum diaphragm to control idle speedup when the air conditioner is on. This unit forces the throttle open enough to raise the idle rpm to the desired level.

Fig. 6-64. Air conditioner idle speedup control. When control solenoid is energized, valve is opened to admit air below throttle plates. (Ford)

WARMING THE FUEL CHARGE

When the air-fuel mixture enters the manifold during the warm-up period, gases from the exhaust manifold are directed to the base of the intake manifold where the carburetor is attached. This warms the fuel charge. When the engine is hot, the gases are directed away from the intake manifold. This action is controlled by the thermostatic MANIFOLD HEAT CONTROL VALVE. Figs. 6-65, 6-66, and 6-67. Carburetor intake air is also heated by means of a thermostatically controlled air cleaner. Fig. 6-95. See Emission Controls, Chapter 8 for additional detail.

Fig. 6-65. Operation of a manifold heat control valve. Notice how hot gases are directed up and around intake manifold passages. (Buick)

Fig. 6-66. Manifold heat control valve. (Plymouth)

Fig. 6-67. Exhaust manifold with heat control valve. Note bimetal spring that closes valve when cold.

HEAT CROSSOVER—V-8 ENGINE

On a V-8 engine, the manifold heat control valve is located in the exhaust manifold on one bank. When cold, the heat control closes and directs some of the hot gases up through the intake manifold. After passing through, the gases flow out the exhaust manifold on the other side. When hot, the valve opens and both exhaust manifolds expel gas directly into the exhaust system. The valve is actuated by a thermostatic spring or as in some models, by a vacuum motor, Figs. 6-68, 6-69, and 6-70.

WATER HEATED MANIFOLD

Some engines pass cooling system water (coolant) through passages in the intake manifold. This pro-

Fig. 6-68. V-8 engine heat crossover. Heat control is closed and hot gases are being directed up through passages in intake manifold. Notice different type of choke stovepipe used. (Oldsmobile)

Fig. 6-69. Sectioned intake manifold (V-8), showing passage for exhaust gases. Carburetor bolts on top of intake risers. (Dodge)

Fig. 6-70. Vacuum motor control of exhaust heat valve. (Chevrolet)

vides a controlled temperature for the fuel mixture. Fig. 6-71 illustrates a water-heated intake manifold for a V-8 engine. The top view shows the complete manifold (for a four-barrel carburetor). The second

sketch shows the intake passages (shaded portion). The bottom sketch shows the flow of water through the manifold.

ELECTRICAL HEATING OF FUEL MIXTURE

Some engines utilize a thin ceramic heating element built as part of the carburetor base to intake manifold spacer. The heating grids are located under the primary bores and provide rapid heating of the fuel mixture during cold startup and driveaway. This improves fuel vaporization and reduces the length of time the choke must be closed. The heater is shut off by a thermostatic switch when the engine reaches a specified temperature. Fig. 6-72 shows one type of fuel mixture heater.

CARBURETOR ICING

It is possible, especially during the warm-up period, for ice to form on the throttle valves. As the nozzles feed fuel into the air horn, it turns into a vapor. This vaporizing action chills the air-fuel mixture and the throttle bores in the throttle valve area.

When the moisture-laden mixture contacts the chilled throttle valve, it condenses, then freezes. This pileup of ice can reach the point where, when the accelerator is released, the engine will stall because no air can pass around the throttle valve.

Fig. 6-71. Water heated intake manifold. Water replaces hot gases in this installation. (Lincoln)

145

Fig. 6-72. This carburetor spacer block has built in electric heater to warm fuel charge passing through primary bores. Heater shuts off after engine warms. (Oldsmobile)

Some heat crossover systems channel a small portion of the hot gases directly through a passage in the carburetor flange. This heats the throttle valve and idle port areas and prevents the formation of ice.

Fig. 6-73 shows the bottom of a four-barrel carburetor. On this model, the vacuum draws air for the automatic choke from a tube running through the heat crossover passage similar to that in Fig. 6-68. The heated air passes through the choke housing, into the carburetor flange, around the primary bores where it is finally drawn into the manifold. This prevents icing. Heated intake air also helps.

ALTITUDE COMPENSATION

When operating at higher elevations, the fuel mixture tends to become overly rich in that the air becomes thinner and contains less oxygen to sustain burning. This problem is overcome by either adjusting the amount of fuel or the amount of air in the mixture.

This adjustment can be controlled by using an aneroid (pressure sensitive sealed bellows) or by an exhaust sensor. The exhaust sensor "senses" an increase in unburned hydrocarbons passing through the exhaust and feeds this information back to a computer. The computer, in turn, sends a signal to an electric solenoid (similar to the setup in Figs. 6-43 and 6-44). The solenoid can then operate a fuel flow control rod, valve, etc., to alter the amount of fuel delivered to the airstream. The setup can be designed to feed additional air instead of lessening fuel flow. The "closed loop" fuel system that employs an exhaust sensor and computer will be covered in detail in Chapter 8.

The aneroid can control either a fuel or air flow valve so as to maintain the proper air-fuel ratio at various altitudes. Fig. 6-74 illustrates the use of an

Fig. 6-73. One type of carburetor icing control. Hot air from choke housing (passes by choke piston through slots in cylinder wall) is drawn through carburetor mounting flange and discharged around base of throttle valves.

Fig. 6-74. Aneroid controlled spring loaded valve compensates for changes in altitude. As altitude increases, aneroid expands opening valve. When engine is cold and regular choke valve closes, auxiliary choke will close to also prevent excess air delivery around choke. (AMC)

aneroid to admit extra air as altitude increases. At lower elevations, atmospheric pressure collapses the aneroid which in turn holds the valve closed. As elevation increases, atmospheric pressure drops and the aneroid expands, pushing the valve open. This admits extra air into the stream of fuel which leans the air-fuel ratio, Fig. 6-74.

VARIABLE VENTURI CARBURETOR

One carburetor design incorporates a special venturi valve that can change the size of the venturi opening. It uses a special venturi valve that is controlled by both engine vacuum and throttle position. The effect is to produce a nearly constant air speed through the venturi. Study the exploded view of a variable venturi carburetor in Fig. 6-75. Note that this has a DUAL venturi valve (one section for each of the two barrels or bores) and that the valve is attached to two metering rods. When the valve position changes, it alters

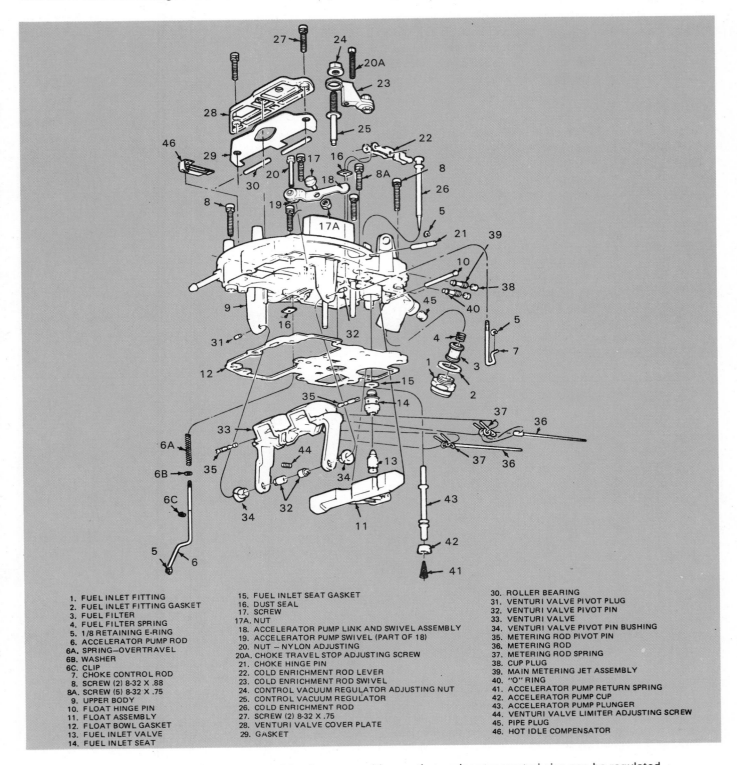

1. FUEL INLET FITTING
2. FUEL INLET FITTING GASKET
3. FUEL FILTER
4. FUEL FILTER SPRING
5. 1/8 RETAINING E-RING
6. ACCELERATOR PUMP ROD
6A. SPRING—OVERTRAVEL
6B. WASHER
6C. CLIP
7. CHOKE CONTROL ROD
8. SCREW (2) 8-32 X .88
8A. SCREW (5) 8-32 X .75
9. UPPER BODY
10. FLOAT HINGE PIN
11. FLOAT ASSEMBLY
12. FLOAT BOWL GASKET
13. FUEL INLET VALVE
14. FUEL INLET SEAT

15. FUEL INLET SEAT GASKET
16. DUST SEAL
17. SCREW
17A. NUT
18. ACCELERATOR PUMP LINK AND SWIVEL ASSEMBLY
19. ACCELERATOR PUMP SWIVEL (PART OF 18)
20. NUT — NYLON ADJUSTING
20A. CHOKE TRAVEL STOP ADJUSTING SCREW
21. CHOKE HINGE PIN
22. COLD ENRICHMENT ROD LEVER
23. COLD ENRICHMENT ROD SWIVEL
24. CONTROL VACUUM REGULATOR ADJUSTING NUT
25. CONTROL VACUUM REGULATOR
26. COLD ENRICHMENT ROD
27. SCREW (2) 8-32 X .75
28. VENTURI VALVE COVER PLATE
29. GASKET

30. ROLLER BEARING
31. VENTURI VALVE PIVOT PLUG
32. VENTURI VALVE PIVOT PIN
33. VENTURI VALVE
34. VENTURI VALVE PIVOT PIN BUSHING
35. METERING ROD PIVOT PIN
36. METERING ROD
37. METERING ROD SPRING
38. CUP PLUG
39. MAIN METERING JET ASSEMBLY
40. "O" RING
41. ACCELERATOR PUMP RETURN SPRING
42. ACCELERATOR PUMP CUP
43. ACCELERATOR PUMP PLUNGER
44. VENTURI VALVE LIMITER ADJUSTING SCREW
45. PIPE PLUG
46. HOT IDLE COMPENSATOR

Fig. 6-75. Variable venturi, number 33, changes position so that carburetor venturi size can be regulated.

fuel flow through the use of the metering rods, see Fig. 6-75.

OTHER CARBURETOR FUNCTIONS

The carburetor may furnish an opening for the distributor vacuum advance line and linkage to operate kickdown switches for automatic transmissions and overdrives. It may have a linkage (TV) rod connection to mechanically activate transmission controls. The carburetor can also have a vacuum port to help control the EGR valve which feeds exhaust gases into the air-fuel mixture in the intake manifold of the engine, plus other special functions on specific applications.

GOVERNORS

Some carburetors are equipped with various types of governors to limit engine speed. These are usually found on heavy equipment such as trucks and buses. Fig. 6-76 shows a schematic view of a centrifugal type governor to control engine speed.

AIRFLOW DIRECTION

Carburetors can be of three basic airflow designs—DOWNDRAFT, UPDRAFT, and SIDEDRAFT.

Your basic carburetor was a downdraft type, Fig. 6-34. Fig. 6-77 shows airflow in typical V-8 intake manifold. Airflow in the various carburetor designs is indicated in Figs. 6-78, 6-79, and 6-80.

SINGLE BARREL

A typical downdraft, single-barrel carburetor is shown in Fig. 6-81. Study the various parts.

Fig. 6-76. Centrifugal governor. Shaft 10 revolves, causing assembly 4 to rotate entire unit. As rate of spin increases, weights 6 swing outward, drawing rounded ends of 2 downward. This shoves 4 down and causes it to press on 9. Friction is lessened by ball bearing 8. As weights continue outward, 9 is depressed and throttle lever is pulled back slowing engine. Return spring 7 attempts to keep throttle shaft 13 in open position. (Continental)

Fig. 6-77. V-8 intake manifold for a two-barrel, downdraft type carburetor. (Oldsmobile)

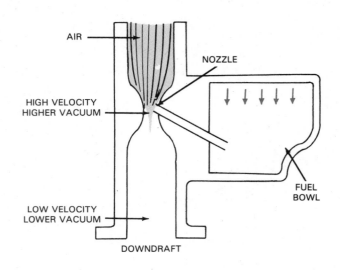

Fig. 6-78. Downdraft carburetor. Very widely used. (Deere & Co.)

A single-barrel SIDEDRAFT carburetor is pictured in Fig. 6-82. Study the fuel flow.

DUAL CARBURETOR

Many engines employ the dual carburetor (referred to as the TWO BARREL). Basically this carburetor is nothing more than single-barrel carburetors mounted side by side. Each barrel has its own discharge nozzle, idle port, accelerator discharge jet, and throttle valve. A fuel bowl, air horn, choke and throttle shaft common to both is used.

Each barrel feeds into a separate intake passage, Fig. 6-77. Notice that one barrel feeds cylinders 1, 4, 6, 7; the other feeds 2, 3, 5, 8.

See typical dual carburetors in Figs. 6-83 and 6-84.

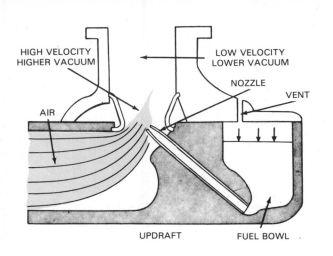

Fig. 6-79. Updraft carburetor. Used basically on small gas engines. (Deere & Co.)

Fig. 6-80. Sidedraft carburetor. Used on a number of engines. (Deere & Co.)

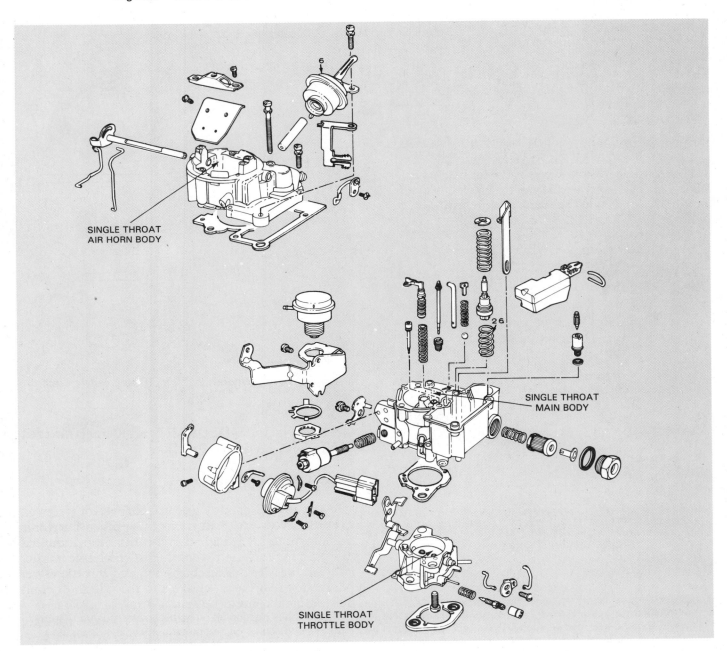

Fig. 6-81. Typical single-barrel, downdraft carburetor. (GM)

1—DAMPER ASSEMBLY. 2—AIR VALVE COVER. 3—VACUUM CHAMBER. 4—DAMPING ELEMENT. 5—SEAL. 6—CONTROL PISTON (AIR VALVE). 7—METERING NEEDLE. 8—METERING JET. 9—FLOAT NEEDLE VALVE. 10—FUEL BOWL. 11—IDLE MIXTURE SCREW. 12—FLOAT. 13—SPRING. 14—THROTTLE VALVE. 15—COMPRESSION SPRING. 16—DAMPER OIL. 17—DAMPER ROD. 18—DIAPHRAGM.

Fig. 6-82. Sidedraft (SU Type) carburetor, using a vacuum-operated piston to control fuel mixture and a single needle valve that provides proper mixture for all operating conditions. Venturi size is variable, depending on control piston position. Study control piston and metering needle action in A, B, C, and D. Note that as control piston and metering needle move upward, venturi area is increased, allowing a greater flow of air along with increased fuel flow made possible when tapered metering needle is raised out of its seat or jet. A—Idling. B—Throttle fully opened—low speed. C—Intermediate speed. D—High speed operation.   (Jaguar, Toyota, Mercedes-Benz)

1—Gasket.	13—Float baffle.	24—Choke link.
2—Intake adapter.	14—Air horn.	25—Air valve rod.
3—Insulator.	15—Air valve.	26—Air valve lever.
4—Throttle body.	16—Air horn gasket.	27—Accelerator pump.
5—Main body.	17—Vent screen.	28—Metering rod.
6—Choke heater cover and coil.	18—Choke valve.	29—Power piston.
7—Needle seat assembly.	19—Pump lever.	30—Idle screw and spring.
8—Spring.	20—Vacuum break and bracket.	31—Fast idle cam.
9—Fuel inlet filter.	21—Idle speed solenoid.	32—Intermediate choke rod.
10—Gasket.	22—Vacuum hose.	33—Pump rod.
11—Fuel inlet fitting.	23—Vacuum break lever.	34—Throttle lever assembly.
12—Float assembly.		

Fig. 6-83. Typical two-barrel, downdraft carburetor. Note main parts—air horn, main body, and throttle body. (Americal Motors)

Fig. 6-84. Assembled view of one type of two-barrel, downdraft carburetor. (Chrysler)

FOUR-BARREL CARBURETOR

Basically, a four-barrel carburetor is a cluster of four single-barrel carburetors. They are arranged in two groups. One group of two barrels is called the PRIMARY side, and the other two are termed the SECONDARY side.

There is wide variation in four-barrel carburetor design. The one illustrated in Figs. 6-85, 6-86, and 6-87 is typical.

Fig. 6-85 illustrates the primary and secondary float circuits. Fuel enters the strainer in the secondary bowl opening. It flows through a passage to the primary side. Notice that the needle valve in the secondary side is spring loaded. The secondary float bowl supplies less gasoline. As it has less drain, it is subject to flooding when road bumps shake the float up and down. The spring pressure allows the float to bounce without the needle valve moving. Some four-barrel carburetors have a single float circuit that serves both sides. Fig. 6-85 illustrates a double float circuit.

A four-barrel idle circuit is shown in Fig. 6-86. Both secondary and primary sections feed fuel during idle. Only the primary idle discharge side is adjustable. Some models feed idle fuel through the primary side only.

Both intermediate and full power throttle positions are illustrated in Fig. 6-87. Notice that in the right-hand view, the primary side is supplying fuel for the intermediate speed ranges. Both the throttle auxiliary valve and the secondary throttle valves are still closed. As long as they remain in this position, fuel will flow from the idle discharge, but none from the secondary main discharge nozzle.

Fig. 6-85. Four-barrel primary and secondary float circuits. Notice the spring-loaded needle valve used in secondary circuit. (Buick)

Fig. 6-86. Four-barrel idle circuits. Both primary and secondary sides feed fuel for idling. Primary side is adjustable; secondary is fixed. (Buick)

Fig. 6-87. Intermediate and full throttle circuits. Note position of auxiliary throttle valve during full power operation (small figure on left side).

As speed is increased, or the throttle is fully opened, the secondary throttle valves will open. The valves can be opened by a vacuum or by mechanical linkage. They normally open when the primary throttle valves have been opened about 40 deg.

When the secondary valves are open and engine speed is around 1400 rpm, the airflow through the secondary barrels reaches an intensity that will force the auxiliary valve open. The auxiliary valves are mounted off-center. When they open, fuel will flow from the secondary discharge tubes. Secondary idle flow will cease (see small left cross section, Fig. 6-87).

Notice that the primary barrels have a choke valve. No choke valve is needed in the secondary barrels since they are closed when starting. Fig. 6-87.

A four-barrel carburetor gives the advantage of a small venturi area at medium speeds, but when full power is needed, the advantages of the large venturi area are available. A four-barrel carburetor is shown in Fig. 6-87A. Fig. 6-88 is an exploded view of still another four-barrel carburetor.

MANIFOLD DESIGN

It is not enough just to carry fuel from the carburetor to the cylinders. Each cylinder should get the same type and amount of fuel mixture. To design an intake manifold to deliver equal amounts of fuel to all cylinders is not easy.

It is essential that the passages in the manifold be as nearly equal in length as possible. In addition, they should be smooth with gentle curves. Fig. 6-77 shows one specific V-8 intake manifold design for a dual carburetor. Another V-8 intake manifold for a four-barrel carburetor, is pictured in Fig. 6-89. Note how large the secondary bores are in relation to the primary.

INTAKE MANIFOLDS

Intake manifolds are designed to carry fuel from the carburetor to the valve ports. They can be made of cast iron or aluminum.

The V-8 engine mounts the manifold between the cylinder heads. The L-head engines bolt the manifold to the side of the block. The I-head bolts the manifold to the cylinder head.

Gas exhaust and water heating of the manifold has been discussed under WARMING THE FUEL CHARGE.

Fig. 6-87A. Two views of a modern four-barrel carburetor. (Plymouth)

A six cylinder manifold passage design is shown in Fig. 6-90.

RAM INDUCTION

By offsetting the carburetors to one side of the engine (V-8 engine), and feeding the fuel mixture through extra long intake manifold passageways, a RAM effect is produced. Due to the inertia of the long moving stream of fuel mixture, it will flow into the cylinder up to the last second the intake valve is open.

A compression wave will travel back and forth through the passage at the speed of sound. If the manifold length is correct, the compression wave will be timed to the opening of the intake valve and the air will "ram" itself into the cylinder. This gives the effect of mild supercharging.

Fig. 6-88. Exploded view of a four-barrel carburetor.   (AMC)

PRIMARY BORES SECONDARY BORES

❷ ❹ ❻ ❽

❶ ❸ HEAT CROSSOVER PASSAGE ❺ ❼

Fig. 6-89. Intake manifold for a V-8 engine. Manifold is designed for a single four-barrel carburetor. Note very large secondary bores. (Cadillac)

HEAD

WELL TYPE CHOKE

VACUUM LINE

CHOKE VALVE

CARBURETOR

FUEL LINE

LONG BRANCH INTAKE MANIFOLD

Fig. 6-90. This six cylinder intake manifold design provides a separate passage for each cylinder. In addition, equal fuel distribution is aided by placing carburetor some distance from engine. (Plymouth)

The ram induction manifold will produce this effect only at certain engine speeds, depending upon the length of the manifold. The manifold is designed to produce this beneficial effect at the normal operating speeds. Fig. 6-91 illustrates the ram type manifold for a V-8 engine. Fig. 6-92 shows "turbocharging action."

AIR CLEANERS

It is essential that air entering the carburetor is clean air. A good air cleaner, properly serviced, will add greatly to the useful life of the engine.

There are three types of air cleaners in general use.

OIL-WETTED POLYURETHANE AIR CLEANER

An older type (not very efficient) oil-wetted air cleaner consists of a housing, copper mesh element and metal support ring. This design draws air through the oil-dampened element.

The modern oil-wetted cleaner utilizes a POLYURETHANE (soft, porous, sponge-like material) element. The polyurethane, when dampened with oil, effectively filters the air. When dirty, it may be cleaned. Fig. 6-93.

OIL BATH AIR CLEANER

An oil bath air cleaner pulls the air down a passageway, forces it to make a sharp bend over a puddle of oil, back up through a mesh, and over and down into the carburetor. The air gains considerable speed as it travels down into the cleaner. When it makes the sharp bend, just above the oil, the heavier

dust particles cannot make the corner and are slammed into the oil where they settle to the bottom. The wool-like mesh stays wet with oil and cleans the air even more.

Note how the air is forced to change directions just above the oil bath in Fig. 6-94. This filter may be cleaned by draining the oil, flushing the element, cleaning the base and refilling to the correct level with the recommended grade of engine oil.

DRY TYPE AIR CLEANER

A dry type air cleaner draws air through a specially treated paper. The paper is pleated accordian style. Fig. 6-95 illustrates a modern filter of this type having a series of ducts (passages) and a thermostat designed to furnish heated air to the cleaner during engine warm-up. The air is drawn from around the exhaust manifold. When the engine is heated the thermostat will close off the source of heated air.

Fig. 6-96 shows an exploded view of a typical dry or paper type air cleaner. Fig. 6-97 pictures a typical paper filter construction.

SUPERCHARGERS

Superchargers are used to increase engine horsepower by forcing more air-fuel mixture into the cylinders. The normal engine depends upon the vacuum created by the pistons to draw the mixture into the cylinders. The supercharger, or as it is sometimes called, "blower," assists the vacuum by raising the pressure of the incoming air. It does this with one of three types of superchargers.

Superchargers can be mounted between the carburetor and manifold or ahead of the carburetor.

Fig. 6-91. Ram induction intake manifold as used on V-8 engine. Carburetors mounted off to one side allow long intake passages across to opposite bank of cylinders. (Plymouth)

Fig. 6-92. Schematic showing operation of a typical turbosupercharger—often termed "turbocharger". Turbochargers increase engine power and efficiency. (Buick)

Due to the increase of air-fuel mixture delivered to the engine (with a resultant increase in power), it is essential that the engine compression and design lend itself to supercharging.

Fig. 6-93. Polyurethane air cleaner element. This filter can be rinsed in solvent, squeezed dry, dipped in oil, squeezed to remove excess oil and placed back in service. (Chevrolet)

ROOTES TYPE SUPERCHARGER

In a Rootes supercharger, a pair of rotors whirling within an enclosure seize air and carry it around and out the opposite side. This type runs about one and a half times faster than the engine. It is a positive displacement type. Fig. 6-98.

Fig. 6-94. Oil bath air cleaner often incorporates a hollow section below oil to assist in muffling sounds of incoming air.

Fig. 6-96. Exploded view of an air cleaner using a dry paper filter element. This cleaner controls temperature of incoming air to some extent—hot air for starting and warm-up, cooler air for normal running. (AMC)

Fig. 6-95. Modern air cleaner with paper type air filter element. Filter must be cleaned or replaced quite often when operated under dusty conditions. If paper element becomes clogged, it restricts incoming air and produces a choking effect on engine. (Ford)

Fig. 6-97. Cutway showing typical pleated paper filter construction. (Wix)

VANE TYPE SUPERCHARGER

The vane type supercharger is also a positive displacement type and works like a vane oil pump. Its operational speed is comparable to that of the Rootes type. Fig. 6-99.

CENTRIFUGAL TYPE SUPERCHARGER

The centrifugal supercharger is a nonpositive type. It has an impeller with series of curved fins or vanes. As impeller is whirled, air is drawn in at center and thrown off the rim. Air is trapped in circular housing which is small at one end and gets progressively larger. See Fig. 6-100. A supercharger driven by the engine exhaust, called "TURBOCHARGER," is shown in Fig. 6-92.

The turbocharger is being used on a number of engines. The additional "boost" (air being forced into the cylinders by raising the pressure of the column of air-fuel mix in the intake manifold) provides increased horsepower, torque and efficiency. Fig. 6-101 shows a cutaway view of a typical turbocharger. Note how the turbine drives the compressor via a shaft connecting the two. Turbochargers spin very fast—up to 120,000 rpm.

Fig. 6-98. Rootes type supercharger. Rotors have minimum clearance between themselves and housing. (John Deere)

LIQUEFIED PETROLEUM GAS

LP-Gas (mixture of butane and propane) is only in the liquid state when highly compressed. When pressure is reduced, it turns into a vapor.

Storage and transportation of LP-Gas is expensive, due to the heavy container necessary to contain and transfer it. LP-Gas is generally used in fleet (large groups of vehicles) operation. Its use is favored by some and certain advantages such as clean burning, low cost, high octane rating, no oil sump contamination, and reduced engine wear are claimed.

LP-Gas is stored in heavy tanks under pressure. It passes from the tank through a filter to a high pressure reducing valve. Gas leaves this valve at pressures from 4 — 15 psi (27.5 — 103.4 kPa). The semiliquid (half vapor, half liquid) fuel then moves into a vaporizer that warms it up and changes it into

Fig. 6-99. Vane type supercharger. Air is drawn in behind one vane and forced around and out by the other.

Fig. 6-100. Centrifugal type supercharger. Spinning impeller draws air in at center and throws it off at rim. Impeller uses series of vanes or fins to throw air.

Fig. 6-101. Turbocharger. Exhaust flow acting on turbine spins compressor. (Peugeot)

all vapor. The vapor travels to a second pressure reducing valve where it is reduced to atmospheric pressure. From here it travels to the carburetor (actually a mixing valve) and on into the cylinders when the engine is started. Fig. 6-102 shows the operational theory of the commonly used "liquid withdrawal" type of LP-Gas system.

GASOHOL, ALCOHOL

Gasohol is a mixture of regular, unleaded gasoline and ethanol alcohol. The mix usually contains around 90 percent gasoline and 10 percent alcohol. A standard fuel system is used. A number of cars have been altered to use 100 percent alcohol.

We will undoubtedly see much progress made in the utilization of alternate (non-petroleum) fuels in the coming years.

SUMMARY

FUEL FLOW

A fuel pump, by means of a diaphragm and check valves, draws gasoline from the tank. The gasoline is drawn out through a pickup tube with a screen on the end. Gasoline then passes through lines to the pump, where it is expelled through a pulsation damper chamber through a filter to the carburetor fuel bowl.

When the fuel level in the bowl raises, a float will begin to close the float needle valve. At a predetermined level, the float will completely shut the float needle valve, and fuel will no longer flow to the carburetor. When fuel is consumed and the level starts to drop, the fuel pump will again fill the bowl.

The fuel pump is operated electrically or mechanically and may have a filter either on, before, or after it.

MIXTURE

For efficient operation an engine such as used in a passenger car requires an air-fuel ratio that is constantly changing. This varied mixture is produced and delivered by the carburetor or a fuel injection system which is detailed in the next chapter.

The carburetor contains a number of circuits designed to produce a proper air-fuel mixture for all engine needs. The general operation of a carburetor is as follows:

When the engine first starts, the choke valve is closed. Vacuum is strong in the area beneath the choke valve, resulting in a very rich mixture by reducing the air supply and increasing the withdrawal of fuel from the bowl. As soon as the engine starts, the choke partially opens. As the engine is idled to warm-up, fuel is fed into the passing airstream by the idle screw port. The choke continues to open. When the engine is hot, it will be fully opened.

When the accelerator opens the throttle valve, the idle screw port fuel delivery is assisted by additional

Fig. 6-102. Schematic LP-Gas fuel system using liquid withdrawal technique (liquid drawn from tank—not vapor). Liquid fuel leaves tank and after passing through two regulators, plus being heated, it is turned into an atmospheric pressure vapor. Vapor enters mixing valve (carburetor) and is drawn into cylinders. (Bendix-Zenith)

fuel coming from the idle port or part throttle holes just above the idle screw port.

As the throttle continues to open, the air speed through the air horn and venturi increases until fuel begins to feed from the main discharge nozzle. At very high speeds where the throttle is wide open or when the car is pulling very hard, additional fuel is administered by a power valve or by a metering rod. During the cruising and full power range, no fuel is fed by the idle port or idle screw port.

To assist in smooth acceleration, an accelerator pump is provided to feed additional gasoline during acceleration only.

Engine speed is controlled by the position of the throttle valve in the carburetor.

Study Fig. 6-103. Follow each circuit and study the parts and operational principle involved.

The air and fuel mixture is delivered to the combustion chambers by means of an intake manifold. The temperature of this mixture is somewhat controlled by heat crossover passages, heated air intake and, in some cases, by running the coolant through passages in the intake manifold. Even distribution of fuel to all cylinders is very important.

CARBURETOR TYPES AND KINDS

There are downdraft, updraft and sidedraft carburetors. Some are single-barrel, some double-barrel, and others have four barrels. All carburetors—despite shape, size and type—attempt to provide as nearly perfect an air-fuel mixture as possible for all engine needs.

SUPERCHARGERS

Superchargers, usually the exhaust driven TURBOCHARGER type, are being used on a number of engines. They increase horsepower and efficiency.

VIEW A—FUEL FLOW (IDLE STAGE)

VIEW B—FUEL FLOW (FAST IDLE STAGE)

VIEW C—MAIN METERING SYSTEM

VIEW D—POWER SYSTEM

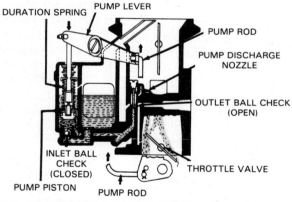

VIEW E—ACCELERATING SYSTEM (DISCHARGING STROKE)

VIEW F—ACCELERATING SYSTEM (RETURN STROKE)

Fig. 6-103. Carburetor circuits or systems. Study each circuit and be certain you understand exactly how it operates and what particular parts are concerned.

OTHER FUELS

LP-Gas, pure ethanol alcohol and a mix of gas and alcohol (Gasohol) are all being used to some degree.

AIR INTAKE

Air entering the carburetor must be cleaned. Failure to clean the air will result in rapid deterioration of the engine. Air is generally cleaned by a dry type air cleaner that utilizes special paper as the filtering element. Cleaners must be serviced regularly to maintain efficiency.

There are many DOORS TO SUCCESS. They are seldom marked "WELCOME—ENTER." You are more apt to find the doors securely locked. Knowledge is the most versatile key. STUDY and LEARN—don't stay "locked out" for the rest of your life.

KNOW THESE TERMS

Fuel mixture, Tank gauge unit, Mechanical fuel pump, Electric fuel pump. Fuel filter, Fuel pulsation, Vapor lock, Air horn, Fuel bowl, Main discharge tube, Venturi, Jets, Choke, Throttle valve, Metering rod, Antipercolator, Accelerator pump, Choke, Float, Throttle return dashpot, Carburetor icing, Intake manifold.

REVIEW QUESTIONS—CHAPTER 6

1. Air is largely made up of _____ and _____.
2. An average fuel-air ratio for normal operation is _____ parts of air to _____ part of fuel.
3. Name the parts that make up a fuel delivery system.
4. A fuel pump uses a diaphragm and one check valve. True or False?
5. The most commonly used fuel pump is the electric type. True or False?
6. Name three elements commonly used to filter fuel.
7. Explain how fuel pulsations are controlled.
8. What is vapor lock?
9. What is a carburetor venturi and how does it work?
10. How is the fuel level in the carburetor controlled?
11. What is a secondary or booster venturi? How does it help?
12. Of what use is the air bleed in a carburetor?
13. What are carburetor jets?
14. Engine speed is controlled by the _____.
15. What is carburetor linkage?
16. Explain how the idle circuit functions.
17. What is provided to assist the idle circuit when the throttle is opened just beyond an idle?
18. What circuit provides fuel for normal cruising speeds? How does it work?
19. Of what value is an antipercolator?
20. Describe the operation of the high speed—full power circuit.
21. What is a "flat spot," and what may be done to cure it?
22. How does the cure for the flat spot operate?
23. Explain the operation of the automatic choke.
24. During the warm-up period, engines must idle fairly fast. A device is provided for this purpose. What is it called and how does it work?
25. If a cold engine becomes "flooded," what mechanism will force the choke valve open?
26. Cars with automatic transmissions usually have a _____ to prevent stalling when the throttle is closed.
27. Of what value is the idle compensator?
28. What are some features that are found in a well designed intake manifold?
29. How can ice form in a carburetor? How is it prevented?
30. What is a dual or double-barrel carburetor?
31. What is a quad or four-barrel carburetor?
32. What are the two most common types of air cleaners?
33. Of what value is a supercharger?
34. The following should be matched. Above are the names of the carburetor circuits. Below are problems. Match the problem with the circuit that will cure it.
    1. Idle circuit.
    2. Low speed circuit.
    3. High speed circuit.
    4. High speed—full power circuit.
    5. Acceleration circuit.
    6. Choke circuit.
    7. Float circuit.
    Engine cold, will not start.
    Bad "flat spot."
    Fuel level too high.
    No power at top speed.
    Accelerator up—engine won't run.
    Engine very rough at speed just above idle.
    Engine rough at cruising speeds.
35. List three safety hints dealing with the fuel system.
36. The turbocharger uses engine exhaust to:
    a. Drive the compressor.
    b. Open the oxygen sensor gate.
    c. Drive the turbine.
    d. Drive the alternator.
37. Late model engines feed heated air to the air cleaner—normal running. True or False?
38. Maximum supercharger rpm is around:
    a. 5,000 rpm.
    b. 120,000 rpm.
    c. 20,000 rpm.
    d. 2,000 rpm.
39. What does "Gasohol" consist of and in what proportions?
40. Which of the following statements does NOT refer to LP-Gas:
    a. Stored in heavy tanks under pressure.
    b. A mixture of butane and propane.
    c. Enters engine cylinders as a liquid.
    d. Uses a special carburetor (mixing valve).

CAMSHAFT

GLOW PLUG

INJECTOR

INTAKE
MANIFOLD

GLOW PLUG
WIRING HARNESS

DIESEL

CAMSHAFT
DRIVE SPROCKET

VALVE

CYLINDER

INJECTION
PUMP

HEAD

PISTON PIN

FLYWHEEL

BLOCK

BELT
TENSIONER

PAN

PISTON

TIMING
BELT

CONNECTING ROD

OIL PUMP

CRANKSHAFT

Cutaway view of a four-stroke cycle, 4-cylinder diesel engine. This 1998 cc (121.9 cu. in.) engine has a compression ratio of 22.7 to 1. It also features an aluminum alloy cylinder head.   (Mazda)

Chapter 7

FUEL SYSTEMS — FUEL INJECTION

After studying this chapter, you will be able to:
- Describe the major parts of a gasoline fuel injection system.
- Describe the major parts of a diesel injection system.
- Identify the parts of gasoline and diesel injection systems.
- Summarize the operating principles of gasoline and diesel injection systems.
- Compare the different types of gasoline and diesel injection systems.

FUEL INJECTION—DIRECT AND INDIRECT

A fuel injection system does NOT use a carburetor. Fuel, under pressure, is sprayed through an injection nozzle in one of three locations. The fuel may be sprayed directly into the cylinder. This is called DIRECT INJECTION. Fuel may be sprayed into either the intake manifold just ahead of the intake valve or into the throttle body at the entrance to the intake manifold. This is termed INDIRECT INJECTION. Current gasoline systems favor the indirect injection method. Fig. 7-1 shows one indirect setup.

Note how fuel enters the intake manifold just ahead of intake valve.

MECHANICAL FUEL INJECTION

Originally, most fuel injection systems were the MECHANICAL type. These used an engine driven injector pump that distributed fuel, under pressure, to fuel injection nozzles where it was then sprayed into the cylinder or into the intake manifold. The pump was precisely timed to the engine intake strokes.

The amount of fuel delivered was controlled basically by the position of the accelerator linkage that in turn actuated a fuel rail (mechanism for controlling injection quantity) within the pump body, Fig. 7-2.

ELECTRONIC FUEL INJECTION

The electronic fuel injection system, like the mechanical type, also delivers fuel, under pressure, to

Fig. 7-1. Cutaway showing location and arrangement of fuel (gasoline) injection nozzle in intake port. (Mercedes)

Fig. 7-2. Note parts of mechanical, intermittent fuel injection system. (BMW)

the injectors. Unlike the mechanical type, however, the electronic system uses no injector pump-distributor setup. It employs an electric fuel pump to provide sufficient pressure to produce a proper injector spray pattern. Although this pressure varies with the system, it runs between 10 and 50 psi (68.9–344.7 kPa) for many and up to around 65 psi (448.1 kPa) for others.

The injector may be opened and closed electrically as in the case of the intermittent systems.

In continuous injection systems, the injector is forced open by fuel pump pressure. The amount of fuel delivered is controlled either by an electronic control device or by an air flow metering valve, depending on the system. We will study each system in detail shortly.

INTERMITTENT FUEL INJECTION—(TIMED)

Some fuel injection systems inject fuel ahead of each valve, as shown in Fig. 7-1, just before and/or during the intake stroke. This system uses one injector for each cylinder involved. Each injector is open for only several milliseconds and is carefully timed to each cylinder intake stroke.

The injector is opened by means of an electric solenoid (magnetic winding). When an electrical current is passed through the solenoid winding, it forms a powerful magnetic field that draws a sealing needle off its seat. This admits a stream of fuel for as long as the injector remains energized.

The injector must emit an even, smooth stream. Fig. 7-3 shows a typical solenoid controlled injector. Remember, the injector is only open while energized.

Fig. 7-3. Solenoid operated fuel injector for use in an intermittent, electronically controlled system. Study construction. 1—Filter. 2—Magnetic winding. 3—Return spring. 4—Magnetic armature. 5—Sealing needle. (Volvo)

INTERMITTENT FUEL INJECTION—(NON-TIMED)

A number of fuel injection systems do not attempt to precisely time each injector to a specific cylinder intake stroke. Some systems energize one-half of the injectors all at once then the entire other half on an alternating basis. Other systems use only two injectors in the entrance to the intake manifold and operate both either at the same time or on an alternating basis.

These non-timed systems spray the mixture into the manifold where it will remain until the intake stroke draws it into the cylinder. Although, at first glance, such systems might appear poorly designed, in actual use, they work very well.

INJECTOR PULSE WIDTH

"Pulsing" an injector refers to energizing the solenoid causing the injector to open. Pulse width is a measurement of how long the injector is kept open—the "wider" the pulse width, the longer the open time. The amount of fuel delivered by a given injector depends upon the pulse width.

CONTROLLING PULSE WIDTH

Pulse width is controlled by an electronic computer that constantly monitors engine speed, load, throttle position, exhaust, temperature, etc. Based on all these incoming signals the computer is constantly adjusting pulse width so as to deliver a correct air-fuel ratio for any given engine demand.

CONTINUOUS FUEL INJECTION

During engine operation, the CONTINUOUS fuel injection system feeds atomized fuel from the injectors ALL THE TIME. The amount will vary to suit engine needs.

The continuous system injectors need no solenoid to open or close them. Fuel pump pressure forces the spring loaded injector open causing fuel to spray into the intake manifold. Study the continuous injector pictured in Fig. 7-4. Note the difference between it and the intermittent injector in Fig. 7-3.

Fig. 7-4. Fuel injector used on a continuous injection system. (Volvo)

TYPICAL SYSTEMS

Although there are a number of design differences between various fuel injection systems, current systems are of either INTERMITTENT or CONTINUOUS INJECTION design.

The intermittent system may be fully electronic controlled or can use an air flow meter in conjunction with a computer. The continuous system can be controlled mechanically without the typical computer-electronic circuitry. See Fig. 7-45.

We will now examine a typical system of each type.

INTERMITTENT ELECTRONIC INJECTION SYSTEM—DIGITAL CLOSED LOOP TYPE

The intermittent "Digital Electronic Fuel Injection" system employs only TWO injectors, Fig. 7-5. Both injectors are mounted on the throttle body directly above the throttle valves. When the engine is running, the injectors are energized alternately.

The throttle body contains both injectors, throttle valves, idle speed control, throttle position sensor and fuel pressure regulator. It mounts on top of the intake manifold, Fig. 7-6.

Fuel pressure to the injectors is maintained at around 10 psi (68.9 kPa) for this specific system. The regulator, incorporated into the throttle body, is typical with a spring loaded diaphragm controlling a valve assembly. When pressure exceeds the regulator setting, the diaphragm is forced down allowing fuel to escape through the valve. Excess fuel is returned to the tank. Fig. 7-7 illustrates the regulator. Note the

Fig. 7-5. Fuel injector used by one type of electronically controlled system. (Cadillac)

Fig. 7-6. Throttle body with injectors. Injectors are energized at same time during cranking and alternately during running. (Cadillac)

Fig. 7-7. This unit will regulate fuel pressure to injector. Excess pressure opens regulator valve and extra fuel passes back to tank. (Cadillac)

injector action. Fig. 7-8 shows regulator action.

An electronic computer, in this case a DIGITAL computer, is used to control the pulsing of the injectors. The computer, often termed electronic control module, receives signals from several sensors that monitor such things as the throttle position, engine rpm, manifold air temperature, coolant temperature, intake manifold pressure, atmospheric pressure, oxygen content of exhaust stream, etc.

Based on the input of information from the various sensors, the control module determines exactly what injector pulse width (time injector is open) is needed. The slightest change in sensor signals causes the control module to instantly change injector pulse width to correspond with engine fuel needs.

In this system, the pump supplies fuel flow and pressure. The regulator controls the pressure. The throttle valves, actuated by the accelerator, determines air flow. The control module, acting on signals from the sensors, determines proper injector pulse width and pulses them accordingly. Pulse width is constantly altered to maintain a very carefully controlled air-fuel ratio. Fig. 7-9 is a schematic of the closed loop digital fuel injection system.

CLOSED LOOP FEATURE

A "CLOSED LOOP" fuel system refers to the fact that the air-fuel ratio control device (carburetor or

Fig. 7-8. Fuel pressure regulator action.   (Lancia)

fuel injector) is sensitive to the oxygen content of the exhaust. The system determines the proper air-fuel ratio and then constantly monitors its exhaust to verify the accuracy of the mixture setting.

Whenever the exhaust sensor determines the oxygen content is off, the system corrects itself to bring the oxygen back to proper levels. The system tries to maintain a "stoichiometric" air-fuel mixture. This is an engineering term for an ideally combustible air-to-fuel ratio. More details on mixtures and ratios are given in Chapter 8.

Fig. 7-9. Schematic showing layout for a closed loop, intermittent electronic fuel injection circuit. (Cadillac)

STOICHIOMETRIC AIR-FUEL MIXTURE

The fuel injection or carburetor fuel system engineer always strives to design a system that will produce as nearly a perfect air-fuel mixture as possible. A "perfect" ratio mixture will burn very cleanly with a minimum of pollutants. Such a mixture is called a "STOICHIOMETRIC" mixture and is around 14.7 parts of air to 1 part of fuel by weight.

INTERMITTENT ELECTRONIC INJECTION SYSTEM—AIR FLOW METER TYPE

The digital closed loop system just discussed, sensed air flow to the engine by means of a manifold absolute pressure sensor, barometric pressure sensor and manifold air temperature sensor.

An AIR FLOW meter is used to detemine air flow on some electronic controlled intermittent systems. A schematic of such a system is illustrated in Fig. 7-10. Study the layout. You will notice the use of an air flow meter as well as a cold start injector. This is also a "closed loop" system.

AIR FLOW METER

The air flow meter contains an air passage into which a spring loaded hinged flap or plate protrudes. As the air moves through the meter on its way to the intake manifold, it forces the hinged plate to swing to the side. As the throttle plates open wider, more and more air moves through the meter. This, in turn,

causes the plate to swing open further.

To prevent troublesome "flutter" (erratic movement) of the hinged plate, a compensating plate is made as an integral part. The compensating plate, working in the confines of the meter, smoothes out sudden plate movements that would cause problems. Fig. 7-11 shows a cross-section of a typical air flow meter. Note bypass to allow sufficient air flow at idle when plate practically closes main passage.

FLOW METER POTENTIOMETER

The air flow meter plate shaft is connected to a potentiometer (a sliding contact resistor device). As the plate swings open, the potentiometer generates an electrical signal proportional to the position of the plate. The electronic control module (computer) receives this signal and adjusts injector pulse width accordingly. Fig. 7-12 shows potentiometer action.

COLD START INJECTOR

This system (along with some others) uses a separate injector that is energized to provide extra fuel for cold starting. A thermostatic time switch energizes the cold start injector only during cranking and even then, only if the engine coolant temperature has fallen to a specified level. The switch is also time sensitive and will close the injector within around 10 seconds with the coolant at its coldest. As coolant temperature increases (still below specified cold level)

Fig. 7-10. Schematic of a somewhat different type of closed loop, intermittent fuel injection system. This setup uses an air flow meter as part of fuel flow control. (Toyota)

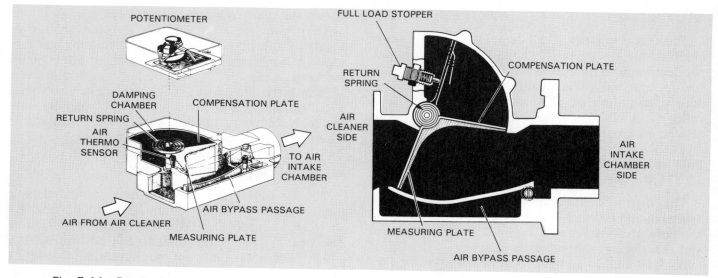

Fig. 7-11. Detail of air flow meter used to measure amount of air flow to engine. Air flow hinged plate actuates potentiometer to create an electric signal to ECU (Electronic Control Unit). (Toyota)

Fig. 7-12. Potentiometer action as air meter hinged plate is forced open by air flow. (Lancia)

Fig. 7-13. Cold start injector. 1—Solenoid winding. 2—Injector return spring. 3—Sliding armature. 4—Seal. 5—Inlet filter. 6—Spray nozzle. (Volvo)

the 10 second open period will be reduced accordingly. A cold start valve is pictured in Fig. 7-13. A thermostatic time switch is illustrated in Fig. 7-14.

THROTTLE VALVE SENSOR

The throttle valve shaft is attached to a throttle valve sensor or switch. The sensor sends an appropriate signal to the control module indicating whether the throttle valve is in the idle or full throttle position, Fig. 7-15.

OTHER SYSTEM COMPONENTS

This system also uses an auxiliary air valve, ignition sensor, coolant sensor and closed loop oxygen sensor. Along with the major control unit, the AIR FLOW VALVE and other parts just covered, combine to produce a functional injection system that can maintain accurate air-fuel ratios over a wide range of operating conditions.

The setup employs one injector per cylinder. The injectors can be energized four at a time in alternating

groups for eight cylinder engines or all at once for six and four cylinder use.

The injectors produce one half of the fuel needed for the intake stroke each time they are energized. It is thus necessary that all injectors be energized or pulsed TWICE for each complete four stroke cycle (one pulse per crankshaft revolution). Study Fig. 7-10. Do you understand what each component does in the overall operation of the system?

REMEMBER:

In intermittent injection systems, RATE OF FUEL FLOW through the injectors remains constant. The total amount of fuel delivered is determined by the LENGTH OF TIME (pulse width) the injectors are held open.

CONTINUOUS INJECTION—MECHANICAL TYPE

The continuous, mechanically controlled injection system feeds fuel through all of the injectors, ALL of the time. In order to control the amount of fuel delivered to the engine for any given need, the RATE OF FLOW through the injectors must be carefully controlled.

The system controls fuel flow, not by means of an electronic control module but by using a fuel distributor, mechanically controlled by a hinged air flow sensor. System operating pressures range from around 50 — 65 psi (344.7 — 448.1 kPa).

The overall continuous injection system is shown in Fig. 7-16. Study it carefully.

PRESSURE SOURCE—THE PUMP

The system pressure is generated by a fuel pump similar to that shown in Fig. 6-21 of the previous chapter. It uses a pressure relief valve to prevent excessive pressure in the event of a pinched line or other blockage. A check valve is located at the outlet. When the pump is switched off, the check closes and maintains system pressure in the lines. The fuel then passes into the fuel accumulator.

FUEL ACCUMULATOR

The fuel accumulator serves several functions. It dampens pressure fluctuations in the system. It muffles fuel pump noise. The accumulator aids in maintaining a residual line pressure over a period of time after the engine is turned off. This aids quick starting and provides protection against fuel vaporizing in the lines due to heat soak (engine heat being transferred to fuel lines). A typical fuel accumulator is illustrated in Fig. 7-17. The fuel enters at inlet and exits at outlet. This creates a pressure on diaphragm causing it to move downward, compressing plunger and spring. When diaphragm has moved down as in B, note extra fuel stored under pressure above diaphragm. When pump is stopped, spring and plunger push against diaphragm to force fuel up through hole in plate above, thus maintaining residual pressure, Fig. 7-17.

Fig. 7-14. Thermostatic time switch. (Lancia)

Fig. 7-15. Throttle position sensor. Throttle shaft is attached to and operates switch. (Toyota)

From the accumulator, fuel moves through a filter on the fuel distributor.

FUEL DISTRIBUTOR

The basic function of the fuel distributor is to deliver fuel to the injectors at whatever rate of flow (amount) is required at any given time. The distributor consists of a fuel control unit and four pressure regulating valves (four-cylinder engine). Study the sectioned view of the fuel distributor in Fig. 7-16. A phantom view showing the four pressure regulating valves is pictured in Fig. 7-18. Study the fuel passageway setup and the spring loaded diaphragm in each pressure regulator.

The control plunger has a recessed groove that is always exposed to line pressure. This permits fuel to flow from this groove into passageways to the lower chamber (under the diaphragm) of each pressure regulating valve, Fig. 7-16. When the control plunger is raised in its bore, this same groove uncovers metering slots leading to the top chambers of the pressure regulating valves. This would then produce an equal pressure above and below the valve diaphragm EXCEPT for the spring forcing the diaphragm down. This extra force causes a pressure differential of around 1.4 psi (9.65 kPa) between the upper and lower chambers. This constant pressure difference is necessary so that the QUANTITY of injected fuel is always proportional to the exposed area of the metering slots. Fig. 7-19 shows a cutaway view of the con-

Fig. 7-16. Schematic of a typical mechanically controlled continuous fuel injection system. Main controls are air flow sensor and fuel distributor. (Saab)

Fig. 7-17. Fuel accumulator action. A—Parts defined. B—Fuel pump forces fuel to move diaphragm and plunger down. C—Pump off, spring pushes up on diaphragm keeping pressure on fuel trapped in system. (Volvo)

Fig. 7-18. Fuel distributor for mechanically controlled continuous injection system. There is a pressure regulating valve for each injector.   (Saab)

Fig. 7-20. Control plunger action—partial engine load condition. Diaphragm has flexed downward small amount allowing moderate fuel flow to injector.   (Saab)

trol plunger and its relationship to the metering slots.

Control plunger action under a partial load condition is shown in Fig. 7-19. Air flow sensor has raised plunger enough to uncover metering slot. Regulator diaphragm has flexed down, opening outlet to injector. Fuel is flowing to injector, Fig. 7-20.

Plunger action under full load is pictured in Fig. 7-21. Note that plunger groove has completely exposed metering slot. Diaphragm has flexed further downward fully opening outlet to injector. Fuel is now flowing at a fast rate to the injector, Fig. 7-21.

Fig. 7-21. Control plunger action—heavy engine load. Diaphragm forced further down increasing fuel flow to injector.   (Saab)

Fig. 7-19. Fuel distributor control plunger. Plunger is raised and/or lowered by the air flow sensor lever arm.   (Volvo)

AIR FLOW SENSOR OPERATES CONTROL PLUNGER

The amount the control rod is raised determines the amount of fuel delivered to the injectors. An AIR FLOW SENSOR is used to actuate the plunger. See Fig. 7-16.

The sensor is pivoted on a shaft and balanced so that a plate attached to the sensor lever arm "floats" in a venturi shaped opening. All air drawn from the air cleaner must pass through this opening. Fig. 7-22 shows an air flow sensor. Note how air must flow through the venturi and thus move sensor plate.

The sensor plate is raised in direct proportion to the air flow through the venturi. Fig. 7-23 illustrates how the sensor plate moves upward as air flow is increased. The upward movement moves the control plunger up causing an increase in fuel delivery. The sensor plate continually monitors air flow so that the air-fuel mixture remains correct for all engine loadings, Fig. 7-23.

The top of the control plunger is subjected to control pressure, Figs. 7-16, 7-23. This constant pressure is designed to smooth out sensor action. Control pressure is determined by a pressure regulator valve, Fig. 7-16.

COLD START INJECTOR

A solenoid operated cold start injector is used to provide additional fuel for cold starting or for hot starting when fuel has vaporized in the lines. A thermostatic time switch controls the length of time the cold start injector is held down. This unit functions much as that covered in the section on intermittent fuel injection.

WARM-UP REGULATOR

When the engine is warm, the warm-up regulator, Fig. 7-16, maintains constant control pressure that pushes down on the control plunger. When the engine is cold, the regulator decreases control pressure thus allowing the sensor to open the plunger an additional amount. This provides extra fuel for cold starts.

REMEMBER:

The mechanical continuous injection system feeds fuel from the injectors all the time. The amount of fuel required is determined by the air valve sensor. The sensor operates the fuel distributor plunger, uncovering the metering slots the exact amount needed to produce the proper fuel flow from the injectors.

Fig. 7-22. Air flow through mechanically controlled, injection system. Air must pass through venturi opening thus forcing air flow sensor plate to swing upward. This action moves control plunger.   (Saab)

Fig. 7-23. Air flow sensor plate action. As air flow increases through venturi, plate is forced upward. Lever arm will raise control plunger thus increasing fuel flow. (Volvo)

DIESEL INJECTION SYSTEM

The automobile diesel engine, primarily due to fuel efficiency, is becoming popular.

The true diesel does NOT use a spark plug to ignite the fuel. Air is drawn into the cylinder and highly compressed. The compression is so high that the compressed air will reach temperatures of 1,000°F (538.2°C). At the precise time the piston has completed the compression stroke, diesel fuel is sprayed into the combustion chamber. The intense heat of the compressed air ignites the fuel, and the power stroke follows.

DIESEL FUEL

Diesel fuel is produced in several grades, 1-D, 2-D, and 4-D. Only 1-D and 2-D are suitable for use in automotive diesel engines.

2-D fuel is generally specified for most engines operating under normal conditions and within normal temperature ranges. It burns well and gives somewhat better mileage than 1-D.

1-D fuel is used only for extreme cold weather (below 20°F, −7°C) or in very special cases of frequent stop, start, and accelerate type service.

DIESEL FUEL CHARACTERISTICS

HEAT VALUE is an indication of the relative amount of power produced by a specific amount of fuel. It is measured in BTUs (Joules) per pound of fuel.

FLASH POINT is the temperature to which the fuel must be heated in order to produce a vapor that will ignite in the presence of a flame.

VISCOSITY is a measurement of the fuel's fluidity (how well it pours). Improper viscosity can affect diesel engine operation by producing poor injector spray patterns.

SULPHUR CONTENT is important in that diesel fuel with a high sulphur content causes premature engine wear as well as causing a varnish to form inside the engine.

CETANE NUMBER RATING is a comparison between the burning characteristics of a specified sample of diesel fuel as compared to that of a test fuel

called CETANE (liquid hydrocarbon).

Some other diesel fuel characteristics are POUR POINT, VOLATILITY and CARBON RESIDUE.

In general, it is very important that only CLEAN, FRESH, WATER FREE fuel of the proper characteristics be used.

OVERALL SYSTEM

A schematic of a typical diesel system layout is shown in Fig. 7-24. Units consist of tank, fuel pump, filter, injection pump, injectors, and the necessary fuel lines.

WATER DETECTOR

Some vehicles are equipped with a WATER DETECTOR that will alert the driver to the fact that water is present in the fuel. The water may then be drawn off. Water is extremely damaging to the injection system, Fig. 7-25.

FUEL FILTER

Fuel must be kept clean to avoid injector system trouble. One type of fuel filter is pictured in Fig. 7-26.

DIESEL INJECTION PUMP

Due to high compression (around 22 to 1) used in diesel engines, the injection pump must be capable of producing high pressures. Pressure ranges vary greatly depending on the pump and engine but can range from 3,000 up to around 15,000 psi (20 685–103 425.0 kPa).

HOW THE INJECTOR PUMP PRODUCES PRESSURE

By using a plunger operating in a cylinder, the pump traps fuel ahead of the plunger. When the plunger is forced up, it builds pressure on the fuel. Pressure will be increased to the point at which the injector will open and inject fuel into the engine. Fig. 7-27 shows the essential parts. Note that the shape of the cam influences TIMING, QUANTITY of fuel and the RATE of injection — all very important to proper operation.

Fig. 7-24. Schematic showing relationship of diesel injection system components. (Pontiac)

Fig. 7-25. Fuel tank water detector alerts driver that water is present in tank. Water is damaging to diesel injection systems. (GM)

Fig. 7-26. One type of diesel fuel system filter. This is a spin-on, disposable cartridge type. (Oldsmobile)

Pumps can use a single plunger pump for each injector or a single pump (often consisting of two or more opposing plungers) to serve all injectors.

There are a number of injector pump designs but the commonly used automotive diesel types may be classified as IN-LINE or DISTRIBUTOR.

IN-LINE INJECTOR PUMP

The in-line injector pump uses a separate cylinder-plunger-cam for each cylinder. They are contained in a straight row in a common housing.

The cams are part of a common camshaft driven by the engine at one-half engine speed. Drive may be by chain, belt, or gear.

Fuel from the fuel pump is fed to all of the plunger assemblies. As the camshaft rotates, the plungers are moved up and down in their cylinders.

174

FUEL PRESSURE
TO NOZZLE

CYLINDER

PUMPING
PLUNGER

SHAPE OF CAM CONTROLS:

1. Quantity — How Far
   Plunger Moves
2. Timing — When
   Plunger Moves
3. Rate — How Fast
   Plunger Moves

REVOLVING
CAM

Fig. 7-27. The cam operated plunger, working in a cylinder, is used to produce pressure in diesel injector pump. (Deere & Co.)

A single control rack or rail with gear teeth along one side, is meshed with each plunger assembly. By moving the control rack, the effective pump action (amount of fuel pumped) of all plungers can be ad-

justed. A typical in-line pump is pictured in Fig. 7-28. Study it carefully and note the location of all parts.

IN-LINE INJECTOR PUMP METERING CONTROL

Each plunger operates in a separate cylinder or barrel. The top section of the plunger has a wide band or groove cutaway. One edge of the cut forms a HELIX (spiral shape). The plunger also has a vertical slot reaching from the top of the plunger down into the cutaway area.

The bottom of the plunger is connected, by means of a flange, to the toothed control sleeve that meshes with the control rack teeth. When the control rack is moved back and forth, the plunger will rotate in the cylinder. Study the arrangement in Fig. 7-29.

METERING CONTROL RACK ACTION— NO PUMPING POSITION

In Fig. 7-30, fuel has moved into the plunger-cylinder area. Control rack has been moved to the extreme left. This rotates the plunger until the VER-

1 Pressure pipe (injection pipe)	12 Tappet spring	22 Tappet guide screw	33 Setting lever
2 Cap nut	13 Plunger vane	23 Injection pump housing	34 Setting lever stop, also adjustment screw with full load stop
3 Pipe union	14 Roller tappet	24 Fuel feed union	
4 Valve spring	15 Clamping jaws (to grip the pipe unions)	25 Control rod guide bearing and start-metering stop	35 Guide lever
5 Seal between pipe union and injection pump housing	16 Suction chamber	26 Camshaft (drive side)	36 Diaphragm pin with pressure pin and compensator spring
6 Pressure valve with pressure valve holder	17 Control bore (feed and return bore)	27 Link stud	37 Diaphragm assembly
7 Pressure chamber	18 Control rod	28 Bearing base-plate with gasket and centering adjustment	38 Vacuum line
8 Plunger ⎤ = forming pump	19 Pin on control sleeve rotating lever	29 Fuel feed pump	39 Diaphragm
9 Cylinder ⎦ element	20 Adjustable clamping piece with guide groove	30 Journal bearing	40 Guide pin
10 Seal	21 Clamp screw	31 Rocker arm	41 Air cleaner and oil filler bore
11 Governor sleeve with steering arm		32 Stop pin for full load stop	

Fig. 7-28. Typical diesel engine in-line injection pump. Study cutaway carefully and learn part names. (Mercedes-Benz)

Fig. 7-29. Pump plunger construction. When control rack is moved, plunger will be forced to rotate by segmented gear sleeve acting on plunger flange. (American Bosch)

Fig. 7-30. Pump plunger in "no pumping" position. Metering control rack moved to non-pumping position. Trapped fuel will flow down vertical slot and out port. No fuel will be delivered to injector. (Deere & Co.)

TICAL slot is aligned with the fuel port. In this position, the camshaft can force the plunger to the top of its travel WITHOUT any pumping action. Since the vertical slot is aligned with the port, all fuel trapped above the plunger will merely squirt down through the slot and out the port. No fuel will be delivered.

METERING CONTROL RACK ACTION— PARTIAL FLOW

Note Fig. 7-31. The control rack has moved partway to the right. This rotated the plunger, moving the vertical slot out of alignment with the ports. When the cam raises the plunger, the plunger will seal off the ports, trapping the fuel in the cylinder.

Continued upward travel will exert pressure on the confined fuel forcing it through the injector nozzle. The QUANTITY of fuel delivered will depend upon the relationship between the cutout helix and the port. When the plunger has raised far enough (straight up with no rotating action) so that the cutout helix uncovers the port, the trapped fuel will again squirt down the plunger vertical slot, through the cutout area and out the port. Keep in mind that the plunger always raises the same distance each time the cam revolves. Pumping plunger LIFT distance is always the same but PUMPING distance depends upon the position of the helix in relation to the port. Note A in Fig. 7-31. This indicates plunger pumping distance for this location of the helix.

METERING CONTROL RACK ACTION— FULL FLOW

The rack, Fig. 7-32, has now been moved to the extreme right. Plunger has rotated further counterclockwise moving vertical slot and helix further away

Fig. 7-31. Plunger in pumping position for moderate delivery. Control rack has moved plunger to a partial flow position. Plunger will force trapped fuel to injector until helix uncovers port. Plunger pumping distance is shown at A. (Deere & Co.)

from port. When cam raises plunger, plunger will close off ports and force fuel through injector. In that the plunger PUMPING distance, B in Fig. 7-32, is now greater, quantity of fuel will be increased. At this setting, pump will deliver maximum flow, Fig. 7-32.

Pump plunger action during entire PUMPING portion of plunger lift, is pictured in Fig. 7-33. Note how fuel is trapped above plunger in B, forced out

Fig. 7-32. Plunger in maximum delivery position. Note long plunger pumping distance B. This produces heavy fuel delivery. (Deere & Co.)

of cylinder in C, and how helix uncovers port in D, stopping pump action.

INJECTOR PUMP DELIVERY VALVE

Fuel flowing from the pump cylinder is forced through a delivery valve on its way to the injector. The fuel flow forces the delivery valve from its seat, A in Fig. 7-34.

Fig. 7-34. Injector pump fuel delivery valve. This valve produces a sudden drop in injector line pressure as soon as fuel delivery ceases. This helps the injector nozzle valve to close without dripping. (Oldsmobile)

When the helix uncovers the cylinder ports, pressure in the pump cylinder drops instantly. This causes the delivery valve plunger to quickly return to its seat, B of Fig. 7-34. In so doing, the volume in the delivery line (injector housing, line to injector and

Fig. 7-33. Pump plunger action during entire pumping cycle. Note how helix has uncovered port in D thus stopping fuel delivery even though full plunger lift travel may raise it still higher. (Deere & Co.)

delivery valve spring chamber) is suddenly IN-CREASED by the amount of the delivery valve plunger travel, C in Fig. 7-34. This increase in volume causes a sudden reduction in delivery line pressure that allows the injector nozzle valve to snap shut quickly and cleanly without dripping. A delivery valve is used on both in-line and distributor type pumps. Fig. 7-34.

DISTRIBUTOR TYPE INJECTION PUMP

The popular DISTRIBUTOR type injection pump is pictured in Fig. 7-35. You will note that a single, double-plunger type pump serves all injector outlets. A single delivery valve is located in the rotor. Study the pump thoroughly and learn all part names.

PUMP CHARGING CYCLE

Fuel enters the TRANSFER PUMP from the in-line fuel pump. From the transfer pump, fuel moves through rotor passages into the pumping chamber and fuel metering valve area. Excess fuel flows through the transfer pump pressure regulator back to the inlet side. For fuel to flow through rotor passages, rotor must turn far enough to align rotor passages with fuel charging ring ports. Cam ring is so positioned as to permit pump plungers to be forced apart by entering fuel. The distance the pump plungers move apart determines how much fuel is delivered. The distance plungers move apart is controlled by the governor operated METERING VALVE, Fig. 7-36.

PUMP DISCHARGE CYCLE

In Fig. 7-37, pump rotor is turning. Angled inlet passages no longer line up with charging ring ports. Fuel is trapped in pumping chamber. Cam ring rollers have been squeezed inward by cams thus forcing two plungers toward each other. As plungers are forced together, the trapped fuel is forced past the delivery valve, into the injector line thus opening injector nozzle and spraying fuel into cylinder.

PUMP FUEL RETURN CIRCUIT

Transfer pump pressure forces fuel through a vent passage in the hydraulic head, Fig. 7-38. Flow

Fig. 7-35. Cutaway view of a distributor type injection pump. Pump creates pressure and distributes fuel from single pump to all injectors. Learn part names and their relationship to overall pump.   (Ford)

Fig. 7-36. Rotary injection pump in charging cycle position. Study fuel flow. Note how opposing plungers are forced outward filling the space between them with fuel. (Chevrolet)

Fig. 7-37. Rotary type injection pump in discharge cycle position. Cams force plungers together. Fuel is pumped through delivery valve to proper injector line.

through the passage is partially blocked by a wire to prevent excessive flow and pressure loss. Any air from the transfer pump flows, with some fuel, through the vent into the governor linkage compartment and then back to the fuel tank, Fig. 7-39.

ELECTRICAL FUEL SHUTOFF

The electrical fuel shutoff, Fig. 7-35, rotates the metering valve to the closed position when the shutoff solenoid is deenergized.

OTHER PUMP FEATURES

The pump can also offer a VISCOSITY COMPENSATING valve that tends to keep pump function the same with either light or heavy (or cold) fuels.

Fuel delivery timing can be automatically advanced or retarded to compensate for engine speed and/or load changes. See advance mechanism in Fig. 7-35.

DISTRIBUTOR TYPE PUMP FUEL INJECTION SYSTEM SCHEMATIC

A schematic of the entire fuel system is shown in Fig. 7-39. Start at the fuel tank and study the various components and their relationship to the overall system.

Fig. 7-38. Injection pump fuel return circuit. (Oldsmobile)

Fig. 7-40 illustrates a pump control setup for one particular system.

INJECTOR TYPES

There are many different injector designs but all are a variation of two basic types—INWARD OPENING and OUTWARD OPENING. Study the action of the two nozzle designs in Fig. 7-41.

One type of injector nozzle is pictured in Fig. 7-42. Is it inward or outward opening? Note the heavy spring 6, keeping the jet needle 1, against its seat. Injection pressure will force fuel down canal 14, to pressure chamber 19 where it will act against the shoulder of the jet needle. When pressure reaches a point high enough to overcome spring pressure, needle will lift off seat and fuel will be sprayed into the cylinder.

SPRAY PATTERN IMPORTANT

Fuel pressure, fuel viscosity, nozzle design, and nozzle condition must all be correct so that a proper spray pattern is formed. Spray patterns will vary depending upon engine design. Fig. 7-43 illustrates the pattern recommended for one particular engine.

METERING VALVE

GOVERNOR SPRING

HOUSING PRESSURE REGULATOR

VENT WIRE ASSEMBLY

HEAD PRESSURE

CAM RING

TRANSFER PRESSURE TAP HOLE PLUG

BALL CHECK ASSEMBLY

AUTOMATIC ADVANCE MECHANISM

GOVERNOR HOUSING LUBE

CHARGING PASSAGE

ROTOR

DELIVERY VALVE

PRESSURE REGULATOR

FILTER

FUEL PUMP

FUEL TANK

TRANSFER PUMP

FILTER

NOZZLE

HIGH PRESSURE DISCHARGE CIRCUIT

TRANSFER PUMP PRESSURE CIRCUIT

HOUSING PRESSURE CIRCUIT

INLET PRESSURE AND RETURN OIL CIRCUIT

Fig. 7-39. Schematic of diesel fuel system employing a rotary type injection pump.   (Oldsmobile)

AUTOMATIC FAST IDLING CONTROL

FUEL INJECTION PUMP

INJECTION PUMP AUTOMATIC STOP CONTROL

ACCELERATOR PEDAL

Fig. 7-40. Injection pump controls as used on one specific installation.   (Peugeot)

Fig. 7-41. Nozzles are of either inward opening or outward opening design. (Deere & Co.)

GLOW PLUGS

To aid in igniting the compressed air-fuel mix during cold starting, automotive diesel engines use glow plugs. The glow plug is an electrically operated device that protrudes into the precombustion chamber. When energized, the glow plug tip heats to a dull red.

1 Jet needle
2 Nozzle assembly
3 Nozzle element
4 Thrust pin
5 Cap nut for fixing injection nozzle
6 Compression spring
7 Nozzle holder
8 Drain hole in the nozzle holder
9 Through-way jointing piece with annular canal for leak-off oil union
10 Hexagon nut for fixing the through-way jointing piece
11 Cap nut for fixing the injection pipe
12 Fuel feed
13 Leak-off oil drain back to fuel tank
14 Pressure canal in the nozzle holder
15 Special washers belonging to compression spring (machined steel disks)
16 Annular groove and feed bores in nozzle element
17 Annular groove and pressure canal in nozzle assembly
18 Mounting thread
19 Pressure chamber in nozzle assembly

Fig. 7-42. One type of inward opening injector design. (Mercedes-Benz)

UNACCEPTABLE SPRAY PATTERN CONE ANGLE TOO WIDE AND FUEL DISTRIBUTION UNEVEN.

UNACCEPTABLE SPRAY PATTERN FUEL NOT BEING ATOMIZED. FUEL BEING INJECTED IN A SOLID STREAM.

ACCEPTABLE SPRAY PATTERN FUEL BEING ATOMIZED. EVEN FUEL DISTRIBUTION.

ENCLOSE SPRAY IN BEAKER

Fig. 7-43. Injection spray pattern is important for smooth, efficient engine operation. (Oldsmobile)

The swirling, highly compressed air-fuel mixture is heated by the glow plug tip. This additional heat causes the mixture to ignite more readily thus helping the engine to start.

Glow plugs are turned on and off automatically on some vehicles. Under most starting conditions, the plugs are energized for a very short period. The engine can be started in seconds after the key is turned on, Fig. 7-44. The glow plugs may still be energized for a very short while following engine startup.

SUMMARY

FUEL INJECTION—GASOLINE

Fuel injection systems, both ELECTRONIC and MECHANICALLY controlled systems, are seeing wider use. Some systems use intermittent injection while others employ continuous injection.

Fuel injection systems provide extremely accurate control of the air-fuel mixture thus increasing engine efficiency while at the same time reducing emission levels. Fig. 7-45.

FUEL INJECTION—DIESEL

Diesel engines are highly efficient and are available on an ever increasing number of autos. They use high pressure injector pumps and inject fuel directly into the precombustion chamber cylinder.

KNOW THESE TERMS

Direct fuel injection, Indirect fuel injection, Mechanical fuel injection, Electronic fuel injection, Timed fuel injection, Intermittent fuel injection, Pulse width, Continuous fuel injection, Closed loop, Stoichiometric mixture, Flow meter, Cold start injector, Throttle valve sensor, Fuel accumulator, Fuel distributor, Diesel fuel grades, Water detector, Diesel injection pump, Control rack, Diesel injectors, Glow plugs.

REVIEW QUESTIONS—CHAPTER 7

1. Most gasoline fuel injection systems inject the fuel directly into the cylinders. True or False?
2. Gasoline fuel injection systems employing a mechanical pump operate on the _____ flow principle:
   a. Continuous.
   b. Intermittent.
   c. Rotating.
   d. All at once.
3. Explain how the solenoid operated gasoline injector operates.
4. The _____ flow injector system feeds some fuel constantly.
5. Electronic fuel injection systems can use either:
   a. One injector per cylinder.

Fig. 7-44. Diesel engine glow plug. Glow plug heats air-fuel mixture in precombustion chamber to assist cold engine startup and initial driveaway. Note how glow plug tip protrudes into precombustion chamber. Injector spray enters this area. (Mazda)

   b. Two injectors for the entire engine.
   c. Both of the above.
   d. None of the above.
6. Normal fuel system pressures exceed 100 psi (689.4 kPa) in the mechanical gasoline injection system. True or False?
7. Fuel pressure regulators operate by opening a spring loaded _____ to relieve excess pressure.
8. What is meant by a closed loop fuel system?
9. A vital component of the closed loop system is the _____ _____.
10. What unit does an air flow meter use to generate an electrical signal?
11. The cold start injector supplies _____ _____ for cold starts.
12. The cold start injector operates continuously during cold weather. True or False?
13. In the mechanically controlled continuous fuel injection system, the air flow sensor moves the _____ _____ to change fuel flow.
14. In the continuous injection fuel distributor, there is _____ pressure regulator for _____ cylinder/cylinders.
15. Diesel injection pumps are of two general types. Name them.

16. Diesel injection systems feed some fuel from the injector nozzle at all times. True or False?
17. What grade of diesel fuel is normally used for average use?
18. Some diesel injection pumps must be carefully timed while others are designed to inject fuel at any time. True or False?
19. Some diesel injection pumps use a control rack to adjust fuel flow. The rack is used to rotate the _____ _____.
20. Explain how the item in question 19 functions to control fuel flow.
21. Rewrite the following sentence, leaving out the wrong words. "Diesel engines use a glow plug that protrudes into the cylinder, precombustion chamber, crankcase."
22. The distributor pump uses a single pump for all the injectors. True or False?
23. The delivery valve:
   a. Prevents system leaks.
   b. Regulates system pressure.
   c. Injects fuel into the hollow control rack.
   d. None of the above.
24. List four diesel fuel characteristics.
25. Diesel injector nozzle designs are of two general types. Name them.

Fig. 7-45. Cutaway view of a rotary engine incorporating electronic fuel (gasoline) injection. This 2-rotor engine produces 135 horsepower at 6,000 rpm. (Mazda)

Modern 180.62 cubic inch (2 960 cubic centimeter), 6-cylinder, fuel injected, turbocharged engine. Many components mounted on top of engine are emission control related. How many can you find and identify?   (Nissan)

Exhaust gases pass around and heat oxygen sensor zirconia element, causing oxygen ions to conduct through element from atmosphere to outer electrode. This, in effect, forms a basic electrochemical cell that develops a voltage between two electrodes. When exhaust gas oxygen content increases (leaner air-fuel mixture), output voltage drops close to zero. A richening of fuel mixture (decreases oxygen content) causes output voltage to rise to around one volt. This voltage output signal is fed to a computer that in turn controls carburetor air-fuel mixture ratio.   (General Motors)

Chapter 8

EXHAUST SYSTEMS AND EMISSION CONTROLS

After studying this chapter, you will be able to:
- Define automotive emissions.
- List the three types of emission controls.
- Explain the operating principles of emission control systems.
- Identify the major parts of emission control systems.

Approximately 99.9 percent of the exhaust from the average car engine (gasoline powered) consists mostly of water, nitrogen, carbon dioxide, and carbon monoxide. About 0.1 percent (one tenth of one percent) of the exhaust is made up of hydrocarbons (unburned gasoline).

Some of these emissions, such as water, oxygen, nitrogen, and carbon dioxide, are of little concern. Others, such as hydrocarbons (HC), oxides of nitrogen (NO_x), and carbon monoxide (CO), can pose a health problem for the nation if uncontrolled.

Hydrocarbon emission into the atmosphere, where it reacts with the sunlight, tends to produce what may be called photochemical (sunlight causing chemical reactions or change) smog.

Excellent progress has been made in the development of a number of emission control devices. These units, when properly installed, serviced and maintained, do an excellent job of reducing harmful emissions. Ongoing research and development in this vital area will undoubtedly bring about further reductions.

EMISSION CONTROL

Emission controls may be divided into three general types; FUEL SYSTEM VAPOR CONTROLS, INTERNAL ENGINE CONTROLS and EXTERNAL ENGINE CONTROLS.

The fuel vapor controls are designed to minimize the escape of gasoline vapors from the carburetor, fuel tank, and filler cap. The vapor control system would also include engine crankcase fume control.

Internal engine controls consist of basic engine design (camshaft design, combustion chamber shape, manifold design, etc.) in addition to the controls determining air-fuel ratio, engine temperature, ignition timing, etc. The purpose here is to promote clean, efficient burning of the fuel mixture within the combustion chamber.

External controls are those such as the catalytic converter and air injection system. They help the exhaust gases to continue the burning process as they move through the exhaust system.

POSITIVE CRANKCASE VENTILATION (PCV)

The combustion process produces many gases, some very corrosive. A great deal of water (almost a gallon of water for each gallon of gasoline) is also formed.

The high pressure in the cylinder during the firing stroke forces some of these gases by the piston rings into the crankcase area. To prevent acid, etc., dilution of the oil, these blow-by gases must be removed.

For many years a simple road draft tube pulled the gases out into the atmosphere. This created significant amounts of air pollutants. The CLOSED POSITIVE CRANKCASE VENTILATION system removes the gases without discharging them into the atmosphere.

By connecting a hose between the engine interior and the intake manifold, engine vacuum will draw the crankcase fumes out of the engine and into the cylinders where the gases will be burned along with the regular fuel charge. A schematic illustrating a typical PCV system is shown in Fig. 8-1.

PCV CONTROL VALVE NEEDED

If allowed to flow into the intake manifold at all times and in any amount, the crankcase gases would upset the basic carburetor air-fuel ratios required for various operating conditions. To prevent this, it is essential that a PCV flow control valve be incorporated into the system. One type of control valve is pictured in Fig. 8-2.

KEY TO PCV SYSTEM

F = FILTERED AIR
B = BLOW-BY GASES
FILTERED AIR + BLOW-BY GASES
COMBUSTIBLE MIXTURE

Fig. 8-1. Schematic illustrating positive crankcase ventilation system. Note how crankcase blow-by gases are drawn into intake manifold where they mix with fuel charge for burning. (GM)

BLOW-BY GASES

Fig. 8-2. Typical PCV valve. Note flow of blow-by gases through valve. (Jeep)

PCV CONTROL VALVE ACTION

When the engine is stopped, no intake manifold vacuum exists and the PCV valve is held closed by spring action, as in A, Fig. 8-3.

During periods of idle or deceleration, vacuum is high. The tapered valve plunger is drawn into the metering opening. This reduces the size of the passageway allowing only a small flow of crankcase gases to the intake manifold. See B, Fig. 8-3.

When the vehicle is operating at a normal load, the vacuum drops off somewhat. This allows the spring to push the plunger partway out of the opening. This increases the opening and gas flow is reasonably heavy, as in C, Fig. 8-3.

Acceleration or heavy loading causes manifold vacuum to drop greatly. The spring instantly pushes the plunger further out of the opening. Crankcase gas flow is now at its heaviest. Look at D, Fig. 8-3.

In the event of a "backfire" in the manifold, the reverse pressure allows the spring to fully close the valve, A in Fig. 8-3, to prevent the flame from traveling into the crankcase. This prevents a possible explosion in the crankcase area.

EVAPORATION CONTROL SYSTEM (ECS)

The evaporation control system (also called evaporative emission control system) is designed to prevent the release of either liquid gasoline or gasoline vapor into the atmosphere.

Although setups vary, a typical system is composed basically of a special pressure-vacuum filler cap, a nonvented (closed to atmosphere) fuel tank, a tank fill limiter, vapor separator, vent line, a charcoal canister, purge valve, and an excess fuel and vapor return line to the tank. A roll-over valve may also be used to prevent fuel leakage from tank in the event the vehicle is rolled and lands upside down.

| ENGINE NOT RUNNING OR IN CASE OF BACKFIRE | IDLING OR DECELERATING | NORMAL OPERATION | ACCELERATION OR HIGH LOAD |

PCV VALVE IS CLOSED.

A

PCV VALVE IS OPEN.
VACUUM PASSAGE IS SMALL.

B

PCV VALVE IS OPEN.
VACUUM PASSAGE IS LARGE.

C

PCV VALVE IS FULLY OPEN.

D

Fig. 8-3. PCV control valve action. As tapered plunger moves out of metering opening, gas flow area is increased. (Toyota)

A schematic of one specific evaporative control setup is illustrated in Fig. 8-4. Study the various parts and their relationship to the overall system.

ECS OPERATION

The fuel tank is sealed with a pressure-vacuum cap. This is a special cap, using both a pressure and a vacuum relief valve, that prevents excessive pressure or vacuum in the tank in the event of system failure. The valves remain closed under normal operating conditions. When pressure exceeds around 0.8 psi (5.52 kPa) or a vacuum forms in excess of 0.1 Hg (0.69 kPa) the valves are activated. See Fig. 8-5.

The fuel tank "breathes" through the vent tube as fuel is consumed or when it expands or contracts from heating and cooling.

The tank shown in Fig. 8-6 is designed so that when it is filled to capacity, there is sufficient air dome above the fuel to permit thermal expansion without forcing liquid gasoline into the vent lines. When filling the tank, the small orifice (hole) in the vent restricter slows down the venting of the tank while filling so that an air dome is present thus limiting fill capacity.

Any vapors in the tank travel through the fuel tank vent tube to the charcoal canister. The carburetor float bowl is also vented to the canister so that bowl vapors generated by "engine off heat soak" (heat from engine transferred to carburetor after engine is stopped), will be forced into the canister.

Study the system portrayed in Fig. 8-6. Note that the bowl vent line is connected to a bowl vent valve. An idle purge and off-idle purge port are provided for the idle purge line.

ECS ACTION

The system is in the engine OFF mode. The bowl vent valve spring has forced the vent valve to the OPEN position. Vapors from the float bowl are moving through the bowl vent line and are entering the canister. Vapors from the fuel tank are also entering the canister.

The canister is filled with highly activated charcoal granules (small particles). When the vapors touch the charcoal, the granules absorb and store the vapors.

As long as the engine remains off, the vapors will be retained by the canister.

Upon starting the engine, vacuum will be formed in the carburetor-intake manifold assembly. This vacuum, working on the bowl vent valve diaphragm, pulls the vent valve up against spring pressure and closes the bowl vent valve.

At the same time, vacuum under the throttle valve will work on the idle purge port and draw fresh air through the charcoal bed. As the air passes over the charcoal, it will pick up the stored vapors and draw them into the carburetor where they will be mixed with fuel charge for burning.

Fig. 8-4. Study parts of an evaporation control system. (AMC)

Fig. 8-5. Pressure vacuum cap. This cap will relieve either excessive pressure or vacuum and thus prevent tank or other system damage. (Chrysler)

As the throttle valve is opened wider, the off-idle purge port will be uncovered and the flow of air through the canister will be increased somewhat. As the engine continues to run, the canister will be purged (cleaned) of vapors.

When the engine is stopped, the canister bowl vent diaphragm will release the valve and the spring will force it open, permitting bowl vapors to once again enter the canister. See Fig. 8-6.

CANISTER CONSTRUCTION

All canisters contain a bed of activated charcoal (carbon). A filter pad can be placed both above and

Fig. 8-6. Schematic of one type of evaporation control system. This setup uses a bowl vent valve. (Buick)

below the charcoal.

Some canisters use only the bowl vent valve and vent the canister directly to the carburetor, as in Fig. 8-6. Fig. 8-7 also illustrates this type. This particular canister uses clean air from the air cleaner. Note that clean purge air enters the top of the canister, passes down through a pipe and moves out and up through

the charcoal. This is called a CLOSED canister. With this setup, as soon as the engine starts, purge air is drawn through the canister, Fig. 8-7.

Another canister design makes use of not only the bowl vent control valve but utilizes a canister purge valve as well, Fig. 8-8. The purge air flow rate is controlled by the size of the orifice in the purge control valve.

A thermal (heat controlled) vacuum switch controls vacuum to the purge valve. When engine operating temperature reaches a specified level, the thermal vacuum valve will apply vacuum to the purge valve and purge air flow will commence. Note that this too is a CLOSED type because clean purge air is drawn in from the air cleaner.

Another, somewhat different canister design is illustrated in Fig. 8-9. This unit uses a control valve that is not a part of the tank. It also draws purge air into the canister through the bottom. This can be referred to as an OPEN canister. A filter pad is used to clean the air.

Some vapor control systems employ two canisters. Such a system is pictured in Fig. 8-10. One canister is used for the bowl vapor storage while the other handles tank vapors only.

LIQUID FUEL CONTROL

It is very important in the closed fuel system, that no liquid fuel be forced into the canister. Evaporative control systems may use an air dome in the tank, a

Fig. 8-7. Cutaway of a vapor storage canister using only a bowl vent valve. Canister purge air is vented directly to intake (induction) system. (Pontiac)

188

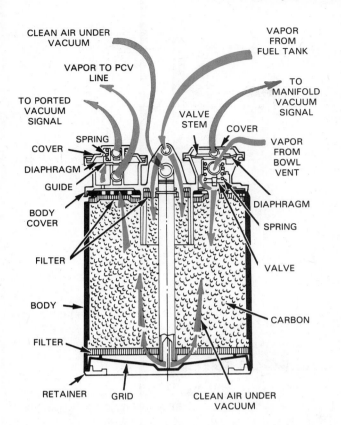

CLEAN AIR UNDER VACUUM

VAPOR TO PCV LINE

TO PORTED VACUUM SIGNAL

COVER

SPRING

DIAPHRAGM

GUIDE

BODY COVER

FILTER

BODY

FILTER

RETAINER

GRID

CLEAN AIR UNDER VACUUM

VALVE STEM

COVER

VAPOR FROM FUEL TANK

TO MANIFOLD VACUUM SIGNAL

VAPOR FROM BOWL VENT

DIAPHRAGM

SPRING

VALVE

CARBON

PURGE & BOWL VENT

VAPOR FROM FUEL TANK

FILTER

CANISTER BODY

CARBON

FILTER

GRID

FILTER

AIR UNDER VACUUM

Fig. 8-8. Closed type vapor storage canister with a thermal vacuum switch controlled purge valve.   (Pontiac)

Fig. 8-9. Vapor canister design that draws purge air up through an external filter at the bottom. Control valve is remotely located. This is an open type canister.   (Pontiac)

BOWL EXTERNAL VENT (HOSE "A")

AIR CLEANER

PORTED VACUUM SIGNAL (HOSE "C")

BACKFIRE RESTRICTOR

VENT VALVE (CAPPED)

BOWL VENT INLET (CAPPED)

CARBURETOR FUEL BOWL

MANIFOLD VACUUM SIGNAL (HOSE "B")

BOWL VENT CONTROL (VALVE NORMALLY OPEN)

TANK VENT INLET (CLOSED)

PURGE AIR INLET

1500 CC CANISTER

SPLASH SHIELD

PURGE AIR

2500 CC CANISTER

HOSE "G"

PCV HOSE (MANIFOLD VACUUM) (HOSE "D")

BALL CHECK VALVE AND TANK RESTRICTOR

SEALED GAS CAP

SEALED GAS CAP

PRESSURE VACUUM RELIEF VALVE

(OPTIONAL AUXILIARY) FUEL TANK

MAIN FUEL TANK

VAPOR

FUEL

ON VEHICLES WITH 20-GALLON (76 LITRES) FUEL TANK, PRESSURE RELIEF VALVE IS PART OF GAS CAP.

Fig. 8-10. Evaporative control system using two-stage canisters. This specific pickup truck system uses one canister for bowl vapors and other for tank vapors. Study connections carefully.   (Chevrolet) vapor separator or liquid check valve to prevent liquid fuel from leaving the tank.

LIQUID-VAPOR SEPARATOR

The liquid-vapor separator unit collects any liquid fuel and drains it back to the tank, preventing it from entering the charcoal canister. The separator is connected to three vent lines—one to each top front corner of the fuel tank and one to the top, center back. See Fig. 8-11. The rear vent standpipe in the separator has a hole near the bottom that permits any liquid fuel that may have been forced into the separator to drain back into the tank.

The liquid-vapor separator is mounted ABOVE the gas tank so that regardless of how steep a hill the car may be on or how much it may be tipped to the side, one vent will be above the fuel level and will be free to pass vapor to canister. Fig. 8-11 pictures an evaporation control system using liquid-vapor separator.

LIQUID CHECK VALVE

The liquid check valve allows tank vapors to pass into the canister under normal conditions. If liquid fuel, however, starts filling up the check valve, the float will be forced to rise. This forces the needle into its seat thus closing off the vent line until the liquid fuel drains back into the tank, Fig. 8-12.

ROLLOVER CHECK VALVE

A rollover check valve can be used to seal off the tank vent line in the event the vehicle is turned upside down in an accident. Some rollover valves also incorporate a liquid separator valve as part of their construction. One form of rollover valve is pictured in Fig. 8-13. When the valve is inverted, the steel ball will force the valve plunger to close off the vent line.

Fig. 8-12. Typical liquid check valve. Fuel entering valve raises float forcing needle to seal off vent line. (AMC)

DIESELING OR RUN-ON

Some engines, due basically to lean mixtures, high operating temperatures, and fast idle speeds, tend to continue running after the ignition key is turned off. This is commonly known as "dieseling" or "run-on." It can produce a considerable amount of pollution.

To prevent dieseling, some engines employ an electric solenoid. When the key is on, the solenoid keeps the throttle valve open far enough for normal idle. When the key is turned off, the solenoid allows the throttle to COMPLETELY CLOSE. This shuts off all air and the engine cannot diesel.

Another setup automatically engages the air conditioning compressor drive clutch for several seconds whenever the key is turned off. This places the engine

Fig. 8-11. This evaporative control system employs a liquid-vapor separator to prevent liquid fuel from being forced into charcoal (carbon) canister. (Toyota)

Fig. 8-13. One type of rollover check valve. (AMC)

Fig. 8-14. One method that has been used to circulate a portion of exhaust gases. This will lower NO$_x$ emissions.

under a small load causing it to slow down and stop without dieseling.

EXHAUST GAS RECIRCULATION (EGR)

When peak combustion temperature exceeds 2,500°F, (1 372°C), the nitrogen in the air mixes with the oxygen to produce oxides of nitrogen (NO$_x$).

By introducing a metered portion of the hot exhaust gases into the intake manifold, the incoming fuel charge will be diluted and flame temperatures lowered. This, in turn, reduces the level of NO$_x$ emissions. Fig. 8-14 shows one method that has been used to admit exhaust gas into the intake manifold. Note how gas flows through floor jets, Fig. 8-14.

The amount of exhaust gas that is recirculated can be controlled by an EGR valve. Such valves are widely used as they can be designed to admit carefully controlled amounts of exhaust gases into the intake air stream. The exact amount will vary according to engine speed and loading.

EGR valves are of two basic types, VACUUM MODULATED (PORTED) and BACK PRESSURE MODULATED.

VACUUM MODULATED (PORTED) EGR VALVE

The vacuum modulated (controlled or regulated) EGR valve incorporates a vacuum diaphragm to actuate the gas flow control valve (often termed pintle). The vacuum tube is connected to a timed (located to operate at a specific point of throttle opening) port in the carburetor air horn that is located just above the throttle valve in the closed or idle position.

When in the idle position, the throttle valve has not uncovered the port and no vacuum is applied to the EGR valve, A in Fig. 8-15. Note the diaphragm spring

Fig. 8-15. Action of the vacuum diaphragm operated EGR valve. Note how the engine vacuum is used to open valve in B.

forces the valve closed and no exhaust gas flow takes place.

When the throttle valve is opened beyond the idle position, the port is uncovered and engine vacuum is applied to the EGR valve. The vacuum causes the diaphragm to raise upward against spring tension. This draws the valve (pintle) upward allowing exhaust gas to flow through the valve into the intake manifold. See B in Fig. 8-15.

The EGR valve remains closed during periods of idle or heavy deceleration (accelerator completely released). Flow is reduced or stopped during heavy acceleration due to momentary low engine vacuum.

A temperature sensitive control is placed between the EGR valve and the carburetor. Below certain temperatures, the EGR vacuum line is closed rendering the EGR valve inoperative.

A schematic, showing how timed port in the carburetor admits vacuum to EGR valve diaphragm, is pictured in Fig. 8-16.

Fig. 8-16. When throttle valve starts to open, timed port is uncovered thus admitting engine vacuum to EGR vacuum diaphragm. This opens pintle valve. (GM)

BACK PRESSURE MODULATED EGR VALVE

Unlike the vacuum modulated EGR valve just discussed, the back pressure modulated valve employs two diaphragms. Some designs use two separate diaphragms while others, such as that pictured in Fig. 8-17, utilize a single diaphragm that serves two separate functions.

The POWER diaphragm portion, A in Fig. 8-17, is secured between the outer edges of the diaphragm plate and the valve stem support housing. The center or CONTROL diaphragm portion divides the chamber formed between the diaphragm plate and valve stem support housing.

The power diaphragm plate is spring loaded. This

action closes the pintle valve when the engine is stopped or when intake vacuum cannot be applied to the power diaphragm.

In A of Fig. 8-17, the engine is operating. Ported or timed vacuum is applied to the power diaphragm. In that the control diaphragm is held down by the valve spring, the control valve is open. As long as it remains open allowing air to enter, a vacuum cannot be formed above the power diaphragm. Until such a vacuum is formed, the power diaphragm will remain down, keeping the pintle valve closed. Although exhaust gases cannot pass the pintle valve, they have moved up through the hollow valve stem and have entered the chamber beneath the control diaphragm. Pressure is building up attempting to force the control diaphragm upward.

The exhaust gas back pressure, B, Fig. 8-17, has finally raised to the point that it has forced the control diaphragm upward causing it to seal off the control valve opening. In that air can no longer pass, vacuum is formed above the power diaphragm. Atmospheric pressure, acting on the bottom of the power diaphragm—valve stem housing assembly, moved the entire unit up thus opening the pintle valve. Exhaust gas now passes into the intake manifold. Fig. 8-17.

AIR INJECTION MAKES COMBUSTION MORE COMPLETE

Hydrocarbon and carbon monoxide emission via the exhaust can be reduced by a more complete burn-

Fig. 8-17. An exhaust backpressure modulated EGR valve. A—Low backpressure, valve closed. B—Exhaust backpressure closes control valve, vacuum forms above power diaphragm plate drawing pintle valve up to open position. (Buick)

ing of the fuel charge.

Following the power stroke, the engine exhaust valve opens to permit exhausting of the burned fuel charge. As the charge passes the exhaust valve, it is still burning. By injecting a stream of fresh air into the burning gases just as they pass the exhaust valve, the burning will be both intensified and prolonged. This increased burning action will tend to burn up a great deal of the normally unburned hydrocarbons, as well as changing a significant portion of the carbon monoxide (poisonous) gas into harmless carbon dioxide. Fig. 8-18 illustrates one setup for injecting air into the area near the exhaust valve.

CARBON MONOXIDE IN EXHAUST

Car engines, despite the use of emission controls, produce poisonous carbon monoxide. Use the same precautions regarding ventilation that apply to a car not equipped with controls.

AIR INJECTION SYSTEM ACTION

A typical air injection system (called Air Injection Reactor, Thermactor, Air Guard, etc.) is illustrated in Fig. 8-19.

Note that the AIR PUMP, Figs. 8-19, 8-20, draws fresh air in through the air cleaner. Some other setups draw air through a separate, smaller filter. The air is mildly compressed. The compressed air is then directed, via a hose, through the air bypass or

DIVERTER VALVE, through a CHECK VALVE and into a DISTRIBUTION MANIFOLD, Fig. 8-19.

AIR PUMP

The air pump or compressor, is of the positive displacement, vane type.

A relief valve limits the amount of pressure the pump can develop. Spring loaded carbon shoes permit sliding contact between the vanes and rotor. The pump is belt driven from the engine. Fig. 8-20 shows a

Fig. 8-18. When air is injected into the exhaust stream, it provides the oxygen needed to keep exhaust gases burning. This helps to reduce emissions of HC and CO. (Nissan)

Fig. 8-19. Typical air injection exhaust emission control system. (Chevrolet)

Fig. 8-20. Cutaway of air injection pump. (Toyota)

cutaway view of a typical air pump. Study the part arrangement.

As each rotating pump vane passes the intake chamber, Fig. 8-21, a charge of air is drawn in. The next vane propels the air charge around into the compression chamber. The compression chamber reduces the volume of the charge thus placing it under compression. Pressurized air is then discharged through the exhaust chamber. Note that the intake and exhaust chambers are separated by the section of housing termed the "stripper," Fig. 8-21.

CHECK VALVE

The one-way check valve, Figs. 8-19, 8-22, is forced open by the air passing through to the distribution manifold. In the event of pump failure or at any time that exhaust pressure may equal or exceed pump pressure, the check valve will seat and prevent backfeeding of hot exhaust into the hoses or pump.

DISTRIBUTION MANIFOLD AND AIR INJECTION TUBES

An air distribution manifold and air injection tube setup for both an in-line and V-type engine is shown in Fig. 8-22. Some other engines incorporate the distribution manifold and injection tubes as an integral part of the cylinder head.

BACKFIRE PROBLEM

Quick closure of the throttle valve permits a momentary continuation of fuel flow. This fuel flow produces a mixture so rich that it will leave a large amount of unburned gasoline following the power (combustion) stroke.

The exhaust, rich in unburned fuel, upon striking the injected stream of fresh air, will flare up into a violent burning action causing a backfire (loud bang in exhaust system).

The backfire problem is cured by using either an ANTIBACKFIRE VALVE, a DECELERATION VALVE or a DIVERTER VALVE.

ANTIBACKFIRE VALVE

The antibackfire valve, Fig. 8-23, will admit a swift rush of air from the air pump into the INTAKE manifold for a very short time (about 1–2 seconds) whenever the throttle is suddenly closed. This air leans out the fuel mixture and prevents backfiring. This setup also prevents the engine from stalling at in-

Fig. 8-21. End view of an air injection pump. Note how outer edges of vanes maintain constant contact with housing wall.

Fig. 8-22. Air distribution manifold and air injection tube setup as used for one specific in-line and V-type engine.

Fig. 8-23. Antibackfire valve admits air to intake manifold upon deceleration. Vacuum diaphragm forces valve open.

tersections, eliminating the need for a throttle closing dashpot on cars equipped with automatic transmissions. Fig. 8-23 illustrates the construction of one type of antibackfire valve.

ANTIBACKFIRE VALVE OPERATION

The air pump is connected to the INLET side of the antibackfire valve. The valve outlet is connected to the intake manifold. Normally, the valve is held closed by spring action, Fig. 8-23.

By connecting the valve (via the signal line connection) to the intake manifold, a vacuum is formed in chamber A and through the small orifice in the check valve, in chamber B as well. In that an equal vacuum now exists on both sides of the valve diaphragm, the valve is kept closed by the return springs.

Upon a sudden closure of the throttle, a very powerful vacuum is instantly formed in chamber A. Because the increase in vacuum has not had a chance to affect chamber B as quickly, chamber B will have a lower vacuum than chamber A at this instant. This forces the diaphragm to open the check valve against spring pressure.

If the throttle remains in the released position, the stronger vacuum will be applied to chamber B through the check valve orifice. With an equal vacuum on each side, the return springs will force the valve shut.

When the car is suddenly accelerated, immediately following sudden deceleration that opened the antibackfire valve, it is important that the flow of air to the intake manifold stops instantly to prevent upsetting the mixture required for proper acceleration.

The acceleration causes a vacuum drop in chamber A, leaving chamber B with a higher vacuum. This draws open the diaphragm check valve, allows spring action to snap the backfire valve closed and cuts off the flow of air and permits smooth acceleration. See Fig. 8-23.

DECELERATION VALVE

The deceleration valve is also actuated by high intake vacuum during deceleration. During periods of deceleration, the vacuum diaphragm will draw the valve down against spring pressure and allow air to bleed (flow) into the intake manifold to prevent backfiring.

The valve incorporates a check and delay valve for rapid chamber pressure balance. Fig. 8-24 shows a deceleration valve in the OPEN mode.

Fig. 8-24. Deceleration antibackfire valve. Valve shown in open position. (GM)

DIVERTER VALVE (BYPASS VALVE)

The diverter valve, Fig. 8-25, is widely used to control engine backfiring.

During periods of deceleration, the high manifold vacuum action on the valve diaphragm, draws the diaphragm upward against spring pressure. This causes the top of metering valve to move against its seat. This closes off pump air flow to the exhaust manifold and "diverts" or "dumps" the air flow downward and out through the internal silencer. This air is vented to the atmosphere on some applications and to the carburetor air cleaner on others. Without the air flow to the exhaust manifold, backfiring will be avoided.

The diverter valve can also divert excess pump air flow during high speed operation. This is accomplished by the built-in relief valve, Fig. 8-25.

Fig. 8-26 illustrates a typical system employing a diverter valve. Note three functions of the diverter valve.

Fig. 8-25. Diverter valve construction. (Oldsmobile)

DUAL FLOW AIR INJECTION SYSTEM

One air injection system applies full pump air flow to the exhaust valve area only during the warmup period. When a specific engine temperature is reached, a vacuum operated air-switching valve diverts a large percentage (not all) of the air to a point further along the exhaust system. This helps the EGR system to function effectively in reducing NOx emissions on this specific installation. Fig. 8-27.

PULSE AIR INJECTION

The PULSE AIR injection system does not use an air pump. It employs the normal exhaust pressure pulsations to draw air into the exhaust manifold.

At the beginning of the intake stroke, just before the exhaust valve closes, a vacuum is formed in that portion of the exhaust manifold. This momentary vacuum pulse draws fresh air in through an air injection tube. Continual alternating vacuum and pressure pulses produce sufficient fresh air flow to significantly increase exhaust burning (oxidization), thus reducing CO and HC emissions.

One setup employing the pulse air principle is shown in Fig. 8-28. Note that a separate air pipe is used for each cylinder on this specific engine. Each pipe has a separate air check valve.

PULSE AIR INJECTION OPERATION

The air injection tubes, A in Fig. 8-29, are connected to distribution (manifold) pipes that lead to an air filter. Some installations use the carburetor air cleaner while others use a separate filter. A one-way air check valve is used in the lines. Study Fig. 8-29. Note that this arrangement also uses four injection tubes.

A somewhat different pulse air system is pictured in Fig. 8-30. Instead of admitting fresh air to all the exhaust port areas, air is drawn into ports number 3, 4 and 5 only.

Air is fed continually (once per vacuum pulse) through pipe C. Air pipes D will allow air to be drawn into exhaust ports 4 and 5 only when INTAKE manifold vacuum is high enough to operate the diaphragm on check valve B assembly. System is shown with all pipes feeding air. Fig. 8-30.

AIR CHECK VALVES ARE VERY IMPORTANT

You will note that the various pulse air systems shown in Figs. 8-28, 8-29, and 8-30 all use air check valves. The check valves open during the vacuum pulse phase but instantly pop shut during the pressure

Fig. 8-26. Air injection system diverter valve functions. 1—Admitting air to exhaust port. 2—Diverting or bypassing air during deceleration. 3—Relieving excessive air pressure during high speed operation. (GM)

Fig. 8-27. Air injection system using an air-switching valve for dual flow injection control.   (Chrysler)

Fig. 8-28. Pulse air injection system uses no air pump. Exhaust pressure pulsations cause fresh air to be drawn in during the low pressure (vacuum) pulsations.   (Buick)

phase. This prevents back-feeding of exhaust gases and insures that when air is drawn in, even in tiny "gulps," it will be fresh air and not a "yo-yo" action of burned exhaust gases in the air pipes.

HEATED INTAKE AIR

In order to assist in proper engine operation when using a lean fuel mixture, the air passing to the carburetor is often heated. This heated air also reduces

carburetor icing and speeds engine warmup.

A thermostatically controlled, vacuum motor (diaphragm) operated damper unit (flapper valve) in the air cleaner intake tube can admit air from either the exhaust manifold heat stove, from the underhood area or from both. Many installations provide either exhaust stove air (heated) or OUTSIDE air piped to the air cleaner through a flexible duct attached to the air cleaner snorkel. Fig. 8-31 shows one typical arrangement.

THERMOSTATICALLY CONTROLLED AIR CLEANER CONSTRUCTION AND OPERATION

A cutaway view of a typical thermostatically controlled air cleaner is shown in Fig. 8-32. Study the construction and the relationship of the various parts. Note that the diaphragm is connected to the control damper unit via linkage. Fig. 8-32.

Fig. 8-33 shows the control damper positioning to regulate intake air temperature. In A of Fig. 8-33, the engine is OFF. With no vacuum in the vacuum chamber, the diaphragm spring pushes the control damper down, closing off the hot air pipe from the manifold heat stove (sheet metal shroud).

In B of Fig. 8-33, the engine is operating but the underhood air temperature is below 85°F (29.4°C). The temperature sensing (thermostatic) spring has closed the air bleed valve admitting full engine vacuum to the vacuum chamber. This draws the diaphragm upward and lifts the damper so that outside air is cut off and hot air is admitted.

When the underhood temperature rises above

Fig. 8-29. Pulse air injection system. Note how vacuum pulsation draws fresh air in through injection tube. Air flow is from carburetor air cleaner. (Saab)

Fig. 8-30. Another pulse air injection setup. Air is fed into number 3 port constantly. Additional air is fed into number 4 port and into number 5 port during periods of high vacuum. (Toyota)

128°F (53.4°C), the sensor bimetal spring opens the air bleed valve. This reduces vacuum in the vacuum chamber to the point the diaphragm spring tilts the damper downward completely closing off the hot air entrance. All air is then taken in through the "snorkel," C of Fig. 8-33.

When the underhood temperature is between 85°F and 128°F (29.4°C–53.4°C), the sensing spring holds the air bleed partially open. This permits both outside and hot air to be drawn into the carburetor, D in Fig. 8-33.

The actual operating temperatures can vary somewhat depending on system design. The idea is to maintain the inlet air temperature somewhere around 100°F to 115°F (37.8°C to 46.1°C).

If, at any time, the engine is heavily accelerated, vacuum to the chamber will instantly drop off permitting the spring to snap the damper downward cutting off hot air and permitting maximum air flow through the snorkel. Look at Fig. 8-33.

CATALYTIC CONVERTER

A catalytic converter (reactor) is a device installed in the exhaust line to significantly lower emission levels of hydrocarbons (HC), carbon monoxide (CO),

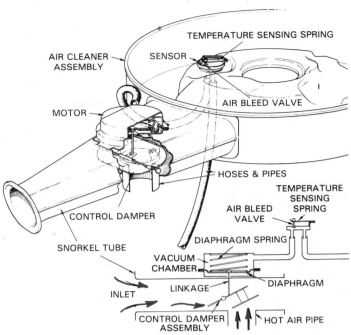

Fig. 8-31. Thermostatically controlled air cleaner is designed to provide temperature control of the air reaching the air cleaner. During cold starts, control provides heated air.

Fig. 8-32. Construction details of common type of thermostatically controlled air cleaner. Damper is blending both hot and cold air. (Buick)

and in the case of some converters, oxides of nitrogen (NO_x).

Converters are of two basic catalyst types—the TWO-WAY (oxidation) and the THREE-WAY (reduction). Both types can employ either a PELLET or MONOLITH design.

TWO-WAY CONVERTER—PELLET TYPE

Thousands of tiny beads or pellets of porous aluminum oxide, covered with a thin coating of platinum (Pt) and palladium (Pd) are placed inside a perforated container. See Fig. 8-34. The container or "core" is then suspended inside the converter shell. Baffles are arranged in such a way that the exhaust gases enter from one side of the perforated core, flow through the pellet bed and out the other end of the converter.

Fig. 8-33. Operation of the thermostatically controlled air cleaner. Study each view and note action of various controls in determining position of control damper.

Converters are made of stainless steel because of the very high operating temperature that can exceed 1,600°F (872°C). The outer shell is lined with a layer of insulation to prevent heat transfer to other areas and to also maintain high catalyst temperatures.

A typical two-way, pellet type converter is illustrated in Fig. 8-34. Study the flow of exhaust through the converter.

TWO-WAY CONVERTER—MONOLITH (HONEYCOMB) TYPE

In place of glass beads, the monolith converter uses a ceramic honeycomb block coated with alumina and treated with a very thin coating of platinum and palladium. The entire exhaust system flows through this treated honeycomb mass.

A monolith converter is shown in Fig. 8-35. Note how exhaust is forced to move through the honeycomb.

TWO-WAY CATALYTIC CONVERTER OPERATION

Catalyst material, in this case palladium and platinum, causes an increase in the rate of a chemical reaction (here, exhaust gas burning). The catalyst itself will not be altered or consumed by the reaction.

The catalytic converter (in some cases two are employed) is placed in the exhaust system between the exhaust manifold and muffler. When the hot gases are forced through the converter, they contact the catalyst coated pellets or honeycomb, depending on the type. The catalyst causes a rapid increase in the exhaust temperature. This in turn causes the carbon monoxide and hydrocarbons to change (by means of an oxidizing process) into water (H_2O) vapor and carbon dioxide (CO_2). The two-way oxidizing converter does not reduce oxides of nitrogen (NO_x).

THREE-WAY, DUAL BED CONVERTER

The THREE-WAY converter uses an additional catalyst bed coated with platinum and rhodium (R). This bed not only helps reduce hydrocarbons and carbon monoxide but also lowers the levels of oxides of nitrogen.

One type of three-way, dual bed monolith converter is shown in Fig. 8-36. Note the use of two separate catalyst beds. They have a space between them into which air from the air injection pump may be forced.

The front bed (inlet end) is treated with platinum and rhodium and is termed a "reducing" catalyst (catalyzes reduction of NO_x). The rear bed is coated with palladium and platinum and is referred to as an "oxidizing" catalyst. Study the construction of three-way converter in Fig. 8-36.

A three-way, dual bed pellet type converter is il-

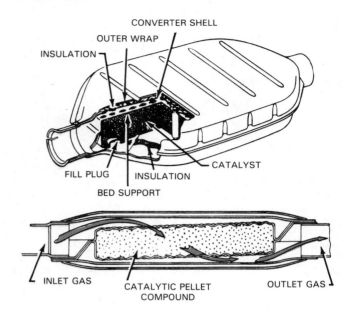

Fig. 8-34. Two-way, pellet type catalytic converter. Note how exhaust is forced to travel through catalyst bed (pellets). (Pontiac)

Fig. 8-35. Two-way monolith type catalytic converter. Catalyst bed is of honeycomb construction to allow exhaust to flow through. (Buick)

lustrated in Fig. 8-37. Note air inlet from air injection pump and exhaust flow pattern.

OPERATION OF AIR INJECTED THREE-WAY CONVERTER

Exhaust gas passes first into the reducing catalyst. Levels of oxides of nitrogen are reduced. There is also some oxidizing of hydrocarbons and carbon monoxide.

Air, from the air injection system, is forced into the space between the catalyst beds. This will supply additional oxygen which in turn will allow a high oxidization heat level.

As the treated exhaust from the first bed moves through the space between beds, it picks up additional oxygen. As it encounters the second oxidizing catalyst, great heat is created and the resultant oxidiz-

Fig. 8-36. Three-way, dual bed monolith catalytic converter. Note secondary air (air from air injection pump) pipe. This converter lowers level of hydrocarbons, oxides of nitrogen and carbon monoxide.   (Ford)

ing process changes the carbon monoxide and hydrocarbons into water vapor and carbon dioxide.

Fig. 8-38 pictures the operation of the dual bed, three-way converter system. Note how air pump is forcing air into the center section of the converter.

In order to prevent excessive heating of the three-way, dual bed converter, the system air control valve will divert air from the converter when engine temperature exceeds 225°F (107°C), during prolonged idle, under deceleration conditions, during wide open throttle, whenever engine is cold and choke forms rich mixture, etc. Fig. 8-39 shows the action of the air control valve when engine temperature is under 126°F (52°C). Note how air is diverted to the

Fig. 8-37. Three-way dual bed pellet type catalytic converter. Air inlet pipe admits air from air injection pump. Note exhaust flow pattern.   (Buick)

exhaust manifold to help in the reduction of carbon monoxide and hydrocarbons that are produced in large amounts during warmup.

Fig. 8-38. Dual bed, air injected, three-way catalytic converter system. Engine temperature exceeds 126° F (52°C). Manifold vacuum is not applied to air control valve and valve is passing pump air into center section of converter. Note exhaust check valve to prevent exhaust from back-feeding into air supply system.   (Ford)

Fig. 8-39. When engine temperature is under 126 °F (52 °C), engine vacuum is applied to air control valve causing it to shut off pump air to converter. Air flow is now diverted to exhaust manifold air injection system. Under some conditions, pump air is bypassed into atmosphere. (Ford)

MULTIPLE CONVERTERS

Some installations employ two catalytic converters. One, often quite small, is located very close to the exhaust manifold. The other can be located downstream in the exhaust system between the manifold and muffler.

CHOKE CONTROL

Although a richer mixture is needed for cold engine startup, it is important that the fuel mixture be leaned (more air—less fuel) as fast as possible. This helps to promote cleaner burning with significant lowering of emissions.

To accomplish this, an electric choke may be used. It may be fully electric or electrically assisted. On fuel injection engines, cold startup mixtures are also carefully controlled.

For full details on electric chokes and other cold start mixture controls, refer to Chapters 6 and 7.

IGNITION TIMING IS VERY IMPORTANT

For cleaner burning of fuel, the spark must occur at the precise time. As timing needs vary with engine temperature, loading, rpm, etc., timing must constantly be altered to match all possible conditions.

Timing control is accomplished through the use of distributor vacuum advance and centrifugal advance mechanisms. In the fully electronic ignition systems, the timing can be adjusted electronically through the input from various sensors.

Spark timing control sensors include those related to gear position, vehicle speed, engine vacuum (load), engine temperature, etc.

One type of engine temperature related spark timing control is pictured in Fig. 8-40. A dual diaphragm vacuum advance is used. When the engine temperature is above 129°F (54°C), the bimetal switching valve (BVSV) admits engine vacuum to the main diaphragm, providing advance. When engine temperature is below around 104°F (40°C), the valve is fully closed. This provides retarded timing to speed up the heating of the three-way converter used with

Fig. 8-40. One form of engine temperature controlled spark timing control. Shown in hot engine mode with BVSV valve open admitting vacuum to main diaphragm of distributor vacuum advance. When engine is cold, BVSV valve closes off vacuum to main diaphragm and spring will retard timing. (Toyota)

this setup.

For extended coverage of ignition timing control, see Chapter 3.

THROTTLE POSITIONERS

The throttle valve may be held open somewhat more during cold engine idle and also during periods of deceleration to improve emission control. One such system is illustrated in Fig. 8-41.

When the engine is cold, BVSV valve is open and no vacuum reaches TP (throttle positioner) diaphragm. Positioner spring pressure holds throttle open. In hot engine idling mode, BVSV is closed. Engine vacuum draws positioner diaphragm back allowing throttle valve to fully close.

When car is cruising, vacuum to positioner is weak allowing it to move outward towards throttle lever. If accelerator is suddenly released, throttle lever strikes positioner and is held open briefly before vacuum can build and pull positioner rod away from throttle lever.

CLOSED LOOP SYSTEM

The closed loop fuel system (covered extensively in Chapter 6 and 7), provides very sensitive and precise control of the air-fuel ratio. This will provide a close to perfect ratio for all operating conditions.

By using an oxygen sensor in the exhaust system, constant monitoring of the combustion process is possible. With the electrical signal generated by the oxygen sensor, along with other sensors, an electronic control module can adjust air-fuel ratio, alter ignition and injection timing, bypass or inject air into the exhaust manifold, inject air into the converter, alter idle speed, etc. Such a system makes possible a sizeable reduction in emissions.

An electronic closed loop system is illustrated in Fig. 8-42. This system, when all components are used, is capable of monitoring up to 15 different items and can, using this information, control nine functions. See Fig. 8-42.

OTHER EMISSION CONTROLS

A great number of other items are emission related and their proper design, maintenance and function are important.

Engine design, cooling system efficiency, tire pressure and construction, engine condition, both from a wear and tune-up standpoint, car weight and shape, exhaust system design, fuel itself, etc., all must be considered in the search for clean air.

CAUTION:

Proper emission reduction is dependent on a carefully balanced and integrated number of emission devices and systems.

Whenever performing tune-up work, adjustments, repairs, etc., keep in mind that very often an adjustment or alteration in one system will affect others. Always follow manufacturer's recommendations and specifications. Do not alter, disconnect or override emission controls.

EXHAUST SYSTEM

Burned gases leave the engine through the exhaust valves and then enter the exhaust manifold. From there, they travel through the exhaust pipe, one or more catalytic converters and mufflers and leave the car via the tailpipe. A resonator can also be incorporated.

The system must be leakproof, free from vibration

Fig. 8-41. Throttle positioner action during cold and hot (normal heat) engine conditions. Study throttle positioner (TP) action. (Toyota)

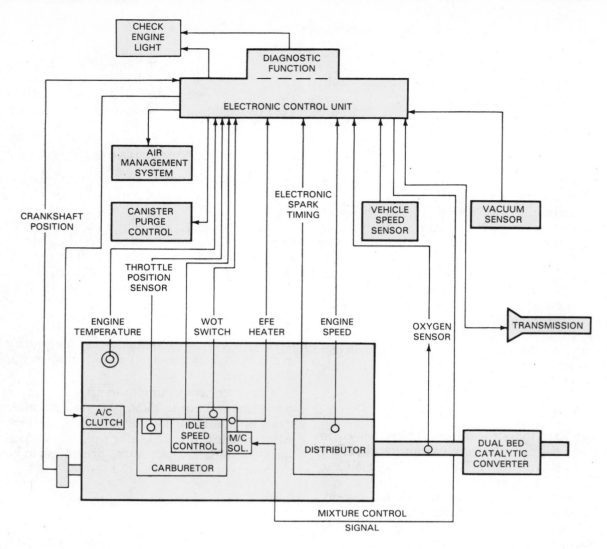

Fig. 8-42. Schematic of a closed loop electronic control system, called "Computer Command Control." With several optional components, such a system can monitor and control a wide range of units and functions. (Chevrolet)

and ample size with smooth curves to prevent excessive back pressure (exhaust gas flow restricted creating system pressure making it harder for cylinders to clear themselves during exhaust stroke). The setup should quiet the exhaust sound to acceptable levels and should discharge the exhaust in a manner that will minimize the possibility of gases being drawn into the vehicle passenger compartment.

SINGLE EXHAUST SYSTEM

In the single exhaust system, only one exhaust pipe is provided. The pipe, converter, and muffler are sized in proportion to the engine displacement. Note the use of an additional "mini" converter in the single system shown in Fig. 8-43.

DUAL EXHAUST SYSTEM

The dual exhaust system employs two separate exhaust lines, each equipped with catalytic converter and mufflers. Fig. 8-44 shows a typical dual arrangement.

Some systems feature dual exhaust pipes from the engine through the catalytic converters then join the pipes so that they use a single muffler and tailpipe.

EXHAUST PIPE

The exhaust pipe is subjected to intense heat and corrosive gases on the inside and to water, road salt, etc., on the outer surface. To provide proper service life, stainless steel is used for the converters and occasionally for some of the piping. Aluminized (coated with a layer of aluminum, inside and out) steel is widely used for both exhaust, tailpipe and mufflers.

MUFFLER DESIGN

There are two basic muffler designs. One uses a series of baffled chambers to dampen the sound. This type is pictured in Fig. 8-45.

The second type, termed "glass pack," "steel pack," etc., is of a straight-through design. This passes the exhaust through a perforated pipe surrounded with metal or glass wool (fiberglass). The straight-through

Fig. 8-43. A single exhaust system. Note additional "mini" catalytic converter. (Plymouth)

Fig. 8-44. One arrangement for a dual exhaust system. Note resonators. (British-Leyland)

Fig. 8-45. A muffler using the baffle principle. (Walker)

muffler is designed to eliminate as much back pressure as possible, Fig. 8-46.

A modification of the straight-through principle is pictured in Fig. 8-47. Instead of using fiberglass, the perforated sections of the pipe are surrounded with sound deadening chambers. This design, termed

Fig. 8-46. A "straight-through" muffler. Heavy fiberglass packing is used around the perforated pipe.

Fig. 8-47. A "chambered pipe" exhaust system in which a series of muffling chambers are incorporated into one system.

"chambered pipe," requires a mininmum of space beneath the car. Fig. 8-47.

RESONATORS

Resonators may also be of the straight-through design. They are small mufflers added near the end of the exhaust system to silence any resonance (continued vibration sound created or sustained within the exhaust system) remaining after the quieting action of the regular exhaust system.

EXHAUST MANIFOLDS

Exhaust manifolds, often constructed of cast iron, should have smooth gentle bends to improve exhaust flow. The manifold is bolted to the head and may contain passageways for air injection. Some manifolds use a gasket while others use metal to metal contact. The manifold may also contain a heat control valve and the oxygen sensor for closed loop fuel systems. Fig. 8-48 illustrates one setup for a six-cylinder engine.

HEAT CONTROL VALVES

The exhaust system also houses the heat control valve. It can be located in the exhaust manifold or in

Fig. 8-48. Six-cylinder exhaust manifold as used on one engine. No gasket is used between head and manifold on this setup.   (AMC)

the exhaust pipe close to the manifold. For full details on these valves, see Chapter 6.

MANIFOLD TO EXHAUST PIPE CONNECTION

An exhaust pipe to manifold connection may be one of several types. A flat surface gasketed connection is shown in Fig. 8-49.

Fig. 8-49. Flat, gasketed exhaust manifold to pipe connection. (Volkswagen)

Another type, using the ball socket principle, is pictured in Fig. 8-50. This connection allows some degree of flexing without breaking either the seal or the manifold-pipe assembly. Note use of springs to maintain pressure, Fig. 8-50.

Fig. 8-51 shows a full ball connector. This also provides some flexing and misalignment without leaking.

SYSTEM HANGERS

The exhaust system is usually suspended on hangers designed to allow system flexing while providing shock protection and sound deadening. Rubber rings,

Fig. 8-50. Semi-ball socket type manifold to pipe connection.   (Cadillac)

Fig. 8-51. Full ball type manifold to pipe connection. 1—Exhaust manifold. 2—Exhaust pipe, spherically flared. 3—Flange. 4—Spherical connection adapter. 5—Self-locking hex head nut. 6—Hex head bolt.   (Mercedes-Benz)

tubes, biscuits, etc., are usually part of the typical hanger assembly. Fig. 8-52 shows one type.

OTHER EXHAUST SYSTEM CONNECTIONS

The exhaust pipe to converter and to muffler connections can be either welded or clamped. All connections must be tight and absolutely leak free. Several types of connections are shown in Fig. 8-53.

SYSTEM HEAT SHIELDING

The modern exhaust system produces a great deal of heat. The system must, for ground clearance, fit quite closely to the floor pan. To prevent heat damage to various undercar components as well as preventing the transfer of heat to the passenger compartment, a great amount of heat shielding is used. This may consist of metal shields around the system, shields under the floor pan and heavy insulation under the floor mats. Fig. 8-53 shows the heat shielding used on one single exhaust system. Study its connections.

SUMMARY

Automotive exhaust emissions of major concern are hydrocarbons, oxides of nitrogen and carbon monoxide.

Emission controls are of three basic types: fuel system vapor control, internal engine and external engine controls.

The positive crankcase ventilation system removes fumes from the crankcase and burns them in the cylinders. The PCV valve controls the flow of gases.

The evaporative control system prevents the escape of both liquid gasoline or vapor into the atmosphere. Vapors are stored in a charcoal canister until the

Fig. 8-52. An exhaust system hanger such as this allows flexing while reducing noise. Note rubber "biscuits." (Volkswagen)

Fig. 8-53. Complete exhaust system showing heat shielding and various connections. (Nissan)

engine is started. They are then drawn off and burned in the engine. Canisters can be of OPEN or CLOSED design.

A portion of the exhaust gas is allowed to move into the intake manifold. This lowers combustion temperatures thus lowering oxides of nitrogen (NO_x). The exhaust gas recirculation (EGR) valve controls the flow of exhaust to the manifold.

EGR valves can be of either BACK PRESSURE (exhaust gas) or VACUUM modulated design.

Air injection systems force a stream of fresh air into the burning exhaust as it leaves the cylinder. This prolongs burning thus reducing hydrocarbon and carbon monoxide emission. An engine driven vane type pump provides the air. Some setups use "pulse" air instead. A check valve prevents exhaust from entering air system in the event of excessive exhaust pressure. A diverter valve is used to prevent engine backfiring during deceleration.

Heated air is drawn into the air cleaner during engine warmup. The thermostatically controlled air cleaner can admit all hot or all cold air or can blend the two together depending on engine temperature.

Catalytic converters reduce exhaust emissions. Converters can use either a pellet bed or a monolith, honeycomb catalyst.

The catalyst, when treated with platinum and palladium, is called an oxidizing catalyst and will change carbon monoxide and hydrocarbons into water and carbon dioxide.

The reducing catalyst is treated with platinum and rhodium. It will reduce the amount of nitrates of oxygen. It will also, to some degree, oxidize hydrocarbons and carbon monoxide.

Two-way converters use an oxidizing catalyst. Three-way converters contain both reducing and oxidizing catalysts.

Some converters utilize a controlled stream of injected air to improve their efficiency. The air injection system can be used as the air source. Systems can use more than one converter.

Proper choke control during engine warmup and driveaway is very important. Electric chokes may be used to speed up opening under certain conditions. Chokes must be carefully calibrated and adjusted.

Ignition timing must be kept within specified limits. Various devices such as a vacuum advance, certrifugal advance, electronic advance, are used to change timing. These units, in turn, are controlled by engine temperature, vacuum, speed, etc.

Throttle positioners can be used to speed up idle during warmup and also to prevent full throttle closing during deceleration. These items are controlled by engine temperature, speed, vacuum, etc. They can be electric or vacuum operated.

Closed loop fuel systems can monitor and control many items such as air-fuel ratio, engine idle, ignition timing, air injection, etc. An oxygen sensor constant-ly monitors the oxygen content of the exhaust and the electronic system instantly makes the adjustments needed to maintain the best air-fuel ratio.

Care must be used when making adjustments on any engine system as adjustments on one system may affect other systems. Follow manufacturer's specifications. Do not disconnect or alter emission controls.

Exhaust systems are usually comprised of an exhaust manifold, catalytic converters, mufflers, resonators, exhaust and tailpipes along with the necessary connections, fittings, and hangers.

Stainless steel is used for converters and some exhaust pipes. Aluminized steel is widely used for the remainder of the system.

Exhaust systems must not leak.

They should quiet the exhaust and discharge it properly to the passing air stream. The system must be secured so as to prevent rattling, overheating of surrounding areas and excessive vibration or twisting force.

Heat shielding is important and must be properly located and attached.

Manifold to exhaust pipe connections can be of many types. The flat connector, the semi-ball, and full ball type connectors are often used.

Fig. 8-54 illustrates a number of typical emission control systems and devices. Starting at A, study each schematic and see if you thoroughly understand what they are for and how they function.

KNOW THESE TERMS

HC, CO, NO_x, PCV, Evaporation control system, Charcoal canister, Liquid-vapor separator, Dieseling, EGR valve, Air injection system, Deceleration valve, Pulse air injection, Thermostatic air cleaner, Catalytic converter, Exhaust system, Muffler, Resonator.

REVIEW QUESTIONS—CHAPTER 8

1. The three major exhaust pollutants are _____, _____ and _____.
2. List the three general types of emission controls.
3. To prevent crankcase fumes from escaping to the atmosphere, engines are equipped with a _____ _____ _____ system.
4. The system in question 3 uses a _____ valve.
5. Crankcase gases are allowed to flow heavily into the intake manifold during engine idle. True or False?
6. Modern fuel tanks use a _____ cap.
7. The vapor control canister is filled with:
   a. Fiberglass.
   b. Felt.
   c. Activated charcoal.
   d. Activated porous ceramic.
8. Vapor control canisters only store engine

Fig. 8-54. Some typical emission control systems. A—Air injection. B—Thermostatically controlled intake air. C—Electronic air-fuel mixture control along with a catalytic converter. Note oxygen sensor. This setup may be referred to as a Closed Loop system. D—PCV (positive crankcase ventilation) system. E—Fuel system vapor control.

crankcase vapors. True or False?

9. Explain how a vapor canister operates.

10. Canisters can be of several types:
    a. Open.
    b. Inverted.
    c. Horizontal.
    d. Closed.
    e. Pressurized.

11. To prevent liquid fuel from entering the canister, fuel systems can use one or more devices. Name two.

12. The _____ _____ valve prevents liquid fuel from flowing through the tank vent line in the event the car is upside down.

13. Lowering the combustion flame temperature helps control the production of:
    a. HC.
    b. NOx.
    c. CO.
    d. AC.

14. The EGR valve admits exhaust gas to the intake manifold at ALL times. True or False?

15. Explain how the EGR system functions.

16. The air injection system forces air into the:
    a. Intake manifold near intake valve.
    b. Exhaust manifold near exhaust valve.
    c. Crankcase.
    d. Vapor canister.

17. Name two devices that can be used on the air injection system to prevent "backfires" during deceleration.

18. What unit provides air for the air injection system:
    a. Fan.
    b. Air pump.
    c. Air cleaner snorkel ram pressure.
    d. Intake system backpressure.

19. Explain how any one of the devices you named in question 17 operates.

20. One air injection system uses the constant pressure fluctuations of the exhaust system as a source of air pressure. What is this system called?

21. Explain the operation of the system in question 20.

22. Air injection systems are equipped with a _____ _____ to prevent exhaust backfeeding into the system.

23. The thermostatically controlled air cleaner admits cool air to the engine during engine warmup. True or False?

24. The thermostatically controlled air cleaner allows somewhat leaner air-fuel mixture during the warmup period. True or False?

25. Catalytic converter catalyst beds may be of either _____ type or _____ type construction.

26. A reducing catalyst can lower _____, _____ _____ and _____ _____ _____ type emissions.

27. The reducing catalyst is coated with _____ and _____.

28. The reducing catalyst lowers what emission more than others.

29. Explain the operation of an OXIDIZING catalyst.

30. List the two emissions controlled by the oxidizing catalyst.

31. Explain the operation of a three-way, air injected catalytic converter.

32. To speed up choke release during engine warmup, some carburetors are equipped with an _____ heated choke.

33. List two ignition distributor timing advance mechanisms.

34. List three engine related factors that affect ignition timing.

35. A throttle positioner is:
    a. A shaft attached to the throttle.
    b. A rivet to secure throttle position.
    c. A device to hold the throttle partially open.
    d. A unit to prevent throttle backpressure.

36. Briefly explain the operating principle of a CLOSED LOOP fuel system.

37. Where is the oxygen sensor located?
    a. In the exhaust system.
    b. In the air intake system.
    c. In the PCV valve.
    d. In the air diverter valve.

38. When doing tune-up or repair work on engine systems, it is important to remember several points regarding emissions. List three.

39. List two types of muffler construction.

40. A resonator is used to:
    a. Reduce exhaust sounds.
    b. Force air into the converter.
    c. Prevent exhaust backpressure.
    d. Alter ignition timing.

41. Modern exhaust systems produce a great deal of heat. When installing catalytic converters, exhaust pipes, etc., all _____ _____ must be in place to prevent damage to adjacent parts.

Chapter 9

ENGINE CLASSIFICATION, PARTS IDENTIFICATION

After studying this chapter, you will learn to:

■ Compare four-stroke and two-stroke cycle engines.
■ Explain the different engine classifications.
■ Describe the operating principles of a rotary type engine.
■ Identify the parts of various engine types.

You have constructed a basic engine, studied parts and their uses and added the ignition, lubrication, cooling and fuel systems. This completes the basic engine.

This chapter is devoted to a study of the various ways in which the basic engine theory and parts are utilized to produce multicylinder engines of several types. Various methods of engine classification as well as different kinds of engines will be discussed.

CYCLE CLASSIFICATION

FOUR-STROKE CYCLE ENGINE

Your basic engine was a four-stroke cycle. For a brief review, study Fig. 9-1. This demonstrates that it takes two complete revolutions of the crankshaft to complete the cycle. As a result, the crankshaft receives one power stroke and must then coast until

INTAKE STROKE—As piston moves down or toward crank-case, intake valve opens and partial vacuum is created in cylinder. Vaporized air-fuel mixture is forced into cylinder by atmospheric pressure.

COMPRESSION STROKE—In-take valve closes. As crank-shaft rotates, piston moves up and compresses air-fuel mixture.

POWER STROKE—Ignition system fires spark plug to ig-nite mixture just before piston reaches top of its travel. Ex-panding gases, which result from burning of fuel, force piston down to turn crankshaft.

EXHAUST STROKE—After fuel charge is burned, exhaust valve opens. Burned gases are forced out of cylinder by upward movement of piston.

Fig. 9-1. Four-stroke cycle principle. This series of events requires two complete revolutions (720 degrees of rotation) of crankshaft. Note that there is ONE power stroke per cycle. (TRW, Inc.)

the next power stroke arrives. The vast majority of automobile engines use the four-stroke cycle engine.

TWO-STROKE CYCLE ENGINE

The two-stroke cycle engine performs the intake, compression, firing and exhaust sequence in ONE REVOLUTION of the crankshaft.

This is accomplished by eliminating the valves as used in the four-stroke cycle engine. In place of the valves, two ports enter the cylinder wall. One is used for the intake of fuel and the other for exhaust.

FUEL MIXTURE CONTAINED IN THE CRANKCASE

The fuel-air mixture is drawn into the crankcase through a REED or a ROTARY valve. Oil is usually mixed with the gasoline to provide lubrication. A passage connects the intake port to the crankcase interior.

SEQUENCE OF EVENTS IN ONE REVOLUTION

Imagine that a charge of fuel is in the cylinder and that the piston is at the bottom of its stroke. As the piston travels up, it closes off both intake and exhaust ports. As it continues upward, it compresses the fuel charge and, at the same time, forms a vacuum in the airtight crankcase.

The vacuum pulls open a small flap-like reed valve and fuel mixture enters the crankcase.

When the piston reaches the top of its stroke, it has compressed the charge and filled the crankcase with fuel mixture. This has all happened in one-half revolution of the crankshaft.

The plug now fires the charge and drives the piston down. Several things happen as the piston plunges downward. The mixture in the crankcase is compressed and the reed valve shuts. The piston is also performing the power stroke.

When the piston has traveled down the cylinder far enough to expose the exhaust port, the exhaust will flow out of the port. As the piston travels down a trifle more, the intake port is uncovered. As the crankcase fuel mixture is compressed, it forces combustible mixture to flow through the intake port into the cylinder.

The piston top is generally shaped to deflect the incoming mixture upward. This helps to fill the cylinder with fresh fuel as well as assist in scavenging (cleaning out) the remaining exhaust gases.

This has all taken place in one revolution of the crankshaft. Every time the piston reaches the top of its travel, it will be driven downward by a power stroke. Study Fig. 9-2.

CERTAIN ADVANTAGES

The two-stroke cycle engine has several advantages that have made it popular for small engine applica-

tions—outboard motors, chain saws, lawn mowers, go-carts, etc.

By eliminating the valves, it also eliminates valve springs, cam followers, camshaft and gears. This enables the engine to be quite compact and light. Machining costs are reduced.

More power per pound of engine weight is available as it fires every stroke. It does not produce twice the power of a four-stroke cycle of comparable size, as some power is lost through compressing crankcase mixture as well as poorer volumetric efficiency (ability to intake fuel).

It can also operate at very high speeds, as there are no valves to "float."

In order to completely scavenge the cylinder, some of the intake fuel also leaves the cylinder. This makes for less fuel ecomony. Despite this fact, the two-stroke cycle is popular.

A two-cycle engine that utilizes an exhaust valve and no mixture in the crankcase will be shown in the section on diesel engines later in this chapter.

REED VALVE OPEN   REED VALVE CLOSED

Fig. 9-2. In left-hand view, piston is traveling upward and has almost reached top of its stroke. It has compressed air-fuel charge trapped above piston. Spark plug has just fired and fuel mixture is starting to burn.

On way upward, piston has drawn fresh fuel mixture into crankcase through reed valve. Fuel vapor contains suspended droplets of oil that lubricate surfaces of moving parts.

In right-hand view, air-fuel mixture has fired and piston is traveling down. It has uncovered intake and exhaust ports, allowing burned gases to escape and fresh charge to enter. Air-fuel mixture flows through intake port because piston, while traveling down, compressed mixture in crankcase.

In two strokes, requiring one revolution, engine has performed all necessary functions to enable it to receive a power stroke for every crankshaft revolution.

WANKEL ROTARY PISTON ENGINE

The Wankel rotary piston engine, although under development for a number of years, has arrived on the automotive scene in significant numbers.

Named after its German inventor, Dr. Felix Wankel, the Wankel rotary piston engine is very powerful for its size.

This engine is also often referred to as a Wankel Engine, Rotary Piston Engine, Rotary Combustion Engine or just Rotary Engine. In the interest of brevity, we shall refer to the engine as a "rotary engine."

CERTAIN ADVANTAGES

The rotary engine has several advantages as compared to the reciprocating piston engines now in popular use. It is considerably smaller and lighter. It is an extremely simple engine, using many less parts. It has no reciprocating (back and forth) motion, produces less vibration and offers significantly more horsepower than a reciprocating engine of comparable size.

Just how widely used the rotary engine will become depends on a great many factors, not the least of which are possible improvements to the standard piston engine, adaptability to future emission control requirements, other possible engine types and public acceptance of the engine.

ROTARY ENGINE CLASSIFICATION

Rotary engines are not classified as four cylinder, six cylinder, etc. In fact, they have no cylinders in the usual sense.

The number of ROTORS used in the engine is the basis for one classification—single-rotor, double-rotor, triple-rotor, etc. They are also referred to as 1-rotor, 2-rotor, 3-rotor, etc.

Although a number of 3-rotor and 4-rotor experimental engines have been built, common usage at this time employs either a 1-rotor or a 2-rotor engine. The 1-rotor engines are used mostly for small gasoline engine applications (snowmobiles, garden tractors, outboards, etc.) and the 2-rotor models for automobiles.

ROTARY CONSTRUCTION

Our coverage will relate to the 2-rotor engine. Remember that the 1-rotor operates exactly the same way; the only difference is that is has just one rotor.

Basically, there are just three moving parts in the 2-rotor engine—the eccentric shaft (also called mainshaft) and the two rotor assemblies. The remainder of the engine consists of two rotor housings, two end housings, two fixed gears, and a center housing. All the housings are held rigidly together with a series of bolts.

ROTOR HOUSING

The rotor housing, usually made of aluminum or nodular iron, has a curved, oblong inner shape. Fig. 9-3. This shape is known as a 2-node EPITROCHOID curve. The space between the inside epitrochoid curve and the exterior is hollowed out to allow passage of coolant. The series of small round holes are for the draw bolts that will secure the center or intermediate housing and the end housings. See Fig. 9-3.

Fig. 9-3. Typical rotor housing. This particular housing is made of aluminum. The inner curve area is covered with a hard chrome plating a few thousandths of an inch thick. (Mazda)

The epitrochoid curve area of the rotor housing is commonly plated with a thin layer of hard chrome, nickel alloy, etc., to produce a smooth, long wearing contact surface for the rotor seals.

This particular housing contains holes for TWO spark plugs and has a peripheral exhaust gas port. Some rotary engines employ ONE spark plug per housing.

ECCENTRIC SHAFT

The ECCENTRIC SHAFT (similar in action to a crankshaft) has TWO eccentric rotor journals. Note that they face exactly opposite (180 deg.) each other. Fig. 9-4. The shaft has two main bearing journals and is drilled for the passage of lubricating oil.

The eccentric shaft passes through the center of both rotor housings and is supported by the main journal bearings located in the end housing. Fig. 9-4.

INTERMEDIATE HOUSING

The rotor housings are separated by an IN-TERMEDIATE housing. This housing has a center

Fig. 9-4. Two-rotor engine eccentric shaft. Note oil holes.

hole through which the eccentric shaft passes. Both sides are ground to provide a smooth, flat surface upon which the rotor side seals operate. The edges are hollow for passage of coolant. On the intermediate housing shown in Fig. 9-5, a fuel mixture intake port is provided on each side. Fig. 9-5.

END HOUSINGS

The open outer end of each rotor housing is covered by an END HOUSING (also called side plate). These housings are hollow to permit the passage of coolant. The side facing the rotor is ground to provide a smooth, flat surface for the rotor outer side seals. It also contains a fuel intake port. Note the fixed (non-moving) gear attached to the center of the side housing shown in Fig. 9-6.

A closeup view of the end housing fixed gear is pictured in Fig. 9-7. This gear bolts to the end housing (both end housings have a fixed gear). It also contains the main bearing and as such, supports the eccentric shaft. Fig. 9-7.

ROTOR

A triangular shaped ROTOR made of special cast iron is used in each rotor housing. The rotor has an

Fig. 9-5. Intermediate (center) housing that separates the two rotors. (Mazda)

Fig. 9-6. One form of end housing. Note fixed gear, flat seal contact surface and the inlet port.

Fig. 9-7. One fixed gear, such as this, is bolted to each side housing. The eccentric shaft journals ride in main bearings in the center of each fixed gear. (Mazda)

inner bearing surface that rides on the eccentric shaft rotor journal. The rotor also has an internal gear (fixed to the rotor) that is in constant mesh with the end housing fixed gear.

The three rotor faces each contain a depression (cutout) that forms the combustion chamber. Both rotor sides as well as each apex (end or tip) are grooved for seals. Fig. 9-8 illustrates a typical rotor along with the seals.

The rotor, mounted on the eccentric shaft, is shown in position in the rotor housing in Fig. 9-9. All three rotor tips just clear the rotor housing epitrochoid surface. Fig. 9-9.

ASSEMBLED ROTARY ENGINE

A cutaway of a typical 2-rotor rotary engine is pictured in Fig. 9-10. Systems, such as carburetion, cool-

CORNER SEAL HOLE
SIDE SEAL GROOVE
BEARING SURFACE
ROTOR FACE
ROTOR INTERNAL GEAR
BALANCE HOLE
ROTOR FACE
COMBUSTION CHAMBER CUTOUT
SIDE SEAL SPRING
SIDE SEAL
APEX SEAL GROOVE
3-PIECE APEX SEAL
APEX SEAL SPRING
LINK BLOCK SPRING
LINK BLOCK

Fig. 9-8. Rotor and rotor seals. (NSU)

ECCENTRIC SHAFT
ROTOR HOUSING
ROTOR TIP
ROTOR HOUSING SURFACE
ROTOR
ROTOR INTERNAL GEAR
ROTOR TIP
ROTOR TIP

Fig. 9-9. Rotor mounted on eccentric shaft and in place in the rotor housing. You can see that each rotor tip almost touches the housing. (Mazda)

215

Fig. 9-10. Two-rotor Wankel rotary piston engine. Study part names and location. Note combustion chamber shape formed in each rotor face. (NSU)

ing, lubrication, etc., are much like that used on the reciprocating piston engine.

Study this illustration very carefully and fix the relative locations of the rotors, eccentric shaft, fixed gear and housing, firmly in mind. Fig. 9-10.

Another 2-rotor rotary engine is featured in Fig. 9-11. This engine uses two spark plugs per rotor. See how the rotor internal gear engages the end housing fixed gear. Fig. 9-11.

ROTARY ENGINE OPERATION

The rotary engine is a four-cycle engine and performs the four distinct strokes involved—intake, compression, power, and exhaust.

Each face of the triangular rotor acts much as a conventional piston in that it draws in the mixture, compresses it, applies the power of the burning charge to the eccentric shaft and exhausts the burned mixture. Instead of a reciprocating action, however, the rotor continually revolves in the same direction as the eccentric shaft.

FIXED GEAR FORCES ROTOR TO REVOLVE AT ONE-THIRD ECCENTRIC SHAFT SPEED

If the rotor were mounted freely on the eccentric shaft rotor journal, the rotor would merely whirl as a fixed part of the shaft and the tips could not follow the epitrochoid rotor housing surface.

By meshing the rotor internal gear with a fixed gear attached to the end housing, when the eccentric shaft turns, it forces the rotor to "walk" around the fixed gear. This "walking" action causes the rotor to revolve around the eccentric shaft rotor journal in the same direction as the eccentric shaft and, at the same time, keeping all three rotor tips constantly close to epitrochoidal wall of rotor housing.

This planetary motion of the rotor constantly changes chamber volume between each rotor face and rotor housing. The change in volume is the principle used for engine operation.

Study the rotor action in A, B, C, D, and E, Fig. 9-12. In A note that the red line on the eccentric shaft and the red dot on the lower rotor lobe are aligned. In B, the eccentric shaft has moved to the right (clockwise)—see red line. The rotor has also moved clockwise but at a slower speed. Follow the alignment of the red line and red rotor dot from A through E. Actually, the eccentric shaft must make THREE complete revolutions in order to turn the rotor ONE full turn. The rotor then, turns at ONE-THIRD eccentric shaft speed. Also note how the chamber volume for each rotor face is changed as the rotor orbits about the fixed gear. Fig. 9-12.

Fig. 9-11. Another 2-rotor rotary engine. Two spark plugs per rotor and a dual ignition system are used on this engine. One plug (the leading plug) fires a fraction of a second before the trailing plug.   (Mazda)

Fig. 9-12. Rotor action within the rotor housing. Rotor internal gear and housing fixed gear are not shown.   (NSU)

PERFORMING THE FOUR-STROKE CYCLE

To better understand just how these different strokes or phases (we shall refer to them as phases so as to differentiate between them and the "strokes" of the reciprocating engine) are accomplished, study the larger bottom sketches, 1 through 5, in Fig. 9-12. We will follow ONE rotor face through the complete cycle. Note that this face lies between rotor tips A and B.

In 1, Fig. 9-12, rotor face A-B has rotated past the intake port. As tip B passed the intake port, the chamber volume rapidly increased. This action formed a vacuum causing fuel mixture to flow into the enlarged chamber area. Note that the chamber is

217

packed with fuel mix at this point. This is the IN-TAKE phase.

In 2, Fig. 9-12, the rotor has turned further to the right and in so doing, chamber size has started to reduce. In that the fuel mixture is now trapped in this rapidly diminishing chamber, COMPRESSION takes place and will continue until rotor face A-B has turned to the position shown in 3. At this point, maximum compression is applied. Note how the chamber size has been greatly reduced, 2 and 3, Fig. 9-12.

When compression is at the maximum, the spark plug ignites the fuel charge, 3, Fig. 9-12. When the charge ignites, the rapidly expanding gases apply pressure to the A-B face of the rotor forcing it to continue walking around the fixed gear. As it rotates, it transmits the power of the burning gas to the eccentric shaft rotor journal causing the eccentric shaft to spin, 4, Fig. 9-12. This is the POWER phase.

The burning gas will continue to revolve the rotor until tip B uncovers the exhaust port. When this happens, the still burning gas, under considerable pressure, will rush out the exhaust port as in 5, Fig. 9-12. This is the EXHAUST phase.

Follow rotor face A-B through 1 to 5 and note how, as the ports are uncovered and the chamber volume changes, each phase of a four-cycle operation is performed.

ALL THREE ROTOR FACES "WORK"

As mentioned, each of the rotor faces (also called flanks) perform a true four-cycle as shown in Fig. 9-12, and as such, become "working" faces. Study the four figures in Fig. 9-13. Note that the direction of engine rotation, as viewed from this end, is COUNTERCLOCKWISE. Fig. 9-12 showed CLOCKWISE rotation.

In 1, Fig. 9-13, face A has just finished the exhaust phase and as the intake port is opened, is set for the INTAKE. Face B is in the COMPRESSION phase

and face C is in the POWER phase.

In 2, Fig. 9-13, face A is now in the INTAKE phase, face B well through COMPRESSION and face C has started the EXHAUST.

As the rotor turns, 3, face A is well into the IN-TAKE, face B has reached maximum COMPRESSION and face C is in the middle of the EXHAUST phase.

Further rotation, as in 4, Fig. 9-13 has caused face A to reach full INTAKE. Face B is now under POWER and face C is completing the EXHAUST phase.

You can easily see from Fig. 9-13 that each rotor face, in turn, will perform the intake, compression, power and exhaust phases and that as each face passes the spark plug, it will have taken in a charge of fuel mix, compressed it and will be ready to apply POWER to the eccentric shaft.

In that the rotor turns one-third eccentric shaft speed, the eccentric shaft will receive ONE power impulse for every ONE revolution of the shaft.

A 2-rotor engine, such as pictured in Figs. 9-10 and 9-11, will produce TWO power impulses for each revolution of the eccentric shaft. This, coupled with the fact that there is no reciprocating motion, produces a very smooth running engine. However, it still must be balanced.

ENGINE MUST BE BALANCED

In order to eliminate vibration, a balance weight on the front of the engine as well as one incorporated in the flywheel, is used to counterbalance the rotor assemblies. Fig. 9-14 illustrates the use of such weights.

COMPRESSION RATIO

The compression ratio of the rotary engine is computed much the same as that for the reciprocating

INTAKE   COMPRESSION   POWER   EXHAUST

Fig. 9-13. All three rotor faces (A—B—C) are constantly working in one phase (intake, compression, power, exhaust) or the other.

Fig. 9-14. Counterbalance weights offset that of the rotor assemblies. The relatively heavy flywheel also smooths out torsional (twisting action) vibration caused by intermittent power impulses.

piston engine. The minimum chamber capacity (full compression) is divided into the maximum chamber (full intake) capacity. Fig. 9-15 shows the minimum and maximum chamber capacities for both a rotary and a reciprocating piston engine. If the minimum chamber capacity was 4 cubic inches and the maximum 32 cubic inches, the compression ratio would be 8 to 1 (minimum into maximum). Fig. 9-15.

ROTOR SIDE SEALS

Both sides of the rotor have spring loaded seals to close the very small running clearance between rotor sides and the housing surface. The seals provide a barrier against compression loss and also control oil consumption. The seals can incorporate a rubber O-ring at the bottom of the seal groove to prevent oil transfer between seal and seal groove.

The side seals operate under conditions much less severe than the tip or apex seals and as such can be made of regular cast iron similar to the material used for conventional piston rings. Typical side seals are shown in Fig. 9-8.

ROTOR APEX SEALS

Tip or apex seals remain in contact with the curved rotor housing walls at all times. They slide across the surface at very high speeds.

In addition to the normal apex seal spring pressure, the seals are forced against the housing wall by gas pressure working in the seal groove and also by the strong inertia force generated by the spinning rotor that literally jams the seals outward at high rpm.

A cross-sectional view of a typical apex seal is pictured in Fig. 9-16. Note the spring, gas, and inertia forces working on the seal.

Despite the problems faced by the apex seals, careful design and the use of special materials such as graphite, carbon, silicon nitride, etc., produce seals with a very long service life.

An apex seal and spring are shown in Fig. 9-17.

A section of a rotor, illustrating an apex seal, corner seal and side seals, is illustrated in Fig. 9-18.

Fig. 9-15. Rotary and reciprocating engine compression ratios are computed the same way. The minimum chamber capacity is divided into the maximum chamber capacity. These particular engines would have a ratio of 8 to 1. (Mazda)

Fig. 9-16. The apex seal is subjected to spring, gas, and inertia pressure. (Mazda)

Fig. 9-17. One type of apex seal and spring.

ROTARY ENGINE CARBURETION AND EXHAUST

The rotary engine uses a conventional fuel system (carburetor or fuel injection) but instead of admitting fuel mixture and exhausting burned gases through valves, ports (holes) are used. The rotor tips, as they revolve, open and close the ports.

SIDE PORT INTAKE

One type of rotary engine uses side ports for the intake system. Each rotor side housing, as well as the intermediate housing, has an intake port. The rotor side seals slide across the port opening. A schematic of the side port design is portrayed in Fig. 9-19.

A cutaway view of a SIDE port intake system is shown in Fig. 9-20. Follow the fuel fixture flow from carburetor, into rotor chamber and on out the exhaust ports. Note the intake ports are located in the side housing and in the intermediate housing while the exhaust ports are located in the rotor housings.

PERIPHERAL PORT INTAKE

A cutaway view of a rotary engine using PERIPHERAL intake ports (intake port, as well as

Fig. 9-18. Section of rotor tip showing juncture of apex, side and corner seals. (Mazda)

Fig. 9-19. Schematic illustrating side port intake. At low speeds, the primary stage ports feed fuel mix. At high speeds, the carburetor secondary system opens and fuel mix enters through both primary and secondary ports. Exhaust port is in the rotor housing.

Fig. 9-20. Fuel mixture flow pattern in the side port intake system. (NSU)

exhaust, is located in the periphery of the rotary housings), is illustrated in Fig. 9-21. Study the fuel flow. In this design, the apex seals slide across both the intake and exhaust ports.

COOLING THE ROTARY ENGINE

Many small rotary engines for snowmobiles, etc., utilize air cooling. In these engines, a blast of cooling air is forced across a series of cooling fins cast into the engine.

The incoming fuel mixture is sometimes employed to assist in air cooling. The fuel mixture is passed from the carburetor through one end housing, through openings in the rotor and eccentric shaft,

Fig. 9-21. Rotary engine using peripheral intake ports. The left hand rotor apex seal is just passing over the intake port. The upper rotor face is just completing its intake phase. The back rotor face is under compression and the bottom face is finishing the exhaust phase. (NSU)

Fig. 9-22. Using the incoming fuel mixture to cool the rotor and eccentric shaft. Note how mixture passes through opening in rotor and shaft.

through the other housing and back around and into the rotor housing through a peripheral port. The fuel mixture, as it flows through the openings, tends to cool both rotor and eccentric shaft. This technique is shown in Fig. 9-22.

Automotive applications of the rotary engine

utilize water cooling. The system incorporates a radiator, water pump, thermostat, and cooling passages through end and rotor housings. The system functions the same as that on a reciprocating piston engine.

A schematic view of a typical rotary engine lubrication system is illustrated in Fig. 9-23. In addition to lubricating all moving parts, the oil helps greatly to

Fig. 9-23. Schematic of a rotary engine lubrication system. An oil cooler is employed. A metering oil pump injects a carefully measured amount of oil into fuel so as to provide a positive and controlled amount of lubrication for apex seals. (Mazda)

keep the rotor within the proper temperature range. By tracing the path of the oil in Fig. 9-23, you will see that oil is pumped through hollow cavities in the rotor and will thus carry off the excess heat.

A cross-sectional view of a rotary engine is shown in Fig. 9-24. Note how the rotor is hollowed out for the passage of oil for cooling.

ROTARY ENGINE EMISSION CONTROL

As with the reciprocating engine, the rotary engine utilizes various emission controls. A typical emission control system for a rotary engine is portrayed in Fig. 9-25.

VALVE LOCATION CLASSIFICATIONS

Engines are also classified according to the valve location. Various arrangements have been used, but modern practice has settled on the I-head, F-head, and L-head. The I-head is the most popular. The names are derived from the resemblance to letters of the alphabet. This will be demonstrated in forthcoming sketches.

L-HEAD

The L-head engine has both valves in the block, and on the same side of the cylinder. A line drawn up through the cylinder and across to the valves will pro-

duce the letter L in an inverted (upside down) position. Fig. 9-26 illustrates the L-head design. Fig. 9-27 shows a cross section of an actual L-head engine.

F-HEAD

The F-head places one valve in the head and one in the block. Fig. 9-28.

Fig. 9-24. Transverse cross-sectional view of a rotary engine. Note hollows in rotor for cooling oil.

Fig. 9-25. Typical rotary engine emission controls. A catalytic converter may also be used in exhaust system. (NSU)

Fig. 9-26. L-head engine. Valves are in the block, both on the same side. Note letter L. (TRW, Inc.)

Fig. 9-27. Transverse cross section of an L-head engine. Both valves are in the block and on same side. (American Motors)

Fig. 9-28. F-head engine. One valve in block, other in the head. Note F. (TRW, Inc.)

Fig. 9-29. I-head engine. Both valves are in head. Note I. (TRW, Inc.)

I-HEAD

In the I-head engine both valves are located in the cylinder head. They may be arranged in a straight line or staggered. Figs. 9-29 and 9-30. This is commonly called a "valve-in-head" engine.

T-HEAD

Your basic engine was of T-head design—both valves in the block and on opposite sides of the cylinder. This design was used to make the illustra-

tions clear. It is not currently being used in automobile engines.

DIFFERENT VALVE TRAIN

Your basic engine was of a type that requires the same valve train as the L-head engine in Fig. 9-27.

When valves are placed in the head, as in the I-head, they are inverted and a somewhat different train is required to operate them. Several techniques may be employed. The schematic in Fig. 9-31 illustrates the use of a very popular rocker arm-push rod

Fig. 9-30. Transverse cross section of an I-head (overhead valve) engine. Both intake and exhaust valves are in the head. (American Motors)

Fig. 9-31. Schematic shows simplified valve train for one cylinder of overhead valve engine.

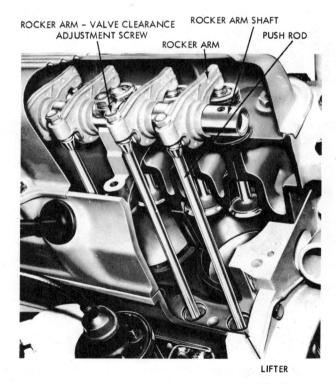

Fig. 9-32. Cutaway view shows a typical valve train used to operate overhead valves. (Plymouth)

setup to actuate the valves. Note how push rod force is transferred in the opposite direction by the rocker arm. Figs. 9-30 and 9-32 illustrate the use of a rocker arm-push rod valve train on an actual engine.

Fig. 9-33 shows a somewhat different rocker arm design. Instead of oscillating on a rocker arm shaft, this type uses a ball arrangement on which the rocker arm pivots. Fig. 9-33.

When the camshaft is mounted "overhead" (above the valves), push rods are not required. The rocker arm setup shown in Fig. 9-34 is operated by the camshaft lobe rubbing directly on the rocker. Zero valve stem to rocker clearance is maintained by a hydraulic valve lash adjuster. Fig. 9-34.

The camshaft lobes can also be arranged to work directly on the valve stems as shown in B, Fig. 9-43.

OVERHEAD VALVE ADJUSTMENT

Some installations provide an adjusting screw in the push rod end of the rocker arm. This screw is moved in or out until the recommended clearance exists between the valve stem and the rocker arm. See Fig. 9-35.

Where hydraulic lifters are used, there is no clearance. The only adjustment necessary is the initial setting to place the lifter plunger at the halfway point

in its travel. Some engines make the initial setting with adjustable rocker arms, while others use push rods that, when installed, provide the proper setting. Push rods of slightly different lengths are available to make minor changes. Fig. 9-36 shows such a setup.

224

Fig. 9-33. Ball type rocker arm. (TRW, Inc.)

Fig. 9-35. Rocker arm with adjustment screw used to set proper valve clearance or "lash." (British-Leyland)

Fig. 9-34. One type of overhead camshaft rocker arm arrangement. Note hydraulic lash adjuster. (Ford)

Fig. 9-36. Nonadjustable rocker arm. This type depends upon precise parts so that, upon assembly, hydraulic lifter plunger will be at midpoint of travel. (Dodge)

HOW DOES THE COMBUSTION CHAMBER AFFECT VALVE LOCATION?

The shape and size of the combustion chamber is very important. A well designed chamber will allow high compression ratios without the occurrence of damaging detonation (violent explosion of the fuel charge). Compression ratios of around 8.5 or 10.5 to 1 were used for many years. Current practice has lowered the ratio to around 8, 8.5, or 9 to 1. This aids emission control.

High compression necessitates squeezing the air-fuel charge into a small area. In order to have this small area, and still allow room for the valves to open, it is necessary to locate the valves in the head. In this position, they may open down into the cylinder. Some pistons have small indentations cut into their tops to allow the valves to clear. Fig. 9-37.

With the L-head engine, sufficient space must be left above the valves to allow full opening. This space naturally becomes part of the combustion chamber. When the piston is on TDC on the compression stroke, this space lowers the compression ratio.

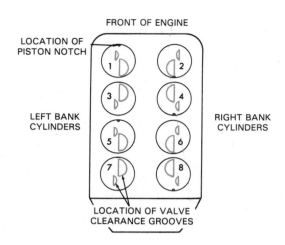

Fig. 9-37. Piston indentations used for valve clearance. Each piston has two small indentations to allow valve heads to clear. (Chevrolet)

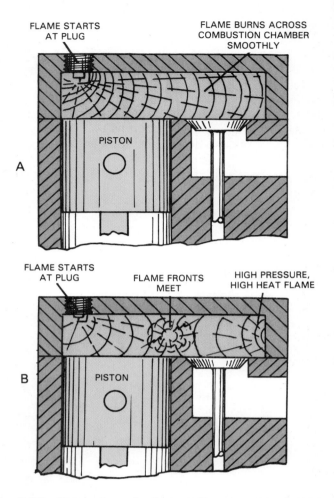

Fig. 9-38. Detonation. A—Proper flame travel. B—Two flame fronts increase burning rate and cause detonation.

WHAT CAUSES DETONATION?

When the highly compressed air-fuel charge is fired, the flame travels from the plug in an outward direction. As the charge continues to burn, pressure greatly increases.

If the pressure in any part of the chamber raises high enough, before the flame reaches it, this area will be hot enough to fire itself. This will produce two flame fronts and thereby increase the burning rate. Instead of firing smoothly, there is a violent explosion that literally slams the piston down. This is very damaging to an engine.

Detonation can be caused by an excessively high compression ratio or by a low grade of gasoline. An overheated valve or bit of carbon, etc., can ignite the "end gas" and cause the formation of the second flame front. Fig. 9-38.

PREIGNITION

Preignition is caused when a glowing bit of carbon, an overheated spark plug, etc., ignites the fuel charge before the spark plug fires. When preignition occurs, the premature explosion attempts to drive the piston down against the direction of rotation.

COMBUSTION CHAMBER DESIGN

Many years ago a man named Ricardo developed a combustion chamber that is still used in the L-head engine.

Ricardo found that by causing a violent turbulence in the compressed fuel charge, and by locating the spark plug near the center, flame travel through the charge was smooth, and compression could be raised considerably without detonation.

He located the combustion chamber over the valves and allowed the piston to come very close to the head. As the piston travels up on compression, it forces the

fuel into the area above the valves. As the piston comes close to the head, the remaining mixture is rapidly squeezed, causing it to shoot into the combustion chamber, setting up a rapid turbulence. The area between the piston top and the head is referred to as the "squish" or "squash" area. Fig. 9-39.

Fig. 9-39. Ricardo principle. When top of piston nears head, trapped air-fuel mixture in "squish" area shoots into combustion chamber, causing turbulence.

HEMISPHERICAL COMBUSTION CHAMBER

The hemispherical type of combustion chamber is compact and allows high compression with very little detonation. By placing the valves in two planes, it is possible to use larger valves, thereby improving breathing.

A HEMISPHERICAL combustion chamber is highly efficient and despite its somewhat expensive nature (shaping chamber, more complex valve mechanism, etc.), it is used on a number of engines. Figs. 9-40, 9-41, and 9-43.

Fig. 9-41. Cross-sectional view showing engine using a hemispherical combustion chamber. Lobes on the double overhead camshafts operate directly against the valve stem caps. (Fiat)

Fig. 9-40. Hemispherical combustion chamber. Valves are set in two planes. (TRW, Inc.)

WEDGE SHAPE COMBUSTION CHAMBER

Another widely used combustion chamber shape is the WEDGE. When properly designed, it is quite efficient.

When the wedge shape is incorporated in the head, a flat top piston will produce a desirable "squish" effect. When the top of the engine block is machined at an angle of around 10 deg., it is possible to build the cylinder head flat. The combustion chamber wedge is formed by the angled cylinder and a piston with an inverted V top. This setup will also produce a "squish" effect.

The spark plug is generally located at one corner of the wedge. This provides a smooth flame travel and loads (presses down) the piston gradually. You can see by studying Fig. 9-42, that when the charge is first ignited, it presses on only a portion of the piston. This partial pressure starts the piston down smoothly. As soon as the piston has moved a little, the flame front spreads across the entire piston dome and full thrust is applied. This provides a smooth loading feature.

The engines in Figs. 9-30, 9-45, and 9-47 use a wedge chamber formed in the head.

NOTICE COMBUSTION CHAMBER

As you study the various engines illustrated in this chapter, notice the types of combustion chambers used. Study the valve arrangement and piston shape.

OVERHEAD CAMSHAFT

Some engines mount the camshaft over the head. Either one or two shafts can be used. This eliminates

Fig. 9-42. Wedge combustion chamber. Notice that head is flat and cylinder block is machined at an angle—approximately 10 deg. Valves are set in a plane.

227

CAMSHAFTS

HEMISPHERICAL CHAMBER

CAMSHAFT

ROCKER ARM

HYDRAULIC LASH
ADJUSTER

WEDGE
COMBUSTION
CHAMBER

A

B

Fig. 9-43. Engines using overhead camshafts. A—Uses a wedge combustion chamber with all valves in one plane. Hydraulic lash adjuster maintains zero clearance at all times. B—Uses a hemispherical combustion chamber. Two camshafts are employed. Note how cams actuate valves.

the added weight of the rocker arms and push rods that may tend to make the valves "float" at high speeds. Figs. 9-41 and 9-43.

CYLINDER CLASSIFICATION

Cylinder placement gives rise to another method of engine classification. Many arrangements have been used, but only those in popular use today will be covered in this text.

IN-LINE ENGINE

In in-line engines, the cylinders are arranged one after the other in a straight line. They are in a vertical position, or near vertical. Fig. 9-44. The number of cylinders most commonly used is either four or six. Until the popular adoption of the V-8, an eight cylinder in-line was used. A few five cylinder in-lines are now produced.

The eight cylinder in-line is no longer in common use due primarily to its great length and the fact that under high compression operation, it had a tendency to actually flex or bend. Torsional vibration would set up unless the crankshaft was unusually heavy and the block itself would tend to twist.

V-TYPE ENGINES

The V-type engine places two banks or rows of cylinders at an angle to each other—generally 90 deg.

The V-type engine has certain advantages: short length, extreme block rigidity, heavy crankshaft, low profile that is conducive to low hood lines.

Extremely high compression ratios can be used in the V-type engine without block distortion under load. The short, heavy crankshaft is resistant to torsional vibration. The shorter block permits a reduction in car length with no sacrifice in passenger room.

For many years V-8, V-12, and V-16 engines were of the flat-head (L-head) design, but current practice on V-6, V-8, and V-12 (V-16 engines are not currently in production) engines is to use the valve-in-head (I-head) setup. Figs. 9-45 and 9-64.

HORIZONTAL-OPPOSED ENGINES

This type of engine is like taking a V-type engine and flattening the V until both banks lie in a horizontal plane.

The advantage here is an extremely low overall height, which makes this engine ideally suited to in-

Fig. 9-44. Cutaway view of a typical six cylinder, in-line, overhead valve engine. Valves are actuated by push rods operating rocker arms. (Triumph)

stallations where vertical space is limited. Fig. 9-46 shows a horizontal-opposed engine. It is an air-cooled, six cylinder version.

SLANT OR INCLINED TYPE ENGINE

In reality an inclined type engine is an in-line engine with the cylinder block slanted to one side. The engine in Fig. 9-47 illustrates this type. Notice that by slanting the engine, space is provided to utilize a long branch, ram type intake manifold.

OTHER CYLINDER ARRANGEMENTS

There have been many methods used in locating cylinders. Fig. 9-48 shows one other type. This is termed a RADIAL engine, which has been very popular for aircraft use.

FIRING ORDER

Firing order refers to the sequence in which the cylinders fire. Firing orders are given from front to

rear. The order in which the engine must fire is determined by the number of cylinders and the arrangement of the crankshaft throws. Firing order for Chevrolet cars for example is: four cylinder 1-3-4-2; six, 1-5-3-6-2-4; V-8, 1-8-4-3-6-5-7-2. The Buick 3.0 litre (181 cu. in.) is 1-6-5-4-3-2.

COOLING CLASSIFICATION

As you have learned, engines are either liquid-cooled or air-cooled. Both types of cooling are used in American and foreign made engines. Countless numbers of air-cooled engines are used to operate saws, mowers, scooters, etc.

Both types have advantages and disadvantages but, when correctly designed, both function properly.

FUEL CLASSIFICATION

You have also learned that automobile engines can use gasoline, LP-Gas (propane), diesel, alcohol or gasohol (mixture of gasoline and alcohol). Gasoline powers the majority of cars but diesel is gaining rapidly in popularity. Gasohol is seeing wider use.

Both gasoline and LP-Gas utilize the same basic type of engine. One of the principal differences is in carburetion. The true diesel does not use a carburetor

and needs no ignition system. Due to the pressures and stresses involved, diesel engines are very sturdily built. The theory of diesel engines was covered in the DIESEL INJECTION section. Diesel engines are either two or four-stroke cycle types.

TWO-STROKE CYCLE AND FOUR-STROKE CYCLE DIESEL ENGINES

A two-stroke cycle diesel engine is somewhat different than the gasoline engine of this type discussed earlier in this chapter. The two-stroke cycle diesel engine utilizes an exhaust valve. No fuel mixture enters the crankcase. The supercharger forces air into the cylinder intake ports. Fig. 9-49 shows the two-stroke cycle operation in a diesel engine. Notice that air rushing in through cylinder liner ports helps scavenge the cylinder by flowing out the exhaust passage for a portion of the piston travel. As air only enters, there is no loss of fuel.

Fig. 9-50 shows a typical four-stroke cycle, four cylinder automotive diesel engine. A five cylinder diesel is also used. See Figs. 9-66 and 9-67. Refer to Chapter 7 for further details regarding diesel fuel injection system operation.

GAS TURBINE ENGINE

A great deal of research is being carried on in an endeavor to adapt the gas turbine engine to meet modern automotive needs. The gas turbine has proved to be effective for both aircraft and heavy trucking use.

The big advantage of the gas turbine is its freedom

Fig. 9-45. Cross section of typical V-type engine. Angle between cylinder banks is often 90 deg. as shown here. (Dodge)

Fig. 9-46. Cross section of horizontal-opposed engine. Air-cooled engine has a very low profile, making it adaptable to limited space.

Fig. 9-47. Cross section of a slant or inclined engine. By slanting engine, overall height is reduced allowing for a long branch intake manifold. Car hood height can also be lowered. (Toyota)

from excessive vibration and its simplicity of design. With proper development and adequate adaptation, the gas turbine has great potential. Fig. 9-51 is a schematic of a gas turbine.

Notice that the turbine is divided into two basic sections—the GASIFIER section and the POWER section.

The compressor, in the manner of a centrifugal supercharger, forces air into the burner section. As the fuel is burned, it leaves the burner area at high speed. It passes through the gasifier nozzle diaphragm and is directed against the gasifier turbine blades.

This drives the gasifier turbine at high speed. Since it is on the same shaft as the compressor, the gasifier turbine drive the compressor at the same high rpm.

After leaving the gasifier turbine, the hot gases are directed through a second set of stationary blades. These blades direct the gases against the power tur-

Fig. 9-48. Radial engine. All connecting rods are fastened to master rod. This design has been used for many years in aircraft—very successfully.

AIR ENTERING COMBUSTION CHAMBER
THROUGH CYLINDER LINER PORTS

AIR BEING COMPRESSED WITH
THE EXHAUST VALVE CLOSED

CHARGE OF FUEL BEING INJECTED
INTO COMBUSTION CHAMBER

EXHAUST TAKING PLACE AND
CYLINDER ABOUT TO BE SWEPT
WITH CLEAN SCAVENGING AIR

Fig. 9-49. Two-stroke cycle diesel engine operation. (Detroit Diesel Engine Div.—General Motors)

bine, causing it to spin at high speed.

The power turbine drives transmission reduction gears to lower the rpm to a usable level.

If desired, the gases can be carried through other power turbines until all residual (what is left) power is utilized.

EXPERIMENTAL ENGINES

The search for better engines is never ending. Many ideas have been tried and adopted, others have failed. There are several types of engines such as the Stirling,

gas turbine, steam, stratified charge, different adaptations of the rotary, etc., under development at the present time. Much experimentation and testing is being done on electrically driven cars. Whether or not these types of engines will find successful application as automobile power plants, only time will tell.

ENGINE MOUNTING

It is common practice to mount the engine on resilient rubber pads. This isolates engine vibrations and prevents their transfer to the car body. It also

INJECTOR   GLOW PLUGS

INJECTOR PUMP

INJECTOR PUMP
DRIVE CHAIN

Fig. 9-50. A four cylinder, four-stroke cycle automotive diesel engine. Compression ratio is around 22 to 1. Maximum engine speed (without load) is 4,750 rpm.   (Peugeot)

eases torque (twisting strain) loading of the drive line.

The "three point" suspension is popular. This method uses one mount on either side of the engine near the front and one at the back, usually under the transmission. An alternate plan is two; one on either side near the back, with one at the front. The front mount would be near the center of the engine.

It is advisable to support the engine somewhat up on the sides to minimize torque deflections. Fig. 9-52 illustrates a typical mounting pattern. Small shock absorbers are sometimes employed, especially on diesel engines, to further control vibration.

DANGER!

ENGINE REMOVAL AND INSTALLATION CAN BE QUITE DANGEROUS. MAKE CERTAIN THAT ALL LIFT EQUIPMENT IS IN GOOD CONDITION. SECURE THE LIFT STRAP OR CHAIN WITH STRONG BOLTS, WITH THE BOLT THREADS TURNED IN DEEPLY. IF A STUD IS USED, MAKE SURE THE NUTS ARE SCREWED ON FAR ENOUGH TO HOLD.

MOUNT THE PULLER STRAP TO A SPOT THAT WILL WITHSTAND THE PULLING

Fig. 9-51. Schematic showing operation of a gas turbine engine.

STRAIN AND ALLOW THE ENGINE TO BALANCE.

WHEN PULLING, OR INSTALLING, KEEP CLEAR OF THE ENGINE AT ALL TIMES. WATCH HANDS AND FINGERS WHEN GUIDING IN OR OUT.

PLACE ENGINE ON THE FLOOR OR ON AN ENGINE STAND IMMEDIATELY. NEVER WORK ON AN ENGINE THAT IS SUPPORTED IN MIDAIR BY THE LIFT.

REMEMBER ENGINES ARE HEAVY AND MUST BE HANDLED WITH UTMOST CARE!

IDENTIFICATION AND CLASSIFICATION

The remainder of this chapter is devoted to engine classification and parts identification. Study ALL the engine figures in this chapter very carefully. Make certain you know the names and uses of all parts. It is most important that you build a complete and accurate mental image of the various types of engines, and the relationship of one part to the other.

As you study each figure, ask these questions:
1. Is this engine air or water-cooled?
2. Is this a V-type, in-line, or opposed engine?
3. Does it burn gasoline or diesel fuel?
4. If gasoline, does it have an updraft, downdraft or sidedraft carburetor?
5. Is it an L-head, F-head, or I-head?
6. What type of combustion chamber design is used?
7. Is it a four-stroke cycle or a two-stroke cycle?
8. How many cylinders does it have?
9. Do I know the names and uses of all the parts?
10. Do I know the working relationship of one part to another?

Fig. 9-52. Engine mounts and mounting pattern. This is a typical three point suspension pattern.   (Plymouth)

In addition to knowing the names and uses of all parts, be certain to test your knowledge of the various systems by identifying the cooling, lubrication, ignition, and fuel systems. Figs. 9-69, 9-70, 9-72, 9-73.

SUMMARY

Engines can be classified in many ways. The most commonly used classifications are by CYCLE, VALVE LOCATION, CYLINDER ARRANGEMENT, FUEL USED, COOLING and NUMBER OF CYLINDERS.

The vast majority of auto engines are of the four-stroke cycle type. The two-stroke cycle is generally used in small utility engines. Both have advantages and disadvantages.

The I-head (overhead valve or valve-in-head)

Fig. 9-53. Longitudinal view of V-8 engine. Note use of timing and oil pump drive chains.   (Mercedes-Benz)

engine is in almost universal use today.

The most commonly used combustion chamber shapes are the WEDGE and the HEMISPHERICAL.

Detonation during high compression can be stopped by proper fuel and combustion chamber design. Ricardo, in early experiments, set forth some basic principles of design that are still incorporated in modern engines. He found that it was essential to provide turbulence in the compressed charge.

The V-8, V-6, in-line four and six cylinder, and four or six cylinder horizontal-opposed engines, dominate the field of engine design and use.

The diesel two-stroke cycle engine differs from the small gasoline engine of the same type. The diesel incorporates an exhaust valve, a supercharger and a conventional crankcase.

Experiments with new and different types of engines are always in progress. Further development of existing engines is also taking place. Considerable research is being done on steam, gas turbine and electric drive autos.

The Wankel rotary piston engine uses a triangular shaped rotor that revolves inside an epitrochoid shaped housing. It operates on the four-cycle princi-ple. It has no reciprocating action and as a result, is very smooth running. The rotary is a simple engine with very few moving parts (rotor and eccentric shaft) in the basic engine.

Engines are mounted on rubber, generally using the three point suspension system.

Engine removal and installation can be dangerous—be careful!

Mechanics, like engines, are classified in many ways. A good engine is developed by hard work, study, experimentation and experience. Top-notch mechanics are developed the same way. If you desire to be the very BEST, always apply these rules. If not, you may end up in the low horsepower, "blockhead" classification.

KNOW THESE TERMS

Two-stroke cycle, Wankel, L-head, F-head, I-head, T-head, Detonation, Preignition, Hemispherical chamber, Wedge chamber, Overhead camshaft, In-line, V-type, Horizontal-opposed engine, Slant engine, Firing order, Gas turbine, Engine mounts.

Fig. 9-54. Exploded view of engine and related parts. (Datsun)

Fig. 9-55. Engine employing TWO spark plugs per cylinder. Note use of overhead valves and hemispherical combustion chamber. (Nissan)

Fig. 9-56. Longitudinal cross section of a typical six cylinder, overhead valve engine. Study all parts.   (Toyota)

Fig. 9-57. Cutaway view of a 4-cylinder, overhead camshaft, in-line engine. This engine uses a ribbed timing belt.   (Datsun)

Fig. 9-58. Four cylinder, in-line, overhead camshaft engine. Note use of timing chain to operate camshaft. This engine slants a few degrees from vertical. (BMW)

Fig. 9-59. Cutaway view of a Ford 1.6 litre, electronic fuel injected engine. Study various parts. Note use of hemispherical combustion chambers. (Ford)

Fig. 9-60. Four cylinder, in-line engine. (Fiat)

Fig. 9-61. Cutaway of an in-line, six cylinder engine using an overhead camshaft. (BMW)

Fig. 9-62. Fuel injected, in-line six cylinder engine. (BMW)

Fig. 9-63. This is the Plymouth slant six engine. Notice how it is inclined from the vertical.

AIR CLEANER

COIL

CARBURETOR

HOT AIR PICKUP

INTAKE MANIFOLD

VALVE SPRING

ROCKER ARM

VALVE

HYDRAULIC VALVE LIFTER

HEAD

EXHAUST MANIFOLD

BLOCK

CYLINDER

WATER JACKET

PISTON

PISTON PIN

CAMSHAFT

CONNECTING ROD

STARTER

CRANKSHAFT

CRANKSHAFT COUNTERWEIGHT

OIL PAN

DIPSTICK

OIL PICKUP

Fig. 9-64. Cross section of Cadillac V-type engine.

INTAKE OPEN

FUEL INJECTOR

INTAKE CLOSED

EXHAUST CLOSED

INTAKE CLOSED

EXHAUST CLOSED

INTAKE CLOSED

EXHAUST VALVE OPEN

GLOW PLUG

CONNECTING ROD

PISTON

A   CRANKSHAFT   B   C   D

Fig. 9-65. Four-stroke cycle diesel engine principle. A—Beginning of intake stroke. Intake valve opens and piston draws air into cylinder. B—Compression stroke. Both valves closed. C—Firing stroke. Fuel is injected and then ignited by heat of compression, thus driving piston down. Both valves closed. D—Exhaust stroke clears burned gases from cylinder through open exhaust valve. Complete cycle takes four strokes requiring two revolutions of crankshaft.   (Champion)

Fig. 9-66. Four cylinder diesel engine. Note use of drive belts instead of gears or chains. (VW)

Fig. 9-67. Cutaway of a V-8 diesel engine. (Oldsmobile)

Fig. 9-68. Four cylinder, valve-in-head engine. 1—Rings. 2—Piston. 3—Piston pin. 4—Connecting rod. 5—Connecting rod bolt. 6—Connecting rod insert (upper) bearing. 7—Connecting rod cap. 8—Connecting rod insert (lower) bearing. 9—Oil pan gasket. 10—Oil pan. 11—Oil pump. 12—Cylinder head assembly. (Honda)

Fig. 9-69. Cutaway of a Chevrolet V-8 engine.

Fig. 9-70. Four cylinder, in-line engine. Note use of a timing belt driven overhead camshaft. Engine is an inclined or slant (leans to one side) design. (Chrysler)

HOW THE CVCC ENGINE OPERATES

❶ INTAKE STROKE

During the intake stroke, a lean mixture is drawn through the main intake valve into the main combustion chamber. At the same time, a rich mixture is drawn through the auxiliary intake valve into the pre-chamber.

❷ COMPRESSION STROKE

At the end of the compression stroke, a rich mixture is present in the pre-chamber, a moderate mixture is formed in the main combustion chamber near the pre-chamber outlet, and a very lean mixture is present in the remainder of the combustion chamber.

❸ IGNITION

When the spark plug fires, the rich mixture in the pre-chamber is easily ignited. The flame from the pre-chamber ignites the moderate mixture.

❹ POWER STROKE

The flame area is further extended to burn the lean mixture in the main combustion chamber. The formation of carbon monoxide is minimized because of this lean mixture.

KEY
▨	LEAN MIXTURE
▩	MODERATE MIXTURE
▦	RICH MIXTURE
▨	FLAME AREA
░	HOT GASES

❺ BOTTOM DEAD CENTER AND EXHAUST STROKE

The stable and slow burning during the combustion cycle has two desired effects:

(1) The low peak temperature minimizes the formation of oxides of nitrogen.

(2) The high average temperature reduces hydrocarbon emissions.

The hot gases exit through the exhaust valve, and oxidation continues in the manifold.

Fig. 9-71. Honda CVCC engine incorporates a small, auxiliary intake valve in each cylinder to produce an engine that will operate on a very lean air-fuel ratio. Study sequence of events.   (Honda)

Fig. 9-72. Exploded view of a four cylinder, in-line engine, external parts.

1—Generator pulley.	22—Cylinder block drain.	43—Engine left hand front mount.
2—Generator cooling fan.	23—Fan blades.	44—Engine front plate.
3—Dipstick.	24—Fan and water pump pulley.	45—Gasket.
4—Dipstick guide.	25—Water pump bearings and seals.	46—Crankcase and cylinder block.
5—Distributor shaft bushing.	26—Water pump.	47—Tappet cover.
6—Water temperature gauge element.	27—Gasket.	48—Front main bearing cap.
7—Thermostat housing.	28—Spacer.	49—Cork seal.
8—Gasket.	29—Seal.	50—Pan drain plug.
9—Thermostat.	30—Water pump shaft key.	51—Front main bearing stud.
10—Rocker cover.	31—Shaft.	52—Pan gasket.
11—Heater pipe.	32—Welch plug.	53—Sump.
12—Rocker cover gasket.	33—Generator bracket.	54—Center main bearing cap.
13—Cylinder head.	34—Oil pressure gauge connection.	55—Oil return pipe.
14—Intake manifold.	35—Core plug.	56—Rear main bearing.
15—Gasket.	36—Fan belt.	57—Fuel pump.
16—Intake manifold heating plate.	37—Oil seal.	58—Oil pressure relief valve.
17—Intake and exhaust manifold gasket.	38—Timing cover bolt.	59—Vacuum advance line.
18—Core plug.	39—Timing chain cover.	60—Breather pipe.
19—Cylinder head gasket.	40—Gasket.	61—Gasket.
20—Manifold washer.	41—Generator swinging link.	62—Engine rear plate.
21—Exhaust manifold.	42—Engine right hand front mount.	

REVIEW QUESTIONS—CHAPTER 9

Check YOUR horsepower rating by answering the following questions:

1. List the strokes in a four-stroke cycle engine—in their proper order.
2. List the strokes needed in the two-stroke cycle engine. Explain the sequence of events during these strokes.
3. What are the basic differences between four-stroke cycle and two-stroke cycle engines?
4. Explain where the valves are located in I-head, F-head, and L-head engines.
5. For what development in engine design is Ricardo well known?
6. Using cylinder arrangement, list the three most popular engines in use today.
7. What is detonation and how is it caused?
8. What is preignition and how is it caused?
9. List some factors that must be used when developing a good combustion chamber.
10. What combustion chamber is in widespread use today?

11. Why do some engines use an overhead camshaft?
12. What determines an engine's firing order?
13. Engines are mounted on _____.
14. Most engines are mounted using the _____ _____ suspension principle.
15. In fuel classification, what three principal fuels are concerned?
16. How does the two-stroke cycle diesel differ from its gasoline counterpart?
17. List five important points to consider in the SAFE removal and installation of an engine.
18. Did you study all of the illustrations in this chapter? Can you identify various systems? Do you know names and function of all the parts?

19. In the rotary engine, the rotor turns _____ to every _____ turns of the eccentric shaft.
20. Explain the basic difference between the rotary and the reciprocating piston engine.

DID THE APPLICANT GET THE JOB?

Imagine you are a garage owner and you have just interviewed someone seeking a job as mechanic in your shop. If you asked the Review Questions and received the answers you gave, WOULD YOU HIRE THE APPLICANT?

We hope this person got the job. If not, how would you handle the rejection?

Fig. 9-73. Inclined, four-cylinder overhead valve engine. Study this illustration carefully. Can you name all the major parts and explain their function? (British-Leyland)

Chapter 10

ENGINE TESTS, MEASUREMENTS

After studying this chapter, you will be able to:
■ Recall engine measurement formulas.
■ Solve basic engine measurement problems.
■ Develop an understanding of engine ratings.

Everyone has heard the word horsepower, but very few people, including many mechanics, understand exactly what it means and how it is computed.

WHAT IS HORSEPOWER?

Many years ago, people recognized the need for devising a yardstick with which to measure the work-producing ability of the gasoline engine. Since horses had been used to do the work for so long, it was natural to compare the power developed by the early engine to that produced by a horse.

The work ability of an average draft horse had long been the standard unit of work measured in foot-pounds. WORK can be defined as a force applied to a body that causes the body to move. The amount of work done can be computed by multiplying the distance the body moved by the force (weight of body). This answer would be in FOOT-POUNDS (joules).

It was found, for example, that the average draft horse could lift one hundred pounds, three hundred and thirty feet in one minute. If one pound is lifted one foot in one minute, one FOOT-POUND of work would be done. The horse lifted 100 pounds 330 feet in one minute. So using the work formula (distance moved × force weight), we find the horse performed work at the rate of 33,000 FOOT-POUNDS (44 741J) per minute.

The RATE at which work is performed is termed POWER. This then became the standard measure for one HORSEPOWER. Fig. 10-1.

HORSEPOWER FORMULA

To find engine horsepower, the total rate of work in foot-pounds accomplished is divided by 33,000. If a machine lifts 100 lbs. 660 ft. per minute, its total rate of work would be 66,000 ft. lbs. Dividing this by 33,000 ft. lbs. (1 horsepower) you will find that the machine is rated as 2 horsepower (hp). Your formula would be:

$$\frac{\text{Rate of work in ft. lbs.}}{33,000 \ (1 \ hp)} =$$

$$\frac{\text{Distance moved} \times \text{force}}{33,000} = \frac{D \times W}{33,000} = hp$$

This formula may also be used to determine the horsepower required to perform a specific task. Let us assume that you wanted to lift buckets of earth from an excavation. The loaded bucket weight is 5,000 lbs., and you want to raise it 15 ft. per minute. Using your formula:

$$hp = \frac{D \times W}{33,000} = \frac{15 \times 5,000}{33,000} = \frac{75,000}{33,000} = 2.27 \ hp$$

Fig. 10-1. Horsepower. Ability to perform work at rate of 33,000 ft. lbs. per min. = 1 horsepower.

249

The minimum amount of horsepower (disregarding friction) required would be 2.27.

POTENTIAL HORSEPOWER

If a certain engine burns a specific fuel at a certain rate, and if all the heat of the burning fuel could be converted into useful power, you would have the ideal engine. Unfortunately, engines have not reached this level. In fact, even the best engines are relatively inefficient in that the usable power falls far short of the potential.

Engine efficiency can be broken down into THERMAL EFFICIENCY and MECHANICAL EFFICIENCY. Any comparison between different engines on an efficiency basis must be conducted under identical situations. Weather, altitude, temperature, speed, etc., all affect the test results.

THERMAL EFFICIENCY

Engine thermal efficiency (heat efficiency) is based on how much of the energy (ability to do work) of the burning fuel is converted into useful horsepower.

The heat generated by the burning fuel drives the piston down, producing the power stroke. Much of this heat is lost to the cooling system, some to the lubrication system and a great deal to the exhaust system. The thermal efficiency of the average engine is around 25 percent. This means that the engine is losing approximately 75 percent of the fuel's heat energy. Fig. 10-2.

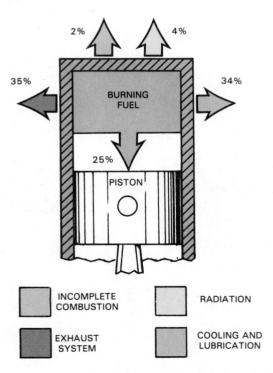

Fig. 10-2. Average engine thermal efficiency is around 25 percent. Note loss to incomplete combustion, exhaust, radiation, cooling, and lubrication.

FORMULA FOR THERMAL EFFICIENCY

The generally accepted formula for computing BRAKE THERMAL EFFICIENCY is:

$$\text{Brake Thermal Efficiency} = \frac{\text{Brake Horsepower (bhp)} \times 33{,}000}{778 \times \text{Fuel Heat Value} \times \text{Weight of Fuel Burned Per Minute}}$$

The 778 is Joule's equivalent, the fuel heat (calorific) value is based on the Btu (British thermal unit) per pound.

MECHANICAL EFFICIENCY

Mechanical efficiency is based on the relationship of power developed within the engine, and actual brake horsepower delivered at the crankshaft. Fortunately, mechanical efficiency is better—around 90 percent. This means that 10 percent is lost to friction within the engine. Engine friction is not constant but increases with speed.

FORMULA FOR MECHANICAL EFFICIENCY

The formula is:

$$\text{Mechanical Efficiency} = \frac{\text{Brake Horsepower}}{\text{Indicated Horsepower}} = \frac{\text{bhp}}{\text{ihp}}$$

PRACTICAL EFFICIENCY

When dealing with auto engines, you are primarily interested in horsepower delivered at the drive wheels.

Every pound of gasoline that enters the engine has the ability to do a certain amount of work. There are many factors that rob energy before it gets to the drive wheels. If you figure the potential energy in a pound of fuel as 100 percent, you may get as little as 15 percent delivered to the drive wheels. Fig. 10-3 illustrates some of these energy losses.

INDICATED HORSEPOWER

The indicated horsepower (ihp) is a measure of the power developed by the burning fuel within the cylinders.

In order to compute ihp, it is necessary to find the pressures within the cylinder for the intake, compression, power and exhaust strokes. A measuring device gives a constant reading of the pressures. This is placed on an indicator graph.

The next step is to establish a mean effective pressure (mep). This is done by taking the average pressure during the power stroke and subtracting the average pressure during the other three strokes. Once the mep is determined, the following formula is used to determine the indicated horsepower:

Indicated Horsepower (ihp) = $\dfrac{PLANK}{33,000}$

P — mep in lbs. per sq. in.
L — length of the stroke in feet
A — cylinder area in sq. in.
N — power strokes per min. $\dfrac{rpm}{2}$

K — number of cylinders

Indicated horsepower ratings do not reflect losses from friction, heat, etc.

IF YOU POUR A POUND
OF GAS IN ENGINE

YOU GET APPROXIMATELY
15% OF ENERGY WITH WHICH
TO PROPEL CAR.

POWER
TO
PROPEL
CAR 15%

| ENGINE FRICTION 8% | COOLING SYSTEM 30% | EXHAUST SYSTEM 32% | RADIATION 4% | WHEELS TIRES DRIVE LINE 10% | INCOMPLETE COMBUSTION 1% |

Fig. 10-3. Practical efficiency. Energy leaks out between engine and drive wheels, demonstrating some factors involved. Percentages are approximate and change from engine to engine, and also from conditions under which engine is operated.

MEAN EFFECTIVE PRESSURE—BMEP, IMEP

Mean effective pressure is of two distinct types—BMEP (Brake Mean Effective Pressure) and IMEP (Indicated Mean Effective Pressure).

As mentioned, INDICATED MEAN EFFECTIVE PRESSURE is used as part of the formula for determining INDICATED HORSEPOWER. It represents the AVERAGE pressure in the cylinder. Fig. 10-4 illustrates a graph showing the pressure curve in a specific cylinder during all four strokes. Note highest pressure occurs at the peak of the power stroke. Study pressure during other strokes.

BRAKE MEAN EFFECTIVE PRESSURE is calculated by using the horsepower rating as determined by an engine dynomometer.

To calculate the BMEP from any given horsepower rating, the following formula may be used:

BMEP (4-cycle) = $\dfrac{792,000 \times hp}{\text{Eng. rpm} \times \text{cu. in. displacement}}$

BMEP (2-cycle) = $\dfrac{792,000 \times hp \times 2}{\text{Eng. rpm} \times \text{cu. in. displacement}}$

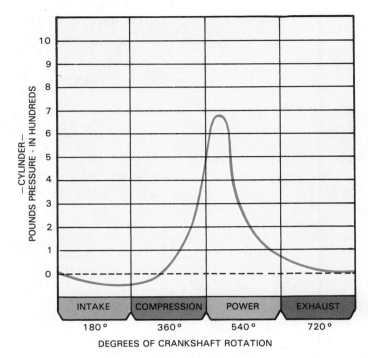

Fig. 10-4. Cylinder pressure graph showing pressure in a specific cylinder during all four strokes. Such pressures are used to determine the cylinder indicated mean effective pressure (IMEP).

BRAKE HORSEPOWER

Brake horsepower (bhp) is a measurement of actual usable horsepower delivered at the engine crankshaft. Brake horsepower is not constant but increases with speed. An early method of measuring crankshaft horsepower made use of a device called a PRONY BRAKE. Fig. 10-5.

The formula for determining brake horsepower on the Prony Brake is:

Fig. 10-5. Prony brake. Prony brake is used to measure bhp. A clamping device grasps spinning flywheel. Clamp is tightened until a specific rpm, with throttle wide open, is reached. At this point, weight reading on the scale is taken. By knowing scale reading (W), distance from center of crank to arm support (L), and rpm of flywheel (R), it is possible to compute bhp.

$$bph = \frac{2\pi \times R \times L \times W}{33,000}$$

$$bph = \frac{R \times L \times W}{5,252}$$

R — Engine rpm.
L — Length from center of drive shaft to point where beam presses on scale.
W — Weight as registered on scale.

The modern method of testing and determining brake horsepower is by using an ENGINE DYNAMOMETER or a CHASSIS DYNAMOMETER.

One type of engine dynamometer uses a large generator (dynamo) to which the engine is attached. The engine drives the generator and by placing an electrical load in the circuit, bhp at various rpm can be determined. Fig. 10-6.

Fig. 10-6. Engine dynamometer. This schematic demonstrates general idea of dynamometer. Generator dynamo can be loaded until engine rpm is at a certain point with throttle wide open. By using instrument readings, horsepower can be calculated.

Another popular type of engine dynamometer utilizes a water brake power absorption unit that attaches directly to the engine. Fig. 10-7.

The chassis dynamometer is used to measure bhp at the drive wheels. The car drive wheels are placed on two rollers and the engine is engaged. As the wheels turn the rollers, the rollers are loaded (made increasingly difficult to turn). By computing the amount of loading the wheels can handle, it is possible to determine bhp at the drive wheels. This is practical efficiency that is meaningful to the average motorist.

Chassis dynamometers are becoming quite popular. Many of the larger garages are installing them for use in engine tuning and testing. Fig. 10-8.

GROSS AND NET HORSEPOWER RATINGS

Under S.A.E. (Society of Automotive Engineers) specifications, a GROSS brake horsepower rating is the maximum horsepower developed by an engine equipped with only basic accessories needed for its operation. This would include the built-in emission controls, oil, coolant pump and fuel pump. The fan, air cleaner, catalytic converter, alternator, muffler, etc., can be left off.

The NET horsepower rating is the maximum horsepower developed by the engine when equipped with ALL the accessories such as fan, alternator, catalytic converter, muffler, air pump, air cleaner, fuel pump, coolant pump, etc., that it would have when installed in the car. The NET rating is a more informative figure for the car buyer in that it shows the horsepower that will actually be produced in normal usage.

The specified test conditions (29.38 in. Hg. or 99.01 kPa barometric pressure, 85°F [29.46°C] ambient air

Fig. 10-7. Attaching a portable engine dynamometer. Engine is operated with wide open throttle. Dynamometer water brake is adjusted until engine load pulls rpm down to desired level, at which point gauges will indicate bhp being developed. (Go-Power)

Fig. 10-8. Schematic showing operation of a typical chassis dynamometer. This unit measures horsepower delivered to driving wheels. (Clayton)

temperature, 0.38 in. Hg. or 1.28 kPa water vapor pressure or humidity), are the same for both GROSS and NET ratings.

Some other nations use a DIN horsepower rating. This is a NET rating done under slightly different conditions and specifications, so it will vary from ratings used in the United States.

FRICTIONAL HORSEPOWER

Frictional horsepower (fhp) is a measurement of the amount of hp lost to engine friction. It is computed by this formula:

$$fhp = ihp - bhp$$

As mentioned, frictional horsepower is not constant but increases with engine speed. Fig. 10-9.

TORQUE

Engine torque (twisting action) is the ability of the crankshaft to impart a twisting or turning force. It is measured in pounds-feet (newton-metres). If a pipe wrench is placed on a pipe and a pressure of one pound is exerted one foot from the center of the pipe, the torque (Torque = Force × Distance) applied to the pipe would be one POUND-FOOT. Actually, when measuring TORQUE, the reading is given in lbs. ft. When measuring WORK, the reading is given in ft. lbs. Fig. 10-10.

TORQUE AND BHP ARE NOT THE SAME

Engine bhp increases with engine speed. Engine torque increases with engine speed up to the point where, all factors considered, the engine is drawing in the maximum amount of fuel mixture. Torque is greatest here and any additional increase in rpm will cause torque to diminish. Fig. 10-11 compares torque and bhp.

VOLUMETRIC EFFICIENCY

Volumetric efficiency (sometimes referred to as breathing ability) is the measure of an engine's ability to draw fuel mixture into the cylinders. It is determined by the ratio between what is ACTUALLY drawn in and what COULD be drawn in if all cylinders were completely filled.

As engine speed increases beyond a certain point, the piston speed becomes so fast that the intake stroke is of such short duration that less and less fuel mix is drawn in. As torque is greatest when the cylinders receive the largest amount of fuel mix, torque will drop off with a decrease in volumetric efficiency.

Many factors influence volumetric efficiency. Engine speed, temperature, throttle position, intake system design, atmospheric pressure, etc., all help in

Fig. 10-9. Frictional horsepower graph. Notice how an increase in engine rpm causes more friction.

Fig. 10-10. Torque. Torque or twist applied to this pipe would be one pound-foot. This is torque in excess of wrench weight.

Fig. 10-11. Bhp and torque graph for one specific engine. Notice how horsepower increases almost to maximum speed while torque drops off at a much lower rpm. Relationship between torque and bhp will vary depending on engine design. (American Motors)

its determination.

It can be improved by adding a supercharger; straighter, smoother and ram length intake manifold; larger intake valves; better exhaust flow, etc.

A formula used to determine volumetric efficiency is:

$$\text{Volumetric Efficiency} = \frac{\text{Total volume of the charge}}{\text{Total cylinder volume (displacement)}}$$

All tests between engines must be under identical conditions. See Figs. 10-12 and 10-13.

VOLUME THAT COULD BE HELD, CYLINDER VOLUME

VOLUME OF FUEL MIX ACTUALLY DRAWN IN

Fig. 10-12. Volumetric efficiency.

Fig. 10-13. Volumetric efficiency at various speeds. This graph is only approximate; volumetric efficiency will vary from engine to engine. X marks point of highest efficiency and highest torque.

ENGINE SIZE (DISPLACEMENT)

Engine size (not physical dimensions) is related to piston displacement. Piston displacement refers to the total number of cubic inches of space (litres) in the cylinder when the piston moves from the top of its stroke (TDC) to the bottom (BDC). Fig. 10-14.

All related factors being equal, the bigger the engine displacement, the more power produced. To calculate piston displacement, find the area of the cylinder ($0.7854 \times \text{Diameter}^2$) and multiply that

answer by the total piston travel (stroke) from TDC to BDC. This answer is then multiplied by the number of cylinders and you have the total piston displacement in cubic inches. The formula:

$$\text{Piston Displacement} = 0.7854 \times D^2 \times \text{Travel} \times \text{Number of Cylinders}$$

For example you want to find the displacement of a V-8 engine have a cylinder diameter (bore) of 3.875 and a piston travel (stroke) of 3 inches.

$0.7854 \times D^2$ (15015) × Travel (3 inches) × Number of Cylinders (8) = 283.0248 cu. in.

CYLINDER BORE AND PISTON STROKE

As you noticed in the foregoing section, the displacement hinged on the cylinder BORE (diameter) and the piston STROKE. The bore is the diameter of the cylinder. The stroke is the length the piston moves from TDC to BDC. Fig. 10-15

When bore and stroke are equal, the engine is referred to as SQUARE. Modern practice uses a stroke that is shorter than bore diameter. This is referred to as an OVER SQUARE engine.

By reducing the stroke, piston speed is decreased. This prolongs the life of cylinders, pistons and rings.

Let us say that you want to compute the distance a ring slides up and down during one mile of driving. Your hypothetical (make believe) car will have a tire diameter of 30 in., the engine drives 1 to 1 through the transmission (standard transmission—no overdrive), and the differential (rear end) reduces drive line speed 4 to 1 (drive line turns four times for each revolution of the wheels).

The circumference of the tire (6.283 × Radius) would be 94.245 inches. Reducing circumference to feet, you would have 7.85. If the tire rolls 7.85 feet

ORIGINAL WATER   ADDITIONAL WATER

Fig. 10-14. Piston displacement: A—If you were to fill cylinder with water when piston is on TDC; B—Next, place piston on BDC; C—Then, measure additional water required to fill cylinder, you would have cylinder displacement in cu. in. Space from top of piston, when piston is on TDC, is called clearance volume. This space is occupied by water in A.

per revolution, it will make 672.61 revolutions per mile.

The engine rpm would be four times that of the wheel rpm, so this would give 2690.44 engine rpm per mile. As the rings slide up and down for each stroke (3 in.), this would be a total of 6 in. per engine revolution. With 2690.44 rpm per mile, the rings would slide 1345.22 ft. for every mile of travel.

The same engine with a 6 in. stroke would slide the rings twice as far. This shows that the short stroke decreases wear. Not only is sliding distance less, but speed at which rings slide is greatly reduced.

Fig. 10-15. Engine bore (cylinder diameter) and stroke (distance piston moves in traveling from top dead center to bottom dead center). Connecting rod journal offset or "throw" determines length of stroke.

COMPRESSION RATIO

Compression ratio is the relationship between the cylinder volume (clearance volume) when the piston is on TDC, compared to the cylinder volume when the piston is on BDC. Fig. 10-16.

Compression ratios range from 5 or 6 to 1 to slightly over 11 to 1 (8.5 to 1 about average) for gasoline engines, 22.5 to 1 for diesels.

To a certain degree, the higher the compression ratio in an engine, the more power it will develop. Such being the case, the question is, "Why not raise the compression a great deal on all engines?"

One reason this is impractical is that engine fuels of today will not let us. When a fuel mixture is compressed, heat energy is developed. The temperature at which the air-fuel mixture will ignite itself sets a limit on the amount it can be satisfactorily compressed. Another trouble is that when the compression ratio of

an engine is too high, the result is detonation, or knocking of the engine.

Effective emission control, at least at the present time, has required that compression ratios be lowered from 10 or 10.5 to 1 down to about 8 or 8.5 to 1.

SUMMARY

Horsepower is a measure of the rate at which work is performed. One horsepower is the ability to perform work at the rate of 33,000 foot-pounds per minute.

Engines are relatively inefficient. Efficiency is based on THERMAL and MECHANICAL efficiency. Thermal refers to heat efficiency which is not good. Most engines are about 25 percent efficient under the thermal basis, and about 90 percent efficient on a mechanical basis.

On a practical efficiency basis, only about 15 percent of the total potential energy of the fuel is used to drive the wheels.

Energy is lost to the cooling, lubrication, and exhaust systems as well as to engine, drive line, and wheel friction.

Indicated horsepower is a measure of the power developed by the burning fuel within the cylinders. This ihp is not what is delivered by the crankshaft. Crankshaft horsepower is termed brake horsepower and is measured by a dynamometer. Frictional horsepower is a measure of the horsepower lost to engine friction. Net bhp ratings are taken with all normal accessories on the engine. Gross bhp figures are with some accessories (fan, cleaner, generator, etc.) removed.

Engine brake horsepower and torque are not the same. Brake horsepower increases with rpm until maximum is reached. Torque increases to the point where volumetric efficiency is greatest and any additional speed will cause it to diminish. Torque is a measure of the engine's twisting or turning force at the crankshaft.

Volumetric efficiency refers to how well the engine

Fig. 10-16. Compression ratio. Cylinder volume in A totals 8. When piston is on TDC, cylinder volume totals 1. Volume in A is 8, volume in B is 1; compression ratio is 8 to 1.

is able to draw in fuel mixture. It is different from engine to engine, speed to speed, and is influenced by a number of other factors.

Engine size is usually given in cubic inches or litres. The number of cubic inches or litres of cylinder space is computed on piston displacement. Cylinder bore and stroke are determining factors in cubic inch or litre computations.

Compression ratios are important in that, when high, they improve power and economy. Current ratios have been lowered somewhat (to improve emission control) to around 8 or 8.5 to 1 for gasoline engines. Diesel engines remain about 22.5 to 1.

The science of engine testing and measurement is very complicated, and in its true sense, lies in the realm of engineering. To expect even the best mechanics to be completely familiar with it would be most foolhardy.

It is important that the student of auto mechanics be familiar with basic items in the field. The chapter you have just read will provide you with a knowledge of the more common factors. Make certain you understand them and, for your own benefit, make up some problems that will utilize the formulas given.

REMEMBER

The training and background of the superior mechanic represents hundreds of hours of study in all phases of auto mechanics. This expert knows the HOW, WHEN and WHY of automotive service and sustains a never-ending search for information and knowledge. The auto mechanic who takes pride in this work is to be respected and admired.

KNOW THESE TERMS

Potential horsepower, Thermal efficiency, Mechanical efficiency, Practical efficiency, Indicated horsepower, Brake horsepower, Dynamometer, Prony brake, Gross horsepower, Net horsepower, Frictional horsepower, Torque, Volumetric efficiency, Engine size, Cylinder bore, Cylinder stroke, Compression ratio.

REVIEW QUESTIONS—CHAPTER 10

1. What is horsepower?
2. How is horsepower computed? Give the formula.
3. Engine efficiency can be classified as _____ and _____.
4. Give the formula for both efficiency classifications.
5. What is indicated horsepower?
6. What is brake horsepower?
7. The _____ is now used to determine brake horsepower.
8. Explain the difference between GROSS and NET brake horsepower.
9. Does the S.A.E. rating indicate true brake horsepower?
10. The difference between indicated horsepower and brake horsepower is classified as _____ horsepower.
11. What is torque?
12. Are brake horsepower and torque one and the same?
13. To what does the term volumetric efficiency refer?
14. Give the formula for volumetric efficiency.
15. Piston displacement means _____.
16. What is meant by bore and stroke?
17. How is compression ratio figured?
18. What is WORK?
19. The rate at which work is done is referred to as _____.
20. What would you say if someone asked, "What is meant by the cubic inch rating of an engine?"
21. What is ENERGY?

If you had answered all the above questions correctly—even if you had to refer back to do it—you have the stuff it takes. CONGRATULATIONS!

Chapter 11

ENGINE CLUTCHES

After studying this chapter, you will be able to:
- Explain clutch operation.
- Name the different types of clutches.
- List the various clutch release mechanisms.
- Define the basic parts of a clutch.
- Identify the parts of a clutch.

WHAT IS A CLUTCH?

A clutch is a mechanism designed to connect or disconnect the transmission of power from one working part to another.

There are many types of clutches. All accomplish the same general purpose. This chapter concerns the clutch used on modern automobiles with standard transmissions. Its function is to connect or disconnect the flow of power from the engine to the transmission and drive line.

OF WHAT USE IS A CLUTCH?

A clutch is used to transmit engine power to the transmission in a manner that will allow the car to start out in a smooth fashion. The clutch is used to facilitate the shifting of transmission gears. It also can be used to allow the engine to operate, when the car is stopped, without placing the transmission in neutral (out of gear).

HOW IS A CLUTCH MADE?

The clutch in popular use is the single plate, dry disc type. It consists basically of six major parts— flywheel, clutch disc, pressure plate, springs, pressure plate housing or cover and the linkage necessary to operate the clutch. To best illustrate basic clutch construction and operation, each part will be discussed in order.

FLYWHEEL

In addition to its use to smooth out engine operation and provide a base for the starter ring gear, the flywheel forms the foundation on which the entire clutch is attached.

The clutch side is machined smooth to provide a friction surface. Holes are drilled into the flywheel to provide a means of mounting the clutch assembly. A hole in the center of the flywheel allows a bearing to be installed (this hole in many cases is actually drilled in the crankshaft).

The bearing in the center of the flywheel will act as a support for the outboard end of the transmission input shaft (sometimes called "clutch shaft"). It is referred to as a "pilot bearing." This may be either a ball bearing or a bronze bushing. Both must be provided with lubrication. Fig. 11-1.

STARTER RING GEAR

HOLE FOR CLUTCH COVER BOLTS

SMOOTH AREA FOR CLUTCH DISC

FLYWHEEL TO CRANKSHAFT FASTENER

PILOT BUSHING FOR TRANSMISSION INPUT SHAFT

CRANKSHAFT

RECESS TO ALLOW ROOM FOR CLUTCH DISC HUB MECHANISM

FLYWHEEL

STARTER RING GEAR

Fig. 11-1. Cross-sectional view shows typical flywheel design. Flywheel provides foundation on which clutch assembly is built.

CLUTCH DISC

The clutch disc is round and constructed of thin, high quality steel, with a splined (grooved) hub placed in the center. The hub splines engage splines on the transmission input shaft. The clutch disc can move back and forth on the shaft, but when the disc is turned, the shaft must turn also.

Both sides of its outer edge are covered with friction material. It is often made of asbestos, (see asbestos warning in Chapter 20), cotton and copper wires either woven or molded together. It is riveted to the disc.

To assist in smooth engagement, the disc outer edges are often split and each piece cupped. The friction material is riveted to these segments. When the disc is compressed, these cupped segments act as a spring-like cushion.

The inner hub and thin outer disc are fastened together in such a manner as to alow a certain amount of radial (circle around the center) movement between them. This movement is controlled by stop pins. Coil springs act as a drive unit between hub flange and outer disc. These springs act as a dampening device, soften the torque thrust when the outer disc is pressed against the flywheel, and transmit this thrust to the hub. Torsional vibration is controlled by a molded friction washer between clutch hub flange and outer disc.

Fig. 11-2 illustrates the edges of the cupped segments. Notice how the facing (friction material) is riveted to the segments. A typical clutch disc is shown in Fig. 11-3.

Fig. 11-3. One type of clutch disc. Note splined hub and arrangement of torsional coil springs that cushions shock of engagement. (Chevrolet)

Fig. 11-4. Pressure plate. Pressure plate is spring loaded and presses clutch disc against flywheel.

Fig. 11-2. Edge view of clutch disc. Notice how segments are cupped to produce cushion effect that assists in smooth clutch engagement. A—Cupped segment. B—Rivet. C—Lining.

PRESSURE PLATE

The clutch pressure plate is generally made of cast iron. It is round and about the same diameter as the clutch disc. One side of the pressure plate is machined smooth. This side will press the clutch disc facing area against the flywheel. The outer side has various shapes to facilitate attachment of springs and release mechanisms. Fig. 11-4.

PRESSURE PLATE ASSEMBLY

In addition to the pressure plate itself, there are a number of coil springs, (or diaphragm), a cover, and

release levers. The springs are used to provide pressure against the pressure plate. Various numbers of springs are used, depending on the type of service for which the assembly is designed. The springs push against the clutch cover and pressure plate. Fig. 11-5.

The release levers are designed to draw the pressure plate away from the clutch disc. One end of the release lever engages the pressure plate. The other end is free and is designed to be pressed inward. Between the two ends, the lever is hinged to the clutch cover by means of an eyebolt.

There are generally three release levers. Some levers are of the semi-centrifugal type. This type has a weight added to its outer end. As the clutch assembly spins, centrifugal force will act upon these weights and cause them to exert additional pressure against the pressure plate. This assists the springs. Release lever location and action is shown in Fig. 11-6.

The clutch cover bolts to the flywheel and acts as a base for the springs. The pressure plate release lugs pass through slots in the cover, allowing the cover to drive the pressure plate.

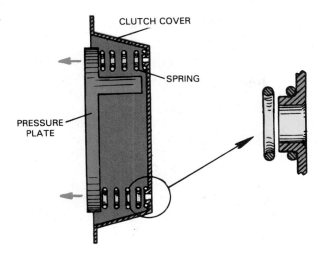

Fig. 11-5. Clutch springs—coil type. Size and number of springs vary with clutch design.

Fig. 11-6. Release lever action. A—Release lever free, pressure plate engaged. B—Release lever pushed inward, drawing pressure plate away from flywheel. C—Weight added to centrifugal type release lever. When clutch revolves, weight is thrown outward, adding to spring pressure.

Most flywheel and pressure plate assemblies are marked, so that upon reassembly they may be bolted together without disturbing the flywheel balance. At the factory, the flywheel and clutch pressure plate assembly are bolted together and balanced. After balancing, they are marked so the balance may be retained. The flywheel, clutch disc, pressure plate, release levers, springs and cover are shown in their respective positions in Fig. 11-7.

Fig. 11-7. Clutch units in their relative positions. Arrows indicate balance marks that must be aligned when assembling. (American Motors)

CLUTCH RELEASE LEVER OPERATING MECHANISM

Another essential part of the clutch is the release lever operating mechanism. This consists of a ball bearing referred to as a "throw-out" bearing. This bearing is mounted on a sleeve or collar that slides back and forth on a hub that is an integral part of the transmission front bearing retainer.

The throw-out bearing is filled with grease at the factory and ordinarily need not be serviced during its useful life. Another type throw-out bearing that is used on many foreign cars is the graphite type. This type employs a ring of graphite to press against a smooth plate fastened to the clutch levers. Fig. 11-8.

Fig. 11-8. Clutch throw-out bearings. A—Ball bearing type. B—Graphite type.

The throw-out bearing sleeve is moved in and out by a throw-out fork. This fork is usually pivoted on a ball head stud. A return spring pulls the fork back toward the transmission. Fig. 11-9.

When the free end of the throw-out fork is pulled rearward, the inner end will push the throw-out bearing against the clutch release levers. If sufficient pressure is applied to the fork, the release levers will draw the pressure plate back, releasing the clutch disc. As the throw-out bearing contacts the whirling release fingers, the bearing will rotate. The sleeve is held still by the clutch throw-out fork. The action of the entire throw-out assembly is shown in Fig. 11-10.

Fig. 11-9. Clutch throw-out fork. Fork engages throw-out bearing, pivots on ball stud.

Fig. 11-10. Clutch throw-out assembly. When clutch throw-out fork is moved in direction A, throw-out bearing is moved in direction B. When throw-out contacts release levers, pressure plate will retract. When clutch throw-out fork is fully released, there must be clearance at C to prevent bearing from being turned constantly by whirling levers.

CLUTCH HOUSING AND INPUT SHAFT (CLUTCH SHAFT)

The clutch housing, made of cast iron or aluminum, bolts onto the engine. The housing surrounds the flywheel and clutch mechanism. The bottom section of some housings is open, while other housings form a complete enclosure. Housings usually have openings in them to allow circulation of air to cool the clutch. The transmission can either bolt to the housing, or be an integral part of it.

The transmission input shaft passes through the clutch mechanism, and its outboard (outer) end is supported by the clutch pilot bearing. The shaft is splined near the end, and the clutch disc rides on it at this point. Fig. 11-11.

Fig. 11-11. Clutch housing and input shaft, showing flywheel, clutch disc and hub. Remainder of clutch mechanism is now shown. This housing forms full enclosure. Notice how outboard end of input shaft is supported by pilot bearing pressed into flywheel.

COMPLETE ASSEMBLY

Fig. 11-12 shows the entire clutch mechanism in an exploded view. Notice the use of the graphite throw-out bearing and the full enclosure clutch housing. The transmission input shaft is not shown.

Fig. 11-13 pictures a cross section of a clutch fully assembled. The transmission clutch shaft is shown in place. Both pilot and throw-out use the antifriction ball bearing setup.

HOW DOES A CLUTCH WORK?

Remember that the flywheel, clutch cover, release levers and pressure plate all revolve as a single unit. The transmission input shaft and the clutch disc are splined together, forming another unit.

The only time the clutch disc will turn (car standing still) is when it is pinched between the flywheel and pressure plate. When the release levers draw the pressure plate away from the flywheel, the clutch disc

1—Flywheel.
2—Locating pin.
3—Clutch plate with lining.
4—Pressure plate.
5—Release lever pin.
6—Release lever retainer.
7—Release lever.
8—Release lever plate.
9—Pressure plate spring.
10—Clutch cover.
11—Cover bolt.
12—Fork and lever seal.

13—Retaining plate screw.
14—Release bearing.
15—Release bearing retainer spring.
16—Seal retaining plate.
17—Fork and lever thrust washer.
18—Fork and lever shaft bushing.
19—Clutch fork and lever.
20—Fork and lever shaft bushing.
21—Fork and lever thrust washer.
22—Clutch to gearbox bolt.
23—Starter cover screw.
24—Cover.

25—Clutch to gearbox bolt.
26—Split pin for drain hole.
27—Clutch housing.
28—Fork and lever shaft.
29—Taper pin.
30—Eyebolt nut.
31—Release lever strut.
32—Eyebolt.
33—Anti-rattle spring.
34—Flywheel to crankshaft bolt.
35—Lockwashers.

Fig. 11-12. Exploded view—clutch assembly. Only one release lever is shown—there are three. Number of springs used will vary from five to seven in average clutch. (British-Leyland)

will stand still while everything else continues to revolve. When the pressure plate travels back toward the flywheel, the disc is seized and forced to turn the transmission input shaft. Fig. 11-14.

1—Engine flywheel.
2—Drive disc.
3—Pressure plate.
4—Eye bolt.
5—Strut.
6—Anti-rattle spring.
7—Release lever pin.
8—Adjusting nut.
9—Release lever.
10—Release bearing and support assembly.
11—Trans. drive gear bearing retainer.
12—Release fork ball stud.
13—Retainer.
14—Clutch release fork.
15—Pressure spring.
16—Cover.
17—Input shaft.
18—Engine crankshaft.
19—Pilot bearing.

Fig. 11-13. Cross section—assembled clutch. Study this and learn names of clutch parts. (GMC)

DIFFERENT PRESSURE PLATE SPRING

Instead of a number of coil springs, another type of clutch uses a diaphragm type spring. General clutch construction is the same. The basic difference is in the pressure plate spring.

The diaphragm spring is round and quite thin. It is made of high quality, heat-treated steel. It is constructed with a dished profile to produce the necessary spring effect. A number of fingers radiate from the center where they terminate in a solid edge.

Fig. 11-14. Clutch operation—simplified. A—Flywheel, pressure plate, springs, and clutch cover are revolving. Clutch disc and clutch shaft are stopped as pressure plate is disengaged. B—Pressure plate engaged—seizes clutch disc and entire unit revolves.

261

One application cuts six of the fingers somewhat shorter to assist in cooling. The remaining twelve are left full length. Fig. 11-15. Another version bends the six fingers upward. Weights are attached and they produce a centrifugal effect to assist spring pressure at high rpm.

The outer edge of the diaphragm engages the pressure plate. The fingers point inward and dish out slightly. Two pivot rings are placed a short distance from the outer edge. The pivot rings are secured by means of a stud to the clutch cover. One pivot ring is on the outside of the diaphragm, one on the inside.

The pressure plate is driven by three double spring steel straps. The straps are riveted to the cover and bolted to the pressure plate.

The throw-out bearing contacts the ends of the fingers. The fingers then act in the place of release levers, Fig. 11-16. A cutaway view of a diaphragm clutch arrangement is illustrated in Fig. 11-17.

Fig. 11-17. Cutaway of complete clutch assembly. This unit employs a diaphragm spring. (Plymouth)

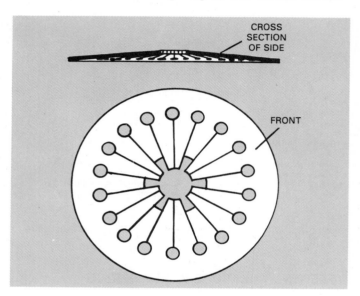

Fig. 11-15. Diaphragm spring. Note short fingers for cooling.

1—Pilot bearing.
2—Facing.
3—Disc.
4—Facing.
5—Dampener spring plate rivet.
6—Dampener spring outer plate.
7—Driven member stop pin.
8—Dampener spring.
9—Dampener spring plate.
10—Pressure plate.
11—Retracting spring bolt.
12—Pressure plate retracting spring.
13—Spring pivot ring.
14—Clutch spring.
15—Spring retainer bolt.
16—Spring retainer bolt nut.
17—Spring pivot ring.
18—Throw-out fork.
19—Release bearing and support assembly.
20—Fork ball head stud.
21—Ball retainer.
22—Cover.

Fig. 11-16. Exploded view—diaphragm spring clutch. This type of clutch uses fingers of diaphragm to act as release levers.

HOW DIAPHRAGM CLUTCH WORKS

When the throw-out bearing applies pressure to the diaphragm fingers, the entire diaphragm is bent inward. The action can best be described as the same sort of effect as squeezing the bottom of an oil can. The inner pivot ring prevents the outer edge of the diaphragm from moving inward, so when the center of the diaphragm is pressed inward, the outer edges pivot outward. When the fingers are released, the diaphragm resumes its original position. Study Fig. 11-18 which demonstrates diaphragm action.

Fig. 11-19 shows the position of the diaphragm when the clutch is engaged. Notice how the fingers point outward, causing the diaphragm to pivot on the outer pivot ring. This action presses the diaphragm outer edge tightly against the pressure plate. The clutch disc is held firmly.

Now study Fig. 11-20. The throw-out bearing has pressed the fingers in. The diaphragm now pivots on inner pivot ring, and the outer edges lift the pressure plate away from the clutch disc. The disc is free and the clutch is disengaged.

Pressure plate, cover and diaphragm assembly are pictured in Fig. 11-21. A complete diaphragm clutch assembly is shown in Fig. 11-22.

Fig. 11-18. Diaphragm spring action. Dotted line shows diaphragm in disengaged position. Notice how outer edge moves back and forth, depending on position of fingers. (Chevrolet)

Fig. 11-20. Diaphragm spring clutch in disengaged position. Throw-out bearing has bent clutch diaphragm fingers inward. This pulls outer edge back, retracting pressure plate and leaving clutch disc free. (Chevrolet)

Fig. 11-19. Diaphragm spring clutch in engaged position. Disc is pinched between pressure plate and flywheel. Note spring pressure produced by diaphragm at outer edges. (Chevrolet)

Fig. 11-21. Diaphragm clutch pressure plate assembly. Arrows indicate retracting springs and fasteners. (Chevrolet)

Fig. 11-22. Cutaway of a diaphragm clutch. Note use of clutch flex cable to operate throw-out fork. Learn part names and locations. (Volvo)

OTHER TYPES OF CLUTCHES

There have been a great number of clutches designed and used over the years. The two shown in this chapter completely dominate the automotive field today. Some heavy-duty type car and truck clutches utilize extra springs and two clutch discs with a second pressure plate, smooth on both sides, sandwiched between them.

CLUTCH PEDAL LINKAGE

There are two principle methods used to actuate the clutch throw-out fork. One system incorporates the use of links, levers and rods or cables connected between the clutch pedal and throw-out fork. When the pedal is depressed, the force is transmitted to the fork. Fig. 11-23 illustrates a fairly simple hookup.

The other system utilizes hydraulic control of the fork. On many cars, due to design, the mechanical linkage required to operate the fork would be extremely complicated. The hydraulic control simplifies the job.

Fig. 11-23. One mechanical clutch linkage arrangement. When clutch pedal is depressed, clutch throw-out fork is actuated. (Plymouth)

264

When the clutch is depressed, it actuates a small master cylinder. Fig. 11-24. The pressure created in the master cylinder is transmitted to a "slave" cylinder bolted near the fork. The slave cylinder is connected to the fork with a short adjustable rod. When pressure is applied to the slave cylinder, it operates the fork. An exploded view of one type of hydraulically operated clutch setup is shown in Fig. 11-25.

Both master and slave units are of simple design. Regardless of position or obstructions, they are easily connected with hydraulic tubing. The principles of hydraulics will be discussed in the chapter on BRAKES.

SELF-ADJUSTING CLUTCH

Some vehicles employ the use of a SELF-ADJUSTING CLUTCH linkage setup.

The self-adjusting mechanism used with a mechanical arrangement is generally attached to the clutch pedal and mounting bracket, Fig. 11-26. The cable that is used with this clutch cannot be made shorter or longer by cutting.

The position of the clutch cable may be altered by adjusting the position of the quadrant (toothed type ratchet) in relation to the clutch pedal. This unit keeps proper cable tension and makes adjustments as the clutch lining wears down. The pawl is shown in engagement with the quadrant teeth in Fig. 11-26.

When the clutch pedal is in the normal driving posi-

Fig. 11-24. Hydraulic clutch control. Clutch pedal movement builds pressure in the master cylinder that in turn actuates the slave cylinder. (Toyota)

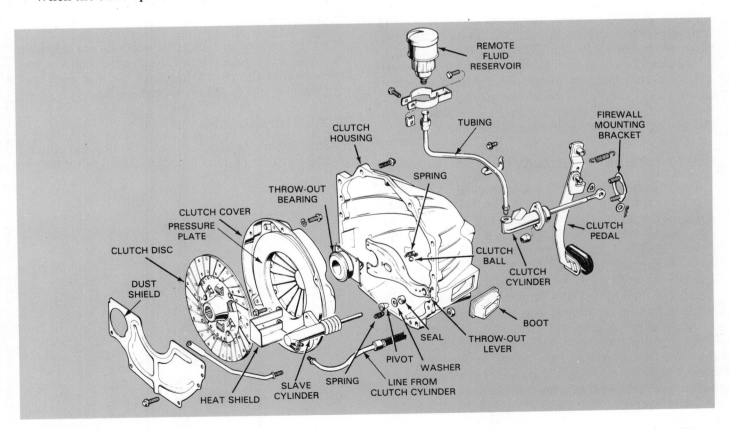

Fig. 11-25. Exploded view of clutch assembly. This unit uses a hydraulic piston to actuate throw-out lever. (AMC)

Fig. 11-26. Self-adjusting clutch mechanism. Note teeth on quadrant and pawl. (Oldsmobile)

Fig. 11-27. Exploded view of a self-adjusting clutch setup. Note clutch cable and how it is attached to quadrant. (Oldsmobile)

tion (not depressed), the pawl is held away from the quadrant with a metal stop located on the bracket. In this position, the quadrant hub spring works against the spring force being applied at the throw-out (release) bearing. The cable is now in a "balanced" state with correct tension being applied.

As the clutch pedal is depressed, the pawl will travel away from the metal stop. At this point, the pawl spring will push the pawl down and into engagement with the quadrant teeth. Continued depression of the pedal pulls on the cable, which in turn, forces the throw-out bearing against the fingers or levers in the pressure plate, releasing the clutch.

As the pedal is released, the quadrant returns to its resting position and the pawl is disengaged from the quadrant by the metal stop. The cable is once again in a "balanced" state of even tension. As the lining wears off the clutch disc, the pawl will engage a different tooth on the quadrant, providing proper compensation for the "extra travel." Fig. 11-27 shows an exploded view of a self-adjusting cable system.

CLUTCH PEDAL "FREE TRAVEL"

Free travel of the clutch pedal is most important. When the clutch pedal is released, the throw-out bearing must not touch the release levers. It must clear for two reasons. As long as it touches, it will continue to rotate. This will shorten its useful life. Also, if the throw-out bearing is not fully released, it may bear against the release levers hard enough to partially disengage the clutch. Any removal of pressure plate force will cause the clutch to slip. When slippage occurs, the clutch facing will overheat and burn up.

All manufacturers specify the amount of free travel that must be allowed. Free travel, or pedal travel, means how far the clutch pedal can be depressed before the throw-out bearing strikes the release levers.

Free travel is easy to check. Depress the clutch with one finger. You will find that it moves very easily for about an inch or inch and a half. It will then seem to

strike something, and you will have to push harder to move it past this point. The hard point was where the release levers and throw-out bearing made contact.

The distance you moved the pedal from the full out position until it became hard to push is the free travel. Free travel is set by adjusting the clutch linkage. Do not adjust the clutch assembly. Fig. 11-28.

CLUTCH COOLING

By their very nature, clutches generate considerable heat. You will notice that all clutch covers have openings and that the clutch housings are also provided with openings to facilitate air circulation.

RIDING THE CLUTCH

Some drivers develop the habit "riding the clutch" (resting left foot on clutch pedal). The natural weight

Fig. 11-28. Clutch free travel. Follow manufacturer's recommended setting.

of the leg will cause the throw-out bearing to strike the release levers. Any additional pressure may even cause the clutch to slip. Clutch pedals are to be used only when needed. Keep foot off!

WILL A CLUTCH EXPLODE?

Clutches in racing and other competition engines can, and sometimes do, explode. The high rpm sets up tremendous centrifugal forces. If the clutch fails, parts are thrown outward in a violent fashion. The clutch housing will be shattered and the driver endangered.

WARNING!

IN ANY VEHICLE USED FOR COMPETITION, IT IS IMPERATIVE THAT A SCATTER SHIELD BE USED TO PROTECT THE DRIVER IN THE EVENT OF CLUTCH FAILURE!

A scatter shield is a piece of heavy steel plate that covers the clutch housing. It should extend down the sides to prevent parts from striking anyone standing nearby. It must be bolted securely into place.

BE CAREFUL!

NEVER WORK ON A CLUTCH ASSEMBLY, WHEN IN THE CAR, WITHOUT FIRST DISCONNECTING THE BATTERY. OTHERWISE, IF THE STARTER IS ACCIDENTALLY OPERATED, SEVERE DAMAGE COULD BE INFLICTED ON YOUR HANDS.

SUMMARY

A clutch is necessary to assist in smooth starting, shifting gears and allowing the car to be stopped without putting the transmission in neutral.

The clutch is designed to connect or disconnect the transmission of power from one working part to another—in this case, from the engine to the transmission.

Automobile clutches in use today are of the single plate, dry disc type. One type uses coil springs as a means of loading the pressure plate. Another type uses a diaphragm spring.

The flywheel, clutch disc, pressure plate, springs, clutch cover and operating mechanism linkage make up the primary parts of the typical clutch.

In operating position (engaged), the clutch disc is held firmly between the flywheel and pressure plate. When the flywheel turns, the disc turns the transmission input shaft to which it is splined.

To disengage the clutch, the clutch pedal is depressed. Either through mechanical or hydraulic linkage, the throw-out fork pushes the throw-out bearing into contact with the pressure plate release levers. The levers draw the pressure plate away from the clutch disc to release it. When the disc is freed, the flywheel and pressure plate assembly continue to rotate, even through the disc and input shaft are not moving.

There are two principal types of throw-out bearings, the ball bearing type and the graphite type. Most cars use the ball bearing type.

The clutch disc is designed to assist in smooth engagement by torsion springs in the hub assembly as well as cupped segments to which the friction facing is riveted.

Clutch free pedal should be adjusted according to the manufacturer's specifications. Some clutches are self-adjusting. The others must be manually (by hand) adjusted as lining wears down. Never ride the clutch. Study the cutaway of the clutch-transmission assembly in Fig. 11-29.

KNOW THESE TERMS

Flywheel, Clutch disc, Pressure plate, Release lever, Input shaft, Clutch diaphragm, Clutch springs, Clutch linkage, Free travel, Clutch explosion.

REVIEW QUESTIONS—CHAPTER 11

Every chapter in this book is an important link in your chain of learning. Remember: A CHAIN IS NO STRONGER THAN ITS WEAKEST LINK!

KNOW the answers to the following questions:
1. Define the word clutch.
2. What are the three main uses of the clutch?
3. Name the major parts that make up the clutch.
4. Of what use is the pressure plate?
5. What is the clutch disc?
6. What part does the flywheel play in the clutch assembly?
7. Release levers are pivoted on an _____ bolt.
8. Two types of springs are used to load the pressure plate. Name them.
9. The clutch cover is bolted to the _____.
10. The pressure plate is driven by the _____.
11. Name two types of throw-out bearings.
12. What is the semi-centrifugal release lever?
13. The _____ operates the throw-out bearing.
14. What are the two ways of actuating the throw-out fork?
15. Explain the operation of the diaphragm spring.
16. What kind of release levers are used in the diaphragm clutch?
17. What is clutch pedal free travel?
18. How is free travel adjusted?
19. Even though most competition engines use heavy-duty "beefed up" clutches, what additional unit must be installed to safeguard driver and spectators?
20. Working on the clutch, while in the car, can be dangerous. It is wise to always _____

Fig. 11-29. Cutaway of a complete clutch and manual transmission assembly. (Peugeot)

before starting the job.

21. Most clutches have aligning punch marks. What are they for?
22. What is meant by riding the clutch?
23. What is the transmission input shaft?
24. How is the outboard end of the transmission input shaft supported?
25. What are splines?
26. What two parts of the clutch and transmission are splined together?
27. Of what use is the clutch housing?
28. Explain how the clutch disc is designed to assist in

smooth clutch engagement.

29. From what type material is the facing used on the clutch disc made?
30. Explain HOW a clutch works during engagement and disengagement—step by step, naming the parts involved and their function.
31. What is meant by the term "self-adjusting" clutch?
32. The hydraulic type clutch linkage works in a similar fashion to that of automobile brakes. True or False?

Chapter 12

MANUAL TRANSMISSIONS AND TRANSFER CASES

After studying this chapter, you will be able to:
■ Explain how a manual transmission operates.
■ Describe the operating principles of a transfer case.
■ Identify the basic parts of a manual transmission.
■ Name the components of a transfer case.
■ Trace power flow through transmission gears.

The average engine would have power enough to operate a car without a transmission provided the car operated on reasonably level roads and maintained sufficient speed. When the car must be started from a standstill, or when attempting to negotiate steep grades, the engine would not provide sufficient power and the car would stall.

Much less torque is required to move a car rolling on level ground than is necessary to drive the same car up a steep hill. Fig. 12-1.

THE ENGINE NEEDS HELP

To enable the engine to increase torque to the drive line, it is obvious that a torque multiplier (transmission) is needed. Fig. 12-2.

Fig. 12-1. Torque required—car on level ground. Torque is the twisting force on axle—as shown by hand. (Chevrolet)

Fig. 12-2. Torque required—car on steep grade. Original amount of torque is now insufficient, so it is necessary to increase torque by means of a torque converter or multiplier. The twisting force of hand is multiplied through use of transmission gears. (Chevrolet)

By using a torque multiplier, it is possible to adapt the available power of the engine to meet changing road and load conditions.

HOW IS TORQUE MULTIPLIED?

If you (an engine) exerted all your strength (power) and still failed to lift a certain object (drive a car), you could multiply your strength by using a lever and fulcrum, Fig. 12-3.

If you weigh 200 lbs. and get on the lever 5 ft. from the fulcrum, a force of 1,000 ft.-lbs. will be exerted. Then, if a weight of 500 lbs. is placed on the other end of the lever 1 ft. from the fulcrum, it would exert a force of 500 ft.-lbs. By using a simple torque converter or multiplier, you can now raise 500 lbs. with ease. How much weight could you raise in Fig. 12-4?

If you weigh 200 lbs. and want to lift 4,000 lbs. you would have to stand 20 ft. from the fulcrum. In order to raise the weight a short distance, it is mandatory

Fig. 12-3. Lever and fulcrum. Weight of 200 lbs. at A will raise weight of 500 lbs. at B because original weight is multiplied by using a lever and fulcrum.

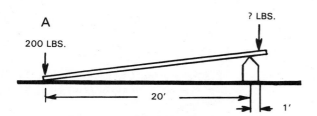

Fig. 12-4. Problem: If you are standing on the lever at A, how much weight will you be able to lift?

Fig. 12-5. Lever travel. If the speed with which you depress the lever remains constant, the more you multiply your strength and the slower the weight will rise. To raise 4,000 lbs., it is necessary to depress the lever 20 ft. to raise the weight 1 ft.

Fig. 12-6. Principle of gear torque multiplication. The larger the driven gear in relation to the driving gear, the greater the torque multiplication. As torque is increased, driving gear must turn more times to turn driven gear once.

that you depress the end of the lever a distance 20 times as much as the distance the weight has been raised. See Fig. 12-5.

You will note that as your (engine's) strength (torque) is increased, the speed with which the weight (car) is moved becomes slower. This is true, since you will find it necessary to depress the lever a greater distance as you move farther from the fulcrum.

From a study of this simple lever and fulcrum, it is possible to make these deductions:

1. If the speed of an engine remains constant and its torque is multiplied, the engine will lift more weight but will take longer to do it.
2. If the speed of an engine remains constant and its torque is reduced, it will lift less weight but will lift it faster.

Therefore, as engine torque multiplication increases, the car road speed will decrease and as torque multiplication decreases, the car road speed will increase—engine rpm remaining constant.

TORQUE MULTIPLICATION THROUGH GEARS

The same principle used in the lever and fulcrum example is used in automotive transmission gears. Consider the fulcrum as the car drive shaft; the amount of weight to be lifted as the torque required to turn the shaft; the engine torque as the person's weight; the body of the gear as the lever. Then it is easy to see how the gear multiples the torque. Fig. 12-6 shows this principle.

You can see that as the size of the gear is increased, the same amount of pressure on a tooth will produce an increase in torque. In A, Fig. 12-6, the driving gear tooth is 1 ft. from the center of the shaft. If it were pushing down with a 200 lb. force, the driving tooth

would be exerting a 200 ft. lb. push on the tooth of the driven gear. As the driven tooth is 4 ft. from the center of the drive shaft, it would exert an 800 ft. lb. force on the drive shaft. In B, the force of the driving gear would be the same, but as the driven tooth is now 2 ft. from the center, it would exert a force of only 400 ft. lbs. on the drive shaft.

TRANSMISSION GEAR RATIOS

The average car transmission provides the driver with a choice of three forward speeds: DIRECT

DRIVE (no torque multiplication), SECOND GEAR (approximate ratio of 2 to 1) and a LOW GEAR (approximate ratio of 3 to 1). By selecting one of the ratios, it is possible to operate the car under all normal conditions.

Ratios vary from car to car, depending on engine horsepower and car weight. A reverse gear is also incorporated. The reverse ratio is about the same as the low gear. (Engine turns three times to transmission output shaft once.)

Torque is multiplied even more through the differential gears. This will be discussed in a later chapter.

Many cars are equipped with four and five-speed transmissions to provide even a wider range of gear ratios. A typical four-speed ratio could be: 1st gear, 2.52 to 1; 2nd gear, 1.88 to 1; 3rd gear, 1.46 to 1; 4th gear, 1.00 to 1; reverse 2.59 to 1. A typical five-speed transmission ratio could be: 1st gear, 3.287 to 1; 2nd gear, 2.043 to 1; 3rd gear, 1.394 to 1; 4th gear, 1.00 to 1 (direct drive, one to one); 5th gear, 0.853 to 1 (acts as an overdrive).

TRANSMISSION GEARS

Transmission gears are made of high quality steel, carefully heat-treated to produce smooth, hard surface gear teeth with a softer but very tough interior. They are drop-forged (machine hammered into shape) while red hot. The teeth and other critical areas are cut on precision machinery.

The teeth on transmission gears are of two principal types, spur and helical. The helical gear is superior in that it runs more quietly and is stronger because more tooth area is in contact. Helical gears must be mounted firmly, since there is a tendency for them to slide apart due to the spiral shape. Fig. 12-7.

There must be some clearance between the gear teeth to allow for lubrication, expansion and possible size irregularity. This clearance is very small (a few thousandths of an inch). Fig. 12-8 illustrates backlash (clearance between face and flank areas) and also gives gear tooth nonmenclature.

There are many other types of gears. Those that are used on the automobile will be discussed where they apply to a unit under study.

TRANSMISSION CONSTRUCTION AND OPERATION

A typical transmission consists of a cast iron or an aluminum housing, four shafts, bearings, gears, synchronizing device and a shifting mechanism. Fig. 12-9 shows the four shafts and bearings in their relative positions in the housing.

To show how the transmission works, the four shafts with gears are shown in Fig. 12-10. By studying the illustration, you will see that the transmission is in neutral. Notice that the input or clutch shaft is turning, but the output or main shaft is standing still. Also note that the input shaft gear is always driving

Fig. 12-8. Elementary gear tooth nomenclature. Pitch line or pitch diameter is true diameter used in calculating exact ratios. Outside circle is full diameter of gear. Root circle is minimum diameter of gear.

Fig. 12-7. Gear tooth shapes. A—Helical. This tooth is cut at an angle to the centerline of the gear. B-Spur. Cut straight across (parallel to gear centerline). C—Left side, helical; right side, spur. (Land-Rover)

Fig. 12-9. Housing shafts and bearings. 1—Clutch pilot bearing. 2—Input shaft bearing. 3—Input shaft. 4—Countershaft supported in housing. 5—Countershaft. 6—Reverse idler shaft supported in housing. 7—Housing. 8—Output shaft roller bearing. 9—Output shaft. 10—Output shaft ball bearing. 11—Input shaft gear teeth. Input and output shafts turn. Countershaft and reverse idler shaft remain fixed.

271

Fig. 12-10. Transmission in neutral. Input shaft 13, is revolving. Input gear 1 is driving entire cluster gear. Cluster gear 8 is driving reverse idler gear 7. Output shaft 6 is not moving as both sliding low and reverse gear 5 and sliding high and second gear 4 are in neutral positions. 2—Splined stub. 3—Splined recess on sliding gear 4. 6—Output shaft is splined to allow gears to be shifted back and forth. 8—Cluster reverse idler gear. 9—Cluster low gear. 10—Cluster second gear. 11—All cluster gears connected to this cluster body. 12—Large constant mesh cluster gear. 14—Countershaft. 15—Cluster bearing.

the counter or cluster gear. The cluster gear revolves on roller bearings.

The cluster gear assembly has four gears all cut on the same steel blank. They are: large gear—drive gear, next in size—second speed gear, next—low speed gear, smallest—reverse gear. When the input shaft is turning, the cluster gear also turns, but in an opposite or counter direction.

The reverse idler gear turns when the cluster gear is turning. The reverse idler rides on a bushing between it and the reverse idler shaft. There are two gears that are always in contact; input shaft gear and cluster drive gear; cluster reverse gear and reverse idler gear. These are called constant mesh gears.

The output shaft is splined and two gears are placed on it. Both gears are free to move back and forth on the splines. The smaller of the two is the second speed gear. Notice that it has a splined recess in its face. This splined recess is designed to slip over a splined stub protruding from the input shaft. Notice the action of this splined recess when the transmission is placed in high gear. Fig. 12-13.

The larger sliding gear is the low and reverse gear. It can be shifted into mesh with either the reverse idler gear or the low cluster gear. Study Fig. 12-10, and trace the flow of power (indicated by arrows).

FIRST OR LOW GEAR

The clutch is depressed, thus releasing the clutch disc. The input shaft and cluster gear will stop turning. The output sliding low gear is shifted forward, and meshed with the cluster low gear. The output second gear is left out of mesh.

When the clutch is engaged, the input shaft will turn the cluster gear. The cluster gear will revolve at a slower speed. The cluster low gear, being smaller than

the output shaft low sliding gear, will turn the output shaft at even a slower speed. The output shaft speed will be roughly one-third that of the input shaft, giving a gear reduction of three to one. This reduction multiplies the engine torque but gives less forward speed. Fig. 12-11.

SECOND GEAR

When ready for second gear, the clutch is depressed to break the flow of power from the engine. Low sliding gear is moved to a neutral position, and second sliding gear is meshed with the cluster second gear. The clutch is then released and the flow of power, with less torque multiplication, is resumed.

Notice that the cluster second gear is larger in proportion to the sliding second gear. The gear reduction is now less (around 2 to 1) and torque falls off but speed picks up. Fig. 12-12.

HIGH GEAR

When the car attains sufficient speed, the clutch is again depressed. Sliding second gear is moved forward until the splined recess has slipped over the splined stub on the input shaft. Low sliding gear remains unmeshed. When the clutch is released, the transmission is in high gear with no torque multiplica-

Fig. 12-11. Transmission in low gear. Sliding low and reverse gear has been shifted forward and is meshed with cluster low gear. Output shaft is now turning. All gears that are in mesh with another gear are shown with simulated teeth.

Fig. 12-12. Transmission in second gear. Sliding low gear has returned to neutral position. Sliding second gear moved into mesh with cluster second gear. Output shaft now turns faster.

tion. The input and output shafts are locked together through the splined stub and recessed second gear. This gives direct drive through the transmission. See Fig. 12-13.

REVERSE

The sliding second gear is placed in the neutral position. The low reverse sliding gear is moved back until it engages the reverse idler gear. As the reverse idler is revolving in the same direction as the input shaft, it will impart a reverse rotation to the output shaft. The gear reduction or torque multiplication is comparable to that of the low gear, around three to one. Fig. 12-14.

SYNCHRONIZING MECHANISM

Once the car is in motion, the drive line will turn the output shaft continuously. As a result, the sliding gears will be whirling. When an attempt is made to mesh them with any of the cluster gears (which tend to stop when the clutch is depressed), the gear teeth will be subjected to damaging impact forces. The sound of "grinding" gears, when shifting, results from the sliding gear teeth literally smashing against the cluster gear.

It is obvious that for one gear to mesh with another

quietly and without damage, both gears must be rotating at nearly the same speed. Most transmissions are equipped with a device called a synchronizer. Its job is to move ahead of the unit that is to be meshed, seize the other unit and bring the rotational speed of both units together. Once both units are rotating at the same speed, they may be meshed.

Fig. 12-15 is a simplified version, illustrating the principle of the synchronizing device. A is the input shaft and it is stopped with the clutch disengaged. In order to mesh whirling splined hub B on output shaft C with the splined recess D in input shaft, it will be necessary to start input shaft turning. Notice cone ring E that is an extension of hub B. The ring is supported on pins that fit into holes in the hub. The ring is held out by springs G.

As sliding hub B is moved toward splined recess D, ring E will touch cone-shaped bottom H of recess. As the hub is moved closer to recess, the springs G will force cone ring E tightly against the bottom of cone recess. As the cone ring is whirling, it will impart torque to the input shaft and start it turning. As the hub moves closer, spring pressure increases and cone ring will be jammed into cone recess with enough force to spin input shaft at nearly the same speed of whirling hub B. The hub may then be meshed into recess with no grinding or shock. Fig. 12-15.

The simplified synchronizer as shown in Fig. 12-15, would be for direct (high) drive. By putting a cone ring (called blocking ring or synchronizing cone) on both sides of the hub, Fig. 12-16, it could be shifted

Fig. 12-13. Transmission in high gear. Sliding second gear has moved toward input until splined recess in gear engages splined stub on input shaft. Sliding low gear is in neutral position. Input and output shafts are locked together and drive is direct.

Fig. 12-14. Transmission in reverse gear. Sliding second gear has returned to neutral. Low and reverse sliding gear are meshed with reverse idler gear. Output shaft now rotates in a reverse direction. Ratio is about same as low gear.

Fig. 12-15. Simplified synchronizer. As clutch hub B is shifted toward splined recess D, cone ring E will strike cone recess and spin input shaft. Hub B is then meshed into splined recess D without grinding. Cone ring pins and springs are forced into clutch hub.

the other way and engage splined recess in the output shaft second gear. For this arrangement, the second gear would no longer be a sliding gear and would not be splined to the output shaft.

The second gear would become a constant mesh gear and would be turned whenever the cluster gear is revolving. It would rotate on the output shaft either on a bushing or roller bearings. Fig. 12-16.

When high gear is desired, the sliding clutch hub would be shifted into the input shaft recess as shown in Fig. 12-15. For second gear, the clutch hub would be shifted back until meshed with the second gear. When the hub engages the second gear, the output shaft would be locked, through the clutch hub, to the second gear; and the output shaft would be driven by the cluster second speed gear driving the locked output shaft second gear. Both shifts would be quiet, as the synchronizer would equalize or synchronize their speeds before meshing. Fig. 12-16.

Study the synchronizer illustrated in Fig. 12-17. This popular type, splines the hub to the shaft but does not permit end movement of the hub. The clutch sleeve is shifted forward or backward on the hub. This action forces (by means of inserts) the blocking rings to equalize gear speeds before the clutch sleeve engages the other gear to lock gear to hub through clutch sleeve.

Low gear is generally used for starting. Since gears are stopped when the car is not in motion and the clutch is depressed, synchronizing the low gear is not absolutely necessary. Current practice, however, is toward full synchronization for all forward gears. This permits low or first gear to be engaged while the vehicle is still in motion.

Fig. 12-17. One popular type of synchronizer unit. Hub is splined to output shaft. Clutch sleeve moves back or forth on hub as needed to connect hub with proper gear.   (Ford)

VARIOUS TYPES OF SYNCHRONIZER DEVICES

There are several types of synchronizer units used today. All use a cone (blocking ring) that precedes the movement of either the clutch hub or, in many cases, the clutch sleeve. The cone engages a tapered surface on the part to be engaged to synchronize the speed before meshing.

As you study the transmissions in this section, determine what type of synchronizer is used and how it works.

THREE-SPEED SYNCHROMESH TRANSMISSION

NEUTRAL

Fig. 12-18 shows a typical synchromesh transmission in neutral. Notice that the input shaft drives the cluster gear, which in turn drives the constant mesh second speed gear. As the second gear turns on the output shaft, no power is transmitted. This transmission uses the strut-type synchronizer. Notice that the clutch sleeve is in a neutral position. The sliding low and reverse gear is also in a neutral position.

LOW GEAR

Fig. 12-19 illustrates the transmission in low or first gear. The clutch sleeve is still in the neutral position, but the sliding low and reverse gear has been shifted into mesh with the cluster low gear. Power is transmitted (follow arrows) from the input shaft to cluster, to sliding low gear, to output shaft.

SECOND GEAR

Fig. 12-20 shows the transmission in second gear. The sliding gear has been moved to a neutral position. Notice that the clutch sleeve has been shifted back, until it engages the splines or small teeth on the second gear. As the clutch sleeve is splined to the clutch hub which, in turn, is splined to the output shaft, the second gear is locked to the output shaft. The input shaft drives the cluster gear, the cluster drives the second speed gear, and the second speed gear drives the output shaft through the clutch sleeve and hub.

Fig. 12-16. Constant mesh second gear with synchromesh in high and second gears. Output shaft second gear 7, is free to rotate on output shaft 10. A roller bearing or bushing is provided at 9. A snap ring 8 keeps second gear from moving back and forth. When synchromesh hub 5 is moved into second gear splines 6, second gear is locked to output. 1—Input shaft. 2—Supported inner end of output shaft. 3—Input splines. 4—Cone synchronizer ring. 11—Cluster second gear. 12—Countershaft. 13—Cluster assembly. 14—Cluster drive gear.

Fig. 12-18. Synchromesh transmission in neutral. Power flow is from input gear to cluster drive gear to output constant mesh second gear. As synchromesh clutch sleeve is in neutral, constant mesh second gear will revolve on output shaft and no power will be transmitted beyond this point. (Pontiac)

Fig. 12-19. Synchromesh transmission in low gear. Power flow is from input gear to cluster drive gear, from cluster low gear to output sliding low and reverse gear. As sliding gear is meshed, power is transmitted to output shaft. (Pontiac)

Fig. 12-20. Synchromesh transmission in second gear. Power flow is from input gear to cluster drive gear. From cluster drive to cluster second gear to constant mesh output second gear. As clutch hub has engaged teeth or splines on second gear, second gear is locked to output and will transmit power. (Pontiac)

HIGH GEAR

Fig. 12-21 shows the transmission in high gear. The sliding gear is still in a neutral position. The clutch sleeve has been shifted away from the second gear and has engaged the small teeth on the input shaft. As this locks the input and output shafts together, the power flow is direct. The cluster is driven and still turns the second gear which is free to turn on the output shaft.

REVERSE GEAR

Fig. 12-22 illustrates the transmission in reverse gear. The clutch sleeve is in the neutral position. The sliding gear has been moved into mesh with the reverse idler gear. The input shaft turns the cluster; the cluster drives the reverse idler; the idler drives the sliding gear in a direction opposite to engine rotation. This will cause the output to drive the car backward.

SHIFT MECHANISM

The transmission is shifted by means of shifter forks that ride in a groove cut into the clutch sleeve and sliding gear. The forks are attached to a cam and shaft assembly. Spring loaded steel balls pop into notches cut in the cam assembly to hold the shift mechanism into whatever gear is selected. The shafts pass through the housing or housing cover and are fastened to shift levers. Fig. 12-23.

The shift levers can be operated via linkage attached to a steering wheel shift control or to a floor shift stick. Some transmissions operate the shift forks by means of a floor shift stick that enters the transmission housing and engages sliding shift fork rails. The shift stick is pivoted in a ball-like assembly. Figs. 12-24, 12-25, and 12-26 illustrate three different shift mechanism arrangements.

Transmissions have also been shifted by means of electric solenoids, oil pressure, and by vacuum. The three shown are in universal use.

COMPLETE TRANSMISSION— CROSS SECTION

Fig. 12-27 illustrates a typical three-speed transmission. Both high and second gear have synchromesh. Notice the bearing locations and the method used to secure all shafts. Second is a constant mesh gear turn-

Fig. 12-21. Synchromesh transmission in high gear. Clutch hub has now engaged splines on the end of input shaft. This will lock input and output shafts together and power is transmitted straight through. Cluster is driven but will not transmit power.   (Pontiac)

Fig. 12-22. Synchromesh transmission in reverse gear. Clutch sleeve has now been returned to a neutral position. Sliding low and reverse gear has been meshed with reverse idler gear. Input gear drives cluster. Cluster drives reverse idler and reverse idler drives output shaft in reverse direction.   (Pontiac)

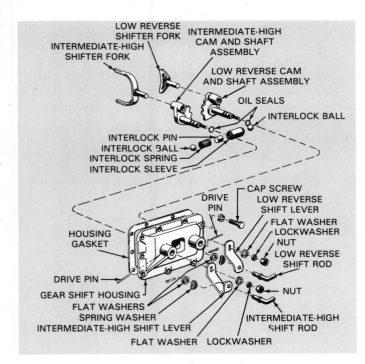

Fig. 12-23. Gearshift housing assembly—exploded view. Shifter forks engage low and reverse sliding gear and clutch sleeve. Forks are actuated by moving shift levers. Each fork must be returned to neutral before other can be moved. This is accomplished by interlock pin. Interlock balls hold cam into whatever position it has been placed. (Mercury)

Fig. 12-24. Steering column gearshift. Study all parts, names, and locations. Note that gearshift lever linkage is inside column.

ing on a bushing on the output or main shaft. Fig. 12-28 illustrates the gear drive positions in a fully synchronized, three-speed transmission.

ASSEMBLED TRANSMISSION—CUTAWAY

The transmission shown in Fig. 12-29 is of a heavy duty, four-speed, fully synchronized design. All gears are in constant mesh, and shifting is accomplished by actuating the sliding clutch sleeves through means of shifter forks.

Fig. 12-25. Four-speed transmission floor shift. Notice use of additional lever to actuate reverse gear. (Chevrolet)

Fig. 12-26. Floor shift. This type of shift mechanism is incorporated into transmission top cover. 1—Shift fork. 2—Shift rail. 3—Shift fork. 4—Shift rail. 5—Slot for end of shift stick. 6—Shift stick end. 7—Pivot ball. 8—Stick. When end of stick 6 enters slot 5, it must be pulled to one side in order to move shift rail. Interlock pin arrangement prevents both rails from moving at once. Each rail, after being shifted, must be returned to neutral before other rail will move. Another setup, consisting of spring-loaded detent balls, holds each rail into whatever gear is selected.

THREE-SPEED TRANSMISSION— EXPLODED VIEW

An exploded view of a three-speed, fully synchronized (all forward speeds) transmission is shown in Fig. 12-30. Study all the parts and their construction. Learn their names.

FOUR-SPEED TRANSMISSION

Fig. 12-31 shows an exploded view of a four-speed transmission. Note that all forward gears are synchronized. Gear teeth are helical cut, with the exception of the reverse sliding gear and rear reverse idler gear. Learn the names, location, and use of all parts. Study

Fig. 12-27. Typical three-speed synchromesh transmission. Note synchronizer construction. Pressure is applied to cones by shifter flange. When pressure reaches a certain point, clutch hub will move into engagement with either high or second gear splines or teeth.   (Dodge)

Fig. 12-28. Gear drive positions in a fully synchronized (all forward gears) transmission. N—Synchronizer clutch sleeve in neutral position.   (Pontiac)

the gear drive positions for various speeds.

See Fig. 12-33 for the gear drive positions of a typical four-speed transmission.

FIVE-SPEED TRANSMISSION

Fig. 12-32 shows a cutaway view of a five-speed transaxle. Fig. 12-34 pictures a standard five-speed transmission. Study the parts and learn their names. An exploded transaxle is shown in Fig. 12-35.

Fig. 12-36 depicts the power flow (red lines) through the various gear ranges of one type of five-speed transmission. Study them carefully.

FOUR-WHEEL DRIVE TRANSFER CASES

Transfer cases are units used on vehicles equipped with four-wheel drive. They provide power to both the front and rear axle assemblies when needed.

There are basically two types of transfer cases,

PART-TIME and FULL-TIME. Figs. 12-37 and 12-45 show an overall view of four-wheel systems.

PART-TIME TRANSFER CASE—CONSTRUCTION

The part-time transfer case housing is made of cast iron or aluminum. Power is transmitted through a series of gears and/or chains. Most incorporate a high and low range, which provides approximately a 1 to 1 (high range) or 2.6 to 1 (low range) gearing arrangement. Fig. 12-38 shows an exploded view of one type of part-time case. Study parts, learn names, and their locations.

PART-TIME TRANSFER CASE—OPERATION

The part-time (normally in 2-wheel drive, in 4-wheel drive part-time) transfer case is generally shifted with a floor mounted lever or levers.

Input torque from the transmission is transmitted

278

1 — Input shaft.
2 — Retaining ring (bearing to shaft).
3 — Retaining ring (bearing to case).
4 — Pilot bearing.
5 — Fourth speed blocker ring.
6 — 3-4 synchronizer.
7 — Third speed synchronizer blocker ring.
8 — Third speed gear.
9 — Second speed gear.
10 — Second speed blocker ring.
11 — 1-2 synchronizer.
12 — Transmission case.
13 — First speed synchronizer blocker ring.

14 — First speed gear.
15 — Rear bearing.
16 — Speedometer gear.
17 — Vent cap.
18 — Output shaft.
19 — Intermediate shifter lever.
20 — Rear oil seal.
21 — Rear extension.
22 — Retaining ring (bearing to shaft).
23 — Belleville washer.
24 — Spacer.
25 — Spacer.
26 — Retaining ring (bearing to extension).
27 — Thrust washer.

28 — Cover screw.
29 — Spacer.
30 — Roller bearing.
31 — Spacer.
32 — Countergear or cluster gear.
33 — Magnet.
34 — Cover.
35 — Spacer.
36 — Roller bearing.
37 — Spacer.
38 — Cluster gear shaft.
39 — Thrust washer.
40 — Input shaft main drive gear bearing.

Fig. 12-29. Cutaway of a fully synchronized four-speed transmission.   (Chevrolet)

through the gear train by the input gear. Fig. 12-39.

When the case is in 2H (2-wheel drive, high range) torque goes from the input gear to the planetary gearset assembly. This assembly revolves as a unit. Torque then flows (red line) to the mainshaft through the planetary carrier that is splined to the mainshaft. From the mainshaft, torque travels to the rear yoke, which is also splined to the mainshaft, then on to the rear drive line and rear axle. Fig. 12-39. In two-wheel drive, high range, the sliding clutch stays in neutral. No torque is flowing to the driven sprocket.

When the case is shifted in 4H (four-wheel drive, high range), input torque from the input gear is transmitted through the mainshaft in the same manner as two-wheel drive, high range. The sliding clutch has now been moved into mesh with the mainshaft clutch gear. Torque now flows through the drive sprocket to the driven sprocket by means of the drive chain.

In that the driven sprocket is attached to the front output shaft, torque now travels to the front drive line and axle setup. Fig. 12-39.

In 4L (four-wheel drive, low range), torque flow through the case is almost identical to four-wheel

drive, high range. The only difference is that the annulus gear is moved into mesh with the lockplate. Because the lockplate is bolted to the case, the annulus gear is held and cannot turn. The planetary pinion gears now rotate about the inside of the annulus gear. This produces a low range gear reduction of about 2.6 to 1. A power flow schematic of a part-time case is pictured in Fig. 12-39.

WARNING! Part-time transfer cases should not be operated in four-wheel drive when on dry, hard surfaced roads.

FULL-TIME TRANSFER CASE—CONSTRUCTION

Unlike the part-time transfer case, this unit delivers power to the front and rear axle assemblies all the time (full-time).

The case is constructed from either aluminum or cast iron. Power is transmitted through a series of gears and a chain.

Most cases include a high and low range. High range is approximately 1 to 1 and low range is 2 to 1. Fig. 12-40 shows an exploded view of a full-time transfer case. Learn part names and locations.

Fig. 12-30. Three-speed transmission—exploded view. (Pontiac)

1—Cover.
2—Cover fastener.
3—Gasket.
4—2nd and 3rd gear shifter fork.
5—Setscrew.
6—Interlock spring.
7—Interlock pin.
8—Shift rail.
9—Setscrew.
10—Shift rail.
11—Interlock pin.
12—1st and reverse gear shifter fork.
13—Setscrew.
14—Shift lever.
15—Seal.
16—Retainer fasteners.
17—Bearing retainer.
18—Seal.
19—Gasket.
20—Shift lever.
21—Pin.
22—Spring.
23—Case.
24—Gasket.
25—Lock washer.
26—Extension to case fastener.

27—Extension housing.
28—Bushing.
29—Seal.
30—Blocking ring.
31—Synchronizer spring.
32—Clutch sleeve.
33—Second and high synchronizer assembly.
34—Synchronizer hub and insert.
35—Spring.
36—Blocking ring.
37—Second gear.
38—First gear.
39—Blocking ring.
40—Spring.
41—Reverse sliding gear and first speed clutch sleeve.
42—First and reverse gear synchronizer assembly.
43—Insert.
44—Spring.
45—Bearing retaining snap ring.
46—Snap ring.
47—Input shaft bearing.
48—Input shaft and main drive gear.
49—Output shaft inner support bearing.
50—Snap ring.
51—Snap ring.

52—Thrust washer.
53—Output shaft.
54—Snap ring.
55—Countershaft.
56—Lock pin.
57—Thrust washer.
58—Thrust washer.
59—Cluster gear bearing.
60—Cluster or counter gear.
61—Cluster gear bearing.
62—Thrust washer.
63—Thrust washer.
64—Snap ring.
65—Snap ring.
66—Snap ring.
67—Snap ring.
68—Output shaft bearing.
69—Speedometer drive gear.
70—Seal.
71—Reverse idler gear bushing.
72—Reverse idler.
73—Bushing.
74—Thrust washer.
75—Reverse idler shaft.
76—Thrust washer.
77—Lock pin.

FULL-TIME TRANSFER CASE—OPERATION

This particular full-time transfer case features a differential unit that is somewhat like a drive axle differential. It compensates for the different speeds between the front and rear axles which is caused during turning and driving over irregular surfaced terrain. By compensating for these different items, the case will permit the vehicle to be continuously operated (in four-wheel drive) on hard and dry surfaced highways. For more information on how the differential works, see Chapter 16.

Fig. 12-31. Four-speed transmission—exploded view. This transmission provides synchromesh for 1st, 2nd, 3rd, and 4th gear. In this synchronizer design, synchronizer hub does not move. When clutch hub sleeve is shifted, it forces cone-shaped blocking ring with it. Blocking ring engages other part on a similar taper and synchronizes the two. Additional pressure on clutch sleeve causes it to slip on clutch hub inserts (these are what move blocking rings) and it engages splines on other part. When disengaged, it snaps back into notch in middle of hub inserts, causing them to release pressure on blocking ring. Learn names of all parts. Study them and be certain you know their functions. Note vent to allow air to escape, or to enter, as transmission heats up and cools down. (Ford)

OTHER TRANSFER CASE DESIGNS

QUADRA-TRAC

Quadra-Trac can have high and low range, a neutral position, and four-wheel lock position to be used when the vehicle is immobile because of excessive wheel spin.

This transfer case allows full-time operation in four-wheel drive. The differential assembly consists of a side gear, rear output shaft and a viscous coupling (a torque biasing limited slip unit) and differential pinion gear unit. This differential also operates like a standard differential. Fig. 12-41 illustrates an exploded view of a Quadra-Trac case.

Power flow through the Quadra-Trac unit can be seen in Fig. 12-42. Study it carefully.

SELECT DRIVE TRANSFER CASE

This particular transfer case is designed to be used on some cars equipped with four-wheel drive. The unit is pictured in Fig. 12-43.

The select drive case allows fully differentiated four-wheel drive and also two-wheel drive. The driver may select either two-wheel, or four-wheel drive by means of a mode selector.

The mode selector is a vacuum switch, which allows the driver to engage or disengage the front drive axle and transfer case by means of two vacuum shift

Fig. 12-32. Cutaway view of a five-speed transaxle assembly. Note differential and drive axle assembly. (Mazda)

Fig. 12-33. Gear drive positions in a typical four-speed transmission. Forward gears are all synchronized. (Buick)

282

motors. An overall view of the select drive vacuum control system is shown in Fig. 12-44.

SUMMARY

The engine must have a transmission (torque multiplier) to adapt its available torque to meet changing road and load conditions. See Fig. 12-45.

Torque multiplication is accomplished through the use of transmission gears. By arranging a movable set of various sized gears, it is possible to secure any reasonable degree of torque multiplication.

Most transmissions give four or five forward gear ratios and one reverse.

Transmissions are generally equipped with helical gears to assure longer life and quieter operation. One gear (low) may be of the sliding type, or all forward gears may be of constant mesh design. A synchromesh unit is designed to provide smooth gear shifting without clashing or grinding. The transmission consists of the input and output shaft assemblies, the cluster gear and the reverse idler assembly. All are housed in a strong steel or aluminum housing. The gears are selected either by a floor shift or steering wheel column shift control.

The shafts revolve on roller and ball bearings. The second speed gear and reverse idler gear are sometimes mounted on bronze bushings. The input and output shafts are secured by means of snap rings and bearing retainers. End play in the cluster gear is controlled by the use of bronze and steel thrust washers.

The transmission housing can be bolted to the clutch housing or cast as an integral part.

The transmission housing often acts as a base for the rear engine mount.

The transmission is lubricated by filling the housing partially full of heavy transmission gear oil. As the gears whirl, they throw the oil to lubricate all parts. Leakage is controlled by oil seals at both front and rear ends.

NOTE:

When shifting the transmission, it is wise to hesitate in the neutral range for a brief moment. The synchromesh unit depends upon a limited amount of friction to synchronize the speeds. By hesitating a moment, and then shoving the stick smoothly into the desired gear, the synchromesh unit will have time

Fig. 12-34. Cutaway view of a Peugeot five-speed transmission. Note two-piece housing and shifting linkage arrangement. (Peugeot)

1.	CLUTCH AND DIFF. HOUSING	
2.	CLUTCH SHAFT BUSHING	
3.	INPUT SHAFT OIL SEAL	
4.	DRIVE SHAFT OIL SEAL	
5.	STRAIGHT KNOCK PIN	
6.	TRANSAXLE CASE	
7.	DRAIN PLUG	
8.	GASKET	
9.	MAGNET	
10.	BEARING RETAINER	
11.	REAR COVER	
12.	GASKET	
13.	INPUT SHAFT	
14.	INPUT SHAFT FRONT BEARING	
15.	3RD GEAR ASSEMBLY	
16.	3RD/4TH SYNCHRONIZER ASM.	
17.	SYNCHRONIZER SLEEVE	
18.	CLUTCH HUB	
19.	INSERT	
20.	INSERT SPRING	
21.	3RD/4TH BLOCKER RING	
22.	4TH GEAR ASSEMBLY	
23.	3RD NEEDLE BEARING	
24.	4TH NEEDLE BEARING	
25.	4TH COLLAR	
26.	4TH GEAR THRUST WASHER	
27.	INPUT SHAFT REAR BEARING	
28.	5TH GEAR	
29.	INPUT SHAFT END NUT	
30.	OUTPUT SHAFT	
31.	OUTPUT SHAFT FRONT BEARING	
32.	1ST GEAR ASSEMBLY	
33.	1ST/2ND SYNCHRONIZER ASSEMBLY	
34.	REVERSE GEAR	
35.	CLUTCH HUB	
36.	INSERT	
37.	INSERT SPRING	
38.	1ST/2ND BLOCKER RING	
39.	2ND GEAR ASSEMBLY	
40.	1ST NEEDLE BEARING	
41.	2ND NEEDLE BEARING	
42.	2ND COLLAR	
43.	3RD/4TH OUTPUT GEAR	
44.	KEY	
45.	OUTPUT SHAFT REAR BEARING	
46.	OUTPUT SHAFT BEARING SHIM	
47.	INPUT SHAFT BEARING SHIM	
48.	5TH GEAR THRUST WASHER	
49.	5TH NEEDLE BEARING	
50.	5TH COLLAR	
51.	5TH GEAR ASSEMBLY	
52.	5TH SYNCHRONIZER ASSEMBLY	
53.	SYNCHRONIZER SLEEVE	
54.	CLUTCH HUB	
55.	INSERT	
56.	INSERT SPRING	
57.	5TH BLOCKER RING	
58.	INSERT STOPPER PLATE	
59.	OUTPUT SHAFT END NUT	
60.	REVERSE IDLER GEAR ASM.	
61.	REVERSE IDLER SHAFT	
62.	STRAIGHT PIN	
63.	REVERSE IDLER SHAFT BOLT	
64.	GASKET	
65.	CLUTCH FORK SHAFT ASM.	
66.	CLUTCH RELEASE BEARING	
67.	RELEASE BEARING SPRING	
68.	CLUTCH SHAFT BUSHING	
69.	CLUTCH SHAFT SEAL	
70.	CLUTCH PRESSURE PLATE ASM.	
71.	CLUTCH DISK ASSEMBLY	

Fig. 12-35. Exploded view of a five-speed transaxle. Learn part names and locations.   (Oldsmobile)

Fig. 12-36. Power flow through a five-speed transmission.   (Peugeot)

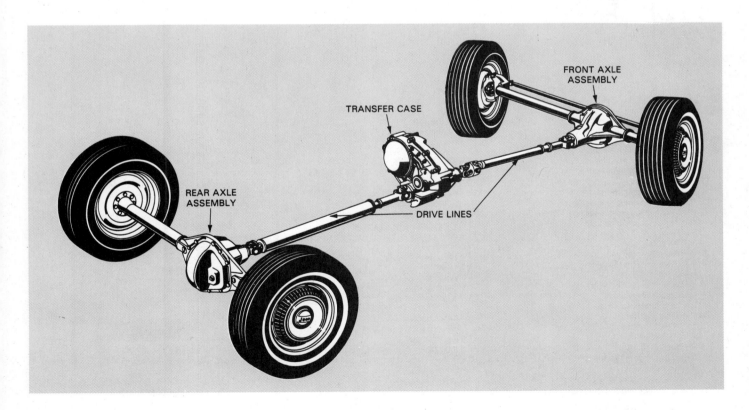

Fig. 12-37. Overall view of one type of four-wheel drive, drive train. Note transfer case which supplies power to both axle assemblies when engaged. Four-wheel drive aids vehicle control and performance in sand, snow, mud, etc.   (Jeep)

Fig. 12-38. Exploded view of a typical part-time, four-wheel drive transfer case. Note use of a drive chain (49) to transmit power from drive sprocket (16) to driven sprocket (50), and planetary gear assembly (5). Learn part names and locations.   (Jeep)

1—Input gear thrust washer.
2—Input gear thrust bearing.
3—Input gear (from transmission).
4—Mainshaft pilot bearing.
5—Planetary assembly.
6—Planetary thrust washer.
7—Annulus gear.
8—Annulus gear thrust washer.
9—Needle bearing spacers.
10—Mainshaft needle bearings (120).
11—Needle bearing spacer.
12—Thrust washer.
13—Oil pump.
14—Speedometer gear.
15—Drive sprocket retaining ring.
16—Drive sprocket.
17—Sprocket carrier stop ring.
18—Sprocket carrier.
19—Clutch spring.
20—Sliding clutch.
21—Thrust washer.
22—Mainshaft.
23—Mainshaft thrust bearing.
24—Annulus gear retaining ring.
25—Mode fork.
26—Mode fork spring.

27—Range fork inserts.
28—Range fork.
29—Range sector.
30—Mode fork bracket.
31—Rear case.
32—Seal.
33—Pump housing.
34—Rear retainer.
35—Rear output bearing.
36—Bearing snap ring.
37—Vent tube.
38—Rear seal.
39—Rear yoke.
40—Yoke seal washer.
41—Yoke nut.
42—Drain and fill plugs.
43—Front output shaft rear bearing.
44—Front output shaft rear thrust bearing race (thick).
45—Case magnet
46—Front output shaft rear thrust bearing.
47—Front output shaft rear thrust bearing race (thin).
48—Driven sprocket retaining ring.
49—Drive chain.
50—Driven sprocket.

51—Front output shaft.
52—Front output shaft front thrust bearing race (thin).
53—Front output shaft front thrust bearing race (thick).
54—Front output shaft front bearing.
55—Front output shaft front thrust bearing.
56—Operating lever.
57—Washer and locknut.
58—Bearing sector shaft seal retainer.
59—Range sector shaft seal.
60—Detent ball, spring, and retainer bolt.
61—Front seal.
62—Front yoke.
63—Yoke seal washer.
64—Yoke nut.
65—Input gear oil seal.
66—Input gear front bearing.
67—Front case.
68—Lock mode indicator switch and washer.
69—Input gear rear bearing.
70—Lockplate.
71—Lockplate bolts.
72—Case alignment dowels.

286

to function.

So-called "speed shifting" is very injurious to the synchromesh gears, and for that matter, the entire drive train. Speed shifting may be justified when a vehicle is entered in competition. At any other time, it is considered the mark of a poor driver, generally one who knows nothing of how a car is built. Good drivers and good mechanics (good mechanics are almost always excellent drivers) have a sincere respect for the work and skill involved in good machinery.

Some vehicles are equipped with transfer cases which provide a means of driving front and rear axles at the same time. This allows part-time or full-time, four-wheel drive.

KNOW THESE TERMS

Torque multiplication, Gear ratio, Synchronizer, Cluster gear, Sliding gear, Input shaft, Output shaft, Shift fork, Shift mechanism, Part-time transfer case, Full-time transfer case.

REVIEW QUESTIONS—CHAPTER 12

Do not leave this chapter until you can answer the following questions. If you must go back and reread certain sections, this may slow you down; but remember—as torque goes up, speed goes down.

1. Of what value is a transmission?
2. How does a transmission multiply torque?

Fig. 12-39. Schematic showing power flow through a part-time transfer case. This unit is same as that pictured in Fig. 12-37. Note that in 2H, power from transmission travels through input gear to rear axle. No torque is delivered to front axle at this time.   (Jeep)

Fig. 12-40. Exploded view of a full-time transfer case. Note drive chain and differential (open type) assembly. See Chapter 16. (Ford)

1 — Mainshaft rear bearing spacer — short (2).
2 — Side gear.
3 — Viscous coupling and differential assembly.
4 — Mainshaft rear pilot roller bearings (15).
5 — Mainshaft O-ring.
6 — Rear output shaft.
7 — Oil pump.
8 — Speedometer gear.
9 — Differential end play shims (selective).
10 — Mainshaft needle bearings (82).
11 — Mainshaft rear bearing spacer.
12 — Clutch gear.
13 — Clutch gear locating ring.
14 — Drive sprocket locating ring.
15 — Drive sprocket.
16 — Side gear clutch.
17 — Mainshaft thrust washer.
18 — Mainshaft.
19 — Clutch sleeve.
20 — Mainshaft thrust bearing.
21 — Annulus gear retaining ring.
22 — Annulus gear thrust washer.
23 — Annulus gear.
24 — Planetary thrust washer.
25 — Planetary assembly.
26 — Mainshaft front pilot bearing.
27 — Input gear.
28 — Input gear thrust bearing.
29 — Input gear thrust bearing race.
30 — Input gear oil seal.
31 — Input gear front bearing.

32 — Front case mounting stud (6).
33 — Front case.
34 — Lock mode indicator switch gasket.
35 — Lock mode indicator switch.
36 — Input gear rear bearing.
37 — Low range lockplate.
38 — Shift rail.
39 — Range selector.
40 — Range fork.
41 — Range fork insert.
42 — Range fork pads.
43 — Mode fork spring.
44 — Mode fork pads.
45 — Mode fork insert.
46 — Mode fork.
47 — Shift rail spring.
48 — Mode fork bracket.
49 — Rear output shaft bearing.
50 — Rear output shaft bearing seal.
51 — Rear case.
52 — Wiring clip.
53 — Spline bolt.
54 — Rear output bearing.
55 — Rear retainer.
56 — Vent.
57 — Output shaft oil seal.
58 — Rear yoke.
59 — Yoke seal washer.
60 — Yoke locknut.
61 — Vent chamber seal.
62 — Fill plug and gasket.

63 — Drain plug and gasket.
64 — Rear case bolt.
65 — Washer (2).
66 — Case alignment dowel.
67 — Front output shaft rear bearing.
68 — Magnet.
69 — Front output shaft rear thrust bearing race (thick).
70 — Front output shaft rear thrust bearing.
71 — Front output shaft rear thrust bearing race (thin).
72 — Driven sprocket retaining snap ring.
73 — Drive chain.
74 — Driven sprocket.
75 — Front output shaft.
76 — Front output shaft front thrust bearing race (thin).
77 — Front output shaft front thrust bearing.
78 — Front output shaft front thrust bearing race (thick).
79 — Front output shaft front bearing.
80 — Washer.
81 — Locknut.
82 — Operating lever.
83 — Range sector shaft seal retainer.
84 — Range sector shaft seal.
85 — Detent ball.
86 — Detent spring.
87 — Detent retaining bolt.
88 — Front output shaft seal.
89 — Front yoke.
90 — Lockplate bolts.

Fig. 12-41. Exploded view of another type of full-time, four-wheel drive transfer case. Note viscous coupling, limited slip unit. (Jeep)

Fig. 12-42. Schematic showing power flow through the Quadra-Trac case. Note that power is supplied to the front and rear axles "full-time" in both low and high range. (Jeep)

Fig. 12-43. This is an exploded view of a full-time, select-drive transfer case. Note magnet used to catch and hold any ferrous (iron) particles in fluid. Particles could cause premature wear on bearings, chain, etc. (AMC)

3. Why is gear action very similar to a lever and fulcrum?
4. Name the various gears that are available in a standard transmission.
5. What are the approximate ratios of these gears?
6. Explain how the transmission works in each gear.
7. Name the various parts of a gear tooth.
8. Two types of gear teeth are generally used. They are the _____ type and the _____ type.
9. Name the four shafts used in the transmission.

10. How are these shafts turned or driven?
11. What is a synchromesh unit?
12. How does synchromesh work?
13. What lubricates a transmission?
14. What is a constant mesh gear?
15. Explain how gears are shifted.
16. What secures the various shafts to prevent them from working in or out?
17. How is the end play in the reverse idler gear and cluster gear controlled?

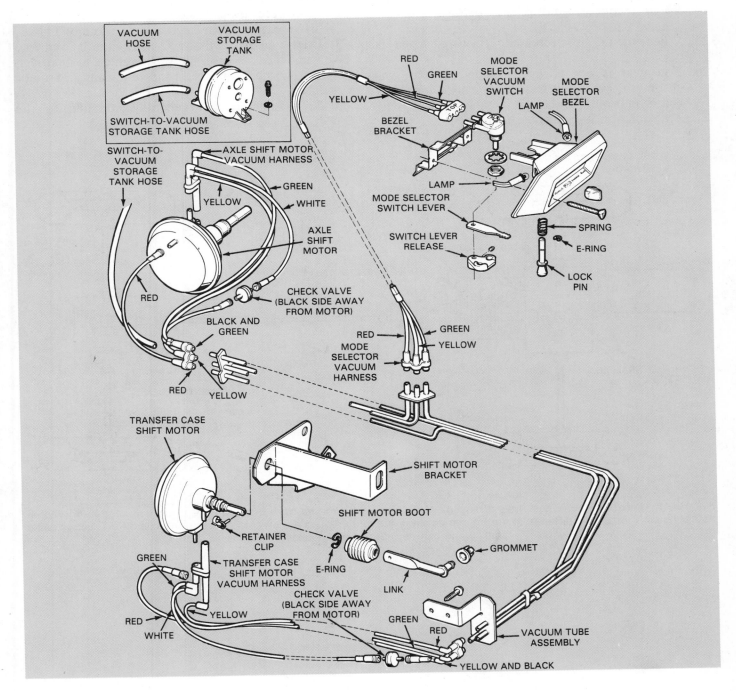

Fig. 12-44. Schematic showing overall view of vacuum control system used with a select-drive transfer case setup. Note two vacuum motors which do the shifting when activated by mode selector vacuum switch. (AMC)

18. What supports the inner end of the output shaft?
19. What holds the shifter fork cam in place after a shift is made?
20. Why are four and five-speed transmissions sometimes used?
21. How is the outer end of the input shaft supported?
22. The inner bearing on the input shaft is a bronze bushing. True or False?
23. Reverse idler gears are always supported on roller bearings. True or False?
24. When torque is multiplied, forward speed is _____.
25. When torque is decreased, forward speed is _____.
26. Low gear is not always provided with a synchromesh. Why is it less important to have low gear synchronized?
27. Transmission housings are made of _____ or _____.

28. The transmission housing often provides a base for the _____.
29. Why is speed shifting considered foolish by expert drivers?
30. If the tooth of the driving gear were pushing on the tooth of the driven gear with a force of 100 ft. lbs., how many ft. lbs. of torque would be applied to the driven gear shaft if the driven gear pitch circle diameter is 1 ft.?
31. List the gear ratios for a typical five-speed transmission.
32. Five-speed transmissions can provide an overdrive feature when in fifth gear. True or False?
33. Briefly describe what a transfer case is used for.
34. Some transfer cases allow the vehicle to be driven on dry, hard surfaced roads constantly. True or False?
35. Transfer cases are generally attached to the _____.

Fig. 12-45. Part-time four-wheel drive arrangement. Power is transmitted from 5-speed transmission to central differential. Power flows from central differential, through drive shaft and on to rear axle. Power is sent to front axle differential by pinion shaft when central differential is locked. (Audi)

Chapter 13

TRANSMISSION OVERDRIVES

After studying this chapter, you will be able to:
■ Identify the major parts of a transmission overdrive.
■ List the advantages of an overdrive.
■ Describe the operating principles of an overdrive.

When the standard transmission has been shifted into high gear, the ratio between engine and drive shaft is one to one. When cruising at 55 mph (88.5 km/h), the engine would be turning about 2,600 rpm (depending on tire size and differential gear ratio).

Given sufficient horsepower, a road that is fairly level and a reasonable road speed, the engine could propel the car with a lower overall gear ratio. To take advantage of this fact, an overdrive unit is offered by several car makers.

WHAT IS AN OVERDRIVE?

An overdrive can be an additional gear in a manual transmission or a mechanical unit that bolts to the rear of the transmission. In Fig. 13-1, the overdrive

Fig. 13-1. Cross-sectional view of a five-speed manual transmission in which fifth gear is an overdrive gear. Gear ratios are: First—3.287 to 1. Second—2.043 to 1. Third—1.394 to 1. Fourth—1.000 to 1 (direct drive, one to one). Fifth—0.853 to 1. Fifth gear overdrive allows engine rpm to drop while maintaining same road speed. This generally improves both engine life and fuel economy. Can you figure out the different gears involved in each speed selection? (Toyota)

INPUT SHAFT

OUTPUT SHAFT

293

(fifth) gear gives a gear ratio of a 0.853 turn of the input shaft to one turn of the transmission output shaft. A planetary gear unit bolted to the rear of the transmission (see following pages) accomplishes much the same thing by providing a gear ratio of around 0.7 to 1.0. See Fig. 13-2.

VALUE OF AN OVERDRIVE

The first advantage of the overdrive is that it reduces engine speed around 30 percent while still maintaining the same road speed. The reduction in engine speed gives increased fuel mileage, reduces engine noise and prolongs engine life. An overdrive works satisfactorily provided:

1. That the engine has sufficient power to propel the car in overdrive gear without "lugging" (straining to pull).
2. That reasonable road speed is maintained.
3. That the road is fairly level.

An overdrive will not guarantee higher top speeds (illegal on the highway). As car speed increases, wind resistance raises quickly. At very high speeds, the wind will produce a resistance to forward motion comparable to that of climbing a long grade (hill). This can easily upset the advantage of a higher gear, and performance could be improved by shifting into direct (high) gear.

OVERDRIVE CONSTRUCTION AND OPERATION

PLANETARY PINION CARRIER

The standard transmission output shaft is made somewhat longer so it will extend into the overdrive housing. It has a splined end that drives a planetary

INPUT TURNS — OUTPUT TURNS

3	TRANSMISSION LOW GEAR	1
2	TRANSMISSION SECOND GEAR	1
1	TRANSMISSION HIGH GEAR	1
.7	TRANSMISSION HIGH GEAR — OVERDRIVE GEAR	1

Fig. 13-2. Various gear ratios. Notice how addition of overdrive lowers ratio.

pinion carrier with three planet pinion gears. The term planetary comes from the fact that the pinions revolve, in orbital fashion, around a central or sun gear, like planets revolve around the sun. Fig. 13-3 illustrates the carrier and pinions. For study purposes, only two of the three pinions are shown and the unit is somewhat simplified.

SUN GEAR

A sun gear (termed sun because planet pinions revolve around it) assembly is installed on the output shaft. One end has helical teeth that are meshed with the pinion gears. This is the sun gear proper. The sun gear assembly is NOT splined to the transmission output shaft but is free to turn. The other end has a continuation of the helical teeth upon which a balk (stop) gear is placed. When required, it is possible to stop the sun gear by holding the balk gear with a steel plunger termed a pawl. (More on this later.)

An additional set of teeth, similar to the sun gear proper, are cut on the sun gear assembly. A flange is also cut on the assembly, to provide a spot for a shift fork to move the sun gear unit in toward the planet carrier far enough so the additional teeth will mesh with internal teeth cut in the transmission side of the planet carrier. When the sun gear assembly is shifted toward the carrier, these two units will mesh, thus locking carrier and sun gear units together. The sun gear proper is always in mesh with the planet pinion, even when the sun gear lock-up teeth are removed from mesh with the carrier. Fig. 13-4.

INTERNAL GEAR

A large ring gear with internal teeth surrounds the planet carrier and meshes with the planet pinions. The internal gear is splined to, and becomes a solid part of, the overdrive output shaft. Fig. 13-5.

PLANETARY GEARSET

You now have the essential parts for what is termed a planetary gearset. It consists of a sun gear, planet pinion gears and carrier, and an internal gear. Fig. 13-6.

USING THE PLANETARY GEARSET TO PRODUCE AN OVERDRIVE RATIO

When the pawl (steel plunger) stops the balk gear, the sun gear is held stationary. The planet pinion carrier will be turned by the transmission output shaft. As the planet carrier revolves, the pinions are forced to walk (roll around) around the sun gear. As they are also meshed with the internal gear (which is part of overdrive output shaft), the internal gear is forced to rotate faster than the carrier. By the time the carrier has made .7 of a turn, the internal gear will have made a complete turn. As the carrier is on transmis-

Fig. 13-3. Planet pinion carrier. A—Cross-sectional view of carrier. Note that carrier hub is splined to transmission output shaft. B—View of entire carrier. Two of three pinions are shown.

Fig. 13-4. Sun gear assembly. Sun gear meshes with planet pinions. Balk gear is splined on. Sun gear assembly can turn on transmission output shaft when desired. Planet pinions shown are part of planet carrier assembly.

Fig. 13-5. Internal gear. Internal gear surrounds and meshes with planet pinion gears. Only two are shown. Ring gear is held to ring gear body by snap ring. Both units spline together.

Fig. 13-6. Planetary gearset. A—End view of gearset. B—Showing ring gear body and output shaft. C—Exploded view.

sion output shaft, and the internal gear is on overdrive output shaft, the planetary gearset has allowed engine speed to drop 30 percent and still maintain the same road speed. Figs. 13-7 and 13-8.

OTHER FUNCTIONS OF THE PLANETARY GEARSET

The planetary gearset can be used to multiply torque, decrease torque, drive direct with no multiplication or produce a reverse rotation. How

Fig. 13-7. Overdrive effect. A—Sun gear stopped. Pinion gear walking around sun gear, forcing internal gear to move in same direction. B—Pinion has walked 90 deg. Notice how internal gear has gained. It is traveling faster than pinion carrier.

Fig. 13-8. Relationship between rpm of pinion carrier and internal gear. Every time transmission output shaft turns pinion carrier .7 of a turn, internal gear is forced to rotate a full turn. This causes overdrive output shaft to revolve faster than transmission output shaft. (Chevrolet)

this is done will be covered in the next chapter since the automatic transmission makes full use of the planetary gearset.

OVERDRIVE LOCKED OUT

When the use of the overdrive is not wanted, it may be placed in the LOCKED-OUT STAGE. When any two of the three planetary members are locked together, the planetary action is stopped, and the entire assembly revolves as a solid unit.

The overdrive is locked out by shifting the sun gear assembly until its additional lock-out teeth mesh with internal teeth on engine side of the planet carrier. See Fig. 13-9.

SOMETHING MISSING?

If the sun gear assembly is shifted out until the lock-out teeth are free of the pinion carrier, and the pawl is not holding the sun gear stationary, what type of drive would we have?

Fig. 13-9. Overdrive locked out. Sun gear assembly has been shifted until sun gear lock-out teeth have engaged carrier lock-out teeth. This locks two members of planetary gearset together and gearset will drive as a solid unit with no planetary action.

Trace the power flow. The transmission output shaft will turn the pinion carrier. It will take torque to move the internal gear, as it is part of the output shaft. As a result, the whirling pinions will walk around in the internal gear, and the sun gear will be spun backward. Type of drive—NONE! Fig. 13-10.

MISSING PART—ROLLER CLUTCH

Fig. 13-11 illustrates the principle of the roller clutch. Notice that it consists basically of three parts, the splined inner hub with tapered cams on the outside surface, a series of hardened steel rollers (one per cam surface) and an outer ring or race. As used in an overdrive, the rollers are contained or held in position with a steel cage. A spring is incorporated to assist in the functioning of the unit as a clutch.

Fig. 13-10. Unit will not drive. Internal gear is being held by output shaft. Engine is spinning pinion carrier. Pinions are walking around in internal gear, causing sun gear to revolve backwards. No torque is transmitted to internal gear and car will not move. (Chevrolet)

Fig. 13-11. Roller clutch action. In A, hub is being driven by transmission output shaft. Rollers have traveled up cams and have seized outer race thus driving it. In B, accelerator has been released and inner hub has slowed down. This causes rollers to travel back down cams and release outer race. Outer race will now freewheel or overrun hub. (Chevrolet)

The inner hub is the driving part; the outer race is the driven part. When the cam hub receives driving torque, the rollers are forced up the cam surfaces until they are wedged tightly against the outer race. The outer race will then be driven. When the driving torque is removed from the hub, the rollers disengage and return to their low positions, freeing the outer race. The race may continue to turn while the hub turns slowly or even stops. This action is referred to as FREEWHEELING. The outer race will be driven only when the speed of hub exceeds that of race. Figs. 13-11 and 13-12.

OVERDRIVE ROLLER CLUTCH

A roller clutch is splined to the transmission output shaft in back of the splined pinion carrier. The internal gear body forms the outer race. When the transmission output shaft is turning faster than the internal gear, and the sun gear is free, the clutch rollers will drive the internal gear body. When the sun gear is stopped, the planetary action will drive the internal gear and body faster than the carrier and clutch hub, and the clutch will remain disengaged. Fig. 13-13.

OVERDRIVE CONTROLS

Sun gear unit is shifted by fork, shift rail and cam lever arrangement. Overdrive may be locked out (sun gear splines or lock-out teeth shifted into mesh with carrier) by driver, by moving control lever via mechanical linkage arrangement.

The shift rail extends into the transmission. It is so arranged that when the car is shifted into reverse, the overdrive shift rail is moved, locking out the overdrive. This is necessary to back the car when the overdrive is in the overdrive position. A slot in the overdrive shift rail will also prevent the pawl from engaging blocking gear when overdrive is locked out.

The pawl is operated by an electric solenoid. The solenoid is energized by an electric current actuated by a governor controlling a relay. When car speed is around 30 mph (48 km/h), the governor closes a set of contact points, energizes the relay which in turn energizes the solenoid, causing it to attempt to push the pawl into the balk gear. Fig. 13-14.

Fig. 13-13. Overdrive roller clutch. Drive is through transmission output shaft, to clutch hub, to rollers, to ring gear body, to overdrive output shaft. When accelerator is released, transmission output shaft will slow down, rollers will retract, and overdrive output will freewheel.

Fig. 13-14. Basic overdrive controls, Top sketch—Sun gear assembly has been shifted into lock-out position. Cam lever has been turned until it has drawn shift rail and fork to right, 2. Pawl is blocked by rail at 1. When sun gear assembly moves, balk gear and ring remain fixed. They slide on balk gear teeth. A—Showing how rail clears pawl when moved to left. B—Showing action of cam lever in shifting rail. Spring 3, furnishes force to keep rail moving to left. R—When transmission is placed in reverse, pressure on rod at R, forces sun gear into lock-out position.

Fig. 13-12. Roller clutch (often called "overrunning clutch"). Notice how rollers are contained in thin steel cage. This forces them to act as a unit. Outer race has been cut away to show hardened steel rollers.

BALK RING

A balk ring, Fig. 13-15, is attached to the balk gear hub in such a fashion as to allow the gear to rotate while the ring is held stationary by the tip of the solenoid pawl. There is a controlled amount of friction between the gear and the ring.

When in overdrive, and before the pawl has stopped the sun gear, the drive is through the roller clutch. As the balk gear is turning, the block or balk ring will rotate until stopped by the pawl. When the governor energizes the solenoid, the pawl will shove in. However, it will be unable to move since the balk ring is interfering with its movement. When the driver releases the accelerator, the roller clutch will disengage. As the internal gear walks the pinions around the sun gear, the sun gear will slow down. When the transmission input shaft rpm is 70 percent that of the overdrive output shaft, the sun gear will be stopped. As engine speed decreases, the sun gear will begin to rotate in a reverse direction. Since there is friction between the balk gear and balk ring, the ring will be pulled backward to expose an opening through which the pawl will snap. The balk gear will stop and the

Fig. 13-15. Balk gear and balk ring action. Sketch at left shows pawl being held out by balk ring (also called blocker ring). Balk gear (also called sun gear control plate) is still being turned. Right hand sketch shows how balk ring has been pulled up when balk gear began reverse rotation. Opening in balk ring is lined up to allow pawl to snap in and lock balk gear. This stops sun gear assembly and produces overdrive effect. (Chevrolet)

Fig. 13-16. Complete overdrive unit. Learn names of parts and proper locations: 1—Sun gear teeth for balk gear. 2—Balk gear. 3—Sun gear shift groove or collar. 4—Pinion carrier assembly. 5—Internal gear. 6—Planet pinion gear. 7—Roller clutch with roller cage. 8—Roller clutch inner hub. 9—Overdrive output shaft. 10—Speedometer drive gear. 11—Output shaft bearing. 12—Roller clutch roller. 13—Cam lever rod. 14—Shift fork. 15—Solenoid. 16—Shift rail. 17—Pawl. 18—Balk ring. 19—Transmission output shaft. (Chevrolet)

transmission is in overdrive. All this happens in a second or so.

COMPLETE OVERDRIVE UNIT

Fig. 13-16 shows a cutaway of a complete overdrive unit. Study all parts and learn their names. Remember that when desired, the sun gear rotates on the transmission output shaft. Number 1 in the illustration shows the teeth upon which the balk gear 2 rides. These teeth are cut the full length of the sun gear unit with a portion removed. In this way, the teeth serve as sun gear teeth, lock-out teeth, and balk gear teeth.

Note the action of the shift rail. The lever 13 has been moved to allow the rail to move into overdrive position with sun gear lock-out teeth clear of carrier, and solenoid pawl free of shift rail.

EXPLODED VIEW—COMPLETE OVERDRIVE

Fig. 13-17 illustrates the overdrive in an exploded view. Notice the solenoid and governor assemblies. The retractor spring forces the shift rail and fork to

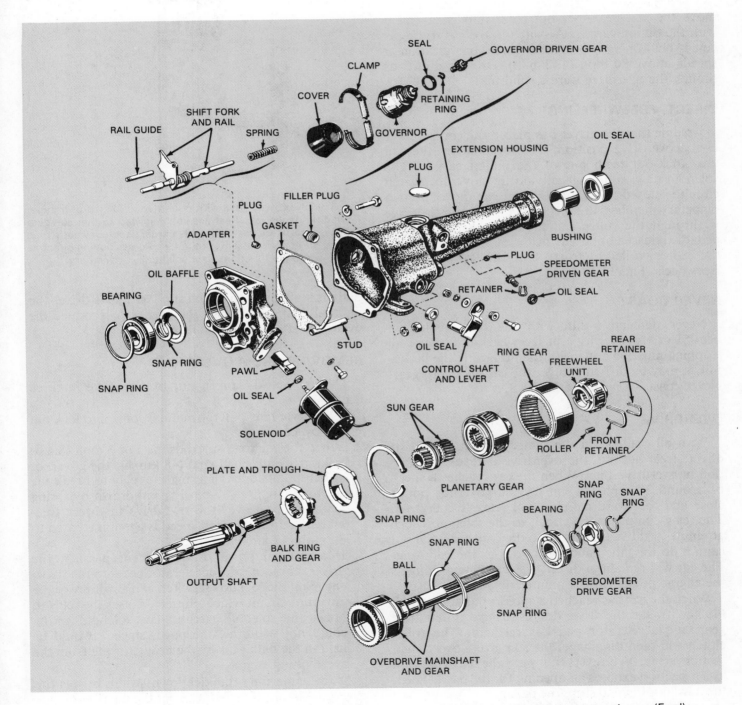

Fig. 13-17. Exploded view of a typical overdrive. Study each part, its name, location, and construction. (Ford)

the left, when the shift lever is moved to overdrive. The internal gear and internal gear body are splined together and are held with the large snap ring.

OVERDRIVE DRIVE STAGES

LOCKED-OUT

When overdrive is not desired, it is placed in the locked-out position. Fig. 13-18. Locking out is accomplished by the driver, who moves a dash control to operate the shift rail lever.

The lever causes the overdrive shift rail and fork to move the sun gear lock-out teeth into engagement with the pinion carrier. A switch in the governor circuit is held open to prevent solenoid energization at speeds above 30 mph (48 km/h). Drive is direct, as though the overdrive were a solid unit.

DIRECT, FREEWHEELING

Assume that the driver has placed the control lever in the overdrive position. The lever moves the sun gear lock-out teeth out of the pinion carrier. The solenoid pawl is disengaged and the governor switch circuit is closed. Now the sun gear can move, no two planetary members are locked together, and the drive is through the roller clutch. When the accelerator pedal is released at speeds below 30 mph (48 km/h), the clutch rollers retract, and the car coasts or freewheels. Fig. 13-19.

NEVER COAST

Never descend a hill with the transmission in neutral or the overdrive in freewheeling because all stopping must be done with the brakes. If the brakes fail, it may be difficult to get the car back into gear. Never coast – it is DANGEROUS!

OVERDRIVE

With all controls in the same position as that of direct, freewheeling, the overdrive is ready to function in overdrive gear. When the car reaches a speed of around 30 mph (48 km/h), the governor points close and the overdrive electrical relay is energized. The relay completes the circuit to the solenoid which attempts to shove the pawl into the balk gear. Since it cannot do this, the pawl is held out by the balk ring. The car will remain in direct, freewheeling as long as the engine power flow is uninterrupted.

When the car has reached a speed of about 30 mph (48 km/h), and the driver desires the use of overdrive gear, the accelerator pedal is released. The roller clutch will then disengage; the sun gear slows down, then reverses. As it reverses, it pulls the balk ring with it. This action exposes an opening for the pawl. Then, the pawl pops in and stops the balk gear. The sun gear can no longer turn, and the drive is through the carrier

Fig. 13-18. Power flow with overdrive in locked-out stage. Pawl disengaged, sun gear assembly shifted so that sun gear lock-out teeth are meshed with carrier lock-out teeth thus locking sun gear and carrier together. Power flow is direct as overdrive functions as a solid unit. (Mercury)

pinions walking around the sun gear. This drives the internal gear faster than the carrier to produce the overdrive effect. See Fig. 13-20.

REMOVING FROM OVERDRIVE

The car may be taken out of overdrive in three ways:

1. The driver may pull the manual control to lock out the overdrive.
2. When the car road speed drops 4 or 5 mph (6.4 to 8.0 km/h) under 30 mph (48 km/h), the governor switch points open, causing the relay to break the solenoid circuit. The pawl is withdrawn by spring action. This leaves the overdrive in direct freewheeling until the road speed is again increased to 30 mph (48 km/h).
3. If additional power is desired for passing, the driver may move the accelerator pedal to the floor, engaging the kickdown switch. This will break the governor circuit which, in turn, causes the relay to break the solenoid circuit. The solenoid spring could not withdraw the pawl, since it would be held in the balk gear by the heavy torque from the accelerating engine.

At the same time the kickdown switch breaks the governor circuit, it also shorts out the distributor side of the coil primary by shunting the circuit to ground

Fig. 13-19. Power flow with overdrive in direct, free-wheeling stage. Drive is direct, through roller clutch. When accelerator is released, car will coast or freewheel. (Mercury)

Fig. 13-20. Power flow with overdrive in overdrive stage. Sun gear stopped by pawl. Planet pinion carrier revolving. Pinions walking around sun gear, driving internal gear faster than carrier. (Mercury)

in the solenoid housing. This causes the engine to quit, and as soon as the torque thrust is removed, the pawl pops out and frees the sun gear. As the solenoid pawl assembly pulls into the solenoid body, the ground circuit from the coil is broken, and the engine begins to run again. The drive is now direct through the roller clutch. This whole operation, after the kickdown switch is depressed, takes but a fraction of a second.

After passing, the accelerator is released. The kickdown switch reestablishes the governor circuit. The governor energizes the relay, the relay energizes the solenoid, and the pawl once again stops the sun gear. The unit is then in overdrive.

Fig. 13-21 shows a schematic drawing of overdrive electrical parts and circuits. Study it carefully. Notice the ground points A are open when the solenoid is inactive.

At B, the wire to the solenoid divides into two coil circuits, the PULL-IN coil and the HOLD-IN coil. When the solenoid is energized, the pull-in coil draws the pawl plunger down. Once down, the pull-in winding circuit is broken and the plunger is held down by the hold-in coil.

CONSTANT DRIVE OVERDRIVE

Unlike the overdrive just discussed, the constant drive does not freewheel. The unit is either in DIRECT or OVERDRIVE. It is controlled by hydraulic pressure generated by a small pump within the unit itself. The assembly is attached directly to the rear of the regular transmission. Study the cutaway shown in Fig. 13-22.

An exploded view of a very similar overdrive design is featured in Fig. 13-23. Note the relationship of all parts.

DIRECT DRIVE MODE

Fig. 13-24 illustrates the overdrive unit in the DIRECT DRIVE mode. The cone clutch is being jammed against annulus by heavy spring pressure. This locks the sun gear (sun wheel) to the annulus

Fig. 13-21. Schematic of typical overdrive electric control circuit. Examine each circuit in diagram. Note two windings in solenoid. (Chevrolet)

Fig. 13-22. Cutaway of a hydraulically operated, constant drive (no freewheel mode) overdrive. Study part relationships carefully. (British-Leyland)

causing the planetary setup to revolve as a solid unit. Drive is through the one-way (unidirectional) clutch. Deceleration torque is through the planet gear-sun gear-carrier assembly. Note that the cone clutch is free of the brake ring. Fig. 13-24.

OVERDRIVE MODE

To produce the overdrive effect, the overdrive control position is selected. This causes oil pump pressure to build in the pistons. As the pistons move, they overcome the spring pressure. This forces the cone clutch to jam against brake ring. This stops the sun gear, causing the planet gears to "walk" around the sun gear. As they walk, they are also being carried around on the planet carrier. This combined action causes the annulus to speed up, thus producing the overdrive effect. Study the power flow and position of the various units. Fig. 13-25.

CLUTCH APPLY PISTON ACTION

A schematic of the overdrive hydraulic system in the OVERDRIVE mode, is shown in Fig. 13-26.

Before the solenoid can be energized on this setup,

the switch must be on, car speed above 38 mph (61 km/h) and transmission in third gear.

Note that the solenoid is energized. This admits residual oil pressure to the bottom of the relief valve piston. The piston moves up and compresses the relief valve springs. This raises system pressure to around 540 psi (3 723 kPa), forcing clutch apply pistons to move cone clutch against brake ring. Fig. 13-26.

OTHER OVERDRIVE ASSEMBLIES

An overdrive gear is often built into both automatic and manual transmissions. Fig. 13-1 shows a typical arrangement for a manual setup. For additional information on "built-in" overdrives, refer to Chapters 12 and 14. Look at Fig. 13-27.

SUMMARY

The overdrive is a unit that is attached to the rear of the transmission. It reduces engine speed about 30 percent while maintaining the same road speed. It accomplishes this advantage by using a planetary gearset.

The overdrive proper consists of the transmission

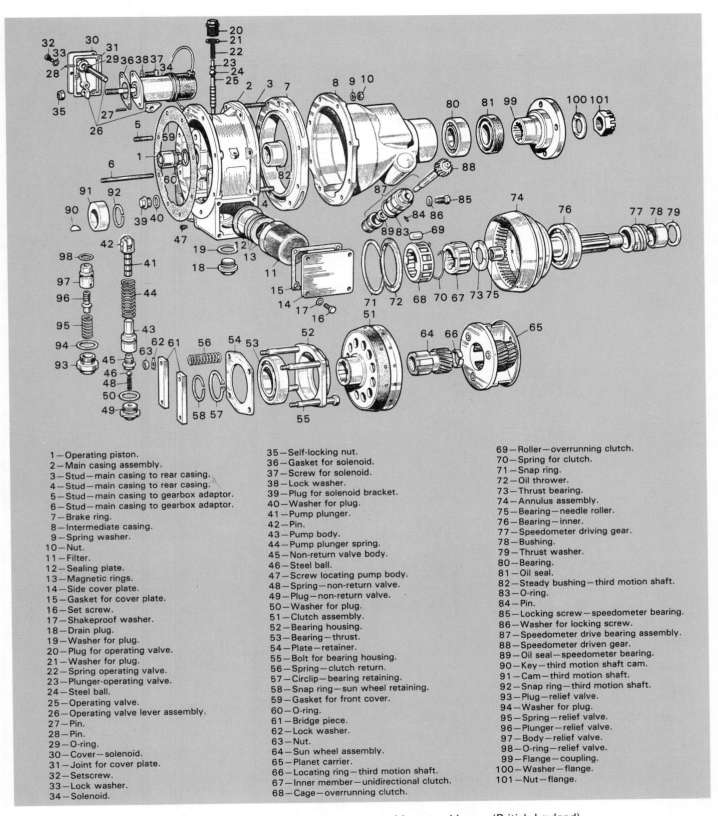

Fig. 13-23. Exploded view of a constant drive overdrive. (British-Leyland)

1—Operating piston.
2—Main casing assembly.
3—Stud—main casing to rear casing.
4—Stud—main casing to rear casing.
5—Stud—main casing to gearbox adaptor.
6—Stud—main casing to gearbox adaptor.
7—Brake ring.
8—Intermediate casing.
9—Spring washer.
10—Nut.
11—Filter.
12—Sealing plate.
13—Magnetic rings.
14—Side cover plate.
15—Gasket for cover plate.
16—Set screw.
17—Shakeproof washer.
18—Drain plug.
19—Washer for plug.
20—Plug for operating valve.
21—Washer for plug.
22—Spring operating valve.
23—Plunger-operating valve.
24—Steel ball.
25—Operating valve.
26—Operating valve lever assembly.
27—Pin.
28—Pin.
29—O-ring.
30—Cover—solenoid.
31—Joint for cover plate.
32—Setscrew.
33—Lock washer.
34—Solenoid.

35—Self-locking nut.
36—Gasket for solenoid.
37—Screw for solenoid.
38—Lock washer.
39—Plug for solenoid bracket.
40—Washer for plug.
41—Pump plunger.
42—Pin.
43—Pump body.
44—Pump plunger spring.
45—Non-return valve body.
46—Steel ball.
47—Screw locating pump body.
48—Spring—non-return valve.
49—Plug—non-return valve.
50—Washer for plug.
51—Clutch assembly.
52—Bearing housing.
53—Bearing—thrust.
54—Plate—retainer.
55—Bolt for bearing housing.
56—Spring—clutch return.
57—Circlip—bearing retaining.
58—Snap ring—sun wheel retaining.
59—Gasket for front cover.
60—O-ring.
61—Bridge piece.
62—Lock washer.
63—Nut.
64—Sun wheel assembly.
65—Planet carrier.
66—Locating ring—third motion shaft.
67—Inner member—unidirectional clutch.
68—Cage—overrunning clutch.

69—Roller—overrunning clutch.
70—Spring for clutch.
71—Snap ring.
72—Oil thrower.
73—Thrust bearing.
74—Annulus assembly.
75—Bearing—needle roller.
76—Bearing—inner.
77—Speedometer driving gear.
78—Bushing.
79—Thrust washer.
80—Bearing.
81—Oil seal.
82—Steady bushing—third motion shaft.
83—O-ring.
84—Pin.
85—Locking screw—speedometer bearing.
86—Washer for locking screw.
87—Speedometer drive bearing assembly.
88—Speedometer driven gear.
89—Oil seal—speedometer bearing.
90—Key—third motion shaft cam.
91—Cam—third motion shaft.
92—Snap ring—third motion shaft.
93—Plug—relief valve.
94—Washer for plug.
95—Spring—relief valve.
96—Plunger—relief valve.
97—Body—relief valve.
98—O-ring—relief valve.
99—Flange—coupling.
100—Washer—flange.
101—Nut—flange.

output shaft, overdrive output shaft, roller clutch, sun gear unit, planet pinion carrier, planet pinions, and the internal gear that is splined to the output shaft.

A series of mechanical and electrical controls are provided to enable the driver to actuate the overdrive.

There are three drive stages:

1. LOCKED-OUT stage in which the sun gear lock-

Fig. 13-24. Schematic showing overdrive unit in direct drive. Spring pressure high, very low oil pressure, causes cone clutch to jam against annulus. Follow power flow arrows. (British-Leyland)

Fig. 13-25. Overdrive unit in overdrive mode. High hydraulic pressure overcomes springs and causes cone clutch to move away from annulus and jam against brake ring. Follow power flow arrows. (British-Leyland)

Fig. 13-26. Hydraulic system action during overdrive mode. Note high system pressure has moved apply pistons. (AMC)

out teeth are meshed with the planet carrier, causing the unit to function as a solid piece.

2. DIRECT, FREEWHEELING where the sun gear lock-out teeth are free of the carrier, the pawl is disengaged and drive is transmitted through the roller clutch. When power is removed, the car coasts or freewheels.

3. OVERDRIVE stage in which the pawl engages the balk gear, stopping the sun gear. Sun gear lock-out teeth are clear of the pinion carrier. Drive is through the planet pinion carrier to pinions, to internal gear, to output shaft.

The overdrive may be shifted into direct at any time by depressing the accelerator pedal to the floor. At speeds below 30 mph (48 km/h), the overdrive will drop into direct, freewheeling.

KNOW THESE TERMS

Lugging, Planetary pinion carrier, Sun gear, Overdrive ratio, Roller clutch, Balk ring, Overdrive drive stages.

REVIEW QUESTIONS—CHAPTER 13

Knowledge is life's planetary gearset. It lets you slow down a little, while still maintaining the same "road speed." As you would with the overdrive—NEVER COAST.

Intelligence is the ability to learn. Knowledge is what is learned. Intelligence without knowledge is like a car without an engine—WORTHLESS! Learn all you can!

By knowing the answers to the following questions, you will have made your understanding of the next chapter much easier. It deals with automatic transmissions which make full use of the planetary gearset.

1. An overdrive is _____ _____ .
2. What does it do?
3. Is an overdrive suited to ALL cars?
4. If so or if not—why?
5. The overdrive will give a speed reduction (for the engine) of about _____ percent.
6. For what is the sun gear assembly used?
7. How does the internal gear transmit power?
8. Why is the gearset called a planetary gearset?
9. The unit connecting the sun gear and the internal gear is called a _____.
10. The balk gear is splined to the _____.
11. What is the use of the balk gear?
12. Why is it necessary to have a roller clutch?
13. How does the roller clutch function—and when?

14. The pinion carrier is splined to the _____ _____.
15. The roller clutch is splined to the _____ _____.
16. The solenoid is used to actuate the _____.
17. When the sun gear lock-out teeth engage the pinion carrier, the overdrive is in direct, free-wheeling. True or False?
18. When the pawl is disengaged and the sun gear lock-out teeth are free of the pinion carrier, the overdrive is locked out. True or False?
19. At about what speed will the overdrive kick in or become operative?
20. Name the three ways in which the unit may be taken out of overdrive.
21. What is the kickdown switch for?
22. The overdrive governor operates the overdrive shift fork and rail. True or False?
23. Draw a diagram of the overdrive electrical circuits. Indicate and name the units involved.
24. To back the car, it is necessary to _____ the overdrive.
25. Where is the overdrive fastened?
26. Explain the complete operation involved in the three overdrive stages.

CLUTCH ASSEMBLY

DIFFERENTIAL ASSEMBLY

TRANSMISSION

Fig. 13-27. Cutaway view of a five-speed, manual transaxle assembly. (Toyota)

Cross-sectional view of a two-speed Toyoglide automatic transmission.   (Toyota)

Chapter 14

AUTOMATIC TRANSMISSIONS

After studying this chapter, you will be able to:
■ Describe the parts of an automatic transmission.
■ Explain how an automatic transmission functions.
■ Identify the major components of an automatic transmission.
■ Compare the different types of automatic transmissions.

Like the standard transmission, the automatic transmission is designed to adapt the power of the engine to meet varying road and load conditions. In this case, however, the transmission does this automatically. Instead of three set forward gear ratios, it can produce an infinite number of ratios between engine and wheels.

The automatic transmission eliminates the clutch pedal and, instead of a solid type conventional clutch, it utilizes a fluid coupling between the engine and transmission.

After the driver has selected the necessary range (speed or ratio selection) by shifting a lever or pushing a button, the transmission shifts itself up or down depending on road speed, throttle position and engine loading.

BASIC CONSTRUCTION

Basically, in addition to the metal housing, the automatic transmission assembly consists of:
1. A fluid coupling or torque converter to transmit power from the engine to the transmission proper.
2. One or more planetary gearsets and shafts to secure the necessary forward and reverse speeds.
3. A series of brake bands and multiple disc clutches designed to control the planetary gearsets.
4. Hydraulic servos and pistons to actuate the bands and clutches.
5. One or more oil pumps to provide the necessary hydraulic pressure.
6. Numerous valves (control, check, pressure regulation, balanced, transition, downshift, etc.), all designed to control, direct and administer hydraulic pressures throughout the transmission.
7. Some means of cooling the oil.
8. Manual control system used by the operator to select certain speed ranges; high, low, etc.

FLUID COUPLING

The fluid coupling utilizes a special lightweight oil to transmit engine power from one member to another.

For purposes of illustration, imagine cutting a hollow steel doughnut down the center, Fig. 14-1. You now have two halves, each shaped like the unit shown in Fig. 14-2.

Fig. 14-1. Cutting a hollow steel doughnut.

Fig. 14-2. One half of the steel doughnut.

TORUS

Each half, or member, is called a TORUS. Vanes or fins are placed in each torus. The vanes are straight and are spaced at equal intervals. Fig. 14-3.

The two torus members are fastened to shafts. One member to an input, the other to an output shaft. They are placed face to face with a slight clearance between them. Fig. 14-4.

As indicated in Fig. 14-4, the flywheel holds the driving torus. A thin housing from the flywheel also extends around the driven member. An oil seal is placed between the transmission shaft and this housing. The housing is filled with oil.

You will also notice that the driven member is splined to the transmission or output shaft. The shaft is supported by a pilot bushing in the crankshaft. When the crankshaft turns the flywheel, the driving member and housing will spin. The driven member is entirely free since there is no mechanical connection between it and the driving member.

VANES OR FINS

Fig. 14-3. Vanes are placed in each torus. Notice that vanes are straight and equally spaced. In an actual torus, a greater number of vanes are used.

DRIVING MEMBER   DRIVEN MEMBER

CRANKSHAFT

TRANSMISSION SHAFT

FLYWHEEL   VANES

Fig. 14-4. Torus members in place. One torus member is fastened to each shaft. Notice how transmission shaft is supported by bushing in end of crankshaft.

HOW FLUID COUPLING FUNCTIONS

Imagine two fans facing each other, at reasonably close range. If one fan were plugged in, the air blast from the driving fan would cause the other fan to spin. Air is the medium of power transfer. Since the two fans are not in an enclosed area, the power transfer would not be very efficient. Fig. 14-5.

The fluid coupling works on somewhat the same principle as the fan. However, oil is used instead of air, and since the driving and driven torus are mounted very close together in an enclosed space, power transfer is excellent.

If oil were placed in a horizontal torus, and if the torus were spun, the vanes would carry the oil around at high speed. This motion of oil would be referred to as a ROTARY motion. The centrifugal force set up by the whirling would cause the oil to fly outward and upward. Fig. 14-6.

If the driven torus were placed above the driving torus, the oil that is thrown out would strike the vanes in the driven torus. After striking the vanes it would travel up, over and back down into the driving torus. As the driving torus is whirling, it would be thrown outward and upward back against the vanes of the driven torus. This around and around motion of the oil is termed VORTEX flow. The same action takes place when the torus members are in the vertical position. Figs. 14-7, 14-8, and 14-9.

As the speed of the driving torus is increased, the

Fig. 14-5. Coupling drive using fans and air. Air from driving fan will cause other fan to spin.   (Chevrolet)

OIL

A

TORUS

OIL

B

TORUS

Fig. 14-6. Oil action in torus. A—Cutaway of torus at rest. Oil is level. B—Torus is spinning. Oil is thrown outward and is directed upward by curved torus edge.

Fig. 14-7. Start of vortex flow. When driving torus starts to spin, oil is thrown out, up into driven torus, around and back into driving torus. This action, around and around, is termed vortex action.

Fig. 14-9. Rotary and vortex flow. (Pontiac)

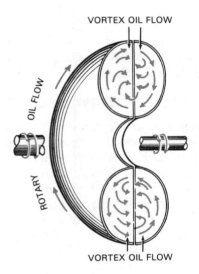

Fig. 14-8. Rotary and vortex oil flow.

Fig. 14-10. Use of a split ring to smooth vortex flow. Top view illustrates split ring as installed in a torus. Vanes are cut away to receive ring. A shows how oil vortex flow is guided and smoothed by split ring. B shows turbulence present in center when split ring is not used.

rotary and vortex flow of the oil becomes more violent. This will cause the driven torus to turn faster and faster.

Finally the speed of the driver and driven members will become equal. At this point the rotary flow is constant, but there is little or no vortex flow. You will remember that vortex flow is caused by centrifugal force throwing the oil outward. If both members are whirling at the same speed, each member will attempt to throw oil into the other, canceling the vortex flow.

SPLIT RING

To assist the oil in maintaining a smooth vortex flow, a hollow ring is sometimes placed in each member. The oil is guided around, and there is less tendency for the oil to work against itself in the center area. Fig. 14-10.

FLUID COUPLING EFFICIENCY

The fluid coupling effects a smooth transfer of power from the engine to the transmission.

At high engine speeds, the coupling is very efficient. It gives a one to one ratio between driven and driving members. At medium speeds the coupling is not quite as effective. At low engine speeds there is little power transfer.

This allows the coupling to act as a clutch. When engine speed is low, there is no power transfer. This is the same as having a conventional clutch in the disengaged position. As engine speed is increased, power transfer becomes more effective. All jerking and roughness is eliminated by the use of the fluid coupling. This provides smooth takeoff and reduces wear and strain on the drive train.

The fluid coupling cannot increase torque above that produced by the crankshaft.

When the engine is accelerating, the driving torus transmits engine torque to the driven torus. When coasting, the driven torus becomes the driver and allows the engine to act as a brake.

TORQUE CONVERTER

A torque converter is similar to the fluid coupling but there is one very important difference. The fluid coupling can transmit all available engine torque, but it cannot multiply this torque. The torque converter can and does multiply engine torque. The amount of multiplication depends on the type and design of converter used, as well as road and engine speeds.

The ability to multiply torque makes it possible to reduce the number of gears in the transmission.

The torque converter uses a driving and driven torus but, in this case, they are generally referred to as the pump (driver) and the turbine (driven). In some cases, more than one pump and turbine are used. The pump is sometimes referred to as the impeller.

VANES

The converter blades or vanes are curved to facilitate proper vortex flow. The pump vanes are curved one way, and the turbine blades the other. Fig. 14-11.

STATOR

The secret of torque multiplication lies in the use of one or more STATORS. Fig. 14-12.

A stator is a small, wheel-like arrangement that is inserted between the pump and turbine. The job of the stator is to intercept the oil thrown off by the tur-

PUMP VANES   TURBINE VANES

FLUID COUPLING VANES

Fig. 14-11. Fluid coupling and torque converter vanes. Torque converter vanes are curved. Fluid coupling vanes can be straight. (Chevrolet)

Fig. 14-12. One type of stator. (Ford)

bine and redirect the path of this oil so it will enter the pump smoothly. The stator is mounted between the pump and the turbine. As the pump begins to spin, oil is thrown outward into the curved vanes of the turbine. The oil then circulates around through the turbine vanes. Instead of being discharged back into the pump vanes (as in fluid couplings), the oil is first passed through the stator.

In the fluid coupling, which uses no stator, torque transmission and multiplication efficiency is reduced by having turbine oil enter the pump at various angles, depending on speed and load conditions. This poor entry angle can work against the pump and absorb valuable torque.

The stator is mounted on a stationary shaft, and is allowed to spin in the direction of the pump. Any attempt to rotate the stator against pump rotation, causes it to lock to the shaft.

SPRAG AND ROLLER ONE-WAY CLUTCHES

Stator locking action is produced by using either a roller or a sprag one-way (overrunning) clutch. The roller clutch is described in Chapter 13.

The sprag clutch is similar to the overrunning type used in the overdrive. Instead of using round rollers that walk up a tapered step to lock up the clutch, the sprag clutch uses a flat unit with curved edges. When the outer race is turned one way, the sprags tip and present their narrow diameter. This allows the outer race (fastened to stator) to turn.

When the stator attempts to rotate in the opposite direction, the sprags tip the other way and present the long diameter. This causes them to jam between the two races, locking them together and preventing rotation in this direction. Fig. 14-13. Note location of stator one-way clutch. Fig. 14-12. See roller clutch in Fig. 14-20.

TORQUE MULTIPLICATION

As the pump discharges oil into the vanes of the turbine, the force of the oil tends to turn the turbine. In A, Fig. 14-14, you see a wheel (turbine) with cups (vanes) attached. Oil is being sprayed into the cup by

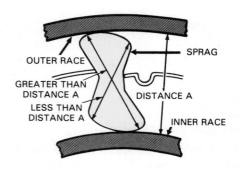

Fig. 14-13. Cross section showing sprag clutch construction. (Cadillac)

Fig. 14-14. Torque multiplication by using a stator.

a pressure gun (pump).

The oil strikes the cup (vanes) and exerts some force. The force, however, is not enough to cause the heavy wheel to turn. You can see that the oil is striking one side of the cup, then is directed around and out (vortex action). Obviously a great deal of potential force of the oil is being lost.

In B, Fig. 14-14, a stationary curved piece (stator) has been placed so the oil is redirected into the cup (vane). The oil can now strike the cup and, instead of leaving, will continue to circulate back into the cup. The torque produced by the oil in A, has been increased in B, by adding the extra torque that was lost when the oil left the cup. By redirecting the stream of oil, the torque has been multiplied. This is the job of the stator.

As the wheel (turbine) turns faster and faster, it will finally approach the speed of the oil stream (pump). Look at C, Fig. 14-14. When this happens, the cup will be moving at about the same speed as the oil stream. In this case the oil will not fly out of the cup and cannot be redirected. Torque multiplication is no longer possible. TORQUE MULTIPLICATION IS ONLY POSSIBLE WHEN THERE IS A DIFFERENCE IN THE SPEED OF THE PUMP AND TURBINE! THE GREATER THE DIFFERENCE—THE GREATER THE MULTIPLICATION, A, B, and C, Fig. 14-14.

NEWTON'S LAW

Newton's law says: "For every action there is an equal and opposite reaction."

Applying Newton's law to the torque converter, we find three areas of action and reaction caused by the oil flow. A—Pump, B—Stator, C—Turbine. Look at Fig. 14-15.

As the stator blades are held in a fixed position during the torque multiplication period, the reaction of these blades to the oil flow is to direct the force in the same direction as that of pump A.

Using Newton's law, the reaction of the turbine blades on the oil stream will be equal to the force exerted by both pump A and stator B. If A is the action force of the pump, B the reaction force of the stator,

Fig. 14-15. Newton's law as applied to converter forces. Force of pump A, plus force of stator B, combine to produce force C, which is greater than original force A.

and C the reaction force of the turbine, then: C = A + B.

The original force A has been increased by B, giving a reaction force of C that is greater than A. In short, original torque A has been multiplied to C. See Fig. 14-15.

WHY CONVERTER BLADES ARE CURVED

The pump vanes are curved in such a manner as to direct the vortex flow leaving the vanes in a direction that will exert as much force as possible against the turbine vanes. The leading edge (part of the vane where oil first enters), or inner portion of the pump vane, is curved to assist smooth reentry of oil being discharged by the stator.

The turbine blades are curved in an opposite direction. This curve produces two favorable functions. When pump oil is thrown against the turbine vanes, the curved leading edge (that portion where oil first enters) assists in a smooth entry. This reduces breakup of the smooth oil stream and prevents a buildup or damming effect that reduces entry oil velocity.

The last portion of the turbine vane is curved to increase the turbine energy absorption by deflecting the oil stream as much as possible. The more it is deflected, the more energy it will give up to the deflecting object.

Fig. 14-16 illustrates this principle. Note in A, Fig. 14-16, that a stream of oil is striking a flat vane. Notice how the stream is broken up. This imparts a

Fig. 14-16. Oil stream deflection. Bending direction of oil stream so a maximum amount of oil stream energy will be absorbed by deflecting object.   (Dodge)

Fig. 14-18. Oil transfer with a stator. As oil leaves turbine vanes, it strikes stator vanes. As stator is locked, vanes bend oil stream so it enters pump at proper angle. It will now assist pump as it will enter with some initial velocity.

small force to the vane. In B, Fig. 14-16, the leading edge of the vane has been curved. The oil stream is now entering in a smooth fashion and will retain its velocity. However, no greater force is imparted to the vane. In C, Fig. 14-16, the last portion of the vane has been curved to provide a much greater deflection of the oil stream.

As the oil stream velocity was maintained by the curved leading edge, oil stream deflection by bending the last portion will now provide a much greater absorption of energy by the vane.

STATOR IS NECESSARY

Since the curved turbine blades discharge oil in a direction opposite to pump rotation, the work of the pump would be hampered since oil could not reenter the pump blades in a smooth manner. As a result, vortex flow would be impaired and torque transmission would fall off. Fig. 14-17.

Fig. 14-17. Oil transfer without stator. As oil leaves turbine blades and attempts to reenter pump, oil works against pump rotation. Oil is entering at wrong angle.

The stator blades are curved at an angle that will intercept the oil leaving the turbine blades smoothly. At the same time, this adds to the force of the pump and increases vortex velocity. Fig. 14-18.

A in Fig. 14-19, shows how the oil stream from the curved turbine blades is redirected by the stator so it enters the pump vanes with an initial velocity. B in Fig. 14-19 illustrates the same action.

Stator vanes, as well as a roller overruning or one-

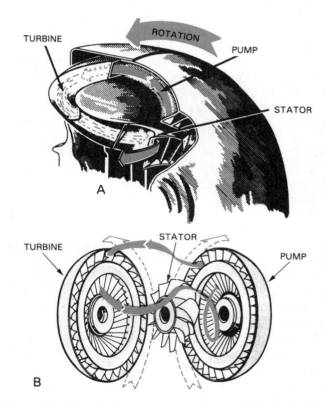

Fig. 14-19. Stator action. A—Stator bends oil stream leaving turbine blades in direction that will allow it to enter pump with initial velocity. B—Follow oil flow from pump to turbine, stator, and back into pump. Note how stator redirects oil into pump in direction of pump rotation.   (Dodge, AMC)

way clutch, are shown in Fig. 14-20. The one-way clutch hub is stationary and the stator can turn only in the direction shown by the arrow.

VARIABLE PITCH STATOR

To further increase the usefulness of the stator, and to adapt it to different load requirements, one type of

Fig. 14-20. Stator. One form of stator. This unit uses a one-way roller clutch. Notice that stator can turn in one direction only.

Fig. 14-21. Variable pitch stator. Pitch or angle of stator blades can be changed to meet different requirements. (Buick)

stator is built with adjustable vanes. It is referred to as a VARIABLE PITCH stator. Fig. 14-21.

VORTEX FLOW

Vortex flow in the torque converter is much faster than that of the fluid coupling. This is accomplished by: the initial velocity of pump oil reentry provided by the stator; the curved vanes; smooth turbine oil entry. The higher the vortex flow velocity, the greater the torque transfer.

As road speed builds up, the turbine speed approaches that of the pump. Vortex flow is slowed down and the torque converter acts much like the fluid coupling. Figs. 14-22 and 14-23 illustrate the vortex flow during torque multiplication, and during the fluid coupling condition.

OTHER VARIATIONS

Some converters use a pump, turbine and one stator. Others use a pump, turbine and two or more stators. Another type uses a pump, three turbines, a small inner stator and a larger outer stator. Some use two pumps. All are designed to facilitate torque transfer and multiplication. The pump, turbine and one stator design is in common use today.

Fig. 14-22. Torque converter—vortex flow. Vortex flow is very rapid in torque converter. This is especially true at stall. (Chevrolet)

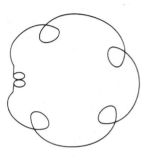

Fig. 14-23. Vortex flow at coupling point. Vortex flow has almost stopped when coupling point is reached. Coupling point is when pump and turbine are traveling at same speed and torque multiplication is no longer possible. (Chevrolet)

TORQUE CONVERTER IN ACTION

When the car is standing still with the transmission in DRIVE range and engine idling, there is very little transfer of torque from pump to turbine.

AT STALL

As the engine is accelerated, pump speed rapidly increases. Oil is thrown into the turbine with increasing force, A, Fig. 14-24. Leaving the turbine, the oil strikes the stator, B, Fig. 14-24. As the stator is forced backward by the oil, the one-way clutch will lock it up. The oil is then diverted, and enters the whirling pump, C, Fig. 14-24. As this vortex flow increases in speed, more and more torque is applied to the turbine. Fig. 14-24.

The maximum torque multiplication is delivered when the pump has reached its highest velocity, and the turbine is at stall (standing still). This condition is shown in Fig. 14-25. Notice that this converter uses two stators. Both are in operation.

INCREASING SPEED

As the turbine begins to turn, torque multiplication tapers off. When turbine speed increases, the oil leaving the trailing edges of the turbine will change its angle so it begins to strike the rear face of the primary stator.

This change of angle is caused by the fact that even though the oil is being thrown toward the stator, the turbine is moving by the stator faster than the oil is moving toward the stator.

Fig. 14-24. Oil travel path. Oil is thrown from pump into turbine at A. Oil leaving turbine strikes stator at B, and is deflected into pump at proper angle, and with initial velocity at C. (Pontiac)

Fig. 14-25. Torque converter—at stall. Stall condition, as illustrated, will provide maximum amount of torque multiplication. Turbine and both stators are stopped and pump is spinning very fast. (Plymouth)

If you parked your car (turbine) alongside a target (stator), you could throw a rock (oil) backward and strike the target (stator blade). Say that you threw the rock at 50 mph, it would strike the target (stator blade) on the front face at 50 mph.

Then, if you drove the car (turbine) past the target (stator blade) at 100 mph and threw a rock, instead of striking the target, the rock would actually travel away from the target at about 50 mph. If there was a row of targets (stator blades), instead of striking the front face of the one you aimed at, the rock would ac-

tually strike the rear face of one of the other targets.

A similar action takes place with the turbine oil. As the turbine rotary speed surpasses the vortex velocity, the oil strikes the back of the stator blades causing the stator to start freewheeling. This causes the primary stator sprag clutch to uncouple, and the primary stator will freewheel with the turbine. As the secondary stator angles still deflect the oil, it remains stationary. Fig. 14-26.

Fig. 14-26. Torque converter—increasing car speed. Turbine is starting to approach pump or impeller speed. One stator is freewheeling and other is still stopped and is deflecting oil into pump. (Plymouth)

CRUISING SPEED

As car speed reaches the cruising range, the turbine speed approaches that of the pump.

The angle of oil discharge from the turbine causes the oil stream to strike the back of both primary and secondary stators. Both stators are now freewheeling and there is no torque multiplication.

Vortex flow is slow and the converter is performing much like a fluid coupling. This condition is known as the COUPLING POINT. Fig. 14-27.

TORQUE MULTIPLICATION CURVE

The ratio between torque multiplication with the turbine at STALL and the COUPLING POINT is illustrated in Fig. 14-28. Notice how torque multiplication drops off as turbine speed increases.

INFINITE GEAR RATIOS

The torque converter provides an infinite number of ratios as opposed to the standard transmission's three or four ratios. This provides a smooth flow of power that automatically adjusts to varying load conditions, within limit of unit. See Fig. 14-29.

PLANETARY GEARSETS

As you learned in the overdrive section, a planetary gearset can be used to step up the speed of the output

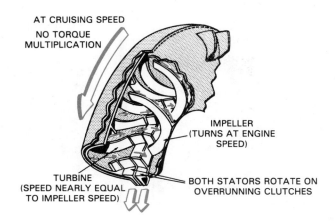

AT CRUISING SPEED
NO TORQUE MULTIPLICATION

IMPELLER (TURNS AT ENGINE SPEED)

TURBINE (SPEED NEARLY EQUAL TO IMPELLER SPEED)

BOTH STATORS ROTATE ON OVERRUNNING CLUTCHES

Fig. 14-27. Torque converter—cruising speed. Pump and turbine are turning at about same speed and both stators are freewheeling. Vortex flow is almost nil. This is referred to as coupling point. (Plymouth)

TORQUE INCREASE

2 TO 1 RATIO

1 TO 1 RATIO

TORQUE INCREASE CHART (PUMP AT 1500 RPM)

TORQUE INCREASE CURVE

COUPLING POINT

TURBINE SPEEDING UP

TURBINE STALLED

TURBINE DRIVEN AT 9/10 PUMP SPEED

Fig. 14-28. Torque curve chart. (Mercury)

LOW

HIGH

OVERLAPPING GEAR RATIO

Fig. 14-29. Torque converter provides an extensive number of possible gear ratios. (Chevrolet)

INTERNAL GEAR

SUN GEAR

PLANET PINIONS

PLANET CARRIER

SUN GEAR

INTERNAL GEAR

Fig. 14-30. Typical planetary gearset. (Cadillac)

shaft to reduce torque. The planetary gearset can also be used to reduce output speed, thereby increasing torque. The gearset can transmit motion at the same torque, and can be used to reverse torque. The automatic transmission makes full use of these features of the planetary gearset.

The planetary gearset is compact. Its gears are in constant mesh. It is quiet and strong. Fig. 14-30 illustrates a typical planetary gearset. Learn the names of all parts.

TORQUE INCREASE—LARGE

If the planetary gearset internal gear is held, and power is applied to the sun gear, the planet pinions are forced to turn and walk around the internal gear. This action causes the pinion carrier to revolve at a lower speed than the sun gear. Torque increase is large. Fig. 14-31.

TORQUE INCREASE—SMALL

If the sun gear is held, and the internal gear is driven, the planet pinions must walk around the sun gear. This causes the pinion carrier to move slower than the internal gear, and torque will increase. See Fig. 14-32.

SUN GEAR DRIVES

INTERNAL GEAR HELD

PLANET CARRIER DRIVEN

Fig. 14-31. Planetary gearset in large torque increase. (Cadillac)

SUN GEAR HELD

INTERNAL GEAR DRIVES   PLANET CARRIER DRIVEN

Fig. 14-32. Planetary gearset in small torque increase.
(Cadillac)

SUN GEAR DRIVES

INTERNAL GEAR TURNS IN   PLANET CARRIER HELD
OPPOSITE DIRECTION

Fig. 14-34. Planetary gearset in reverse.   (Cadillac)

TORQUE TRANSMISSION—CONSTANT

When any two members of the gearset are locked together, planetary action is stopped. Under these conditions, the gearset will revolve as a solid unit, providing a means of torque transmission with no increase or decrease. Fig. 14-33.

TORQUE TRANSMISSION—REVERSE

By holding the planet carrier and driving the sun gear, the planet pinions are forced to rotate about their pins. This causes them to drive the internal gear in a reverse direction at a reduced speed. Fig. 14-34.

USE OF THE PLANETARY GEARSET IN A TYPICAL AUTOMATIC TRANSMISSION

Detail 1, Fig. 14-35, shows the start of a planetary gearset as used in a two-speed transmission. Notice that the primary sun gear and shaft are one piece, and they are splined to the converter turbine. The arrow indicates the constant direction of rotation for the

TWO MEMBERS LOCKED TOGETHER

Fig. 14-33. Planetary gearset in direct drive.   (Cadillac)

sun gear and shaft.

In detail 2, Fig. 14-35, the output shaft, planet carrier (one piece), one long and one short pinion have been added. The long and short pinions always rotate in the direction of the arrows. The long pinions are in constant mesh with both the sun gear and the short pinions. At this point, drive is not yet possible.

Detail 3, Fig. 14-35 illustrates the addition of a forward sun gear and flange. The integral flange and forward sun gear are free to turn independently of the primary sun gear and shaft. The forward sun gear is in constant mesh with the short pinions.

A brake drum has been placed on the forward sun gear flange, and a brake band surrounds the drum. If the band were applied (squeezed against the drum), the drum would be stopped. This would stop the forward sun gear. As the shaft turns the primary sun gear, it drives the long pinions counterclockwise. The long pinions turn the short pinions clockwise. The short pinions then walk around the stationary forward sun gear, turning the pinion carrier and output shaft at a ratio of 1:75 to 1 in this transmission.

BRAKE BANDS

A brake band is a steel band that encircles the drum. It is usually faced with a bonded friction lining. One end of the band is secured. The other end is fastened to a servo actuating rod. When the band is tightened, it will stop the drum.

SERVO OPERATES BAND

A hydraulic piston called a SERVO is used to apply the band. It consists of a cylinder in which is placed a piston. An opening is provided at one end to admit oil. The piston is held in the released position by a spring pressing against the piston.

When oil, under pressure, is admitted to the cylinder, the piston is forced forward, either ac-

Fig. 14-35. Step-by-step construction of two-speed automatic transmission gearset. (Ford)

tuating the band through direct contact or by actuating linkage. When the oil pressure is reduced, the spring will return the piston and the band will release.

Some servos have openings on both sides of the piston. In this case, oil can be used to assist in servo release. Other servos have two pistons.

Fig. 14-36 is a schematic drawing of a typical servo. This unit acts directly on the band through a piston rod or stem.

The servo in Fig. 14-37 is of the direct acting type. Note the band adjusting screw and how the piston may be applied and released by oil pressure.

ACCUMULATOR PISTON

Often an accumulator piston is used to assist the servo in engaging the band quickly and smoothly. Fig. 14-38 illustrates one type. Note use of lever and strut design.

Fig. 14-36. Schematic of one type of band servo. (Cadillac)

Fig. 14-37. Direct acting servo. Note that oil pressure may be applied to either side of piston, causing it to move in direction desired. (Ford)

Fig. 14-38. One type of accumulator piston.

Oil entering the cylinder presses on the large apply piston. As the apply piston is held back by a spring, oil enters a small check valve and pushes on the accumulator piston.

Being small in diameter, the accumulator piston is not held back by a spring. It moves outward against the actuating lever rapidly but with light pressure. After the actuating lever has started to engage the band, it takes additional pressure to provide further band application. The large apply piston will move forward. Its pressure is added to that of the accumulator and the band is applied firmly.

The accumulator piston gives a fast, soft application that is immediately followed by additional heavy pressure for firm engagement. Not all servos use the accumulator piston.

Oil pressure and its control will be covered later in this chapter.

CLUTCH

Detail 4, Fig. 14-35, shows the addition of a multiple disc clutch. The clutch hub is splined to the primary sun gear shaft. A stack of clutch discs (the number varies) is arranged in alternate fashion. The driving discs are splined to the clutch hub; the driven discs are splined to the clutch drum.

A piston in the clutch drum squeezes the plates together when oil pressure from the transmission is applied to the piston. A heavy spring releases the discs when oil pressure drops.

When the clutch is applied, the discs are pressed together to lock the clutch hub and drum together. The clutch hub is splined to the primary sun gear shaft, and the drum is part of the forward sun gear. With the clutch applied, both primary and forward sun gears will be locked together. This stops all gear action and the parts revolve as a solid unit. The transmission is in direct or high gear. A typical clutch is shown in Figs. 14-39, 14-40, and 14-41.

Fig. 14-39. Pair of multiple disc clutches. One is released by a coil spring, other is released by disc type spring. (Ford)

INTERNAL GEAR FOR REVERSE

Detail 5, Fig. 14-35, shows the addition of a ring or internal gear that is in constant mesh with the short pinions. An additional band and actuating servo are provided to either stop or release the internal gear. This is the reverse band and servo.

With low band and high gear clutch released, and reverse band applied, the internal gear will be held. This causes the short pinions to walk around, pulling the pinion carrier with them and imparting reverse motion to the output shaft.

NEUTRAL AND PARK

Detail 6, Fig. 14-35, illustrates the transmission in neutral and park. Notice the parking pawl that engages teeth on the planet carrier. This locks the output shaft, and prevents the car from rolling when parked.

The use of a torque converter makes it possible to have only two forward ratios, direct and low. Common practice, however, favors the use of three or four

Automatic Transmissions

Fig. 14-40. Multiple disc clutch schematic. Note that hydraulic pressure is not acting on the clutch apply piston. With no oil pressure, clutch release springs separate clutch discs. Clutch hub turns but cannot drive output shaft—drum assembly. (GM)

Fig. 14-41. Multiple disc clutch. Oil pressure is now acting against clutch apply piston. Piston overcomes spring pressure and squeezes clutch discs and plates tightly together. In that some discs are attached to drum output shaft assembly and others to hub (in an alternating arrangement), squeezing action locks hub and drum together. Hub now turns output shaft. (GM)

forward ratios or ranges. This provides better mileage and performance. Study the illustration in Fig. 14-35 until you have learned the action in each gear.

PRINCIPLES ARE THE SAME

There have been numerous types of automatic transmissions. Some utilize a fluid coupling, others

have torque converters. Designs encompass two, three, and four speed ranges. Even through construction and design have varied, and still does, the general operating principles are much the same. Each automatic transmission uses a torque converter, or fluid coupling, to transmit torque to one or more planetary gearsets. These gearsets are controlled by servos and clutches that are actuated by oil pressure. The pressure is controlled by various devices.

CONTROL SYSTEM

For purposes of illustration, you will now "build" a simple control system for a two-speed automatic transmission.

OIL PUMP

There have been several types of pumps used in automatic transmissions. One is the variable output, VANE type. Output is altered by moving the outer vane cylinder. Fig. 14-42.

Another, in current use, is the ROTOR pump. Study the exploded view in Fig. 14-43.

Fig. 14-42. Variable output vane oil pump. Pump is shown in position that will produce maximum output. Note that slide is up. (Pontiac)

Fig. 14-43. A rotor oil pump. (AMC)

319

Still another widely used pump is the "internal-external" GEAR pump. Look at Fig. 14-44.

The start of your oil actuating and control system will be the gear oil pump drawing oil from the transmission oil sump or pan. The pressure output of the pump is controlled by a pressure regulator valve. When pressure exceeds the amount required, the valve opens and bypasses oil back to the sump. This produces constantly regulated main line pressure. See Fig. 14-45.

MANUAL CONTROL VALVE

The next addition is a manually operated control valve that will allow the driver to cut off, or open, the main line pressure. Fig. 14-46.

Fig. 14-46. Manual control valve. Valve is shown in open position.

Fig. 14-44. A—Note action in transmission internal-external gear oil pump. B—Exploded view of gear type oil pump. (Toyota)

Fig. 14-45. Gear oil pump and pressure regulator. (GMC)

LOW RANGE

From the manual control valve, the main line will go to the low range band servo. To place the car in the low range, the driver merely opens the manual valve via linkage. As the engine turns the input shaft, the oil pump will build up pressure. The oil pressure will travel to the servo and tighten the band. When the car is accelerated, torque will be imparted and the car will move forward in the LOW range. Fig. 14-47.

HIGH RANGE

Another line must be added. This will run from the main line to a shifter valve. It will leave the shifter valve and branch out. One line will go to the high range clutch unit, another to the low range servo. In Fig. 14-48, you can see that the main line pressure has traveled to the shifter valve. The low range circuit is not shown.

HOW SHIFTER VALVE IS OPENED

GOVERNOR

You will note an opening on the right end of the shifter valve marked "oil passage from governor."

As the car moves forward in low range, the output shaft spins a governor unit. Oil pressure from the main line is piped to the governor unit, then to the shifter valve. When the car is not moving, the governor weight is in and oil pressure is stopped at the governor. Fig. 14-49.

As the car gathers road speed, the governor unit will spin faster and faster. At a predetermined speed, the governor valve will open and oil pressure will travel to the shifter valve. See A, Fig. 14-50. Note governor in B, Fig. 14-50.

When governor pressure reaches a certain level, the tension of the shifter spring will be overcome and the shifter valve will open. Fig. 14-51 shows the governor pressure building up against the shifter valve.

Fig. 14-47. Low range. When manual valve is opened, oil under pressure from pump travels via main line to servo. Oil will press on servo piston, causing it to tighten band. Car is now in low range.

SHIFT RANGE CHANGES

When the manual valve is opened, oil pressure actuates the low band servo. The car will then move forward in low range. Oil pressure also travels to the shifter valve and the governor. Fig. 14-52.

When the car reaches a predetermined road speed, the governor will have opened enough to allow oil pressure to flow to the shifter valve and force it open. When the shifter valve opens, oil pressure flows to the clutch and band servo units.

As the pressure builds up in the clutch, a corresponding pressure builds up in the servo. As the pressure from the shifter valve is working on two pistons of the servo, as opposed to the pressure from the manual valve working on one servo piston, the servo will be forced to move to the left and free the low band.

When the servo pistons stop moving to the left, the

Fig. 14-48. Schematic of shifter valve. Valve is shown in closed position. (GMC)

Fig. 14-49. Schematic of governor valve in closed position. Note that main line oil pressure cannot pass governor valve. (GMC)

Fig. 14-50. A—Schematic of governor valve in open position. Note main line oil pressure is now passing through valve. B—Cross section of a different type of governor. 1—Driven gear. 2—Primary weight. 3—Spring. 4—Valve. 5—Secondary weight. (GMC)

pressure in the clutch unit will build up rapidly, thus locking the clutch unit. The transmission is now in high range and will remain there until car speed falls below the shift point. When this happens, governor pressure is lost, clutch disengages and manual valve pressure reapplies low band servo. All this is done automatically. Fig. 14-53 shows the circuit in HIGH range.

SHIFT POINT SHOULD VARY

The point at which the transmission upshifts into high and downshifts into low range is controlled by the governor. These points are always constant.

It is very desirable to have the shift points vary according to load requirements. For rapid acceleration, the transmission should stay in low range longer.

Fig. 14-51. Governor pressure acting on shifter valve. Governor weight has been thrown out by centrifugal force. Governor valve is open and main line pressure is passing through governor to shifter valve.   (Lincoln)

Fig. 14-53. High range—schematic. Road speed has opened governor. Governor pressure opens shifter valve. Main line pressure now flows through shifter valve to offside of both servo pistons and to clutch. Servo releases and clutch applies. Transmission is now in high range.

Fig. 14-52. Low range—schematic. Manual valve open. Pressure to low band servo. Pressure to governor. Pressure to shifter valve. Governor closed; no pressure to open shifter valve. Shifter valve closed; no pressure to offsides of low band servo or clutch.

When attempting to pass at low speeds just above the downshift point, it is desirable to have the downshift occur when needed.

DELAYING THE UPSHIFT

You will notice a spring in the shifter valve in Fig. 14-51. As mentioned, the spring tension is overcome by governor pressure at a certain road speed. By plac-

ing a regulator plug to the left of the spring, and then connecting linkage to the throttle, it is possible to vary the spring tension.

When the throttle is depressed, the regulator plug is forced against the spring, increasing its tension. The car must gain more road speed to boost governor pressure, to overcome shifter spring tension. This will delay the upshift from low to high range. Fig. 14-54.

THROTTLE VALVE

Instead of moving the regulator plug by mechanical means, a throttle valve is used. The throttle valve is connected to the foot throttle through linkage. This rod is often referred to as the TV (throttle valve) rod. When the throttle is depressed, the throttle valve is moved and transmits oil pressure to the regulator plug. The amount of pressure depends on the distance the throttle is moved.

The throttle valve is an application of the spool balanced valve. Pressure is admitted to the valve at A, Fig. 14-55. It travels around the small spool section and exits through B. It is bypassed to chamber C at the spool end D. The pressure pushes on the shifter valve regulator plug and on the spool at D, Fig. 14-55.

Spring pressure E is controlled by the TV rod. When the throttle opening is small, spring pressure E is light. Oil pressure at D forces the spool to the right against the light spring pressure.

As the spool moves to the right, it starts to block opening A. As opening A size is reduced, the oil pressure entering the valve is also reduced.

If the spring is pushing to the left with a pressure of 15 lbs., the spool will be forced to the right until the entrance A is small enough to admit oil at 15 lbs. pressure. The valve will then be balanced. If spring pressure is increased, it will force the spool to the left, increasing opening A and oil pressure will build up in C. This will force the spool to the right until opening A is again closed far enough to balance oil pressure with spring pressure.

FORCED DOWNSHIFT

Another valve (it can be part of the throttle valve) is provided to admit high main line pressure to the shifter valve. This valve is sometimes called the T valve.

When the driver depresses the accelerator almost to the floor, the throttle valve strikes a detent plug and

Fig. 14-54. Shifter valve regulator plug. Throttle pressure will change spring tension and cause shifter valve to open under various pressures. (GMC)

Fig. 14-55. Throttle valve. Oil pressure balances spring pressure by moving spool until opening A admits proper pressure. TV rod adjusts spring pressure.

spring. When the accelerator is pressed beyond this point, the TV rod forces the T valve open. This directs main line pressure to the off side of the shifter valve. The shifter valve will close, cutting off pressure to the clutch and off side of the band servo. Now the servo will be actuated by manual valve pressure, and the low range band will tighten. This places the car in low range before road speed is slow enough to cause sufficient drop in governor pressure. This is called a forced downshift. Fig. 14-56.

Fig. 14-56. Forced downshift. When TV rod forces throttle valve rod in at A, main line pressure passes through T valve to offside of shifter valve. This additional pressure overcomes governor pressure and shuts shifter valve. Transmission will now downshift.

VACUUM MODULATOR

Makers now use a vacuum modulator in preference to the TV rod. The modulator utilizes engine vacuum, a very reliable indicator of engine loading. Therefore, the modulator provides very accurate means of controlling the throttle valve (also called modulator valve).

The vacuum modulator consists of a container separated into two areas by a flexible diaphragm. A spring forces the diaphragm rod to apply pressure to the throttle valve to increase TV pressure. In operation, engine vacuum causes the diaphragm to move away (against spring pressure) from the throttle valve, lowering the pressure. As engine loading varies, vacuum fluctuates. So the modulator is constantly altering throttle valve pressure in accordance with engine vacuum. See A, Fig. 14-57.

An altitude sensitive modulator is illustrated in B, Fig. 14-57. It incorporates an evacuated (air removed) bellows. The collapsing bellows tends to force the diaphragm toward the throttle valve. At sea level, the collapsing force is highest, adding to diaphragm pressure and raising TV pressure. As altitude increases, the collapsing force lessens and TV pressure is decreased.

The altitude compensating bellows provides a more

Fig. 14-57. A—Vacuum modulator controlling throttle valve by varying pressure on the push rod. B—Altitude sensitive modulator. Note evacuated bellows. (Ford)

uniform shift feel regardless of elevation. Look at B in Fig. 14-57.

COMPENSATOR VALVE

To add to the pressure on the band during heavy acceleration, a compensator valve is often used. This valve is controlled by foot throttle pressure on the throttle valve. During rapid acceleration (when torque is heavy), the compensator valve admits additional pressure to the band servo. Fig. 14-58.

COMPLETE CONTROL CIRCUIT

Fig. 14-59 shows the complete hydraulic system as used in one model of the Chrysler TorqueFlite, three-speed automatic transmission. Trace each circuit and study its construction and application. A similar transmission is illustrated in Fig. 14-60.

HYDRAULIC CONTROL CIRCUITS

The various oil circuits are extremely compact, and every possible means is used to avoid open tubing. Many of the shafts and other units are drilled to carry oil. Figs. 14-61 and 14-62. Most of the control valves are housed in one compact control valve body. An exploded view of the many components of a control valve body is shown in Fig. 14-63. Also, see Fig. 14-64.

Fig. 14-58. Compensator valve. Heavy throttle pressure opens compensator valve, admitting additional pressure to operate servo. Compensator pressure acts on on side of second servo piston.

OIL COOLING

Transmission oil is generally cooled by circulating it, via tubes, to a unit housed in the lower radiator. In cross-flow radiators, the tubes are connected to the right or left hand side tank. Fig. 14-65.

LUBRICATION

The transmission is lubricated by special oil which circulates through the unit. Never use any oil but AUTOMATIC TRANSMISSION FLUID, TYPE "A", SUFFIX "A." The container will be marked AQ - ATF - (several numbers) - A. Some makers specify an exact fluid (such as Dexron II, Ford Type F, CJ Type, etc.) for their own transmission. ALWAYS FOLLOW THESE RECOMMENDATIONS!

SHIFTING

The transmission may be placed in any desired range by moving a gearshift lever, usually located on the steering column. This moves a selector lever on the transmission. The range indicator with a sliding arrow shows the operator which range is "in." See Fig. 14-66.

A console floor shift mechanism is shown in Fig. 14-67. A push-button shift control also has been used.

DIFFERENT TYPES OF AUTOMATIC TRANSMISSIONS

Automatic transmission design has grown quite sophisticated, resulting in a more compact, smoother acting and highly reliable unit.

The use of the straight fluid coupling, once popular, has been replaced with the more efficient torque converter.

Torque converters have used both multiple turbines and stators. Current practice uses the basic converter design consisting of one pump, one turbine and a single stator. The stator is generally of FIXED PITCH (angle cannot be changed) construction.

The transmission and torque converter, as used in some front wheel drive cars, are separated. The

Fig. 14-59. Complete hydraulic control for a TorqueFlite, 3-speed transmission. (Chrysler)

Fig. 14-60. Cutaway view of a THM 180C automatic transmission. Learn part names and their locations.   (Pontiac)

Fig. 14-61. Cutaway of a Peugeot 3-speed automatic transmission. Study part arrangement.   (Peugeot)

torque converter drives the transmission via a link belt (chain) assembly.

Figs. 14-68, 14-69, 14-70, and 14-71, illustrate the clutch and band action in a two-speed transmission. Study the power flow in each range.

A cutaway view of a three-speed transmission is illustrated in Fig. 14-72.

A four-speed transmission is shown in Figs. 14-73, 14-74, and 14-75.

Fig. 14-76 illustrates the Ford "torque-splitter" transmission. Note its very unique design and see how many components you can identify.

Figs. 14-77 and 14-78 show cutaways of a three-speed transmission.

Another three-speed transmission design is illustrated in Fig. 14-79.

The clutch and band action of one three-speed transmission is shown in Fig. 14-80. Study the action and power flow in each range.

Figs. 14-81, 14-82, and 14-84 feature front wheel drive transaxle setups.

Study all the transmission illustrations. Make certain you know the various part names and can explain their basic functions.

Fig. 14-62. Sun gear shaft showing drilled passageways. (Ford)

Fig. 14-63. Exploded view of control valve body. (Ford)

Fig. 14-64. A General Motors 200-4R automatic transmission. This four-speed unit provides an overdrive ratio in top range. It also utilizes a converter lockup clutch. (GM)

LOCKING CONVERTER

The normal converter allows some slippage, even at cruising speeds. This is due to the fact that the only connection between pump and turbine is the transmission fluid.

To prevent this slipping action, and thus improve fuel economy, a number of converters are equipped

Fig. 14-65. Method of cooling transmission oil. This side view shows oil cooler located in right-side radiator tank. (Cadillac)

Fig. 14-66. Column gearshift linkage. (Ford)

with a lockup feature. When the lockup unit is activated, the pump (impeller) and turbine are mechanically locked together. To allow a lockup condition, most setups are arranged so that the transmission must be in high range, speed above around 35 to 40 mph (56–64 km/h) and in a cruise condition (no hill, acceleration, or other engine loading situation).

There are several lockup designs. A schematic of one type is pictured in Fig. 14-83. Study A carefully. Note part names.

LOCKUP OPERATION

Before lockup, the turbine and pump (impeller) are mechanically free of each other and drive is through

Fig. 14-67. A console (floor) gearshift linkage arrangement. (Plymouth)

Fig. 14-70. Transmission in direct drive range. Forward clutch applied. Low band and reverse clutch released.

Fig. 14-68. Schematic illustrates Pontiac two-speed transmission action in neutral. Clutches and band are released.

Fig. 14-71. Transmission in reverse. Reverse clutch applied. Low band and forward clutch released.

Fig. 14-69. Transmission in low range. Note power flow. Low band is applied while clutches are released.

Fig. 14-72. Cutaway of an automatic transmission as used by BMW. How many parts can you identify? (BMW)

1. TORQUE CONVERTER
2. DIRECT DRIVE SHAFT
3. FRONT PUMP SEAL
4. FRONT PUMP 'O' RING
5. FRONT PUMP BODY
6. FRONT PUMP GASKET
7. FRONT PUMP DRIVE GEAR
8. FRONT PUMP DRIVEN GEAR
9. STATOR SUPPORT – FRONT PUMP
10. INTERM. CLUTCH PISTON INNER LIP SEAL
11. INTERM. CLUTCH PISTON OUTER LIP SEAL
12. FRONT PUMP BUSHING
13. INTERM. CLUTCH PISTON
14. INTERM. CLUTCH PISTON RETURN SPRINGS & RETAINER
15. INTERM. CLUTCH EXTERNAL SPLINE STEEL PLATES (SEL.)
16. INTERM. CLUTCH INTERNAL SPLINE FRICTION PLATES
17. INTERM. CLUTCH PRESSURE PLATE
18. NO. 1 THRUST WASHER (FRONT PUMP) SELECTIVE
19. STATOR SUPPORT SEAL RINGS (REV. CLUTCH)
20. STATOR SUPPORT SEAL RINGS (FWD. CLUTCH)
21. OVERDRIVE BAND
22. INTERM. OWC RETAINING SNAP
23. INTERM. OWC RETAINING PLATE
24. INTERM. OWC OUTER RACE
25. INTERM. ONE-WAY CLUTCH ASSY.
26. REVERSE CLUTCH DRUM
27. REVERSE CLUTCH PISTON SEAL (OUTER)
28. REVERSE CLUTCH PISTON
29. REVERSE CLUTCH PISTON SEAL (INNER)
30. THRUST RING
31. REVERSE CLUTCH PISTON RETURN SPRING
32. RETAINING SNAP RING
33. REVERSE CLUTCH FRONT PRESSURE PLATE
34. REVERSE CLUTCH INTERNAL SPLINE FRICTION PLATE
35. REVERSE CLUTCH EXTERNAL SPLINE STEEL PLATE
36. REVERSE CLUTCH REAR PRESSURE PLATE
37. REVERSE CLUTCH RETAINING RING (SEL.)
38. NO. 2 THRUST WASHER (REV. CLUTCH)
39. TURBINE SHAFT
40. FORWARD CLUTCH CYLINDER & TURBINE SHAFT
41. FORWARD CLUTCH PISTON SEAL (OUTER)
42. FORWARD CLUTCH PISTON SEAL (INNER)
43. FORWARD CLUTCH PISTON
44. FORWARD CLUTCH PISTON RETURN SPRING
45. RETURN SPRING RETAINER
46. RETAINING SNAP RING
47. WAVED PLATE
48. FORWARD CLUTCH EXTERNAL SPLINE STEEL PLATE
49. FORWARD CLUTCH INTERNAL SPLINE FRICTION PLATE
50. FORWARD CLUTCH PRESSURE PLATE
51. RETAINING SNAP RING (SELECTIVE)
52. NO. 3 NEEDLE BEARING (FWD. CLUTCH)
53. FORWARD CLUTCH HUB
54. NO. 4 NEEDLE BEARING
55. REVERSE SUN GEAR & DRIVE SHELL ASSY.
56. NO. 5 NEEDLE BEARING
57. FORWARD SUN GEAR
58. CENTER SUPPORT RETAINING RING
59. FORWARD SUN GEAR PRECISION BUSHING
60. CENTER SUPPORT PLANETARY
61. PLANETARY OWC CAGE SPRING & ROLLER ASSY.
62. PLANETARY ASSY.
63. REVERSE BAND
64. DIRECT CLUTCH HUB
65. NO. 7 NEEDLE BEARING (DIRECT CLUTCH INNER)
66. RETAINING SNAP RING (SELECTIVE)
67. THRUST SPACER
68. DIRECT CLUTCH PRESSURE PLATE
69. DIRECT CLUTCH INTERNAL SPLINE PLATES
70. DIRECT CLUTCH EXTERNAL SPLINE PLATES
71. RETAINING SNAP RING
72. RETURN SPRING & RETAINER
73. DIRECT CLUTCH PISTON
74. DIRECT CLUTCH PISTON SEAL (INNER)
75. DIRECT CLUTCH PISTON SEAL (OUTER)
76. RING GEAR & PARK GEAR
77. DIRECT CYLINDER
78. OUTPUT SHAFT SMALL (2) STEEL SEAL RINGS (DIRECT CLUTCH)
79. NO. 8 NEEDLE BEARING (DIRECT CLUTCH OUTER)
80. OUTPUT SHAFT
81. OUTPUT SHAFT LARGE (4) STEEL SEAL RINGS
82. OUTPUT SHAFT HUB
83. RETAINING SNAP RING (O.P.S. HUB TO O.P.S.)
84. RETAINING SNAP RING (O.P.S. HUB TO RING GEAR)
85. REAR CASE BUSHING
86. NO. 9 NEEDLE BEARING (REAR CASE)
87. CASE ASSY.
88. NEUTRAL START SWITCH
89. VENT CAP
90. GOVERNOR COUNTERWEIGHT
91. BODY ASSY. – GOVERNOR
92. PLUG GOVERNOR
93. SLEEVE GOVERNOR
94. SCREEN ASSY. – GOV. OIL
95. SPRING GOV. VALVE
96. VALVE GOVERNOR
97. BODY GOVERNOR
98. BOLT (GOVERNOR BODY TO COUNTERWEIGHT)
99. CLIP – (GOVERNOR COVER TO GOVERNOR BODY)
100. BOLT (GOVERNOR COVER TO GOVERNOR BODY)
101. COVER – GOVERNOR VALVE BODY
102. RETAINING SNAP RING (GOVERNOR ASSY. TO O.P.S.)
103. EXTENSION HOUSING BRACKET
104. EXTENSION HOUSING BUSHING
105. EXTENSION HOUSING
106. EXTENSION HOUSING SEAL
107. BOLT (EXT. HSG. TO CASE) M6-12.5 X 30 (6 REQ'D.)
108. PIPE PLUG – 1/8-27 DRY SEAL
109. OVERDRIVE SERVO PISTON RETURN SPRING
110. OVERDRIVE SERVO PISTON
111. OVERDRIVE SERVO PISTON SEAL
112. OVERDRIVE SERVO COVER SEAL RINGS
113. OVERDRIVE SERVO COVER
114. RETAINING SNAP RING (O/D SERVO TO CASE)
115. REVERSE SERVO PISTON RETURN SPRING
116. REVERSE SERVO PISTON (SELECTIVE)
117. REVERSE SERVO COVER
118. RETAINING SNAP RING (REV. SERVO TO CASE)
119. 3-4 ACCUMULATOR VALVE SEAL
120. 3-4 ACCUMULATOR VALVE
121. 3-4 ACCUMULATOR VALVE RETURN SPRING
122. 3-4 ACCUMULATOR COVER
123. 3-4 ACCUMULATOR COVER SEAL
124. RETAINING SNAP RING (3-4 ACCUM. TO CASE)
125. 2-3 ACCUMULATOR VALVE SEAL (SMALL)
126. 2-3 ACCUMULATOR VALVE
127. 2-3 ACCUMULATOR VALVE SEAL (LARGE)
128. 2-3 ACCUMULATOR VALVE RETURN SPRING
129. 2-3 ACCUMULATOR COVER
130. RETAINING SNAP RING (2-3 ACCUM. TO CASE)
131. PARK PAWL SHAFT
132. GUIDE CUP
133. PARK PAWL RETURN SPRING
134. MANUAL LEVER
135. GROMMET
136. THROTTLE LEVER OIL SEAL
137. ATTACHING NUT & LOCK WASHER – M8 X 1.25
138. THROTTLE LEVER (OUTER)
139. PARK PAWL
140. PARK PAWL ACTUATING ROD
141. MANUAL LEVER (INNER)
142. ROLL PIN – 1/8 X 0.95 GROOVED
143. DETENT SPRING
144. ATTACHING NUT (MANUAL LVR) – M14 X 1.5 HEX
145. THROTTLE LEVER (INNER)
146. THROTTLE TORSION SPRING
147. VALVE BODY REINFORCEMENT PLATE
148. SEPARATOR PLATE GASKET (UPPER)
149. SEPARATOR PLATE
150. SEPARATOR PLATE GASKET (LOWER)
151. VALVE BODY (MAIN CONTROL)
152. FILTER & GROMMET ASSY. – OIL PAN
153. OIL PAN GASKET
154. OIL PAN
155. BOLT (OIL PAN TO CASE) – M8-1.25 X 15 (17 REQ'D.)
156. OIL FILTER GASKET
157. BOLT (VALVE BODY TO CASE) M6 1.0 X 30 (8 REQ'D.)
158. BOLT (VALVE BODY TO CASE) M6 1.0 X 40 (17 REQ'D.)
159. BOLT (SCREEN TO VALVE BODY) M6 1.0 X 16 (3 REQ'D.)
160. BALL (GOVERNOR DRIVE)
161. SPRING (ANTI CLUNK)
162. GROMMET
163. OIL SEAL ASSY.

Fig. 14-73. Exploded view of a Ford four-speed automatic transmission. Study parts, names, and their relationship to overall unit. (Ford)

Fig. 14-74. Mercedes-Benz four-speed automatic. Study parts carefully. How many can you identify?
(Mercedes-Benz)

Fig. 14-75. Four-speed automatic transmission with overdrive in fourth gear. Unit is equipped with a lockup converter that
is actuated in fourth gear. How many parts can you name?   (Ford)

CLUTCHES

TORQUE CONVERTER

SPLITTER GEAR

DIFFERENTIAL DRIVE GEAR

DIFFERENTIAL GEARING

PLANETARY GEARSET

Fig. 14-76. Ford split-torque, three-speed automatic transaxle. Note "splitter gear." This arrangement divides engine torque in second and drive gears. In second gear, 38 percent of the torque transmission (output) is through the converter and 65 percent mechanically. In drive, 93 percent of torque is transmitted mechanically with only 7 percent through the converter. This prevents most converter slippage.   (Ford)

CONVERTER PUMP

PUMP ASSEMBLY

FORWARD CLUTCH

DIRECT CLUTCH

FRONT BAND

INTERMEDIATE CLUTCH

INTERMEDIATE SPRAG

CENTER SUPPORT

ROLLER CLUTCH

REAR BAND

OUTPUT CARRIER AND INTERNAL GEAR

STATOR ROLLER CLUTCH

OUTPUT SHAFT

SUN GEAR

SPEEDOMETER DRIVEN GEAR ASM.

REAR INTERNAL GEAR

REACTION CARRIER

SUN GEAR SHAFT

DETENT SOLENOID

MAIN SHAFT

STATOR SHAFT

CONTROL VALVE ASM.

TURBINE SHAFT

TURBINE

STATOR

MANUAL SHAFT

FILTER ASSEMBLY

Fig. 14-77. Turbo-Hydramatic 400, three-speed transmission.   (GM)

Fig. 14-78. Turbo-Hydramatic 350 automatic transmission. This is a three-speed unit employing four multiple disc clutches, two planetary gearsets, two roller clutches, and an intermediate overrun band.　(Chevrolet)

the fluid. There is NO contact between turbine and clutch friction surface. Action is like that of a conventional converter. See B, Fig. 14-83.

When lockup conditions are all present, transmission fluid will move through a passage in the transmission input shaft. It will flow into the space between the turbine and clutch apply piston. Piston will move, engage clutch friction surface to lock pump and turbine together. This action is shown in C, Fig. 14-83.

SUMMARY

The automatic transmission shifts in accordance with speed and load conditions.

It uses one or more planetary gearsets to produce the desired gear ratios. Multiple disc clutches and bands are used to control gearsets, Fig. 14-84.

The clutches and bands are actuated by hydraulic pressure produced by one or two oil pumps. The oil pressure is directed and controlled by a series of valves. Distribution is via oil passageways in the various units.

Definite speed ranges such as drive, low, reverse, etc., can be selected by the driver through mechanical linkage connected to a control valve in transmission.

Power transmission from engine to transmission is through a fluid coupling or a torque converter.

The torque converter can multiply the engine

torque, thereby giving a wide range of power. The amount of multiplication is dependent on converter design and position between "stall" and "coupling point."

Lubrication is provided by special transmission oil as it circulates through the unit.

Oil is cooled by piping it to a cooler unit in one of the radiator tanks.

A complete study and mastery of the automatic transmission involves a great deal of material. This chapter has endeavored to give you a working knowledge of the basic principles involved. For further study, manufacturers' shop manuals are an excellent source of information.

KNOW THESE TERMS

Fluid coupling, Torus, Torque converter, Stator, One-way clutches, Stall, Planetary gearsets, Brake bands, Accumulator piston, Clutch, Oil pump, Manual control valve, Governor, Throttle valve, Vacuum modulator, Compensating valve.

REVIEW QUESTIONS—CHAPTER 14

1. What unit eliminates the conventional clutch as used on standard transmission installations?
2. What is a planetary gearset?
3. Name the parts in a planetary gearset.

Fig. 14-79. Ford C6, three-speed transmission.   (Ford)

CLUTCHES AND THE BAND ARE RELEASED
NEUTRAL

THE INTERMEDIATE BAND IS APPLIED. THE REVERSE AND HIGH CLUTCH DRUM, THE INPUT SHELL, AND THE SUN GEAR ARE HELD STATIONARY.

THE FORWARD CLUTCH IS APPLIED. THE FRONT PLANETARY UNIT RING GEAR IS LOCKED TO THE INPUT SHAFT.
SECOND GEAR

BOTH THE FORWARD AND THE REVERSE AND HIGH CLUTCH ARE APPLIED. ALL PLANETARY GEAR MEMBERS ARE LOCKED TO EACH OTHER AND ARE LOCKED TO THE OUTPUT SHAFT.

HIGH GEAR

THE FORWARD CLUTCH IS APPLIED. THE FRONT PLANETARY UNIT RING GEAR IS LOCKED TO THE INPUT SHAFT.

THE LOW AND REVERSE CLUTCH (LOW RANGE) OR THE ONE-WAY CLUTCH (D1 RANGE) IS HOLDING THE REVERSE UNIT PLANET CARRIER STATIONARY.

FIRST GEAR

GEAR RATIOS	
FIRST 2.46:1	
	SECOND 1.46:1
	HIGH 1.00:1
	REVERSE 2.17:1

THE REVERSE AND HIGH CLUTCH IS APPLIED. THE INPUT SHAFT IS LOCKED TO THE REVERSE AND HIGH CLUTCH DRUM, THE INPUT SHELL, AND THE SUN GEAR.

THE LOW AND REVERSE CLUTCH IS APPLIED. THE REVERSE UNIT PLANET CARRIER IS HELD STATIONARY.

REVERSE

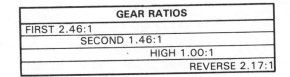

Fig. 14-80. Transmission action during various speed ranges in Ford C6, three-speed transmission.

Fig. 14-81. A front wheel drive automatic transmission. This three-speed unit transfers torque from turbine shaft to transmission input shaft via a drive chain. (Oldsmobile)

4. A planetary gearset can be used to _____ or _____ torque and it can also be used to _____ the direction of rotation.
5. What unit is used to stop the planetary internal gear?
6. The planetary gearset can be used to transmit torque as a solid unit by _____ any two _____ of the gearset together.
7. The action in question 6 is accomplished by applying oil pressure to what unit?
8. What is a fluid coupling?
9. How does a fluid coupling work?

Fig. 14-82. Three-speed automatic transaxle (transmission and drive axle make up an integrated assembly). (Toyota)

Fig. 14-83. Operation of a lockup torque converter. A—Lockup clutch design. B—Lockup apply piston has released and unit is unlocked. In this mode (condition or stage), it will operate as a standard torque converter. C—Apply piston has moved against clutch friction surface thus locking converter. In this mode, it will operate as a solid drive unit with no slippage between turbine and pump (impeller).

10. What is the principal difference between a fluid coupling and a torque converter?
11. The fluid coupling can multiply torque. True or False?
12. The vanes in a torque converter are straight. True or False?
13. Fluid motion in both the torque converter and the fluid coupling is in two directions. One motion is called the _____ flow, the other the _____ flow.
14. Of what value is the split ring in the fluid coupling and torque converter.
15. What is a stator?
16. How does a stator work?
17. The fluid coupling uses a stator. True or False?
18. The stator can revolve in one direction only.

What stops its rotation in one direction?

19. Why must the stator revolve in one direction only?
20. What is the stall point?
21. Explain what we mean by coupling point.
22. Why are torque converter vanes curved?
23. What is a servo and what does it do?
24. A multiple disc clutch uses a servo to actuate it. True or False?
25. What value is there in the use of an accumulator piston?
26. There are two types of oil pumps in general usage in the automatic transmission. Name them.
27. What is a shifter valve?
28. What opens the shifter valve?
29. What controls the source that opens the shifter valve?
30. Explain the action when the simple two-speed automatic transmission is placed in Low Range; in High Range.
31. What unit is used to delay the upshift?

32. How is downshift accomplished?
33. Draw a sketch showing how a spool balance valve works.
34. To apply extra pressure on the brake band during heavy acceleration, a _____ valve is often used.
35. What lubricates an automatic transmission?
36. SAE 20W MS engine oil will work well in an automatic transmission. True or False?
37. Explain, step-by-step, how a typical two-speed automatic transmission functions. Start with the shift lever in neutral.
38. When all other lockup conditions are present, converter lockup will take place in:
    a. Low range.
    b. High range.
    c. Reverse.
    d. Neutral.
39. The lockup converter prevents slippage between the pump and turbine. Explain how it functions.

① Transmission	⑫ Drum hub assembly	㉓ Side gear
② Rear clutch	⑬ Bearing housing	㉔ Pinion gear
③ Front clutch	⑭ Output gear	㉕ Pinion shaft
④ Connection shell	⑮ Turbine shaft	㉖ Differential gear case
⑤ Rear clutch hub assembly	⑯ Oil pump shaft	㉗ Ring gear
⑥ Planetary carrier	⑰ Bearing cover	㉘ Oil seal
⑦ Sun gear	⑱ Oil seal	㉙ Side bearing housing
⑧ Low and reverse brake	⑲ Torque converter	㉚ Control valve
⑨ One-way clutch	⑳ Converter housing	㉛ Oil pan
⑩ One-way clutch inner race	㉑ Oil seal	㉜ Oil pump
⑪ Planetary carrier	㉒ Speedometer drive gear	

Fig. 14-84. Cutaway of a 3-speed automatic transaxle assembly. (Mazda)

Chapter 15

DRIVE LINES

After studying this chapter, you will be able to:
- List the basic parts of an automobile drive line.
- Explain the function of each drive line part.
- Describe various types of drive lines.

In order for the transmission output shaft to drive the differential pinion gear shaft, it is necessary to connect these two units by means of a propeller shaft. Fig. 15-1.

PROPELLER SHAFT MUST BE FLEXIBLE

When the rear wheels strike a bump or a hole, the rear axle housing moves up or down in relation to the frame. As the transmission is more or less solidly fixed to the frame, it becomes obvious that to allow the rear axle to move up and down, the drive line or propeller shaft must be able to flex. Fig. 15-2.

UNIVERSAL JOINT IS NEEDED

It is clear that a solid drive line would be bent and finally broken as the angle of drive changes. To allow the drive line, or propeller shaft, to move without breaking, a flexible joint is used. This is called a UNIVERSAL JOINT. Fig. 15-3.

By using a universal joint, torque can be transmitted constantly even though the rear axle is moving up and down. Fig. 15-4.

TYPES OF UNIVERSAL JOINTS

The cross and roller, sometimes called CARDAN, is in common use. It consists of a center cross, often referred to as a SPIDER, and two yokes, frequently called KNUCKLES. The yokes surround a needle

Fig. 15-2. Propeller shaft must flex. A represents normal operating angle of propeller shaft. B shows how bump forces differential up. Notice how propeller shaft angle changes. Since transmission is fixed to frame, propeller shaft must flex.

Fig. 15-1. Connecting transmission and differential. Top view showing propeller shaft hookup.

Fig. 15-3. Simple universal joint. Shaft A is transmitting torque in horizontal plane. Shaft B is transmitting same torque, but at different angle. Yokes swivel around ends of cross, imparting a degree of flexibility to universal joint.

339

Fig. 15-4. Universal joints in action. As rear axle moves up and down, universals allow drive angles to change without binding propeller shaft.

Fig. 15-6. Cross and roller universal joint employing injection molded plastic "rings" to secure bearing cup or bushing to slip yoke. Plastic is forced into an injection hole and flows into ring groove cut in bushing and yoke. The plastic hardens and secures bushing. (Oldsmobile)

bearing roller bushing assembly. The roller can be retained in the yoke by using snap rings, injected molded plastic rings, U-bolts, bolted plates, etc. The roller needles surround the cross ends. These cross ends are called TRUNNIONS.

This setup allows the yokes to swivel on the cross with a minimum amount of friction. Fig. 15-5 shows an exploded view of a typical cross and roller universal joint. A cutaway view of another cross and roller is pictured in Fig. 15-6. Note that this particular setup employs injection molded plastic "rings" to secure the bearing cup or bushing in the yoke.

An enlarged view of the cross or spider is shown in Fig. 15-7. Notice that the trunnions are smoothly finished. A hollow in each trunnion leads to the center of the cross. A grease fitting is placed in the center. When lubricated, grease will flow out to each

Fig. 15-7. Universal joint cross with bushing and roller assemblies. Note grease channel in each trunnion. (Spicer)

needle roller.

A phantom view of a cross and roller joint is shown in Fig. 15-8. Typical cross and roller joint installations are pictured in Fig. 15-17.

BALL AND TRUNNION UNIVERSAL JOINT

Another type of universal, called the ball and trunnion, is sometimes used. This universal, in addition to allowing the drive line to bend, also allows fore and aft (forward and backward) movement of the propeller shaft.

A ball and trunnion joint is illustrated in Fig. 15-9. The cross pin is inserted in the hole in the ball on the end of the propeller shaft. The ball and roller assembly mounts on the ends of the cross pins. The round ball slides back and forth in a round hole in the center of the joint body. The rollers also slide and tip in grooves in the outer body.

Fig. 15-5. Exploded view of a typical cross and roller universal joint. (AMC)

340

Fig. 15-8. Phantom view of a cross and roller universal joint. (Dana Corp.)

The cutaway, Fig. 15-10, shows the ball and trunnion in the assembled position.

DRIVE LINE CHANGES LENGTH

As the rear axle moves up and down, it swings on an arc that is different from that of the drive line. As a result, the distance between transmission and rear axle will change to some extent.

SLIP JOINT

To allow the drive line to adjust to these variations in length, a slip joint is often used. The forward end of the propeller stub shaft has a series of splines cut

Fig. 15-9. Exploded view of ball and trunnion universal joint. Boot, clamp and grease cover protect universal joint from water and dust. Centering buttons prevent end movement of pin, ball and needle rollers. (Plymouth)

Fig. 15-10. Assembled ball and trunnion universal joint. Ball and trunnion joint is shown on right end. Left joint is conventional cross and roller.

into it. The universal yoke sleeve has corresponding splines cut into it. The yoke sleeve is slipped over the splined propeller shaft stub, and the universal is bolted to the transmission output shaft. The shaft can move fore and aft by sliding in the yoke sleeve splines. Fig. 15-11.

As mentioned, the ball and trunnion universal allows fore and aft movement, so a slip joint is not necessary when this type of joint is used.

Fig. 15-12. Typical propeller shaft. Yokes are welded to hollow shaft. Note sliding yoke on one end. This allows drive line to adapt to changes in length as suspension moves up and down. (Toyota)

Fig. 15-11. Universal joint incorporating a slip joint in yoke.

PROPELLER SHAFTS

The propeller shaft is generally hollow to promote light weight and of a diameter sufficient to impart great strength. Quality steel and aluminum, in a few cases, are used in its construction. Some have a rubber mounted torsional damper.

The universal yoke and splined stub (where used) are welded to the ends of a hollow shaft. The shaft must run true, and it must be carefully balanced to avoid vibrations. The propeller shaft is often turning at engine speeds. It can cause great damage if bent, unbalanced or if there is wear in the universal joints. Fig. 15-12.

HOW DO THE WHEELS DRIVE THE CAR?

When the propeller shaft turns the differential, the axles and wheels are driven forward. The driving force developed between the tires and the road is first transferred to the rear axle housing. From the axle housing, it is transmitted to the frame or body in one of three ways:

1. Through leaf springs that are bolted to the housing and shackled to the frame.
2. Through control or torque arms shackled (bolted, but free to swivel) to both frame and axle housing.
3. Through a torque tube that surrounds the propeller shaft, which is bolted to the axle housing and pivoted to the transmission by means of a large ball socket (sometimes referred to as a torque ball). See Fig. 15-13.

HOTCHKISS DRIVE

The Hotchkiss type of drive is used when the rear axle drive thrust is transmitted to the frame through the springs or via control arms.

The Hotchkiss drive consists of an open propeller shaft secured to the transmission output shaft and differential pinion gear shaft. Front and rear universal joints are used. If both joints are of the cross and roller type, a slip joint must be provided.

The main task performed by the Hotchkiss drive is that of transferring output shaft torque to the differential. Wheel drive thrust is NOT transmitted to the drive line. A typical Hotchkiss drive is pictured in Figs. 15-1, B in 15-13, and 15-14. The Hotchkiss drive is in widespread use today.

Fig. 15-13. Methods used to transfer driving force from rear axle housing to car frame. A—Force transmitted through leaf springs. B—Transmitted through control rods. C—Transmitted through torque tube.

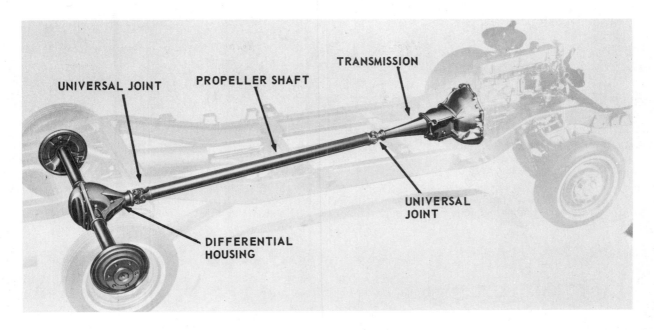

Fig. 15-14. Typical Hotchkiss drive setup. In this particular car, drive thrust from rear axle housing is transmitted to frame via control arms. (Chevrolet)

TWO-PIECE HOTCHKISS

To reduce excessive propeller shaft length (with resultant problems of vibration and installation), a two-piece propeller shaft is often used. In this type of installation, it is necessary to have a center support bearing for the shafts. This support consists of a ball bearing held in a dustproof housing that is, in turn, supported by the frame. Rubber is generally incorporated in the mount to reduce noise and vibration transfer to the frame. The rubber will also allow some movement of the shaft without binding.

Fig. 15-15 illustrates a typical center support bearing. Note that the front propeller shaft rests in the

Fig. 15-15. One type of propeller shaft center support bearing. A dust protected ball bearing, mounted in rubber, is used to support two shafts where they meet. (GMC)

rubber cushioned bearing. The splined stub allows slip joint action at this point.

Both front and rear shafts in a two-piece Hotchkiss drive are pictured in Fig. 15-16. The center support is also on rubber mounts. Note the use of three universal joints. Fig. 15-17 shows several types of propeller shaft and universal joint assemblies.

TORQUE TUBE DRIVE

When the rear axle housing thrust is not carried to the frame through the springs or by control rods, a torque tube drive is used.

The torque tube is a hollow steel tube that reaches from the transmission to the rear axle housing. One end of the torque tube is secured to the axle housing by a ring of bolts. The other, or forward end, is fastened to the transmission through a torque ball arrangement.

The propeller shaft runs through the torque tube. The transmission end has a universal joint, located inside the torque ball. The rear end of the propeller shaft is splined to the pinion gear shaft.

All housing drive thrust is carried through the torque tube to the torque ball, to the transmission, to the engine, and then on to the frame through the engine mounts. The car is literally being shoved forward by the torque tube pressing on the engine.

The torque tube is often braced by metal strut rods fastened to the axle housing and extending out some distance to the torque tube. On some installations, a center support bearing is located midway in the torque tube to steady the propeller shaft.

The universal joint located inside the torque ball receives lubrication from the transmission oil. Oil is

Fig. 15-16. Two-piece Hotchkiss drive—assembled. This setup uses three universal joints; two on one shaft, one on other. Rubber cushioned center support is used where shafts connect. (American Motors)

Fig. 15-17. Various propeller shaft and universal joint assemblies. A—Four wheel drive. B—Yoke, top view. C—Front wheel drive axle shaft constant velocity joint. D—One-piece shaft. E—Exploded view of cross and roller joint. F—Two-piece propeller shaft. G—Yoke, side view. H—Shaft made up of two separate tubes, bonded together with rubber to help eliminate torsional vibration. I—Two-piece shaft. J—Universal joint assembled. (Volvo, Toyota, British-Leyland, Renault)

kept from running into the torque tube by an oil seal. A typical torque tube arrangement is shown in C, Fig. 15-13. A modified torque tube, cross and roller setup, is pictured in Fig. 15-18.

One make of car has used a two-piece torque tube that allows a bend in the tube to facilitate a beneficial drive angle. Fig. 15-19. This type uses a front universal in the torque ball and a second joint where the two torque tubes are bolted together. The torque tube is little used today.

Fig. 15-18. One form of torque tube drive. This setup uses a short torque tube from differential housing to the central joint assembly (where tire drive thrust is transmitted to the frame). A conventional Hotchkiss drive is used from the central joint to the transmission. (Opel)

Fig. 15-19. Two-piece torque tube. A second universal, located where two torque tubes meet, is used. Front universal is not shown. (Buick)

UNIVERSAL JOINT CAN CAUSE FLUCTUATING SHAFT SPEED

If a conventional universal joint is driving at an angle and the speed of the driving shaft is constant, the speed of the driven shaft will rise and fall. Even though the driven shaft is turning the same number of turns per minute, its speed will fluctuate. Actually, the driven shaft speed will rise and fall two times for every revolution. This is due to the fact that the angle of drive is not equally divided between the two shafts. Figs. 15-20 and 15-21.

UNIVERSAL JOINT YOKES MUST BE IN SAME PLANE

When using a universal joint on each end of a propeller shaft, the disturbing shaft speed fluctuation can be greatly reduced if both universal joint yokes are in the same plane (lined up). Fig. 15-22 illustrates speed fluctuations by means of a speed fluctuation chart.

With the joint yokes in the same plane, the torque of the driving shaft will be transmitted to the pinion shaft in a smoother manner. The propeller shaft speed will rise and fall from the front joint action, but the fluctuation will be cancelled out by the action of the rear joint. Fig. 15-23.

CONSTANT VELOCITY UNIVERSAL JOINT

There are several different types of universal joints designed to produce even transfer of torque without

Fig. 15-20. Schematic showing principle of constant velocity universal joint. A illustrates necessary location for ball socket that will keep angle of drive evenly divided between shafts 1 and 2. B shows coupling yoke and ball socket. Note how both shafts form same angle—3 and 4. (Chevrolet)

Fig. 15-21. Shaft speed fluctuates as drive angles change. Were you to chart speed of X as it moves around one revolution, you would find that it accelerates through D, decelerates through A, accelerates through B, and once again decelerates through arc or distance C. These speed fluctuations are caused by drive angle changes that do not divide angle equally between both shafts connected by universal joint.

ONE REVOLUTION OF PROPELLER SHAFT

30°

SPEEDS OF
DRIVEN SHAFT
FOR DRIVING
SHAFT SPEED OF
1000 RPM

1200
1100
1000
900
800

0 ◄ACCELERATION► 90 ◄DECELERATION► 180 ACCELERATION ► 270 ◄DECELERATION► 360
DEGREES OF ROTATION

CONVENTIONAL UNIVERSAL JOINT
SHOWING FLUCTUATIONS

CONSTANT VELOCITY UNIVERSAL
JOINT, NO FLUCTUATIONS

Fig. 15-22. Speed fluctuation chart. As universal joint turns, angle formed by cross changes. It never divides angle equally between two shafts, (except for one brief moment as cross angle shifts from one extreme to other). This causes acceleration-deceleration fluctuation that transmits torque in a jerky fashion. Dotted line illustrates even speed when constant velocity (later) universal joint is used. Undulating line (waving) represents speed fluctuation achieved with conventional type universal joint.

SAME
PLANE

YOKE

PROPELLER
SHAFT

YOKE

Fig. 15-23. Universal joint yokes must be in same plane.

speed fluctuations. They are commonly referred to as constant speed or constant velocity universal joints. These joints provide an extremely smooth power transfer.

Constant speed transfer is made possible by special design of the joint that automatically divides angle of drive equally between two shafts. Fig. 15-24 shows an exploded view of one widely used design. A cutaway of an assembled joint is featured in Fig. 15-25. Fig. 15-26 pictures a one-piece propeller shaft utilizing two constant speed universal joints.

SUMMARY

Drive lines can be of two general types, Hotchkiss and torque tube. The torque tube currently enjoys little use.

Fig. 15-24. Exploded view of a constant velocity universal joint arrangement. Note centering assembly. (Chrysler)

Fig. 15-25. Cutaway of assembled constant velocity joint. Study centering ball and seat arrangement. (GM)

Fig. 15-26. A one-piece propeller shaft incorporating a constant velocity universal joint at each end. This produces a very smooth transfer of torque. (Cadillac)

When the rear axle housing drive thrust is carried by the springs or control arms, an open shaft Hotchkiss drive may be used. It will use two or more universal joints. The propeller shaft may be of two-piece design.

If the drive line must carry the drive thrust, the torque tube system is employed. A propeller shaft, using one or more universal joints, is enclosed in a steel tube. The tube carries the thrust.

Universal joints are of two basic types, the cross and roller and ball and trunnion.

As drive line angles change, it is necessary to utilize a slip joint to allow fore and aft movement of the propeller shaft.

Drive lines must operate at high speeds. Therefore, they must be accurately constructed and carefully balanced. See Fig. 15-17.

Some universal joints are lubricated upon construction and are sealed for life. Other types utilize a grease fitting for periodic lubrication.

To prevent speed fluctuation transfer to the pinion shaft, it is essential that both front and rear propeller shaft yokes be in the same plane.

Constant velocity universal joints are used to provide smooth torque transfer without speed fluctuations.

KNOW THESE TERMS

Propeller shaft, Universal joint, Cross and roller, Ball and trunnion, Slip joint, Hotchkiss drive, Torque tube drive, Constant velocity universal joint.

REVIEW QUESTIONS—CHAPTER 15

1. What is the name of the unit that connects the transmission output shaft to the differential pinion gear shaft?
2. As the rear axle housing moves up and down in relation to the transmission, what unit allows the necessary flexing of the drive line?

3. What are two common types of drive?
4. When the drive thrust is through the springs, a _____ type of drive may be used.
5. When the drive thrust is not carried by the springs or control arms, the _____ drive must be used.
6. Name two types of universal joints.
7. The _____ and _____ universal joint will allow fore and aft movement of the propeller shaft.
8. When the _____ and _____ universal joint is used, it is necessary to incorporate a _____ _____ in the drive system.
9. Most propeller shafts are solid. True or False?
10. Wheel drive thrust is carried to the frame in three ways. Name them.
11. What advantage is there in making the propeller shaft in two pieces?
12. What is a torque ball in a torque tube drive setup? What is its purpose?
13. Some propeller shafts use a constant velocity universal joint on both ends. True or False?
14. What would happen if the two propeller shaft universal yokes were not in the same plane?
15. Why must the drive line be carefully balanced?
16. In a two-piece drive line, a _____ bearing must be used.
17. What is a constant velocity universal joint? Where is it commonly used?
18. How does the constant velocity universal joint stop shaft speed fluctuations?
19. Universal joint friction is reduced by using _____ _____ in the yoke bushings.
20. How are universal joints lubricated?

Fig. 15-27. Phantom view of front engine-rear drive setup. This particular vehicle incorporates an air suspension system, four-speed overdrive transmission, and a four-wheel disc braking system. How many systems can you identify?　(Ford Motor Co.)

Chapter 16

DRIVE AXLE ASSEMBLIES

After studying this chapter, you will be able to:
- Explain the construction of different types of drive axle assemblies.
- List the parts of various drive axles.
- Compare the differences between a rear wheel and front wheel drive axle assembly.
- Describe the operating principles of drive axle assemblies.

Drive axle assemblies have several important functions. They must hold the wheels on, keep them upright, allow them to be turned (in front, on four-wheel drive and front-wheel drive vehicles) and propel the wheels forward or backward. They must drive the wheels in such a manner that one can turn faster than the other, yet both must receive torque.

Drive axle assemblies must absorb the driving force of the wheels, and transmit it to the frame through springs, control rods, etc. The axle assembly provides an anchorage for springs, supports the weight of the vehicle and forms the foundation upon which the wheel brakes are mounted. Obviously, the axle assemblies must be well constructed, using quality materials.

CONSTRUCTION

The rear axle basic assembly may be broken into several major sections: housing, axles, differential. Combined, these form the basic unit.

HOUSING

The axle housing is usually made of stamped steel parts welded together. Or, the center section of the housing may be made of cast steel. Two basic types have been used: the BANJO type housing (in wide use) and the SPLIT housing (little used) consisting of two or more pieces. Both types are shown in Fig. 16-1.

AXLES

Two steel axles are placed inside the housing. Their inner ends almost touch; and, in some cases, they do touch. The outer ends protrude out of the housing and form a base upon which the wheels, hubs, etc. are attached. The inner ends are splined and are supported by the differential assembly. The outer ends are supported in roller or ball bearings. Fig. 16-2.

Fig. 16-1. Axle housings. A—One-piece banjo type (so named because of resemblance to musical instrument). B—Three-piece split type housing. Sections are bolted together.

Fig. 16-2. Rear axles. Axle inner end supports are not shown. Housing is banjo type. Axle outer ends have not yet been formed.

ATTACHING WHEEL HUBS

Two methods are employed to secure the wheel hubs to the axle. One method employs a taper on the axle end; the other forms the axle end into a flange upon which the wheel is bolted. Fig. 16-3.

TYPES OF AXLES

Live axles (axles that turn with the wheels) are of three basic types: full-floating, three-quarter-floating and semifloating. Most cars utilize the semifloating axle. Most trucks have full-floating axles. If the axle breaks, the wheel will not come off. The three types are illustrated in Fig. 16-4.

DRIVING THE AXLES

The rear wheels of a vehicle must turn at different speeds when rounding the slightest corner (outside wheel must roll farther). Therefore, it is necessary to employ a unit called a DIFFERENTIAL to drive the axles so both axles receive power, yet they are free to turn at different speeds.

THE DIFFERENTIAL

A splined axle side gear is placed on the inner splined end of each axle. The axle side gear is sup-

Fig. 16-4. Axle types. A—Semifloating. Axle drives, retains and supports wheel. Outer end is supported by bearing. B—Three-quarter-floating. Axle drives and retains wheel. Housing supports load via a bearing in hub that contacts housing. C—Full-floating. Axle drives wheel. Housing-hub bearings support load and retain wheel. Note double-locking nuts that draw hub and tapered roller bearings together. All inner ends are supported in differential.

ported by the differential case. The side gear is free to turn in the case. Fig. 16-5.

As shown in Fig. 16-5, the differential case may be turned. It will revolve about the axle side gears. The differential pinion shaft will turn with the case, but the axle side gears will not be driven.

By bolting a large ring gear to the differential case, and connecting it to a ring gear pinion gear and shaft, it will be possible to turn the case. The propeller shaft will be attached to the ring gear pinion shaft.

When the propeller shaft turns the ring gear pinion, the pinion will turn the ring gear. The ring gear, in turn will revolve the differential case and pinion shaft. The axle side gears will still NOT TURN. By adding two differential pinion gears (the differential pinion shaft will pass through these gears) that mesh with the side gears, the revolving case will turn the axle side gears with it. Figs. 16-6 and 16-7.

DIFFERENTIAL ACTION

The propeller shaft turns the ring gear pinion shaft. The ring gear pinion turns the ring gear which, in turn, revolves the differential case. When the case turns, the differential pinion shaft turns with it. As the differential pinions are mounted on this shaft, they are forced to move with the case. Being meshed with the axle side gears, the pinions will pull the axle side gears along with them.

When the car is moving in a straight line, the ring gear is spinning the case. The differential pinions and axle side gears are moving around with the case, with no movement between the teeth of the pinions and axle side gears. The entire movement is like a solid unit.

When rounding a turn, the case continues whirling

Fig. 16-3. Attaching wheels and hubs. A—Tapered end of axle will wedge into a tapered hole in wheel hub. Key will prevent axle rotation in hub. B—Flanged axle end. Wheel is bolted directly to axle flange. This method is widely used.
(John Deere)

and pulling the pinions around on the shaft. As the outer wheel must turn faster, the outer axle side gear is now moving faster than the inner axle side gear. The whirling pinions not only pull on both axle side gears, but now begin to rotate on their shaft, mean-

Fig. 16-5. Axle side gears. Axle side gear is free to turn with axle inside differential case. Pinion shaft turns with case. Axle side gear is splined to axle end. See right-hand axle gear.

Fig. 16-6. Differential unit. Two differential pinions are pulled around by differential pinion shaft. When case is revolved, pinions will turn axle side gears. Since these are splined to axles, axles will now turn with case.

Fig. 16-7. Cutaway view of a rear axle differential unit. (Ford)

while walking in the axle side gears. This allows them to pull on both axle side gears, while at the same time, compensating for difference in speed by rotating around their shaft. This action is shown in Fig. 16-8.

You can see in Fig. 16-8, detail A, the car is moving in a straight line. The pinion is pulling both gears, but it is not turning. In B, the right side axle gear is moving faster than the left axle gear. The pinion gear is still moving at the same speed. It is still pulling on both gears, but has now started to turn on the pinion shaft. This turning action, added to the forward rotational speed of the shaft, has caused the right-hand side gear to speed up and actually begin to pass the pinion shaft. Study Figs. 16-9 and 16-10. The reverse walking effect on the left-hand side gear has caused it to slow down. The differential action adjusts itself to any axle speed variation.

If one wheel begins to slip, the axle on firm ground will stand still. The case continues spinning the pinions, but they will merely walk around the stopped axle gear and impart the torque to the spinning axle. A special traction differential is often used to over-

Fig. 16-10. Differential action during a turn. Pinion gears rotate in opposite directions and "walk" around in the side gear thus driving them in the same direction but at different speeds. (American Motors)

Fig. 16-8. Differential action. A—Axle side gears, pinion gear and shaft revolve as a unit—straight line driving. B—Axle side gears move forward but at different speeds. Pinion gear 3 is turning on shaft. Notice that dot 2 has moved ahead of pinion shaft. Dot 1, even though it is moving forward, is doing so more slowly. It is moving slower than pinion shaft. This would be the axle on inside of turn.

Fig. 16-9. Differential action during straight ahead driving. Note pinion gears do not rotate and they drive both side gears at the same speed. (American Motors)

come this tendency. It will be covered later in this chapter.

DIFFERENTIAL CARRIER AND BEARINGS

A heavy and rigid section is bolted to the housing. It contains the pinion gear, shaft, and bearings. This is termed the DIFFERENTIAL CARRIER. Two large bearing holders are provided to support the spinning differential case. These are termed CARRIER BEARINGS. In some applications, the carrier is made as a solid part of the axle housing.

All the component parts of the axle housing, axles and differential, are shown in Fig. 16-11.

An assembled view of a differential is shown in Figs. 16-7, 16-12, and 16-13.

SPECIAL TRACTION DIFFERENTIAL

To avoid the loss of driving force that occurs when one wheel begins to slip, special differentials are designed to automatically transfer the torque to the wheel that is not slipping. This enables the car to continue its forward motion. Although there are several variations, all employ the principle of a friction device (clutch plates or a cone clutch) to provide some resistance to normal differential action.

CHRYSLER SURE-GRIP

The Chrysler Sure-Grip differential is basically a standard model, but with several important additions. The axle side gears are driven not by two differential pinions but by four. This requires two separate pinion shafts.

The two shafts cross, but are free to move in-

1. Differential pinion shaft	20. Carrier bearing adjuster lock	39. Pinion shaft bearing
2. Differential pinion thrust washer	21. Lock bolt split washer	40. Pinion shaft bearing cup
3. Differential pinion gear	22. Lock bolt	41. Adjusting shim
4. Axle side gear	23. Ring gear to case bolt	42. Pinion shaft bearing
5. Side gear thrust washer	24. Ring gear to case bolt lock	43. Pinion shaft bearing cup
6. Axle thrust block	25. Differential case	44. Shim
7. Thrust block spacer	26. Grease seal	45. Ring gear pinion gear
8. Carrier bearing cup	27. Nut	46. Ring gear
9. Carrier bearing cone and rollers	28. Lock washer	47. Axle
10. Axle	29. Bolt	48. Carrier to housing bolt (cap screw)
11. Axle outer bearing	30. Gasket	49. Housing bolt lock washer
12. Wheel hub key	31. Shim	50. Pinion shaft grease seal
13. Cotter pin	32. Grease fitting plug	51. Carrier bearing cap lock washer
14. Axle nut	33. Differential pinion shaft lock pin	52. Carrier bearing cap screw
15. Washer	34. Bearing spacer	53. Differential carrier and carrier bearing cap
16. Axle outer bearing cup	35. Cotter pin	54. Carrier to housing gasket
17. Grease seal	36. Lock nut	55. Housing vent
18. Carrier bearing adjuster	37. Washer	56. Housing
19. Ring gear to case bolt nut	38. Pinion shaft flange	57. Fill level plug

Fig. 16-11. Exploded view of one type of rear axle assembly. Study all parts and learn names. Notice relationship of one part to other. (Dodge)

dependently of each other. The shaft outer ends are not round, but have two flat surfaces that form a shallow V. These ramp-like surfaces engage similar ramps cut in the differential case. Fig. 16-14.

A series of four clutch discs are used in back of each axle side gear thrust member. Two of these discs are splined to the differential case, and two are splined to the thrust member. The thrust member is splined to the axle. When the thrust members push outward, the clutch discs are forced together, locking the axle to the case. Figs. 16-15 and 16-16.

SURE-GRIP DIFFERENTIAL OPERATION—BOTH AXLES TURNING AT THE SAME SPEED

When the propeller shaft drives the pinion gear, the torque thrust is transmitted to the ring gear. As the ring gear drives the differential case, the pinion shafts are forced to rotate with the case.

The differential pinions encounter resistance when they attempt to turn the axle side gears. This resistance is transferred to the pinion shafts that are driving the pinions. As both ends of each pinion shaft are seated in tapered ramps, and since they have some "play" at this point, this forces the shafts to slide up the ramp surfaces. This sliding movement moves both

shafts in an outward direction. As each shaft moves outward, it moves its pinions in the same direction. The pinions press against the pinion thrust members, forcing them to lock up the clutches. This is the ac-

Fig. 16-12. Cross section of a rear axle assembly. Note thrust washers behind axle side gears and differential pinions. Differential carrier is an integral part of axle housing. Axle end is flanged for wheel attachment. (Oldsmobile)

Fig. 16-13. Hypoid drive rear assembly—banjo housing, semifloating axle, tapered and keyed wheel hub, demountable differential carrier.

Fig. 16-14. Pinion shafts and case ramps. Notice that shafts fit together but are free to move outward. A—End view of a pinion shaft at rest in bottom of case ramp. B—When case pulls on pinion shaft, pinion end slides up ramp. This forces pinion shaft in an outward direction and moves pinion gear outward thus locking clutch. Both shafts react but in opposite directions.

Fig. 16-16. Cross section of Sure-Grip differential. Pinion thrust members are moved against clutch units by pinion gears.

tion when the car is traveling in a straight line. See Fig. 16-17.

AXLES TURNING AT DIFFERENT SPEEDS

When the car turns a corner, the inner shaft slows down. When this happens, the pinion gears will start turning on their shafts. They will walk around the slower shaft and speed up the other shaft. This walking causes the outer shaft to rotate faster than the differential case, allowing the pinion shaft on the outer

Fig. 16-15. Cutaway of Sure-Grip differential. See how pinion shafts fit in case ramps. Note clutch unit (one on each side) splined to case and to axle. (Chrysler)

Fig. 16-17. Sure-Grip operation when vehicle is moving in straight line. Both pinion shafts are in outer positions, locking up clutch units. Differential pinions are not walking and both shafts are receiving equal torque. (Chrysler)

side to slide down its ramp. This releases the pressure on the outer clutches and lets the differential unit operate much like the standard model. Fig. 16-18

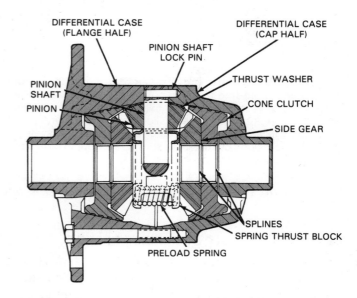

Fig. 16-18. Sure-Grip operation when vehicle is moving around corner. Left axle has slowed down, pinions walk and release pressure on outer or right-hand clutch assembly. Left-hand axle, or inner axle, is receiving greatest torque.

shows differential action when one axle is moving faster than the other. Note that the slower moving axle is receiving most of the torque since it remains clutched to the case.

This type of differential will provide better traction than the standard differential. It is particularly useful when roads are slippery and is also valuable in producing fast acceleration. A high-powered engine will often cause one wheel to spin during acceleration when using a standard differential.

A somewhat different traction differential, Fig. 16-19, uses cone clutches under coil spring pressure. A cross-sectional view is pictured in Fig. 16-20.

Fig. 16-20. Cross-sectional view of Buick Positive-Traction differential. Construction is similar to Oldsmobile's Anti-Spin unit.

Fig. 16-19. Oldsmobile Anti-Spin traction type differential. Cone clutches are splined to axle ends. Coil spring pressure forces cones into tight engagement with case.

The Oldsmobile Anti-Spin differential, shown in Fig. 16-19, uses the pressure of the coil springs to force the clutch cones into tight engagement with the case. This action tends to lock the axles to the case. In order for differential action to occur, the cones must be forced to slip. If one wheel slips, the other will still receive some driving force via the cone. The Positive-Traction differential in Fig. 16-20 functions in a similar manner.

Another positraction differential is illustrated in Fig. 16-21. Construction is similar to that in Figs.

Fig. 16-21. Exploded view of a Cadillac "Positraction" differential. Note guides on clutch disc packs. These stop discs from rotating. (Cadillac)

16-19 and 16-20 except disc clutches are employed instead of cone clutch.

HYPOID GEARING

To facilitate lowering the propeller shaft tunnel in the floor of the car, and to allow lowering the body of the car, many ring gear pinion gears enter and drive the ring gear somewhat below the centerline of the axles.

This gearing setup, using a modified spiral bevel gear, is referred to as HYPOID gearing. A special hypoid lubricant is necessary to prevent premature wear due to the sliding, wiping action that takes place between the ring and pinion gear teeth. Figs. 16-22 and 16-23.

Study the construction used in the pinion shaft assembly in Fig. 16-23. Take note of the two tapered roller bearings used to support the shaft. This type of bearing withstands both radial (forces working at right angles to the shaft) and longitudinal (lengthwise) thrust.

Fig. 16-22. Hypoid gearing. Pinion gear engages ring gear below axle centerline. (Chevrolet)

Fig. 16-23. Typical hypoid gearing—cross section. Note how pinion gear engages ring gear below axle centerline.

SPIRAL BEVEL GEARING

Another type of ring and pinion gearing uses the spiral bevel gear. This type of pinion gear meshes with the ring gear at the axle centerline. The spiral tooth shape allows an overlapping tooth contact that makes for quiet operation, as well as added strength. Before one tooth rolls out of contact with another, a new tooth contact is made. This distributes the torque load over several teeth. Figs. 16-24 and 16-25.

The cross section, in Fig. 16-25, shows the path of the churning lubricant (see arrows). Notice how it is thrown up and forward where it drops down and flows back, lubricating the ring gear and pinion gear, pinion bearings, etc.

SPUR BEVEL

More antiquated, as far as differential gearing is concerned, is the spur bevel. You will notice that the

Fig. 16-24. A—Bevel (spur) gears. B—Spiral bevel gears. Spiral bevel locates pinion gear in line with axle or ring gear centerline. (Chevrolet)

teeth are straight. This type of gear is somewhat noisy and does not offer the strength of the spiral bevel. It works well, however, for differential PINION gears. A, Fig. 16-24 and 16-26.

Fig. 16-25. Cross section of differential using spiral bevel gearing. Drive pinion gear engages ring gear in line with axles.

RING AND PINION

The tooth contact position, as well as clearance and back lash (distance one gear will move back and forth without moving the other gear), is of critical importance. Ring and pinions are always matched, and must be installed as a pair. NEVER REPLACE ONE WITHOUT THE OTHER. Fig. 16-27 illustrates tooth clearance, backlash, as well as other gear tooth nomenclature.

Correct and incorrect ring and pinion tooth contact patterns are shown in Fig. 16-28. The correct contact pattern is very important for strength, wear, and quiet operation.

These patterns are brought out by coating the teeth (after cleaning) with Prussian blue or white lead compound. The gears are revolved in both directions, and contact pattern becomes visible. The drive side is side that contacts when the pinion is driving the ring. The coast pattern is when the ring is driving the pinion.

Fig. 16-26. Spur bevel gearing. Pinion on axle centerline. Gears are straight cut.

Fig. 16-27. Gear tooth nomenclature. Toe is small part of gear that faces inward. (Chevrolet)

Fig. 16-28. Gear tooth contact patterns.

GEAR RATIO

A considerable reduction is effected as the ring gear has several times the number of teeth as that of the pinion. The difference is expressed as a ratio. Gear ratios vary but commonly cover a range of around 2.56:1 to nearly 4 to 1. Higher ratios (4.56:1, 5.10:1, etc.) are available for truck use.

When ratios are even (3.00:1, 4.00:1, etc.) the same teeth on the pinion would contact the same teeth on the ring every third or fourth revolution of the pinion. Any tooth damage or imperfection would then tend to be transferred to the constantly mating tooth, with the possibility of a short service life. To avoid this, most ratios are uneven (2.56:1, 2.78:1, etc.). The uneven ratio prevents frequent contact between the same teeth, providing a varying contact-wear pattern.

Lower ratios will cut down engine speed, but produce poorer acceleration. The correct ratio is determined by a careful consideration of the car weight, the type of service it will have, the engine horsepower, transmission gearing, and whether or not an overdrive is incorporated.

SWING AXLES

Some rear axles use a standard differential, but the differential housing is bolted to the frame. The rear wheels are mounted on swinging arms, and the axles are open and use a universal joint at each end. This setup allows the rear wheels to be individually sprung, and does offer some benefits over the solid axle housing. Some setups use one universal per axle. Others place the axle shafts in articulated (movable) housings. Fig. 16-29 and 16-33.

A partial view of the swing axle as used in the Chevrolet Corvette is shown in Fig. 16-30. Note how the differential carrier is bolted to the frame. The axle

Fig. 16-29. Swing axle—rear view. Schematic of swing axle. Note two inner universal joints. Each wheel is free to move up and down by itself. Swing arms are pivoted on inner ends only. Outer ends are bolted to wheel assembly. This requires only one universal per axle. Differential housing is bolted to frame.

Fig. 16-30. Corvette swing axle arrangement. Differential carrier is bolted to frame. Universal joint at each end of axle shafts permit wheel up-and-down movement.

drive shaft universal joints permit the wheels to move up and down. Note transverse (across car) leaf spring.

PLANETARY GEAR DIFFERENTIAL

One type of front wheel drive has used a planetary differential to reduce the space needed. Figs. 16-31 and 16-32.

The pinion gear (drive pinion) turns a ring gear. The ring gear turns an internal gear. The internal gear is meshed with the outer pinions, and the outer pinions to the inner pinions. The inner pinions engage the sun gear which is splined to the RIGHT-HAND axle. The planetary pinions rotate on shafts passed through the planet pinion carrier.

When the internal gear is revolved, it pulls the outer pinions around with it, thus driving the sun gear (right axle) and planet carrier (left axle). As long as the car is traveling in a straight line, the planet pinions do not move.

PLANETARY DIFFERENTIAL ACTION

During a right turn, the left wheel travels faster than the right. The internal gear drives the pinion carrier through the pinions. The sun gear cannot drive the right axle at the same speed as the left due to the resistance between the right tire and the road. As a result, the planet pinions walk around the sun gear, permitting the left wheel to travel faster. Fig. 16-31.

When the car makes a left turn, the planet pinion carrier is prevented from turning at the same speed as the sun gear, by the tire-to-road friction of the left tire. The planet pinion carrier is then forced to walk around the internal gear, allowing the right axle to travel faster than the left. Fig. 16-32.

LUBRICATION

A special heavy oil is used in rear axle housings. The viscosity will be around SAE 90. Special hypoid oils are used in hypoid assemblies. Another special oil

Fig. 16-32. Planetary gear differential action during a left turn. Right axle is traveling faster than left. Carrier walks around internal gear.

is required for traction type differentials.

In operation, oil circulated by the ring gear is thrown over all the parts. Some installations make use of troughs to guide the returning lubricant to special spots, such as the ring and pinion contact area, and also to the pinion bearings.

The lubricant is retained by gaskets and oil seals. A drain plug is provided at the bottom of the housing, and a filler plug is located partway up the side of the housing. NEVER FILL THE HOUSING ABOVE THE LEVEL OF THIS UPPER PLUG.

Some axle outer bearings are lubricated by the housing lubricant. Others have a lubrication fitting by which wheel bearing grease may be injected at recommended internals. NEVER USE A PRESSURE GREASE GUN ON THESE FITTINGS. GREASE MAY BE FORCED BY THE SEALS AND ENTER THE BRAKES. USE A HAND GUN AND APPLY GREASE SPARINGLY. Other types use a bearing filled with grease and sealed at the factory. Enough lubricant is provided to last the normal life of the bearing.

TRANSAXLE

Many vehicles now incorporate front wheel drive. To accomplish this, a different differential, drive axle, and transmission arrangement is used. This system is called a TRANSAXLE. An overall view of a transaxle setup with engine attached, is shown in Fig. 16-33. Transaxles are also used on some rear wheel drive arrangements.

TRANSAXLE CONSTRUCTION

The housing which contains the clutch or torque converter, (manual or automatic transmission) and differential assembly is generally constructed of aluminum or magnesium. The housing can be of a two or three piece design depending upon application.

Fig. 16-31. Planetary gear type differential action during a right turn. Left axle is traveling faster than right. Planet pinions walk around sun gear. (Oldsmobile)

Fig. 16-33. One type of manual transaxle arrangement. Engine, clutch, transmission and axle components fit closely together. Note that engine is mounted in a transverse position.   (Plymouth)

A cutaway view of one type of manual transaxle is depicted in Fig. 16-34.

Another manual transaxle assembly is pictured in Fig. 16-35. Study the part relationships to one another.

TRANSAXLE OPERATION

Power (torque) is fed to the transmission input shaft, via clutch or torque converter. The power then travels through the transmission and is carried to the differential assembly by gears or belts (chains). It then passes through the differential gears, through the axles, on to the wheels.

Differential action is the same as discussed earlier in this chapter.

FRONT DRIVE AXLES—TWO-WHEEL DRIVE

Many of today's two-wheel drive cars use a front drive axle arrangement.

One type of front wheel drive is shown in Fig. 16-36. This particular system uses an automatic trans-

axle to supply power to the front drive axles. Note the use of independent front suspension.

FRONT DRIVE AXLES—FOUR-WHEEL DRIVE

Vehicles equipped with four-wheel drive use a front drive axle. Torque is supplied to the front axle by the transfer case (see Chapter 12) and front propeller shaft.

Some front-wheel drive vehicles are also equipped with four-wheel drive. They use a live axle assembly in the rear.

These axle assemblies can be of a one-piece (Banjo) housing setup or independent suspension type (open axles). A one-piece, front drive axle unit is illustrated in Fig. 16-37.

FRONT DRIVE AXLES—FOUR-WHEEL DRIVE—CONSTRUCTION

Construction of most front drive axles used on four-wheel drive vehicles is basically the same as the rear axle. Fig. 16-38 shows an exploded view of one

Fig. 16-34. This illustrates one type of 4-speed, manual transaxle. Note two-piece case construction and gear relationships. Learn part names and locations. (Plymouth)

Fig. 16-35. Cutaway view of a 5-speed manual transaxle. This unit attaches to an engine which is longitudinally mounted (parallel with vehicle). (Citroen)

Fig. 16-36. A cross section view of an automatic transaxle, front-wheel drive setup. Gear ratios for this transmission are: 1st gear, 2.69 to 1; 2nd gear, 1.55 to 1; 3rd gear, 1.00 to 1 and reverse is 2.10 to 1. Study all parts carefully. (Plymouth)

Fig. 16-37. Overall view of a solid front drive axle housing. Note use of hydraulic steering damper (two-way shock absorber). This unit aids in eliminating road, tire, etc., vibration and shocks that can be transmitted to steering wheel. (Chevrolet)

type of front axle.

There is one major difference. Front axle assembly must also incorporate a means of allowing the wheels to be turned as well as driven. This is done by using a yoke and steering knuckle assembly, Fig. 16-39. The wheel components are attached to the yoke, which is welded into place on the axle housing. To allow the drive axle to be turned with the steering knuckle, a universal joint is used, Figs. 16-38 and 16-39.

FRONT DRIVE AXLE—FOUR-WHEEL DRIVE—OPERATION

The front axle operates in the same fashion as the rear except for steering of the wheels. For differential and axle operating principles, refer to the front of this chapter.

SUMMARY

The axle assemblies provide a base for springs, hold the vehicle up, provide a foundation for the brakes,

Fig. 16-38. Exploded view of a front drive axle. Study different parts and learn their locations in relation to one another. (Ford)

Fig. 16-39. Cross-sectional view of a front drive axle steering knuckle arrangement. Steering knuckle swivels on ball studs. Ball studs are securely bolted to yoke, which in turn, is welded to axle housing. Note universal joint on axle which allows it to drive and swivel with steering knuckle. (GMC)

hold the wheels in line and drive the front and/or rear wheels while allowing them to turn at different speeds.

The axle assembly is broken into three basic units: the axles, the differential and the housing.

Axles are of three types: semifloating, three-quarter-floating, and full-floating.

The differential contains axle side gears, pinions, a pinion shaft and the case itself. The differential drives both axles while allowing their speeds to vary. A special traction differential improves the performance of the differential under adverse conditions.

The differential unit is supported by the differential carrier, and it revolves in tapered roller bearings. A large ring gear is bolted to the case. A pinion gear, supported on a shaft in the carrier, drives the ring gear.

The rear axle assembly is lubricated by a rather heavy (SAE 90 average) lubricant. Limited slip units require special lube. Transaxle arrangements also must use a specific lubricant. Follow manufacturer's specifications for proper lubricant type and viscosity.

Many vehicles use transaxle front drive arrangements. These units house the clutch or torque converter, manual or automatic transmission and differential assembly, and are bolted to the engine.

On vehicles equipped with four-wheel drive, a front drive axle must be used. This, when receiving power from the transfer case, along with the rear axle driv-ing, enables the vehicle to go over rough and soft terrain such as rocks, mud, sand, etc.

Figs. 16-40, 16-41, 16-42, and 16-43 show parts of several types of drive axle assemblies.

KNOW THESE TERMS

Axle housing, Axle, Wheel hub, Differential, Differential carrier, Carrier bearing, Sure-grip differential, Hypoid gearing, Spiral bevel gearing, Spur bevel, Ring and pinion, Gear ratio, Swing axles, Planetary gear differential, Transaxle, Four-wheel drive.

REVIEW QUESTIONS—CHAPTER 16

Like a traction differential, the ability to apply one's efforts where they will do the most good will push a person much further along the road to success. When you study, really "lean" into it. See if you can get through the following questions without getting "stuck."

1. List seven functions of the rear axle assembly.
2. For purposes of study, the rear axle assembly can be broken into three basic units or sections. Name them.
3. What are the two types of housing? Which one is more often used?
4. The outer ends of the axles run in bronze bushings. True or False?
5. Describe two methods of attaching the wheel or

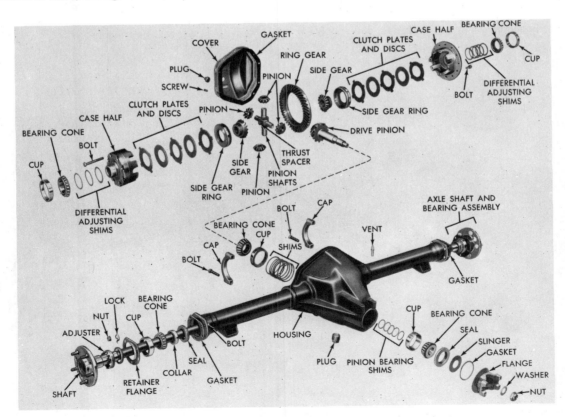

Fig. 16-40. Exploded view of a complete rear axle assembly. Note use of a traction type differential. (Plymouth)

wheel hub to an axle.

6. Name the three different types of axles and describe them.

7. Why is a differential necessary?

8. Name the parts that make up the differential assembly.

9. Describe the action of the differential in straight-line driving.

10. Describe the action of the differential when rounding a corner.

11. What is the purpose of the differential carrier?

12. How is a differential case supported in a carrier?

Fig. 16-41. Fully independent rear drive transaxle arrangement. Note use of toe link rods. They enable correct rear wheel alignment to be obtained. (Pontiac)

Fig. 16-42. Rear axle assembly. This unit employs a torque tube drive line. Note use of a three-piece, split housing. (Peugeot)

13. Of what use is the special traction type of differential?
14. What parts do you find in the traction differential that you do not find in the standard model?
15. Explain the action of the traction differential when rounding a corner.
16. What is a hypoid gear setup as used in the differential?
17. Why is a hypoid used?
18. What is a spiral bevel gear?
19. What advantages does the spiral bevel gear have over the spur bevel?
20. Backlash is the amount of wear in the teeth. True or False?
21. To determine tooth contact patterns, it is necessary to coat the gear teeth with some sort of marking material such as white lead. True or False?
22. The toe part of the ring gear tooth is that part which faces the inside of the gear. True or False?
23. How do you determine the gear ratio used in the rear axle?
24. What factors limit your choice of gear ratio?
25. What type of rear axle uses universal joints and open axles?
26. A good quality engine oil is quite satisfactory as a rear axle lubricant. True or False?
27. How is the rear axle lubricant contained or kept in the housing?
28. Explain how the rear axle assembly is lubricated.
29. Outer rear wheel bearings are lubricated in three ways. Name them.
30. Briefly, what does the term transaxle mean?
31. Transaxles can be used on both front and rear wheel drive cars. True or False?
32. Transaxle housings are usually constructed of _____ or _____.
33. A transaxle sends power (torque) to the differential by two means. Name them.
34. Front wheel drive cars do not use independent front suspension. True or False?
35. On four-wheel drive vehicles, the _____ _____ provides power to the front axle.
36. On the front of four-wheel drive vehicles, the _____ _____ and axle _____ _____ allow the wheels to be turned.
37. Four-wheel drive vehicles can use both _____ and _____ front axle setups.

Fig. 16-43. Exploded view of left and right drive axle assemblies. These axles are used in setups such as shown in Fig. 16-41. Learn part names and their locations. 1—Dust cover. 2—Drive shaft and Birfield joint. 3—Boot band. 4—Birfield joint band. 5—Boot band. 6—Double offset joint boot. 7—Boot band. 8—Circlip. 9—Double offset joint cage. 10—Double offset joint inner race. 11—Ball. 12—Snap ring. 13—Double offset joint outer race. 14—End plate. 15—Inner shaft. 16—Bearing. (Chrysler)

Phantom view of Peugeot 505 reveals unibody construction, torque tube drive shaft, suspended differential, and independent wheel suspension front and rear. This model features strut type front suspension. Swing axles with trailing arms and sway bar are used at rear. (Peugeot)

Chapter 17

FRAMES, BODIES, SPRINGS, SUSPENSION SYSTEMS

After studying this chapter, you will be able to:
- Name the different types of vehicle frames.
- Describe the function and operation of chassis springs.
- List the various types of suspension systems.
- Explain the operation of suspension system components.

If the axles were bolted directly to the frame, every rough spot in the road would transmit a jarring force to the car. Freeway speeds and riding comfort would be impossible.

You know that the modern auto does ride well. Its ability to negotiate rough roads and handle well at freeway speeds is a direct result of a properly designed suspension system.

The object of any suspension system is to allow the body of the car to travel forward with a minimum amount of up-and-down movement. It also permits the car to take turns with little roll or tendency to break frictional contact (skidding) between the tires and the road. Even though the tires and wheels must follow the road contour, the body should be influenced as little as possible. Fig. 17-1.

FRAMES

In order to provide a rigid structural foundation for the car body, and to provide a solid anchorage for the suspension system, a frame of some sort is essential. There are two types of frames in common use today: the separate steel frame to which the body is bolted at various points; the integral body and frame in which the frame and body are built as a unit and welded together.

INTEGRAL FRAME

In the integral type frame (also called unit or unibody), the various body sections are used as struc-

Fig. 17-1. Car body must be insulated against road shock. Blue dotted line shows how car body moves forward smoothly despite rapid up-and-down motion of wheels.

tural strength members to help support and stiffen the entire unit. All sections are welded together. In some cases, the rigid body has reinforced points to which the suspension system is attached. Others use a partial frame, front and rear, to which the engine and suspension systems are fastened.

An example of the unit body construction using a partial frame, is shown in Fig. 17-2.

An underside view of the unit body construction is illustrated in Fig. 17-3. Notice the short stub frame in the front end, securely bolted to the unit body. Body rails are used in the rear to form an attachment point for the rear springs.

CONVENTIONAL FRAME

The conventional type of frame is constructed as a separate unit, and the body is bolted to it at various points. Rubber insulator blocks are used between the frame and the body attachment points to minimize the transfer of bothersome vibrations.

The conventional frame must be quite rigid, since the suspension system, engine, and body depend upon the frame to support and keep all units in alignment.

The frame may be constructed of steel members, cold riveted together (so that rivets will not shrink upon cooling and allow lateral movement between parts), or the frame members may be welded. The structural members are usually of the channel or box type. Fig. 17-4.

Fig. 17-2. Integral body and frame (unit) construction. By using body sections as strength members, great ridigity is secured. With this type of construction, a full length frame is not required. All sections are welded together. (Toyota)

FORE-STRUCTURE ASSEMBLY   UNDER-BODY OUTER RAILS

UNDER-BODY FLOOR PAN

Fig. 17-3. One type of unit body construction, as viewed from underneath. There is no full length frame. Note how partial frames are used as an attachment base for front and rear suspension components. (Pontiac)

Viewed from the top, the commonly used frame would resemble those shown in Fig. 17-5.

SPRINGS

In many cases, a suspension system uses two or more different types of springs. There are four types of springs in general use today: leaf, coil, torsion bar and air springs.

SEMIELLIPTICAL LEAF SPRING

The semielliptical leaf spring has been used for many years. It consists of a number of flat steel springs, of varying lengths, bolted together into a single unit. The spring is fastened to the front or rear axle by means of U-bolts. The ends of the spring are

Fig. 17-4. Frame cross sections. A—Channel. B—Boxed channel. C—Boxed U-channel. B is welded. C is riveted.

shackled to the frame. The top leaf, called the main leaf, has the ends curled around to form the spring eyes. Some springs also curl the second leaf ends around the eye to provide both additional strength and safety. See Figs. 17-6, 17-8, and 17-12.

When the spring is bent downward, the leaves slide against each other. The same action takes place on the rebound (springs snapping back to their original shape). To prevent squeaks, and to ease spring action, special neoprene rubber or nylon inserts are often used between the ends of the leaves. The springs then flex these small rubber pads. Other leaf springs are covered with metal casings and are filled with grease.

Several rebound clips are placed around the spring leaves at various points. These clips prevent the leaves from separating when the spring rebounds upward. Fig. 17-6 illustrates one-half of a semielliptical spring. Rebound clips and the leaf rubber pad inserts are also shown.

Fig. 17-7 shows how the spring is fastened to the axle. Notice the use of rubber pads to eliminate spring vibration transfer. The spring center bolt passes through the spring, keeping the leaves properly spaced in a lengthwise position. the top of the center bolt fits into a depression in the mounting pad, pinning the spring firmly to the axle mounting pad when the U-bolts are tightened.

One end of the spring is mounted on a pivot shackle that will allow no fore and aft movement. The other end must be on a hinge type shackle to allow the spring to shorten and lengthen as it flexes up and down. Fig. 17-8.

Most spring shackles are of similar design but use three different materials to reduce friction.

Fig. 17-5. Frame shapes: A—Platform construction is similar to unitized construction. B—Perimeter frame is separate from body and forms a perimeter border that surrounds passenger compartment. C—X-type frame is named because of its shape. Frame has a stiff front and rear section along with a rigid center section. D—Unitized with bolt-on stub frame, strong stub frame holds the engine, accessories, power train, and running gear. E—Ladder frame is similar to the perimeter frame, but the rails do not completely encompass the passenger compartment. (Blackhawk)

Fig. 17-6. Partial view of semielliptical leaf spring. Center bolt serves to keep leaves in line and properly spaced. (MG)

Fig. 17-7. Spring to axle housing mounting. Note use of rubber "isolator" blocks. (Dodge)

RUBBER-BUSHED SHACKLE

A rubber-bushed shackle uses a rubber bushing between the spring eye and the spring eye bolt. The spring and bolt do not touch. The pivoting motion is absorbed by the flexible rubber. This type requires no lubrication. Fig. 17-9.

THREADED SHACKLE

The shackle bolts, in the shape of a U, are passed through the spring eye and through the spring hanger. These bolts are threaded full length. A steel bushing, threaded inside and out, is started on the bolts, then screwed in until it bottoms. Grease is inserted through a grease fitting. This type of shackle provides a wide wearing surface, prevents side motion and retains grease well. Fig. 17-10.

BRONZE-BUSHED SHACKLE

A bronze bushing is inserted between the spring eye and bolt. It must have periodic lubrication. One type of bronze bushing is illustrated in the top half of the hinge shackle, shown in Fig. 17-11.

A complete semielliptical spring is shown in Fig. 17-12. The left end pivots in spring hanger. Right end is supported on a hinge shackle. Rubber bushings are used in both ends.

SINGLE LEAF SPRING

A single leaf, semielliptical spring is shown in Fig. 17-13. The spring is fairly long and wide, is made of either steel or fiberglass, and is quite thin even in the thicker center section. The entire spring consists of ONE leaf.

The use of leaf springs has been generally confined

Fig. 17-8. Flexing causes a variation in spring length. 1—Stationary spring hanger. 2—Hinge type shackle. In A, normal load may produce this spring shape. In B, spring has been compressed. End 1 has merely pivoted but end 2 has moved out as spring lengthens. Difference in length is shown at C.

Fig. 17-9. Rubber-bushed spring shackle. Bushings are in two parts. A metal sleeve fits inside bushings, and shackle bolt passes through this sleeve. When shackle bolts are tightened, rubber bushings are somewhat compressed, causing them to expand and grip both spring eye and bushing sleeve tightly. All movement is taken within rubber bushings. (Chevrolet)

Fig. 17-10. Threaded U-shackle. Threaded sections of U pivot in steel bushings. Steel bushing is stationary in hanger and in spring eye.

to the rear suspension on the modern auto. The car in Fig. 17-38 (front wheel drive) uses a dead (does not drive) rear axle with single leaf rear springs.

COIL SPRINGS

Coil springs are made of special spring rods, heated and wound in the shape of a spiral coil. They are then carefully tempered to give the proper tension. One end is secured to the frame, the other to the axle or suspension device. Pads are used on the ends to prevent vibration transfer. Fig. 17-14.

TORSION BAR SPRING

The torsion bar spring consists of a relatively long spring steel bar. One end is secured to a nonmovable mounting. The other end is free to turn.

A lever arm, at right angles to the bar, is secured to the free end. This lever arm is fastened to the suspension device. When the wheel strikes a bump, and the lever arm is pushed upward, it will twist the long bar. The bar will have resistance to twisting that has been

Fig. 17-13. Single leaf spring. Long, wide and quite thin. Entire spring is made up of one leaf.

Fig. 17-11. Bronze-bushed shackle. Bronze-bushed part of shackle is shown in top half of shackle. Bottom half is rubber bushed. A—Spring or shackle hanger. B—Bronze bushing. C—Spring bolt. D—Shackle side link. E—Steel bushing. F—Rubber. G—Steel bushing. H—Spring bolt. I—Spring eye.

Fig. 17-14. Coil spring. Each end is bolted to mount. Rubber or fabric pads are used at ends.

Fig. 17-12. Complete semielliptical leaf spring. Not shown is rear axle housing to which spring is fastened via the two U-bolts. (Lincoln)

carefully calibrated to the load forces it is designed to bear. Fig. 17-15 illustrates a simplified form of the torsion bar spring.

AIR SPRING

The air spring consists of a hollow steel container with a flexible diaphragm stretched across one end. The diaphragm extends upward part way into the container. The steel dome is fastened to the frame. The diaphragm is secured, via a plunger, to the axle.

The dome is filled with air, forcing the diaphragm and plunger partially down. The spring action is imparted by the diaphragm, flexing up and down against the compressed air inside the dome. An air compressor is used to furnish air to the dome units. Fig. 17-16 illustrates a typical air spring.

Fig. 17-15. Torsion bar spring. When lever arm is moved up or down, it must twist long torsion bar. An anchor mount secures fixed end to frame. Support bearing holds free end. Both anchor and free end are square. This type of spring can be used in front or rear, or both.

Fig. 17-16. Air spring. Proper air pressure in steel container is furnished by air compressor. Leveling valve keeps spring at proper height.

SPRING OSCILLATION

When the vehicle is traveling in a level, forward motion and the wheels strike a bump, the spring (regardless of type used) is rapidly compressed. The compressed spring will attempt to return to its normal loaded length. In so doing, it will rebound, causing the body of the car to be lifted. Since the compressed spring has stored up energy, it will rebound past its normal length. The upward movement of the car also assists in rebounding past the normal length.

The weight of the car will push the spring down, but since the car is traveling downward, the energy built up by the descending body will push the spring below its normal loaded height. This causes the spring to rebound again. This process, called spring oscillation, is repeated a little less each time until the car is finally still. Fig. 17-17.

SHOCK ABSORBER CONTROL ACTION

To overcome spring oscillation, a dampening device, called a SHOCK ABSORBER, is used. Many types of shock absorbers have been designed and used (vane type, opposed piston, gas pressurized, etc.). Most popular, front and rear, is the hydraulic double direct-acting or telescoping shock. Such shocks are often referred to as airplane type shocks.

Fig. 17-17. Spring oscillation. When wheel strikes bump, spring is compressed. Even though wheel returns to level roadway, spring oscillates. Oscillation gradually diminishes and finally stops. (Ford)

One end of the shock is mounted to the frame; the other end is attached to the axle. When the spring attempts to compress or rebound, its action is hindered by the shock absorber.

As the frame attempts to rise and fall in relation to the axle, the shock must telescope out and in. The shock's resistance to telescopic movement hinders this up-and-down motion. Instead of a long series of uncontrolled oscillations, the spring action is smoothed out, and the car will quickly return to its normal loaded level.

SHOCK CONSTRUCTION AND OPERATION

The telescopic shock absorber consists of an inner cylinder, outer cylinder, piston and piston rod and, in some cases, an outer dust and rock shield. A series of valves, in the piston and at the bottom of the inner cylinder, control the movement of the hydraulic fluid within the shock.

Fig. 17-18 illustrates a typical telescoping shock absorber in three positions. The left-hand illustration shows the shock at rest with the car at normal loaded

EXTENSION STROKE

SHOCK ABSORBER AT REST

COMPRESSION STROKE

DUST SHIELD

OIL SEAL

PISTON ROD

TOP PLUG

RESERVOIR TUBE

PRESSURE TUBE

FLUID UNDER PRESSURE

FLUID ESCAPES THROUGH PISTON VALVE INTO LOWER PART OF PRESSURE TUBE

PISTON VALVE

FLUID ESCAPES THROUGH PISTON VALVE INTO UPPER PART OF PRESSURE TUBE

FLUID UNDER PRESSURE

ADDITIONAL FLUID DRAWN IN THROUGH BASE VALVE FROM RESERVOIR TUBE TO COMPENSATE FOR DISPLACEMENT OF PISTON ROD

BASE VALVE

EXCESS FLUID WHICH CANNOT BE ACCOMMODATED IN UPPER PART OF PRESSURE TUBE DUE TO DISPLACEMENT OF PISTON ROD IS FORCED THROUGH BASE VALVE INTO RESERVOIR TUBE

Fig. 17-18. Shock absorber action—at rest, compression, rebound. Study each illustration and determine shock action shown in each.

height. Notice that the inner cylinder (pressure tube) is completely filled with fluid, while the outer cylinder (reservoir tube) is only partially filled. The piston is near the midpoint of its travel in order to allow up-and-down movement.

The middle illustration, Fig. 17-18, shows the action of the shock during spring compression. Note that the piston and piston rod have moved down in the pressure tube, forcing the fluid to pass through the piston valve into the upper section of the pressure tube. Since the piston rod occupies space formerly filled with fluid, some fluid must be displaced through the base valve into the reservoir tube. The valves are calibrated to cause a certain resistance to the passage of fluid. Although the fluid passes through the valves quite easily when the shock is compressed slowly, any increase in compression speed causes a rapid buildup of resistance. The shock thus cushions the violence of the spring compression.

The right-hand illustration, Fig. 17-18, shows shock action during spring rebound. The piston is forced upward in the pressure tube, and the fluid trapped above moves down through the piston via a different valve. To compensate for the reduced amount of piston rod now in the pressure tube, additional fluid is pulled in from the reservoir tube through the base valve.

The shock action on rebound is similar to that of compression, although some shock valves are calibrated to provide more resistance on rebound than on compression. Note the rubber grommets (washers) used to fasten the shock.

Fig. 17-19 shows a typical mounting setup for a telescoping shock absorber. The top end is fastened by rubber grommets to the frame. The bottom is bolted to the lower arm of the front suspension system. The movement of the suspension arm, up and down, will operate the shock.

Some shock absorbers can be set to provide a soft, normal or a firm action; others provide this feature automatically. Fig. 17-20 illustrates a type that can be set by hand.

FRONT END SUSPENSION SYSTEMS

There are three basic front end suspension systems in use today:

1. Solid axle, leaf spring type.
2. Independent suspension using long and short swinging arms.
3. Independent suspension—MacPherson strut type.

There are various adaptions of these systems, but all use the same basic principle.

Fig. 17-20. Adjustable shock absorber. This particular shock also incorporates an overload or booster spring. When adjustment knob is turned, internal valving is altered to change hydraulic resistance to movement. (Armstrong)

SOLID AXLE

Use of the solid front suspension has been confined largely to trucks. This system uses a solid steel dead axle (does not turn with wheels) with a leaf spring at each side. The wheels swivel on each end via a pivot arrangement between the axle and the wheel spindle. Fig. 17-21 and 17-22. A solid axle housing, four-wheel drive setup is pictured in Fig. 17-23.

Any up or down movement of either front wheel causes a vertical tipping effect of both wheels because they share a common axle. This effect upsets the steering geometry as well as imposes a twisting motion to the frame. Fig. 17-22. One exception to this is the Twin-I-Beam front axle used in some Ford light trucks. In this setup, two beams are used. Each one can pivot independently. Fig. 17-35.

Fig. 17-19. Shock absorber mounting. (Dodge)

Fig. 17-21. Solid front axle suspension. Spring shackles are fastened to frame. Note I-Beam type axle setup. (Ford)

Fig. 17-22. Tipping effect of solid front axle.

Fig. 17-23. One type of solid front axle. The housing is hollow and contains driving axles. It is used in the front of a four-wheel drive vehicle. Note hydraulic steering stabilizer. (Toyota)

INDEPENDENT FRONT WHEEL SUSPENSION

With independent suspension, each front wheel is free to move up and down with a minimum (least attainable) effect on the other wheel. There is also far less twisting motion imposed on the frame.

This effect is achieved by using two arms at each side of the frame. The upper arm is considerably shorter than the lower, giving rise to the term LONG AND SHORT ARM SUSPENSION.

The inner ends of both arms are pivoted to the frame via threaded bushings (same principle as threaded U-shackle). Or, as currently in wide usage, rubber bushings. The outer ends are attached to the steering knuckle by threaded bushings or a ball joint.

When one wheel strikes a bump, it is deflected upward. This allows it to travel up or down without af-

fecting the other wheel. Fig. 17-24.

By calculating the positioning and lengths of both upper and lower arms, it is possible for the wheel assembly to move up or down with a minimum of tipping (change in camber angle, which will be described later). Fig. 17-25 shows inner pivot points 1 and 2, on typical long and short arm suspension. Note the different arcs transcribed by each arm.

Fig. 17-24. Action of individual front wheel suspension system. Wheel B has been deflected upward. Long and short arms pivot and coil spring is compressed. Wheel A is not affected.

Fig. 17-25. Upper and lower arm pivot arcs of individual front wheel suspension system.

Various examples of the threaded bushing and rubber bushing arm pivots are shown in accompanying illustrations. The threaded bushing outer arm pivots, knuckle support, steering knuckle, and spindle assembly are shown in Fig. 17-26.

INDEPENDENT FRONT SUSPENSION, USING COIL SPRING

Figs. 17-27 and 17-28 show typical independent front suspensions, using rubber bushing arm pivots. The coil spring top rests in a cup-like spot against the frame. The bottom of the coil is supported by a pad on the lower control arm. The top of each telescoping shock is fastened to the frame; the bottom is attached to the lower control arm.

When the wheel strikes a bump, it is driven upward. This causes arms to pivot upward, compressing spring and shock. Note rubber bumpers used to limit arm travel and to soften the blow when limit is reached.

Fig. 17-26. Upper and lower control arm pivot pins and threaded bushings.

Fig. 17-28. Exploded view of long and short arm syspension. Study parts, construction and locations.   (Cadillac)

For steering purposes, the front wheel steering knuckle pivots on ball joints.

Fig. 17-26 shows the older type of independent suspension system that utilized threaded pivot bushings on both the inner and outer arm ends. Note use of kingpin for steering pivot.

An exploded view of a current type of front suspension system (one side) is shown in Fig. 17-28. Notice that the spindle or steering knuckle pivots on BALL JOINTS. Rubber bushings are used for the control arms. Look at Fig. 17-27.

Threaded bushings and kingpins have been supplanted by rubber bushings on the control arm inner ends and by attaching the outer ends to the spindle assembly by means of ball joints. The ball joint allows the arms to pivot when they travel up and down. In addition, they allow the steering knuckle to pivot from side to side for steering, Fig. 17-29, eliminating the kingpin type pivot.

A detailed view of the ball joint steering knuckle

and ball joints is shown in Figs. 17-30 and 17-31. In 17-30, notice how the knuckle and spindle assembly pivots in the ball joints.

The coil spring can be mounted on top of the upper control arm, with the upper end supported in a tall

Fig. 17-27. Independent front wheel suspension, using long and short control arms and coil springs. Note stabilizer bar.   (GM)

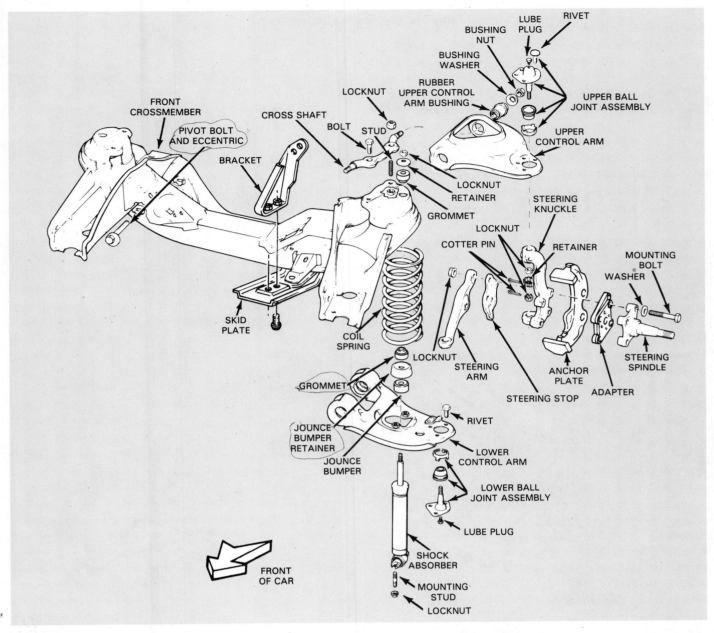

Fig. 17-29. Exploded view of a coil spring, independent front suspension setup. (AMC)

Fig. 17-30. A ball joint steering knuckle. Steering knuckle pivots on ball joints for steering action. (British-Leyland)

housing that is an integral part of the body and frame. Fig. 17-32.

Another type of popular coil spring front suspension is the MacPherson strut type illustrated in Fig. 17-33 and 17-34. In this setup, the coil spring mounts on top of a heavy duty strut and pedestal assembly.

Also unusual is Ford's Twin-I-Beam front suspension on light duty trucks. It utilizes coil springs placed between the I-beam axles and the vehicle's frame. See Fig. 17-35.

DANGER!

WHEN DISMANTLING A COIL SPRING FRONT SUSPENSION SYSTEM, MAKE CERTAIN THE CONTROL ARM IS SECURED TO PREVENT IT FROM SLAMMING DOWNWARD WHEN DISCONNECTED. WHEN EITHER THE

Fig. 17-31. Cross section—upper and lower ball joints. (Plymouth)

Fig. 17-32. Coil spring mounted above upper control arm. Note narrow lower control arm and strut used to provide fore and aft bracing. (AMC)

Fig. 17-33. A MacPherson strut type front suspension. Wheel assembly pivots about long strut as well as moving up and down on strut. Shock absorber is built as an integral part of strut. (BMW)

INNER OR OUTER END IS DISCONNECTED, THE TERRIFIC FORCE OF THE PARTIALLY COMPRESSED COIL SPRING IS UNLEASHED, AND IT WILL PROPEL THE ARM DOWNWARD WITH LETHAL FORCE. Fig. 17-36.

TORSION BAR FRONT SUSPENSION

A torsion bar, Fig. 17-37, is located on each side of the frame in the front of the car. The lower control arm is attached to the torsion bar free end. When the wheel is driven upward, it must move the lower control arm upward, thus twisting the long spring steel bar. Fig. 17-37.

Fig. 17-38 shows a view of torsion bar suspension as used on Oldsmobile Toronado. Also see Fig. 17-3.

Fig. 17-39 illustrates a similar setup for hinging the lower control arm. Notice that the arm pivots on a stub shaft. The torsion bar fits into the end and does not support the arm. It merely produces spring resistance to up-and-down movement.

REAR SUSPENSION

The use of coil springs and the leaf springs dominates rear suspension systems. Fig. 17-40 illustrates a typical suspension system utilizing coil springs. The rear axle housing is mounted on springs and is attached to a set of upper and lower control arms.

The control arm pivot points are rubber bushed. One end of the arm is connected to the housing, the

Fig. 17-34. Study the parts in the MacPherson strut suspension and compare them to Fig. 17-33.

Fig. 17-36. When dismantling front suspension system, be careful.

Fig. 17-35. Ford Twin I-Beam front suspension as used on light duty (1/2, 3/4, and 1 ton) trucks. Each axle is free to pivot up and down without affecting the other. (Ford)

Fig. 17-37. Simplified torsion bar front suspension. When wheel spindle moves up or down, torsion bar must be twisted. Torsion bar anchor is bolted to frame. Both lower control arm support and upper control arm pivot support are fastened to frame by using support brackets.

Fig. 17-38. Oldsmobile front wheel drive Toronado suspension system. Note use of torsion bars in front and a dead axle with single leaf springs in rear. (Oldsmobile)

Fig. 17-39. Lower control arm pivot. Control arm rides on stub shaft. Basically, this is the same torsion bar principle as in Fig. 17-38. (Dodge)

other to the frame. The arm arrangement allows the rear axle housing to move up and down but prevents excessive fore-and-aft and side-to-side movement.

The shock absorbers in Fig. 17-40 are STRADDLE mounted (tops of shocks are closer together than bottoms). In addition to controlling spring action or oscillation, straddle mounting assists in controlling side movement between frame and axle housing, and it also helps to resist tipping on turns.

There are other variations in the use of control arms. Some use a centrally located upper arm as well. Fig. 17-41 illustrates a semi-independent rear suspension which incorporates a twisting cross beam axle setup.

Fig. 17-40. Coil spring rear suspension system. Fore-and-aft movement, as well as axle housing rotation, is controlled by both the upper and lower control arms. Lateral control rod, along with angled shock absorbers, prevents excessive side-to-side movement. (Toyota)

Fig. 17-41. One type of semi-independent twisting cross beam rear axle setup. Each wheel assembly is semi-independent from the other and is controlled by a coil spring and shock absorber. (Chrysler)

The axle connects to the car underbody and holds the wheels in correct alignment.

DANGER!

WHEN SUPPORTING A CAR BODY WHILE REMOVING THE REAR AXLE, WORKING ON THE SUSPENSION SYSTEM, ETC., MAKE CERTAIN THE CAR IS SECURELY BLOCKED. A CAR IS HEAVY AND CAN EASILY CRUSH A CARELESS MECHANIC—BLOCK IT SAFELY.

INDIVIDUALLY SUSPENDED REAR WHEELS

As mentioned earlier, some rear end setups bolt the differential housing to the frame, and drive the rear wheels through open (or enclosed) axles, using universal joints to allow flexibility. These assemblies may use a suspension system similar to the long and short arm front suspension. The swing axle suspension in Fig. 17-42, uses pivoted trailing arms with a transverse leaf spring. Note differential carrier is bolted to frame. Other setups utilize coil springs or torsion bars.

TYPE OF DRIVE

The type of drive, Hotchkiss or torque tube, must be considered in the selection of the proper design for the rear suspension. With the open Hotchkiss drive, some method of controlling rear axle housing twist must be incorporated. As the wheels are driven forward, the axle housing tends to revolve in the opposite direction. As a result, the housing must be held in position by some controlling device. If leaf springs are used, they will control the torque twist, and impart the drive force to the frame. If coil or air springs are used, trailing arms and other control arm designs must be incorporated since the springs themselves are incapable of handling these forces.

With the torque tube drive system, the twisting and driving forces are controlled by the torque tube. However, it is still necessary to use control arms when the coil or air spring is used, because some means must be provided to control side-to-side movement.

STABILIZER BAR

To overcome the tendency for car bodies to lean on corners, a stabilizer bar is usually incorporated in the suspension system. Made of spring steel, the stabilizer passes across the frame and is secured to the frame in two places. The outer bar ends are bent around and back. These outer ends are fastened to the lower control arms (when used in front) through short linkage arms.

Fig. 17-43 illustrates a stabilizer bar and its location on the frame. The two bushing brackets on the forward straight part of the bar fasten it to the frame. The short linkage that connects it to the control arms

Fig. 17-42. Swing axle type of rear suspension. Note the use of a transverse leaf spring. U-joints on axle drive shafts allow independent wheel movement in an up-and-down direction. (Chevrolet)

is shown in an exploded position.

Fig. 17-44 shows one side of a stabilizer bar. Notice how it is connected directly to the lower control arm, thus eliminating additional linkage.

STABILIZER ACTION

As long as the frame dips up and down in a level manner, the stabilizer bar does not affect its action. When the frame attempts to tip, one end of the bar must be bent down, and the other up. This imparts a twisting force to the bar, and it resists the rolling, tipping action. In so doing, it helps to keep the car level. Fig. 17-45.

SPRUNG WEIGHT

Sprung weight refers to the weight of all parts of the car that are supported by the suspension system. The frame, engine, body, etc., all make up the sprung weight.

UNSPRUNG WEIGHT

Unsprung weight refers to all parts of the car that are not supported by the suspension system, wheels, tires, steering knuckles, rear axle assembly, etc.

The ideal situation is to have the unsprung weight as small as possible in relation to the sprung weight. The unsprung weight will then have minimum effect on the riding characteristics of the car.

LUBRICATION

Where chassis grease is needed for the suspension system, grease fittings are provided. Many newer cars have joints that utilize "Teflon" (plastic material) in their construction. This, coupled with special grease

Fig. 17-43. Stabilizer bar mounting. Note various parts and how they are related. (AMC)

Fig. 17-44. Stabilizer bar connections. Other end of bar (not shown) is mounted in the same manner. (Chevrolet)

Fig. 17-45. Stabilizer bar action. In A, frame is moving up and down, but is not tipping. Bar offers no torsional resistance. In B, frame is tipping to right, pressing down on 1 and lifting up on 2. Bar must be twisted to allow this action. Resistance to twisting will minimize rolling or tipping motion of frame.

and excellent seals, has extended greasing intervals to as much as 30,000 miles (48 270 km). Other setups are lubricated for the normal operating life of the vehicle.

Chassis grease is a rather light and sticky type of grease that is compounded to enter fittings readily, lubricate well, adhere to the moving parts and resist water.

Where rubber bushings are used, grease is not necessary. In fact, grease should not be used since it has a deteriorating effect on the rubber.

AUTOMATIC LEVELING CONTROL

The automatic level control is designed to maintain a nearly constant rear curb height (distance from bumper, frame, etc., to ground) regardless of load changes (to 500 lbs. or 227 kg) over the rear axle.

The leveling installation consists of a vacuum-operated air compressor, air tank, pressure regulator valve, leveling valve (height control valve), special shock absorbers, and the necessary tubing and hose.

LEVELING CONTROL NEEDS AIR PRESSURE

The air pressure for the level control is furnished by a two-stage, vacuum-operated compressor. Fig. 17-46. A schematic cross section of the air compressor is

Fig. 17-46. Exploded view of vacuum-operated air compressor used to supply air to the automatic level control system. (Buick)

pictured in Fig. 17-47. For the intake stroke, the sliding distributor valve (operated by linkage attached to piston) applies engine vacuum to compartment B and atmospheric pressure to compartment A. This forces the diaphragm to move the piston toward the reservoir. This opens check valve 1, and fills the first stage with air.

When the piston reaches the end of the intake stroke, it causes the distributor valve to admit vacuum to compartment A, and atmospheric pressure to compartment B. This moves the piston back toward check valve 1, causing it to close. As the piston continues its movement, it compresses the air ahead of it. The air, being under pressure, travels through the hollow piston opening and check valve 2, allowing the air to enter the second stage cylinder. When the piston has completed its stroke, the distributor valve again reverses the vacuum to the opposite side of the diaphragm (compartment B) and the piston is forced to travel toward check valve 3. As it travels, it does two things:

1. It compresses the air in the second stage cylinder. This closes valve 2 and opens valve 3, allowing the compressed air to flow into the reservoir. At the same time, a fresh charge of air is drawn in through valve 1.

Fig. 17-47. Vacuum-operated air compressor action. As diaphragm forces piston toward reservoir, fresh air is drawn in through check valve 1. Air is compressed in second stage cylinder and forced through check valve 3, into reservoir. Reverse stroke forces air from first stage cylinder through hollow cylinder into second stage cylinder. (Pontiac)

2. The compressor piston cycles (moves back and forth) until the pressure built up in the reservoir is equal to the pressure generated by the piston in the second stage cylinder.

When this point is reached, a balanced condition exists and the compressor will not operate until some air has been used by the system. The balance pressure for the unit in Fig. 17-46 would be between 150 and 275 psi (1 034 and 1 895 kPa), depending upon altitude. Fig. 17-47.

Air pressure from the reservoir to the system is limited to a maximum of about 125 psi (861 kPa) by the pressure regulator valve. This protects the leveling valve and shock absorbers from damage. Fig. 17-48.

LEVELING OR HEIGHT CONTROL VALVE

A leveling valve is bolted to the vehicle frame. An overtravel lever, Fig. 17-49, is connected via linkage to the rear axle housing or to the control arm. As weight is added or removed, the distance between the frame and axle changes. This change in distance actuates the overtravel lever, causing the control valve to either admit more air to the shocks (weight added) or to exhaust air from the shocks (weight removed).

Fig. 17-50 illustrates leveling valve action when a load is added to the car. The overtravel lever is forced upward, causing the control shaft arm to open the intake valve. This admits air to the shocks. Shocks will raise car until frame-to-axle distance is the same as it

Fig. 17-50. Control valve action when a load is added to car. Car curb height is decreased, causing overtravel lever to move upward to open intake valve and pass compressed air to shock absorbers. (Buick)

was before the load was added. At this point, the overtravel lever will cause the valve to close.

To prevent sudden changes in frame-to-axle distance (brought about by bumps) from actuating the control valve, a time delay mechanism is built into the valve. Fig. 17-51. Note that the overtravel lever, during a rapid movement, turns around the control valve shaft without moving it. The spring loaded plunger, which normally rests flatly on the shaft moves back to allow this overtravel lever movement. The delay piston, riding in a cylinder filled with silicone fluid, retards rapid movement of the valve shaft lever. The normal delay is from 4 to 18 seconds.

Fig. 17-48. Pressure regulator valve.

Fig. 17-49. Automatic level control valve is actuated by overtravel lever. (Pontiac)

Fig. 17-51. Rapid movement of overtravel lever cannot revolve control valve shaft. In order to turn, shaft must move piston through silicone fluid. Piston will move, but slowly.

SPECIAL SHOCKS

Special shock absorbers (called Superlift shocks by several makers) are basically a normal shock absorber with a rubber boot added. The boot forms a seal between the inner and outer shock sections, thus forming an air chamber. Fig. 17-52.

When air from the control valve is admitted to the shock air chamber, the shock is forced to lengthen. This action raises the car. Exhausting air from the shocks lowers the car. A minimum air pressure, around 8–15 psi (55.1–103.4 kPa), is maintained in the shock at all times to prevent boot friction.

A schematic of the entire automatic level control system is illustrated in Fig. 17-53.

LEVELING SYSTEM—ELECTRIC COMPRESSOR

Some automatic leveling systems utilize an electrically driven compressor. Fig. 17-54 shows an exploded view of such a compressor.

Fig. 17-52. Special Superlift shock absorber used with level control system. Note rubber boot. (Buick)

A schematic of a leveling system using an electric compressor is pictured in Fig. 17-55. Study the arrangement of the various parts. Note the air dryer attached to the compressor.

The air dryer serves a dual purpose. It contains a drying type chemical (silica) that absorbs moisture from the air. This prevents rust formation in the shocks. The moisture is returned to the air when the system is being exhausted (air being released). This cycling procedure gives the drying chemical a long service life.

The dryer also contains a valving setup that maintains a predetermined amount of air pressure of around 10–20 lbs. (68.9–137.8 kPa). This pressure provides an improved ride and prevents rubber boot friction, Fig. 17-56.

MANUAL LEVELING CONTROL

This system incorporates two air adjustable shock absorbers, attached to the rear suspension and connected with flexible tubing.

Air pressure for raising the shocks is generally obtained from an outside source such as a service station and is admitted through the air valve.

To deplete the shocks of unwanted air (lower vehicle curb height) the air valve core is depressed allowing air to escape, Fig. 17-57.

SUMMARY

Car bodies must be suspended on some type of spring devices to isolate them, as much as possible, from the irregularities of the road. The body and frame unit must be rigid and strong to provide secure anchorage for the suspension system, and also to provide positive alignment and the securing of all parts.

Some cars use separate frames, while others use the integral frame and body type of construction. Where the separate frame is used, it is constructed of steel channels and cold riveted together. It has various cross members to provide mounting and bracing points.

Fig. 17-53. Schematic of automatic level control system. (Cadillac)

Fig. 17-54. Exploded view of a single piston electrically driven air compressor used to furnish air for level control system. (Pontiac)

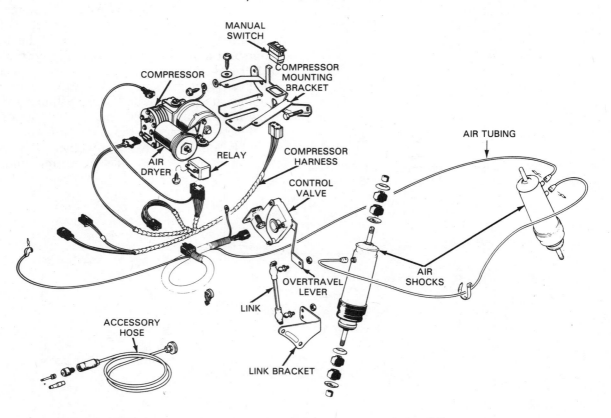

Fig. 17-55. Level control system using electrically operated compressor. (AMC)

Fig. 17-56. Level control system dryer unit. Note use of silica as a drying agent. (Oldsmobile)

There are four types of springs used to suspend the car: leaf spring, coil spring, torsion bar and air spring.

Modern practice uses individual wheel suspension on the front of the car. This is accomplished by mounting the wheel assembly on the ends of pivoting control arms. Any of the four springs can be used in this system.

Common practice is still utilizing the solid rear axle housing with coil, leaf or air springs. Various combinations of control arms are used, depending on the type of drive. The individually suspended swing type rear axle is finding increased application, especially among foreign imported cars.

Hydraulic shock absorbers are used to control spring oscillation. Stabilizer bars help prevent tipping

Fig. 17-57. Manual level control setup. By either raising or lowering air pressure in the shocks, car level can be adjusted to desired height. (AMC)

or rolling on corners. Track bars keep the body and rear axle in alignment.

Fig. 17-58 illustrates a chassis incorporating independent front suspension and dead axle rear suspension. Also, note the components in Figs. 17-59, 17-60, and 17-61.

Fig. 17-58. A chassis employing independent front axle and dead axle rear suspension. (Honda)

Fig. 17-59. Schematic view of an air spring suspension system. Necessary air pressure to operate air springs is provided by an electric compressor. Compressor is triggered to start or stop by electrical signals from control module. Control module is activated by electric signals from three height sensors, connected between suspension and body. Any distance fluctuations between suspension and body (weight added or removed from vehicle) will cause system to add or deplete air in springs to maintain predetermined ride height. (Ford)

Fig. 17-60. Leaf spring rear suspension system. Springs control axle housing rotation, fore-and-aft and side-to-side movement. Angled shock absorbers also help control side-to-side movement. (Toyota)

KNOW THESE TERMS

Integral frame, Conventional frame, Semielliptical leaf spring, Shackle, Coil spring, Torsion bar, Air spring, Spring oscillation, Shock absorber, Solid axle, Independent suspension, Stabilizer bar, Sprung weight, Unsprung weight, Automatic leveling control.

REVIEW QUESTIONS—CHAPTER 17

A thorough background of training will provide the mechanic with a lifetime "suspension system" that will afford fine protection from the rough spots to be found in the "road" of economic fluctuations. A carpenter without tools is helpless, a car without an engine is worthless, and it is obvious that an auto mechanic without training is worse than no mechanic at all. A poorly trained mechanic will spend more time looking for, rather than working at, a job!

In whatever work you may choose, do your best to be the best—STUDY, PRACTICE AND WORK.

1. What is the basic job of the suspension system?
2. Describe the integral frame and body type of construction.

Fig. 17-61. One type of front wheel drive suspension. Note use of MacPherson strut suspension and rack and pinion steering. Use of low drag disc brakes and radial tires relieves some rolling friction, making vehicle more fuel efficient.

3. Name three types of separate frames.
4. The semielliptical spring is wound in the shape of a coil. True or False?
5. What type of spring uses spring shackles?
6. List three types of material used as bearings in spring shackles.
7. Both front and rear shackles must be of the hinge type. True or False?
8. Rebound clips are used to control spring rebound. True or False?
9. Describe the method of mounting a semielliptical spring.
10. Are ALL semielliptical springs made with more than ONE leaf?
11. Describe a coil spring.
12. How are coil springs mounted?
13. Explain how the torsion bar spring differs from the coil spring.
14. Both ends of the torsion bar are anchored to the frame. True or False?
15. Is it possible to use torsion bar springs at both front and rear?
16. What is the principle of the air spring?
17. What unit provides air for the air spring system?
18. Explain how a level control system maintains a constant rear curb height, even though weight to 500 lbs. (227 kg) is added above rear axle.
19. What is spring oscillation?
20. How does the shock absorber control spring oscillation?

21. Describe the action of the shock absorber on both compression and rebound strokes.
22. The most popular type of shock absorber in use on cars today is the _____.
23. How are shock absorbers mounted?
24. The solid front axle is generally used on _____.
25. What is one of the great advantages of the independent front wheel suspension system?
26. Name the basic parts used in the independent front wheel suspension system.
27. Describe the action of the independent front wheel suspension system.
28. Explain the action of the ball joints used on the outer ends of the suspension control arms.
29. List two very real dangers when working on the suspension system.
30. Why is a stabilizer bar necessary?
31. How does the stabilizer bar work?
32. Explain the difference between sprung and unsprung weight.
33. Rubber bushed shackles should never be oiled. True or False?
34. Some of the newer type of suspension joints can forego greasing for periods up to 30,000 miles (48 270 km). True or False?
35. If you are planning to become a mechanic, or even if you are just "interested" in learning about cars, are you doing all you can to learn?

TREAD CONTACT WITH ROAD
UNDERINFLATION

UNDERINFLATION

SHOULDERS OF TREAD WORN

IRREGULAR DEPRESSIONS

MULTI-PROBLEM

ONE SIDE OF TREAD WORN

CAMBER WEAR

TREAD CONTACT WITH ROAD

PROPER INFLATION

TREAD CONTACT WITH ROAD
OVERINFLATION

OVERINFLATION

CENTER OF TREAD WORN

FEATHERED EDGE

TOE-IN WEAR

FINS

SHOULDER OF TREAD
WORN AND SCUFFED

ROUGH SURFACE

CORNERING WEAR

Some common tire wear patterns. Tires must have correct air pressure and be properly aligned and balanced. (Pontiac)

Chapter 18

WHEELS, HUBS, TIRES

After studying this chapter, you will be able to:
- Describe basic wheel, hub, and tire construction.
- Identify the different types of automotive tires.
- Recall tire and wheel size designations.
- Select appropriate tire inflation and rotation procedures.

The drop center, steel disc type wheel is in common use today. Fig. 18-1. It is made in two sections. The outer part forms the rim. The center section (often called "spider") is riveted or spot welded to the rim. The center portion has four, five or sometimes six holes used in mounting the wheel to the wheel hub.

The center section of the rim is "dropped" to allow the tire to be removed. When one bead of the tire is placed in the dropped area, it is then possible to pull the opposite bead off the rim.

Some rims have safety ridges near the lips of the rim. In the event of a blowout, these ridges tend to keep the tire from moving into the dropped center, then coming off the wheel. Fig. 18-2.

Fig. 18-2. Safety rim. Note safety ridge on each side of wheel which retains tire in case of a flat or blowout (ruptured tire). (Chrysler)

The wheel must be manufactured to relatively close tolerances. When mounted, it must run within acceptable limits. Fig. 18-3.

WHEEL BOLTS TO HUB

The wheel is bolted to a hub, either by lug bolts that pass through the wheel and thread into the hub, or by studs that protrude from the hub. In the case of studs, special nuts are required.

Some cars use left-hand threads (nut or bolt turns counterclockwise to tighten) on the driver's side, and

Fig. 18-1. Typical drop center wheel. Center section (spider) can be riveted or welded to the rim. Note drop center section to permit tire removal. Lightweight cast or forged aluminum wheels are finding increased use. (American Motors)

RUNOUT NOT TO EXCEED 1/16 IN.
(1.59 mm) TOTAL INDICATOR READING

DIAL
INDICATOR

Fig. 18-3. Wheel must be true. In upper illustration, left-hand arrow indicates surface to be checked to determine side movement; right-hand arrow indicates area checked for out-of-roundness. Wheel is spun and these areas are checked with a dial indicator that reads movement in .001 in. (0.025 mm). Runout should not exceed 1/16 or .0625 in. (1.587 mm). (Chrysler)

Fig. 18-4. Front wheel and tire assembly. Safety ridges are used to prevent tire from leaving wheel when flat. Note the use of MacPherson strut front suspension. (Toyota)

right-hand threads (turn clockwise to tighten) on the passenger's side. Other cars use right-hand threads on both sides.

CAUTION!

WHEN A WHEEL IS REMOVED AND REPLACED, MAKE CERTAIN THE WHEEL LUGS, OR NUTS, ARE TIGHTENED SECURELY OR THE WHEEL MAY COME OFF IN SERVICE!

A complete wheel, tire, and hub assembly is shown in Fig. 18-4. Study the illustration carefully.

FRONT WHEEL HUBS

Front wheel hubs revolve about the steering knuckle spindle on either ball or tapered roller bearings. A nut on the end of the spindle draws the bearings up and removes excessive play between the bearings and hub.

A special safety washer is used between the nut and the bearing. It passes around the spindle and has a

metal tab that rides in a groove in the threaded area of the spindle. When the hub and bearing spin, the rotating motion is not transferred to the nut, but is stopped by the washer since the tab prevents the washer from turning. A cotter pin is always passed through the castellated (slotted) nut and the spindle. Some adjusting nuts are staked into position by denting a thin lip on the nut itself. The lip is forced into a special groove in the spindle thread area. The method allows for near perfect bearing adjustment. A new nut MUST be used each time bearing service is performed. Fig. 18-5 illustrates a staked nut.

A hub arrangement for one type of front wheel drive is pictured in Fig. 18-6, A. The hub is splined to the outer drive shaft and is held in place by a locknut. The shaft (and hub) revolve in a special double-row ball bearing.

Compare the hubs shown in Fig. 18-6. Fig. 18-7 shows the spindle nut, cotter pin and safety washer.

QUICK-CHANGE WHEELS, SPECIAL HUBS

Some sports cars feature quick-change wire wheels. The outer rim is similar to the steel disc type but, in-

Fig. 18-5. Staking a hub nut: A—Tool is struck with hammer causing nut lip to be bent into spindle groove. B—Length and depth of proper stake. C—Finished staked nut.   (Plymouth)

Fig. 18-6. Study various types of wheel bearings. A—Double-row ball bearing for front-wheel drive. B—Ball bearing front wheel hub. C—Tapered roller bearing front wheel hub.

stead of a steel disc center, wire spokes are used. The wire wheel slides onto a splined hub and is retained by a single quick release or knock-off spinner nut. The wheel and tire assembly can be changed merely by removing the nut. The wheel then pulls off. To replace, merely reverse the procedure. Fig. 18-8 illustrates this type. Notice the spines on the hub and inside the wheel center section. The knock-off nut is also shown.

FRONT HUB LUBRICATION

Wheel hub bearings use a quality, high temperature grease. Fig. 18-6, C, shows the location of this grease. Notice that the hollow hub is not completely filled. The bearings are thoroughly packed.

CAUTION!

ALWAYS INSTALL SAFETY WASHER AND PUT IN A NEW COTTER PIN WHEN REINSTALLING A FRONT WHEEL HUB.

REAR HUBS

One type of rear wheel hub is formed by upsetting the end of the axle itself. The wheel is then bolted directly to the axle flange. Fig. 18-9.

The other setup uses a separate hub that is secured to the tapered axle end by means of a nut and key. The key fits in a groove cut in both the hub and axle. The key is used to prevent the hub from slipping on the axle. Fig. 18-10.

TIRES AND TIRE CONSTRUCTION

Tires serve two main functions. They provide a CUSHIONING ACTION that softens the jolts caused by road irregularities. In this respect, they are actually serving as part of the suspension system. They also provide PROPER TRACTION. Traction enables the car to drive itself forward, provides a means of steering, and allows reasonably fast stopping. Therefore, quality tires are essential to safe vehicle operation.

Tires are constructed of various types of rubber, fabric and steel wire. The fabric casing plies (made of rayon, nylon, polyester, etc.) provide the shape and lend strength to the tire. The plies are impregnated (filled) with rubber. Fig. 18-11.

Fig. 18-7. Exploded view of a typical front wheel assembly. Safety washer, used between outer bearing and spindle nut, is found on all cars. It must always be in place. (Ford)

Fig. 18-8. Quick-change wheel and hub assembly. A single quick release nut allows wheel removal. (British-Leyland)

Fig. 18-9. Integral axle flange hub for rear wheel. Inner bearing retainer prevents axle from slipping through bearing and out of differential housing. (Ford)

The plies are wrapped around steel bead wires, which provide strength to prevent the tire from opening up and leaving the wheel. Filler strips reinforce the bead section.

Fig. 18-10. Detachable rear axle wheel hub. Hub is kept from turning on tapered axle end by a key. (Jeep)

Fig. 18-11. Typical belted bias tire construction. This specific tire uses four sidewall plies (bias arrangement) and two belts beneath tread. (Goodrich)

The fabric plies may be applied in a crisscross (bias) pattern. This is termed BIAS PLY construction. A cutaway of a bias type tire is shown in A, Fig. 18-12.

Another construction method, called BELTED BIAS, uses a bias ply sidewall (two or more plies) plus several layers of tread reinforcing plies directly beneath the tread area. These plies form a continuous "belt" around the tire, Fig. 18-11 and B, Fig. 18-12.

Another tire rapidly growing in popularity is the

Fig. 18-12. Typical tire construction: A—Bias ply (sidewall plies crisscrossed, no belts). B—Belted bias (sidewall plies crisscrossed, belts beneath tread area). C—Radial (sidewall plies parallel with each other and at right angles to tread centerline, belts under tread area). (Firestone)

RADIAL PLY type. This design arranges the casing ply, or plies, so that the cords lie at right angles to the tire tread centerline. Several layers or belts of reinforcing plies (fabric or steel) are placed beneath the tread section. The radial tire permits flexing with minimal tread distortion, gives longer tread life, better traction, softer ride at medium and high speeds, and has less rolling resistance. See C, Fig. 18-12.

PLY RATING AND LOAD RANGE

Ply rating is a general indicator of load-carrying ability. It does not necessarily indicate the actual number of plies used. A two-ply/four-ply rating tire has the same load-carrying ability as a tire utilizing four-ply/four-ply rating construction.

Many cars today are equipped with two-ply/four-ply rating tires. Fig. 18-13 illustrates a cross section of both a two-ply/four-ply rating and a four-ply/four-ply rating tire. Note thicker cords in the two-ply tire.

LOAD RANGE is an indicator of a tire's load capacity as well as number of plies and as such, maximum air pressure that may be used. Load range B indicates a four-ply, C a six-ply and D an eight-ply.

In addition to the load range, all tires must be marked with the size, maximum load and air pressure, DOT (Department of Transportation) number, ply and material identification, construction type (radial, belted-bias, etc.). Fig. 18-14.

Tire treads and sidewalls are made of rubber. Entire tire is placed in mold and vulcanized (heated until rubber is sticky and all parts bond together). The mold imparts sidewall and tread design. Fig. 18-11 shows details of tire construction.

TIRE GRADING

Most tires now being produced will be graded by a Uniform Tire Quality Grading System (UTQGS).

The tire will be graded with a series of numbers and letters, showing the three basic areas of importance—treadwear, traction and temperature resistance.

TREADWEAR is assigned a number grade, example 90, 100, 120, 130, etc. A particular tire with a treadwear grade of 150 should provide 50 percent more mileage than a treadwear tire of 100.

TRACTION is graded on three levels: A, B, and C.

Fig. 18-13. Two-ply/four-ply rating tire has same load capacity as four-ply/four-ply rating. Note how much thicker two-ply cords are than those in four-ply.

Fig. 18-14. All tires must be marked showing maximum load carrying capacity and pressure, size, load range, ply construction and material identification, manufacturer's number and construction type. (Firestone)

397

A offers the best traction on wet roads, while C offers the least amount of traction.

TEMPERATURE RESISTANCE, like traction, is also graded on three levels: A, B, and C. Grade A offers the highest resistance to heat generation, while C offers the least.

TUBELESS TIRES

The modern automobile tire is tubeless (no rubber inner tube is used). The tire and rim form a leakproof unit. The tubeless tire often has a thin bonded rubber lining. The bead area has tiny sealing grooves. Tire and rim must be in good condition to hold air properly. Fig. 18-15.

Fig. 18-16. A—Valve stem construction. Rubber stem body houses core. B—Valve core action. Valve cap acts as second seal against air leakage, as well as preventing entry of dust. (Cadillac)

Fig. 18-15. Tubeless tire construction. Soft rubber liner prevents air leaks into plies. This particular tire is a four-ply/four-ply rating. Note width in relation to height, indicating a very low profile design.

Air is admitted to the tubeless tire by means of a valve stem placed in the rim. Fig. 18-16, A. Valve stem core action is shown in Fig. 18-16, B.

TIRE SIZE

For many years, tire size was related to cross-sectional width (width measured from outside of one sidewall to outside of other) and diameter across beads when mounted on rim.

The advent of the low-profile tire has made it necessary to alter tire size designations somewhat so as to indicate correct load ratings.

Super, low-profile or "wide oval" tires (extremely wide in relation to section height) use series designation that indicates the relationship between section height and width. Section height and width are illustrated in Fig. 18-15. A "70 series" means average section height is 70 percent of width. Letter prefix (D,

E, F, G, etc.) denotes size range—an E being a larger section than a D, and F a larger section than an E, etc. Some current sizes in tires of this type are D70-14 (D, size section, height 70 percent of section width, and 14 in. across the beads), E70-14, H70-15, etc. Note difference in super, low-profile tire, as opposed to more conventional tire. Metric tire size is shown in Fig. 18-17.

SPECIAL TIRES

There are various special safety, and high-speed tires available. The high-speed tire often utilizes steel

Fig. 18-17. Metric tire size breakdown. Size (P255-50V-R16 for example) will be molded into tire sidewall area. See Fig. 18-14 for location. (Chevrolet)

wires in the outer ply-tread area to control distortion caused by centrifugal force. One type of safety tire uses an inner two-ply nylon shield. Both inner and outer areas are filled with air. When the outer chamber is punctured, the inner chamber will support the tire for a number of miles.

Tires with various treads are available. Some are designed for normal highway driving, others for snow, mud, ice, etc.

Most cars now being produced are offered with a COMPACT spare tire. The tire is designed to save space in the luggage area and is much lighter in weight. This aids in overall vehicle fuel economy and makes it much easier to handle when changing a flat.

The compact spare is for "TEMPORARY USE ONLY" and should only be used to replace a flat until the regular can be repaired or replaced. The spare should NOT be "rotated in" with the other tires. When replacing this spare tire, only mount it on the special type rim supplied with the tire. Do not use hubcaps, wheel covers, etc., on the rim while being used, damage to the rim, tire or vehicle may result. Keep inflated to recommended pressure printed on the sidewall. See Figs. 18-18 and 18-19.

Fig. 18-18. Compact spare tire. Tire is designed to be light, small, and used only as a temporary tire. (Toyota)

TIRE RUNOUT

Tires must run reasonably true to prevent vibrations and unbalance. Fig. 18-19 shows one set of runout limits. Notice that tire runout is not as critical as wheel runout. As the tire is flexible, it can absorb some of its own inaccuracy.

TIRE BALANCE

To operate smoothly, it is essential that a tire and wheel be properly balanced. Tire unbalance will cause poor ride, excessive tire wear and result in steering and suspension unit wear due to continual shaking.

The two major effects of unbalance are WHEEL TRAMP (tire and wheel hopping up and down), and WHEEL SHIMMY (shaking from side to side).

Tires must be in STATIC and DYNAMIC balance.

STATIC BALANCE

When a tire is in proper static balance, the weight mass will be evenly distributed around the axis of rotation. If the wheel is raised from the floor and spun several times and always stops in a different place, it is statically balanced.

If the wheel revolves until one side is down, it is obvious that this side is heavier than the opposite or upper side. The tire and wheel is statically unbalanced. Static unbalance is corrected by clipping lead weights to the rim edge opposite the heavy side. Fig. 18-20.

DYNAMIC BALANCE

Dynamic balance is achieved when the centerline of the weight mass is in the same plane as the centerline of the wheel.

Study Fig. 18-21. You will see that the centerline of the weight mass is not in the same plane as the centerline of the wheel. When the wheel spins, centrifugal force will attempt to bring the weight mass centerline into the wheel centerline plane.

Weight mass, Detail 2, will attempt to move to the left. Weight mass 3 will attempt to move to the right. As the wheel revolves, the weight masses will reverse their positions: 2 will move to the right; 3 to the left. Each half turn of the wheel will reverse weight mass position. The resultant struggle, as the weight masses

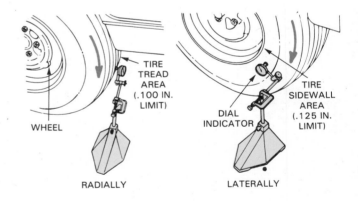

Fig. 18-19. Wheel and tire runout must be within limits specified by manufacturer. Note the use of a dial indicator to take precise readings. (American Motors)

Fig. 18-20. A—Static balance weight. B and C—If more than one weight is necessary, it is essential that they be evenly distributed on each side of light area (indicated by small vertical line). (Plymouth)

attempt to enter the wheel centerline plane, will cause shimmy or wobble. The wobble will cause tire, suspension, and steering wear. Fig. 18-21.

Dynamic unbalance is corrected by adding lead wheel weights to both sides of the rim, until weight masses 1 and 4 equal weight masses 2 and 3. When the weight mass centerline is in the same plane as the wheel centerline, the assembly is dynamically balanced. Fig. 18-22.

Fig. 18-21. Dynamic unbalance. A is a front view and B is a top view. (Plymouth)

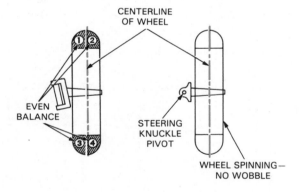

Fig. 18-22. Dynamic balance. Note absence of wheel wobble when dynamic balance is achieved.

PROPER TIRE INFLATION IS IMPORTANT

Car manufacturers determine the proper tire size and pressure after extensive research. Car weight, type of suspension system and horsepower, are all taken into consideration. A tire that is too small will be overloaded. A tire that is too large will add to the unsprung weight, upsetting the suspension system balance.

Proper inflation pressure is important in four ways: traction, riding comfort, fuel mileage, and tire mileage. An overinflated tire will ride hard, produce excessive wear in the tread center area and will not present the full tread for traction use.

Underinflation will wear the outer edges of the tread area. It will cause tire heating, produce mushy steering, and will not properly present the full tread area for traction. Fig. 18-23 shows how the tread contacts the road when underinflated, properly inflated, and overinflated. Fig. 18-24 shows an inflation pressure conversion chart.

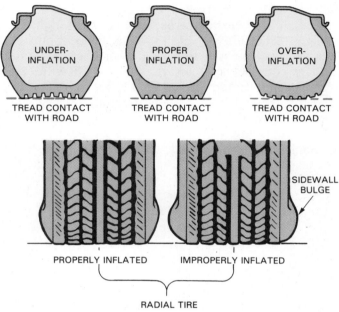

Fig. 18-23. Inflation effect on tire and tread contact. Proper road contact can only be obtained with correct inflation. Notice the slight difference in sidewall bulge between the properly and improperly inflated radial tire. (Chevrolet & Ford)

DANGER!

WHEN INFLATING A TIRE MOUNTED ON A RIM WITH A DEMOUNTABLE RIM FLANGE, SUCH AS USED ON MANY TRUCKS, ALWAYS PLACE A CHAIN OR CAGE AROUND THE TIRE AND WHEEL ASSEMBLY. FACE THE DEMOUNTABLE RIM FLANGE DOWN OR AWAY. MAKE CERTAIN THE RIM IS SECURELY IN THE RIM GROOVE. WHEN INFLATING SUCH SETUPS, THESE RIMS HAVE BEEN KNOWN TO FLY OFF WITH LETHAL FORCE. DON'T TAKE CHANCES. Fig. 18-25.

Fig. 18-26 graphically illustrates the effect of inflation on tire wear.

HIGH SPEEDS AND OVERLOADING PRODUCE HEAT AND EXCESSIVE WEAR

The relationship between car speed, overloading and tire temperature is shown in Fig. 18-27. Note how the heat goes up faster when a given tire is subjected to a 20 percent overload as opposed to the normal

kPa	PSI	kPa	PSI
140	20	215	31
145	21	220	32
155	22	230	33
160	23	235	34
165	24	240	35
170	25	250	36
180	26	275	40
185	27	310	45
190	28	345	50
200	29	380	55
205	30	415	60
Conversion: 6.9 kPa = 1 psi			

Fig. 18-24. Typical tire pressure conversion chart. psi = pounds per square inch. kPa = kilopascals (metric pressure measurement). See "Useful Conversion Tables" in the back of this text for exact conversion figures. (Chevrolet)

Fig. 18-26. Inflation wear graph. Notice that over-inflation is also detrimental to tire wear. (Lincoln)

Fig. 18-25. Demountable rim flange. If not properly placed, demountable flange may fly off when inflating tire.

load. When tires operate at 250–275°F (121–135°C), they lose a great deal of strength and wear resistance.

High speed driving also affects tire tread wear. Higher speeds result in higher tire temperatures and increased tread wear. At 80 miles per hour, for example, tire temperatures build to the critical level, even under normal load. See Fig. 18-27.

TIRES SHOULD BE ROTATED

To compensate for inevitable variations in individual tire wear, it is advisable to rotate the tires about every 5,000 miles (8 046.5 km). Fig. 18-28 illustrates a recommended rotation pattern for both 4 and 5 tire rotation. Note that radial tires are NOT changed from one side of car to the other.

SUMMARY

The drop center, steel disc type wheel is commonly used on modern cars. Wheel is stamped from steel stock, riveted together and fastened to wheel hub using four to six bolts.

The front wheel hubs rotate on ball or tapered roller bearings, and are lubricated by wheel bearing grease.

Fig. 18-27. Speed, load, and temperature graph. At high speeds, a small speed increase causes a large increase in the temperature. Note how overload raises temperature and reduces tire life. (Rubber Mfrs. Assoc.)

Rear wheels are bolted to integral or detachable hub. A few sports cars use quick-change wheels. These require special hubs.

Tires are an important part of the suspension system. They also provide the traction necessary for driving and braking, Figs. 18-29 and 18-30.

Rubber, fabric, and steel wires are used in tire construction. Special safety type tires are available. A wide variety of tread designs are manufactured.

Most tires are the tubeless type in which an air seal is provided by the tire and rim.

The most popular passenger car tire is of two-ply/four-ply rating construction. Ply rating is determined NOT by the number of actual plies but by load-carrying ability. Newly manufactured tires are being graded by the Uniform Tire Quality Grading System.

Tires and wheels must run true, and they must be balanced statically and dynamically. Special lead wheel weights are used in balancing a tire and wheel assembly.

Proper tire inflation is vital to good steering, riding quality, and tire life.

High speeds are ruinous to tire life. Excessive speed promotes heating with a resultant loss of tire strength and wearing quality. Safe vehicle operation is also drastically reduced.

Tires should be rotated every 5,000 miles (8 046.5 km).

Always double-check when mounting wheels on a car to make certain they are bolted on securely. If inflating truck tires—BEWARE OF THE RIM FLANGE!

KNOW THESE TERMS

Dropped center, Hub, Safety ridge, Tread, Sidewall, Bead, Spindle, Wheel bearing, Bias ply, Belted bias, Radial ply, Load range, Tubeless, Tire size, Tire runout, Static balance, Dynamic balance, Inflation pressure, Tire rotation pattern.

REVIEW QUESTIONS—CHAPTER 18

1. Name the type of wheel most widely used today.
2. How is this wheel constructed and what material is used?
3. What is a safety rim? How does it work?
4. What safety precaution, other than supporting the car in a safe manner, should be used when mounting wheels?
5. What is the purpose of a wheel hub?
6. What is the major difference between a front wheel hub and a rear hub?
7. Hub bearings, when used, are either of the _____ or _____ type.
8. What different feature is offered by the quick-change hub?
9. Hubs are lubricated by using lightweight engine oil. True or False?
10. Name the three major parts of a tire.
11. Wire beads are used to give a tire better traction. True or False?
12. A four-ply rating means that a tire contains four actual layers of cord or plies. True or False?
13. How can a tire without an inner tube hold air?
14. Air is injected into the tire through a valve stem and core assembly. True or False?
15. Describe two types of special tires.
16. Static unbalance causes shimmy. True or False?
17. Dynamic unbalance is when the centerline of the weight mass coincides (lines up) with the centerline of the wheel. True or False?
18. List four reasons why tires must be properly inflated.
19. How can a truck rim flange injure and even kill a careless mechanic?
20. How does high speed affect tire life?
21. Draw a diagram showing how tires should be rotated.
22. Tires should be rotated every _____ miles.
23. Draw a cross section of a typical tire and name the various parts.
24. Describe the difference between the construction of a conventional tire and that used in a radial tire.
25. A D70-14 is a larger tire than the F70-14. True or False?
26. What is meant by the term Uniform Tire Quality

Fig. 18-28. Tire rotation recommendations as used by one manufacturer. Note that radial tires are only moved from front-to-back or back-to-front on the same side. Cross-switching (which reverses tire rotation) should not be done on radials. (Chevrolet)

Grading System?

27. Compact spare tires are used for saving luggage space. True or False?

Remember — you to will go faster and further when your training is properly "balanced." Theory, prac-tice, experimentation are all important and must not be neglected. A sound education made up of study in many fields, such as Math, English, History, etc., is essential to every student of Auto Mechanics. Learn all you can, while you can.

HARD CORNERING
UNDER INFLATION
LACK OF ROTATION

INCORRECT WHEEL ALIGNMENT
TIRE CONSTRUCTION NON-UNIFORMITY
REAR WHEEL HEAVY ACCELERATION

Fig. 18-29. Radial tire wear patterns and probable causes for excessive wear. (Chevrolet)

Fig. 18-30. A—Cross sectional view of a tire showing how puncture sealing compound plugs hole as nail is removed. B—Compact spare tire. Keep properly inflated. C—Tire and wheel "match mounted." Radially "stiffest part" or "high spot" of tire is matched to "low spot" on wheel. This provides smoothest obtainable ride. Tire balance mark is placed opposite valve stem for future reference. D—Tire placard, generally found on driver's door jam, recommends proper tire size and correct inflation along with maximum vehicle load. These placards are for specific cars. Do not use information from one label, and apply it to another type of vehicle. (Pontiac)

Cutaway showing construction of a typical rack and pinion steering system. Study part arrangement.
(Peugeot)

High-mounted rack and pinion steering arrangement. This particular vehicle utilizes unibody construction. The car body acts as a frame. (Chevrolet)

Chapter 19

FRONT WHEEL ALIGNMENT AND STEERING SYSTEMS

After studying this chapter, you will be able to:
- Identify the major parts of an automotive steering system.
- Explain the purpose for each part of an automotive steering system.
- Describe the principles of wheel alignment.
- Compare the different types of steering systems.

The front wheels turn when the spindle steering knuckle units swivel, either on BALL JOINTS or on KINGPINS. Figs. 19-1 and 19-2 illustrate both the kingpin (sometimes called spindle bolt) and the ball joint. Modern practice on passenger vehicles favors the use of the ball joint.

ALIGNMENT IS IMPORTANT

It is not enough to merely place the front wheels on hubs, stand them up straight and devise a method of

Fig. 19-1. Exploded view—spindle assembly. This unit utilizes a solid I-beam axle. Spindle assembly swivels on a kingpin (spindle bolt). Currently, this construction is limited to some trucks. (Ford)

Fig. 19-2. Ball joint steering knuckle assembly. No kingpin is used in this setup. The steering knuckle swivels on two ball joints. Note centerline drawn through the ball joints. (Mercedes Benz)

swiveling them from left to right. The car could be driven, but it would steer poorly. At higher speeds, it would become dangerous to handle; tire life would be short. To secure easy steering, sure handling, smooth operation and good tire wear, several front wheel alignment factors must be considered.

CASTER

Everyone is familiar with the common caster used on furniture. You may have wondered why the little wheel always swivels around and trails obediently behind a chair or dresser leg. The reason is simple.

Referring to Fig. 19-3, you will see that the centerline about which the caster swivels strikes the floor ahead of the caster wheel. If the caster attempts to move to either side, the point of resistance between the caster and the floor will be to the side of the swivel centerline. As the caster is encountering some resistance to forward motion, it will not move until the moving weight mass actually drags it forward. It cannot be dragged forward until all the "slack" is taken up. In this case it will not move straight forward until it is directly in back of the swivel centerline.

Fig. 19-4 illustrates how resistance to forward motion forces a trailing object (caster wheel) to line up behind the moving swivel line.

Fig. 19-3. Chair leg caster. Centerline of swivel axis contacts floor ahead of caster wheel contact.

Fig. 19-4. Caster effect. Table leg in B starts to move to right. Caster wheel is off to one side and encounters a rolling resistance that forces it to line up and trail directly behind table leg in C.

CASTER ANGLE AS APPLIED TO STEERING SYSTEM

By tilting the top of the kingpin (or, in case of ball joint, top of steering knuckle) toward the rear of the car, the centerline of the swivel, or steering point, will be in front of the point at which the tire encounters the road. As this places the point of resistance to forward motion behind the steering centerline, the wheel is forced to track behind, automatically lining up with the moving car. This is referred to as POSITIVE CASTER. Fig. 19-5.

Positive caster tends to force the wheels to travel in

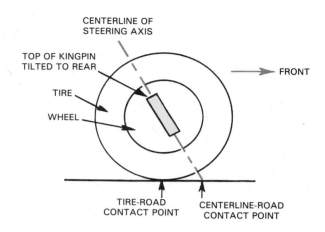

Fig. 19-5. Positive caster. Steering axis (swivel axis) strikes road in front of tire-road contact (caster contact, Fig. 19-3). Wheel will trail behind steering axis centerline-road contact. (Tilt is exaggerated.)

a straight ahead position. It also assists in recovery (wheels turning back to straight ahead position after making a turn). On late model cars, there is often little or no positive caster. Positive caster makes it more difficult to turn the wheels from the straight ahead position than when no caster angle is present.

Another effect of positive caster is a mild tipping effect when cornering. When making a right-hand turn, the right-hand wheel will cause the steering knuckle to raise slightly, while the left-hand wheel will allow the knuckle to lower. This creates a tipping effect, and it is obvious that raising the side of the car on the inside of the turn will have an adverse effect on its cornering ability. When the wheels are turned to the left, the left side raises and the right side drops.

NEGATIVE CASTER

To ease turning, many cars employ a negative caster angle (tipping top of steering knuckle to front of car). This will ease steering and cause a mild banking effect when cornering (side of car on inside of turn will drop and outside will raise). Proper tracking is still provided by kingpin or steering knuckle inclination (to be discussed later). Fig. 19-6.

CAMBER

Positive front wheel camber is provided by tipping the tops of the wheels out. When viewing the car from the front, the top of the wheels are farther apart than the bottom. In short, the centerline (CL) of the wheel is no longer in a vertical plane (straight up and down). Look at Fig. 19-7.

If the tops of the wheels are closer together than the bottoms, the camber is considered negative.

Positive camber places the centerline of the wheel closer to the centerline of the kingpin, or steering axis, where both intersect the road. This assists in reducing the tendency of the front wheels to toe-out (spread

Fig. 19-6. Negative caster. Steering axis centerline strikes road behind tire-road contact point. (Tilt is exaggerated.)

Fig. 19-7. Positive camber. When viewing car from front, tops of wheels are farther apart than bottom. (Camber angle is exaggerated.)

apart at front) and materially lessens road shock to the steering system. Most cars use a small amount of positive camber (less than one degree).

KINGPIN OR STEERING AXIS INCLINATION

The top ball joints of the steering knuckles are closer together at the top than the bottom. The steering axis (view from front of car) places the centerline of the steering ball joints nearer to the centerline of the wheel. Fig. 19-8.

When the center line of the wheel is to the outside of the center line of the steering axis (where they intersect road), the wheels tend to toe-out. This is caused by the road-tire resistance pushing back on the spindle, causing it to swivel backward on the ball joints. Fig. 19-9.

When the centerline of the wheel intersects the road at a point inside the intersection of the steering axis centerline, the wheels tend to toe-in (fronts of tires are closer together than backs). Fig. 19-10.

Steering axis inclination helps to bring the centerline of the wheel and the steering axis centerline closer together where they intersect the road surface. This also causes suspension shocks to be transmitted to and absorbed by the heavy inner spindle and

Fig. 19-8. Steering axis inclination. Front view, driver's side wheel and spindle assembly. Note how top ball joint is closer to center of car than bottom ball joint. This tips steering axis centerline as shown. Steering axis inclination angle is shown at A. (Angles are exaggerated.)

Fig. 19-9. Toe-out effect. A is front view, showing centerline (CL) of wheel striking road to outside of point where CL of steering axis strikes or intersects road. B is top view showing how wheels are forced to toe-out when vehicle moves forward. Arrows 1, 2, and 3 represent direction of force pushing car forward. Arrows 4 and 5 represent forces of resistance to forward motion of wheels. As resistance forces are outside of steering axis-road intersection, wheels toe-out. (Angles are exaggerated.)

Fig. 19-10. Toe-in effect. You will note that CL of wheel now intersects road inside of point where steering axis CL strikes road. Resistance to forward motion will now cause wheel to swing or toe-in when the car moves forward. (Angles are greatly exaggerated.)

knuckle assembly. Fig. 19-11.

Steering axis inclination also helps the car wheels follow the straight ahead position. This tracking effect is caused by the fact that whenever the wheels are turned from the straight ahead position, the car is actually lifted up. Remember that the wheel spindle, when turned, is moved about the steering axis. As the axis is tilted, the spindle will move in a downward direction. Since a downward movement of the spindle is impossible (it is supported by wheel assembly), the steering knuckle is forced upward. This will raise the car a small amount. The effect is similar on both sides.

The weight of the car will tend to force the spindles to swivel back, returning the wheels to the straight ahead position. Fig. 19-12.

Fig. 19-12. Lifting effect of steering axis inclination. A—Steering axis CL. B—Spindle CL. C—Path of spindle end as wheel is turned. Note that as spindle revolves, it travels downward. Since it cannot come nearer to road (wheel holds it up), steering axis area will be lifted. This action affects both wheels regardless of turning direction.

Fig. 19-11. Suspension shock transfer. Load force, transmitted in a vertical plane, will now strike heavy inner end of spindle. Camber and steering axis inclination bring this about. A shows that distance between wheel centerline and steering axis centerline intersection is reduced by camber and steering axis inclination. Resistance to forward motion is now closer to steering axis, reducing shock transfer to tie rods and steering system. (Angles are exaggerated.)

Fig. 19-13. Steering knuckle angle. If steering axis angle is changed, camber angle must also change.   (Cadillac)

STEERING KNUCKLE ANGLE

The steering knuckle angle is determined by the arc formed between the steering axis and the centerline of the spindle. Fig. 19-13 illustrates the steering knuckle angle, as well as positive camber and the steering axis. You will notice that the steering axis inclination angle, and the camber angle, are directly dependent upon each other.

TOE-IN

Toe-in is accomplished by placing the front of the wheels closer together than the back, when viewed from the top.

When a wheel is cambered, the tire engages the road at an angle. Since the tire will adapt itself to the road, the rolling edge of the tire will not be at right angles to the centerline of the wheel. This will cause it to roll as though it were cone shaped, tending to roll outward while moving forward. Fig. 19-14.

To compensate for this roll out (as well as toe-out

Fig. 19-14. Camber toe-out tendency. A—Straight ahead path tire should take. B—Path tire actually takes. When wheel is cambered (exaggerated), surface of tire will engage road at an angle. Tire will adapt itself to road, producing cone shape with apex at C. Tire will then roll on path B just as though it were a cone.

tendencies produced when steering axis intersects road inside CL of wheel), the wheels must be adjusted for toe-in.

This toe-in, generally 1/8 to 1/4 in. (3.18 to 6.35 mm), compensates for the wheel toe-out tendencies plus any wear or play in the steering linkage that would allow additional toe-out. Proper toe-in will allow the tires to move forward without a scrubbing, scraping action between tire and road.

Excessive toe-in, or toe-out, will cause rapid tire wear as shown in Fig. 19-15.

Fig. 19-15. Toe-in and toe-out wear.   (Cadillac)

TOE-OUT ON TURNS

When a car turns a corner, the inner wheel must turn on a shorter radius (smaller circle) than the outer wheel. As a result, the wheels must automatically toe-out on turns to allow the inner wheel to cut more

sharply. This essential action is accomplished by bending both steering arms so they angle slightly toward the center of the car. Fig. 19-16.

When the wheels are turned, the steering arm on the inside of the turn swivels more sharply, due to the angle of the arm at this point. Fig. 19-17 illustrates the difference in wheel angles while turning. Note that when straight ahead, the wheels are set for toe-in.

SLIP ANGLES

When a car rounds a corner at high speed, the actual path taken by the tires is somewhat different than

Fig. 19-16. Steering arms. Steering arms A are angled inward. If centerlines B were continued, they would meet somewhere near differential.

Fig. 19-17. Above. Toe-out on turns. Note that inner wheel on a curve always turns a few degrees more sharply than outer wheel. Below. Toe-in is set with wheels in straight ahead position.   (Buick)

if centrifugal force was not present.

As the wheels turn around a corner, they create a cornering force that endeavors to move the car in the exact direction the wheels are aimed. This cornering force is counteracted by centrifugal force, and the actual path the wheels take is determined by a balance between cornering and centrifugal forces. The difference in the actual path and the path with no centrifugal force is the SLIP angle.

The greater the slip angle, the more rapid the tire wear. Fig. 19-18 depicts slip angles.

Fig. 19-18. Cornering slip angles. Actual center of turn is different from theoretical turning center with no slip angle.

STEERING GEOMETRY

The term STEERING GEOMETRY is often used to describe the various angles formed by the front wheel alignment setup. In other words, caster, camber, toe-in, steering axis inclination, etc., are sometimes collectively referred to as steering geometry. The term FRONT WHEEL ALIGNMENT refers to the same thing.

STEERING GEOMETRY ADJUSTMENTS

Various means are provided for adjusting the different front wheel alignment angles. Eccentric bushings in the outer ends of the threaded bushing control arms enable the steering knuckle support to be tipped in or out. The knuckle support can be tipped forward or backward by turning the threaded bushing.

Shims are provided under the anchor ends of the ball joint support arms. By adding or removing shims, proper adjustment, in or out, forward or backward, is possible.

Toe-in is set by adjusting the tie rods (to be covered later).

On vehicles using a solid front axle, the kingpin inclination and the camber angles are built into the axle assembly. If these angles vary from their initial factory setting, the axle itself must be bent to reset the angles.

STEERING SYSTEM

The steering system is designed to allow the driver to move the front wheels to the right or left, with a minimum of effort, and without excessive movement of the steering wheel.

Though the driver can move the wheels easily, road shocks are not transmitted to the driver. This absence of road shock transfer is referred to as the NONREVERSIBLE feature of steering systems.

The system may be divided into three main assemblies—the steering gearbox with steering wheel and connecting shaft, the spindle assembly-steering arm units, and the linkage necessary to connect the gearbox to the steering arms. Fig. 19-62 illustrates a steering column setup.

STEERING ARMS

The steering arms are either bolted to the spindle assembly or forged as an integral part. As mentioned, they are angled toward the center of the car to provide toe-out on turns. The outer ends of the steering arms have a tapered hole to which the tie rod ball sockets are attached.

When the steering arms are moved to the right or left, they force the spindle assembly to pivot on the ball joints, or on the kingpins, depending on which is used. Fig. 19-19.

STEERING LINKAGE

Linkage is necessary to connect the steering gearbox pitman arm to the steering arms.

Several variations have been used in assembling the

Fig. 19-19. Steering arms are sometimes referred to as steering knuckle arms or spindle arms. (Chrysler)

linkage to produce the desired effect. The most commonly used arrangement today is the parallelogram type of linkage. It is so named because when viewed from the top, it assumes somewhat the shape of a parallelogram. Fig. 19-20.

Note that linkage shown in Fig. 19-19 is also of the parallelogram type.

Fig. 19-21. Ball socket connection. If spring on either side of ball stud seats breaks, it cannot collapse enough to allow socket seats to spread apart and drop ball stud. Even if both springs break, seats cannot move apart enough to drop stud. Seat spreading is controlled by steel blocks inside spring. (Ford)

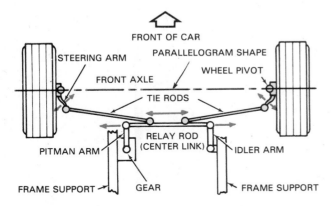

Fig. 19-20. Parallelogram linkage. Schematic top view of parallelogram steering linkage setup. Notice how axle, steering arms and tie rods form shape of a parallelogram. Arrows indicate movement of parts. (Chevrolet)

by means of a ball socket. Two types of ball socket connections are pictured in Figs. 19-21 and 19-22.

THE LINKAGE TRAIN

PITMAN ARM

Starting at the gearbox, there is an arm called a pitman arm. This arm can be made to swing from side to side (cross steering) or from front to back (fore-and-aft steering). In the case of the parallelogram linkage train, it swings from side to side. The pitman arm is moved by the gearbox cross shaft. The pitman arm (also called steering gear arm) is shown in Figs. 19-19, 19-27, 19-30, and 19-31.

CENTER LINK

The pitman arm is attached to a long bar, called a center link, relay rod, or connecting link, Fig. 19-19,

IDLER ARM

The opposite end of the center link is affixed, by means of a ball socket, to an idler arm. The idler arm pivots about a support bolted to the frame, and it is arranged so it is parallel to the pitman arm. A typical idler arm is shown in Fig. 19-23.

TIE RODS

Two tie rods, Fig. 19-19, are used to connect the steering arms to the center link. The ends are connected by ball sockets, similar to those shown in Figs. 19-21 and 19-22.

One end of each tie rod is adjustable, so tie rod length can be changed to adjust toe-in. One type of adjustable tie rod end is shown in Fig. 19-24. A typical tie rod adjustment procedure is pictured in Fig. 19-25.

Tie rods usually are of equal length and about the same length as the lower control arms. As the frame (to which center link is fastened via pitman arm and

Fig. 19-22. Different types of ball socket tie rod ends. B uses a nylon bearing, while A and C employ a metal-to-metal bearing surface.

Fig. 19-23. Typical idler arm. This model uses a threaded bushing arrangement. The support bolts to the frame. (Oldsmobile)

Fig. 19-24. Adjustable tie rod end. Ball socket can be screwed in or out of tie rod. When proper adjustment is procured, it is retained by tightening clamp on tie rod. This will bind tie rod threads against those of ball socket end.

Fig. 19-25. Tie rod adjustment. This type uses a double end sleeve with two clamps. (Mercury)

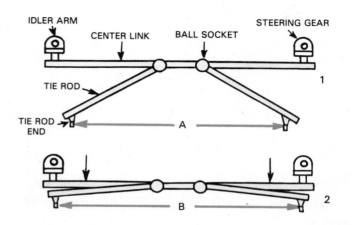

Fig. 19-26. Center link and tie rods should be nearly parallel. (1) Setup with tie rods and center link not parallel (front view). Notice distance A between tie rod ends. When body of car dips downward (2), center link is carried down with frame. Tie rod ends are fastened to steering arms and cannot move down. As center link travels down, angle between link and rods narrows. Tie rod ends must spread out (distance B), forcing steering arms out and toeing wheels in. When car is at normal curb height, link and rods should be almost parallel, as in (2). In this position, link can move up and down with a minimal effect on toe-in and toe-out.

idler arm) raises and lowers, there will be minimum disturbance in toe-in, toe-out.

The center link and the tie rods should be as near parallel as possible (when viewed from front). This will help eliminate toe-in and toe-out changes, as the frame raises and lowers. Fig. 19-26.

A complete linkage system (parallelogram pattern) is shown in Fig. 19-27.

An exploded view of parallelogram linkage used in another system is shown in Fig. 19-28.

A different linkage arrangement, called CENTER STEERING, is illustrated in Fig. 19-29. Notice that an intermediate steering arm replaces the parallelogram center link. A drag link rod connects the steering arm to the pitman arm. This pitman arm has fore-and-aft movement.

Another type of linkage arrangement used on a truck solid axle is shown in Fig. 19-30. Notice that the tie rod is one piece and is connected at each end to the steering or spindle arms. A drag link, working fore and aft, connects the pitman arm (sometimes referred

to as steering sector shaft arm) to an extension on the spindle. When the drag link swivels this spindle, the action is transferred to the other spindle by the tie rod.

STEERING GEARBOX

The steering gearbox is designed to multiply the driver's turning torque so the front wheels may be turned easily and resist the transfer of road shock to the driver. The torque developed by the driver is multiplied through gears, then is transmitted to the wheel spindle assembly via linkage.

Present day autos use either manual or power steering gear setups.

Fig. 19-27. Top view—parallelogram linkage. Each tie rod can be adjusted without changing toe-in or toe-out of opposite wheel. This allows a proper setting and leaves steering wheel in straight ahead position.   (Oldsmobile)

Fig. 19-28. Exploded view—parallelogram steering linkage. Steering arms in this setup are an integral part of spindle assembly. (Mercury)

MANUAL OR STANDARD STEERING GEARBOX

The standard steering gearbox consists of a long steel shaft with a worm gear on one end and the steering wheel on the other. Fig. 19-31.

A pitman arm shaft passes at right angles to the worm gear. The inner end of the pitman shaft (also called cross shaft, roller shaft, sector shaft, gear shaft, etc.) engages the worm gear either through gear teeth, a round steel peg, a roller gear, or a notched arm that passes around a peg affixed to a ball nut that rides on the worm. Fig. 19-31.

The worm gear end of the steering shaft is supported by ball or roller bearings on each side of the worm. These bearings remove end and side play in the worm. Bearing adjustment is provided by shims.

The pitman arm shaft operates in bushings or needle bearings. There is an adjustment screw to control worm and pitman shaft clearance.

A cast housing surrounds and holds all parts in alignment. The housing is partially filled with gear oil for lubrication. Seals prevent the escape of lubricant and keep out dust and dirt. The housing is bolted to the frame or some rigid area. The steering shaft passes up through a steering column to the steering wheel.

Fig. 19-31 shows one type of steering gearbox. The tapered peg, 10, rides in the worm grooves. When the worm is revolved, it causes the peg to follow along the worm grooves, imparting a turning motion to the pitman shaft assembly. Splines in the pitman arm attach it securely to the pitman shaft.

Fig. 19-32 is a cross section of the RECIRCULATING BALL WORM AND NUT GEARBOX. Instead of a taper peg riding in the worm grooves, this type uses a nut that rides up and down the worm. Ball bearings ride half in the worm and half in the nut. When the worm is turned, the ball bearings impart an axial (lengthwise of shaft) thrust to the ball nut. As the nut is prevented from turning, it will then travel up or down, depending on the worm direction.

As the ball bearings roll along and one by one,

Fig. 19-29. Center steering linkage. An intermediate steering arm (sometimes called a bell crank) is used to change fore-and-aft movement of drag link to a cross movement of tie rods.

Fig. 19-30. Steering linkage. This drawing portrays a typical linkage setup on a solid axle, light truck application. Steering arm (spindle arm) on driver's side acts as a bell crank. (Ford)

1—Top cover.	10—Follower peg.	19—Worm gear.
2—Capscrew.	11—Steering box.	20—Bearings.
3—Adjusting screw.	12—Inner column.	21—Races.
4—Locknut.	13—Steering box bracket.	22—Gasket.
5—Filler plug.	14—Oil seal.	23—Adjusting shims.
6—Washer.	15—Dust excluder.	24—End cover.
7—Gasket.	16—Pitman arm.	25—Seal.
8—Adjusting screw stop.	17—Washer.	26—Nut.
9—Follower peg screw.	18—Castellated nut and cotter pin.	27—Capscrew.

Fig. 19-31. Exploded view—worm and tapered pin (follower peg) steering box. (British-Leyland)

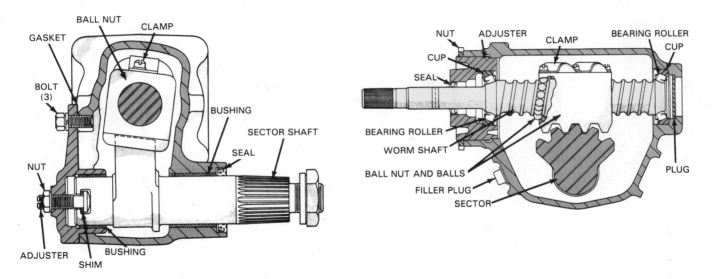

Fig. 19-32. Cross sections of a recirculating ball worm and nut steering gearbox. Study part names, location, and function. (Dodge)

come to the end of the groove in the nut, they are forced through a return tube. Eventually, they reenter the nut groove at the opposite end, which accounts for the name, recirculating ball worm and nut.

One side of the nut has gear teeth cut into it. The pitman arm sector gear teeth engage the nut teeth. When the nut travels up or down, the pitman shaft is forced to rotate. The recirculating ball worm and nut reduces friction to a very low level, making it a very popular type of gearbox. Study Fig. 19-32. Notice the bearing and pitman shaft adjustments. Fig. 19-33

shows a cutaway view of another recirculating ball worm and nut.

Fig. 19-34 shows a different version of a recirculating ball worm and nut. Notice the ball return tube. The pitman shaft engages the ball nut by means of a slotted sector riding on the ball nut peg.

A WORM AND ROLLER gearbox is shown in Fig. 19-35. The pitman shaft engages the worm by means of a roller with gear teeth cut around it. The roller is mounted on antifriction bearings. As the roller is free to turn, the friction developed in a wiping gear action is bypassed. When the worm is rotated, the roller teeth follow the worm and impart a rotary motion to the pitman shaft.

Fig. 19-36 illustrates a pitman shaft and roller in detail.

A RACK AND PINION steering gear is pictured in Figs. 19-37 and 19-39. A steering shaft from the steering wheel fastens to the pinion shaft universal joint. When the pinion is turned, it forces the rack to move, either to the right or left. The ends of the rack are connected to the steering arms by a flexible joint and a short tie rod. All gear rack movement is then transferred directly to the steering arms.

STEERING SHAFT UNIVERSAL JOINTS

Many applications make use of one or more universal joints in the steering shaft. This enables the shaft to be located at various convenient angles without moving the gearbox. It also relieves the mounting stress and deflecting (bending) forces sometimes encountered in a solid shaft.

In addition, the universal joint dampens steering shock and vibration transfer to the steering wheel. Fig. 19-38 shows a mounted gearbox with a flexible U-joint attached to the worm shaft. The steering shaft is shown in phantom (faint, indistinct) view.

Fig. 19-33. Cutaway of a manual recirculating ball worm and nut steering gearbox. Note universal coupling. (Plymouth)

Fig. 19-34. Exploded view—recirculating ball worm and nut steering gearbox. 1—Felt bush and washer. 2—Outer column. 3—Paper gaskets (joint washers). 4—Shims. 5—Shims. 6—Spring cap. 7—Filler plug. 8—Top cover. 9—Steering box. 10—Double coil spring. 11—Damper button. 12—Guide roller. 13—Rocker shaft. 14—Nut. 15—Steel balls (lower track). 16—Ball return tube. 17—Steel balls (nut). 18—Rocker shaft bush. 19—Oil seal. 20—Drop arm (swing lever). 21—Steel balls (upper track). 22—Upper track. 23—Spacer. 24—Inner column and worm.

Fig. 19-35. Cross sections of a worm and roller manual gearbox. (Toyota)

Fig. 19-36. Pitman shaft roller. Needle bearings are used to reduce friction between three-tooth roller and pin upon which it turns. (Chrysler)

Fig. 19-37. Rack and pinion steering gearbox. Both ends of rack are connected to steering arms by means of tie rods. (Peugeot)

416

STEERING GEAR REDUCTION

The amount of gear reduction found in the various gearboxes depends on vehicle type, weight, steering characteristics (fast or slow) desired, and the ultimate use of the vehicle.

Gearbox ratios will vary from 15:1 to 24:1. Steering wheel movement will average from 4 to 6 turns from full left to full right for standard manual gearboxes.

POWER STEERING

Power steering is designed to reduce the steering wheel turning effort by utilizing hydraulic pressure to bolster (strengthen) the normal torque developed by the steering gearbox. It should ease steering wheel manipulation and, at the same time, offer some resistance so that the driver can retain some "road feel."

ROAD FEEL

Road feel is the feeling imparted to the steering wheel by the wheels of a car in motion. This feeling is very important to the driver in sensing and predetermining vehicle steering response. A good driver can tell when the front wheels are approaching the walk (slipping sideways) point or if more or less turning effort is required to stabilize the car body on turns, in winds, etc. Complete and effortless power steering would rob the driver of this valuable road feel.

To maintain road feel, power steering systems require some wheel effort, approximately 1 to 3 lbs. pull on the steering wheel rim.

TWO GENERAL TYPES OF POWER STEERING

Power steering systems are of two general types. One type controls and utilizes the hydraulic pressure directly within the steering gearbox housing. The other type uses a hydraulic cylinder and control valve attached to the linkage system. This second type uses a conventional standard gearbox. Both systems use a hydraulic pump, generally belt driven by the engine, to produce the necessary hydraulic pressure.

In both the self-contained and linkage types, a control valve is actuated by driver steering effort. This valve admits oil, under heavy pressure, to one side or the other of a hydraulic piston. The pressure the oil creates against the piston is transferred to either the pitman shaft, or to a direct connection to the steering linkage, which assists the driver in manipulating the front wheels.

SELF-CONTAINED POWER STEERING UNIT

The self-contained unit places the control valve mechanism, power piston, and gears in an integral unit. Pressure developed by the unit is applied to the pitman shaft.

Fig. 19-38. Steering shaft flexible universal joint. Adjustments for worm bearing and cross shaft are shown. Note alignment marks at base of universal joint. (Chevrolet)

There are several different models of the self-contained type, but all share many basic design principles. They may be divided into two general catagories, the in-line and the offset. The in-line is in popular use today.

IN-LINE, SELF-CONTAINED POWER STEERING UNITS UTILIZING A PIVOT OPERATED, SLIDING SPOOL VALVE

Study Figs. 19-40 and 19-41. Notice that all the basic elements of the conventional manual steering gear are used. A pitman shaft (steering gear cross shaft) engages a recirculating ball nut that rides on a typical worm gear or shaft.

The basic difference is the addition of a reaction unit, a pivot lever, a valve body and the utilization of the ball nut as a power piston.

HOW IN-LINE UNIT WORKS

In operation, oil under pressure from the pump enters the valve body via the inlet passage. When no effort (above 1 to 3 lbs.) is being applied to the steering wheel, the reaction unit is centered and the pivot lever is straight up and down. This keeps the spool valve in a neutral position.

Two round washer-like springs (pressure plate) hold the center thrust bearing race, Figs. 19-40 and 19-41, in a neutral position. The center thrust bearing is attached to the worm shaft, by being secured between two thrust bearings, which are in turn affixed to the worm shaft by a shoulder on the left end and a locknut on the right. The bearings revolve with the worm shaft, but the center thrust bearing remains still. The center thrust bearing can move up or down

Fig. 19-39. Rack and pinion steering systems: A—One type of manual rack and pinion steering setup. Note the tube and housing assembly, breather tube and cutaway of the tie rod end. B—An exploded view of a manual rack and pinion steering assembly. C—A cutaway view of the pinion shaft and steering rack. D—One type of manual rack and pinion steering incorporated on a front wheel drive vehicle. Note MacPherson strut suspension. (AMC, Honda, Peugeot)

with the worm shaft, but not around with it.

The lower end of the pivot lever rests in a cutout in the center thrust bearing. When the center thrust bearing is in the neutral position, the pivot lever is straight up and holds the spool valve in the neutral position. Fig. 19-42, A.

With the spool valve in the neutral position, oil is fed to both sides of the power piston and to both reaction rings.

Oil also works its way around the balls between the power piston and the worm shaft. This oil collects in the hollow formed between the left end of the worm shaft and the left end of the power piston. This pressure created on the worm shaft end is counter-balanced by pressure created on the worm shaft balancing ring, Fig. 19-40.

In the neutral position, oil pressure is equalized on

all sides, and no hydraulic pressure is applied to the pitman shaft by the power piston.

LEFT TURN

When the steering wheel is turned to the left, the worm shaft attempts to impart motion to the power piston. As the power piston has a rack of teeth that engage the pitman arm teeth, the resistance to turning offered by the wheels holds the power piston still.

As the power piston does not want to move, the worm shaft (which has some lateral play, or looseness) will start to screw out of the power piston. As it screws out just a few thousandths of an inch, it moves the center thrust bearing race with it. The center thrust bearing race will then move the bottom of the pivot lever to the right. This causes the top of

Fig. 19-40. Cross section of a power steering unit. This is self-contained, in-line type.

the pivot lever to move the spool valve to the left.

When the spool valve moves to the left turn position, Fig. 19-42, B, it opens the left turn oil passageway and oil travels to the left turn power chamber.

The right turn passageway can no longer receive pressurized oil, but has opened to allow the oil to be returned from the right turn power chamber. Look at Fig. 19-43.

As soon as the spool valve is moved to the left, two things happen. Oil flows to the left turn power chamber and exerts a force on the power piston. Since the right turn power chamber oil is no longer pressurized, the power piston will be forced to the left. This squeezes the right turn power chamber oil out through the oil return passageways, back to the pump reservoir.

As the oil pressurizes the left turn power chamber, it also feeds to the right side reaction ring. This creates pressure that attempts to return the center thrust bearing to the neutral position. The round reaction springs also try to force it back to the neutral position.

These two forces on the center thrust bearing "fight" against the driver's turning force on the wheel and produce the essential road feel.

As soon as the driver's turning force no longer exceeds the reaction ring and spring pressure plate pressure, the center thrust bearing will be forced back to the neutral position. This pivots the spool valve to neutral and equalizes the pressure on each side of the power piston.

RIGHT TURN

A right turn will produce the same action, only the spool valve moves to the right and oil pressure is applied to the right turn power chamber.

The worm shaft is connected to the steering shaft, Fig. 19-41, by a flexible connector. This connector allows the necessary worm shaft end movement.

Maximum pump pressure for this unit is around 950 psi (6 550 kPa). Oil leakage is prevented by neoprene rubber O-rings that ride in grooves.

Study Figs. 19-40 through 19-43. Trace oil flow patterns. Study the various parts and their actions.

OIL INLET
SPOOL VALVE
BY-PASS RELIEF PASSAGE
OIL OUTLET
LEFT TURN POWER CHAMBER
PIVOT LEVER
BACK-PRESSURE VALVE AND SPRING
PRESSURE PLATE
RECIRCULATING BALL CIRCUIT
POWER PISTON

STEERING SHAFT
FLEXIBLE COUPLING
COLUMN JACKET SUPPORT
WORM SHAFT BALANCING RING
LEFT TURN REACTION RING
CENTER THRUST BEARING RACE
RIGHT TURN REACTION RING
CYLINDER HEAD
WORM SHAFT
RIGHT TURN POWER CHAMBER

CROSS SHAFT
SECTOR GEAR

STEERING GEAR
CROSS SHAFT

FRAME SIDE RAIL

ADJUSTING WEDGE

STEERING ARM

Fig. 19-41. Cutaway of a self-contained, in-line power steering unit. Note use of adjusting wedge to secure proper gearbox alignment. (Plymouth)

OFFSET POWER STEERING GEAR

In the SELF-CONTAINED OFFSET type of unit, the additional force offered by the pressurized oil is not applied to the ball nut assembly (as just discussed). Instead, it is applied to the pitman shaft by a power piston rod working in a separate power cylinder. The power piston has a rack of gear teeth cut in one side that mesh with a separate set of pitman sector teeth.

There have been several designs used for the offset type power steering gear. Fig. 19-44 depicts one type.

TO RESERVOIR
PUMP PRESSURE IN
SPOOL VALVE
A
TO PISTON
PIVOT LEVER

TO RESERVOIR
PUMP PRESSURE IN
B
TO PISTON
RETURN FLOW

Fig. 19-42. A—Spool valve in neutral position. Note that spool valve is centrally located and pressurized oil is passing to power piston through both piston outlets. B—Spool valve in left turn position. Valve has moved to left. Right piston outlet is cut off from source of pressurized oil. Return flow will now pass up through right side piston outlet. (Plymouth)

Fig. 19-43. Oil flow during left turn. Study oil flow for this turn position. A right turn is merely a reversal of this when spool valve is moved to right by valve actuating lever.

Notice that the pitman shaft sector teeth are built on both sides. The ball nut presses on one sector, and the power piston rack engages the other set of sector teeth.

IN-LINE UNIT WITH TORSION BAR AND ROTATING SPOOL VALVE

A popular type of in-line, self-contained power steering unit is shown in Fig. 19-45. It employs a

Fig. 19-44. Offset, self-contained power steering unit. In this type, power piston operates in an offset cylinder and applies force to pitman shaft through a second set of pitman shaft teeth (power sector).

Fig. 19-45. Power steering gearbox employing a rotary valve to control oil flow to the power rack-piston.　(Cadillac)

spool valve, but instead of sliding back and forth, the spool rotates a small amount inside the valve body. This type may be referred to as an open-center, rotary type, three-way valve. The spool valve is a very close fit in the valve body.

The steering shaft is connected to a coupling, which in turn is splined to the lower stub shaft. Fig. 19-45. The stub shaft passes through and is pinned to the spool valve. The stub shaft is pinned, at the outer end, to a torsion bar (tempered steel bar designed to twist or spring a certain amount when a turning force is applied). The inner end of the stub shaft floats (is free) on the bar.

The inner end of the torsion bar is pinned to the valve body cap. The valve body cap, in turn, is pinned to the worm shaft. A pressure line and return line from steering pump attach to gear valve housing.

Oil pressure in the pressure cylinder will run around 125 psi (861.87 kPa) for normal driving, about 400 psi (2 758 kPa) maximum for cornering, and up to 1,000–1,200 psi (6 895–8 274 kPa) for parking. Study the construction of the unit, Fig. 19-45.

ROTARY VALVE ACTION, STRAIGHT AHEAD

When the car is traveling straight ahead and no appreciable turning effort is applied to the steering wheel, the torsion bar holds the spool valve in the neutral position. In this position, the spool valve is aligned to cause oil entering the valve body from the pressure port to pass through the slots in the spool valve. From the spool valve, oil flows to the oil return port. No pressure is applied to either side of the power rack-piston. Oil flow is pictured in Fig. 19-46 and in A, Fig. 19-49.

Fig. 19-46. Oil flow through rotary valve when in neutral position. Study valve construction.　(Oldsmobile)

Fig. 19-47. Oil flow through rotary valve in right turn position.

Fig. 19-48. Oil flow through rotary valve in left turn position.

ROTARY VALVE ACTION, RIGHT TURN

When the steering wheel is moved to the right, a turning force is applied to the stub shaft and through the pin to the torsion bar. Remember that the inner end of the torsion bar is pinned to the valve body cap (valve body cap is pinned to valve body, which is pinned to worm shaft). The resistance of the front wheels to movement causes the turning effort to twist or deflect the torsion bar. As the bar twists, the stub shaft revolves enough to cause the spool valve to rotate.

As the spool valve rotates to the right, the right turn grooves are closed off from the return grooves and open to the pressure grooves. The left turn spool grooves are opened more to the return grooves and closed to the pressure grooves. This action permits oil flow to the right turn power chamber. The oil pressure forces the power rack-piston upward, applying additional turning force to the pitman shaft sector teeth.

On this particular unit, the initial power assist will start with about a 1 lb. pull on the rim of the steering wheel. This turns the valve about .3 of 1 deg. Full power assist will result with about 3 1/2 lbs. pull on the steering wheel, rotating the spool about 4 deg. See Fig. 19-47 and B, Fig. 19-49.

ROTARY VALVE ACTION, LEFT TURN

Moving the steering wheel to the left twists the torsion bar in the opposite direction, causing the spool valve to rotate to the left. This closes off the left turn grooves from the return grooves and opens them to the pressure grooves. The right turn slots are closed to pressure and opened to return. Oil flows to the left turn power chamber and forces the power rack-piston downward. Fig. 19-48 and C, Fig. 19-49.

Fig. 19-49. Oil flow through rotary valve and power rack-piston nut action during straight ahead, right turn and left turn positions.

WHAT HAPPENS IF TORSION BAR BREAKS?

In the unlikely event the torsion bar should break, the stub shaft is connected to the worm shaft (some movement is allowed to permit torsion bar action) by two tangs that will still provide manual turning force.

ROTARY VALVE ACTION

An exploded view of a rotary valve power steering gear is shown in Fig. 19-50.

LINKAGE TYPE POWER STEERING

The linkage power steering system employs a power cylinder and control valve to provide the power assist. This system uses a conventional manual gearbox. A pitman arm actuates the power cylinder control valve. Fig. 19-51.

One end of the power cylinder is attached to the frame; the other end is connected to the steering linkage relay rod. The relay rod is attached to the control valve, which is connected to the power cylinder by high pressure hoses.

The end of the pitman arm is formed into a ball, which is placed in the control valve assembly in a ball socket arrangement. Pressure of the pitman shaft ball, either to the right or left, actuates the control

valve. The control valve then transmits oil pressure to one side or the other of the power cylinder piston. Figs. 19-52 and 19-53.

Road feel and control valve operation are based on much the same principles as the integral type control valve. Study Figs. 19-51, 19-52, and 19-53. Follow the

Fig. 19-51. Linkage type power steering—neutral position. Pitman arm ball actuates control valve. (Mercury)

Fig. 19-50. Exploded view of a power steering gear utilizing a rotary spool valve. Study part relationship. (American Motors)

Fig. 19-52. Linkage type power steering—right turn position. Pressure from pitman arm ball has moved control valve, allowing pressurized oil to enter one side of power cylinder. Piston cannot move, so cylinder is forced away from pressurized side and exhausts oil from other side. This force is transferred to linkage to assist driver.

Fig. 19-53. Linkage type power steering—left turn position. Control valve has moved in other direction, reversing pressurized area in power cylinder. Power cylinder is now moving to right and will pull on linkage.

oil flow and valve action in neutral, right, and left-hand turns.

POWER CYLINDER AND CONTROL VALVE IN ONE UNIT

Another type of linkage power steering system incorporates the power cylinder and control valve in one unit. The pitman arm moves the control valve, admit-

ting oil pressure to the power cylinder. The road feel in this system is produced by the force required to move valve spool, which is centered by oil pressure.

Fig. 19-54 illustrates a linkage power steering system. Fig. 19-55 pictures an integral power steering system.

POWER STEERING PUMPS

A power steering pump is belt driven by the engine. It can be mounted as a separate unit or built as an in-

Fig. 19-54. Linkage power steering system—top view. Study arrangement of parts.   (Mercury)

STEERING GEAR

PUMP UNIT

OIL RESERVOIR

Fig. 19-55. Integral power steering system—top view. Self-contained, offset type is shown.   (Lincoln)

tegral part of the front engine plate and driven directly by the crankshaft.

The returned oil is forced into a reservoir from which the oil flows down into the pump proper.

The oil is pumped by a vane, rotor, roller vane, or a slipper vane pump. The maximum pressure (about 1,000 psi or 6 895 kPa) is regulated by a control valve. The oil (Type-A automatic transmission fluid) provides the lubrication for the pump and steering mechanism. Fig. 19-56 shows a typical vane oil pump.

Fig. 19-57 shows vane operation in another vane pump. Notice that some oil, under pressure, is admit-

ted behind the vane ends to force them outward to contact the pump ring walls. Cutaway of a vane pump is pictured in Fig. 19-61.

Another type of power steering pump, the SLIPPER VANE, is shown in Fig. 19-58. The vanes are spring-loaded to hold them in contact with the wall.

See cutaway of a ROLLER VANE pump, Fig. 19-59; ROTOR pump, Fig. 19-60, and a GEAR PUMP, Fig. 19-62.

POWER STEERING UNITS CAN BE OPERATED MANUALLY

In the event of pump pressure failure, power steering systems can be operated manually with somewhat more pressure than required with conventional steering gearbox.

CAUTION!

THE STEERING SYSTEM IS OF CRITICAL IMPORTANCE IN THE SAFE OPERATION OF THE CAR. IT MUST BE SERVICED AND INSPECTED ON A REGULAR BASIS.

WHENEVER REPAIRS ARE MADE, MAKE CERTAIN ALL PARTS FIT. THEY MUST BE PROPERLY ADJUSTED AND SECURE.

IF A PART IS BENT OR WORN, NEVER WELD, HEAT OR STRAIGHTEN IT. THROW IT AWAY—UNDER NO CIRCUMSTANCES CHEAT ON SAFETY!

SUMMARY

To insure easy and safe handling of a car, the front wheels must be properly aligned. Several angles must be considered.

RETURN TO PUMP INLET

OIL FILTER

RETURN LINE FITTING

VALVE SPRING
CHAMBER
CONTROL
VALVE

OUTLET PORT

PUMP RING
VANE
ROTOR

INLET OIL PASSAGE

NO PRESSURE
PRESSURE
RETURN

Fig. 19-56. Vane type power steering pump. Follow oil flow pattern.

Fig. 19-57. Vane type power steering pump. (GMC)

Fig. 19-58. Slipper vane power steering pump. Slippers are spring-loaded to insure wall contact. Metering pin allows heavy oil flow to gear during lower engine rpm, but reduces oil flow at higher rpm (above 3,000 rpm) to reduce fluid temperatures. (Plymouth)

Camber is when the tops of the wheels are not the same distance apart as the bottoms. Positive camber spaces the tops farther apart than the bottoms, while negative camber spaces the tops closer together than the bottoms.

Caster is achieved by tilting the kingpin, or the steering axis, either forward or backward. When the top of the axis is tipped toward rear of car, the caster is positive. When the top is tipped toward front of car, the caster is negative.

Steering axis inclination is produced by tipping the top of the steering axis in toward the center of the car.

Toe-in is when the wheels are closer together at the front than the rear. Toe-out is when the wheels are closer together at the back than the front.

The angle formed between the steering axis and the center line of the spindle is called the steering knuckle angle.

Toe-out on turns is accomplished by angling the steering arms in toward the center of the car.

When cornering, the actual path taken by the car,

and the path upon which the wheels are aimed, are different. This difference is expressed in terms of a slip angle.

The front wheels swivel from left to right on either a kingpin or a ball joint arrangement.

Steering linkage is provided to transfer the force from the pitman arm to the steering arms. The most popular arrangement for this linkage is the parallelogram. This linkage consists of a center link, tie rods and idler arm.

The various linkage parts are connected by means of ball sockets. This allows a swiveling movement without end play.

The newer type of linkage ball sockets use a special grease and excellent sealing, in combination with a special plastic bearing area, to allow extended lubrication intervals.

Cars use either a standard, manual steering gearbox or a power steering unit.

Some popular types of gearing used in both types of boxes are the recirculating ball worm and nut, worm and sector, worm and taper pin, and worm and roller. The most widely used is the recirculating ball worm and nut. The rack and pinion steering is seeing sharply increased usage.

There are two general types of power steering. One type is self-contained, with all hydraulic pressure applied to the pitman arm shaft. The other type uses a standard type gearbox with a power cylinder attached to the linkage system. The self-contained type is currently in widespread usage.

Both kinds of power steering systems are actuated by oil pressure. The pressurized oil is admitted to either side of the power cylinder as controlled by a valving setup.

Road feel is maintained by the use of a torsion bar, balanced oil pressure and return springs. The system

Fig. 19-59. Cutaway of a roller vane power steering pump. (Mercury)

427

Fig. 19-60. Rotor type power steering pump. Trace oil flow pattern and note how oil is returned to reservoir through filter. (Lincoln)

RETURN PORT

SINGLE HOLE ORIFICE

PRESSURE PORT

PRESSURE RELIEF VALVE

FLOW CONTROL VALVE

RETURNING FLUID

FLUID UNDER PRESSURE

uses oil pressure to assist the driver only when the pull on the steering wheel exceeds 1 to 3 lbs. The second the turning effort on the steering wheel falls to this amount, the oil pressure is equalized on both sides of the power piston.

Oil pressure is provided by a high pressure oil pump that is generally belt driven by the engine. The pumps can use the vane, rotor, roller vane, or a slipper vane pump unit. Automatic transmission fluid or a special power steering fluid provides lubrication for both the steering gearbox and the pump. The pump is connected to the power unit by high pressure hose.

KNOW THESE TERMS

Caster, Negative caster, Camber, Steering axis inclination, Toe-in, Toe-out, Slip angles, Steering arm, Steering linkage, Pitman arm, Center link, Idler arm, Tie rods, Steering gearbox, Steering gear reduction, Power steering, Road feel, Power steering pump, Rack and pinion steering.

REVIEW QUESTIONS—CHAPTER 19

If, when reading, a person stumbles over a new word and, instead of looking up the pronunciation and meaning, goes merrily along the way, you can assume that the person's vocabulary will not improve. The same goes for the student of auto mechanics. When you see a new word, a new part, a new idea, or a new theory, STOP AND FIND OUT WHAT IT MEANS, HOW IT WORKS, AND WHY IT WORKS.

1. The front wheels swivel on either a _____ or a _____ setup.
2. Why is proper wheel alignment very important?
3. What is caster?
4. Why is it used?

Fig. 19-61. Cutaway of a vane type power steering pump. (Cadillac)

5. Define the meaning of camber.
6. What effect does camber have on the steering system?
7. Kingpin, or steering axis inclination, affects the steering in what way?
8. What is toe-in?
9. Of what particular use is toe-in?
10. When turning a corner, one side of the car raises while the other lowers. What is the reason for this?
11. How is toe-out on corners produced?
12. What is slip angle?
13. The term steering geometry refers to what?
14. The most popular type of steering linkage arrangement is the _____.
15. Name the linkage parts used in the above linkage arrangement.
16. Give the uses of these parts.
17. What type of steering system (self-contained or linkage) is in popular use today?
18. The _____ _____ steering gearbox reduces friction to a very low level and is therefore widely used.
19. What is a worm and sector type of gearbox?
20. Explain how a worm and roller gearbox works.
21. Of what value are U-joints as used in a steering shaft?
22. What is a self-contained power steering gearbox? How does it differ from the other type? What is the other type?
23. What is road feel and how is it maintained in the power steering systems?
24. Oil pressure for the power steering system is produced by what unit?
25. Pressures run up to _____ pounds.
26. Explain the actions involved in a typical power steering unit for straight ahead position, left turn, right turn.
27. What type of fluid is used in power steering systems?
28. Explain the action of a typical power steering pump.
29. Starting with the steering wheel, name all major parts, in order, between the steering wheel and the steering arms.
30. Name some safety factors that must be considered whenever work is done on the steering system.
31. If a power steering unit fails, what happens?
32. What is a ball socket, how is it made, and what use does it serve?
33. Rack and pinion steering makes use of a worm and roller assembly to assist rapid rotation. True or False?

Fig. 19-62. Exploded view of a gear type power steering pump. Note flow control-relief valve which maintains an output pressure of 925-1,095 psi (6 375-7 545 kPa). (Honda)

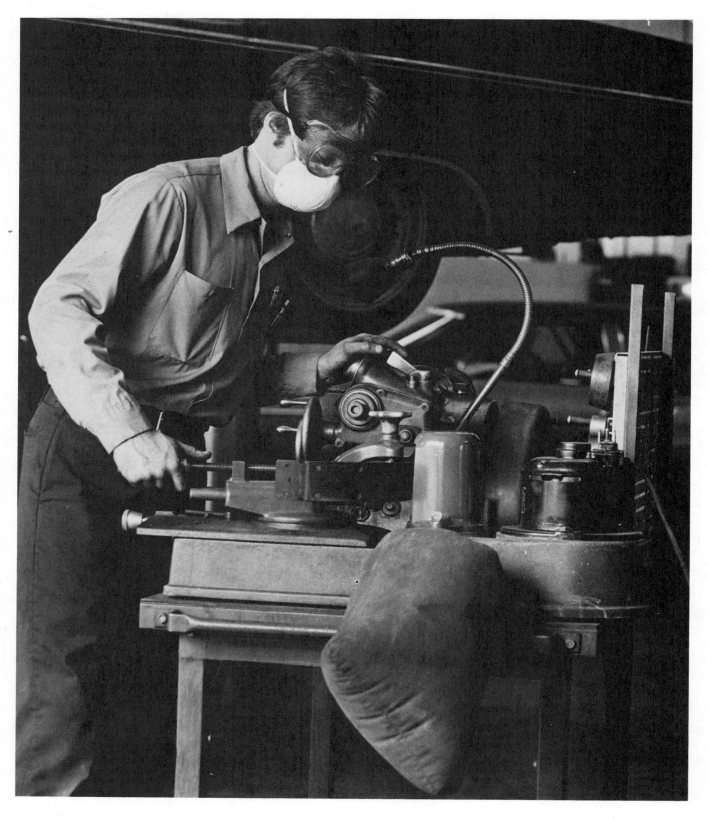

When working with automotive brakes, take safety precautions to prevent brake lining dust from entering your lungs. Brake dust can contain asbestos, a very powerful cancer causing substance. Note the vacuum system and filter mask being worn by this mechanic.

Chapter 20

AUTOMOBILE BRAKES

WARNING: BRAKE FRICTION MATERIALS CONTAIN ASBESTOS—A KNOWN CARCINOGEN (A SUBSTANCE THAT CAN CAUSE CANCER). GRINDING LININGS, CLEANING BRAKE ASSEMBLIES, ETC., CAN PRODUCE SMALL AIRBORNE PARTICLES OF ASBESTOS. THESE ARE EASILY INHALED BY THE MECHANIC. BREATHING THESE PARTICLES MAY CAUSE CANCER.

OBSERVE THE FOLLOWING RULES:
1. Never use compressed air to blow brake assemblies clean. Use a vacuum source or flush with water.
2. Equip brake shoe grinders with an efficient dust removal system. Turn on system whenever grinder is in operation.
3. When some exposure might be unavoidable, wear an approved filter mask.

After studying this chapter, you will be able to:
- List the safety precautions to follow when working on an automotive brake system.
- Identify the basic parts of a brake system.
- Explain the function for each part of a brake system.
- Describe the principles used during brake system operation.

The modern car uses HYDRAULIC BRAKES as a stopping medium. A special fluid (hydraulic brake fluid), confined in rubber flex hose and steel tubing lines, is used to transmit both motion and pressure from the brake pedal to the wheels.

How the braking system works will be discussed, but first you must have a basic knowledge of hydraulics.

HYDRAULICS—THE SCIENCE OF LIQUID IN MOTION

A liquid, under confinement, can be used to: transmit pressure; increase or decrease pressure; transmit motion.

AIR IS COMPRESSIBLE

Air confined under pressure will compress, thereby reducing its volume. Fig. 20-1.

LIQUIDS CANNOT BE COMPRESSED

When a liquid is confined and placed under pressure, it cannot be compressed. A, Fig. 20-2, shows a cylinder filled with oil. A leakproof piston is placed on top of the oil. When a downward force is applied, as shown in B, the force will not compress the oil.

LIQUIDS CAN TRANSMIT MOTION

In Fig. 20-3, you will see that any movement of piston A will cause piston B to move a like amount.

Fig. 20-1. Air is compressible. There is no pressure on piston in A. In B, pressure has forced piston down, compressing air trapped in container.

Fig. 20-2. Liquids cannot be compressed. When pressure is applied to piston in B, it does not compress liquid.

Fig. 20-3. Liquids can transmit motion. Above. Both pistons are at rest. Below. Piston in left cylinder has been forced down. When it traveled down, it forced liquid into other cylinder. Since other cylinder is same size, its piston will be raised equal distance other piston was lowered.

LIQUIDS CAN TRANSMIT FORCE

If a 200 lb. force is placed on piston A, Fig. 20-4, piston B will support 200 lbs. Both pistons are the same size.

PASCAL'S LAW

Pascal, an early French scientist, stated, "When pressure is exerted on a confined liquid, it is transmitted undiminished." Fig. 20-5 illustrates Pascal's Law. Notice that the original pressure force is the same at all outlets.

LIQUIDS CAN INCREASE FORCE

When a force is applied to piston A, Fig. 20-6, it can be increased if it is transmitted to a larger piston B. If piston A has a surface area of 1 sq. in., the 200 lb. force on piston A represents a pressure of 200 lbs. per square inch (psi).

According to Pascal's Law, this 200 psi force will be transmitted undiminished.

If piston B has a surface area of 20 sq. in., piston A will exert a 200 lb. force on each square inch of piston B. This would produce a mechanical advantage (MA) of twenty, and the original 200 lb. force would be increased to 4,000 lbs.

Fig. 20-4. Using a liquid to transmit force. A 200 lb. force on piston A is transmitted, via liquid, to piston B.

Fig. 20-5. When pressure is exerted on a confined liquid, it is transmitted undiminished. Force on piston has created a pressure of 50 psi (lbs. per square inch), upon liquid in pressure cylinder. Notice that all gauges read the same throughout the system. Pressure is transmitted undiminished to all parts. If gauge A reads 50 psi, gauges B, C, D, and E will also read 50 psi.

Fig. 20-6. Liquids can be used to increase force. A 200 lb. force on piston A (piston area of 1 sq. in.) is increased to 4,000 lbs. on piston B (piston area of 20 sq. in.).

The force may be further increased by either making piston A smaller or piston B larger.

LIQUIDS CAN DECREASE FORCE

If force is applied to piston B, the original force of 200 lbs. would have to be raised to 80,000 lbs. to produce a pressure of 4,000 lbs. on piston A. By applying the force to the large piston transmitting it to the smaller, the force increase has been reversed and the original force, as applied to the piston, will be diminished. Remember that the force involved per square inch is transmitted undiminished. Pressure producing ability of this psi force can be increased or decreased by applying it to a large or to a small area. Notice in Fig. 20-7, that pressure in the pump cylinder, and pressure in the lifting cylinder, are the same. Yet, the force applied to the pump piston has been increased many times on the head of the lift.

A HYDRAULIC JACK

Fig. 20-7 shows how a fluid, using the principle illustrated in Fig. 20-6, can be used to produce a powerful lifting force.

When the jack handle raises piston A, piston A will form a vacuum, this will draw check valve 1 open and

Fig. 20-7. Simple hydraulic jack. If piston B has an area 100 times greater than piston A, ram will lift 100 times more than whatever pressure is generated by piston A.

HYDRAULIC PRINCIPLES APPLIED TO CAR BRAKING SYSTEM

Basically, the car hydraulic system consists of a master cylinder (containing piston A, Fig. 20-8), rubber hose and steel tubing to form connecting lines, and one or two wheel cylinders (containing pistons B, Fig. 20-8) for each wheel.

When the driver depresses the brake pedal and exerts a force on the master cylinder piston, this force is transmitted, undiminished, to each wheel cylinder. The wheel cylinder pistons transfer this force (increased or decreased, depending on piston area) to the brake shoes.

When the master cylinder piston A moves, the wheel cylinder pistons will move until the brake shoes engage the revolving brake drum. Further movement is impossible. Any attempt to depress the master cylinder piston beyond this point will transmit pressure, not motion.

HYDRAULIC BRAKE FLUID

Hydraulic brake fluid is used to transmit motion and pressure to the wheel cylinders and disc brake caliper pistons.

Some of the more important characteristics of a quality brake fluid are:

1. Maintains even viscosity (thickness) throughout a wide temperature variation and does not freeze at coldest possible temperature vehicle system may encounter.

close check valve 2. When the handle is depressed with a force that exerts 200 lbs. pressure (or any force) on piston A, check valve 1 will close, check valve 2 will open and 200 psi will be transmitted to piston B.

If piston B has a surface area one hundred times greater than the 1 sq. in. area of A, piston B will raise a weight of 20,000 lbs.

Fig. 20-8. Schematic of a simple brake system (hydraulic system). When foot pressure is applied to pedal, master cylinder piston creates pressure, thus causing wheel cylinder pistons to move outward.

2. Boiling point of the brake fluid must be above the highest operating temperature of the brake system parts.

3. Fluid should be hygroscopic (ability to absorb and retain moisture) to prevent internal freezing of parts.

4. Should act as a lubricant for pistons, seals, cups, etc., to aid in reducing internal wear and friction.

5. Fluid must not corrode the metal parts of the system. It must not deteriorate the rubber parts.

A recent development is SILICONE brake fluid. It is believed that this fluid will offer extended service life and top performance under a wide range of operating conditions.

Never mix different fluids. DO NOT install silicone fluid in a glycol-based (standard brake fluid) system without first removing ALL of the old fluid.

CAUTION!

Hydraulic brake fluid is POISON. Keep it away from skin, eyes, etc.

MASTER CYLINDER

The master cylinder is the central unit in which hydraulic pressure is developed. Pressure of the driver's foot on the brake pedal is transmitted, via various linkage arrangements, to the master cylinder piston. As the piston is forced forward in the cylinder, it pushes brake fluid ahead of it. Since the brake lines and wheel cylinders are filled with brake fluid, the piston is acting upon a solid column of fluid.

When the wheel cylinder pistons have pressed the brake shoes against the drums, fluid movement ceases and pressure rises according to the force on the master cylinder piston.

Fig. 20-9 illustrates brake pedal linkage, master cylinder, lines, and brake assemblies. Four systems are shown in one schematic.

MASTER CYLINDER CONSTRUCTION

Most master cylinders are manufactured of cast iron or aluminum and contain brackets with holes for mounting.

Modern practice leans heavily upon fire wall mounting (metal wall between driver and engine compartment). With the master cylinder in this location, it can be inspected and serviced easily, and it is less apt to become contaminated by water and dirt. It is operated by a suspended pedal. Fig. 20-10.

Fig. 20-9. Schematic of hydraulic brake system. Study general layout of parts and their names. Note that four different brake designs are illustrated. In practice, brake designs are paired, front and rear. (Raybestos)

Fig. 20-10. Fire wall mounting of power brake assembly. Note use of suspended brake pedal. (Bendix)

BRAKE FLUID RESERVOIR

The master cylinder generally has an integral reservoir, or reservoirs in double-piston (dual) master cylinders, for brake fluid. This will provide additional fluid, when needed, to compensate for minute leaks, lining wear requiring more fluid movement, etc. The reservoir cover is vented (has an air hole in it) to allow expansion and contraction of the fluid without forming pressure or vacuum. A rubber diaphragm contacts the fluid and follows the level up and down. The diaphragm excludes dust, moisture, etc.

A typical reservoir cover is illustrated in Fig. 20-19.

CYLINDER

A cylinder with a very smooth wall is provided in the master cylinder. This cylinder contains two aluminum pistons. The cylinder is connected to each reservoir by two ports (holes), the compensating port and intake or breather port, Figs. 20-11 and 20-13.

Fig. 20-11. Typical dual master cylinder setup. This one uses a nylon reservoir and aluminum cylinder body. Note how this setup is angled. (Delco)

PISTON ASSEMBLY

Two close fitting aluminum pistons are placed in the cylinder. The inner face of the piston presses against a rubber PRIMARY cup. This cup prevents leakage past the piston. The outer piston end has a rubber SECONDARY cup to prevent fluid from leaving the master cylinder. The inner piston head has several small bleeder ports that pass through the head to the base of the rubber primary cup.

Both piston assemblies rest in the cylinder. They are retained by a stop plate and/or a snap ring in the end of the cylinder. Pressure is applied to the pistons by means of a push rod that connects to the brake linkage. See Figs. 20-11, 20-12, 20-13.

CHECK VALVES AND PISTON SPRINGS

The check valve is of a two-way design, illustrated in the section on master cylinder operation, Figs.

Fig. 20-12. Exploded view of an aluminum master cylinder with nylon reservoir and screw on reservoir caps. Study part names and locations.   (Plymouth)

Fig. 20-13. Master cylinder fluid level. Air space is important so that reservoir fluid can expand without spewing out or creating pressure in system. Flexible diaphragm will normally ride on top of fluid. Note double-piston construction. (Bendix)

20-14 and 20-17. In operation, the piston forces fluid through the check valve into the brake lines. When the brake is released, pressure from the brake shoe return springs forces fluid back against the check valve. This pressure will force the entire check off its seat allowing fluid to return to the cylinder, Fig. 20-17. A check valve is not used with disc brakes.

The check valve coil spring returns the check to its seat when the spring pressure (around 10 psi or 68.9 kPa) is greater than the pressure of the returning fluid. This keeps pressure in the lines. This STATIC pressure will prevent the entry of air, dust, etc., into the brake system. It also assures a solid column of fluid so that movement of the master cylinder piston is immediately transferred to the wheel cylinder pistons.

Study the return spring location in the cross section of the master cylinder in Fig. 20-11.

Fig. 20-12 illustrates another master cylinder. Study the part arrangement and construction.

MASTER CYLINDER RESERVOIR FLUID LEVEL

The master cylinder reservoir should be filled to within 1/2 to 1/4 in. (12.7–6.35 mm) of the top of the reservoir, depending upon manufacturer's recommendations.

Fig. 20-13 illustrates this, as well as the entire master cylinder. Note that a separate reservoir is used for each piston.

DUAL MASTER CYLINDER OPERATION, RELEASED POSITION

Fig. 20-14 shows the master cylinder in the released position. The primary piston is pushed back against the stop plate. There is static pressure in the brake line and wheel cylinder.

The brake shoe return springs have pulled the shoes

away from the drum. The shoes, in turn, have compressed the wheel cylinder pistons. The primary cups are free of the compensating ports; the breather port is open to the center section of the primary piston. No pressure is present within the master cylinder itself. Look at Fig. 20-14.

DUAL MASTER CYLINDER OPERATION, BRAKES APPLIED

When pedal pressure is applied to the primary piston by means of the push rod, it moves forward and blocks off the compensating port, sealing the fluid in front of it. As the piston continues to move forward, it will transmit fluid pressure to either front or rear wheel cylinders and to the base of the secondary piston. This causes the secondary piston to move forward, block off its compensating port and apply pressure to the other wheel cylinders. Note that pedal pressure in Fig. 20-15 has moved both pistons and has created pressure to both chambers. Note how pressure in the front (secondary piston) chamber is applying the brake shoes. Study check valve action.

BRAKE RELEASE, START

When the driver removes his or her foot from the brake pedal, push rod pressure is removed from the pistons. The check valve impedes the sudden return of the fluid. As the pistons start to move outward in the cylinder, they will move faster than the fluid can return through the lines. This creates a mild vacuum in the pressure chambers and fluid will flow through the bleeder holes in the head of the pistons. This fluid will bend the lips of the cups away from the cylinder wall, and fluid will flow into the cylinder ahead of the pistons.

This action also allows brakes to be PUMPED up. Pumping is the repeated application of the pedal in

Fig. 20-14. Dual master cylinder in the fully released position. Primary piston fully against stop plate, compensating ports open. No pressure in master cylinder. Static pressure maintained in drum brake lines by check valve. Brake lining is not touching drum. (Buick)

Fig. 20-15. Dual master cylinder in applied position. Both compensating ports are closed and pressure is generated in the brake lines. Pressure has forced wheel cylinder pistons outward moving shoe lining against brake drum. (Buick)

quick movements. It is used when one full application fails to expand the shoes until they touch the drum. This condition is caused by faulty brake adjustment or worn brake shoes. Both are dangerous and should not be tolerated.

The flow of fluid through the bleeder holes will also prevent the possible entry of air by keeping the cylinder filled at all times. Fig. 20-16.

BRAKE RELEASE, FINISH

When pressure drops in the master cylinder, the brake shoe return springs retract the shoes. As the shoes retract, they squeeze the wheel cylinder pistons together. This, in turn, forces the brake fluid to flow back into the master cylinder.

The returning fluid forces the check valve off its

seat, and fluid flows into the master cylinder.

As the pistons return to their fully released position against the stop plate, the primary cups uncover the compensating ports and any excess fluid will flow into the reservoir.

When the piston return spring pressure is again greater than the pressure of the returning fluid, the check valve seats and maintains the desired static pressure in the system. See Fig. 20-17.

DUAL MASTER CYLINDER PROVIDES PROTECTION

For years, one real danger in the typical hydraulic brake system with a single piston master cylinder was the fact that a line rupture, blown wheel cylinder,

Fig. 20-16. Master cylinder at the start of fast release. Note how fluid flows through bleeder holes in the head of the piston. This forces rubber seal cup away from cylinder walls to allow fluid to bypass piston which prevents a mild vacuum from retarding the piston withdrawal. (Buick)

Fig. 20-17. Master cylinder at the finish of brake release. Both pistons have uncovered their compensating ports. As the brake shoes are retracted, they squeeze the wheel cylinder pistons together and the fluid is forced back through the lines, through the check valve and into the master cylinder reservoir. Note check valve action. (Buick) etc., could cause a sudden and complete loss of braking. To prevent this, the DUAL MASTER CYLINDER (also referred to as a TANDEM or DOUBLE-PISTON master cylinder) was developed and is now in universal use in this country. Figs. 20-11, 20-12, 20-13, and 20-19.

DUAL CYLINDER—RELEASED POSITION

When the brake pedal is in the released position, both pistons are retracted. Each has fluid in front of it and the compensating ports are open. Look at A, Fig. 20-18.

DUAL CYLINDER OPERATION— APPLIED POSITION

When pedal pressure is applied to the primary piston, it moves forward and blocks off the compensating port, sealing the fluid in front of it. As it con-

Fig. 20-18. Dual master cylinder operation. A—Released position. B—Applied position. C—Front system failure—still provides brake pressure to rear. D—Rear system failure—still provides pressure to front. (Mercedes)

tinues to move forward, it will transmit fluid pressure to the front wheel cylinders and to the base of the secondary piston. This causes the secondary piston to move forward, block off its compensating port and apply pressure to the rear wheel cylinders. Note that pedal pressure in B, Fig. 20-18, has moved both pistons and has created pressure to both front and rear wheel cylinders.

DUAL CYLINDER OPERATION, FAILURE IN FRONT WHEEL PORTION

A failure in the front wheel portion of the system would allow fluid to escape from the system and prevent pressure buildup. Note in C, Fig. 20-18 that the primary piston moves in, forcing fluid from the burst portion of the system until the primary piston strikes the secondary piston. Additional pedal movement will cause the primary piston to physically move the secondary piston forward, transmitting normal brake pressure to the rear wheels.

DUAL MASTER CYLINDER OPERATION, FAILURE IN REAR WHEEL PORTION

If the rear brake system fails, the primary piston will force the secondary piston in until the secondary piston strikes the end of the cylinder. The primary piston will then apply normal pressure to the front system as in D, Fig. 20-18.

The dual master cylinder, by providing separate systems for the front and rear brakes, will provide some braking force regardless of line failure. Although both front and rear systems could fail at the same time, such an event is highly unlikely.

Fig. 20-19 shows an exploded view of another dual master cylinder. Study the part names and locations.

QUICK TAKE-UP MASTER CYLINDER

The quick take-up master cylinder is used with the diagonal split brake system. Opposite front and rear brakes are both operated by the primary or secondary piston only. This master cylinder, Fig. 20-20, operates in the same manner as the standard cylinder, with several exceptions. Proportioners (proportioning valves) and a warning light switch are attached directly to the cylinder. However, the most important feature is the quick take-up valve, Fig. 20-20.

QUICK TAKE-UP OPERATION—APPLICATION

The quick take-up design supplies a large volume of brake fluid to the brakes during the initial (beginning) brake application. This low pressure fluid quickly supplies the increased fluid displacement requirements caused by no-drag, front caliper pistons (pulled away from disc by seals and retracted to their resting place), brake shoes, and lining.

At the start of the initial brake application, C in

Fig. 20-19. Exploded view of a dual master cylinder arrangement. Note the removable steel reservoir and fluid filters. (Chevrolet)

Fig. 20-21, more brake fluid is displaced in the primary, low pressure chamber than the high pressure chamber. This is caused by a larger diameter in the low pressure chamber than is present in the high pressure chamber. Fluid is forced around the outer edge of the primary piston lip seal and into the high

pressure chamber. From here, it travels to the wheel brake units.

Because equal pressure and displacement must be maintained in both systems, the primary piston moves a smaller amount than the secondary piston. This compensates for the larger amount of fluid moved from the low pressure space of the primary piston to the high pressure space.

As low pressure displacement requirements are reached, pressure will increase in the primary piston low pressure chamber until the spring-loaded ball check valve inside the quick take-up opens. This permits fluid to travel into the reservoir, A in Fig. 20-21. After this quick take-up operation phase is finished, the cylinder functions as a conventional dual master cylinder.

QUICK TAKE-UP OPERATION—RELEASING

As the brakes are released, the master cylinder springs return the pistons faster than fluid can travel back through the system. This creates a vacuum in the low and high pressure chambers, if vacuum is not relieved. Fluid will pass around the seal lip of the piston cups to relieve the vacuum. The primary low pressure area vacuum will be compensated for through a bypass groove in the quick take-up valve.

The primary piston is compensated by fluid traveling from the reservoir through the small, diameter holes of the quick take-up valve, B in Fig. 20-21. The

Fig. 20-20. Cutaway view of a "quick take-up" master cylinder. Study part names, construction and locations. (Delco)

Fig. 20-21. ''Quick take-up'' master cylinder operation. A—Operation as conventional master cylinder after quick take-up phase has finished. B—Releasing. C—Beginning of quick take-up application. Note fluid flow in all three steps (red arrows). (Delco)

secondary piston is compensated by fluid traveling from the reservoir through the compensating port and by-pass hole, on into the high and low pressure areas.

PRESSURE DIFFERENTIAL WARNING SWITCH

On systems employing the dual master cylinder, failure of either front or rear systems will allow the brake pedal to travel closer to the floorboard before applying the brakes.

Either a mechanical or hydraulic switch is utilized to operate a warning light to alert the driver that the pressure in one system is low or gone. The mechanical switch is triggered by excessive brake travel. The hydraulic switch is operated by a difference in pressure (around 80—150 psi or 551.6—1 034.2 kPa) between the front and the rear system.

One type of hydraulic pressure differential switch is

shown in Fig. 20-22. A drop in pressure on either side will allow the piston assembly to move toward the side with low pressure. This will bring the edge of the piston cutout into contact with the switch terminal thus completing the circuit and energizing the warning light.

BRAKE LINES

The master cylinder is connected to the wheel cylinders by high quality, double thickness, steel tubing. The tubing is copper plated and lead coated to prevent rust and corrosion.

Fig. 20-22. One type of pressure differential switch used to alert driver that brake pressure in either front or rear wheel system is gone. (Chevrolet)

DON'T TRUST IT!

NEVER REPLACE A BRAKE LINE WITH COPPER TUBING OR INFERIOR STEEL TUBING. THAT A CAR'S BRAKES BE GOOD IS ABSOLUTELY ESSENTIAL. USE HIGH QUALITY BRAKE TUBING!

Brake tubing, where connections are made, uses a double lap flare or special I.S.O. flare. Fig. 20-23 illustrates one type of double lap flaring tool.

VIBRATION MUST BE ELIMINATED

The brake lines must be secured, by use of clips, along their path. At no point must they be free to vibrate. Vibration will cause metal fatigue with ultimate line failure.

FLEXIBLE HOSE

It is necessary to use a flexible, HIGH PRESSURE hose to carry fluid to each front wheel cylinder or caliper cylinder, and to connect the metal brake tubing from the rear axle to the body. As the wheels move up and down in relation to the frame, this hose

Fig. 20-24. Flexible brake hose. To disconnect brake line, hold nut 2 and loosen nut 1. Notice the use of retaining clips to keep line secured to mounting brackets. (Toyota)

Fig. 20-23. Brake tubing flares. A—Start of flare. B—Flare being finished. C—Completed flare with nut in place. D—I.S.O. flare. E—Double lap flare assembled in wheel cylinder. (Bendix)

prevents line breakage. Fig. 20-24 shows a flex hose leading from the brake line on its way to the front wheel brake cylinder. Note that the line and hose, where connected, are securely held in a bracket.

Fig. 20-25 illustrates a typical hydraulic service brake system. A distributor fitting carries the line fluid to both front and rear brakes.

WHEEL CYLINDER, PURPOSE

The wheel cylinder is used to transmit the master cylinder pressure to the brake shoes and force them outward against the drum. One wheel cylinder (two, in some systems) is used at each wheel.

WHEEL CYLINDER CONSTRUCTION

The wheel cylinder assembly is of rather simple construction. It consists of a cast iron housing, two

aluminum pistons (sintered iron pistons are sometimes used), two rubber cups, cup expanders (in some applications) a light-weight coil spring, two push rods and two rubber dust boots.

The cylinder is drilled to provide an entrance for a bleeder screw (covered later) and the brake line connection. The cylinder is usually bolted to the brake backing plate (covered later). Study Figs. 20-26 and 20-27 carefully.

SINGLE-PISTON CYLINDER

In cases where two wheel cylinders are used per wheel, the cylinders are generally of the single-piston type. Since each cylinder operates one of the shoes, it is necessary to direct the pressure in only one direction. Fig. 20-28.

STEPPED CYLINDER

When it is desired to transmit more pressure to one of the shoes than to the other, the wheel cylinder is built with a stepped cylinder. One-half of the cylinder is of one size, and the other half is another size. Recalling the section on hydraulics, you can see that each half would exert a different pressure on its brake shoe. Fig. 20-29.

WHEEL CYLINDER OPERATION

When master cylinder forces fluid into wheel cylinder, the two pistons move apart. Push rods, or

Fig. 20-25. Typical service brake system. (Bendix)

Fig. 20-26. Cross section of typical double-piston wheel cylinder. Stamped metal expander cups at each end of spring tend to keep lips of rubber cups in constant contact with cylinder wall. (Oldsmobile)

Fig. 20-27. Exploded view of typical double-piston wheel cylinder. (Lincoln)

links, connect each piston to a brake shoe. As pistons move outward, they force shoes against drum. Study the simplified illustration in Fig. 20-30. Also see Figs. 20-14 and 20-15.

You will notice the cup design in the wheel cylinder is similar to the primary cup in the master cylinder. When the fluid exerts pressure against the cup, the flanged edges are pressed tightly against the cylinder. See A, Fig. 20-30.

HYDRAULIC SYSTEM MUST BE FREE OF AIR

As air is compressible, any air in a hydraulic system would render the system unfit for service. Air must be removed, so each wheel cylinder is provided with a

Fig. 20-28. Single-piston wheel cylinder. (Dodge)

Fig. 20-29. Stepped wheel cylinder. Note difference in cylinder diameter—A being larger than B. Piston in cylinder A will exert more force than piston in cylinder B.

bleeder screw. The bleeder screw is threaded into an opening leading into the center of the wheel cylinder.

Pressure is applied on the master cylinder, and the bleeder screw is loosened. This allows trapped air to escape. Then the bleeder screw is tightened before pressure is removed from the master cylinder. This process is repeated at each wheel cylinder until all air is removed.

A typical bleeder screw is shown in Fig. 20-31. When the screw is loosened, the tapered point uncovers the bleeder hole. This permits air to move up around the point, through the cross hole and out the center passageway. When the screw is tightened, the point seals the opening.

One method of bleeding brakes is shown in Fig. 20-32. One end of a rubber hose is connected to the bleeder screw. The other end is inserted in a partially filled jar of brake fluid. As the air leaves the end of the hose submerged in the fluid, air bubbles rise. Air cannot be drawn back into the system.

CAUTION!

USE HIGH QUALITY BRAKE FLUID ONLY. IT SHOULD MEET OR EXCEED SAE RECOMMENDATION J 1703 AND CONFORM TO

Fig. 20-30. Simplified wheel cylinder action. Fluid, under pressure, enters wheel cylinder and, by pressing on rubber cups, forces pistons and push rods outward.

Fig. 20-31. A—Wheel cylinder showing bleeder screw. B—Cutaway of bleeder screw.

Fig. 20-32. Bleeding hydraulic system with a pressurized bleeder tank. Note air bubbles appearing in glass jar, as fluid forces air from lines. (Bendix)

MOTOR VEHICLE SAFETY STANDARD 116. ANY MINERAL OIL SUCH AS KEROSENE, GASOLINE, ETC., IN EVEN THE SMALLEST AMOUNTS, WILL SWELL AND DESTROY THE RUBBER CUPS IN THE SYSTEM.

WHEEL BRAKE ASSEMBLY

The hydraulic system can be termed a brake actuating device. The wheel brake assemblies form the second part of the braking system.

Each wheel assembly consists of a brake backing plate, a set of brake shoes with clips, return springs, etc., and a brake drum.

BACKING PLATE

A round, stamped steel disc is generally bolted to the end of the axle housing in the rear, (disc brakes in front, drum brakes rear). This disc, called the backing plate, is used as a foundation upon which the wheel cylinder and brake shoe assembly is fastened. The backing plate is rigid and cannot move in any direction. Fig. 20-33.

BRAKE SHOE ASSEMBLY

Most wheel brake assemblies use two brake shoes. These shoes are of stamped steel and have brake linings either riveted or bonded (glued) to the outer surface.

Although of similar design, there are some minor differences in the shapes of the shoes. All utilize a T-shape cross section. The web is used to give the shoe rigidity. When forced against the drum, it will exert braking pressure over the full lining width and length. Fig. 20-34. The ends of the brake shoes may be free-floating, or they may have one end fastened to an anchor.

Brake return or retracting springs are used to pull the shoes together when hydraulic pressure is released. Small spring clips of various designs are used to keep the shoes against the backing plate to insure shoe alignment and prevent rattle. Study the arrangement of parts in Fig. 20-35.

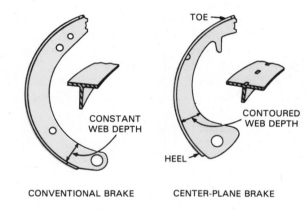

Fig. 20-34. Two brake shoe designs. (Dodge)

Fig. 20-33. Typical brake backing plate. Backing plate forms a foundation for brake shoes and wheel cylinder. (Raybestos)

BOOT PISTON
CUP
BLEED SCREW
SHOE HOLD-DOWN PIN
ANCHOR BOLT NUT
CUP PISTON
WHEEL CYLINDER BODY
SPRING
BOOT
WHEEL CYLINDER BODY BOLTS
ANCHOR BOLT BUSHING
CAM PLATE
PRIMARY SHOE
ADJUSTING HOLE COVER
UPPER SHOE-TO-SHOE SPRING
SHOE LINKS
SHOE HOLD-DOWN SPRING
SHOE HOLD-DOWN PIN
LOWER SHOE-TO-SHOE SPRING
BACKING PLATE
ANTI-RATTLE SPRING
AUTOMATIC ADJUSTER CABLE
FLAT WASHER
ANCHOR BOLT
SHOE HOLD-DOWN SPRING
CABLE GUIDE
PIVOT SCREW
ADJUSTING NUT
ADJUSTER LEVER PIVOT PIN
THRUST WASHER
SECONDARY SHOE
ADJUSTER LEVER RETURN SPRING
PARKING BRAKE LEVER
SOCKET
AUTOMATIC ADJUSTER LEVER

Fig. 20-35. Backing plate and brake shoe assembly. (Dodge)

A backing plate and shoe assembly is shown on a front wheel spindle steering knuckle in Fig. 20-36. This is the two cylinder, single-piston type. Each shoe pivots on one end; the wheel cylinders shove the other end outward.

PRIMARY SHOE

The PRIMARY (forward or leading) brake shoe is the shoe that faces toward the front of the car. It often has different lining than the other shoe.

SECONDARY SHOE

The SECONDARY (reverse or trailing) brake shoe is the shoe that faces the rear of the car.

BRAKE LINING

Brake lining is generally made from asbestos fibers impregnated with special compounds which bind them together. At present, the most widely used lining is molded (asbestos fibers ground up and pressed into shape). Current developments in lining, however, incorporate the use of synthetic fibers, iron powders, steel fibers, ceramic and metallic powders, etc. For heavy-duty braking, special metallic lining, very resistant to brake fade. is offered. SEE BRAKE DUST WARNING – BEGINNING OF CHAPTER!

FORWARD
BACKING PLATE
ANCHOR PIN
SINGLE PISTON CYLINDER
BRAKE SHOE
SINGLE PISTON CYLINDER
SHOE
ANCHOR PIN
SHOE GUIDE SPRING

Fig. 20-36. Backing plate and shoe assembly in place. Note this setup uses two single-piston wheel cylinders. Eccentric anchor pins adjust to center shoes with drum and also hold wheel cylinders in place. (Bendix)

BRAKE DRUM

The brake drum bolts to the wheel hub between the hub and the wheel. It completely surrounds the brake shoe assembly and comes very close to the backing plate so that water and dust will be excluded.

The center section is of stamped steel construction,

while the outer braking rim is of cast iron. An aluminum outer rim is sometimes used to aid in cooling. When aluminum is used, a cast iron braking surface is fused to the aluminum rim.

The outer rim is cast to the steel center section. Cooling fins are often cast into the rim. Fig. 20-37. The braking area of the drum must be smooth, round and parallel to the shoe surface.

When the wheels turn, the drum revolves around the stationary brake shoes. Some drums have a stiff spring stretched around them, on the outside rim, which helps to reduce drum vibration.

A complete wheel brake assembly is pictured in Figs. 20-38 and 20-39. Study these drawings carefully. Note how the brake drum meets the backing plate (dust shield). The plate edge covers the drum for a short distance to provide a good seal.

HOW BRAKE ASSEMBLY WORKS

When master cylinder operation creates pressure in the wheel cylinder, the wheel cylinder pistons and links shove the brake shoes outward into contact with the revolving brake drum. As the shoes cannot revolve, they will stop the drum and wheel.

The kinetic energy (energy stored up in a moving object) in the moving car is converted into heat by the brakes. A fast moving car has tremendous energy. To bring it to a stop will produce a great amount of heat. This heat is given off, mostly to the surrounding air, by the brake drums. Some will pass to the shoes and to the backing plate.

BRAKE FADE

When brake lining becomes overheated, it loses a great deal of its frictional properties. Even hard pedal pressure will not produce fast, even stops.

Some cars, designed for fast and rigorous driving, use special metallic linings that have great resistance to fade.

BRAKE SHOE ARRANGEMENT

There are many arrangements used in mounting brake shoes. Several popular ones are illustrated in this chapter. Some utilize a servo action (one shoe helps to apply other), as well as a self-energizing action (using frictional force to increase shoe-to-drum pressure).

SERVO ACTION, SELF-ENERGIZING BRAKES

Servo and self-energizing action is produced by hooking the heel of the primary shoe to the toe of the secondary shoe. When the wheel cylinder forces the top ends of the shoes out against the drum, the forward shoe will tend to stick to the revolving brake drum and be carried around with it. As the primary shoe attempts to revolve, it will jam the secondary shoe against the single anchor pin. This stops both

Fig. 20-37. Sections of typical brake drums. Note cast iron inner liner when aluminum is used to facilitate cooling.

Fig. 20-38. Cross section showing front wheel, drum brake assembly. Backing plate assembly (backing plate, wheel cylinder, shoes, springs, etc.) is bolted to spindle assembly. (Toyota)

shoes and produces a binding effect that actually helps the brake shoes apply themselves. This servo and self-energizing action reduces the amount of pedal pressure necessary. Study Fig. 20-40.

Note, in Fig. 20-40, how the primary shoe attempts to rotate in the direction of the drum. Since the adjusting screw connects it to the toe of the secondary shoe, the heel of the secondary shoe is jammed against the anchor pin. The arrows illustrate the braking force direction. When the car is traveling in reverse, the secondary shoe applies the primary shoe.

The primary shoe on self-energizing brakes generally has a smaller amount of lining and, usually, it is of a different composition. The secondary shoe does more of the braking; less is needed on the primary shoe.

Fig. 20-39. Cross section of complete wheel brake assembly. Note how shoe friction lining engages drum. Backing plate laps over drum outer edge to help prevent entry of water, dirt, etc.   (Peugeot)

Fig. 20-41. Servo action, self-energizing brake. Primary shoe (left) has a short lining when used in this setup. (Wagner Electric Corp.)

Fig. 20-40. Servo action, self-energizing brake. Primary shoe starts to move with drum and in so doing, applies secondary shoe.   (Buick)

A servo action, self-energizing brake assembly is shown in Fig. 20-41. Note that the primary shoe has less lining. This is a rear wheel brake. The star wheel at the bottom is used to adjust the shoes to keep them close to the drum. Figs. 20-41 and 20-42.

DOUBLE ANCHOR BRAKE

Notice that each shoe is anchored at the bottom. Fig. 20-43. The primary shoe is self-energizing; the rear shoe is not. Spring clips at the outer ends hold the shoes against the backing plate.

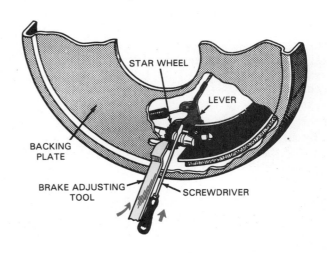

Fig. 20-42. Star wheel shoe adjuster. Special brake adjusting tool engages star wheel teeth to make initial brake adjustment. By moving handle one way or the other, adjuster can be shortened or lengthened to adjust shoe-to-drum clearance. Screwdriver is being used to keep automatic adjuster lever out of engagement with star wheel.   (Plymouth)

SINGLE ANCHOR, SELF-CENTERING BRAKE

The brake shown in Fig. 20-44 has no servo action, but the primary shoe is self-energizing. It is self-centering in that the shoe anchor does not fix the location of shoes in any specific relationship to the drum. The shoes can move up or down until centered. The brakes in Fig. 20-41 are also self-centering.

DOUBLE ANCHOR, DOUBLE CYLINDER BRAKE

In the brake assembly in Fig. 20-45, the free end of each shoe is actuated toward the direction of rotation, and both shoes are self-energizing. Two single-piston cylinders are used.

Brake adjustment is provided by eccentrics. A in

Fig. 20-43. Double anchor brake. Each shoe is fastened to a separate anchor. Shoe-to-drum alignment is secured by rotating eccentric shaped anchor pins.

Fig. 20-44. Single anchor, self-centering brake. Shoe ends, where they butt against anchor, are free to move up or down and automatically align with drum. (Raybestos)

Fig. 20-45. The anchors, B, are also eccentrics so that the shoes may be centered in relationship to the drum.

SELF-ADJUSTING BRAKES

Modern brake systems utilize a device that automatically adjusts the drum-to-lining clearance as the linings wear down. Manual adjustment is provided by turning the star wheel with a special adjusting tool.

The adjustment systems are of three general types: cable, link, and lever. Some systems operate only when braking in reverse; others, when braking in a forward direction, and still another operates when braking in either direction.

A special adjustment lever is attached to one of the brake shoes in such a manner that it is free to pivot back and forth. One end engages the teeth in the star wheel, while the other is attached to a link or a cable. Figs. 20-46 and 20-47. The cable, or the link, is attached either to the anchor (adjustment will take place when braking in one direction only) or to the

Fig. 20-45. Double anchor, double cylinder brake. Apply pistons move each shoe in such a way as to make them self-energizing. (Raybestos)

other brake shoe (will function when braking in either direction). A spring holds the adjustment lever in a downward position.

Study the construction of the cable type adjuster in Fig. 20-46. This particular unit passes the actuating cable up over the anchor and attaches it to the secondary shoe, causing it to function when braking in either direction.

When the brakes are applied, in a forward direction for example, the shoes move out until they contact the rotating drum. They will then move around with the drum until the secondary shoe heel engages the anchor. The small out and around movement tightens the actuating cable, and it pulls upward on the adjustment lever a small amount. When the brakes are released, the shoes are retracted, causing the actuating cable to become slack and the return spring pulls the adjustment lever back down. This action is repeated during each brake application.

The amount of lever movement is very small, and

Fig. 20-46. Cable type automatic brake adjuster. This specific setup works when braking in both directions.

Fig. 20-47. Lever type automatic brake adjuster. This unit functions only when braking in reverse.

normally the cable will not draw the lever up far enough to engage a new tooth on the star wheel. When sufficient lining wear has taken place, however, the out and around movement will be enough to cause the cable to draw the lever up to the next tooth on the star wheel. When the brakes are released, the return spring will draw the lever down, forcing it to rotate the star wheel one tooth.

This adjustment action will take place during the entire life of the lining. Fig. 20-46 depicts a typical cable operated adjustment system.

A lever type adjuster is shown in Fig. 20-47. Since the actuating link is attached to the anchor, it will operate only in one direction. On this unit, where the lever is pivoted to the secondary shoe, it functions only during reverse braking.

The link type adjuster is very similar to the cable type. The utilization of links (wires) instead of the cable is the basic difference. Fig. 20-48.

Fig. 20-48. Link type automatic brake adjuster. This unit functions during reverse braking.

BRAKING RATIO

When a car is stopped, there is transfer of weight to the front of the car (notice how front end dips down during quick stops). This weight transfer forces the front tires more tightly against the road while it relieves the rear tires somewhat.

To compensate for this effect, and to also take advantage of it, the front brakes usually are designed to produce more stopping power than the rear. An average ratio would be: Front brakes—55 to 60 percent. Rear brakes—40 to 45 percent of the stopping force.

DISC BRAKE

The DISC brake differs from drum brakes in the use of a heavy disc or rotor. The disc is bolted to and revolves with the wheel hub. The disc, Figs. 20-49 and 20-50, may be solid or slotted for improved cooling.

The brake CALIPER generally houses one or two pistons. Others have up to four pistons. The three piston setup uses two small pistons on one side of the disc and a larger one on the opposite side. Most four piston arrangements incorporate two pistons of equal size on each side of the disc.

The caliper is bolted to the spindle, dust or splash shield on some models. Brake friction pads are so arranged that when hydraulic pressure is built up behind the pistons, the pads will be forced against the disc, providing braking effort. A typical disc brake is pictured in Fig. 20-49.

Another type of caliper uses a single piston on one side only. This caliper is free to slide sideways to allow brake pads to align with disc. Fig. 20-50.

Fig. 20-49. Typical front wheel disc brake. Disc brake has excellent cooling characteristics, making it highly resistant to brake "fade." (Plymouth)

Fig. 20-50. Cross section of disc brake, showing caliper construction. This is a single piston, sliding caliper setup. (Dodge)

CALIPER CONSTRUCTION AND OPERATION

The heavy, rigid brake caliper, of one or two piece construction, contains one, two (one each side), three, or four (two each side) hydraulic cylinders. The caliper is bolted securely to the spindle.

Pistons, which can be constructed from cast iron, aluminum, or plastic, are fitted to the caliper cylinders with the outer ends resting against friction pads. Rubber boots exclude the entry of dirt and moisture.

One design allows the brake pads to drag VERY LIGHTLY against the rotating disc at all times. Another type operates with only a minimal pad to disc clearance (about .005 in. or 0.13 mm).

A hydraulic line from the master cylinder leads to one side of the caliper. The other side will receive pressure through a crossover (external) line or bypassing the fluid internally through the casting as shown in Fig. 20-52.

The brake lining, or friction pads, are self-centering and press on each side of the disc with equal pressure. Study the caliper construction illustrated in Fig. 20-50.

An exploded view, showing caliper construction, is pictured in Fig. 20-51. Note that the friction pad or lining is affixed to a metal brake shoe. Fig. 20-52 shows a sectioned view of a similar unit.

The caliper piston shown in Fig. 20-53 operates against a snug seal ring snapped into a groove in the cylinder wall. When the brake is applied, the piston moves outward. In so doing, it stretches the seal to one side. A in Fig. 20-53. When brake pressure is released, the seal returns to its normal position, B. This seal "roll" action pulls the piston back around .005 in. (0.13 mm), providing a small amount of pad (lining)-to-disc clearance. As the lining pads wear, the piston moves out through the seal, automatically keeping the proper pad to disc clearance.

A cutaway view of a caliper, using the seals to withdraw the pistons upon brake release, is pictured in Fig. 20-52.

Current practice in this country, when disc brakes are employed, is to place discs on the front with con-

Fig. 20-51. Two-piece disc brake caliper, using four apply pistons. (Bendix)

Fig. 20-52. Cutaway of a four-piston caliper. Note piston seals and ventilated disc which aid cooling. (Bendix)

Fig. 20-53. Piston seal pulls piston back, providing pad-to-disc clearance. A—Brake applied. Piston moves outward and stretches seal. B—Brakes released. Seal rolls back to original shape, drawing piston back with it.

ventional drum brakes on the rear. However, some models are offered with disc brakes on all four wheels.

Study the various disc brake parts and assemblies pictured in Fig. 20-54.

METERING VALVE

In order to insure that the back drum brakes apply at about the same time as the front discs, and that the drum brakes do an equal amount of work during light stopping, a metering valve is placed in the line to the disc brakes.

The metering valve prevents brake fluid movement to the discs until a specified psi has built up in the system (75—125 psi or 517—862 kPa). By the time system pressure reaches this point, the force of the heavy drum brake shoe retracting springs has been overcome, and the shoes are starting to contact the drum. The metering valve then opens and allows fluid pressure to apply the disc brakes. A typical metering valve is illustrated in Fig. 20-55. Note that it is part of a combination valve that also incorporates a brake warning switch and a rear wheel proportioning valve. No residual pressure is maintained in the front disc system.

PROPORTIONING VALVE

Another valve, called a proportioning valve, can be placed in the line to the rear wheels. This valve limits the amount of pressure to the rear drum brakes to prevent rear wheel lockup during rapid stops. The amount of pressure to the rear wheels is directly proportional to the amount of pressure developed within the master cylinder. Fig. 20-56 illustrates a system using metering and proportioning valves. See Fig. 20-55 also.

Disc brakes are highly efficient and resist brake fade (loss of lining-to-disc friction due to

overheating) to a high degree. This is due to the disc rotating in the open air and to the smaller friction area. Despite the fact that the disc is exposed to water and dirt, the disc brakes work well and without grabbing, during wet or dry operation.

Due to the relatively small friction area, disc brakes require somewhat higher hydraulic pressure than conventional drum brakes. This condition is amplified by the lack of either a servo or self-energizing action found in some drum brakes.

EMERGENCY OR PARKING BRAKES

Two types of emergency brakes are in general use. One type uses a mechanical linkage system to operate the rear brake shoes. The other type uses a brake drum fastened to the transmission output shaft to apply stopping force through the drive line and axles. The transmission emergency brake is no longer in general use on automobiles.

BRAKE SHOE EMERGENCY OR PARKING BRAKE

A foot pedal or a dash mounted handle is connected through linkage and cables, to both rear wheel brake assemblies. When the emergency brake is placed in the ON position, the cables pull a lever in each rear brake assembly.

The top of the lever is bolted to one shoe, and one end of a strut (steel bar) is notched into the lever below the top bolt. The other end of the strut is notched into the opposite shoe. The emergency brake cable is attached to the lower end of the lever. See Fig. 20-57.

When the cable pulls the bottom of the lever toward the left, the lever forces the strut to the left until the strut presses the shoe against the drum. At this point, continued movement of the lever causes the lever to pivot on the strut, moving the top of the lever, and the shoe to which it is bolted, to the right until that shoe engages the drum. Further lever movement will now apply force to both shoes.

Fig. 20-54. Various disc brake assemblies. A—Three piston. B—Single piston caliper. C—Cross section showing relationship of caliper to disc or rotor. D—Four piston caliper. E—Ventilated disc and inboard and outboard brake plate and lining assembly. Note pad (lining) wear indicator. When pad is worn, indicator strikes disc making noise to warn driver. F—Sliding and fixed caliper braking action. G—Dual (two) piston caliper. H—Solid or nonventilated disc.
(Delco, EIS, Girling)

Fig. 20-55. This combination valve incorporates a metering valve (left portion), a pressure differential switch (center portion) and a proportioning valve (right portion). Metering valve blocks fluid pressure to front disc brakes until a certain pressure has been reached. This assures that rear drum brakes are applied. (Buick)

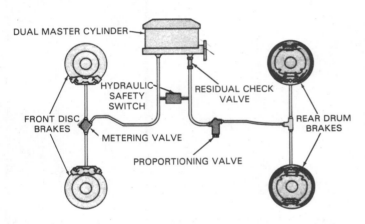

Fig. 20-56. Disc brake system shown employs a proportioning valve, a metering valve and a safety switch (pressure differential switch). (Ammco)

DRIVE LINE EMERGENCY BRAKE

The drive line emergency uses a brake drum mounted on the end of the transmission output shaft. Two stationary brake shoes are mounted inside. The emergency linkage cable operates a lever that applies these shoes much as the rear wheel shoes are applied.

When the drum is stopped, it holds the drive line stationary, and the car (when both rear wheels are on the ground) cannot roll. A in Fig. 20-58.

PARKING BRAKE—DISC TYPE

Some vehicles equipped with disc brakes incorporate an integral parking brake mechanism in the caliper. The caliper is similar to the front caliper in operation and design. The parking brake is actuated by a lever located on the inboard side of the caliper. The lever is moved by the parking brake cable.

As the lever is applied, it rotates the actuator screw which forces the piston assembly against the shoe and

Fig. 20-57. Rear wheel emergency brake assembly. Rear cable pulls on brake lever, thus causing strut to spread and apply brake shoes. (Bendix)

lining. Continued application moves the caliper, bringing the outboard shoe and lining into contact with the disc, thus firmly holding it in position. An exploded view of this caliper setup is in Fig. 20-59.

EMERGENCIES WILL ARISE

ADJUSTMENT OF THE EMERGENCY OR PARKING BRAKE IS OFTEN NEGLECTED. KEEP THE EMERGENCY BRAKE PROPERLY ADJUSTED, ALL LINKAGE FREE AND LUBRICATED. IT WILL BE EASIER TO USE WHEN IT IS REALLY NEEDED!

BRAKE LIGHTS

Brake lights are operated either by a hydraulically operated switch placed somewhere in the brake line, or by a mechanically operated switch actuated by the brake pedal.

Fig. 20-58. Two types of drive line emergency brakes. A—Internal type uses two brake shoes operating against inside of drum. B—External type draws a friction-lined band against outside of drum to prevent car from moving when both wheels are on ground. (Bendix)

Fig. 20-59. Exploded view of a rear caliper using an integral parking brake arrangement. Study part names and locations. (Pontiac)

VACUUM OPERATED POWER BRAKES

Many cars are equipped with power brakes. Such brakes are designed to reduce the amount of pedal pressure necessary to stop the car. Another feature is that pedal travel (distance from release position to full brake application) can be shortened. This makes it possible to have the pedal approximately the same distance from the floor board as the accelerator pedal. The driver, to apply the brakes, merely pivots the foot from the accelerator pedal to the brake pedal. The power brake unit is an additional part that operates in conjunction with the regular brake system already discussed.

HOW POWER BRAKE IS CONSTRUCTED

A power brake unit is built to take advantage of the vacuum produced in a car engine. In the case of diesel engines, a vacuum pump (engine or electrically driven) is used in that diesels do not provide sufficient vacuum for efficient vacuum power booster operation.

In very elementary terms, it is a closed cylinder with a piston inside. One side of the piston is connected to the master cylinder piston. The other side is connected to the brake pedal. A vacuum control valve is placed between the brake and the piston.

The vacuum control valve admits vacuum to one side of the piston, while the normal atmospheric pressure is allowed to exist on the other. This valve can also allow atmospheric pressure to reach both sides of the piston. Fig. 20-60.

Fig. 20-60. Schematic of a simplified power brake. Engine vacuum is admitted through vacuum inlet. Control valve A can apply either vacuum or atmospheric pressure to B section of booster cylinder. As shown, brake pedal is being applied. Pedal linkage has caused control valve A to cut off atmospheric pressure and to apply vacuum to B side. Atmospheric pressure is forcing piston and push rod to right, building pressure in master cylinder.

HOW THE POWER BRAKE WORKS

When the driver presses the brake pedal down, the vacuum control valve closes off the atmospheric pressure to the brake cylinder side of the piston. Further movement of the brake pedal opens a vacuum inlet passage to this same side. As there is atmospheric pressure on one side of the piston and a partial vacuum on the other, the piston will be forced toward the vacuum side. Since the piston is connected to the master cylinder piston, it will apply pressure to the brake system.

The power brake has three stages of operation:
1. Brakes released (released position).
2. Applying brakes (applied position).
3. Holding constant apply pressure (holding position).

TYPICAL POWER BOOSTER

Study the sectional view in Fig. 20-62. This is the same unit as the one pictured in Fig. 20-63. Use it for identifying part names and when studying booster operation in Fig. 20-63.

VACUUM AND ATMOSPHERIC SUSPENDED BOOSTER

In reference to vacuum and atmospheric (air) suspension, the vacuum suspended power booster has a vacuum existing on both sides of the diaphragm or piston when the booster is in the released position. When the booster is applied, atmospheric pressure is admitted to one side to cause the necessary movement of the piston. See schematic B in Fig. 20-61.

An atmospheric suspended booster has atmospheric pressure on each side of the piston in the released position. To cause booster action, vacuum is admitted to one side. See schematic A in Fig. 20-61.

RELEASED POSITION

With engine running and brakes fully released, the valve operating rod and valve plunger are moved to the right by the rod and plunger return spring. Fig. 20-63, A. This presses the right end of the valve plunger against the face of the poppet valve, closing off the atmospheric port. The vacuum port is open and a vacuum is formed on both sides of the diaphragm plate (side to left of diaphragm is subjected to constant vacuum regardless of valve plunger position).

With a vacuum on both sides, the diaphragm return spring moves the diaphragm plate to the right, releasing all pressure on the master cylinder. Look at Fig. 20-63, A.

APPLIED POSITION

When the driver depresses the brake pedal, the valve operating rod is moved to the left. Fig. 20-63, B.

Fig. 20-61. Atmospheric and vacuum suspended power booster. (Wagner)

Fig. 20-62. Typical power booster. 1—Master cylinder. 2—Vacuum check valve. 3—Grommet. 4—Diaphragm. 5—Diaphragm plate. 6—Rear shell. 7—Diaphragm spring. 8—Reaction plate. 9—Valve plunger. 10—Bearing seal. 11—Poppet valve. 12—Poppet valve spring. 13—Poppet retainer. 14—Dust boot. 15—Valve operating rod. 16—Filter and silencers. 17—Valve rod and plunger return spring. 18—Mounting stud. 19—Air valve lock plate. 20—Diaphragm. 21—Front shell. 22—Push rod seal. 23—Cylinder-to-shell seal. 24—Hydraulic push rod. 25—Adjusting screw. (GMC)

This causes the valve plunger to move to the left. As the plunger moves, it will compress the valve return spring and move the poppet valve into contact with the vacuum port seat in the valve housing. This closes the vacuum port leading to the right side of the diaphragm.

Further application of the brake pedal will cause the valve rod to force the valve plunger away from the poppet, OPENING the atmospheric port. As the port is opened, atmospheric air will rush into the area to the right of the diaphragm (control vacuum area) and force the diaphragm plate to the left. This, of course, applies pressure to the master cylinder push rod. (Note how rubber reaction disc is compressed.)

BRAKE FEEL

As the diaphragm plate builds up hydraulic pressure in the brake system, a reaction pressure is transmitted back through the master cylinder hydraulic push rod. The compressed rubber reaction disc transmits this reaction pressure to both the diaphragm plate and the valve plunger. The pressure on the plunger valve tends to force it to the right (without moving diaphragm plate), causing the valve to close off the atmospheric port. The movement of the valve plunger is transmitted to the valve operating rod and on to the brake pedal. This provides the driver with "brake feel," to accurately determine the amount of braking effort being exerted.

This reaction force is directly proportional to pressure created within the master cylinder. Some power boosters use a reaction plate and levers, diaphragms, etc., instead of the rubber disc. Study the reaction disc in Fig. 20-63, A. Note that it is not compressed, and that a portion engages the valve plunger. Compare this with the compressed reaction disc in Fig. 20-63, B.

RUNOUT POINT

The vacuum runout is that point where a full vacuum has built up all the pressure possible on the power piston or diaphragm plate. If the driver desires more pressure than a full vacuum can produce, additional pressure can be exerted on the pedal. This will hold the vacuum port wide open and transmit all of the driver's effort directly to the master cylinder piston.

Generally, wheel lockup (brake shoes will seize brake drum so tightly, tires will stop revolving and will slide) will occur before the vacuum runout point is reached.

HOLDING POSITION

As long as the driver increases pedal pressure, the valve plunger will move to the left. When the driver exerts the desired amount of pressure, plunger movement will cease. The reaction force, transmitted to the reaction disc, will force the valve plunger (without moving diaphragm plate) a slight amount to the right. This shuts off the atmospheric port. The vacuum port also remains shut.

Fig. 20-63. Note power booster action. A—Released position. Vacuum is on both sides of diaphragm. Spring moves diaphragm to right. Pressure not applied to master cylinder. B—Applied position. Poppet valve closes vacuum port and valve plunger moves to left, opening port. Atmospheric pressure forces diaphragm plate toward vacuum side. C—Holding position. Both vacuum and atmospheric ports are closed. This will retain degree of braking desired. (GMC)

When this balanced condition occurs, the right side of the diaphragm plate will be subjected to a specific and unchanging amount of atmospheric pressure. This maintains a constant pressure in the brake system.

If additional pedal force is applied, the atmospheric valve is reopened, causing the diaphragm plate to exert additional pressure on the master cylinder. It will maintain this pressure until pedal and reaction forces are again balanced.

If the pedal is released, the atmospheric port is closed and the vacuum port opened and both sides of the diaphragm plate are subjected to a vacuum. As this removes any force from the plate, the diaphragm return spring will push the plate and valve assembly to the right of the booster cylinder.

Fig. 20-63, C shows a power booster in the holding position. Both vacuum and atmospheric ports are closed. Note how the reaction disc has moved the valve plunger a little to the right (in relation to diaphragm plate), as compared with the applied position in Fig. 20-63, B. This action closes the atmospheric port. Fig. 20-63, C.

OTHER BOOSTER TYPES

There are many variations in booster design, however, the basic principles are much the same.

The heavy-duty tandem booster, shown in Fig. 20-64, uses two diaphragm plates to increase booster-to-master cylinder pressure.

A reaction plate and lever setup, to provide "brake feel," is illustrated in Fig. 20-65. Counterforce from the master cylinder push rod exerts a force on the reaction plate. The plate transfers this force to the

Fig. 20-64. Typical dual (tandem) power booster in the applying stage. (Bendix)

Fig. 20-65. Power booster employing reaction plate and levers to create "brake feel." Note reservoir seal. (Chevrolet)

levers, causing them to tip to the right and move the air valve (valve plunger) to the right to close off the atmospheric port. This movement is transmitted to the brake pedal through the push rod.

PISTON TYPE BOOSTER

Boosters discussed so far have been of the diaphragm type and are in popular use today. Some boosters have used a sliding piston instead of a diaphragm and plate. A sealing ring is used around the piston to provide an airtight seal. This arrangement is pictured in Fig. 20-66.

BELLOWS TYPE BOOSTER

The bellows booster (it gets its name from rubber bellows construction) works on the same principle of vacuum and atmospheric pressure, but no cylinder and piston are used.

When vacuum is admitted to the bellows, the entire unit draws together. In Fig. 20-67, the right side is bolted to the fire wall. When the unit draws together, the left end moves toward the fire wall. This particular bellows booster applies pressure to the brake pedal above its pivot point.

PISTON TYPE BOOSTER ATTACHED TO BRAKE PEDAL

Fig. 20-68 illustrates a piston booster attached to a brake pedal. The booster is in the applied position, forcing the brake pedal out at A and in at B to actuate the master cylinder.

EXPLODED VIEW OF A DIAPHRAGM BOOSTER

An exploded view of a typical diaphragm power booster (similar to one shown in Figs. 20-63, A, B,

Fig. 20-66. Power booster using a sliding piston instead of a diaphragm and plate. Note piston seal. (Wagner)

Fig. 20-67. Bellows type vacuum booster. When vacuum is applied to bellows, bellows shortens in a lengthwise direction to apply necessary pressure. (Bendix)

Fig. 20-68. Power booster attached to brake pedal. This setup applies booster pressure to brake pedal instead of directly to master cylinder. End result is similar—reduced foot pressure. (Plymouth)

and C) is pictured in Fig. 20-69. Study the part names and location.

HYDRAULIC POWER BOOSTER

The hydraulic power booster (also called "Hydro-Boost") is used on some vehicles. This is a popular unit on some diesel engine setups.

As the name implies, the hydraulic booster is operated by hydraulic pressure. The power steering pump is generally used as the source of pressure. Some heavy duty units employ an electro-hydraulic emergency pump as a back up source in the event the power steering pump becomes inoperative.

The setup consists basically of a hydraulic pressure source, the hydraulic booster and a master cylinder. Fig. 20-70 depicts a typical arrangement.

As with the vacuum booster, the hydraulic booster

Fig. 20-69. Exploded view of a typical single diaphragm vacuum power booster. 1—Rear housing mounting brackets (truck). 2—Push rod boot. 3—Foam and felt air filter-silencers. 4—Rear housing. 5—Rear housing seal. 6—Diaphragm. 7—Air valve push rod assembly. 8—Air valve lock. 9—Diaphragm plate. 10—Reaction disc. 11—Piston rod. 12—Diaphragm return spring. 13—Front housing. 14—Front housing seal. 15—Grommet. 16—Check valve. (Chevrolet)

Fig. 20-70. Hydraulic booster system. Note in this application that the pump also supplies pressure for power steering. Booster is attached to master cylinder. (EIS)

Fig. 20-71. Hydraulic booster (Hydro-Boost) system showing fluid flow lines. Fluid from pump flows through booster on its way to power steering gear. (Bendix)

is coupled directly to the master cylinder. Movement of the brake pedal operates the booster valving causing the booster to exert pressure on the master cylinder primary piston. A schematic of brake pedal arrangement and fluid flow is shown in Fig. 20-71.

HYDRO-BOOST—RELEASED POSITION

In the fully released position, Fig. 20-72, power steering fluid flow is basically through the booster power section on to the steering gear. No pressure is built up by the booster. Study the part arrangement in Fig. 20-72.

HYDRO-BOOST—APPLIED POSITION

As the brake pedal is depressed, the input rod and piston are forced forward. This action causes the lever to move the spool forward (towards master cylinder) thus admitting more fluid into the space behind the power piston. As pressure builds, the power piston is forced forward actuating the master cylinder.

The amount of pressure exerted by the booster (up to its maximum output) is proportional to the pressure exerted on the brake pedal. Brake feel is provided by fluid pressure generated in the space between the inboard end of the input rod and the power piston. This pressure creates a force that attempts to force the input rod back against pedal pressure. This

gives the driver the needed feel so that correct foot pressure may be exerted. Fig. 20-73.

ACCUMULATOR PROVIDES EMERGENCY PRESSURE

A spring loaded (can also contain gas under pressure) accumulator is filled with fluid and is pressurized whenever the brakes are applied. In the event the power steering pump runs dry or the drive belt breaks and pressure is lost, the accumulator will still retain enough fluid and pressure to provide one to around three hydro-boost brake applications.

Even after the accumulator charge has been depleted, the brakes can still be operated by using pedal pressure only. As with all boosters that become inoperative, stopping distance will be noticeably in-

Fig. 20-72. Cross section view of one hydro-boost design. Study part location. Booster is in the fully released position. (GMC)

Fig. 20-73. Hydraulic booster in applied position. Lever has moved spool forward raising pressure behind power piston. Piston moves forward to exert pressure on master cylinder piston. (Bendix)

creased. Fig. 20-74 shows an exploded view of a slightly different hydro-boost unit. Note the accumulator.

ACCUMULATOR WARNING!

Do not attempt to work on an accumulator without special tools and training. THEY CONTAIN VERY STRONG SPRINGS AND PRESSURIZED GAS AND CAN FLY APART WITH LETHAL FORCE. DO NOT APPLY HEAT TO AN ACCUMULATOR. FOR PROPER DISPOSAL, FOLLOW MANUFACTURER'S INSTRUCTIONS.

VACUUM RESERVOIR

As long as the engine is running, vacuum is available for the booster. The second the engine stops, the

vacuum is gone. To provide several brake applications without engine vacuum, a vacuum reservoir may be incorporated in the booster system. A separate reservoir, with a vacuum check valve, may be used. This type is shown in Fig. 20-75.

Another common technique places a check valve in the booster body itself. Even though engine vacuum may be lost, enough vacuum will be retained in the booster body to provide one or more power assisted stops. Carefully study the check valve arrangement in Fig. 20-63.

BOOSTER FAILURE

In the event the booster or the vacuum fails, the brakes may still be applied by foot pressure alone. It

Fig. 20-74. Exploded view of a hydraulic booster. Note accumulator that retains pressure for one or more brake applications in the event pump pressure is lost. (Chevrolet)

Fig. 20-75. Vacuum reservoir tank. Reservoir allows one or two brake applications after engine vacuum is gone. (Plymouth)

Fig. 20-76. Two dual or "split" braking system designs. A—Typical front and rear setup is widely used. Note how each master cylinder piston serves only one set of brakes. B—Diagonal setup where each piston serves one front and one rear brake on opposite sides. Other designs such as right side-left side, dual front-dual rear, etc., have been used. (EIS)

will require somewhat more pressure than when the booster is working, but the system will still function. Stopping distance will be greatly increased.

DUAL "SPLIT" BRAKE SYSTEM

As you have learned, the dual master cylinder provides two separate (often called "split" or "twin") braking systems. In the event one system suffers a failure (burst hose, cracked line, etc.) the other will still provide some braking. Although braking distance is significantly increased, the dual system provides an important margin of safety.

Systems may be arranged so that one master cylinder piston provides pressure for the front brakes, the other the rear. See A in Fig. 20-76.

Another arrangement is the diagonal split system in which one master cylinder piston operates one front brake and one rear brake, but on opposite sides, Fig. 20-76, B.

A dual split system is pictured in Fig. 20-77 and 20-79. This system uses pressure from both master cylinder pistons for both front brakes. Note that each front caliper has TWO independent pistons. The rear brake assemblies receive pressure from one (secondary) piston only. Note "remote" (mounted away) master cylinder reservoir used on this setup. It has a "low fluid level" warning circuit, Fig. 20-77.

ANTI-SKID SYSTEM

Fig. 20-78 is a schematic of a typical two wheel (rear wheels) anti-skid braking system. Other optional systems are also available. The anti-skid system permits rapid straight line stops by preventing rear wheel lockup. Some systems affect all four wheels.

SUMMARY

Liquids, under confinement, can be used to transmit motion and to increase or decrease pressure. Air is compressible. Liquids are not. Pascal's Law states,

"When pressure is exerted on a confined liquid, it is transmitted undiminished."

The brake system can be divided into two principal parts, hydraulic system and wheel brake assemblies.

When the brake pedal is depressed, the master cylinder piston compresses brake fluid in the master cylinder. This causes fluid to move in the brake lines. This fluid movement will expand the wheel cylinders and calipers, causing them to apply the brake shoes and pads to the brake drums and discs. Both movement and pressure are used in the hydraulic system.

Cars now employ double-piston or dual master cylinder. This provides a separate braking force for front and back wheels, Fig. 20-79.

Brake lines are made of double thickness, plated steel. No other material is satisfactory. Flexible hoses are used in both the front and in the rear.

There are two basic types of wheel cylinders: single-piston type and double-piston type. Wheel cylinders can also be of stepped construction.

All air must be expelled from a hydraulic system.

LOW FLUID WARNING
SWITCH

REMOTE
RESERVOIR

SECONDARY
PISTON

PRIMARY PISTON

MASTER CYLINDER

← FRONT

Fig. 20-77. "Split" braking system employing dual (separate) front and single rear setup. Some front braking is always possible unless both piston output systems fail.

brake fade and grabbing. The use of the disc necessitates incorporating a proportioning and a metering valve into the system. The metering valve prevents disc application until a definite line pressure is reached while the proportioning valve controls pressure to the rear wheels.

There are two types of emergency or parking brakes in general use. One operates the regular service brake shoes, generally in the rear. The other uses a drive line brake.

Power brakes are used on many cars today. The power brake is essentially the regular brake system with a vacuum or power booster added, to make braking easier for the driver.

There are three basic types of vacuum operated power boosters: piston, diaphragm and bellows types. The diaphragm type is in common use today. They may be either vacuum or atmospheric suspended. All work in essentially the same manner. Atmospheric pressure can, upon application of the brake pedal, be applied to one side of the piston. With atmospheric pressure on one side and vacuum on the other, the piston is forced to move in the direction of the vacuum. As it moves, it applies force either to the master cylinder piston or to the brake pedal itself.

A valve setup is used to control the admission of atmospheric pressure and the application of the vacuum. The booster works in three stages: released, being applied, holding.

The power booster is designed to provide a braking feel for the driver. This is essential in controlling the amount of brake pressure.

The vacuum runout point for a booster is when full vacuum is applied and the booster has exerted all possible pressure on the system.

A vacuum reservoir is provided so that one or two brake applications can be made after the engine stops. Some systems provide a small electric motor driven pump to produce sufficient vacuum for brake application. This works only when the engine is off.

Hydraulic power boosters are also used. They employ pressure from the power steering system.

OF ALL THE PARTS OR SYSTEMS OF THE AUTOMOBILE, THE BRAKES RATE AS ONE OF THE MOST IMPORTANT FROM A SAFETY STANDPOINT. THEY MUST BE SERVICED AND INSPECTED ON A REGULAR BASIS. ANY DEFECTIVE PART MUST BE REPLACED AT ONCE.

The removal of this air is termed BLEEDING.

Never use any fluid other than high quality brake fluid in the system. Anything else is likely to ruin the rubber cups and make the brakes inoperative.

The wheel brake assembly consists of a backing plate, brake shoes and springs, and a brake drum. The backing plate is attached in a rigid manner, and the brake shoes are attached to the backing plate. The shoes are arranged so they may be expanded by the wheel cylinders. As the shoes expand, they will stop the brake drum and wheel.

There are two brake shoes per wheel. There is one primary shoe and one secondary shoe. Some shoes are arranged so that servo action assists in applying the brakes.

Brake shoe servo action is when one shoe helps apply the other. Self-energizing shoes are arranged so shoe-to-drum friction helps apply the shoe.

Some shoes are self-adjusting; others may be adjusted periodically to compensate for shoe lining wear.

The front brakes generally provide somewhat more braking force than the rear brakes. This is to compensate for the transfer of weight to the front during stops.

The disc brake provides high resistance to both

KNOW THESE TERMS

Hydraulics, Pascal's Law, Master cylinder, Check valve, Wheel cylinder, Pressure differential switch, Brake line, Brake hose, Bleeder screw, Backing plate, Brake shoe, Primary and secondary shoe, Brake lining, Brake drum, Brake fade, Disc brake, Caliper,

Fig. 20-78. Schematic showing one type of anti-skid (rear wheels only) braking system. When rear wheel rpm starts to slow down below usual rpm for a given road speed, transmission sensor (on rear wheels on some models) sends an electrical signal to electronic controller, causing modulator to cut off pressure to rear wheel brakes. This releases brakes and prevents lockup. As soon as wheel rpm is what it should be in proportion to car road speed, sensor causes modulator to restore full braking pressure. This on-off braking cycle takes place in about 1/3 of a second. Front wheel brake pressure remains constant. By cycling rear brake pressure, rapid straight line stops are possible. (Cadillac)

Metering valve, Proportioning valve, Emergency brake, Power brakes, Power booster, Brake feel.

REVIEW QUESTIONS—CHAPTER 20

When disassembling, inspecting, repairing, then reassembling automotive components, always study each part. Notice how it is made, of what, how it performs its particular job, its relationship to the entire unit. Only in this way will you develop the keen insight into part design and automotive engineering principles that are a MUST for mechanics that aspire to be the best.

1. Air is not compressible. True or False?
2. Liquids can transmit both _____ and _____.
3. What is Pascal's Law?
4. Explain the workings of a simple hydraulic jack.
5. If a 100 lb. force is applied to a piston with 1 sq. in. of area, how much pressure would a piston with an area of 10 sq. in. exert, if both of these pistons rested with an airtight seal on a column of oil? Assume that both cylinders or columns are connected via a pipe.
6. What is the purpose of a master cylinder?
7. Explain how a master cylinder works in the released position, in the applied position, quick release, and final release positions.
8. The master cylinder reservoir must be filled to within about _____ of the reservoir cover or covers.
9. The reservoir cover must be vented. True or False?
10. Why must a reservoir be provided?
11. Of what use is the master cylinder check valve?
12. Brake lines must be made of _____.
13. Brake lines, where connections are made, must have a _____ flare.
14. Name the parts of a wheel cylinder.
15. Wheel cylinders are generally fastened to the brake drum. True or False?
16. Of what use is flexible high pressure brake hose?
17. Name two types of wheel cylinders.
18. Why are some wheel cylinders of stepped construction?
19. Bleeder screws are furnished in the brake lines. True or False?
20. How does the shape of the rubber pistons in the

master cylinder and wheel cylinders help them to seal?

21. A small amount of air in the brake system is permissible. True or False?
22. Kerosene is a satisfactory substitute for brake fluid in an emergency. True or False?
23. Of what use is the backing plate?
24. Give the names of the two brake shoes used in each wheel assembly.
25. Why are brake shoe retracting springs used?
26. Brake lining is made of _____.
27. What part of the wheel assembly dissipates the greatest amount of heat?
28. Explain what happens in the wheel assembly when the master cylinder builds up pressure in the brake lines.
29. What is brake fade?
30. Explain servo action. What is meant by self-energizing?
31. What unit is used to keep brake shoes in close contact with the drum?
32. What are two types of emergency brakes?
33. How does a power brake work?
34. Explain the action of the power booster in the released, applied and hold positions.
35. How is brake feel provided in a power booster?
36. Name three types of power boosters.
37. Of what use is a vacuum reservoir tank?
38. Of what value is the double-piston or dual master cylinder?
39. A proportioning valve is used with disc brake systems. True or False?
40. The metering valve in disc (front wheels only) brake systems:

a. Controls pressure to rear wheels.
b. Controls pressure to front wheels.
c. Prevents both front and rear systems from simultaneous failure.
d. Prevents disc brake application until line pressure reaches a certain point.
41. What does vacuum suspended mean when referring to power booster? Atmospheric suspended?
42. What type of power booster is in popular use today:
a. Bellows.
b. Diaphragm.
c. Piston.
d. Bellows-piston.
43. The hydraulic brake booster normally utilizes pressure generated in the _____ _____ system.
44. List four characteristics of a good brake fluid.
45. Very briefly explain the operation of the "quick take-up" master cylinder.

WARNING!

BRAKE LINING DUST SHOULD NEVER BE INHALED. THESE MINUTE PARTICLES OF ASBESTOS, WHEN DRAWN INTO THE LUNGS, CAN CAUSE CANCER. WHEN GRINDING LINING, CLEANING BRAKE ASSEMBLIES, ETC., USE CARE TO AVOID BREATHING THE DUST. HAVE PROPER VENTILATION. NEVER CLEAN WITH AN AIR HOSE. HAVE A DUST DISPOSAL SYSTEM ON GRINDER AND WHEN NEEDED, WEAR A SUITABLE RESPIRATOR!

Fig. 20-79. Overall view of a dual diagonal braking system. (Honda)

Chapter 21

ELECTRICAL SYSTEM FUNDAMENTALS

After studying this chapter, you will be able to:
- Describe the principles of electricity and electronics.
- Name the values used when measuring electricity.
- List the basic types of electrical circuits.
- Explain the effects of magnetism.
- Describe the construction and operation of an automotive battery.
- Explain the major parts and operating principles of a starting system and a charging system.

The field of electricity covers a wide and complicated range. Much is known about electricity and much remains to be discovered. A thorough coverage of electricity is not within the scope of this text on auto mechanics. However, a basic understanding of electrical fundamentals and their application to the auto, is a MUST for all students of auto mechanics.

A BAFFLING FORCE

We have learned to control electricity, predict its actions and harness it in many ways. No person has literally seen it flow through a wire. For many years no one was even sure of the direction it moved or what actually did move.

THE ELECTRON THEORY

The accepted theory regarding electricity is termed the ELECTRON THEORY. This theory has explained many of the strange behavior patterns as well as opening the way to many new discoveries, not only in electricity, but in other fields as well.

The electron theory is based on the assumption that electrical phenomenon (fact which may be observed) is produced by a flow of electrons from one area to another. It also states that the flow of electrons is caused by having an excess number in one area, and a shortage in the other. The area with the surplus electrons is referred to as NEGATIVE and the area in short supply, the POSITIVE.

MATTER

Anything that takes up space and has mass is considered matter. Matter can be a solid, a liquid or a gas.

MOLECULE

A molecule is the smallest portion that matter can be broken down to, and still retain all the properties of the original matter. The molecule is made up of atoms.

ATOMS

There are around one hundred different types of atoms. Various combinations of these atoms will produce different molecules of matter.

A molecule of pure water is made up of one atom of oxygen and two atoms of hydrogen. Both oxygen and hydrogen are gases.

All matter is made up of either different atoms, or the same type of atoms. Fig. 21-1 illustrates a progressive breakdown of matter.

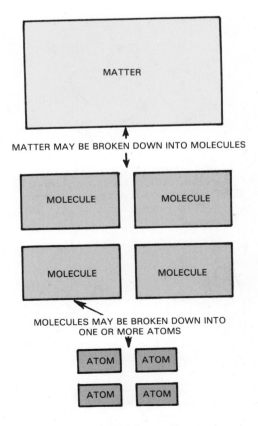

Fig. 21-1. Breakdown of matter.

STRUCTURE OF THE ATOM

The atom itself is made up of neutrons, protons, and electrons.

The electron is a negatively (−) charged particle. The proton is a positively (+) charged particle. The neutron is a neutral particle with no charge.

Protons and neutrons form the center, or nucleus, of the atom. The electrons rotate rapidly around this nucleus. As unlike charges attract each other, the electrons are held in their orbital path. They will not draw in any closer, because the centrifugal force built up by their whirling flight counterbalances the mutual attraction force. Fig. 21-2.

There can be many different atoms, each with a different number of protons, neutrons and electrons. Every atom has the same number of electrons as it has protons. Protons and neutrons are alike in any type of atom. The number of neutrons, protons, and electrons, and their arrangement, produces different types of matter.

A simple atom is that of hydrogen. The hydrogen atom consists of a single neutron and a single proton. A more complex atom is that of copper. This atom consists of 34 neutrons, 29 protons, and 29 electrons. Fig. 21-3.

FREE ELECTRONS

You will notice in Fig. 21-4 that the electrons move in different size orbits. The inner orbits contain what

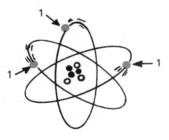

Fig. 21-2. Structure of atom. Electrons, 1, are whirling about nucleus. Solid dots in nucleus represent neutrons. White dots are protons.

Fig. 21-3. Two different atoms. A—Simple hydrogen atom consisting of one proton and one electron. B—More complex copper atom has 34 neutrons, 29 protons and 29 electrons.

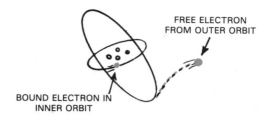

Fig. 21-4. Free and bound electrons. Free electron in outer orbit has been knocked from its path.

is referred to as BOUND electrons. The outer orbits contain the FREE electrons.

The bound electrons are so named because it is difficult to force them from their orbits. The outer free electrons can be more readily moved from their orbits.

POSITIVE AND NEGATIVE CHARGE ATOMS

If some of the free electrons are moved out of their orbit, the atom will have more protons than electrons. This will give the atom a positive charge. If the electrons are returned, until they equal the number of protons, the atom will become electrically neutral. If a surplus of electrons are present, the atom becomes negatively charged.

A negatively charged body will repel electrons, while the positively charged body will attract electrons. Fig. 21-5.

CURRENT

An electrical current is a mass movement of electrons through a conductor (wire). They may be likened to water flowing through a pipe. The amount of electrons passing any given point in the circuit in one second determines the amount of current flowing. The amount of current flow is measured in AMPERES.

Before a current will flow, there must be a surplus of electrons at one end and a scarcity at the other end of the conductor.

CURRENT FLOW

Fig. 21-6 illustrates a schematic of a simple circuit utilizing a battery as the source. Note that the elec-

Fig. 21-5. Negative and positive charge atoms. Atom with negative charge repels electrons. Positive charged atom attracts electrons.

Fig. 21-6. Current flow. Electrons move from negative post through conductor, on to positive post. (Prestolite)

tron flow is from negative to positive.

The battery, through chemical action (covered later), has built up a surplus of electrons at the negative post and a lack of electrons at the positive post. As soon as the copper wire (conductor) is connected to both posts, current (electrons) will flow from the negative to the positive post.

On their way from the negative post, the electrons will pass through the light bulb. As the filament in the bulb creates a resistance to the flow of electrons, it will heat up until it is white hot and glows. After passing through the filament, the electrons pass on to the positive post.

When an electron leaves the negative source, this single electron does not speed through the conductor. It strikes an adjacent electron and knocks it from its orbit. This electron strikes its neighbor and knocks another electron from orbit. As one electron knocks another out of orbit, it replaces the one it knocked out.

To help illustrate this action, imagine placing enough corks in a pipe to fill it from end to end. If you push one cork (electron) into one end of the pipe (conductor), one cork (electron) will pop out the other. As soon as one cork presses on the column of corks, its movement is transmitted through the column. Even though it enters only a small distance, its influence is felt at the other end almost at once. See Fig. 21-7.

VOLTAGE (Electromotive Force—EMF)

As mentioned, current flow is produced by having a difference in electrical potential, or pressure, at each end of a conductor (one end with surplus of electrons and other lacking electrons).

This pressure differential (also known as elec-

tromotive force—EMF) causes the current to flow. To keep the current flowing, it is necessary to maintain the electrical pressure or, as it is commonly called, VOLTAGE.

In the automotive electrical system, voltage is produced either by a battery (electrochemical action) or by a generator (electromagnetic action).

The amount of pressure or voltage is measured in VOLTS. The higher the voltage, the more current flow it can create. Cars commonly use a 12 volt system.

The battery in A, Fig. 21-8, is dead. Both negative and positive sides have a balanced electron condition. There is no voltage or pressure difference.

In B, Fig. 21-8, the battery is charged. The negative side has great numbers of surplus electrons, while the positive side has a deficiency. When a wire is connected across the terminals, the voltage will cause current to flow from negative to positive.

RESISTANCE

When current flows through a conductor, it meets resistance. A relatively poor conductor offers greater

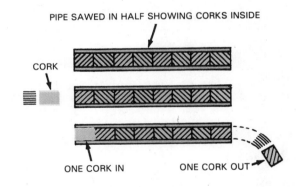

Fig. 21-7. Cork (electron) in a pipe (conductor). Even though cork has just entered pipe, it causes a chain of pressure that results in a different cork being forced out opposite end.

Fig. 21-8. Battery voltage. A—Battery discharged, no voltage, no current flow. B—Battery charged, normal voltage, electrons massed on negative side. Current (electrons) flow through conductor.

resistance than a good conductor.

As the electrons attempt to flow, they bump into other atoms in the conductor. This causes a heating effect. As the conductor heats up, the movement of the atoms becomes more agitated. This further increases the number of collisions. If current flow is increased, the conductor will become hotter and hotter until it will literally burn up.

This heating action is one of the great uses for electricity. Such things as lights, electric burners, heaters, etc., make use of resistance found in conductors. In order to function, the type of conductor and amount of voltage and current flow must be carefully balanced, so the wire will reach a specific desired heat.

A large conductor, of a given material, will offer less resistance than a smaller one. The longer the conductor, the greater its resistance. The amount of resistance in a conductor is measured in OHMS. See Fig. 21-9.

Fig. 21-10. Using an ammeter to check current flow. Ammeter is connected in series with circuit.

Fig. 21-9. Resistance in a conductor. As electrons attempt to move through conductor, they strike atoms. This deflects them and in effect resists their efforts to pass through conductor.

Fig. 21-11. Using a voltmeter to check circuit voltage. Voltmeter is connected in parallel with circuit.

TEST GAUGES

To measure the rate of current flow in amperes, a gauge called an AMMETER is used. The ammeter is connected in series with the circuit. Fig. 21-10.

Voltage is determined by using a VOLTMETER. The voltmeter is connected across the circuit. See Fig. 21-11.

Resistance in ohms is calculated by using an OHMMETER. The ohmmeter test leads are connected across the resistance being measured. Fig. 21-12.

MATERIALS USED FOR CONDUCTORS

Because it has a great number of free electrons, and is relatively inexpensive, copper is widely used as a conductor. There are other materials, such as silver, that are better conductors than copper. Since they are expensive, their use is limited to certain units in an automotive system.

ELECTRICITY MUST HAVE A PATH

In order for electrons to flow, they must have a path or conductor. If more than one path is available,

Fig. 21-12. Using an ohmmeter to check load resistance. Note that circuit is open to prevent damaging ohmmeter. Ohmmeter has its own source of current. Ohmmeter circuit is hooked directly to the load.

current will flow in the one with the least resistance. As you learned in the chapter on the Ignition System, air itself will act as a conductor when voltage is high enough.

To make certain current flows where desired, the conductors in the car's electrical system must be insulated.

INSULATORS

Any material in which the atoms have more than four electrons in their outer orbit will make a good insulator. Since electrons tend to be bound, and resist being knocked from their orbit, current cannot flow.

Glass, ceramics, plastics, rubber, fiber, etc., are excellent insulators. All are used in automotive electrical systems. The wiring itself uses a rubber or plastic coating to prevent the escape of electrons to adjacent metal parts or to other wires. Spark plugs use ceramic insulators. Switches, relays, etc., use fiber, rubber, glass, etc., for specific points where insulation is required.

CIRCUITS

A circuit consists of a power source, a unit to be operated and the necessary wiring to provide a path for electron flow. The circuit must be complete in order to function.

SIMPLE CIRCUIT

A very basic circuit, Fig. 21-13, consists of a power source (battery), a single unit to be operated (bulb) and connecting wires. The current flows from the negative terminal through the conductor, through the unit, and then on through the second conductor to the positive terminal of the battery. It then passes from the positive terminal to the negative terminal through the inside of the battery.

Fig. 21-13. A simple circuit. Current flows from negative to positive through the unit.

SERIES CIRCUIT

A series circuit consists of two or more resistance units that are so wired that the current has but one path to follow. To flow, and complete the circuit, the current must pass through each resistance unit.

As each resistance unit impedes the rate of current flow (amperes), the total amount of resistance offered by all units will determine the amperage flow. The more units added to a specific circuit, the more the resistance, with a resultant lowering of current flow.

If amperage flow is checked at several points in a series circuit, all readings will be the same.

VOLTAGE DROP

As the available voltage is lowered by each resistance unit, the voltage will drop as the units occur. The voltage may be up to a full rated 12 volts at the battery, but will become progressively lower farther out on the circuit. Study Fig. 21-14. Notice that the current must pass through one unit to get to another, that the ampere flow is the same throughout, that the voltage is dropping, and that if any one resistance unit is broken or burned out (wire severed), the current cannot flow.

Fig. 21-14. A series circuit. If ammeter were inserted in circuit at B, C, D, and E, all readings would be same. If voltmeter were installed across or between B and A, it would show full battery voltage. If connected between B and C, it would show a voltage drop (less voltage). If connected between B and D, it would show still more drop.

Any type of circuit will have a certain amount of normal voltage drop. Even the conductor itself somewhat impedes electron flow. When voltage drop becomes excessive, poor unit operation will result. Voltage drop is controlled by using the proper size wires, ample source voltage, proper insulation and clean connections.

PARALLEL CIRCUIT

The parallel circuit consists of two or more resistance units connected in such a way as to allow current flow to pass through all units at once. This eliminates the necessity of the current going through one before reaching the other. Also, if one unit is burned out, the others will still function.

If you were to measure the total resistance in a parallel circuit, you would find it to be less than any one of the unit resistances. You will recall that in the series circuit, the current has to pass through the resistance units, one after the other. This gave a resistance to current movement that was equal to the sum of all the units. In a parallel circuit, the current has several units that it can pass through, actually reducing the total resistance in relation to any one unit resistance value.

EQUAL VOLTAGE

Equal voltage is applied to all resistance units in a parallel circuit. The amount of current flow through each unit will vary according to its individual resistance, but the total current flowing will equal the sum of the current flowing through all the units. See Fig. 21-15.

SERIES-PARALLEL CIRCUIT

A series-parallel circuit is essentially one in which the series and the parallel circuits are combined. It requires the connecting of three or more resistance units in a combination series and parallel hookup.

To determine the resistance of this circuit, the total resistance of the parallel circuit is added to that of the series portion. Current flow will be determined by the total resistance.

Voltage drop will be the drop across the parallel circuit, plus that of any series resistance unit. Fig. 21-16.

STEEL STRUCTURE ACTS AS ONE WIRE

A circuit requires one wire from the source to the unit, and one wire from the unit back to the source.

In an automobile where the body, engine, etc., are made of steel, it is not necessary to have a two-wire circuit. The steel structure of the car can act as one of the wires. One of the battery posts (negative post in this country) is connected (grounded) to the steel framework of the vehicle. The other post or terminal (positive) is connected to the various electrical units with an insulated wire. Fig. 21-17 illustrates the frame being used in place of a wire.

GROUND SYMBOL

When looking at wiring diagrams, where the circuit is connected to the steel structure of the vehicle, you

Fig. 21-15. A parallel circuit. Voltage across 1—1, 2—2, and 3—3 would be equal. Current flow in amperes at A, B, and C would depend upon unit. Current flow at D would equal sum of current flowing through A, B, and C. Total resistance of A, B, and C would be less than any single one.

Fig. 21-16. Series—parallel circuit. Units A and D are in series. Units B and C are in parallel.

Fig. 21-17. Using car frame as one wire in a circuit. Battery and electrical unit are grounded to the frame. Electron flow is from the negative (—) battery terminal to the frame, from the frame to the headlamp and back to the battery through the closed switch.

will see a ground symbol. This symbol indicates that the circuit is assumed, and is not actually drawn. See Fig. 21-18.

OHM'S LAW

Ohm's Law can be expressed in three different ways:

1. Amperes equals volts divided by ohms ($I = \frac{E}{R}$).
2. Volts equals amperes multiplied by ohms (E = IR).
3. Ohms equals volts divided by amperes ($R = \frac{E}{I}$).

Ohm's Law, in its three forms, can be used to find any one unknown factor when the other two are known. A handy form in which to remember Ohm's Law in its three applications is illustrated in Fig. 21-19.

Fig. 21-18. Ground symbol. In top circuit, wire A, (indicating steel structure of car) has been drawn in. In bottom circuit, ground symbols B have eliminated drawing wire A portion of circuit.

Fig. 21-20. Magnetic domains. In A, magnetic domains are small, and they are surrounded by atoms that are not aligned. In B, metal is magnetized and domains enlarged and line up. Combined force creates a strong magnetic field. Note that N and S poles are aligned.

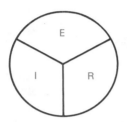

Fig. 21-19. Handy form of Ohm's Law. Try three combinations using this form.

LINES OF FORCE

The first thing to remember about the term MAGNETIC LINES OF FORCE is that it is a term used to describe the invisible force involved.

If a simple bar magnet is placed under a sheet of glass, and fine iron filings are sprinkled on the surface of the glass, the filings will line up in accordance with the so-called lines of force. Fig. 21-21.

MAGNETISM

A great deal remains to be learned about the strange force termed MAGNETISM. It is probably best understood by observing some of its effects and powers.

One theory regarding magnetism states that electrons rotating about the nucleus contain the essentials of magnetism. These electrons not only rotate about the nucleus, but also spin on their own axes (electron spins). Even though each electron creates a very weak magnetic field, the electrons are orbiting in so many directions that one field tends to cancel out the other field.

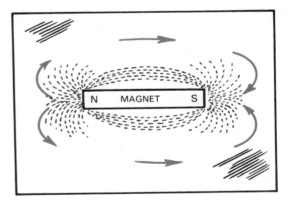

Fig. 21-21. Lines of force around a bar magnet. Lines of force leave N pole and travel along magnet, then enter S pole.

DOMAINS

In an unmagnetized material, there are many minute sections in which the atoms line up to produce a magnetic field. As these magnetic domains are scattered through the material in all directions, one domain tends to cancel out the force of the next one.

To magnetize material (such as steel), it is necessary to orient or line up these domains so that most of them point in the same direction. This is done by placing the steel in a strong magnetic field produced by a current passing through a coil of wire (covered later).

The domains will grow in size as they move into alignment. This growth involves lining up neighboring atoms so the magnetic effect is increased. Look at Fig. 21-20.

The lines of force leave the north (N) pole of the magnet, and enter the south (S) pole. They then pass from the south to the north pole through the body of the magnet.

Notice the effect produced on the iron filings when a horseshoe magnet is placed under the glass. The glass should be tapped to allow the filings to line up. Fig. 21-22.

LINES OF FORCE DO NOT CROSS EACH OTHER

You will note that these fine lines of force do not cross. The lines tend to be drawn in as nearly a

Fig. 21-22. Lines of force around a horseshoe magnet.

straight line as possible, and at the same time they push each other apart.

UNLIKE POLES ATTRACT, LIKE POLES REPEL

If two bar magnets are shoved together with unlike poles on the approaching ends, they will snap together. If the approaching ends have similar poles, they will repel each other. If forced together, they will snap apart when released.

By studying Fig. 21-23, you will see that the magnetic force lines are leaving the north pole. Remember that these lines tend to draw into as straight a line as possible, yet they will not cross as one line repels the other. As the two magnets near each other, the force lines leaving the N pole of magnet number one, instead of swinging up and back to their own south pole, leap across the gap to the other closer south pole of magnet number two. The lines leaving the N pole of magnet number two, will now swing

Fig. 21-23. Unlike poles attract. In A, both magnets are apart and lines of force assume their normal state. In B, magnets approach each other causing force lines from N pole of magnet No. 1 to enter S pole of magnet No. 2. This draws them together, as in C, and the two magnets act as one bar magnet

along both magnets to reach the south pole of magnet number one. As the lines stretch as tightly as possible, the magnets cling tightly to each other. They have, in effect, become one long bar magnet. Fig. 21-23.

When like poles near each other, the magnetic lines entering each pole will repel each other and will refuse to cross. This causes each magnet to push away from the other, until the force fields are far enough apart to become too weak to cause further movement.

Magnetic lines of force will follow metal more readily than air. If a metal bar is placed across the ends of a horseshoe magnet, the force lines follow the bar from N to S pole.

ELECTRICAL SYSTEM, BATTERY

An electric current can be produced chemically by means of a battery.

The typical 12 volt battery is constructed of six elements, Fig. 21-24. The element itself is made up of two groups of plates. One group forms the positive group; the other, the negative group. The plates (number can vary with battery capacity but will not affect open circuit voltage) are lined up with space between, then welded to a post strap. Both groups are sandwiched together so that a negative plate adjoins a positive plate—neg., pos., neg., pos., etc.

Insulating separators of nonconducting microporous (tiny pores) rubber, cellulose fiber or some other type of material are placed between each set of plates. The separators have vertical grooved ridges to allow the electrolyte (mixture of sulphuric acid and distilled water) to move about freely. The separators prevent the plates from touching each other and short-circuiting.

ELECTROLYTE

The battery is then filled (slightly over the top of the plates) with an electrolyte solution made up of

Fig. 21-24. Battery element. Each group is welded to plate strap casting. Note how separators are inserted between all plates. (Chevrolet)

about 64 percent distilled (pure) water and 36 percent sulphuric acid by weight. Fig. 21-25.

POSITIVE PLATE

The positive plate grid (wire-like, skeletal framework of the plate, made of lead and antimony or of lead and calcium) is filled with lead peroxide. The lead peroxide is in sponge form, which allows the electrolyte to penetrate the plate.

H_2O	H_2SO_4	ELECTROLYTE
64% WATER SP.GR. = 1.000	36% ACID SP.GR. = 1.835	ELECTROLYTE SP.GR. = 1.270

Fig. 21-25. Battery electrolyte. Note specific gravity of water compared to electrolyte solution. (Deere & Co.)

NEGATIVE PLATE

The negative plate grid is filled with porous lead, plus expanders to prevent the lead from returning to an inactive solid state. Fig. 21-24 illustrates an element consisting of positive and negative plates, with separators, being sandwiched together.

The six elements are assembled in a hard rubber or plastic (such as polypropylene) battery box or case. The case has partitions to divide it into six compartments or CELLS. Fig. 21-26.

Fig. 21-27 shows how each element is fitted into the individual cells. Note how each element is joined to the others by a lead cell connector or strap. As each element produces around 2 volts, Fig. 21-24, when

Fig. 21-27. Elements in place in their cells. Elements are connected in series by lead straps. Note total voltage of 12 volts. (Chevrolet)

they are connected in series, 12 volts will be produced.

Fig. 21-28 shows the elements in place in the battery box. After installation, each element was connected to its neighbor by a cell connector lead strap. Note side terminal connectors.

Another battery is shown in Fig. 21-29. Note how the elements are kept away from the floor of the con-

Fig. 21-26. Battery box or container. Note cell dividers and raised bottom (element rests).

Fig. 21-28. A 12V battery is shown, with elements in place, cell connector straps attached to elements and cover installed. Note side terminals. (Delco)

COVER HEAT SEALED TO CASE

TERMINAL POST

POLYPROPYLENE COVER AND CASE

SAFETY VENT

CELL DIVIDER

LEAD-CALCIUM GRID

SEPARATOR

ELEMENT REST

CELL CONNECTOR

ELEMENTS

Fig. 21-29. Sectioned view of complete 12V battery. Learn names of all parts.   (Prestolite)

tainer. This allows room for shedding plate material to deposit in the form of sediment. If this sediment touches the plates, it will cause a short circuit.

Fig. 21-30 illustrates all the various battery components and how they are joined together to produce the battery.

HOW A BATTERY FUNCTIONS

The battery does not actually "store" electricity. When charging, it converts electricity into chemical energy. Chemical action of electrolyte, working on active material in the plates, causes a transfer of electrons from positive plates to negative plates. When battery is placed in a closed (completed) circuit, surplus of electrons at negative post flows to positive post. An electric current is produced. The battery is now converting chemical energy into electricity. Fig.

21-31 shows battery action in a simple 2 volt cell. Note electron flow through conductor.

As the current flows, the battery starts discharging. The sulphate in the electrolyte combines with the plate materials, forming lead sulphate. As the current continues flowing (constantly growing weaker), the electrolyte becomes weaker and weaker. Finally the battery is completely discharged.

BATTERY CHEMICAL ACTION REVERSES

By passing an electric current back into the battery (with a battery charger or car alternator) in a reverse

CONTAINER

ELECTROLYTE

2 VOLT BATTERY CELL

Fig. 21-31. A simple 2 volt battery cell. Note current (electron) flow through conductor.   (GM)

GRID

ACTIVE MATERIAL & MANUFACTURING PROCESS

PLATE

CONNECTOR

GROUP

POSITIVE GROUP

NEGATIVE GROUP

SEPARATORS

ELEMENT

ELEMENTS

CONTAINER

ONE PIECE COVER

ELECTROLYTE

VENT CAPS

12 VOLT BATTERY

Fig. 21-30. Battery construction. Note how elements are joined by cell connector straps.   (Firestone) direction, the chemical action is reversed. The sulphate leaves the plates and returns to the electrolyte in the form of sulphuric acid, and the plates revert to lead peroxide and sponge lead. After charging for a sufficient time, the battery will become fully charged. Figs. 21-32 and 21-33.

Fig. 21-32. Battery charge. (Ford)

Fig. 21-33. Battery discharge. (Ford)

SPECIFIC GRAVITY OF THE ELECTROLYTE

When the battery is fully charged, the specific gravity (relative weight of a given volume of a certain material as compared with an equal volume of water) of the battery is around 1.280. This is determined by drawing the electrolyte up into a HYDROMETER. Fig. 21-34.

The depth at which the float rests in the electrolyte determines its specific gravity. The higher the float, the higher the charge. The float is marked, and the mark at the top of the electrolyte is read. Fig. 21-35

shows how to read a hydrometer; also how various stages of discharge affect the specific gravity.

It is not possible to use a hydrometer on many of the maintenance free batteries as caps are not always provided. Battery state of charge is often indicated by a float device built into the battery.

Such a unit is pictured in Fig. 21-36. It contains a small green or other color ball that floats when the electrolyte specific gravity is within a certain range. Below this range, the ball sinks. When the ball is floating, it shows as a bright green dot indicating the battery is 80 percent charged.

When the ball sinks, the unit shows up dark, indicating the battery is discharged. If a light yellow color is visible, it indicates the electrolyte level is too low. Fig. 21-36.

TEMPERATURE CORRECTION

When reading a hydrometer, remember that the temperature of the electrolyte affects the specific gravity. Many hydrometers have built-in thermometers with temperature correction scales. Fig. 21-37.

TEMPERATURE INFLUENCES BATTERY EFFICIENCY

The chart in Fig. 21-38 illustrates how temperature affects the efficiency of a battery.

BATTERIES CAN FREEZE

The electrolyte in batteries, if discharged too much, can freeze and the battery will burst. The freezing

Fig. 21-34. Hydrometer. Electrolyte is being drawn up into glass barrel of hydrometer. (Plymouth)

1.280   1.150

CORRECT METHOD OF READING HYDROMETER. EYE ON LEVEL WITH LIQUID SURFACE. DISREGARD CURVATURE OF LIQUID AGAINST GLASS PARTS. DO NOT TILT HYDROMETER WHILE READING. KEEP FLOAT VERTICAL.

HIGH FLOAT (LEFT) MEANS HIGH SPECIFIC GRAVITY. LOW FLOAT MEANS LOW SPECIFIC GRAVITY.

ACID
WATER

SPECIFIC GRAVITY 1.260-80

SPECIFIC GRAVITY BELOW 1.230-50

FULLY CHARGED
ACID IN WATER GIVES ELECTROLYTE SPECIFIC GRAVITY OF 1.270.

GOING DOWN
AS BATTERY DISCHARGES, ACID BEGINS TO LODGE IN PLATES. SPECIFIC GRAVITY DROPS.

SPECIFIC GRAVITY 1.200-20

SPECIFIC GRAVITY 1.140-60

UNSAFE!
BATTERY HALF DISCHARGED. MORE ACID IN PLATES, LESS IN ELECTROLYTE. STARTING FAILURE IN SIGHT IF BATTERY IS ALLOWED TO REMAIN IN CAR.

DISCHARGED
ACID ALMOST ENTIRELY IN PLATES, LEAVING WEAK ELECTROLYTE BEHIND. SPECIFIC GRAVITY LOWER, ALMOST THAT OF WATER.

Fig. 21-35. Specific gravity as related to battery state of charge. As battery charge falls off, float sinks lower and lower into electrolyte.

point, depending on specific gravity, is illustrated in Fig. 21-39.

DISCHARGE RATE

A battery without being charged, will not last indefinitely. Fig. 21-40 shows the typical current load for modern cars. The alternator must produce suffi-

SIGHT GLASS

GLASS TUBE

GREEN BALL

BATTERY TOP

BATTERY TOP

DARK GREEN DOT VISIBLE CHARGED

DARK GREEN DOT NOT VISIBLE DISCHARGED

LIGHT OR YELLOW ELECTROLYTE LEVEL LOW

Fig. 21-36. Built-in battery charge indicator. Sight glass or "eye" color indicates state of charge. (Chrysler)

°F   SPECIFIC GRAVITY POINTS TO ADD OR SUBTRACT

71°C 160 — 32
65.5°C 150 — 28
60°C 140 — 24
54.5°C 130 — 20
49°C 120 — 16
43°C 110 — 12
37.5°C 100 — 8
32.5°C 90 — 4
27°C 80 — 0
21°C 70 — 4
15.5°C 60 — 8
10°C 50 — 12
4.5°C 40 — 16
-1°C 30 — 20
-6.5°C 20 — 24
-12°C 10 — 28

ADD TO READING | SUBTRACT FROM READING

EXAMPLE 1
HYDROMETER READING 1.260
ELECTROLYTE TEMPERATURE ..... -6.5° (20°F)
SUBTRACT SPECIFIC GRAVITY .... -.024
CORRECTED SPECIFIC GRAVITY IS 1.236

EXAMPLE 2
HYDROMETER READING 1.225
ELECTROLYTE TEMPERATURE ... 37.5°C (100°F)
ADD SPECIFIC GRAVITY .... +.008
CORRECTED SPECIFIC GRAVITY IS 1.233

A FULLY CHARGED RELATIVELY NEW BATTERY HAS A SPECIFIC GRAVITY READING OF 1.275 PLUS OR MINUS .010

Fig. 21-37. Temperature correction chart for hydrometer use. (Plymouth)

cient current output to cover all possible electrical needs.

IDENTIFYING BATTERY TERMINALS

The positive post of the battery, which is usually marked with a POS, or +, is somewhat larger than the negative post. Its top is sometimes painted red. The negative post is the smaller of the two, and is often painted green or black. It is marked with a NEG, or −.

BATTERY CAPACITY RATINGS

There are several standards or ratings set up around battery performance. Three of the most commonly

BATTERY EFFICIENCY AT VARIOUS TEMPERATURES	
TEMPERATURE	**EFFICIENCY OF A FULLY CHARGED BATTERY**
26.7°C — 80°F.	100%
10°C — 50°F.	82%
−1.1°C — 30°F.	64%
−6.7°C — 20°F.	68%
−12.2°C — 10°F.	50%
−17.8°C — 0°F.	40%
−23.3°C — −10°F.	33%

Fig. 21-38. Temperature affects battery efficiency. It is obvious why a fully charged battery is a must for cold weather starting. (Ford)

TYPICAL CURRENT LOAD OF MODERN CARS (IN AMPERES)		
SWITCH	**ACCESSORY SWITCH LOAD**	**MAX. VEHICLE OPERATING LOAD**
Parking	4 to 8	—
Low-Beam Headlamp	8 to 14	—
High-Beam (4) Headlamp	12 to 18	18
Heater	6 to 7	—
Windshield Wiper	2 to 3	3
Air Conditioner	10 to 15	15
Radio	0.4 to 1.8	1.8
Ignition—Standard	3	—
Ignition—Transistorized	8 to 12	12
Alternator Field	3 to 5	5
Total		54.8
Summer Starting		100 - 400 Amperes*
Winter Starting		225 - 500 Amperes*

*Values vary with engine size, engine temperature, and oil viscosity.

Fig. 21-40. Typical current load for various electrical units. Load will vary somewhat depending upon type of ignition system, radio, etc. (Prestolite)

used are: 20-HOUR RATING (ampere-hour capacity), RESERVE CAPACITY and CRANKING PERFORMANCE.

20-HOUR RATING

The 20-hour rating is used to determine the lighting ability of a battery. The test is conducted as follows:

A new, fully charged battery at a temperature of 80°F (26.7°C), is discharged at a rate equivalent to one-twentieth of its published 20-hour capacity in ampere-hours. It is discharged at this rate until the terminal voltage drops to 10.5V (5.5V for a 6 volt battery). The hours of discharge required to drop the terminal voltage to 10.5V, multiplied by the discharge rate in amperes, determines the ampere-hour capacity of the battery and its 20-hour rating.

If a 12 volt, 120 ampere-hour battery (advertised rating) is to be tested, it will be discharged at one-twentieth of its advertised rating, or, in this case, 6A. To pass the test, this battery should withstand 20 hours of 6A discharge before terminal voltage drops below 10.5V. Fig. 21-41.

RESERVE CAPACITY RATING

Battery RESERVE CAPACITY is a measurement of the length of time (in minutes) that the battery will continue to supply current to the car's electrical system following a failure of the charging system.

To arrive at the rating, a new, fully charged battery at 80°F (26.7°C), is discharged at a constant rate of 25A until the battery cell voltage drops to 1.75V. The length of time, in minutes, it takes for this voltage reduction becomes the rating. See Fig. 21-42.

CRANKING PERFORMANCE

Battery drain is very heavy during engine cranking (especially cold weather, cold engine conditions). The CRANKING PERFORMANCE rating provides an indication of just how large a discharge load (in amperes) that a battery can provide in a period of 30 seconds.

The test entails using a new, fully charged battery at 0°F (-17.8°C). The battery is discharged at the highest constant rate possible that will maintain a cell voltage (under load) of at least 1.2V at the end of 30 seconds.

BATTERY CAPACITY

Plate size, number of plates and amount of acid in the electrolyte determine battery capacity. The heavy

SPECIFIC GRAVITY	FREEZING POINT DEGREES F.	DEGREES C	SPECIFIC GRAVITY	FREEZING POINT DEGREES F.	DEGREES C
1.100	+18	−8	1.220	−31	−35.0
1.120	+13	−11	1.240	−50	−46
1.140	+8	−13	1.260	−75	−59.4
1.160	+1	−17	1.280	−92	−69
1.180	−6	−21	1.300	−95	−71
1.200	−17	−27			

Fig. 21-39. Specific gravity affects freezing point. (GMC)

Fig. 21-41. Battery manufacturers' 20-hour rating discharge.

Fig. 21-42. Typical battery reserve capacity discharges. (Battery Council International)

amperage draw starting capacity of a battery depends to a great extent on the total area.

BATTERY VOLTAGE

Battery voltage is determined by the number of cells (compartments containing elements). Each cell has an open circuit voltage of 2.1V. Three such cells produce a 6V battery; six cells, a 12V battery.

CAUTION!

Some batteries (not maintenance free) may occasionally need water added to the electrolyte. Do not overfill. Always use DISTILLED water. some tap waters contain harmful chemicals that will reduce the life and efficiency of a battery. (Freezer and refrigerator frost, when melted, makes a good source of distilled water.)

DRY-CHARGED BATTERY

The dry-charged battery is popular because it is shipped with the plates charged and the battery dry. If this battery is kept in a cool, dry spot, it will last a long time and, unlike the wet battery, does not utilize trickle charging (charging constantly at a very low rate).

When the battery is delivered to the customer, the electrolyte is added and, in this way, the buyer gets a NEW battery even though it has been stored for some time.

DANGER—ACID BURNS!

BATTERY ELECTROLYTE IS A STRONG ACID. IT CAN BE HIGHLY INJURIOUS TO THE EYES, SKIN, AND CLOTHING. IF ACCIDENTALLY SPLASHED WITH ACID, FLUSH AFFECTED AREA WITH LARGE AMOUNTS OF WATER. FOLLOW IMMEDIATELY BY BATHING AREA IN A MIXTURE OF BAKING SODA AND WATER. SODA, BEING AN ALKALI, WILL NEUTRALIZE THE ACID. WHEN WORKING WITH BATTERIES, BE CAREFUL!

DANGER—BATTERIES CAN EXPLODE!

Never bring a spark or open flame near a battery. When charging, the battery gives off hydrogen and oxygen gas. This gas, which is highly explosive, fills the space above the plates and even the atmosphere immediately surrounding the battery. When a battery explodes, it can throw lethal quantities of acid in all directions. BE CAREFUL!

JOB OF THE BATTERY

The main purpose of the battery is to supply current for the ignition system and starter motor UNTIL the car is running. When the engine starts, the alternator supplies the electrical needs of the car and recharges the battery.

ELECTRICAL SYSTEM, GENERATOR

The generator is an electromagnetic device driven by the engine. It is used to produce electricity to meet the needs of the electrical system. It also keeps the battery charged.

GENERATOR USES MAGNETISM TO PRODUCE ELECTRICITY

When a wire is passed through a magnetic field, voltage is generated in the wire. If the wire is part of a closed circuit, current will flow. Fig. 21-43.

If the wire is passed through the magnetic field in the opposite direction, the current flow in the wire will be reversed.

Fig. 21-43. Inducing voltage in a wire. In 1, wire is stationary. No current is flowing. In 2, wire is being drawn swiftly through magnetic lines of force (in direction A). Wire, as it passes through field, will have voltage induced in it. As it makes a complete circuit, current flows (see needle on ammeter).

The amount of current produced in the wire will depend on two factors:
1. Strength of magnetic field.
2. Speed at which wire cuts or moves through field.

As the wire cuts the field, the lines of force are distorted or bent around the leading side. You will notice in Fig. 21-44 that the arrow around the wire indicates the direction in which the magnetic field moves around the wire.

LEFT-HAND RULE FOR CONDUCTORS

By placing your left hand, with the fingers wrapped around the wire in the direction of the magnetic field, your thumb will point in the direction the current is moving.

Fig. 21-44. Wire cutting through a magnetic field. Wire is passing through field in direction A. Note how lines of force are bent as wire moves through field. Two arrows arround wire indicate direction in which magnetic field moves around wire. Using left-hand rule for conductors (Fig. 21-45), you will see that any current flow in the wire would be directly away from you.

By the same token, if you know the direction the current is moving, grasp the wire with the left-hand thumb pointing in the direction of current flow. Your fingers will point in the direction the magnetic field is moving. Fig. 21-45.

ELECTRICITY PRODUCES MAGNETISM

If a current carrying coil is placed around a bar of steel, the bar will become magnetized. The more turns of wire and the stronger the current, the more powerful the magnet.

This principle is used in the generator and in other items of equipment such as relays, voltage regulators, starter solenoids, etc. Fig. 21-46.

LEFT-HAND RULE FOR COILS

You can determine either polarity (which end is N, which end is S) by grasping the coil so the fingers of

Fig. 21-45. Left-hand rule for conductors. Thumb points in direction of current flow and fingers wrap around conductor in direction of magnetic field.

Fig. 21-46. An electromagnet. When current is passed through coil surrounding iron bar, bar becomes magnet. Notice how bar attracts and holds nails while current is flowing.

the left hand wrap around the coil in the direction the current is moving. The thumb will then point to the north pole. If the pole is known, grasp the wire with the thumb pointing in the direction of the N pole, and the fingers will point in the direction the current is flowing. Fig. 21-47.

ELECTROMAGNET CORE

By placing a soft iron core within the coil, the magnetic force lines are concentrated and strengthened. As there is less magnetic reluctance (resistance) in the core than in the air, the force lines will follow the core. How the generator makes use of this principle will be explained.

Fig. 21-47. Left-hand rule for coils. (Motorcraft)

ALTERNATING CURRENT GENERATOR

If a looped wire is rotated between two magnets (pole shoes), it will have voltage induced in it. If the wire is part of a closed circuit, current will flow. If each end of the wire loop is connected to a round ring (slip ring), the loop can rotate in the field and at the same time, remain in contact with the remainder of the circuit. Each end of the rest of the circuit is attached to a carbon brush (block of carbon) that rubs against the slip ring. Fig. 21-48 shows the action of an alternating current (AC) generator. Notice that a voltmeter is placed across the circuit.

In A, Fig. 21-48, the loop is cutting through the field in a counterclockwise direction. This means that the top part of the right-hand side of the loop is the leading edge, while the bottom side is the leading edge on the other half. This causes the magentic lines to wrap around the loop in one direction in one half, and the other direction in the other half. This creates a current flow in the direction of the arrows. Notice that the voltmeter has swung to the right, indicating that voltage is now being generated.

In B, Fig. 21-48, the loop has continued turning until it is out of the magnetic force field. As the loop is not cutting any lines, it creates no voltage, and no

Fig. 21-48. Alternating current generator. This shows action of a single loop. Actual generator uses many loops. (Prestolite)

current flows.

When the loop again passes through the field, the part of the loop moving up through the force lines will be moving down through the force lines, and vice versa. As this reverses the direction the force lines wrap around the loop, the voltage again rises, but the direction of current flow is reversed. This is termed alternating current and is similar to that used in your home.

You will notice in C, Fig. 21-48, that the voltage starts at zero, rises to a peak, falls to zero, reverses directions, rises to a peak and falls again. This all takes place in one complete revolution of the loop.

DIRECT CURRENT GENERATOR

The older, direct current (DC) generator operates on the same principle as the AC generator. The main difference is that the current moves in one direction only. This is accomplished by splitting a single ring (commutator) and connecting the circuit brushes to it in such a manner that when the loop has passed out of the field and is ready to reverse, the brushes connect with opposite halves of the ring.

The DC generator shown in Fig. 21-49 starts out at zero voltage, rises to a peak as the loops cut through the strongest part of the field, drops to zero and before it can reverse, starts rising to a peak again with the current traveling in the same direction.

GENERATOR NEEDS MORE LOOPS

With only one loop passing through the field, the voltage produced is erratic. You noticed in Figs. 21-48 and 21-49, that the voltage rose and fell. By adding more loops, the voltage would not fall back to zero because one loop will be leaving the field while another is entering.

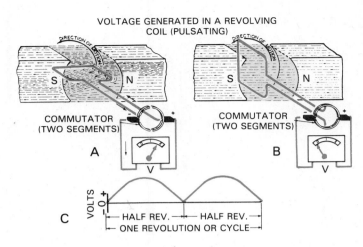

VOLTAGE GENERATED IN A REVOLVING COIL (PULSATING)

Fig. 21-49. Direct current generator. Note how each commutator is split into two sections.   (Prestolite)

As more loops are added, the voltage fluctuations will smooth out. A higher voltage can be produced with more loops. Fig. 21-50 illustrates the effect of adding another loop. Notice that the commutator is now split into four pieces (segments). The brushes contact the commutator segments at exactly the right time to prevent current reversal. Note the graphic illustration of the resultant voltage and the voltage variation.

POLE SHOES

A car generator does not use permanent magnets. Instead, it incorporates two pole shoes. Many turns of wire are wound around the pole shoes. When current passes through these windings, the pole shoes become electromagnets. The more current that flows, the stronger the field. These coils are called FIELD

COILS or FIELD WINDINGS.

The two field windings are connected together in series and wound so that one pole shoe becomes the north pole and the other the south pole. Fig. 21-51 shows the two pole shoes, field frame, and field winding. Only one turn of wire is shown for the field winding; actually, there are many turns.

ARMATURE

The loops (armature windings) that are to rotate in the magnetic field, are wound on a special laminated (many pieces) holder called an armature.

The armature is supported in bearings set in end plates. Generally a ball bearing is used at the pulley end and a bronze bushing at the other end. The armature is turned by placing a pulley on one end and driving it with a V-belt from the crankshaft pulley. Figs. 21-52, 21-53, and 21-54.

COMMUTATOR

The segments of the commutator are fastened to the armature, and the ends of the armature windings are soldered to the segments. The armature segments are insulated from the armature and from each other. The mica insulation between the segments is undercut (cut below level of commutator) to prevent excessive wear of the carbon brushes. See Figs. 21-52, 21-53, and 21-54.

BRUSHES

Two carbon brushes, in spring-loaded holders, are attached to the end plate. Some generators mount the holders in the frame. The brush held in an insulated holder picks up the voltage developed by the armature windings. This insulated brush is connected to

Fig. 21-50. Effect of adding a loop to DC generator. Commutator now contains four segments. Note how voltage pulsation is smoothed out by use of extra loop.   (Prestolite)

Fig. 21-51. Field windings and pole shoes of simplified generator. In actual generator, field windings consist of many turns of wire.   (Lincoln)

Fig. 21-52. Exploded view of typical DC generator. Learn names and location of all parts. 1—Brush. 2—Brush springs. 3—Thrust washer. 4—Commutator. 5—Field coil. 6—Spacer. 7—Driving end bracket. 8—Field frame. 9—Armature. 10—Field terminal. 11—Brush holder. 12—Commutator end bracket. 13—Field terminal nut and washers. 14—Terminal.

Fig. 21-53. Exploded view of a typical DC generator. (Ford)

Fig. 21-54. Cross section of typical DC generator. (American)

the armature (ARM.) terminal of the generator by a short wire.

The other brush holder is grounded to the frame, completing the circuit. The spring pressure on both holders causes the brushes to remain in firm contact with the commutator at all times.

DC GENERATOR CIRCUITS

Although today's cars use an AC generator (alternator), we will devote some space to the study of the DC generators used on thousands of vehicles. Such study will also aid in a thorough understanding of the AC generator circuit that will be covered shortly.

Two types of DC generator circuits were widely used. Both types attach the insulated brush to the ARM. terminal. The main difference is in the grounding of the field windings. One type grounds the field externally, A, Fig. 21-55. The other is grounded internally, B, Fig. 21-55.

HOW GENERATOR WORKS

When the generator armature first begins to spin, there is a weak residual magnetic field in the soft iron pole shoes. As the armature spins, it begins to build voltage. Some of this voltage is impressed on the field windings through the generator regulator. This impressed voltage builds up a stronger winding current, increasing the strength of the magnetic field. The increased field, in turn, produces more voltage in the armature. This builds more current in the field windings, with a resultant higher armature voltage. When the voltage has reached an acceptable peak, further increase is prevented by limiting the amount of voltage impressed on the field windings. A schematic view of a simple generator is shown in Fig. 21-56.

GENERATOR COOLING AND LUBRICATION

Most generators use small fans on the pulley ends for cooling. Such a fan draws a stream of cooling air through the generator. Fig. 21-57.

Lubrication is provided by applying light engine oil to oil holes. The holes lead to a felt wick that administers the oil to the bearings. Avoid over oiling, as the excess oil will be thrown onto the commutator.

DC GENERATOR REGULATOR

It is necessary to control both the voltage and the current produced by the generator. This is done by incorporating a voltage and current regulator in the generator circuit.

Fig. 21-55. Generator circuits. Circuit A is most widely used of two. A grounds field externally in regulator. B runs field current through regulator to field coils, then grounds circuit inside generator. (Motorcraft)

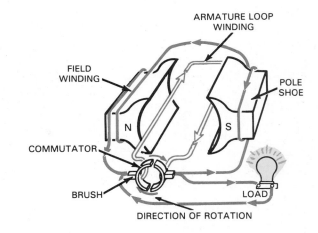

Fig. 21-56. Simple generator. (GMC)

Fig. 21-57. Air cooling generator. Pulley fan draws air through generator body. (Motorcraft)

Excessive generator output will damage the battery, burn out the lights and damage other units in the electrical system.

The generator described in the last few paragraphs is termed a shunt generator. As such, it has no internal method of controlling its output. Therefore, it must be controlled by a regulator.

REGULATOR CONSTRUCTION AND OPERATION

The commonly used regulator has three separate control units. One unit controls the voltage (voltage regulator), another controls the current output (current limiter), and the third connects and disconnects the generator from the battery circuit (circuit breaker or cutout relay).

CIRCUIT BREAKER OR CUTOUT RELAY

The circuit breaker or cutout relay is a simple magnetic make-and-break switch. It is used to connect the generator to the battery circuit when generator voltage builds up to the desired value. It will disconnect the generator when the generator slows down or stops. This prevents the battery from discharging through the generator.

A soft iron core is magnetized to pull down a hinged armature. When the armature is pulled down, it closes a set of contact points and completes the circuit. When the core field is broken, the spring pulls the armature up, breaking the contacts and opening the circuit.

A fine wire from the generator circuit is given many turns around an iron core (shunt winding) and is then grounded. A heavy wire from the generator is given a few turns around the coil and is connected to the upper contact point. The other contact point is connected to the battery circuit.

When the generator first starts turning, the cutout armature keeps the contact points open. As generator voltage builds up, an ever increasing magnetic field is created by the current flowing through the fine windings around the core. When cut-in voltage is reached, the shunt magnetic field is strong enough to pull the armature down and close the contacts. This connects the generator to the battery circuit and current flows from generator to battery. This also causes the heavy windings to add to the magnetic pull of the fine winding.

When the generator slows down or stops, battery voltage will exceed generator voltage, and current will flow from battery to generator. This reversal of current direction in the large winding reverses its magnetic field, which works against that of the fine winding. This reduces magnetic pull on the armature, and the armature spring pulls the contacts open, breaking the circuit. This prevents the battery from discharging through the generator.

When generator voltage builds up again, the armature will be drawn down, and the generator will again be connected to the circuit. Fig. 21-58.

VOLTAGE REGULATOR CONSTRUCTION

The external end of the field coil circuit is connected to one of the voltage control unit contact points. The other point (regulator armature point) leads directly to ground. A spring keeps the armature point against the other point, completing the field coil circuit.

A shunt circuit going to ground through a resistance unit is placed just ahead of the points. When the points are closed, the field circuit takes the easy route to ground through the points. When the points are open, the field circuit must pass through the resistance to get to ground.

An iron core, similar to that of the circuit breaker, is placed directly beneath the armature. A coil of fine wire (one end connected to ground, other end to generator armature circuit in circuit breaker) is placed around the core. Fig. 21-59.

Fig. 21-58. Schematic of a cutout relay. Current passing through both heavy generator wire coil and shunt coil will magnetize iron core, causing it to keep armature pulled down. This allows current from generator to pass through battery. Follow arrows.

VOLTAGE REGULATOR ACTION

When the generator is operating (if battery is low or a number of electrical units are operating), the generator voltage may stay below that for which the control is set. In this event, the flow of current from the generator through the core shunt coil will be too weak to pull the armature down, and the generator field will continue to go to ground through the points. This will complete the field circuit, with no resistance, and the generator will continue to build up voltage.

If some of the electrical load is removed or if the battery becomes charged, the generator voltage will

Fig. 21-59. Voltage regulator unit. Trace movement of current in field circuit. Note that voltage has not yet reached a point high enough to cause electromagnet to pull contact points apart.

increase until it reaches the unit setting. At this point, current flow through the core shunt coil will be high enough to pull the armature down and separate the points.

When the points separate, the field circuit must flow through the field resistance unit. This cuts down the current flow to the generator field coils and weakens the generator magnetic field. This immediately cuts down generator output. When output drops, the current flow through the shunt winding drops, and the armature closes the points. When the points close, field resistance is removed and output goes up.

This cycle is repeated over and over, and the points actually have a vibrating action. They open and close about 50 to 200 times per second. This action then controls or limits the maximum voltage that the generator can produce.

The voltage regulator limits maximum voltage. The condition of the battery and the electrical load actually control the amount of voltage produced. The voltage regulator only comes into play when the generator attempts to exceed predetermined voltage limits. Fig. 21-60 illustrates voltage regulator action. The top illustration shows the points closed when generator voltage is low. When it reaches regulator limits, the points open and the field circuit passes through the resistor. Study each illustration and trace the flow of current in each case.

CURRENT REGULATOR OR LIMITER

Even though generator voltage is controlled, it is possible (when battery is low or a heavy load is on) for generator current to run extremely high. This would overheat the generator and it would soon be ruined. The current, as well as the voltage, must be limited.

CURRENT REGULATOR CONSTRUCTION

A current regulator is built in much the same fashion as the voltage regulator. Instead of a shunt

SYSTEM VOLTAGE LOW
CONTACTS CLOSED
FIELD CURRENT FLOWS DIRECT TO GROUND
GENERATOR VOLTAGE AND OUTPUT INCREASE

SYSTEM VOLTAGE HIGH
CONTACTS OPEN
FIELD CURRENT FLOWS THROUGH RESISTANCE
GENERATOR VOLTAGE AND OUTPUT DROP

Fig. 21-60. Voltage regulator action. Top view shows regulator action when generator voltage is below that for which regulator is set. Bottom view shows regulator action when generator voltage attempts to exceed proper setting. (Motorcraft)

coil of fine wire, a lesser number of turns of heavy wire is wrapped around the core. This heavy wire is connected in series with the generator armature circuit. In operation, the field circuit passes through the current limiter points on its way to the voltage regulator points. See thin black line in Fig. 21-61.

CURRENT REGULATOR ACTION

For purposes of explanation, imagine the generator speed as fairly slow, voltage low and little current flow. Both the current regulator points and the voltage regulator points are closed, and the field circuit is completed without passing through any resistances.

As generator speed increases, current output goes up. If the battery is low and generator voltage remains low, the voltage regulator points remain closed.

Current flow increases up to the setting of the unit. At this time, current flow through the heavy coil windings will cause the core to draw the armature down, opening the current regulator points. In order to be complete, the field circuit must pass through a resistor. This lowers current output. Points close, output increases. When points open, output drops. The points vibrate open and closed fast enough to produce a very smooth flow of current.

When current flow is low and voltage reaches the voltage regulator setting, current regulator points remain closed but voltage regulator points open and close, limiting the voltage.

Either the voltage regulator or the current regulator can function, but they cannot function at the same time. In order for the field circuit to reach ground

without passing through a resistance, both sets of points must be closed.

Study Fig. 21-61 and trace the field circuit through both current and voltage regulator units. Follow the armature circuit through the current regulator coil to the cutout relay and on to the battery. Note the field resistances. One of the resistance units becomes part of the field circuit when either the voltage regulator or current regulator points are open. The other resistance unit is connected to the cutout unit.

When either point set opens, there is a reduction in field current. This causes an induced voltage (similar to action in ignition coil) in the field coils. The resistances, in addition to increasing field circuit resistance, also help prevent arcing at the points. Study Figs. 21-61 and 21-62.

DOUBLE CONTACT VOLTAGE REGULATOR

Another type of regulator uses a double set of contact points on the voltage regulator unit. When the bottom contacts are touching, the field circuit is completed without passing through a resistance unit.

As voltage builds up, the armature moves down and neither upper nor lower contacts are touching. This inserts a series resistance into the field circuit.

As generator speed and field current build up beyond the control of the series resistance, the armature is pulled down, bringing the upper contacts together. This short circuits the field, bringing the voltage within controlled limits. A double contact gives longer service with higher generator output loads than a single contact type. It also allows higher field currents with lower generator speeds. This is shown in Fig. 21-63.

Fig. 21-61. Three unit generator regulator. Trace out all circuits until you understand function of each.

Fig. 21-62. Typical regulator. Regulator cover is not shown. (Plymouth)

TEMPERATURE COMPENSATION

By using bimetallic hinge strips on the circuit breaker (cutout relay) and current regulator, it is possible to allow increased current flow during cold operation. As the system warms up, contact armature resistance changes and current flow is lowered. One type uses a special magnetic shunt that lowers the magnetic pull on the voltage regulator armature when the unit is cold. This alows the voltage to increase until enough magnetic pull is developed to separate the points. When the unit is hot, most of the magnetic

Fig. 21-63. Double contact voltage regulator is shown in position it would assume when generator voltage is below that of unit setting. Field circuit is going directly to ground.

field acts on the contact armature, and voltage is reduced.

Regulator coil magnetic efficiency varies from cold to hot. This must be controlled by temperature compensating devices. Fig. 21-64 shows how one type of regulator is temperature compensated.

AIR GAP

The term REGULATOR AIR GAP refers to distance between contact armature and top of iron core that is magnetized to draw the armature down.

DC GENERATOR POLARITY

POLARITY can be defined as the directional flow of current leaving the generator. When the generator is stopped, a certain amount of residual magnetism remains in the pole shoes. The polarity of the shoes at this time, depends on the direction of current flow in the field coil windings prior to stopping.

If, during generator testing, current is accidentally caused to flow in an opposite to normal direction, the pole shoes will change polarity. N becomes S, and S becomes N. When the generator is installed and the engine started, the reversed polarity will cause current to flow in the wrong direction.

The reversed current flow will damage the cutout relay points by doubling system voltage at the points (generator and battery will be in series). The operating coil magnetic strength will be insufficient to hold the cutout points closed. As a result, they will vibrate and burn. In time, they will actually weld together, and the battery will discharge through the generator. A dead battery, as well as possible damage

VOLTAGE REGULATOR TEMPERATURE
COMPENSATED TO PERMIT HIGHER
VOLTAGE WHEN SYSTEM IS COLD.
TO CHARGE A COLD BATTERY
REQUIRES HIGHER VOLTAGE.

CURRENT REGULATOR TEMPERATURE
COMPENSATED TO PERMIT HIGHER
CURRENT WHEN SYSTEM IS COLD.
EXTRA CURRENT IS NEEDED IN
COLD WEATHER.

CIRCUIT BREAKER TEMPERATURE
COMPENSATED TO KEEP
OPERATION WITHIN CORRECT
LIMITS THROUGHOUT WIDE RANGE
OF TEMPERATURE.

COLD — LESS MAGNETIC PULL ON
ARMATURE REQUIRES HIGHER
VOLTAGE TO OPEN CONTACTS.

HOT — MORE MAGNETIC PULL ON
ARMATURE REQUIRES LOWER
VOLTAGE TO OPEN CONTACTS.

Fig. 21-64. Regulator temperature compensation. (Motorcraft)

to the generator, will result. To prevent this, the generator should be polarized before starting the engine.

GENERATOR POLARIZING

When a DC generator has been disconnected and reinstalled, it must be polarized prior to starting the engine.

When the generator grounds the field circuit externally, A, Fig. 21-55, the generator is polarized by connecting a jumper wire across the Gen. and Bat. terminals of the regulator. Hold one end of the wire against the generator terminal, and scratch the other end across the battery terminal. This one flash causes current to flow through the field coil in the proper direction, insuring correct polarity.

To polarize the internally grounded field circuit, B, Fig. 21-55, DISCONNECT the field lead from the regulator and momentarily scratch it on the battery terminal of the regulator.

Remember this rule for polarizing generators—ALWAYS PASS CURRENT THROUGH THE FIELD COILS IN A DIRECTION THAT WILL CAUSE THE GROUND SIDE OF THE COILS TO BE CONNECTED TO THE GROUND SIDE OF THE BATTERY.

Remember, always polarize a generator after installation!

OTHER TYPES

There are other types of DC generators such as the split field, third brush, etc. Since their uses are limited, they will not be discussed in this text.

A TEAM

The generating system is made up of the battery, generator and regulator. All are dependent on each other. In order for the generating system to function properly, all parts must be in proper working order. The action of any one part is governed by the action of the other two parts.

AMMETER

An ammeter is installed in the generating system to measure the flow of electricity (in amperes) to or from the battery. The ammeter will let the operator know if the battery is being charged, and the rate of charge. The ammeter is connected into the circuit in series. Fig. 21-61 illustrates the ammeter in a typical system.

GENERATOR INDICATOR LIGHT

An indicator light located on the instrument panel may be used instead of an ammeter. When the generator is charging, the light is off. When the generator is not charging, the light will come on. The light does not tell how much the generator is charging. Fig. 21-65 shows the wiring circuit for a typical generator indicator light.

ALTERNATING CURRENT (AC) GENERATOR

The AC generator (also called an alternator) is widely used on cars today.

The modern car has made heavy demands on the electrical system. This, coupled with the fact that much driving is of the stop-and-go city type, has made it difficult to maintain the battery in a fully charged state. A DC generator is not very efficient in slow traffic and at idling speeds.

An AC generator provides a better output at lower engine speeds and, in the heavier models, provides a very high output at cruising speeds. A typical AC generator used in a Toyota charging system is shown in Fig. 21-66.

SEVERAL BASIC DIFFERENCES

The alternator delivers alternating current (AC), while the DC generator delivers direct current (DC).

The DC generator spins the armature (output) coils inside of two or more stationary field coils. The AC generator spins the field coil inside a set of stationary stator windings (output).

The AC generator field is excited (current passed through it) by connecting it to a battery. The current draw is relatively light, around 2 amps. It varies with generator size.

ALTERNATOR CONSTRUCTION

As mentioned, the alternator spins a field coil with alternating N and S poles inside the stator windings. A round iron core is placed on a shaft, and the field winding is placed around the core. Two iron pole pieces are slid on the shaft. They cover the field winding and are arranged so the fingers are interspaced. The fingers on one pole piece all form N poles. The fingers on the other form S poles. As the fingers are interspaced, they form alternate N—S—N—S poles. Fig. 21-67 shows the complete rotor assembly in exploded form.

Fig. 21-68 shows a simple rotor turning inside a single conductor (stator winding). As the rotating

Fig. 21-65. Generator charge indicator light. (Cadillac)

Fig. 21-67. AC rotor assembly. Pole pieces and field winding assembly are pressed on shaft. (Delco-Remy)

Fig. 21-66. Schematic showing charging system circuit. Study part arrangement. (Toyota)

Fig. 21-68. Schematic of simple AC generator. Magnetic field cuts through stator windings. (Delco-Remy)

rotor magnetic fields cut through the conductor, voltage is generated and current flows in the complete circuit. As the alternating N and S pole fields pass around the conductor, the current will alternate; first one direction and then the other.

A small motorcycle alternator stator and rotor are shown in Fig. 21-69. In this installation, the rotor is fastened to the engine crankshaft and whirls inside the stator assembly. Notice the stator is made up of laminated iron rings. The stator reduces field reluctance, thereby intensifying the magnetic field. See Fig. 21-69.

Fig. 21-69. Small motorcycle alternator. (Lucas Ltd.)

Direct current from the battery is fed through the field coil by using brushes rubbing against slip rings. One end of the field coil is fastened to the insulated brush, while the other end is attached to the grounded brush.

Figs. 21-70 and 21-71 illustrate an AC generator using slip rings. As the pole fields pass through the conductor in Fig. 21-70, voltage is imparted in the conductor, and current flows in one direction. In Fig. 21-71, the rotor turns 180 deg., and the N pole and S pole are at opposite positions. This causes current to flow in the opposite direction.

An exploded view of one type of alternator is shown in Fig. 21-72. Note the end plates or covers containing bearings that support the rotor shaft. The stator and stator windings are supported by the covers.

Another alternator is featured in Fig. 21-73. Study the part names and relationship.

A cross-sectional view of a typical alternator is given in Fig. 21-74. Study the location of the various components. The use of DIODES will be explained shortly.

An assembled alternator is illustrated in Figs. 21-75, 21-76, 21-77. The alternator is mounted in a manner similar to that of the DC generator.

An end and sectional view of an alternator employing a built-in regulator is shown in Fig. 21-77. Note battery, field, and sensing terminals.

Fig. 21-70. Schematic of a simple single-phase AC generator. Brushes contact slip rings. (Delco-Remy)

Fig. 21-71. Schematic of simple single-phase AC generator. You will notice that pole pieces have reversed position they assumed in Fig. 21-70. This causes reversal of current in load line or conductor.

THREE-PHASE AC

The stator windings are made up of three separate windings. This produces what is known as three-phase AC. When only one winding is used, single-phase current results. A curve illustrating single-phase AC current flow is shown in Fig. 21-78, A.

Fig. 21-78, B, illustrates three-phase AC. Notice that the distance between high points in the output is shorter.

DIODES

The electrical system of the car is designed to utilize DC, so the AC flow from the alternator must be rectified (changed) to DC. This is accomplished by using an outside rectifier or, as is generally done, by passing the AC flow into silicon diodes.

490

Fig. 21-72. Exploded view of one type of alternator (AC generator). Learn names and location of parts. (Nissan)

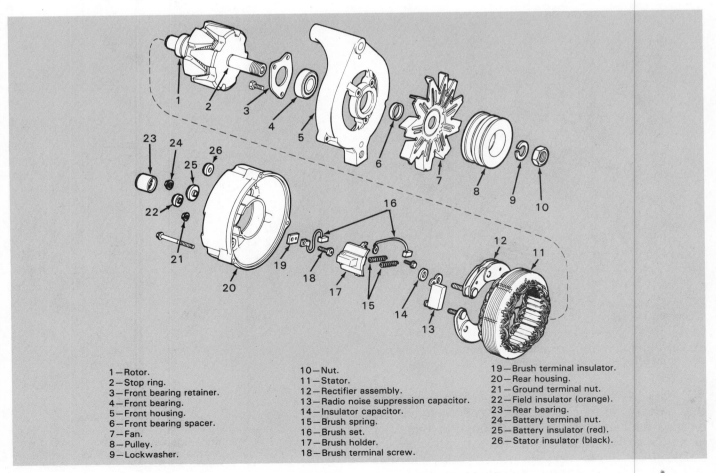

1—Rotor.
2—Stop ring.
3—Front bearing retainer.
4—Front bearing.
5—Front housing.
6—Front bearing spacer.
7—Fan.
8—Pulley.
9—Lockwasher.

10—Nut.
11—Stator.
12—Rectifier assembly.
13—Radio noise suppression capacitor.
14—Insulator capacitor.
15—Brush spring.
16—Brush set.
17—Brush holder.
18—Brush terminal screw.

19—Brush terminal insulator.
20—Rear housing.
21—Ground terminal nut.
22—Field insulator (orange).
23—Rear bearing.
24—Battery terminal nut.
25—Battery insulator (red).
26—Stator insulator (black).

Fig. 21-73. Exploded view of alternator. (Jeep)

Fig. 21-74. Cross section of typical alternator or AC generator. (Cadillac)

Fig. 21-75. Cutaway of assembled alternator. Note how carbon brushes touch slip (collector) rings. (AMC)

Diodes have a peculiar ability to allow current to flow readily in one direction. When the current reverses and attempts to flow through in the other direction, current flow is stopped.

The diodes or rectifiers are located in one end plate or shield. In the alternator illustrated in Fig. 21-76,

Fig. 21-76. Alternator—end view. (Plymouth)

Fig. 21-77. AC alternator (generator). This model incorporates the regulator into alternator slip ring, end frame assembly. Regulator is a solid state electronic unit. (Chevrolet)

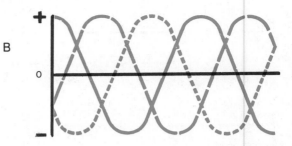

Fig. 21-78. A—Single-phase AC. X represents positive half of wave and Y negative half. B—Three-phase AC. Phase outputs overlap but do not coincide. (Delco-Remy)

three negative polarity rectifiers are pressed into the aluminum end plate. These are on the ground side. Three positive polarity rectifiers are pressed into a heat sink which is insulated from the end plate.

The arrangement of the rectifiers will allow current to flow from the alternator to the battery, but will not allow current flow from the battery to the alternator. This eliminates the need for a generator cutout relay.

The wiring arrangement of the rectifiers is shown in Fig. 21-79. A cross-sectional view of a diode is given in Fig. 21-80. Fig. 21-81 pictures a graphic representation of rectified current flow.

ALTERNATOR OPERATION

When the ignition key is turned on, the battery is connected to the No. 4 terminal of the regulator, Fig. 21-82. Current flow is through both the indicator lamp (ignition terminal of ignition switch) and through the resistor (accessory terminal of ignition switch). Combined current flow is about 1 amp.

From the No. 4 regulator terminal, the current path is through the lower voltage regulator points to the regulator F terminal, then through the alternator field to ground. This current flow excites the field, causing the pole pieces to become electromagnets, and making the "no charge" indicator lamp light.

When the engine is started, it will drive the alter-

Fig. 21-80. Cross section of a diode (rectifier). Current is free to pass one way only. Diode, like a transistor, is a semiconductor (conducts electricity under certain conditions, acts as an insulator under others).

Fig. 21-81. Rectified current flow. This represents three-phase AC current depicted in Fig. 21-78, after it has been rectified. (Delco-Remy)

nator rotor. As the whirling rotor pole force fields cut through the stator windings, an AC voltage is generated.

The initial voltage is impressed from one phase of the stator to the R terminal on the alternator or generator. The R terminal is connected to the No. 2 regulator terminal and from there to the field relay coil winding. Current flow through the field relay coil windings causes the relay points to close. This action

Fig. 21-79. Rectifier wiring arrangement. (Plymouth)

Fig. 21-82. Typical alternator wiring diagram. Note use of a two unit regulator. Study diagram to determine how field relay operates the ''no charge'' indicator lamp. (Pontiac)

Fig. 21-83. Two unit voltage regulator used in AC generator circuit. (Ford)

connects the No. 3 regulator terminal to the lower regulator points. Since the No. 3 terminal is connected to the battery (through starter solenoid), field current flow will be directly from the battery.

At the same time, closure of the relay points impresses full battery voltage on BOTH SIDES of the No. 4 regulator terminal, stopping current flow through the indicator lamp and resistor. This causes the indicator lamp to go out.

In this regulator, the field relay acts as an indicator lamp relay, as well as completing the circuit between the battery and alternator field. Fig. 21-82.

A typical two unit AC generator regulator is illustrated in Fig. 21-83.

Note that the voltage regulator shown in Fig. 21-82 has a double set of contact points. When the alternator is inoperative, a spring holds the bottom contacts together. At lower generator speeds, or when battery or accessory current demand is quite high, the lower contact points remain closed. This permits full current flow (about 2 amps) to the field windings.

As the alternator rpm increases, the voltage at the battery terminal also increases. This causes a heavier current flow through the voltage regulator shunt winding, creating enough magnetic pull to draw the lower points apart. This forces the field circuit to pass through a resistance unit, cutting field current to around 3/4 amp. This, in turn, lowers the value of the pole piece magnetic field, causing a fall off in alternator voltage.

With the lowering of voltage, the current through the voltage regulator shunt winding falls off. This reduces the magnetic pull and allows the spring to once again close the lower points. This opening and closing action is very rapid and will maintain an even voltage setting unless alternator speed becomes too high.

When alternator speed becomes high enough, the 3/4 amp field current (lower points open) will permit the voltage to rise above that desired. The rise in voltage increases the current flow through the voltage regulator shunt windings, intensifying the magnetic pull on the point armature to the point where the upper contact points are drawn together. This grounds the field circuit, stopping ALL current flow in the alternator field windings. Voltage immediately falls off and the upper points open. Voltage increases, and the points close. The vibrating, opening and closing action will limit maximum voltage.

When engine speed is reduced, the lower set of points will limit the voltage satisfactorily. Study the voltage regulator circuit in Fig. 21-82.

Fig. 21-84 shows a wiring diagram of the Delco AC

Fig. 21-84. Wiring diagram for Delcotron (AC generator) charging system using a two unit regulator. (Buick)

generator (called a Delcotron) charging circuit. This setup uses a two unit regulator.

SINGLE UNIT REGULATOR

When an ammeter is incorporated into the charging circuit (instead of an indicator lamp), a single unit regulator will suffice.

Since the diode rectifiers prevent current flow back into the alternator, no cutout relay is required. The alternator current (not voltage) output is self-limiting. Therefore no current regulator is needed. This makes it possible to utilize the single unit regulator (containing only a voltage regulator).

The single unit regulator circuit is pictured in Fig. 21-85. Operation of the voltage regulator is similar to that described in the two unit regulator. Study the circuit. Note the diode rectifiers.

TRANSISTORIZED VOLTAGE REGULATOR

The transistorized, NOT transistor, regulator utilizes a single transistor working in conjunction with a vibrating contact point. The transistor makes it possible for less current to flow across the contact points, prolonging point service life.

TRANSISTOR (SOLID STATE) VOLTAGE REGULATOR

The TRANSISTOR or solid state (no moving parts) voltage regulator is in wide use today. It is compact, provides long service life, accurate control and

Fig. 21-85. Single unit voltage regulator. Note use of ammeter, eliminating need for a field relay.

excellent reliability. The unit may be incorporated into the alternator itself as is shown in Figs. 21-77, 21-86, or it may be remotely mounted.

The transistor regulator, also called electronic regulator, integrated circuit regulator, etc., can utilize such components as transistors, resistors, diodes, capacitors, thermistor, etc.

A charging circuit employing a transistor regulator

Fig. 21-86. Exploded view of an alternator with a built-in voltage regulator.   (Saab)

is pictured in Fig. 21-87. The Zener diode is nonconducting until a specific voltage is reached. At this point, the diode "breaks down" (becomes conductive) and transmits a flow of electricity. This current flow, acting through the transistors, stops the flow of field current to the alternator. This causes the voltage output to fall below diode "break down" voltage, at which time the diode once again becomes nonconductive. This, in turn, stops the current flow to the transistors and allows resumption of field current flow. The cycle is repeated as fast as 2,000 times per second. The thermistor compensates for changes in temperature. Fig. 21-87.

Fig. 21-88. Charging system schematic showing transistor (solid state) voltage regulator. Note diode trio. This unit rectifies current flow from ground through TR1 and the field windings to the stator windings. The bridge rectifier diodes change stator AC voltage to DC output. This regulator is built into the alternator. (AMC)

Fig. 21-87. Charging circuit employing a transistor regulator.

Another charging circuit is illustrated in Fig. 21-88. When stator voltage reaches a certain level, voltage across R3 will increase to the point that it will cause Zener diode D1 to conduct. Forward biased (voltage applied in direction causing current flow) transistor TR2 conducts and transistor TR3 is reverse biased OFF. This turns TR1 OFF. The field current and system voltage immediately decrease with TR1 OFF.

D1 stops conducting when voltage across R3 decreases. This causes transistor TR2 to become reverse biased OFF and transistors TR1 and TR3 forward biased ON. output voltage and field current will increase. This cycle is continually repeated many, many times per second thus holding alternator voltage output to a predetermined level. Fig. 21-88.

Sudden voltage change across R3 is prevented by capacitor C1 and excessive back current through TR1 at high temperature, is prevented by R4. TR1 is protected by D2 that prevents a high induced voltage in the field winding when TR1 is OFF. Voltage control temperature correction is provided by a thermistor (resistance decreases as temperature increases).

The external wiring circuit for one remotely mounted transistor regulator is in Fig. 21-89.

BRUSHLESS ALTERNATOR

Fig. 21-90 illustrates a heavy duty, truck type alternator with built-in voltage regulation. This particular unit, unlike car type alternators, does not employ slip rings and brushes. All conductors carrying current are STATIONARY (do not move). These are regulator circuit components, field winding, stator windings and rectifier diodes.

Study Fig. 21-90. Note stationary (does not turn with rotor) field coil.

STARTER SYSTEM

In order to start the engine, it must be cranked by a starting motor. The starting motor is mounted on the clutch or flywheel housing and operates a small gear

Fig. 21-89. External wiring circuit as used on one charging system employing a remotely mounted (away from alternator) transistor regulator. (Ford)

Fig. 21-90. Heavy duty, truck type alternator with built-in electronic (transistor) regulator. Note stationary field coil and absence of slip rings and brushes. (GMC)

that can be meshed with a large ring gear on the flywheel.

To energize the starter motor, an electrical circuit is completed by the driver. When the starter motor armature begins to turn, the starter gear moves out and engages the ring gear. This spins the flywheel and starts the engine. When the engine starts, the driver breaks the starter circuit by releasing the ignition key switch. This causes the starter gear to move out of mesh with the ring gear.

STARTER MOTOR PRINCIPLES

If a current carrying wire is placed in a magnetic field, the field set up around the wire by the moving current will oppose that of the magnetic field. If the wire is free to move, it will move out of the field. This fact forms the basis for an electric motor. Fig. 21-91.

ARMATURE LOOP

If the conductor is bent in the form of a loop, each side of the loop will set up a magnetic field. Since the current is traveling in opposite directions, the two sides will have opposing fields. Fig. 21-92.

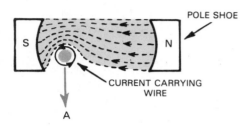

Fig. 21-91. Current carrying conductor in magnetic field. Field around wire (see small arrows) will oppose that of pole field. This will cause wire to be forced out in direction of arrow A.

Fig. 21-92. Armature loop. Note direction of magnetic field on each side of loop.

When the armature loop is placed in a magnetic field, both sides of the loop will oppose the magnetic field, but in opposite directions. This will cause the loop to rotate out of the field. Fig. 21-93.

Fig. 21-93. Armature loop will rotate. Each side of loop has a field moving in opposite directions. These fields oppose pole shoe field causing loop to rotate.

COMMUTATOR SEGMENTS

In order to pass an electrical current into the revolving loop, the loop ends must be fastened to commutator segments (much like DC generator). Copper brushes rub against the turning segments. Fig. 21-94.

One loop would not give the starter motor sufficient power, so many loops are used. The ends of each loop are connected to a copper segment. Fig. 21-95.

Fig. 21-94. Commutator segments. In actual starter motor, many loops and segments are used. Each segment is insulated from shaft and other segments.

Fig. 21-95. Many loops are required. Addition of loops will increase power or torque of starter motor.

The loops are formed over and insulated from a laminated iron core. The ends of all loops are connected to copper commutator segments. The segments are insulated from the shaft and from each other. The core is supported on a steel shaft which, in turn, is supported in bronze bushings.

When current is fed into two of the four brushes, it flows through all the loops and out the other brushes. This creates a magnetic field around each loop. As the armature turns, the loop will move to a position where the current flow reverses. If this were not done, the magnetic field around the loops would push them up out of one side of the field. And when they entered the other side of the pole field, they would be repelled. This constant reversal of current flow is accomplished by the commutator segments moving under the brushes. Two brushes are insulated and two are grounded.

FIELD FRAME AND POLE SHOES

Field pole shoes, four or more, are placed inside a steel cylinder (field frame). Two or more of the shoes are wound with heavy copper strips. Then, when current is passed through the coils, the pole shoes become powerful magnets. The field frame provides a low reluctance magnetic path and further strengthens the magnetic field.

STARTER ELECTRICAL CIRCUITS

The copper loops and field windings are heavy enough to carry a large amount of current with minimum resistance. Since they draw heavy amounts of current, they must not be operated on a continuous basis for longer than 30 seconds. After cranking for 30 seconds, wait a couple of minutes to let the starter motor dissipate some of its heat. A starter heats quickly, so prolonged use can cause serious damage.

Various wiring arrangements are used in starter construction. Detail A, Fig. 21-96 illustrates a four pole, two field winding connected in parallel but in series with the armature. By wiring the field coil in parallel, resistance is lowered, and the field coils produce stronger magnetic fields. The other two poles have no windings but serve to strengthen the field.

Detail B, Fig. 21-96, shows a four pole, four winding setup. Windings are parallel and in series with the armature.

Detail C, Fig. 21-96, pictures a four pole, three winding setup. Two of the windings are in series with themselves and the armature. One winding does not pass through the armature, but goes directly to the ground. This SHUNT WINDING aids with additional starting torque. However, as starter speed increases, the shunt still draws a heavy current and tends to keep starter speed within acceptable limits.

Detail D shows a four pole, four winding setup. Three windings are in series, one is a shunt winding.

Detail E is a four pole, four winding setup with all windings in series.

There are other setups such as the six pole, six windings, etc. The ones illustrated in Fig. 21-96 are most commonly used.

STARTER MOTOR CONSTRUCTION

Fig. 21-97 illustrates, in exploded form, the various parts of a typical starter motor employing a Bendix type drive (not shown). This particular starter has a four pole, three winding circuit. One of the windings is a shunt winding.

Fig. 21-98 shows a cutaway view of a typical starter using an overrunning clutch starter drive. Study construction. Note how the armature shaft is supported at both ends by a bronze bushing.

FLYWHEEL RING GEAR

In order to provide a means for the starting motor to turn the flywheel, a large ring gear is either welded

A

TWO WINDINGS
PARALLEL

B

FOUR WINDINGS
SERIES-PARALLEL

C

THREE WINDINGS
2-SERIES
1-SHUNT

D

FOUR WINDINGS
3-SERIES
1-SHUNT

E

FOUR WINDINGS
SERIES

Fig. 21-96. Starter circuits.   (Motorcraft)

Fig. 21-97. Exploded view of typical starter motor. Learn names and location of all parts. (Mazda)

1—Shift lever.	11—Gasket.	21—Armature.
2—Lever pivot.	12—Shims.	22—Pole shoe.
3—Solenoid plunger.	13—Snap ring.	23—Frame.
4—Steel washer.	14—Bushing.	24—Field winding.
5—Rubber washer.	15—End frame.	25—Drive end frame.
6—Solenoid windings.	16—Adjusting washer.	26—Roller bearing.
7—Contact plate.	17—Brush holder.	27—Pinion.
8—Terminal.	18—Brush.	28—Stop ring.
9—Field lead wire.	19—Brush spring.	29—Snap ring.
10—Fastener.	20—Commutator.	30—Bushing.

Fig. 21-98. Cutaway of starter motor using an overrunning clutch starter drive. Note shift lever and solenoid. (Volvo)

to, or heated and shrunk onto, the flywheel. (Metal ring is heated to expand and while hot is fitted on flywheel. When cool, metal contracts and ring grasps flywheel securely.) Fig. 21-99.

STARTER PINION GEAR

A small gear, called a starter pinion gear, is attached to the starter armature shaft. The pinion gear is much smaller than the ring gear and usually turns 15 to 20 times in order to crank the flywheel one revolution.

PINION ENGAGEMENT

It is necessary to mesh the pinion gear for cranking, and when the engine has started, to demesh (disengage) the pinion.

There are two basic types of pinion engagement devices, and several designs of each basic type. The self-engaging or inertia type is quite popular. The mechanically engaged type is also used.

SELF-ENGAGING STARTER DRIVE, BENDIX TYPE

With the Bendix self-engaging pinion drive, the armature shaft spins and the drive pinion stands still while the threaded sleeve spins inside the pinion. As the sleeve spins, the pinion slides out and meshes with the ring gear. As soon as the pinion reaches its stop, the turning sleeve causes the pinion to turn with it to crank the engine.

The pinion sleeve fits loosely on the armature shaft and is connected to a large spring that is, in turn, fastened to the armature shaft. The spring absorbs the sudden shock of pinion engagement.

When the engine starts, the pinion will spin faster than the armature turns the pinion sleeve. This will reverse its travel on the threaded pinion, and it will spin backward, free of the ring gear. A small coil spring will prevent it from working back into mesh.

Fig. 21-100 illustrates the action of the Bendix type pinion engaging device. In detail 1, the armature shaft and pinion sleeve begin to spin. The stationary pinion is sliding to the left. In detail 2, the sliding action is stopped, and the pinion begins to turn and crank the engine. When the engine starts, detail 3, the pinion is spinning faster than the threaded pinion sleeve. This spins the pinion back out of mesh with the ring gear.

The various parts of a Bendix starter drive are shown in Fig. 21-101. The drive head is attached to the armature shaft.

A Bendix drive, in place on a starter motor, is pictured in Fig. 21-102. Notice the threaded pinion sleeve and pinion. The pinion is weighted on one side, so it will tend to resist being turned until it has slid into mesh with the ring gear.

BENDIX FOLO-THRU

The Bendix Folo-Thru drive has a feature not found on the drive just discussed.

When the pinion slides into mesh with the ring gear, a small, spring-loaded detent pin drops into a notch in the threaded pinion sleeve. This locks the

Fig. 21-100. Bendix starter drive action. (Delco-Remy)

Fig. 21-99. Flywheel ring gear. Ring gear can be cut as an integral part or can be shrunk on. (Citroen)

Fig. 21-101. Bendix starter drive construction.
(Delco-Remy)

Fig. 21-102. Starter motor with Bendix drive.

Bendix in the engaged position and prevents it from being demeshed until the engine speed reaches about 400 rpm. When the engine reaches this speed, the pinion will be spinning fast enough so that centrifugal force will throw the detent pin outward. This action unlocks the pinion, and it will spin out of mesh.

There is a ratchet type clutch drive, detail A, Fig. 21-103, that will allow the pinion to travel faster than the armature shaft. It is the Bendix Folo-Thru drive.

Fig. 21-103. Bendix Folo-Thru drive. Detent pin 5, drops into groove B, and keeps pinion engaged until engine speed is sufficient to throw pin 5 out of groove. 1—Armature shaft. 2—Drive spring. 3—Screw shaft. 4—Control nut. 5—Detent spring and pin. 6—Pinion barrel. 7—Pinion. 8—Anti-drift pin and spring. 9—Setscrew. A—Ratchet. B—Screw shaft detent notch. C—Screw shaft anti-drift slope.

The advantage of this type of drive is that it prevents the pinion from being demeshed until the engine is actually running. With the first type of Bendix drive, if the engine reaches 200 or 300 rpm, then stalls, there could be a problem. The operator may engage the starter again just as the engine stops and it will kick back. If the starter engages the ring gear at this time, serious damage may result to the starter. The Bendix Folo-Thru drive eliminates this possibility.

OVERRUNNING CLUTCH, MECHANICALLY ENGAGED

The overrunning clutch starter drive is engaged with the ring gear by manually operated linkage or an electric solenoid that actuates the shift linkage.

In operation, the pinion is turned by the overrunning clutch. When the pinion is slid into mesh with the ring, the shifting mechanism completes the starter circuit and the one-way clutch drives the pinion.

When the engine starts, the ring will spin the pinion faster than the starter armature is turning. The pinion is free to run faster because the overrunning clutch engages the pinion only when the armature is driving it.

Fig. 21-104 illustrates a typical overrunning clutch starter drive. Study the various views carefully. Note the pinion, drive shell and sleeve assembly, coil spring and shift collar. The coil spring comes into use when the pinion teeth butt against the ring teeth. The actuating lever, or shift lever, will continue to move the shift collar, compressing the spring. When the lever has moved far enough to close the starter switch, the pinion will turn and the compressed spring will force it into mesh with the ring gear.

Fig. 21-104 illustrates an end view showing the spring loaded clutch rollers. When the drive sleeve turns faster than the pinion and collar assembly, the

Fig. 21-104. Overrunning clutch starter drive. Drive rollers lock pinion and collar assembly to drive member when armature shaft is spinning drive member faster than pinion.
(British-Leyland)

rollers are wedged against the pinion, causing it to turn. When pinion speed exceeds that of the sleeve, the rollers retract and the pinion is free of the shell and sleeve assembly.

Fig. 21-105 shows the overrunning clutch drive in place on a starter. Note the solenoid used to operate the shift lever.

STARTER SOLENOID

If an iron core is placed inside a coil of wire, and electric current is passed through the coil, the iron core will be drawn into the coil. Such a unit is called an electric solenoid. A solenoid has many applications and can be used where a push or pull motion is desired.

Fig. 21-106 shows a simple solenoid, and how it can be used to pull on a starter shift lever.

You will note that the solenoid in Fig. 21-106, not only pulled the starter shift lever until the pinion meshed, but it also closed the starter switch after the meshing was almost complete.

STARTER SOLENOID IN OPERATION

Fig. 21-107 shows the starter solenoid in three stages of operation. The disengaged position finds the pinion demeshed. The solenoid plunger is released and no current is flowing.

The partially engaged stage shows current from the starter switch flowing through both the pull-in and the hold-in coils. Both coils are drawing the plunger inward, causing it to pull the shift lever. The pinion is just starting to engage.

The cranking stage shows the plunger pulled into the coil. The pinion is fully engaged. The hold-in coil is operating, but the pull-in winding has cut out. The plunger has operated the starting switch and current is flowing from the battery through the switch and to the starter. Cranking will begin.

When the engine has started, the hold-in coil will cut out and the plunger will move out, retracting the pinion and opening the starter switch. Fig. 21-107.

Starters with self-engaging Bendix type drives generally use a solenoid to open and close the starter switch.

A starter motor employing a solenoid and overrunning clutch drive is shown in Fig. 21-108. Study the solenoid construction.

A somewhat different method of actuating the starter drive is pictured in Fig. 21-109. In this setup, a movable pole shoe is connected to the starter drive shift lever.

When the starter is in the OFF position, one of the field coils is grounded through a set of contacts. When the starter is first actuated, a very heavy flow of current through this field coil pulls on the movable pole shoe. The shoe, in turn, engages the starter drive.

Fig. 21-105. Overrunning clutch starter drive. This starter is engaged by an electric solenoid. Starter increases cranking torque by using reduction gears.   (Chrysler)

When fully engaged, the field coil contacts open and normal starter operation takes place. A holding coil keeps the sliding pole shoe in the engaged position. When current to the starter is interrupted, the pole shoe moves back and disengages the starter drive.

Fig. 21-106. Solenoid used to engage starter drive. In A, the solenoid plunger has moved to right, opening starter switch and retracting starter drive gear. Dash switch is off. In B, dash switch is on, energizing solenoid. Solenoid has drawn plunger into coil. Plunger has engaged drive gear and closed starter motor switch. Starter will now crank engine.

Fig. 21-107. Electric solenoid operation. Note operation in each stage. (Chevrolet)

Fig. 21-108. Sectional view of starter with solenoid operated drive mechanism.

Fig. 21-109. Starter design using one movable pole shoe as a means of actuating the starter drive. (Jeep)

Fig. 21-110. Cross section of typical electric horn. (GMC)

STARTER ACTUATING SWITCHES

In addition to the solenoid operated switch that directs battery current to the starter, it is necessary to furnish current to the solenoid. This is done in several ways. On most cars, turning the key to the fullest travel closes a switch to the solenoid. On older cars, a plunger switch on the dash is used to complete the solenoid circuit. Switches have been used that were operated by the clutch pedal, accelerator pedal, etc. On cars with automatic transmissions, a safety switch is used. To actuate the starter, the drive selector must be placed in Neutral or Park position to complete the circuit through the switch. This prevents the car from being started when the transmission is in gear.

HORNS, LIGHTS, RELAYS AND ELECTRICAL CIRCUITS

The electric horn makes use of an electromagnet, vibrator points, and a diaphragm. Referring to Fig. 21-110, you will see that the electromagnet coil, C, will attract metal washer, A, whenever the contact points are closed. Current flows through the contact points energizing the electromagnet. The electromagnet draws the washer down and, since the washer is attached to rod, B, the diaphragm (thin metal disc) will be bent downward.

When washer, A, moves downward, it causes the points to open and break the circuit. The electromagnet releases the washer and it moves upward, flexing the diaphragm in the other direction. As it moves upward, the points close and the washer is again drawn downward. This cycle is repeated very fast. These small up-and-down pulsations of the diaphragm cause the sound. Sound is magnified by passing it through a long trumpet or a spiral trumpet such as a horn in Fig. 21-110.

RELAY

A relay is an electromagnetic device used to make and break a circuit. The generator cutout relay is one application of this device.

Remember that the farther current is forced to travel, the lower its voltage becomes. If you were to have the horn circuit switch on the steering wheel, it would be necessary to run a wire from the battery, up the steering column, through the switch, down the column and out to the horn. Another possibility would be a wire from the battery to the horn, and from the horn to the switch. The switch in this case would be a ground switch in order to complete the circuit. At any rate, the wire would be unnecessarily long.

By using the relay between the battery and the horn, it is possible to run a wire from the battery to the relay and from the relay to the horn. When the driver actuates the relay, it will complete the circuit and the horn will blow. As this is the shortest possible route, voltage drop will be low.

Fig. 21-111 shows a typical horn circuit using a relay. This particular circuit is inoperative until ignition key is turned on.

When the ignition key is on, voltage is available for the electromagnetic coil, B. When the driver depresses the horn button, the electromagnetic coil circuit is completed and current will flow.

The current flow energizes electromagnet, B. This draws armature, C, down, closing switch points, A. Current will flow through the heavy wire to the relay, across the closed points, on to the horn and to ground. As soon as the horn button is released, the electromagnet is deenergized. The armature pops up, breaking the points, and the horn stops blowing.

By using the relay, it is possible to use a short run

Fig. 21-111. Horn circuit using a relay.   (Dodge)

of heavy wire to avoid voltage drop. It is also possible to actuate the relay from a distance. Headlight relays, when used, are constructed in a similar fashion. See Fig. 21-111.

HEADLIGHTS

The modern headlight is generally of sealed beam construction. The filament, reflector and lens are fused into one airtight unit. Prongs that fit into a wiring socket connector make removal easy.

Fig. 21-112 shows a typical headlamp asembly. Note adjusting screws used to aim headlight.

The halogen bulb headlamp is very popular and provides excellent lighting. A cutaway of one type of halogen headlamp is pictured in Fig. 21-113.

BULBS

Light bulbs used throughout the car are either of the single or double contact type.

Some bulbs have two filaments. This allows the bulb to be used for two separate lighting jobs. The taillight bulb is an example of this type. It is used for both a taillight and stoplight.

Bulbs must be of the proper candlepower or lumen rating (measurement of light intensity) and voltage. Bulbs are also rated by wattage and amperage.

Various bulbs are shown in Fig. 21-114. Note that the sealed beam is actually a large bulb.

HEADLAMP SWITCH

The headlamp switch closes the headlamp circuit; operates the parking lights, taillights, instrument and

Fig. 21-112. Headlamp assembly. Note adjusting screws for headlamp aiming.   (Jeep)

Fig. 21-113. One type of halogen headlamp. Some designs use removable bulbs.   (GM)

Fig. 21-114. Various types of light bulbs. A—Single contact. B—Double contact. C—Midget type. D—Cross section of a typical bulb. 1—Filament. 2—Glass. 3—Brass base. 4—Filament lead. 5—Glass-like cement. 6—Contact. 7—Holding pins. 8—Filament ground lead soldered to brass base. Current travels up from contact through filament, then to ground through brass base. E—Cross section of sealed beam headlamp. Unit is one piece. Reflector is silvered to provide good reflective properties. Lens controls and directs light.

other dash lights, etc. It may be of the push-pull or the turn type. Some cars use a toggle (up-and-down motion) switch. Fig. 21-115 illustrates one type.

FUSES AND CIRCUIT BREAKERS

It is necessary to protect electrical circuits against short circuits (part of circuit accidentally going to ground) that could burn up the wiring. The electrical units must be protected against overloads also.

Fuses and circuit breakers are used to secure adequate protection. When current flow exceeds that for which the circuit is designed, the fuse will "blow" and break the circuit. The circuit breaker points will open and close, constantly breaking the flow of current.

Fig. 21-115. Typical headlamp switch and mounting arrangement. (Dodge)

FUSES

One type of fuse consists of a glass tube with metal end caps. Figs. 21-116 and 21-117. A built-in conductor carries the current from one cap to the other. This conductor is designed to carry a specific maximum load. A newer design is the "ATO-Type" miniaturized fuse. Fig. 21-118. Both use a soft conductor that melts when fuse capacity is exceeded.

A fuse block is shown in Figs. 21-119, 21-120.

FUSIBLE LINK (WIRE)

A circuit may be protected by the use of a special wire, called a FUSIBLE LINK, that acts as a fuse. The wire is covered with HYPALON insulation.

When the fusible link or wire is subjected to an overload, it will begin to heat, causing the insulation to puff up and smoke. If the overload is continued, the hypalon insulation will finally rupture and the fusible link will burn out, breaking the circuit. See Fig. 21-121.

CIRCUIT BREAKER

A circuit breaker feeds the current through a bimetallic strip, a set of points and on through the remainder of the circuit.

When amperage exceeds that for which the breaker is built, the bimetallic strip heats and bends to separate the points. On cooling, it will close and reestablish the circuit. If the overload condition still

Fig. 21-116. Fuse. 1—Glass. 2—Conductor strip. 3—Metal cap.

Fig. 21-117. Fuse. Left—Normal fuse. Right—Overload causes link to melt, breaking circuit. (Toyota)

Fig. 21-118. One type of miniaturized fuse. (Buick)

Fig. 21-119. Typical fuse block or panel. (Chevrolet)

Fig. 21-120. Fuse block utilizing miniature fuses. (Ford)

exists, it will heat and reopen. The circuit breaker will open and close quite rapidly.

This gives it an advantage over a fuse when used on a headlamp circuit. With the fuse, an overload will burn out the fuse and the headlights will go out, and stay out until the fuse is replaced. This could cause an accident. The circuit breaker will cause the lights to flicker on and off rapidly but will still produce enough light to allow the driver to pull safely off the road. Fig. 21-122.

Fig. 21-121. The fusible link prevents system damage due to shorts, overloads, etc. Note, at bottom, how outer insulation has melted off link. Repair requires cutting off burnt link at solder joint and installation of new fusible link. (Oldsmobile)

Fig. 21-122. Circuit breaker. A—Breaker is carrying a normal load. Contact points closed. Circuit complete. B—Breaker overloaded, bimetallic strip heats up. Strip curves upward separating points. Circuit broken.

DIMMER SWITCH

A dimmer switch is located in the headlamp circuit. It is a simple switch that will direct current to one of the two terminals but never to both. One terminal leads to the high beam filament; the other, to the low beam. The high beam terminal also feeds current to the high beam indicator lamp on the dash. Find the dimmer switch in Fig. 21-123.

MANY CIRCUITS

The modern automobile has a large number of electrical circuits. A typical wiring diagram, Fig. 21-123, shows the various lighting circuits from headlamps to taillamps on a late model Buick.

A more complete electrical diagram is illustrated in Fig. 21-124. The electrical circuits, with the addition of many accessory items, are becoming so complex that wiring diagrams are often broken down by sections: starting, charging, body wiring, instrument panel, etc. Study the circuits shown in Figs. 21-123 and 21-124. Can you trace the various circuits?

Fig. 21-123. Typical electrical system diagram, showing Buick headlamp and tail lamp circuits.

GAUGES

Gauges, including oil pressure, temperature, gasoline, and ammeter, were discussed in the chapters covering systems using these gauges. The wiring circuits for several of these gauges are shown in Fig. 21-124. Study the circuit carefully. Locate the gauges and trace their wires back to the car's fire wall. Note how wires are color coded to help when troubleshooting.

CAUTION!

When installing electrical components, make certain they are properly fused. Wires must be insulated, kept from hot areas and must be secured to prevent chafing. When passing through metal parts, install grommets (rubber insulating washers) to protect the wires. Terminals should be clean and tight.

When working on the electrical system, disconnect the battery to prevent accidental short circuiting.

Use great care when repairing headlamp circuits. If the lights suddenly go out, it could be tragic.

Never replace a fuse with a fuse of higher capacity. Never replace a fuse with a bolt, wire, etc. The fuse of correct capacity must be in the circuit.

SUMMARY

ELECTRICAL FUNDAMENTALS

The electron theory states that electricity is caused by a flow of electrons through a conductor. There is a shortage of electrons at one end of the conductor and a surplus at the other. Whenever this condition is present, current will flow.

An atom is made of neutrons, protons, and electrons. The electron is a negative charge of electricity, while the proton is positively charged. The neutron is neutral, electrically.

The free electrons in an atom are those that are relatively easy to "shake" out of orbit. The free electrons are those that cause the current flow.

The pressure that causes current to flow is VOLTAGE. The amount of current flowing is measured in AMPERES. Every conductor will have some RESISTANCE to the movement of electrons.

Insulators are made of materials containing atoms with very few free electrons. The bound electrons resist current flow.

In order for electricity to flow, it must have a circuit or path that is complete. Three circuits are: Series, Parallel, and Series-Parallel.

The lining up or orienting of the magnetic domains in a material is what causes the material to become magnetized.

A magnet is surrounded by lines of force. They leave the magnet at the north pole, and enter the south pole. Like poles repel; unlike poles attract.

BATTERY

A battery is an electrochemical device. It contains positive and negative plates that are connected in such a way as to produce three or six groups or cells. The plates are covered with electrolyte.

A charged battery will amass (gather a great quantity) a surplus of electrons at the negative post. When the battery is placed in a completed circuit, the electrons will flow from the negative post, through the circuit, and on to the positive post.

The battery must be kept charged by passing electricity through it in a reverse direction to that of battery current flow.

Fig. 21-124. A more complete electrical diagram. Note that wires are all color coded to aid mechanic with wire identification. (AMC)

The battery is checked for charge by using a hydrometer to determine the specific gravity of the electrolyte.

Batteries can explode and should never be exposed to sparks or open flame.

The battery is used to supply current for starting the car. Upon starting, the generator will recharge the battery.

Car batteries are of the 12V type.

Be careful of battery electrolyte—it is dangerous!

GENERATOR

The primary job of the generator is to supply the necessary current for the electrical needs of the car and to keep the battery charged.

The generator functions by spinning an armature in a strong magnetic field produced by field coils. As the armature loops spin in the magnetic field, current is induced in the loops. A commutator at one end of the armature is contacted by carbon brushes. The insulated brush picks up the voltage generated by the whirling armature and conducts it to the rest of the electrical system. Both alternating current (most common) and direct current generators are in use.

GENERATOR REGULATOR

It is necessary to control the maximum voltage and current output developed by the generator. This is done by using the generator regulator.

The dc generator regulator contains a cutout relay, voltage and current controls. The ac generator (alternator) regulator does not need a cutout relay.

When either current or voltage output attempts to exceed that for which the generator is designed, an electromagnet breaks a set of contact points, and inserts a resistance in the generator field circuit. With a resistance in the field, voltage and current will lower.

The voltage regulator and the current regulator both operate points in a vibrating manner. As the points vibrate, they produce a smooth, controlled generator output. Either unit can work, but they will not function together.

The battery, generator, and regulator work as a team, and the function of any one unit depends upon the action of the other two.

Battery condition and electrical load determine the current and voltage requirements. The generator produces the required voltage and current, and the regulator controls the generator output on a level consistent with system needs.

STARTER

The starter is used to crank the engine for starting purposes, Fig. 21-125.

The starter motor utilizes a current carrying series of armature loops placed in a strong magnetic field

produced by field coils. As the armature loops are repelled by the magnetic field, the armature is forced to spin. By arranging a sufficient number of loops and connecting them to commutator bars or segments, current in the loops keeps reversing so the repelling force will remain constant. This allows the armature to continue spinning.

The starter uses large copper conductors in both the field and armature circuits. The field and armature are connected in series via four brushes. Since the field strength is very strong, the starter motor will produce enough torque to crank the engine.

Starters draw heavy current loads and therefore heat quite rapidly. They must not be operated continuously for longer than thirty seconds without a brief rest in which to dissipate the heat.

A starter can be energized by closing the starter switch either manually or by using an electric solenoid.

The starter pinion that engages the flywheel ring gear is engaged in two ways. One method uses the Bendix self-engaging type of drive. This type spins a pinion sleeve that causes the pinion to slide out on the sleeve until it engages the ring. The Bendix Folo-Thru is one type of self-engaging drive.

The manual engagement type moves the starter pinion into mesh by means of a shift lever. The lever can be actuated either by a solenoid or mechanically by the driver. When this type starter drive is used, the overrunning clutch is incorporated so that when the engine starts, the pinion will be free to spin until such time as it is drawn out of mesh.

RELAY

A relay is an electromagnetic unit designed to make and break a circuit. The relay can be a distance from the operator and will still function with only a ground wire and switch.

Some relays, such as those used in regulators, are not controlled by the operator.

HEADLIGHTS, FUSES

The headlight circuit is of vital importance. If must be properly maintained.

Fuses are used to protect the car wiring circuits. They must be of the proper size.

MECHANIC IS RESPONSIBLE

Obviously, when a car leaves the shop, the mechanic stays behind. However, the mechanic's care, skill, knowledge, and reputation leave with each car serviced.

If anything goes wrong, and you were the mechanic on the job, you are responsible. The car owner's comfort, peace of mind, and very life may depend on your work. This is a heavy responsibility and one to accept with a great deal of seriousness. Work carefully;

think; use good parts and proper procedures; keep parts clean; avoid the use of slipshod methods and, above all, double-check your work. Remember: A real mechanic is not satisfied with anything but the BEST!

KNOW THESE TERMS

Electron theory, Free electrons, Current, Voltage, Resistance, Ammeter, Voltmeter, Ohmmeter, Series circuit, Parallel circuit, Ohm's Law, Battery, Electrolyte, Battery capacity, Battery voltage, Generator, AC, DC, Voltage regulator, Alternator, Diodes, Starting motor, Starter pinion gear, Starter solenoid, Relay, Dimmer switch, Fuses, Circuit breaker.

REVIEW QUESTIONS—CHAPTER 21

1. What is the electron theory?
2. What is a molecule?
3. Describe the makeup of an atom.
4. About how many kinds of atoms are there?
5. The proton is a negative charge of electricity. True or False?
6. Neutrons orbit around the electrons. True or False?
7. What is a bound electron? A free electron?
8. Explain how electrons flow through a conductor.
9. What is a current of electricity?
10. Current flows from negative to positive. True or False?

Fig. 21-125. This Land-Rover starter motor is designed for rough service. It is waterproofed by means of special seals where housings connect and solenoid attaches. 1—Seals. 2—Solenoid attaching nuts. 3—Solenoid terminals. 4—Starter field terminal. 5—Through-bolt. 6—Commutator cover attaching nut.

11. What is voltage?
12. Define resistance.
13. The flow of electricity is measured in _____.
14. Name the instrument used to check each of the following:
    1. Voltage.
    2. Amperage.
    3. Resistance.
15. What material is widely used as a conductor in the car electrical system?
16. Name and describe three different types of circuits.
17. List several materials that are used for insulation.
18. Draw the symbol for ground.
19. Of what use is Ohm's Law?
20. Explain how a metal bar can be magnetized.
21. What are lines of force?
22. Unlike poles attract; like poles repel. True or False?
23. Magnetic lines of force leave the south pole and enter the north pole. True or False?
24. Describe briefly the construction of a typical automotive battery.
25. The battery contains _____ and _____ plates.
26. A 12V battery will contain three elements. True or False?
27. The battery electrolyte contains _____ and _____.
28. How is a battery charged?
29. What is a hydrometer and what is its use?
30. A battery will have a _____ and a _____ post.
31. How are the battery posts identified?
32. A battery should, when water is needed, be filled with _____ water.
33. What is a dry-charged battery?
34. Battery acid or electrolyte will burn the skin and clothing. True or False?
35. A battery can explode if a spark or flame is brought near. True or False?
36. What is the main job of the battery?
37. The generator is an _____ device.
38. Explain how a generator works.
39. Explain the left-hand rule for conductors; for coils.
40. Name the major parts of the generator.
41. Of what use is the commutator?
42. Generator brushes are made of _____.
43. What are the major differences between the DC and the AC generator?
44. What are the two types of generator circuits in common use on a DC generator?
45. How is generator output controlled?
46. Most generators are oil cooled. True or False?
47. Of what use is the generator regulator?
48. Describe the action of the regulator when controlling voltage, current, and connecting or disconnecting the generator from the battery circuit.
49. The voltage regulator and current regulator can both function at the same time. True or False?
50. What is the double contact voltage regulator? How is it different from the single contact?
51. Does temperature affect the voltage regulator, if so, is there anything done to correct it?
52. What is polarity?
53. Why is it important to polarize a generator after installing?
54. What will happen if the generator polarity is accidentally reversed?
55. How is a generator polarized? There are two methods, depending on the type of circuit. Describe both.
56. How does an ammeter work?
57. Describe the action of the AC generator.
58. How is the AC changed over to DC?
59. What is the main task of the generator?
60. Explain the operation of the starter motor.
61. Name several different starter internal circuits.
62. Of what use is the shunt circuit in the starter motor?
63. Starter motors can be used continuously up to ten minutes before stopping. True or False?
64. Name two types of starter drive mechanisms.
65. Describe the construction and operation of the drive units named in answering question 64.
66. What is a solenoid and what are some of its uses?
67. The electric horn operates by flexing a strong spring. True or False?
68. Draw a simple relay.
69. What is a bulb filament?
70. The dimmer switch is connected in series with the headlamp circuit. True or False?
71. What is the difference between a circuit breaker and a fuse?
72. Draw the following:
    1. Starter circuit.
    2. Generator circuit.
    3. Headlamp circuit.
73. What is a fusible link?
74. When an ammeter is used instead of an indicator light in an AC charging circuit, a field relay must be incorporated in the regulator. True or False?
75. How does the alternator electronic (transistor) regulator differ from the mechanical control type?
76. Cars now use this type generator:
    a. AC generator (alternator)
    b. DC generator
    c. EG generator
    d. Watt generator

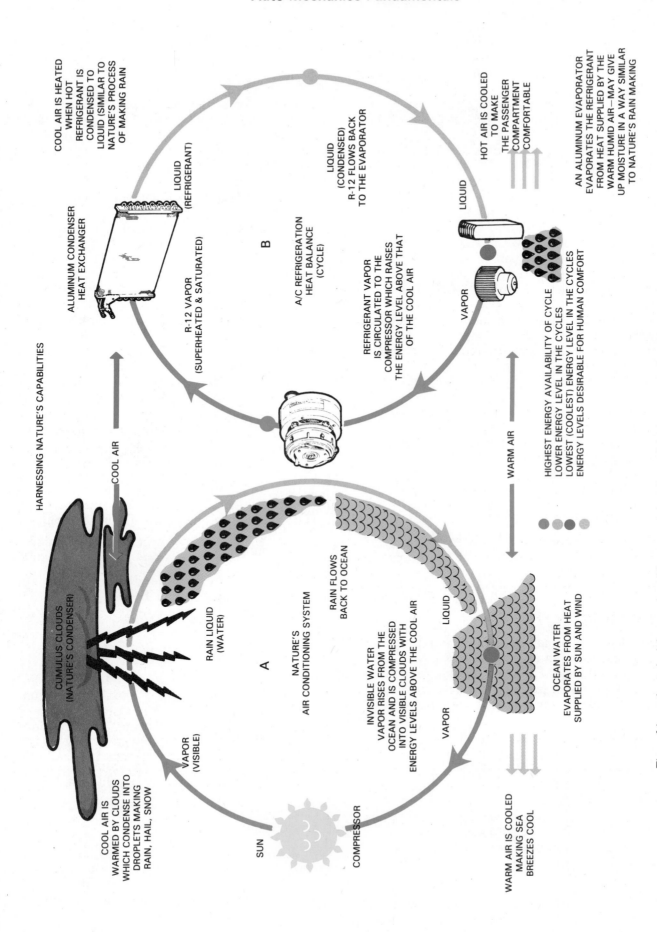

HARNESSING NATURE'S CAPABILITIES

COOL AIR IS HEATED WHEN HOT REFRIGERANT IS CONDENSED TO LIQUID (SIMILAR TO NATURE'S PROCESS OF MAKING RAIN)

ALUMINUM CONDENSER HEAT EXCHANGER

LIQUID (REFRIGERANT)

R-12 VAPOR (SUPERHEATED & SATURATED)

B

A/C REFRIGERATION HEAT BALANCE (CYCLE)

REFRIGERANT VAPOR IS CIRCULATED TO THE COMPRESSOR WHICH RAISES THE ENERGY LEVEL ABOVE THAT OF THE COOL AIR

LIQUID (CONDENSED) R-12 FLOWS BACK TO THE EVAPORATOR

HOT AIR IS COOLED TO MAKE THE PASSENGER COMPARTMENT COMFORTABLE

LIQUID

VAPOR

AN ALUMINUM EVAPORATOR EVAPORATES THE REFRIGERANT FROM HEAT SUPPLIED BY THE WARM HUMID AIR—MAY GIVE UP MOISTURE IN A WAY SIMILAR TO NATURE'S RAIN MAKING

HIGHEST ENERGY AVAILABILITY OF CYCLE
LOWER ENERGY LEVEL IN THE CYCLES
LOWEST (COOLEST) ENERGY LEVEL IN THE CYCLES
ENERGY LEVELS DESIRABLE FOR HUMAN COMFORT

WARM AIR

COOL AIR

CUMULUS CLOUDS (NATURE'S CONDENSER)

COOL AIR IS WARMED BY CLOUDS WHICH CONDENSE INTO DROPLETS MAKING RAIN, HAIL, SNOW

RAIN LIQUID (WATER)

A

NATURE'S AIR CONDITIONING SYSTEM

RAIN FLOWS BACK TO OCEAN

INVISIBLE WATER VAPOR RISES FROM THE OCEAN AND IS COMPRESSED INTO VISIBLE CLOUDS WITH ENERGY LEVELS ABOVE THE COOL AIR

LIQUID

VAPOR

OCEAN WATER EVAPORATES FROM HEAT SUPPLIED BY SUN AND WIND

VAPOR (VISIBLE)

SUN

COMPRESSOR

WARM AIR IS COOLED MAKING SEA BREEZES COOL

The refrigeration principles employed by automotive air conditioning system B, are very similar to those found in nature's own air conditioning, A. Study each cycle. (GM)

Chapter 22

AUTOMOBILE AIR CONDITIONING

After studying this chapter, you will be able to:
- Explain the principles of refrigeration.
- Identify the basic parts of an air conditioning system.
- Describe the operation of each air conditioning system component.
- Compare differences in air conditioning system design.

Automobile air conditioning makes driving far more comfortable in hot weather. It is a method whereby air entering the car is cleaned, dehumidified (excess moisture removed), brought to and kept at a selected temperature.

PRINCIPLES OF REFRIGERATION

The automotive air conditioning system makes use of the principles of refrigeration. Fig. 22-1. To provide a better insight into the functions of the system, it is wise to study some of the basic principles involved.

WHAT IS COOLING?

The term COOLING may be defined as a process of removing heat from an object.

Technically speaking, there is no such thing as cold. When we speak of something being cold, we are really saying that the object is not as hot as something else.

Fig. 22-1. Schematic showing airstream being cleaned, cooled and dehumidified.

COLD actually is a reference to a certain portion of the temperature range. The normal use of the word cold is generally determined by a comparison to the human sense of comfort.

EFFECTS OF HEAT

Heat can be defined as a form of energy that can increase, decrease, or maintain a specific temperature. Some of the more commonly observed effects of heat would be the expansion that takes place when a substance is heated or raised to a higher temperature. The added heat creates a more violent agitation of the molecules, increasing the length of their travel with a resultant increase in physical size.

Water, when heated sufficiently, vaporizes. When heat is lowered enough, water becomes a solid. Wood will reach the ignition point if heat is added, causing it to burn. Water freezing and wood burning are actual changes of state produced by heat.

TRANSFERENCE OF HEAT

Heat may be transferred from one object to another in three ways:
1. Conduction. 2. Convection. 3. Radiation.

CONDUCTION

Conduction is accomplished by actual physical contact between the two bodies. The agitated action of the molecules of the hotter body transfer their actions to that of the cooler body. If a copper wire is held in a flame, the heat of the flame is rapidly conducted through the wire. It travels from molecule to molecule. Some substances transfer heat much more rapidly than others. Fig. 22-2, A.

CONVECTION

Heat can be transferred from one object to another by the air around them. This is one form of convection. As the air heated by the hotter body rises, it comes in contact with the cooler body, raising its temperature.

TRANSFER OF HEAT BY CONDUCTION. HEAT IMPARTED BY BLOWTORCH IS TRANSFERRED FROM ONE END OF ROD TO OTHER END OF ROD BY CONDUCTION.

TRANSFER OF HEAT BY CONVECTION AND RADIATION. AIR ABOVE HOT COALS IS HEATED, RISES, AND TRANSFERS HEAT TO BIRD ON SPIT. A GREAT DEAL OF HEAT IS ALSO TRANS-FERRED TO BIRD BY RADIATION.

TRANSFER OF HEAT BY RADIATION. SUN HEATS EARTH BY TRANSMITTING INFRARED RAYS. CONDUCTION AND CONVEC-TION CANNOT HELP SINCE THERE IS NO PHYSICAL CONTACT OR AIR.

Fig. 22-2. Study three methods of heat transfer. A—Conduction. B—Convection. C—Radiation.

In a room, the air circulation will make a full circle. Even though hot air rises, circulation as it cools will finally bring it to the floor level and heat all objects in the room. Fig. 22-2, B.

RADIATION

Even in the absence of air or physical contact, heat can be transferred through space by infrared rays. (Infrared rays are not visible to the human eye.)

Energy is emitted from molecules and atoms because of internal changes.

When heat is transferred through conduction and convection, the process is relatively slow. Heat transferred by radiation travels at the speed of light.

To get an idea of how heat is transmitted by radiation, assume a body containing heat gives off infrared rays. These rays travel through space and, even though the rays may not contain heat, they have the ability to cause molecules of other substances to increase their speed, and impart heat into the other object. Fig. 22-2, C.

HEAT TRANSFER IS FROM HOT TO COLD

By studying convection, conduction, and radiation, it can be seen that when two bodies are placed in reasonable proximity to each other, the hotter body will give up heat to the colder body. Eventually the hot body will cool, and the cool body will heat, until they reach an equal temperature level.

BTU (BRITISH THERMAL UNIT)

To provide a means of measuring the amount of heat transfer from one object to another, a unit of measurement called the British thermal unit (Btu) was devised. By definition, when one pound of water is heated one degree Fahrenheit, one Btu of heat has been transferred to the water.

LATENT (HIDDEN) HEAT

If heat is imparted to ice, the ice will start to melt. As it is melting, it will not grow warmer even if a great amount of heat is applied to it. This heat that disappears into the ice with no temperature rise, is called LATENT HEAT. It is there, but it cannot be detected.

When a pound of water is heated, it will absorb one Btu for each one degree of temperature rise. It will reach the boiling point at 212°F or 100°C (atmospheric pressure at sea level). Heat applied at this point, even a great amount, will not cause a further increase in temperature. Once again heat is absorbed but is not apparent.

The amount of heat being absorbed to change the water into vapor is great, but if one were to measure the temperature of the vapor, it too would register 212°F (100°C). The heat then, is "hidden" in the water vapor.

When this vapor comes in contact with cooler air, latent heat will transfer to the cooler air and vapor will condense (change back to a liquid). This particular law is known as the LATENT HEAT OF VAPORIZATION LAW.

This latent heat of vaporization (heat transfer involved in changing a liquid to a vapor and vapor back to a liquid) is the basic principle of the refrigeration process used in air conditioning.

PRESSURE AFFECTS BOTH VAPORIZATION AND CONDENSATION TEMPERATURES

Water boils at sea level (unconfined) at 212°F (100°C). If water at 20,000 feet in the air is heated, it will boil at a lower temperature. The pressure on the water at 20,000 feet is less, so the boiling point will be lower. When pressure is raised above normal atmospheric pressure, the boiling point will also rise. The condensation point is likewise affected.

The refrigeration process makes use of this pressure affect on vaporization and condensation. The liquid used in the refrigeration system is generally referred to as REFRIGERANT-12. It is also called by trade names such as Freon-12, Isotron-12, Prestone-12, etc.

REFRIGERANT-12

Refrigerant-12 will boil or vaporize at minus 21.7°F (−30°C) when subjected to zero pounds of pressure (sea level). If the pressure is raised enough, the boiling point can be moved up well beyond the temperature encountered on the hottest day. This low boiling point, plus the fact that it can be passed through the system endlessly without loss of efficiency, makes Refrigerant-12 an ideal refrigeration medium. Fig. 22-3 illustrates the relationship between temperature and pressure.

DANGER!

REFRIGERANT-12 (DICHLORODIFLUORO-METHANE), DESPITE THE FACT THAT IT IS COLORLESS, NONEXPLOSIVE AND NON-FLAMMABLE, MUST BE HANDLED WITH EXTREME CARE. STUDY THE FOLLOWING SAFETY PRECAUTIONS THAT A MECHANIC MUST ALWAYS OBSERVE!

1. KEEP SERVICE AREA WELL VENTILATED.

Remember: Refrigerant-12, at atmospheric pressure and room temperature, is heavier than air. It will displace the air in the room and can cause suffocation. Ample ventilation also helps to prevent poisoning from breathing the fumes caused by allowing refrigerant to contact an open flame.

2. ALWAYS WEAR PROTECTIVE GOGGLES WHEN YOU ARE WORKING ON OR NEAR AN AIR CONDITIONING SYSTEM.

Remember: Refrigerant-12 vaporizes so quickly, it will freeze anything it contacts. If it enters the eyes, serious damage may occur.

3. KEEP STERILE MINERAL OIL AND A WEAK BORIC ACID SOLUTION ON HAND.

Remember: If, by some chance, refrigerant enters the eyes, DO NOT PANIC! Splash large amounts of cold water into the eyes as a means of raising the temperature. Do not rub the eyes. Apply several drops of sterile (clean) mineral oil to the eye. The oil will absorb the refrigerant and help flush it from the eyes. This may be followed by a liberal application of boric acid solution. ALWAYS SEEK THE SERVICES OF A DOCTOR AT ONCE—EVEN IF THE PAIN SEEMS TO HAVE DISAPPEARED.

4. KEEP REFRIGERANT AWAY FROM SKIN.

Remember: If refrigerant contacts the skin, treat in the manner recommended for the eyes.

5. AVOID DISCHARGING REFRIGERANT DIRECTLY INTO SERVICE AREA.

Remember: Refrigerant will vaporize at room temperature and since it is heavier than air, it will settle down. If enough refrigerant is discharged into an area without excellent ventilation, it can displace the air and cause suffocation. When refrigerant is discharged into the service area, it may contact an open flame and produce poisonous phosgene gas.

Always discharge the system into the service area exhaust system. If no such facility is present, discharge the system OUTSIDE of the building.

6. NEVER DISCHARGE REFRIGERANT INTO AN AREA CONTAINING AN OPEN FLAME.

Remember: When Refrigerant-12 comes in contact with an open flame, it produces a poisonous gas (phosgene). In addition to being dangerous to humans, it will tarnish bright metal surfaces.

7. NEVER STEAM CLEAN, WELD, SOLDER, BAKE BODY FINISHES OR, IN ANY WAY,

REFRIGERANT — 12 PRESSURE — TEMPERATURE RELATIONSHIP	(°F)(°C)	(PSIG)(kPa)		(°F)(°C)	(PSIG)(kPa)	
	−21.7 −29.8C	0(ATMOSPHERIC PRESSURE)	0(kPa)	55 12.7C	52.0	358.5
				60 15.5C	57.7	397.8
	−20 −28.8C	2.4	16.5	65 18.3C	63.7	439.2
	−10 −23.3C	4.5	31.0	70 21.1C	70.1	482.7
The table below indicates the pressure of Refrigerant — 12 at various temperatures. For instance, a drum of Refrigerant at a temperature of 80°F (26.6°C) will have a pressure of 84.1 PSI (579.9 kPa). If it is heated to 125°F (51.6°C), the pressure will increase to 167.5 PSI (1154.9 kPa). It also can be used conversely to determine the temperature at which Refrigerant — 12 boils under various pressures. For example, at a pressure of 30.1 PSI (207.5 kPa), Refrigerant — 12 boils at 32°F (0°C).	− 5 −20.5C	6.8	46.9	75 23.8C	76.9	530.2
	0 −17.7C	9.2	63.4	80 26.6C	84.1	579.9
	5 −15.0C	11.8	81.4	85 29.4C	91.7	632.3
	10 −12.2C	14.7	101.4	90 32.2C	99.6	686.7
	15 − 9.4C	17.7	122.0	95 35.0C	108.1	745.3
	20 − 6.6C	21.1	145.5	100 37.7C	116.9	806.0
	25 − 3.8C	24.6	169.6	105 40.5C	126.2	870.2
	30 − 1.1C	28.5	196.5	110 43.3C	136.0	937.7
	32 0C	30.1	207.5	115 46.1C	146.5	1010.1
	35 1.6C	32.6	224.8	120 48.8C	157.1	1083.2
	40 4.4C	37.0	255.1	125 51.6C	167.5	1154.9
	45 7.2C	41.7	287.5	130 54.4C	179.0	1234.2
	50 10.0C	46.7	322.0	140 60.0C	204.5	1410.0

Fig. 22-3. Chart illustrating relationship between pressure and temperature for Refrigerant-12.   (Oldsmobile)

SUBJECT THE AIR CONDITIONING SYSTEM TO EXCESS HEAT.

Remember: Refrigerant when closed to the atmosphere, will build up high pressures with heat. These pressures may easily burst the system or blow out the safety plug, admitting the entire refrigerant charge into the atmosphere.

8. HANDLE REFRIGERANT-12 DRUMS (OR SMALL CANS) WITH CARE.

Remember: If exposed to excess heat (even direct rays from the sun), the drum may blow the safety plug. The protective screw cap should always be over the valve to prevent physical damage. Drums have been known to explode (even when equipped with a safety plug). If tank warming during servicing is needed, use nothing but warm water or warm wet rags. Never use a torch, gas stove, steam cleaner, etc., to heat the tank. Never heat drum above 125°F (52°C).

9. NEVER FILL A TANK COMPLETELY.

Remember: When filling a small tank from a larger one, never completely fill the tank. Allow ample space for refrigerant expansion due to heating. A full tank can be very dangerous.

HOW REFRIGERATION SYSTEM WORKS

Fig. 22-4 illustrates the four basic parts making up the typical refrigeration cycle. Study this schematic and note direction of refrigerant flow as well as the sequence of operations involved. Also note the color code introduced with this illustration for high and low pressure liquid and gas (vapor).

The basic refrigeration system used to air condition automobiles consists of a compressor, condenser, receiver, expansion valve, evaporator, and in many instances, a suction throttling valve. Mufflers may also be incorporated. These various units are connected by high pressure lines. Figs. 22-5 and 22-6 illustrate the fundamental parts of a refrigeration system. Study them carefully.

In order to understand just how a refrigeration system functions, start tracing the flow of refrigerant through the system. Keep in mind that the principle of refrigeration lies in the fact that by controlling the pressure on the refrigerant, we can make it boil, or condense, and thus absorb or give off heat. Start at the receiver.

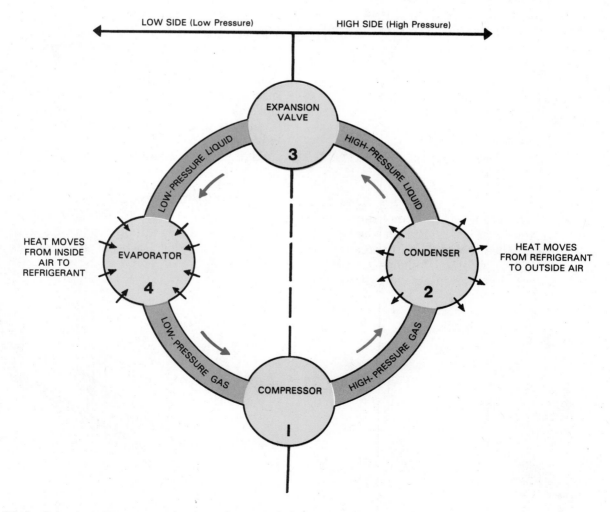

Fig. 22-4. Schematic illustrating the four basic parts employed in the refrigeration cycle. Note refrigerant flow direction. (Deere & Co.)

Fig. 22-5. Schematic of refrigeration system. Arrows indicate direction of refrigerant flow.
(Cadillac)

Fig. 22-6. Schematic of a typical air conditioning system showing refrigerant flow. Study each phase.   (Deere & Co.)

RECEIVER-DEHYDRATOR

The receiver-dehydrator, often called accumulator-drier, filter-drier, etc., is a metal tank that collects liquefied refrigerant as it leaves the condenser. It strains the refrigerant and removes moisture by means of a special desiccant (drying agent).

The receiver may also contain a safety valve. In the event of fire or other overheating, the valve will release the refrigerant charge when pressure in the system exceeds around 500 psi (3 448 kPa), depending on the system. Fig. 22-7.

From the receiver-dehydrator, the high pressure liquid refrigerant is piped to the expansion valve. A SIGHT GLASS is located in the line or in the top of receiver-dehydrator.

SIGHT GLASS

A sight glass serves two functions. It provides a visual means of making an inspection of the refrigerant as it moves to the expansion valve. The presence of bubbles or foam (at temperature above 70°F or 21°C), may indicate the system is low on refrigerant and must be charged (filled). Fig. 22-5.

Some sight glasses also indicate the presence of moisture in the refrigerant. If excess moisture is present, a moisture sensitive element turns pink. If moisture content is within limits, the element remains blue.

EXPANSION VALVE

The Refrigerant-12 arriving at the expansion valve is in a liquid state and is under heavy pressure (100 to 250 psi or 689 to 1 724 kPa).

The expansion valve serves two functions. It meters refrigerant into the evaporator coils, and also reduces the pressure. It must administer the correct amount of refrigerant for all conditions, neither too much nor too little. A typical expansion valve is shown in Fig. 22-8. Study its parts.

Notice that refrigerant from the receiver enters through a fine screen in the high pressure liquid inlet. Further movement of the refrigerant is controlled by the spring-loaded valve.

The action of this valve is controlled by three forces:
1. Valve spring tends to close valve opening.
2. Suction manifold (area at end of evaporator on compressor side) pressure, working through equalizer line, tends to close valve opening.
3. Pressure of thermal bulb tends to open valve.

You will note that a diaphragm is located in the top of the expansion valve. This diaphragm contacts the valve actuating pins. When the valve pins move down, the valve opens. When the pins move up, the valve closes.

If the compressor is started and the system ac-

Fig. 22-7. Receiver-dehydrator. Note strainer and desiccant. (Buick)

tivated, the high pressure liquid refrigerant flows in as far as the needle valve.

As the suction manifold is still warm, considerable pressure is built up in the thermal bulb. This pressure is transmitted to the diaphragm via the capillary tube. The bulb, capillary tube and area above the diaphragm are filled with both liquid and vapor refriger-

Fig. 22-8. Typical expansion valve. This valve is controlled by three forces. 1—Valve spring pressure. 2—Equalizer line pressure. 3—Thermal bulb pressure. (GMC)

ant. Some systems fill this with carbon dioxide.

The thermal bulb pressure on the diaphragm will overcome the pressure of both the valve spring and equalizer tube pressure, causing the diaphragm to flex downward. This downward movement is transmitted to the valve through the actuating pins.

When the valve opens, low pressure refrigerant (liquid) enters the evaporator coils, and warm air passing the coils gives up its heat to the colder refrigerant (around 7°F or −14°C). Refrigerant passing through the evaporator coils begins to boil and, before it leaves the evaporator, completely vaporizes.

Refrigerant vapor leaving the evaporator passes through the suction manifold on its way to the compressor. Even though it is boiling, it is still quite cold. This cools the thermal bulb and reduces its pressure on the diaphragm.

As the refrigerant passes into the evaporator, suction tube pressure is increased. This pressure is applied to the bottom of the diaphragm (through equalizer line) and attempts to move the diaphragm upward.

When the downward pressure of the thermal bulb is nearly equalized by the upward pressure of the suction manifold, the valve spring will close the valve.

When the valve is closed, and refrigerant no longer enters the evaporator, the manifold pressure drops, and its temperature rises. The drop in pressure reduces the upward equalizer pressure on the diaphragm. At the same time, the thermal bulb pressure is increased by the rise in suction manifold temperature. This causes the diaphragm to flex downward, opening the valve and admitting more refrigerant to the evaporator.

By the balance between these three forces, the cooling activity of the evaporator is closely controlled. A slightly different type of expansion valve is shown in Fig. 22-9. The expansion valve, then, strains the liquid refrigerant, reduces the pressure, and meters the proper amount of low pressure refrigerant into the evaporator coils in such a way that a careful balance is maintained between evaporator cooling efficiency and heat load.

EXPANSION TUBE

The EXPANSION TUBE, sometimes called ORIFICE TUBE, Fig. 22-10, is used on the cycling clutch system (covered shortly). Its basic function, much like the expansion valve just covered, is to admit a metered amount of low pressure refrigerant into the evaporator core.

The expansion tube contains a calibrated orifice (opening) that permits the passage of a specified amount of refrigerant. It also utilizes fine filtration screens.

As the high pressure liquid refrigerant moves from the condenser towards the evaporator, it encounters the expansion tube. The tube retards flow and permits only a metered amount of flow through the valve. This action, in addition to controlling the amount of refrigerant entering the evaporator, sharply reduces the pressure.

Study the cross section view in Fig. 22-10.

Fig. 22-10. Expansion tube (orifice tube) admits a metered flow of refrigerant into the evaporator. It also serves to reduce the refrigerant pressure.

THE EVAPORATOR

The evaporator consists of a long tube passed back and forth through numerous cooling fins. The fins are firmly attached to the tube.

An airstream produced by an electric blower, is passed through the cooling fins and around the coils. This air is warmer than the refrigerant and gives up its heat to the fins, coils and then to the refrigerant itself.

As the low pressure refrigerant moves through the evaporator, heat given up by the air passing through the evaporator causes the refrigerant to begin to boil. By the time the refrigerant has passed through the evaporator, it has become a vapor.

Like the latent heat of vaporization found in boiling water vapor, the refrigerant has a great deal of latent heat in its vapor. As the heat is absorbed by the boiling refrigerant, the coils and fins turn cold and in turn cool the air passing over them. This cool air is blown into the interior of the car.

The evaporator dehumidifies (removes moisture) the air passing through the fins. Excess moisture that

Fig. 22-9. A somewhat different type of expansion valve. This valve does not utilize an equalizer line.

may be in the air will condense, as it strikes the cold evaporator fins. This condensation is drained off in the form of water.

Evaporator construction is shown in Fig. 22-11. Note that on this particular unit, an expansion valve is attached to the inlet side. A suction throttling valve is connected to the outlet.

EVAPORATOR TEMPERATURE IS IMPORTANT

The normal evaporator coil temperature varies from around 33°F (.56°C) to 60°F (15.6°C). If the temperature is permitted to drop to 32°F (0°C) or below, condensation that forms on the coils will freeze. Such icing will destroy cooling efficiency.

EVAPORATOR TEMPERATURE CONTROL, THERMOSTATIC SWITCH

Evaporator coil temperature may be controlled by using a thermostatic switch to disconnect the compressor magnetic clutch, when evaporator temperature drops to a critical point. The sensing bulb that operates the switch is placed in contact with the evaporator core. When coil temperature reaches an acceptable level, the switch cuts in the magnetic clutch to once again drive the compressor. Fig. 22-12.

EVAPORATOR TEMPERATURE CONTROL, HOT GAS BY-PASS VALVE

At one time the hot gas by-pass valve was used to control evaporator icing. The hot gas by-pass valve,

Fig. 22-11. Typical evaporator construction. Note that this evaporator is constructed along lines of a cooling system radiator. It is made of aluminum. Study location of each part attached to evaporator. (Cadillac)

Fig. 22-12. Capillary tubing, in contact with evaporator core, controls a thermostatic switch that energizes compressor magnetic clutch. This prevents icing (freezing) of evaporator coils. (Chevrolet)

located on the outlet side of the evaporator, meters a controlled amount of hot, high pressure refrigerant from compressor back into the evaporator outlet. This hot gas joins the vaporized refrigerant leaving the evaporator and is pulled into the compressor. The refrigerant from the hot gas by-pass raises evaporator pressure. The pressure increase raises the boiling point of the refrigerant with a resultant loss in cooling efficiency. This in turn raises the evaporator temperature.

The compressor runs constantly (when AC system is turned on) in systems using the hot gas by-pass valve. A typical system with hot gas by-pass valve is pictured in Fig. 22-13.

EVAPORATOR TEMPERATURE CONTROL, SUCTION THROTTLING VALVE (STV)

The suction throttling valve replaced the hot gas by-pass valve as a means of controlling evaporator temperature. It is installed at the evaporator outlet. Fig. 22-14.

The evaporator outlet pressure acts on the STV piston and, through small bleeder holes, against a diaphragm. Opposing this force is the valve spring and atmospheric pressure on the other side of the diaphragm.

When the evaporator pressure rises to a predetermined level (usually around 30 to 33.5 psi or 207 to 231 kPa), the piston will be moved in an opening direction and pass the excess pressure into the compressor inlet line. When pressure drops, the piston will

Fig. 22-14. Typical suction throttling valve (STV). This valve balances evaporator pressure very accurately at either 30 psi (207 kPa) or at 33.5 psi (231 kPa) controlling evaporator temperature. When engine vacuum is removed from vacuum power unit, small internal spring adds 3.5 psi (24 kPa) pressure to that exerted by valve spring. This will increase controlled pressure to 33.5 psi (231 kPa) and will protect against evaporator icing at high elevations. (Harrison)

close enough to restrict vapor flow to the compressor until pressure builds up to the desired level.

The STV will keep the evaporator pressure balanced very accurately and closely control the evaporator temperature. In Fig. 22-14, note the vacuum power unit. By applying engine vacuum to this unit, valve spring pressure to piston is reduced, allowing the piston to open under less pressure. This lowers evaporator pressure for maximum cooling. See Figs. 22-3 and 22-14.

POA SUCTION THROTTLING VALVE

The POA (Pilot Operated Absolute) suction throttling valve represents an improvement over the suction throttling valve just discussed. It controls evaporator pressure at the desired minimum level regardless of compressor speed, evaporator load or changes in altitude.

Fig. 22-13. Hot gas by-pass valve. Note how by-pass valve feeds hot, high pressure refrigerant back into evaporator outlet. (Buick)

The POA valve, Fig. 22-15, contains a bronze vacuum bellows. The sealed bellows contains almost a perfect vacuum. Since the interior of the bellows has absolutely no pressure, it is referred to as the PILOT OPERATED ABSOLUTE valve.

Note that in Fig. 22-15, the system is off and pressure is equal on both sides of piston (around 70 psi or 482 kPa, ambient air temperature 70-80°F or 21-27°C) allowing spring A to force the piston closed. Since pressure surrounding the bellows is over 28.5 psi (196 kPa), the bellows has contracted. This opens the needle valve and exposes the bellows chamber and head of piston to compressor pressure (lower than inlet or evaporator pressure when system is operating).

When the system is activated, Fig. 22-16, compressor suction starts reducing pressure on the outlet side of the valve. Since the needle valve is still open, pressure will also lower around the bellows and top of the piston. Evaporator pressure will force the piston toward the lower pressure area around the piston head, opening the piston and allowing refrigerant vapor to pass through the valve.

When the pressure surrounding the bellows has lowered to 28.5 psi (196 kPa), the bellows expands and the needle valve closes. Fig. 22-17. Evaporator pressure, entering through an orifice in the piston head, begins to increase pressure on the piston. The piston is still open, valve still closed.

When pressure on both sides of the piston becomes nearly equal, spring A will force the piston closed. The valve remains closed until pressure increases to the point that causes the bellows to contract. Fig. 22-18 shows the POA valve with the piston closed.

When pressure in the bellows area is increased enough, the bellows will contract and the valve will open. This will apply compressor vacuum to the bellows and piston head. The piston will be drawn open as shown in Fig. 22-16. The cycle then starts over and is repeated.

Fig. 22-16. POA valve. System activated. Compressor lowering pressure on outlet side, around bellows and on head of piston. Pressure differential has overcome spring tension and forced piston to open. Needle valve is still open.

Fig. 22-17. POA valve. Outlet pressure around bellows has reduced to 28.5 psi (196 kPa), causing bellows to expand and close needle valve.

COMPRESSOR

The compressor can be of a typical two cylinder, reciprocating piston type, six cylinder AXIAL or the

Fig. 22-15. Schematic of a typical Pilot Operated Absolute Suction Throttling Valve (POA). System is off; pressure is equal on both sides of piston, so spring A has forced piston closed. (Pontiac)

THE PRESSURE SURROUNDING BELLOWS AND ON TOP OF PISTON HAS NOW INCREASED SUFFICIENTLY OVER 28.5 (196 kPa) TO BECOME NEARLY EQUAL (WITHIN 1.3 PSI [8.96 kPa]) OF INLET PRESSURE

1—PRESSURES ON BOTH SIDES OF PISTON NEARLY EQUAL - SPRING TAKES OVER AND PUSHES PISTON CLOSED

NEEDLE VALVE STILL CLOSED

Fig. 22-18. POA valve. Increase in pressure on top of piston has permitted spring to close piston. Pressure in bellows area is still not high enough to contract bellows and open valve.

four cylinder RADIAL type. Figs. 22-19, 22-20, 22-21, 22-22, and 22-23. It is belt driven by the engine. The compressor draws in the low pressure refrigerant from the evaporator and compresses it to around 100–250 psi (689–1 724 kPa), depending on compressor speed and ambient air temperature. Note

that the inlet side of the compressor is generally referred to as the LOW SIDE. The outlet side is referred to as the HIGH SIDE.

When a compressor compresses refrigerant, it also raises the refrigerant temperature. The temperature rise from compression is sufficient to bring the temperature of the compressed refrigerant to above that of the surrounding air. The compressed and heated refrigerant is then forced into the condenser.

Compressor action is illustrated in Fig. 22-19. Note suction and discharge valve action.

Fig. 22-20 illustrates one type of two cylinder, reciprocating piston compressor.

Fig. 22-21 shows a cross-sectioned view of the axial type of compressor. This type uses three, double-ended pistons activated by a wobble or "swash" plate. The design effectively produces a six cylinder compressor.

A cross section of a radial design compressor is featured in Fig. 22-22. This design produces a very compact unit. Fig. 22-23 shows an exploded view of the radial compressor. The pistons work at right angles to the shaft and are spaced around the shaft in a radial fashion.

CONDENSER

A condenser is constructed much like an evaporator. It is mounted in front of the radiator so that an ample stream of air is forced through the cooling fins. Both the fan and forward motion of the car

DOWNSTROKE OF PISTON CREATES VACUUM IN CYLINDER. PRESSURE IN SUCTION LINE FORCES SUCTION VALVE OPEN

PRESSURE IN DISCHARGE LINE HOLDS DISCHARGE VALVE CLOSED

PISTON ON DOWNSTROKE

INTAKE STROKE

PRESSURE IN CYLINDER RAISES DISCHARGE VALVE, GAS FLOWS INTO DISCHARGE PIPE

PRESSURE IN CYLINDER HOLDS SUCTION VALVE CLOSED

PISTON ON UPSTROKE

COMPRESSION STROKE

Fig. 22-19. Pumping action of a typical reciprocating piston type compressor. (Deere & Co.)

Fig. 22-20. Exploded view of a two cylinder, reciprocating piston type air conditioning system compressor. (British-Leyland)

Fig. 22-21. Axial type air conditioning compressor. As swash plate turns, it moves double-ended pistons back and forth. Note magnetic clutch drive pulley. (Buick)

Fig. 22-22. Typical four cylinder radial type Fumpressor construction. (Buick)

Fig. 22-23. Exploded view of a four cylinder radial compressor. (AMC)

cause air to flow through the condenser.

As the hot high pressure Refrigerant-12 gas or vapor passes into the condenser, its temperature is higher than that of the cooling air passing through the condenser. As a result, the refrigerant gives up its heat to the airstream. The compression heat and the latent heat of vaporization both escape.

As the refrigerant passes through the coils, it cools and condenses back into a high-pressure liquid. As it condenses, it flows into the receiver-dehydrator.

The refrigerant must leave the receiver-dehydrator and enter the expansion valve as a liquid. If refrigerant gas is passed to the expansion valve, very little cooling will take place.

A typical condenser is shown in Fig. 22-24. Note inlet line from compressor and outlet line to receiver-dehydrator.

Individual units that make up one car air conditioning refrigeration system are shown in Fig. 22-25. This illustration shows the use of a suction accumulator. It is not used on this system when a six cylinder axial is employed.

Another system, incorporating a muffler and POA suction throttling valve, is pictured in Fig. 22-26. A schematic of a similar system is illustrated in Fig. 22-27. Study each part carefully.

A CCOT (cycling clutch orifice tube) system is shown in Fig. 22-28. The system is controlled by a

Fig. 22-24. Typical condenser. (Fins are not all drawn in.) Unit mounts in front of radiator. (Plymouth)

Fig. 22-25. Air conditioning system. Follow refrigerant flow from receiver-dehydrator, expansion valve, evaporator, suction accumulator (not always used), compressor, condenser, and to receiver-dehydrator.   (Ford)

thermostatic cycling switch.

A capillary tube from the cycling switch relays evaporator temperature to the switch. The switch is designed to cycle the compressor on and off to maintain an evaporator temperature of approximately 32°F to 45°F (0°C to 7°C). This cycling action prevents condensation (moisture) from freezing on the evaporator core.

MAGNETIC CLUTCH

The compressor pulley turns whenever the engine is running. The compressor does not run until the pulley is engaged to the compressor driving shaft.

This engagement is accomplished through the use of a magnetic clutch. Fig. 22-29 pictures one type of magnetic clutch. When the system is turned on, cur-

Fig. 22-26. This air conditioning system employs a POA evaporator pressure control valve (suction throttling valve) to control coil temperature. Note use of a muffler to quiet pumping noises. Sometimes a muffler is used on inlet or suction line as well.   (GMC)

Fig. 22-27. Schematic of an air conditioning system, similar to that shown in Fig. 22-26. Arrows indicate direction of refrigerant flow. (Cadillac)

rent is passed to the electromagnet coil, causing it to attract the armature plate. Through the strong magnetic pull, the armature plate is drawn firmly against the side of the revolving pulley. Effectively locked together, the revolving pulley drives the armature plate which, in turn, drives the compressor.

When the current is stopped, the magnetic pull is broken and flat springs pull the armature plate away from the pulley surface. Note in Fig. 22-29, that the magnetic coil does not revolve. Its magnetic pull is transmitted through the pulley to the armature. The armature plate and hub assembly are fastened to the compressor drive shaft. The magnetic clutch pulley, when not driving the compressor, spins on double-row ball bearings.

MUFFLER

A muffler is often installed on the discharge (high pressure) side of the compressor. The muffler reduces pumping noise and line vibrations. It also smoothes out the surge action produced by the compressor. Note the muffler in Fig. 22-26.

REFRIGERANT OIL

A specific amount (varies with system but often around 6 to 10 oz., 177 to 295 mL), of special refrigeration system oil is placed in the system to provide lubrication for the compressor. Since Refrigerant-12 has great affinity (attraction) for the oil, a certain amount circulates through the system. Viscosity rating will often be 500 or 525. Refrigeration oil is highly refined and must be ABSOLUTELY FREE of moisture.

DISCHARGE AND SUCTION SERVICE VALVES

All automobile air conditioning systems provide discharge and suction service valves. These valves permit the system to be evacuated (emptied), as well as charged (filled) and checked with pressure gauges.

Fig. 22-30 pictures one type of service valve. Sketch 1 shows the valve in a position for evacuating. Number 2 is the operating position. Number 3 is the position used for charging.

Fig. 22-28. Schematic showing refrigerant cycle for a CCOT (cycling clutch orifice tube) system. Note cycling switch. (Cadillac)

529

Fig. 22-29. Magnetic clutch. Pulley revolves whenever engine is running. When current is passed through electromagnet coil, magnetic pull draws armature plate against pulley, driving compressor. (Pontiac)

Fig. 22-30. Typical service valve. 1—Evacuating position. 2—Position for operating. 3—Charging position. Arrows indicate refrigerant flow in the various positions. (American Motors)

Fig. 22-31. Typical Schrader type service valve.

Some systems employ a spring-loaded valve, called a Schrader valve instead of the discharge and suction service valve illustrated in Fig. 22-30. Connections can be made quickly and easily. Fig. 22-31.

SYSTEM PROTECTION—SUPERHEAT SWITCH

A SUPERHEAT SWITCH may be used to prevent damage to the compressor in the event of overheating from loss of refrigerant, loss of oil, etc.

The switch, Fig. 22-32, located in the compressor, senses both system pressure and temperature. When the temperature increases, the sensing tube, filled with a special refrigerant R-114, causes the diaphragm assembly to expand outward thus forcing the electrical contact against the terminal. This completes an electrical circuit.

Low system pressure also affects the closing of the contact. Normal pressure, working on both sides of the diaphragm, tends to make it harder for it to ex-

pand under heat conditions. When system pressure is low, system heat will force the contacts closed even faster. Fig. 22-32.

When the superheat switch contacts close, they complete a circuit causing a flow of electricity through a special thermal fuse. Fig. 22-33. The current causes a heater resistor to heat up. In a very short time, the resistor generates enough heat to melt the fuse. When the fuse melts, current to the compressor clutch is broken and the compressor stops. Study the superheat switch circuit in Fig. 22-33.

COMPRESSOR DISCHARGE PRESSURE SWITCH

A COMPRESSOR DISCHARGE PRESSURE SWITCH is sometimes located in the high pressure discharge line. If discharge pressure drops below a specified level (around 37 psi, 255 kPa), the switch will OPEN and shut off the compressor. Fig. 22-34.

Fig. 22-34. When compressor discharge pressure drops to a specific level, this pressure sensitive switch will turn off compressor. (Harrison)

SENSING TUBE PRESSURE
SYSTEM PRESSURE

Fig. 22-32. Cross section of a superheat switch. Heat causes fluid in sensing tube to expand, thus expanding diaphragm. This will close electrical contact. (Chevrolet)

The switch can also shut off the compressor when ambient air temperature is low (around 25°F, −3.9°C). This is caused by the cold temperature reducing the condenser pressure.

HIGH PRESSURE RELIEF VALVE

The system can be protected against excessive pressure by using a PRESSURE RELIEF VALVE. Fig. 22-35 illustrates one form of relief valve. This unit is located on the receiver-dehydrator. When

system pressure exceeds a certain level (450 to 500 psi, 3 103 to 3 448 kPa), the relief valve will open and vent refrigerant into the atmosphere. As soon as the pressure is relieved, the valve closes.

Another form of pressure relief unit utilizes a pressure sensitive switching device that will shut off the compressor when system pressure exceeds proper limits (around 400 psi or 2 760 kPa on many systems). The switch will close and complete the circuit when the pressure drops to about 290 psi (2 000 kPa).

FAN SWITCH

Some air conditioning systems employ an auxiliary fan in front of the condenser. This will provide additional air flow during hot weather, prolonged idling, etc., conditions. Other autos use an electric fan only, for both condenser and radiator cooling.

Fan switches can be designed as pressure sensitive

Fig. 22-33. Superheat switch compressor protection circuit. Note thermal fuse. (Harrison)

Fig. 22-35. Two possible locations for a high pressure relief valve. Valve protects against excessive system pressure.

or heat sensitive. The pressure type senses system pressure and turns on the electric fan at a specified pressure. The heat sensitive switch activates the electric fan by sensing radiator coolant temperature.

OTHER CONTROLS—WOT SWITCH

Some engines install a WOT (wide open throttle) switch that shuts off the compressor during wide open throttle operation. This relives the engine of the compressor load, thus aiding acceleration and pulling power.

AMBIENT AIR TEMPERATURE CUTOFF SWITCH

The AMBIENT AIR TEMPERATURE CUTOFF SWITCH shuts off the compressor when ambient (surrounding) air temperature drops below a certain point, (around 35°F, 2°C). This will eliminate unneeded compressor operation when air temperatures are low enough.

AIR CONDITIONER AIR FLOW

Many air conditioning systems incorporate a hot water heating core in the setup. By means of a control door, the air can be made to travel through either the heater core or the evaporator. Control of the door may be by manually operated dash controls or, as is becoming increasingly popular, controlled by automatic means.

Some systems pass all air through the evaporator core first. If heating is necessary, heated air is blended in to produce the required outlet air temperature. This method has the advantage of dehumidifying the air, which prevents window fogging during damp weather conditions.

Most systems are arranged so that three air settings are possible:
1. Air within car can be recirculated.
2. All air entering car can be drawn from outside.
3. Some outside air can be mixed with inside air that is recirculating.

A schematic illustrating a typical system air flow pattern is pictured in Fig. 22-36. Note that all incoming air, recirculated or outside, is first passed through the evaporator core. Keep in mind that air flow control systems vary widely depending upon the complexity of the individual system.

AIR CONDITIONING WIRING CIRCUITS

Depending upon the system used, the air conditioning system wiring circuit can vary from relatively simple to reasonably complex. When working on the system or system wiring, follow manufacturer's recommendations for the exact model at hand. Use a wiring diagram when required. Fig. 22-37 illustrates one type.

SUMMARY

Cooling is a process of removing heat from a given object.

Heat is a form of energy that can affect a

Fig. 22-36. Schematic showing air conditioning system air flow. Air amount, direction, blending, etc., are controlled by ducts, doors, flaps, louvers, speed control switches, vacuum controls, etc.

Fig. 22-37. Typical wiring diagram for one specific air conditioning system. Such diagrams are very important in diagnostic and service work.

temperature change in any object.

Heat produces various effects. Expansion, contraction, vaporization, burning, freezing, etc., result from the removal or addition of heat.

Heat transfer occurs through convection, conduction, or radiation. Heat always transfers from a hot object to a colder object.

Latent (hidden) heat is the heat absorbed during a

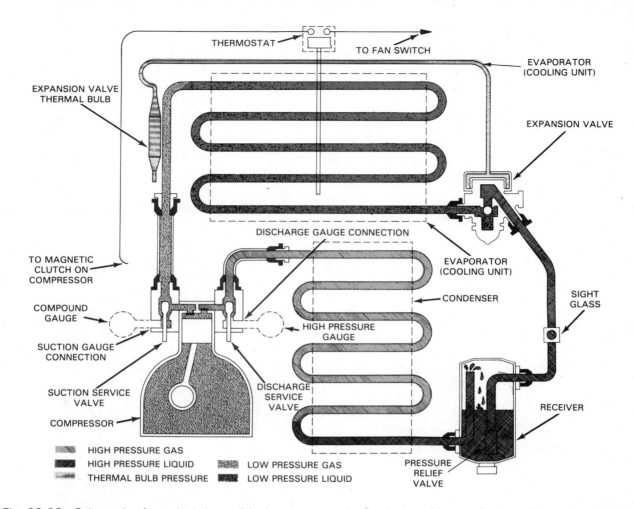

Fig. 22-38. Schematic of a typical air conditioning system cycle. Study the refrigerant flow carefully and note the various changes (high pressure liquid, low pressure liquid, etc.) in the refrigerant as it flows through system. Can you explain the function of all parts and how they operate?

change of state. When water is changed from a liquid to a vapor, a great deal of heat can be applied without a change in temperature. This latent heat is hidden in the vapor.

Refrigerant-12 is the substance used in refrigeration systems. It boils at −21.7°F (−29.9°C) at zero pressure (sea level). It is colorless, tasteless, and heavier than air in either the liquid or vapor state. It must be handled with great care.

The automotive refrigeration system consists basically of a receiver, sight glass, expansion valve, evaporator, suction throttling valve, compressor, muffler, and condenser.

With the system operating, high pressure refrigerant, in a liquid state, collects in the receiver-dehydrator. The receiver-dehydrator removes impurities and moisture from the R-12. From there, the refrigerant moves to the expansion valve. The expansion valve reduces pressure and meters a certain amount of low pressure liquid refrigerant into the evaporator.

As the low pressure liquid refrigerant enters the evaporator, it is warmed by air passing over the coils. As it moves through the evaporator, it begins to boil. More and more heat is absorbed from the passing air.

When refrigerant reaches the evaporator outlet, it is completely vaporized. The vapor is laden with hidden or latent heat.

From the evaporator, the refrigerant vapor is sometimes forced through a suction throttling valve. The suction throttling valve will maintain a regulated evaporator outlet pressure to control evaporator temperature.

After leaving the suction throttling valve, the refrigerant vapor is drawn into the compressor. The compressor raises the pressure of the vapor and, at the same time, causes a rapid rise in temperature. The vapor, on its way to the condenser from the compressor, is under 100 to 250 psi (689 to 1 724 kPa) pressure and is hotter than the ambient (surrounding) air temperature. It still retains all the latent heat of vaporization that it picked up on its way through the evaporator.

When the hot, high pressure refrigerant gas or vapor enters the condenser, it begins to give up heat to the airstream moving over the condenser fins. By the time it passes through the condenser, it has lost sufficient heat to return to the liquid state. Still under heavy pressure from the compressor, the liquid refrigerant travels from the condenser into the

534

receiver-dehydrator. From the receiver-dehydrator, it starts another cycle through the system.

This continual cycling of liquid refrigerant to the evaporator, where it vaporizes and is drawn out, compressed and condensed, produces a steady cooling effect on the air passing through the evaporator core. In this way, heat is taken from air entering the car and is discharged into the atmosphere at the condenser.

The system cools, dehumidifies, and filters air passing into the car. Follow the path of refrigerant through the system. Figs. 22-25, 22-27, 22-28, 22-38.

The superheat switch protects the compressor from excessive heat and system refrigerant loss. The compressor discharge switch is also used to shut off the compressor during a period of low discharge line pressure.

System pressure relief can be accomplished by a pressure sensitive valve or by a pressure sensitive switch.

Fans can be used to provide additional condenser cooling during high heat periods.

Switches can also be used to shut off the compressor during heavy acceleration and during times when ambient air temperature is below certain limits.

Refrigerant-12 is dangerous. Observe all safety precautions when handling drums, or when working on or near the system.

Good mechanics are NEVER satisfied with present levels of skill and knowledge. They CONSTANTLY seek to improve their skills and background of technical information. This requires a good deal of study, listening, and observing.

Take advantage of special automotive classes, read quality automotive magazines and journals, maintain an up-to-date library of top-notch books in your field. Above all, never miss an opportunity to observe, question or listen to, other mechanics in the field. Remember: WHEN YOU THINK YOU KNOW IT ALL—YOU STOP GROWING. IT WILL NOT BE LONG UNTIL THE JOB AT HAND STANDS LIKE A GIANT IN RELATION TO YOUR ABILITY TO PERFORM IT. WHEN THIS HAPPENS, YOUR USEFULNESS AS A MECHANIC IS GONE.

KNOW THESE TERMS

Conduction, Convection, Radiation, BTU, Latent heat, Refrigerant-12, Receiver-dehydrator, Sight glass, Expansion valve, Evaporator, Suction throttle valve, Compressor, Condenser, Magnetic clutch, Muffler, Refrigerant oil, Service valves.

REVIEW QUESTIONS—CHAPTER 22

1. A good air conditioning system will_____, _____ and _____ the air entering the car.

2. What do you really mean when you refer to something as being cold?
3. Name several readily observed effects produced by the addition or removal of heat.
4. What is heat?
5. What is meant by Btu?
6. How is the law of latent heat of vaporization utilized in the refrigeration system?
7. _____ affects both the vaporization and condensation temperature of refrigerant.
8. Heat is transferred from one object to another by _____, _____, and _____.
9. Heat is transferred from a hot object to the colder one. True or False?
10. What is Refrigerant-12?
11. Of what use is the receiver in the system?
12. The sight glass makes it possible to visually inspect the refrigerant for the presence of _____ or _____.
13. The expansion valve performs two important functions. Name them.
14. Explain the function of the evaporator.
15. Why is it necessary to have a compressor in the system?
16. The condenser is used to change the refrigerant from a liquid into a vapor. True or False?
17. Describe the use and action of the magnetic clutch used on the compressor.
18. Name two methods of preventing the evaporator coils from icing up.
19. Of what use are the discharge and suction service valves?
20. List nine safety precautions to be observed when working on or near the air conditioning system.
21. Starting at the receiver-dehydrator, explain just what happens as the refrigerant makes a complete circuit through the system. Describe the areas in which the refrigerant is a vapor and the areas in which it is a liquid.
22. The suction throttling valve is located:
   a. At the inlet to the evaporator.
   b. At the outlet of the evaporator.
   c. At the inlet to the condenser.
   d. At the outlet of the compressor.
23. To provide additional acceleration and pulling power, a switch is often used to break the circuit to the _____.
24. What is the purpose of the superheat switch?
25. Some systems use an ambient air switch to turn off the evaporator when the weather is hot. True or False?
26. Of what use is the electric condenser fan?
27. The orifice type expansion tube reduces refrigerant pressure before it enters the:
   a. Compressor
   b. Condenser
   c. Evaporator
   d. None of the above

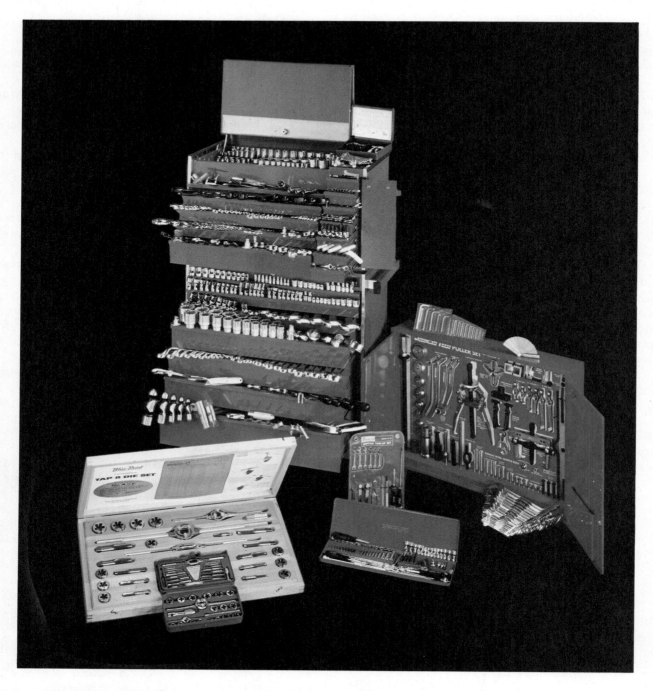

A set of quality hand tools is a must for the mechanic. How many of these tools can you identify?
(Snap-on Tools)

Chapter 23

TOOL IDENTIFICATION, TOOL USE

After studying this chapter, you will be able to:
■ Identify the most common automotive tools.
■ Describe the proper use of automotive tools.
■ List the safety rules to follow when using certain tools.
■ Select the correct tool for the job.

Today's mechanics must be familiar with and understand the use of a large number of tools. Proper tool selection will improve both the quality and speed of any repair operation. Many repair jobs, in fact, would be exceedingly difficult to perform without the right tools for the job.

Good mechanics own a wide selection of quality tools. They constantly strive to add to their collection and take great pride in keeping their tools clean and orderly.

WHAT TO LOOK FOR IN TOOLS

Some mechanics prefer one brand of tools; some, another. You will find, however, that mechanics agree on several important features that will be found in quality tools.

TOOL MATERIAL

The better tools are made of high strength alloy steel and, as such, can be made without a great deal of bulk. These tools are light and easy to use in tight quarters. Heavy, "fat" tools are useless on many jobs.

The quality alloy also gives the tool great strength. Its working areas will stand abuse, and useful life will be greatly extended. Quality material makes it possible for the manufacturer to give a good quarantee on the tool.

TOOL CONSTRUCTION

Quality tools receive superior heat treating. Their openings and working surfaces are held to closer tolerances. Sharp edges are removed and the tools are carefully polished. This imparts a finish that is easy to

wipe clean and a tool that is more comfortable to use.

Tools worthy of a good mechanic will be slim, efficient and properly designed for the job at hand. They will be strong, easy to clean and a pleasure to use. A good guarantee plus efficient service and parts replacement will be offered. This can be an important feature; otherwise usable tools often have to be discarded due to the loss or failure of some minor part that is no longer available.

REMEMBER: In buying tools, you usually get just what you pay for. Fine tools are a good investment.

USE OF TOOLS

Use tools designed for the job at hand. Keep your tools orderly and clean in a good, roll-type cabinet, tool chest and "tote" tray (a small tray that may be carried to the job to keep a few selected tools close at hand). This will assist you in keeping tools in good shape and readily available.

Any tool subjected to rust should be cleaned and lightly oiled. Cutting tools, such as files and chisels, should be separated to preserve the cutting edges. Delicate measuring tools should be placed in protective containers. Keep heavy tools by themselves, and arrange tools so those most often used are handy.

Repeat—KEEP YOUR TOOLS CLEAN. You cannot hope to successfully assemble a fine piece of machinery with grubby tools. The slightest bit of dirt or abrasive that finds its way into moving parts can create havoc when the unit is placed in operation. Tools are a good indication of a mechanic's worth. Dirty, beat up and jumbled tools reveal that the owner has a lot to learn. The quality of this mechanic's finished work is likely to be just as shabby as the tools used on the job.

TYPES OF TOOLS

This chapter does not attempt to cover all the tools used in the automotive trade. Large garages often utilize hundreds of special tools designed for specific jobs, models and units. Basic tools commonly used will be discussed.

HAMMERS

Mechanics find great use for the ball peen, plastic-tipped and brass-tipped hammers. The ball peen is used for general striking work and is available in weights ranging from a couple of ounces to several pounds. Brass and plastic-tipped hammers are used where there is danger of the steel ball peen marring the surface. Fig. 23-1.

Fig. 23-1. Several types of hammers. A—Ball peen. B—Upholstery. C—Plastic-tipped. D—Brass-tipped. (Snap-on Tools)

CAUTION!

BE CAREFUL WHEN USING A HAMMER. DO NOT SWING THE HAMMER IN A DIRECTION THAT WOULD ALLOW IT TO STRIKE SOMEONE IF IT SLIPS FROM YOUR GRASP. KEEP THE HAMMER HANDLE TIGHT IN THE HAMMER HEAD, AND KEEP THE HANDLE CLEAN AND DRY.

CHISELS

Several sizes and types of chisels are essential for cutting bolts, rivets, etc., Fig. 23-2, A. When chiseling, grasp the chisel firmly and strike it squarely. Attempt to keep the fingertips around the chisel body to prevent it from flying from your grasp. On the other hand, avoid grasping it too tightly because a poorly aimed blow may cause serious injury to the hand. You may want to use a chisel holder in some situa-

Fig. 23-2. A—Note chisel and punch assortment. B—Chisel holder, by holding punch or chisel, protects hands when striking with hammer. (Snap-on Tools)

tions. The holder will allow the use of large hammers and greater striking force without the chance of injuring your fingers or hand. One type of chisel holder is shown in Fig. 23-2, B.

Keep the cutting edge of the chisel sharp, and the striking surface chamfered (edges properly tapered) to reduce the danger of mushroom (smashed end) particles flying about. Fig. 23-3. Wear goggles when using a chisel.

The flat cold chisel, illustrated in Fig. 23-3, is used for general cutting. Special chisels such as the cape, half-round and diamond point are used when their shape fits a definite need.

PUNCHES

A starting punch is a punch that tapers to a flat tip. It is used in starting to punch out pins, and to drive out rivets after the heads have been cut off.

Once the pin has been started, the starting punch (because of its taper) can no longer be used. A drift punch, which has the same diameter for most of its length, is used to complete the job.

A pin punch is similar to a drift punch but is smaller in diameter. Fig. 23-4.

Fig. 23-3. Keep chisels in good condition. Chisel in A is in a dangerous condition. B is same chisel after grinding.

Fig. 23-4. Starting and drift punches. Starting punch A is used to start rivet from hole. Drift punch B is used to drive rivet from hole.

An aligning punch, which has a long, gradual taper, is useful to shift parts and bring corresponding holes into alignment. Fig. 23-5.

A center punch is used to mark the material before drilling. It leaves a small, V-shaped hole that assists in aligning the drill bit. A center punch may also be used to mark parts so they will be assembled in the correct positions. Fig. 23-6.

Fig. 23-5. Aligning punch. This punch is shoved through holes in A, then pulled upright and shoved deeper into holes in B. This lines up the two holes.

Fig. 23-6. Center punch is used for marking parts and starting drills.

Be careful when sharpening chisels and punches. Keep the edges at the proper angle and avoid turning them blue (overheating) on the grinder. Overheating will draw (remove) the temper and render the tip soft and uselss. Grind slowly and keep quenching (dipping) the tool in water.

CAUTION!

WEAR GOGGLES WHEN GRINDING OR STRIKING A CHISEL OR PUNCH.

FILES

Commonly used files are the flat mill, half-round, round, square, and triangular. All come in different sizes and with fine-to-coarse cutting edges. Some files have one or more cutting edges. Some files have one or more safe (surface with no cutting edges) sides.

A file should have a handle firmly affixed to the tang. The handle gives a firm grip, and it eliminates the danger of the sharp tang piercing the hand. A typical mill file is shown in Fig. 23-7.

FILE CUT AND SHAPE

When a file has a single series of cutting edges that are parallel to each other, the file is referred to as a single-cut file. A file with two sets of cutting edges that cross at an angle is called a double-cut file. See Fig. 23-8.

A file, from rough to smooth, depends on the number and size of the cuts. Fig. 23-9 illustrates several classifications of cut for both single and double-cut files.

Common file shapes are illustrated in Fig. 23-10. The thin, flat, point file also shown in Fig. 23-10 is used to file distributor and regulator points.

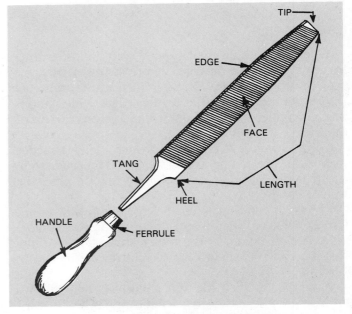

Fig. 23-7. Typical mill file. Single-cut.

Fig. 23-8. Single and double-cut files.

Fig. 23-9. File cuts. Three different file cuts: bastard, second-cut and smooth. (Simonds File Co.)

USING A FILE

When filing, hold the file with both hands. On the forward cut, bear down with pressure sufficient to produce good cutting. On the return stroke, raise the file to avoid battering the cutting edges. One hand is on the handle, while the other hand grasps the tip of the file.

Control the file to prevent it from rocking. Practice is essential. Remember that a file is NOT a crude tool. In the hands of an expert, a file becomes a precision tool.

Choose a file that is correct for the job at hand. Use a coarse cut file on soft material to prevent clogging. A slight drag on the return stroke, when filing soft material, will help keep the cutting teeth clear of filings.

Chalking (rubbing file with chalk) will help remove oil from the file and keep it from clogging. A file card (short bristle wire hand brush) is helpful in cleaning

Fig. 23-10. Nine common file shapes, handy for the mechanic.

the file. An occasional tap of the handle will also help.

Keep file clean and free of oil or grease. Always use a handle! Install by striking handle, file in place, on a solid object. Do not hammer on file; it may break. Some handles screw on.

When you have finished filing, place the file in a dry spot, protected from contact with other files and tools. A good file is a fine tool. Treat it with respect, and you will do more and better work.

There are many files for special purposes, such as those used in body and fender repair. Swiss needle files are miniature files that come in almost all shapes and are very handy for delicate operations.

ROTARY FILES

A selection of rotary files is often found in the mechanic's toolbox. These files are designed to be chucked in an electric hand drill. They are useful in working in "blind" holes, etc., where a normal file is useless. Fig. 23-11.

DRILLS

A twist drill is used by mechanics for drilling holes. Twist drills are available in fractional inch sizes of 1/4 in., 1/2 in., etc. (6.5 mm, 13.0 mm, etc.), letter sizes (A, B, to Z) and number sizes (wire gauge, numbers 1 to 80).

For general auto shop use a set of fractional size drills (29 drills from 1/16 to 1/2 or 1.5 to 13.0 mm), plus a set of number drills (totaling 60, 1 to 60), will usually suffice. A number 1 drill has a diameter of .228 in. The number 60 drill has a diameter of .040 in.

Twist drills with a straight shank are used in hand drills and portable electric drills. For heavy duty power drills, the taper shank drill is often used. See Fig. 23-12.

SHANK CHUCKS IN ELECTRIC HAND DRILL

Fig. 23-11. Rotary file.

Fig. 23-12. Drill shanks.

Drills are commonly furnished in carbon steel and high speed steel. Carbon drills will require more frequent sharpening, and they will not last nearly as long as high speed steel drills.

SHARPENING DRILLS

Different cutting angles are used to make drills more efficient in various metals. Lip clearance angles also vary.

When sharpening a drill, keep in mind that both cutting lips must be the same length and angle. Avoid overheating the drill. If a carbon drill turns blue from overheating, it will be worthless until the blue area of the drill is ground off.

The general purpose drill should have the lips cut at 59 to 60 deg. to the centerline of the drill. Lip clearance should be around 12 deg. Fig. 23-13.

Proper drill grinding must be learned by practice. Use an old drill to practice on. A simple drill grinding gauge is pictured in Fig. 23-14. This gauge will help

you maintain proper lip length and angle.

A drill can be sharpened on either the side or face of the grinder. Start the cut at the leading edge of the lip and finish at the heel. Keep the shank of the drill slightly lower than the tip. The cut is taken with a slight rocking, pivoting motion.

Without starting the grinder, place a new drill against the stone. Move it through the sharpening motion and see how well the stone follows the lip angles. Try your skill on an old drill, then carefully compare it with a new one. Keep at it until you have mastered this skill. If your drills are correctly sharpened, they will cut readily without grabbing. Both lips will produce equal amounts of metal chips. Fig. 23-15.

USING DRILLS

Always securely fasten the piece to be drilled. Chuck the drill, Fig. 23-16, tightly and center punch the spot to be drilled. After the drill has started, apply a small quantity of cutting oil. Oil will make cutting easier, faster and will lengthen drill life. When drilling thin metal or cast iron, oil is not required.

Hold the drill at the proper angle and apply enough pressure to achieve good cutting. When the drill is ready to break through the work, let up on the pressure to avoid grabbing. On thin metal, hold the work down, as well as keep it from turning. Thin work attempts to "climb" up the drill.

SAFETY HINTS

Large portable electric drills develop considerable torque, Fig. 23-17. Make certain you have a firm grip

Fig. 23-13. Drill lip angles. Lengths at A must be equal. Angles should be the same on both sides.

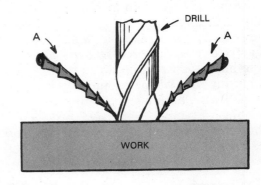

Fig. 23-15. Drill cutting properly. Chips, A, of equal size indicates both lips are cutting.

Fig. 23-14. Using a drill gauge. Gauge checks angle and length of tip. (Starrett)

Fig. 23-16. Twist drills.

Fig. 23-17. Portable electric drills. Note different handle arrangements.

Fig. 23-19. Tapered reamers. (Snap-on Tools)

before engaging the drill.

Never install or remove a drill in a chuck without unplugging the cord. If it is accidentally started when you are grasping the drill or the chuck key, you could be injured.

Keep loose clothing (sleeves, pant legs, ties, etc.) away from the drill.

Always secure the work firmly. If the drill grabs and the work is loose, the work can swing around with a vicious cutting force.

Wear goggles when grinding drills.

Never use a power tool that is not properly grounded, and do not use power tools when standing on a wet surface.

REAMERS

Reamers are used to enlarge or shape holes. They produce holes that are more accurate in size and smoother than those produced by drills. The reamer should not be used to make deep cuts in metal. A cut of a few thousandths of an inch at a time is all that should be attempted.

Some reamers are adjustable in size, while others are of a fixed size. Tapered reamers are handy for removing burrs, assisting in tap starting, etc.

Use cutting oil when reaming. Always turn a reamer clockwise, both when entering and when leaving the hole.

Several different types of reamers are shown in Figs. 23-18 and 23-19.

Fig. 23-18. Reamers. A—Adjustable. B, C—Adjustable with a pilot to help align reamer. D—Kingpin reamer. E—Valve guide reamer. (Snap-on Tools)

IMPACT WRENCH

A power-operated (electric or air) impact wrench is a must for fast work. Parts can be removed and replaced in a fraction of the time required with hand wrenches.

Although the impact wrench in no way replaces hand-operated wrenches, it can be used often and should be included in the tool collection. Various sizes are available. Fig. 23-20 pictures an air-operated impact wrench.

HACKSAWS

The hand hacksaw is a much used tool. It is excellent for cutting bolts, tubing, etc.

Hacksaw blades are generally furnished with 14, 18, 24, or 32 teeth per inch. The 14-tooth blade is handy for cutting fairly thick articles. The 18-tooth blade handles work of medium thickness. The 24-tooth blade is best used on heavy sheet metal,

Fig. 23-20. An impact (power) wrench is a must for every mechanic. This wrench is air-operated. (Skil)

medium tubing, brass, copper, etc. For thin sheet metal and thinwall tubing, use a 32-tooth blade. Fig. 23-21 illustrates typical work for each type of blade.

Blades are made of various material. Some blades are hardened across the full blade width; others have only the tooth edge hardened.

When cutting though alloy steels, select one of the better quality blades, such as high speed (tungsten) steel. These will outwear several of the cheaper blades.

Fig. 23-21. The type of work to be cut determines the best blade tooth per inch selection. These are typical. (Crescent Tools)

USING THE HACKSAW

When hacksawing, keep the blade tight in the saw frame. Make certain the teeth cutting edges face away from the handle. Fig. 23-22. See that the work is held securely to prevent slippage that would result in a broken blade.

Grasp the hacksaw frame firmly, one hand on the grip and the other on the front. Apply enough pressure on the forward stroke to insure cutting, then, raise the blade slightly on the return stroke. Avoid starting the cut on a sharp edge; this may chip the saw teeth.

Try to saw at a speed that will produce 40 to 50 strokes per minute (forward strokes). A little oil will help.

SPECIAL HACKSAWS

The auto mechanic will sometimes find use for a special hacksaw that allows cutting in restricted quarters. A hole saw, operated by an electric drill is

Fig. 23-22. When using a hacksaw, blade must be tight, teeth must face away from handle. Hold work securely and cut at 40—50 strokes per minute.   (Starrett)

also handy for drilling large holes in thin sheet metal. Fig. 23-23.

A conventional hacksaw, as well as two special, tight-quarter saws, are pictured in Fig. 23-24.

VISE

A vise is a work-holding device. A typical bench vise is shown in Fig. 23-25. If the work is easily marred, place special copper covers over the serrated steel jaws.

Fig. 23-23. Hole saws are handy for cutting openings in thin metal, as well as for making large diameter holes.

Fig. 23-24. Hacksaw types. A, B, C—Standard type hacksaw frames. D—Thin junior type for close quarters. E—Jab type will hold broken blade sections. It is handy in restricted areas. F—Hole saw used to drill holes in thin sheet metal.

Fig. 23-25. Typical bench vise.

Keep your vise clean. Oil all working parts. Do not use a vise for an anvil, and do not hammer the handle to tighten the jaws on the work.

TAPS

Taps are used for cutting internal threads. Fig. 23-26. For general garage use, a set of taper, plug, bottom, and machine screw taps should be provided. Each type of tap will have to be provided in both National Fine and National Coarse threads, as well as in the various sizes, 1/4, 5/16, etc.

The taper tap is used to tap completely through the hole. Notice that it has a long gradual taper that allows the tap to start easily.

The plug tap is used to tap threads partway through.

The bottoming tap is used to cut threads all the way to the bottom of a blind hole. The plug tap should precede the bottoming tap, since the bottoming tap will not start well.

The plug tap is the most widely used. It will work satisfactorily, except in the case of running threads completely to the bottom of a blind hole.

Fig. 23-26. Four kinds of taps.

The machine screw tap handles the small diameter, fine thread jobs. Fig. 23-26.

USING THE TAP

After determining the diameter, the number of threads per inch of the screw or stud that will enter the tapped hole, use a tap drill size chart to find what size hole to drill.

For example, suppose you find that you want a threaded hole for a 3/8 stud with coarse (National Coarse) threads. Referring to the chart in Fig. 23-27, you will find the 3/8 N.C. will have 16 threads per inch. Looking directly across from the 3/8 size, you will find that the tap drill size is listed as 5/16. This means that for a 3/8 N.D. stud, you must drill a hole 5/16 in diameter.

If the hole is to be tapped partway through, use a 3/8 x 16 N.C. plug tap. Place the tap in a tap handle, and carefully start the tap in the hole. Place some tap lubricant on the tap. After threading the tap in one or two turns, back the tap up about a quarter to one-half turn to break the chip. Repeat this process as your tapping continues.

Be careful the hole does not clog with chips. It may be necessary to withdraw the tap and remove the chips. Taps are quite brittle. Use them with care, and make certain you use the proper size tap drill.

TAP DRILL SIZES
Recommended for AMERICAN NATIONAL SCREW THREAD PITCHES

COARSE STANDARD THREAD (N. C.) — Formerly U. S. Standard Thread

Sizes	Threads Per Inch	Outside Diameter of Screw	Tap Drill Sizes	Decimal Equivalent of Drill
1	64	.073	53	0.0595
2	56	.086	50	0.0700
3	48	.099	47	0.0785
4	40	.112	43	0.0890
5	40	.125	38	0.1015
6	32	.138	36	0.1065
8	32	.164	29	0.1360
10	24	.190	25	0.1495
12	24	.216	16	0.1770
1/4	20	.250	7	0.2010
5/16	18	.3125	F	0.2570
3/8	16	.375	5/16	0.3125
7/16	14	.4375	U	0.3680
1/2	13	.500	27/64	0.4219
9/16	12	.5625	31/64	0.4843
5/8	11	.625	17/32	0.5312
3/4	10	.750	21/32	0.6562
7/8	9	.875	49/64	0.7656
1	8	1.000	7/8	0.875
1-1/8	7	1.125	63/64	0.9843
1-1/4	7	1.250	1-7/64	1.1093

FINE STANDARD THREAD (N. F.) — Formerly S.A.E. Thread

Sizes	Threads Per Inch	Outside Diameter of Screw	Tap Drill Sizes	Decimal Equivalent of Drill
0	80	.060	3/64	0.0469
1	72	.073	53	0.0595
2	64	.086	50	0.0700
3	56	.099	45	0.0820
4	48	.112	42	0.0935
5	44	.125	37	0.1040
6	40	.138	33	0.1130
8	36	.164	29	0.1360
10	32	.190	21	0.1590
12	28	.216	14	0.1820
1/4	28	.250	3	0.2130
5/16	24	.3125	I	0.2720
3/8	24	.375	Q	0.3320
7/16	20	.4375	25/64	0.3906
1/2	20	.500	29/64	0.4531
9/16	18	.5625	0.5062	0.5062
5/8	18	.625	0.5687	0.5687
3/4	16	.750	11/16	0.6875
7/8	14	.875	0.8020	0.8020
1	14	1.000	0.9274	0.9274
1-1/8	12	1.125	1-3/64	1.0468
1-1/4	12	1.250	1-11/64	1.1718

SPECIAL THREAD (N. S.)

Sizes	Threads Per Inch	Outside Diameter of Screw	Tap Drill Sizes	Decimal Equivalent of Drill
1	56	.0730	54	0.0550
4	32	.1120	45	0.0820
4	36	.1120	44	0.0860
6	36	.1380	34	0.1110
8	40	.1640	28	0.1405
10	30	.1900	22	0.1570
12	32	.2160	13	0.1850
14	20	.2420	10	0.1935
14	24	.2420	7	0.2010
1/16	64	.0625	3/64	0.0469
3/32	48	.0938	49	0.0730
1/8	40	.1250	38	0.1015
5/32	32	.1563	1/8	0.1250
5/32	36	.1563	30	0.1285
3/16	24	.1875	26	0.1470
3/16	32	.1875	22	0.1570
7/32	24	.2188	16	0.1770
7/32	32	.2188	12	0.1890
1/4	24	.250	4	0.2090
1/4	27	.250	3	0.2130
1/4	32	.250	7/32	0.2187
5/16	20	.3125	17/64	0.2656
5/16	27	.3125	J	0.2770
5/16	32	.3125	9/32	0.2812
3/8	20	.375	21/64	0.3281
3/8	27	.375	R	0.3390
7/16	24	.4375	X	0.3970
7/16	27	.4375	Y	0.4040
1/2	12	.500	27/64	0.4219
1/2	24	.500	29/64	0.4531
1/2	27	.500	15/32	0.4687
9/16	27	.5625	17/32	0.5312
5/8	12	.625	35/64	0.5469
5/8	27	.625	19/32	0.5937
11/16	11	.6875	19/32	0.5937
11/16	16	.6875	5/8	0.6250
3/4	12	.750	43/64	0.6719
3/4	27	.750	23/32	0.7187
7/8	12	.875	51/64	0.7969
7/8	18	.875	53/64	0.8281
7/8	27	.875	27/32	0.8437
1	12	1.000	59/64	0.9219
1	27	1.000	31/32	0.9687

Fig. 23-27. Tap drill size chart.   (South Bend Lathe)

What size hole would you drill to tap threads for a 1/2 N.F. bolt? (Answer 29/64.) Figs. 23-27 and 23-28.

DIES

Dies are used to cut external threads. A die of the correct size is placed in a diestock (handle) and turned. Use lubricant, back up every one or two turns, and keep free of chips.

Often dies are adjustable in size, so you can enlarge or reduce (slightly) the outside diameter of a threaded area.

Both taps and dies should be cleaned, lightly oiled and placed in a protective box for storage.

SPECIAL TAPS AND DIES

The mechanic will also find use for a few special taps and dies as illustrated in Fig. 23-29. One form of rethreading tool is shown in A. It is placed on the thread and turned. B shows an internal thread chaser used to clean up dirty or damaged internal threads. A thread restorer, C, is handy for quickly reconditioning external threads. The axle rethreader, D, is placed around the good thread area, clamped shut, and is then turned back over the damaged area.

Nut or rethreading dies, E and F, can be turned on a damaged thread. An ordinary box wrench can be used to turn them. G and H show spark plug hole taps. These are very handy to clean up damaged or carboned plug hole threads. A combination tap and die set for tube flare fittings is illustrated in J. A combination tap and die set is pictured in K.

CLEANING TOOLS

Various cleaning tools are pictured in Fig. 23-30. These different brushes and scrapers provide valuable assistance in the thorough cleaning of parts.

Carbon cleaning brushes that may be operated in a 1/4 in. electric drill are shown in Fig. 23-31. A mandrel, D, is also shown. It is used to hold a small wire wheel.

Fig. 23-28. Tapping operation must be performed carefully. Keep tap square with hole; use lubrication when required and keep backing tap to break chip. Use proper size tap drill.

Fig. 23-29. Taps and dies.

Fig. 23-30. Cleaning tools. A—Sparkproof bristle brush. B—Wire scratch brush. C—Wire brush and scraper combined. D—Flexible fingers carbon scraper. E—Rigid carbon scraper. F, G, H—Scraper blades. J, K—Putty knives.

Fig. 23-31. Power carbon cleaning brushes. D is a mandrel that may be chucked in the electric hand drill to operate a wire wheel.

A wire wheel that may be used on a portable electric drill or mounted on a grinder mandrel is shown in Fig. 23-32.

CAUTION!

ALWAYS WEAR GOGGLES WHEN USING POWER GRINDERS OR WIRE WHEELS.

PLIERS

A mechanic needs a good variety of pliers. Study the pliers shown in Figs. 23-33 through 23-36. Learn the names and uses of each pliers.

Never use pliers in place of a wrench. Use pliers designed for the job. Avoid cutting hardened parts

with your lineman, diagonal or other cutting pliers. Needle nose pliers are delicate; use them carefully.

SCREWDRIVERS

Screwdrivers of various lengths and types are required. The standard, Phillips, Reed and Prince,

Fig. 23-33. A—Needle nose pliers. B—Assorted pliers.

Fig. 23-34. Assorted pliers. A, B—Long nose diagonal cutters. C—Needle nose. D—Duck bill. E—Short needle nose. F—Cutter with long reach cutting jaws.

Fig. 23-32. Power wire wheel.

Fig. 23-35. Vise-grip pliers. A, B—Standard vise-grip. C—Vise-grip bending tool. D—Vise-grip C-clamp. E—Vise-grip welding pliers. F—High leverage cutter for wire and small bolts.

Fig. 23-36. Special purpose pliers. A—Hose clamp pliers. B—Parallel jaw lock ring pliers. C—Lock ring and snap ring pliers. D and E—Brake spring pliers.

Clutch, and Torx-bit tips will cover the various types of jobs ordinarily encountered when servicing cars.

It is wise to have in your tool kit several large and heavy types that will stand some prying and hammering.

The standard tip screwdriver is pictured in Fig. 23-37. It can have a round or square shank.

A number of Phillips tip screwdrivers are shown in Fig. 23-38. Note the stubby screwdriver. It is essential when working in close quarters.

The clutch tip or, as it is sometimes called, the "butterfly," is illustrated in Fig. 23-39.

A set of Reed and Prince tip screwdrivers is shown in Fig. 23-40. At first glance, it looks like a Phillips tip. Close study will show the two tips are of different design.

A Torx-bit type socket set is illustrated in Fig. 23-41. Note the shape of a Torx-bit.

Fig. 23-37. Standard tip screwdrivers.

Fig. 23-39. Clutch tip screwdrivers.

Fig. 23-38. Phillips tip screwdrivers.

Fig. 23-40. Reed and Prince tip screwdrivers.

Fig. 23-41. A—Torx-bit drivers which can be used with ratchets, speed handles, etc. They provide a very positive grip. B—Torx replacement bits. (Vaco Tools)

OTHER TYPES

An assortment of offset screwdrivers makes it easy to remove and drive screws in difficult areas. Look at Fig. 23-42.

The long, thin shank, electrical-type screwdriver is handy for working on small intricate assemblies. Another essential screwdriver is the type designed to hold screws while they are being started.

USING SCREWDRIVERS

As with all tools, use a screwdriver that is designed for the job. Unless the screwdriver is designed for the purpose, do not use a hammer or pry with it.

If the screwdriver tip becomes worn or damaged, grind it slowly to avoid overheating the metal. Attempt to retain the original shape. On the standard tip, do not grind a sharp taper. This will cause the screwdriver to ride up out of the slot.

CAUTION!

WHEN HOLDING SMALL UNITS IN THE HAND, DO NOT SHOVE DOWN ON THE SCREWDRIVER: IT MAY SLIP AND PIERCE YOUR HAND. IF WORKING ON ELECTRICAL EQUIPMENT, SHUT OFF THE CURRENT. WHERE IT IS IMPOSSIBLE TO SHUT OFF THE CURRENT, USE AN INSULATED (FULL LENGTH) SCREWDRIVER AND KEEP YOUR HANDS FREE OF ANY WIRES.

BOX END WRENCHES

The box end wrench is an excellent tool because it grips the nut on all sides. This reduces the chances of

Fig. 23-42. Offset screwdrivers.

slipping with resultant damage to the nut and possibly the hand.

A box wrench is designed with either a 6 or 12-point opening. For general use, the 12-point works well. It allows the wrench to be removed and replaced without moving the handle over such a long swing. For stubborn jobs, damaged nuts, or when there is danger of collapsing the nut, the 6-point will do a better job. It grips the nut across each flat, reducing slippage to a minimum.

The box end wrench is available in either a double offset or a 15 deg. angle offset. Sets in standard size openings, as well as standard lengths, will handle most jobs. Sets are available in midget length for small work in cramped areas. Each end on the box end is a different size.

CAREFUL!

IN USING ALL WRENCHES, PULL, DO NOT PUSH. IF YOU MUST PUSH ON THE WRENCH, PUSH WITH THE PALM OF THE HAND WITH THE FINGERS OUTSPREAD TO AVOID SMASHING THEM IF THE WRENCH SLIPS.

Fig. 23-43 shows several box end wrenches. Detail A has an extra deep offset for additional clearance. B

Fig. 23-43. Box end wrenches. A—Double offset, 12-point. B—Standard offset, 12-point. C and D—Standard offset, 6-point. These are short length box end wrenches.

is a typical double offset. C and D are double offset with 6-point openings. Can you see why the 6-point will grasp the nut or cap screw more securely? These are short length box ends. The standard length is of the same design, but longer.

OPEN END WRENCHES

Open end wrenches are handy but not as dependable as box end wrenches. They grasp the nut on only two of its flats, and are subject to slipping under a heavy pull. There are places, however, where they must be used. Fig. 23-44 illustrates an open end wrench for adjusting valve tappets; it is long with a thin profile. The standard open end wrench is somewhat shorter and of a huskier design.

The open end wrench has the head set at an angle. When the wrench has traveled as far as allowable, it may be flipped over and placed on the nut in an arc of 30 deg. Each end has a different size opening. Open ends are also available with the heads offset more than 15 deg.

COMBINATION BOX AND OPEN END WRENCH

The combination wrench has a box end head on one end and an open end on the other. Generally, the open end is offset 15 deg. from the wrench centerline. Both ends are of the same size.

The combination wrench makes a very convenient tool since the box end can be used both for breaking loose and final tightening. The open end is for faster fastener removal or installation. Fig. 23-45.

Fig. 23-44. Open end wrench.

Fig. 23-45. Combination box and open end wrenches. A—Short length. B—Long length. C—Midget length. D—Large nut size. E—Double offset, both ends set off at a 15 deg. angle from centerline of wrench. (Snap-on Tools)

SOCKET WRENCHES

A socket wrench is very convenient and, in most instances, is faster than the other wrenches.

Sockets are available with 6-point, 12-point, and double-square openings. The 1/4 in. (6.35 mm), 3/8 in. (9.52 mm), 1/2 in. (12.70 mm), and 3/4 in. (19.05 mm), drives will cover a wide range. The drive size refers to the size of the square hole into which the socket handle fits. The larger the drive, the heavier and bulkier the socket.

The 1/4 in. drive is for small work in difficult areas. The 3/8 in. drive will handle a lot of general work where the torque (tightness) requirements are not too high. The 1/2 in. drive is for all-around service. The 3/4 in. drive is for large work with high torque settings.

Sockets are furnished in standard length; also deep sockets for work such as spark plugs requiring a longer than ordinary reach. Swivel sockets are good for angle work. Fig. 23-46.

Sockets should be kept clean, including the inside, and stored according to size.

Fig. 23-46. Sockets. A—Deep, 12-point. B—Deep, 6-point. C—Double-square. D—Standard, 12-point. E—Standard, 6-point. F—Swivel.

SOCKET HANDLES

Various handles are available for sockets. The speed handle is used for fast operation because it can be turned rapidly.

Flex handles in varying lengths allow the socket to be turned with great force, and at odd angles.

Extension bars of different lengths allow the mechanic to lengthen the socket setup to reach difficult areas.

The sliding T-handle varies the handle length. See Fig. 23-47.

The ratchet handle is most versatile. It allows the user to either tighten or remove a nut without removing the socket. On the backstroke, the handle "ratchets." Fig. 23-48.

A ratchet that may be used with the speed handle, flex handle, etc., as well as an adapter that allows the

Fig. 23-47. Socket handles. A—Swivel head speed handle. B—Standard speed handle. C—Extension bar. D—Long flex handle. E—Short flex handle. F—Sliding T-handle.

Fig. 23-48. Socket ratchet handles. A—Short ratchet. B—Long ratchet. C—Ratchet. D—Ratchet adapter. E—Ratchet spinner.

mechanic to spin the socket with fingers until too tight, is also shown in Fig. 23-48.

SOCKET ATTACHMENTS

Many socket attachments are available. Such items as screwdriver heads, drag link sockets, pan screw sockets, crowfoot attachments, Allen wrench heads, etc., all combine to make a socket set a fine tool. A few attachments are shown in Fig. 23-49.

PIPE WRENCHES

Pipe wrenches, both inside and outside, are useful for grasping large or irregular objects. They are strong and exert a powerful holding force. A and B, Fig. 23-50.

CRESCENT OR ADJUSTABLE WRENCH

The Crescent wrench is handy in that it can be adjusted for size. However, it tends to slip, so it is a poor wrench to use for most jobs when other tools are available. When used, adjust the jaws firmly. Also, make certain the wrench is placed so the pull on the handle is toward the bottom side. This relieves heavy pressure on the adjustable jaw. See C, Fig. 23-50.

OTHER USEFUL WRENCHES

The flexible head socket wrench, A in Fig. 23-51, as well as the ratcheting box end, B, are useful additions to the mechanic's toolbox.

Cylinder head wrenches are used for the removal of cylinder head nuts and cap screws. Note the various shapes. Fig. 23-52.

Fig. 23-51. Flex head socket and ratchet box end wrenches. A—Flex head socket. B—Ratchet box.

Fig. 23-49. Socket attachments. A—Weatherhead fitting. B—Handle size adapter. C—Drag link socket. D—Pan screwdriver. E—Crowfoot.

Fig. 23-50. Wrenches. A—Pipe wrench. B—Inside pipe wrench. C—Adjustable wrench. D—Cam-lock wrench.

Fig. 23-52. Cylinder head wrenches.

A stud remover, obviously, is used to remove various studs. Two types are shown in Fig. 23-53.

Allen and fluted wrenches are often used in tightening or removing setscrews, cap screws, etc. They are strong and provide a good grip. Fig. 23-54.

TORQUE WRENCHES

The torque wrench is a MUST for all mechanics. It will enable you to tighten bolts, nuts, etc., to exact torque (tightness) specifications supplied by the manufacturer.

It is of utmost importance that bolts be pulled up to proper specifications. Improper and varying torque on units or assemblies will cause distortion. When certain torque is specified (heads, main, and rod bear-

Fig. 23-53. Stud removers. D—Three jaw stud puller. E—Wedge type stud puller. (Snap-on Tools)

Fig. 23-54. Allen and fluted wrenches. Hex Allen wrench (left) is more popular type.

ings, etc.), use an accurate torque wrench. Fig. 23-55.

Torque wrenches are available in both foot-pound and inch-pound types. The inch-pound wrench is used for delicate low torque applications. Some torque wrenches are available with dual scales on the same wrench. One scale is for foot-pounds and the other for inch-pounds. Still others with dual scales can have one scale for foot-pounds and one for metric values (newton-metres).

Torque wrenches are available in special shapes and sizes. One such wrench is pictured in Fig. 23-56.

PULLERS

Auto mechanics will find use for a wide variety of pullers. They are used for pulling gears, bearings, hubs, etc. An assortment of pullers is shown in Fig. 23-57. Note the various sizes.

Another excellent puller is the slide hammer type. The puller jaws grasp the work, and the weighted slide is banged against the stop. This type of puller is fast and efficient on many types of jobs. Fig. 23-58.

Fig. 23-55. One popular design torque wrench. Torque wrenches insure correct fastener tension.

Fig. 23-56. Small, hand operated, dial indicator (inch-pounds) torque wrench. This wrench is very handy for small jobs such as torquing screws, bolts, etc., used on carburetors, automatic transmission valve bodies, etc.

Fig. 23-57. Pullers. Pullers are available in various styles and sizes.

Fig. 23-58. Slide hammer puller. Slide is hammered on stop to develop powerful pulling force.

SPECIAL PURPOSE TOOLS

Other tools shown in accompanying illustrations are considered special purpose tools. Fig. 23-59 pictures brake service tools. Fig. 23-60 features engine service tools. Some tools for regulator and distributor work are shown in Fig. 23-61.

Useful tire and wheel tools are illustrated in Fig. 23-62. Body tools are shown in Fig. 23-63. Some very handy tools that enable the mechanic to see in difficult areas, as well as remove loose parts where the hand will not reach, are pictured in Fig. 23-64.

A tubing cutter and a tube flaring tool are shown in Fig. 23-65. All tube fittings should be removed and replaced with special tubing flare nut wrenches. They are designed to provide a maximum amount of contact. Slide the open point over the tube and then down on the nut. Fig. 23-66. Miscellaneous hand tools are illustrated in Fig. 23-67.

SOLDERING EQUIPMENT

For soldering all automotive wiring, use ROSIN CORE solder only. Acid core solder leaves a residue that will cause corrosion in electrical units, and should never be used for wiring. Acid core is satisfactory for radiator work.

All parts to be soldered should be clean and bright. Heat the parts with the soldering iron and add solder. Make certain the solder bonds properly. Cool and wipe clean. Tape soldered wiring with plastic tape. Irons are shown in Fig. 23-68.

MEASURING TOOLS

Mechanics are often called on to make PRECISION measurements. To do this, they must have, and understand the use of: an outside micrometer, an in-

Fig. 23-59. Brake service specialty tools. A—Right angle bleeder wrench. B—Bendix eccentric cam wrench. C—Ford eccentric cam wrench. D, E—Offset-head bleeder wrenches. F—Taunus brake wrench. G—Compact car bleeder wrench. H—Datsun brake adjusting tool. J—Bendix brake adjusting tool. K—Pontiac brake adjusting tool. L—Chevrolet brake adjusting tool. M—Star wheel adjusting tool. N—C-washer pliers. O—Three arm hone for brake cylinders. P—Two arm hone for brake cylinders. Q—Parking brake tool.

Fig. 23-60. Piston and cylinder service tools. A—Ring groove cleaner and cutter. B—Ring groove cleaner attachments. C—Ring groove cleaner. D—Piston ring spreader. E, F, G, H—Ring compressors. J, K—Cylinder wall deglazers. L—Deglazer stones. (Snap-on Tools)

Fig. 23-61. Regulator and distributor tools. A—Voltage regulator tools. B—Hex tool for distributor point adjustment. C—Distributor cleaning brush. D—Neon spark tester. E—Distributor point rubbing block surfacers. F—Distributor spring tension tool. G—Distributor point file. H—Regulator point file. J—Point riffler file. K—Flex stones for cleaning points. (Snap-on Tools)

Fig. 23-62. Tire and wheel tools. A—Tire bead remover. B—Wheel lug wrench. C, D—Valve core tools. E—Impact socket. F—Rubber-tipped steel hammer. G—Cross peen hammer. H—Tie rod separator. J—Split rim tool. K, L—Tire removing tools. M—Grease cap tool. N—Hub cap tool.

Fig. 23-63. Body tools. A—Body panel cutter. B—Metal cutting shears. C—Tin snips. D, E, F, G—Door handle tools. H—Door handle pliers. J—Door panel remover. K, L, M, N—Body solder paddles.

Fig. 23-64. Probing tools. Various mirrors and pickup tools for probing into areas that are otherwise inaccessible.

Fig. 23-65. Tubing tools. A—Tubing cutter. B—Tubing flaring tool.

side micrometer, dial gauges, calipers, depth gauges, combination square.

MICROMETER

Both inside and outside micrometers are used to make readings accurate to a fraction of a thousandth of an inch. Fig. 23-69. These precision tools must be kept immaculate. When not in use, keep them wiped

Fig. 23-66. Tubing wrenches. A, B—Six-point. C—Twelve-point.

Fig. 23-67. Other mechanics hand tools. A—Pry bar. B—Cotter pin remover. C, D, E—Cotter pin removers F—Bushing cutter.

Fig. 23-68. Soldering irons. Several types of irons and tips, all electric.

Fig. 23-69. Typical outside micrometer. Note handy decimal equivalents. Learn names of the various parts. (Starrett)

down with an oily rag. When stored, do not allow the spindle end to contact the anvil. Keep them in protective containers.

In use, an outside micrometer is closed around the work until the micrometer may be pulled across the highest point of the work with a slight drag. Never force the micrometer. Both micrometer and work must be clean. Practice on something of a known diameter until you develop the proper "feel."

READING THE MICROMETER

Micrometers are made so that every turn of the thimble will move the spindle .025 in. You will notice that the sleeve is marked with a series of lines. Each of these lines represents .025. Every fourth one of these .025 markings is marked 1, 2, 3, 4, 5, 6, 7, 8, 9. These numbers on the sleeve indicate .100, .200, .300, etc., (one hundred thousandths, etc.). The micrometer sleeve then is marked out for one inch in .025 (twenty-five thousandths inch) markings. They will read from .000 to 1.000.

The tapered end of the thimble has twenty-five lines marked around it. They will read 0, 5, 10, 15, and 20. In that one turn of the thimble moves the thimble edge exactly .025, or one mark on the sleeve,

the distance between marks is determined by reading the thimble line that is even with the long line drawn the length of the sleeve markings.

Look at the markings on the micrometer (mike) in Fig. 23-70. How many numbers are visible on the sleeve? There are three. This 3 indicates that the mike is open at least .300 (three hundred thousandths). You can see that the thimble edge is actually past the 3 but not to the 4. By a careful study you will see that the thimble edge has moved exactly two additional marks past the 3. This means that the edge is lined up two marks past the 3. As each mark represents .025, it is obvious that the edge is actually stopped at .300 plus .050 or .350 (three hundred and fifty thousandths of an inch). In that the thimble edge 0 marking is in line with the line through the sleeve markings, the micrometer is set exactly on .350. The reading then, if this were a one inch mike (reads from 0-1 inch), would be .350.

In Fig. 23-71, A, the micrometer has been opened to a wider measurement. You will see that the thimble edge is no longer exactly on a sleeve marking but is somewhere in between.

How many numbers are visible on the sleeve? There are 5 or .500 (five hundred thousandths). The thimble edge has moved three marks or .075 past the .500 mark. This makes a total of .575. The thimble edge has moved past the third mark. In that the fourth mark is not visible, we know it is somewhere between the third and fourth mark.

Fig. 23-70. Micrometer reads—0.350.

By examining the thimble edge marks, you will see that the twelfth mark is aligned with the sleeve long line. This means that the thimble edge has moved twelve spindle marks past the third sleeve mark. In that each thimble mark is worth .001 (one thousandth of an inch), the thimble has actually moved .012 (twelve thousandths of an inch) past the third sleeve mark. Your reading would be .500 (largest sleeve number visible) PLUS .075 (three sleeve marks past sleeve number) PLUS .012 (twelve thimble marks past third sleeve mark), making a total of 0.587 (five hundred and eighty-seven thousandths of an inch).

Study the readings in Fig. 23-71. Compare your answers with those shown. Make your reading in FOUR steps.

1. Read the largest sleeve number that is visible—each one is worth .100.
2. Count the number of full sleeve marks past this number. Each one is worth .025.
3. Count the number of thimble marks past this last sleeve number. Each one is worth .001. If the thimble marks are not quite in line with the sleeve long line, estimate the fraction of a mark.
4. Add the readings in steps 1, 2, and 3.

The total is the correct micrometer reading.

Fig. 23-71. A—Micrometer reads 0.587. B—0.250. C—0.280. D—0.120. E—0.515-½ or 0.5155.

Micrometers are available in one inch, two inch, three inch, etc., sizes. The range of the mike would actually be zero to one inch, one inch to two inches, two inches to three inches, etc. For example, if you are using a two inch to three inch mike, and your total reading is .094, the actual diameter of the object being measured would be 2.094. If you were using a zero to one inch mike, the diameter would be 0.094.

The inside micrometer is illustrated in Fig. 23-72. It is being used to measure the diameter of a cylinder.

Fig. 23-72. Using an inside micrometer to check cylinder bore size.

METRIC MICROMETER

Except for the sleeve and thimble markings, a metric micrometer looks just like a more conventional inch micrometer. The sleeve and thimble of a metric micrometer are graduated in millimetres, instead of thousandths of an inch. Each line on the sleeve equals 0.50 mm. Each line on the thimble equals 0.01 mm. Two revolutions of the thimble advances the spindle 1.00 mm.

To read a metric micrometer, use the same four steps given for an inch micrometer. For example, look at Fig. 23-73. With the micrometer set as shown, your reading would be:

1. Note 5.00 mm graduation visible.   5.00 mm
2. One 0.50 sleeve line also visible.   0.50 mm
3. Thimble line 28 aligns with sleeve line (28 times 0.01 equals 0.28).   <u>0.28 mm</u>
4. Add these values for measurement.   5.78 mm

Reading 5.78 mm

Fig. 23-73. Reading a metric micrometer.

INSIDE AND OUTSIDE CALIPERS

Calipers are useful tools for rough measurements. Fig. 23-74 illustrates a pair of outside calipers being used to measure the diameter of a shaft.

Fig. 23-75 shows how the inside calipers can be used to measure the size of a hole.

To determine the reading, hold the calipers on an accurate steel rule.

DIVIDERS

Dividers are made somewhat like calipers, but have straight shanks and pointed ends. They are handy for marking circles, surface measurements, etc. Fig. 23-76 shows dividers being used to find the center of a steel shaft.

Fig. 23-74. Measuring diameter of shaft, using an outside caliper. (South Bend Lathe)

Fig. 23-75. Using inside caliper to measure diameter of counterbore.

Fig. 23-76. Dividers being used to find center of shaft. (South Bend Lathe)

DIAL GAUGE OR INDICATOR

A dial indicator is used to read movement in thousandths of an inch. Common uses are checking end play in shafts, backlash in gear teeth, valve lift, shaft runout, taper in cylinders, etc.

Fig. 23-77 shows how a dial indicator is used to check a ring gear for runout. The dial button is placed against the work until the needle revolves about one-half turn. The dial face is set to zero, and the gear revolved in the V-block stand. Any runout (wobble) of the ring gear will cause the dial needle to move. This movement is read in one thousandth of an inch.

DIAL CALIPERS

A dial caliper is a very handy and useful measuring tool. It is capable of taking inside, outside and depth measurements. These instruments are highly accurate and should be handled with care, always return them to the protective container when you have finished.

The dial caliper shown in Fig. 23-78 is capable of measuring objects up to 6 in. (152.4 mm). Each graduation on the bar scale (body) is equal to .100 in. (2.54 mm). The dial is calibrated in .001 in. (0.025 mm). One full revolution of the dial needle equals .100 inch on the bar scale.

A thumb operated roll knob is used so that fine adjustments can be obtained. Any given adjustment can be secured by turning the lockscrew. This prevents the caliper from opening or closing, Fig. 23-78.

FEELER GAUGES

Feeler gauges are thin strips of specially hardened and ground steel. The thickness of each strip is marked in thousandths of an inch. They are used to check clearances between two parts: valve clearance, piston ring end gap, etc. Fig. 23-79.

Space limitations will not permit covering the many specialized tools such as those in Fig. 23-80. The student would be wise to procure catalogs from tool manufacturers. Study the catalogs to learn tool identification and practice.

Fig. 23-77. Checking ring gear runout with a dial indicator.

Fig. 23-78. One type of dial caliper. This particular instrument can measure objects and holes up to 6 in. (152.4 mm) in diameter and depth. Learn the names of the various parts and their locations. (Starrett)

ELECTRICAL TEST INSTRUMENTS

The mechanic must be familiar with and skilled in the use of many electrical testing instruments. The VOLTMETER, AMMETER, OHMMETER, OSCILLOSCOPE, TIMING LIGHT, TACHOMETER, etc., are all very important to proper diagnosis, service, and repair.

Some instruments, such as the magnetic ignition timing device, shown in Fig. 23-81, are designed as individual "hand-held" units. Others like the engine analyzer, pictured in Fig. 23-82, combine a number of instruments into a single stand.

REMEMBER:

GOOD TOOLS make your work easier, faster and more efficient. Use them properly and give them good care. If treated with intelligence, they will give you many years of satisfying use.

KNOW THESE TERMS

Hammer, Chisel, Punch, File, Drill, Reamer, Impact wrench, Hacksaw, Vise, Tap, Die, Pliers, Screwdriver, Box wrench, Open end wrench, Combination wrench, Socket wrench, Extension, Ratchet, Torque wrench, Allen wrench, Puller, Micrometer, Calipers, Dial gauge, Feeler gauge.

REVIEW QUESTIONS—CHAPTER 23

1. What material is commonly used in the construction of quality tools?
2. Name three things to look for when buying tools.
3. Give a few general rules for the use of tools.
4. Name three types of hammers useful to the mechanic.
5. Name several types of chisels the mechanic should have.

Fig. 23-79. Feeler gauges. A—Wire gap gauges. B, C, D, E, F—Various feeler gauges.

6. Of what use are punches?
7. What is the difference between starting, drift and aligning punches?
8. A file with two sets of cutting edges at angles to each other is referred to as a _____ file.
9. Give some safety rules for the use of hammers, chisels, and files.
10. Give two methods that are helpful in keeping a file clean.
11. Drills made of carbon steel will last longer than those made of high speed steel. True or False?
12. For general drilling in steel, what lip angles would you recommend?
13. Describe the procedure to use when sharpening drills.
14. Give some safety precautions to observe when using a portable hand drill.
15. Hacksaw teeth should point away from the handle. True or False?
16. Reamers are used for drilling large holes. True or False?

1—Pinion setting gauge.
2—Pinion setting gauge adaptors.
3—Rear pinion bearing remover.
4—Rear pinion bearing cup installer.
5—Pinion oil seal installer.
6—Differential side bearing puller.
7—Driver handle.

8—Dial indicator set.
9—Pinion oil seal remover.
10—Differential bearing installer.
11—Companion nut socket.
12—Companion flange holder and remover.
13—Axle shaft remover.

14—Pinion oil seal installer.
15—Rear hub puller spacer.
16—Rear hub puller and wedge.
17—Pinion angle gauge (Inclinometer).
18—Bushing service set.
19—End play checking tool.

Fig. 23-80. Specialized tools can make repair operations much easier, faster, and better. This group of tools is designed for drive axle work. (American Motors)

Fig. 23-81. Engine ignition magnetic timing tester. (Marquette)

17. A husky vise will also be useful as an anvil. True or False?
18. If you wish to cut internal threads in a hole, you would use a tap. True or False?
19. If you wish to cut threads on a bolt, you would use a tap. True or False?
20. Describe some useful cleaning tools.
21. When grinding, always wear _____.
22. Name five types of pliers.
23. List six types of screwdrivers.
24. A box end wrench is one of the best to use. True or False?
25. Open end wrenches grip a nut on all but one flat. True or False?
26. Combination box end and open end wrenches have a different size opening on each end. True or False?
27. A spark plug would require a _____ socket.
28. A quarter inch drive set of sockets would be handy for removing head bolts. True or False?
29. Name four types of socket handles.

30. A pipe wrench may be used for gripping a crankshaft journal. True or False?
31. For tightening head bolts, connecting rod bolts, etc., always use a _____ wrench.
32. Describe an Allen wrench.
33. Gears are usually removed by using a _____.

34. See how many other hand tools you can name.
35. Describe how to read a micrometer.
36. Give some general rules for the use and care of tools.
37. Name three different measurements that can be made with a dial caliper.

Fig. 23-82. This engine analyzer incorporates a number of different instruments that help the mechanic make many rapid, accurate tests and measurements. (Allen)

Chapter 24

CAREER OPPORTUNITIES IN THE AUTOMOTIVE FIELD

After studying this chapter, you will be able to:
- Describe the various types of careers available in auto mechanics.
- Compare the different types of specialized mechanics.
- Explain why it is important to finish school before seeking a full-time job as a mechanic.

A VAST FIELD

Our country has been aptly referred to as a "nation on wheels." In fact, the very essence of our economic life and growth is dependent, in a great part, upon the continued improvement and advancement of the automobile.

The automotive field has become so large that today it employs about one out of every seven workers in our nation.

TYPES OF CAREERS AVAILABLE

This chapter will concern itself with careers directly connected with automotive maintenance and repair as found in the modern garage or service center.

CLEANING

In cleaning work, you will be called upon to steam clean the engine and underbody portion of the car. You will wash, and often wax, the exterior finish. Vacuuming, window and upholstery cleaning and installation of seat covers will undoubtedly be delegated to you. Part of your day will be spent in the delivery and moving of cars, plus an occasional assist to the mechanics, parts specialists or other personnel.

Your work in the cleaning department will provide you with an opportunity to demonstrate your ability as a hard working and responsible person. There will be plenty of chances to observe the work involved in other areas and, coupled with additional study, you can prepare yourself for advancement. When ready, you may move from the cleaning to the lubrication department.

MECHANIC, LIGHT REPAIR

Part of the work as a light repair mechanic consists of checking out new cars before delivery. You will go over the entire car to make certain that all systems are functioning and in proper adjustment.

You will probably be responsible for making the normal checkup offered the car buyer after a certain mileage has been reached. At this time you would normally go over the entire car, torque the head bolts, check the timing and valve clearance, inspect the brakes, steering, etc. You would discuss the car's performance with the owner and check up on any complaints regarding its operation.

Training in this job, even though it generally involves minor repair and adjustment, is invaluable if you are interested in the more complicated heavy repair work or, for that matter, in some specialty such as tune-up, brakes, etc.

MECHANIC, HEAVY REPAIR

In the heavy repair department, you will be called on to service, dismantle, check, repair, reassemble, and check engines and units such as transmissions and differentials. See Fig. 24-1. This job will require a great deal of study, practice and experience.

At the start, you probably will work under a qualified and experienced mechanic in this department. Your success in this area will largely depend upon your aptitude (natural ability), interest, ambition and a sincere desire to learn.

Once having mastered the work involved, you will be a valuable asset in any garage and will have placed yourself in a good position for advancement.

SPECIALIZATION

Today, the automobile is steadily incorporating new devices and special features. It is becoming more and more difficult for any one mechanic to attempt the mastery of the entire car. When the volume or work will permit it, specialization in one certain area

Fig. 24-1. A heavy repair mechanic performs major repair work—rebuilding engines being one example. (OTC Tools)

injection system cleaning, adjusting and checking. See Fig. 24-2. Alternator and starter work, as well as electrical wiring, headlights, and other similar jobs are also in this field.

Tune-up work requires a high level of competency. It is a good paying job and will provide an excellent chance for further advancement.

Fig. 24-2. This specialized tune-up mechanic is setting ignition timing. Other duties include spark plug replacement, carburetor adjustment and fuel injection service. (Saab)

will provide customers with faster and more efficient service. The service will be better because the mechanic handling the job will be a specialist in that area.

The specialists will have advanced and concentrated training and experience in a chosen specialty. The full-time work in one area will help the specialist become highly proficient.

LUBRICATION SPECIALIST

The lubrication specialist is involved with lubricating the working parts of the car, checking oil levels in the engine, transmission, differential, changing oil, grease jobs, etc. It includes inspection of battery, brake master cylinder, radiator, and a general inspection of parts critical to safe operation, such as the steering system, springs, shock absorbers, brake lines, parking brake linkage, tires, etc.

Work in this area will provide you with an opportunity to learn a great deal about the various systems on the car. It could pave the way to advancement toward more complicated mechanical service. Most large dealerships have a lubrication specialist.

TUNE-UP SPECIALIST

The tune-up specialist will handle jobs involving ignition system service and repair, carburetor and fuel

DIAGNOSTIC TECHNICIAN

Service centers specializing in diagnostic work are popular. During the diagnosis, each car moves through various inspection areas. Each area has a diagnostician who checks a specific system and indicates the findings on a checklist, as shown in Fig. 24-3. When the car has cleared all stations, the customer is given a summary of recommended services. The head diagnostician also reviews the results and, usually, estimates the cost of the repairs.

The idea behind the diagnostic center is to offer a fast, complete, accurate, and unbiased inspection service. Then, the customer is made aware of any repair or maintenance work that the inspected car may require. The center may or may not have repair facilities. In any event, the customer is free to take the car to any shop for service.

Work in this type of shop requires a high degree of skill within a given specialty. The mechanic may be assigned to a single station or may be asked to work in more than one.

PARTS SPECIALIST

Most garages and service centers of any size find it essential to maintain a rather extensive stock of parts.

Fig. 24-3. Diagnostic technician making notes relative to brake condition. (Bendix Corp.)

Fig. 24-4. Brake service specialist prepares to resurface a rotor on a disc brake lathe. (Ammco)

The ordering, cataloging, storage, and distribution of these parts requires the services of a parts specialist.

The parts specialist must possess a thorough knowledge of all aspects of the service operation. Numerous parts catalogs must be maintained and used. Mechanics must be advised regarding parts modification, parts interchangeability, etc. Regular parts inventories must be taken. The parts specialist is a key figure in the overall garage operation.

BRAKE SPECIALIST

The duties of a brake service specialist involves work such as drum turning, lining installation and truing, shoe adjustment, master and wheel cylinder repair, bleeding, line replacement, parking brake service, disc brake rotor resurfacing, caliper overhaul, and pad replacement. See Fig. 24-4.

Special training in brake trouble diagnosis and power brake units is required.

TRANSMISSION SPECIALIST

This technician will handle all transmission work, both standard and automatic. Look at Fig. 24-5. Necessary skills include testing, diagnosis, disassembly, checking, repair, and reassembly of the transmission. The transmission specialist must have a thorough background of practice as well as special training.

FRONT END SPECIALIST

Wheel balancing, alignment and work on the steering gearbox, linkage, spindles, springs, and control arms falls to the front end specialist. Fig. 24-6. It is this particular mechanic's duty to see that the car steers and handles easily and safely, and that the tires run smoothly and wear properly.

ELECTRICAL SPECIALIST

The modern car makes wide use of electrical units. The electrical specialist will handle work on such items as radios, electric seats, window-operating devices, convertible top power units, instruments, alternators, starters, etc. This job requires an extensive knowledge of electricity and electronics as well as the repair and adjustment of all electrical units.

Fig. 24-5. Transmission mechanic is removing heavy transmission from vehicle using specialized jack. (OTC Tools)

Fig. 24-6. Front end specialist is checking alignment angles on front of vehicle. (Ammco)

AIR CONDITIONING SPECIALIST

This job involves checking, adjusting, and repairing automotive air conditioning systems. Air conditioning is rapidly becoming more popular and will produce many jobs for mechanics with special training in this area.

BODY AND FENDER SPECIALIST

Body and fender work, although not thought of in the general sense of mechanical repair, is an important part of garage work. This is a speciality that requires a great deal of training. As a result, it pays quite well.

The body and fender mechanic will repair damage to the car's metal structure, the upholstering and inside trim. The body and fender specialist will install glass, repair locks, handles, etc. This job requires proficiency in cutting, welding, metal bumping, filling, priming, painting, etc. Within the field of body and fender work, painting is rapidly becoming a specialty of its own.

SUB-SPECIALISTS

In some of the larger garages, mechanics specialize within a specialty. In fuel system service, for example, the work can become involved enough to provide full-time work on carburetor rebuilding.

SUPERVISORY POSITIONS

Most workers, upon entering a particular field, look forward to advancement in pay and position.

This is as it should be, both in the garage and service station fields, as in many other fields.

Advancement depends upon your knowledge and skill as well as a demonstration of your ability to cope with the problems connected with the position.

SHOP SUPERVISOR

The shop supervisor is in charge of the mechanics in the repair department. The supervisor is held directly responsible for the work turned out by the mechanics. This calls for a highly competent mechanic, familiar with and able to perform all jobs that enter the shop.

In larger garages, the supervisor's time will be spent directing the mechanics: checking their work, giving suggestions and, in general, seeing that the shop runs smoothly and efficiently. In a small garage, the supervisor may spend part of the day doing repair work, with the remainder of the time devoted to supervision.

SERVICE MANAGER

The service manager holds a very responsible position. This title is held by the person in charge of the overall garage service operation. The service manager must see that customers get prompt, efficient and fair-priced service. Primary responsibility is to see that customers are pleased and that the mechanics and others in the service department are satisfied and doing good work.

The service manager's job usually entails handling of employee training programs. This requires close cooperation with factory representatives to see that the latest and best service techniques are employed.

The service manager must have an insight into the job itself. This calls for leadership ability, a good personality, training, knowledge, and the ability to work with others.

OVERALL JOB PICTURE

Other jobs found in the modern garage, in addition to those discussed, are shown on the dealer organization chart, Fig. 24-7.

SMALL GARAGE MECHANIC

The mechanic in the small garage will often be called upon to meet customers, diagnose problems, and prepare cost estimates and billings. Training in all aspects of mechanical work done in the garage is required.

WORKING CONDITIONS

The garage of today is a far cry from the crowded, dark, cold, and poorly ventilated garage of yesterday. The modern garage is well lighted, roomy, and pro-

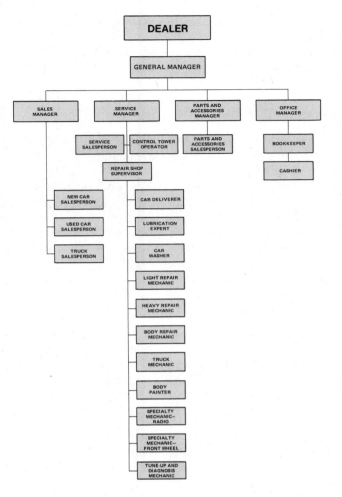

Fig. 24-7. This chart will give you an idea of how a modern automobile dealership is organized.

vides a pleasing place in which to work.

Many modern garages feature lunchrooms, showers, lockers, etc., for their employees. The addition of heavy power equipment has removed much of the sheer labor involved, and also provides easier and more comfortable access to the various parts of the car.

Most mechanics work inside, but when a job incorporates roadside repair, the mechanic may be faced with varying weather conditions.

Many mechanics, especially those in urban areas and in large garages, belong to one of several unions. Among the unions are the International Association of Machinists; the International Brotherhood of Teamsters, Chauffeurs, Warehousemen and Helpers of America; the United Automobile, Aircraft and Agricultural Implement Workers of America.

SALARY

It is difficult to say what salary you can expect. Much depends on type of work performed, location (geographical) of the job, employer, prevailing business conditions, and job supply and demand. All of these exert a definite influence on the salary of mechanics.

Suffice it to say that most mechanics earn a good living and that their salaries are in line with other types of technical jobs.

Many auto mechanics receive a certain percentage of the customer labor charge. As the rates for various jobs are fixed, the skilled mechanic will be able to do more jobs in one day than the unskilled mechanic, and as a result, will earn more money.

When starting to learn the trade under an apprentice program, the student or apprentice mechanic will earn around 55 percent of the journeyman mechanic's income. The rate is gradually increased until the apprentice will earn up to 90 percent of the journeyman rate in the last six months of apprenticeship.

HOURS

Working hours per week may vary from 40 to 48 hours. In some instances, mechanics work beyond these hours. Overtime salary is generally paid for all hours over those set by the union. Holidays and vacations with pay are becoming increasingly available to mechanics.

AVAILABILITY OF EMPLOYMENT

The increasing use of cars, plus the addition of more complex items on the car, has provided a lucrative field for qualified mechanics. If you really learn the trade and are a hardworking, conscientious person, you should be able to readily find employment.

Many small, self-owned shops have been started by mechanics. Many service stations offer light-duty repair and employment possibilities.

On the average, most independent shops and service stations employ one to five mechanics. However, some of the larger garages employ over one hundred people.

About a third of all mechanics work in new and used car dealer garages. Another third work in repair shops that specialize in a multitude of automotive repairs, such as body and fender work, tune-up, brake, front end, radiator work, etc. Other mechanics work for large fleet owners such as the utility companies, dairies, produce companies, and federal, state, county, and city organizations.

If you are sincerely interested in cars, enjoy working on and studying about cars and are in normal health, the chances are good that you would like this work and do well in it.

HOW DOES A PERSON BECOME AN AUTO MECHANIC?

A person develops into an auto mechanic by study, observation, instruction, and experience. High Schools, Trade Schools, Colleges, The Armed Forces, and Apprentice Programs all offer excellent opportunities to acquire the training necessary to gain employment in this field.

Several sound reasons for finishing high school, as well as recommended courses, will be discussed first.

Remember: Many high schools offer fine training programs in Auto Mechanics. Take advantage of them.

STAY IN HIGH SCHOOL

Above all else, GRADUATE FROM HIGH SCHOOL. High school dropouts are considered poor risks by employers and for good reasons.

Facing facts, we know that the vast majority of students who drop out of school do so for one of several reasons. Some of the reasons why students drop out are:
1. They lack the intelligence to compete in school.
2. They are just plain lazy.
3. They are bored and feel that schoolwork does nothing for them.
4. They want to start earning money so that they may feel grown up and independent.
5. They cannot get along with others and rebel against authority.

The actual reasons for dropping out may be any one or a combination of those mentioned. At any rate, the prospective employee usually will have high school graduates applying for the job. If high school graduates are available, why should any employer take a chance on a dropout who did not have what it takes to finish high school.

We know that there are some very fine, intelligent and hardworking students who drop out of school, but the employer is not equipped, nor even inclined, to ferret out these people. Actual practice has shown that, on the average, it is much safer to hire a high school graduate in preference to a dropout.

National figures on salaries and employment show that many dropouts are unemployed a great deal of the time. When they are able to find work, it usually is in low paying jobs. The world today is moving forward at an ever-increasing speed, and there will be little chance for the unskilled and uneducated dropout. STAY IN SCHOOL.

WHAT TO TAKE WHILE IN SCHOOL

Contrary to what many young people in school think, English, Social Studies, Math, and Science are extremely valuable to anyone planning to enter one of the trades.

ENGLISH

The ability to express yourself, both orally and in writing, is important, since you will have many opportunities to meet the public and also to make written reports. The impression you make through your speaking and writing will have a definite bearing on your worth to any employer as well as on your chances for advancement. WORK in your English courses—it will pay off.

MATH

You often hear the statement, "What good does math do—I'm going to be a mechanic?" It does a great deal of good. Mechanics make many precision measurements, customer billings, cost estimates, etc. To fully understand automotive theory requires a good grasp of mathematics. Do not forget that there are many times outside the shop when you will need a reasonable skill in math. Business Math, Algebra, Geometry, and Trigonometry will all be useful tools for your mental toolbox.

SCIENCE

Chemistry and Physics will be invaluable aids in understanding the construction and operation of the automobile. The car embodies the use of Chemistry and Physics in hundreds of applications.

SOCIAL STUDIES

A thorough knowledge of our world, past and present, its people, its problems, its aims, etc., is essential if you hope to make an intelligent contribution to society in general. It will set you apart as a person "in the know" and will allow you to discuss countless things in an intelligent fashion. Your contributions to your work, your country, and your chances of advancement will be greater with study in this area.

English and Social Studies, as well as some Math and Science, are often required courses. Make certain you take and get all you can from them!

OTHER IMPORTANT COURSES

As elective courses, take such things as Mechanical Drawing, Blueprint Reading, Art, Electricity, Machine Shop, Welding, Fundamentals of Auto Mechanics (theory), Auto Mechanics (shop experience), and if offered by your school, On the Job Training in this field.

USE YOUR COUNSELOR AND INSTRUCTORS

This is a big order. To make certain you are on the right track and are getting what you need, see your school counselor. Most high schools, through their guidance office, will provide you with valuable assistance in determining your assets and liabilities, your vocation, the courses necessary, as well as providing you with information on furthering your training after graduation from high school. Talk with your shop instructors, as they can be of great help.

AFTER GRADUATION?

In the event that you desire additional training after graduation, the following areas will prove valuable.

TRADE SCHOOL

There are numerous trade schools across the nation. Many offer excellent courses aimed at teaching the auto mechanics trade. Before selecting any certain school, it is wise to run a careful check on the school itself. You should determine several things:

1. Is the school a reputable institution?
2. Does it offer the courses you need?
3. Does it have top quality instructors and plenty of late model equipment?
4. Does it have a job placement agency?
5. How far along the road to complete training will it take you?
6. What are the costs?
7. Do they offer aid in securing a part-time job if you must work to help pay expenses?

To help you check on these items, contact the school itself, the Better Business Bureau in the city in which the school is located, your High School Guidance Office, the Labor Union to which the mechanics in the area of the school belong, and the Vocational Department of the State Department of Education.

A thorough investigation of the school of your choice will be well worth your time. DO NOT FAIL TO MAKE IT!

ARMED FORCES

If you have decided to join one of the Armed Forces, it may be possible for you to receive training in the field of auto mechanics. The Services have top quality schools. If you have the opportunity to receive the training they offer, plus the experience of enlistment, you will be well on the way to becoming a good mechanic.

If you desire to enter apprenticeship training upon your discharge, most apprentice programs give credit for previous experience and training. How much credit is given will depend on the individual employer or the Joint Apprenticeship Committee involved.

For information regarding training in the Armed Forces, see your local recruiting agent and your High School Guidance Counselor.

APPRENTICE PROGRAM

Many who enter the field of auto mechanics learn the trade by enrolling in an apprentice program.

The apprentice program is designed to teach a specific trade through on-the-job training and study. The apprentice is exposed to, and instructed in, all facets of the trade. The program generally includes some off-the-job training in physics, math, and other related subjects. These classes will be in either a vocational school or, as is sometimes done, taught at the place of business. Correspondence courses are sometimes required.

As apprentices gradually develop skills, they will be exposed to the more technical aspects of the job. In a good training program, the apprentices will learn the trade thoroughly and, upon completion of the apprenticeship, will be highly skilled and valued employees.

HOW TO GET IN THE APPRENTICE PROGRAM

If you are interested in becoming an apprentice, contact employers in the trade you wish to enter. One may have an apprenticeship program and be willing to hire you. The local labor union representing the trade of your choice may be able to help. Many cities have local joint apprenticeship committees. You also may want to contact your local state employment service office.

QUALIFICATIONS ESSENTIAL FOR APPRENTICESHIP

You should have a sincere interest in the trade, be willing to study, observe, take instruction and WORK! You should have average or above ability to work with your hands in addition to your head. Although high school dropouts are sometimes placed, many programs prefer high school graduates.

Learning a trade will equip you with valuable skills and place you in demand. The national apprenticeship program is a fine way in which to master your trade.

ADDITIONAL INFORMATION

If you are interested in the field of auto mechanics, and think you would like to learn the trade, ask your high school guidance counselors for all the information they have available. They will be glad to help even if you have dropped out or graduated. In addition, write to the following sources for very informative booklets that can aid in your career decision:

MOTOR VEHICLE MANUFACTURERS
ASSOCIATION OF THE U.S., INC.
300 New Center Building
Detroit, MI 48202

NATIONAL AUTOMOBILE DEALERS
ASSOCIATION
8400 Westpark Drive
McLean, VA 22102

U.S. DEPARTMENT OF LABOR
Bureau of Apprenticeship and Training
Washington, D.C. 20006

The following car manufacturers, as well as others, may be able to provide you with brochures, booklets, etc. All offer training programs and are glad to explain each program. If you desire booklets or pamphlets only, write to the Manager, Educational Publications Department, at the company address. For training program information, address:

AMERICAN MOTORS CORPORATION

College Graduates:
Training Supervisor
American Motors Corporation
27777 Franklin Road
Southfield, MI 48034

High School, Vocational School Graduates:
Manager, Personnel Department
American Motors Corporation
27777 Franklin Road
Southfield, MI 48034

CHRYSLER CORPORATION

College Graduates:
College Recruitment Services
Personnel Department
Chrysler Corporation
Chrysler Center
P.O. Box 857
Detroit, MI 48288

High School, Vocational School Graduates:
Manager, Personnel Department
Chrysler Corporation
Chrysler Center
P.O. Box 857
Detroit, MI 48288

FORD MOTOR COMPANY

Placement and College Recruitment
Ford Motor Company
The American Road
Dearborn, MI 48121

GENERAL MOTORS CORPORATION

Salaried Placement Personnel
General Motors Corporation
General Motors Building
Detroit, MI 48202

CERTIFICATION

The National Institute for Automotive Service Excellence (NIASE) Certification Program offers a practical way to provide qualified mechanics with the recognition and improved status they deserve. NIASE gives tests and certifications in automobile repair, heavy duty truck (and bus) repair, body repair, and in painting and refinishing. You may receive credit for school shopwork. For information, write:

NIASE
1825 K Street, N.W.
Washington, D.C. 20006

PLAN YOUR CAREER EARLY

Do not "float" through high school wondering what you want to do. Make every effort to set your sights on a goal: college, technical school, armed forces, apprenticeship, etc.

Guidance counselors will be able to help determine your real talents and can give helpful information and guidance in choosing an appropriate career.

Start your high school career by taking subjects that will allow you to select a college, commercial, vocational, etc., course in your Junior or Senior year. By doing this, you will not sell yourself short if you change your plans. You will then have a background of studies that will enable you to go any one of several ways.

DO NOT BECOME A LOST ART

There is little room in this fast moving age for unskilled labor. Unless you learn a trade, you may find yourself out of work most of the time and when you do get employment you may be poorly paid and perhaps not in work of your choice.

SEE YOUR AUTO SHOP INSTRUCTOR

Have you been thinking about a career in auto mechanics? Discuss your ideas and plans with your auto mechanics instructor, who is vitally interested in this field and is in good position to answer your questions.

REMEMBER THESE WORDS

THINK, PLAN, STUDY, WORK, LEARN, PRACTICE, QUESTION. These are good words and are most significant to anyone entering a trade. If you decide to be a mechanic, decide to be the BEST. If you do, these words will become very familiar to you.

KNOW THESE TERMS

Lubrication work, Specialization, Tune-up specialist, Diagnostic technician, Parts specialist, Brake specialist, Transmission specialist, Front end specialist, Electrical specialist, Body and fender specialist, Shop supervisor, Service manager, Apprentice program.

The modern automobile is a highly complex mechanism. Proper service, diagnosis, and repair requires highly trained mechanics. Many specialize in one particular area such as fuel systems. Study this illustration carefully and see how many areas you can identify that lend themselves to specialization. (Cadillac)

METRIC TABLES

SOME COMMON ABBREVIATIONS/SYMBOLS

ENGLISH		METRIC	
UNIT	ABBREVIATION	UNIT	SYMBOL
inch	in	kilometre	km
feet	ft	hectometre	hm
yard	yd	dekametre	dam
mile	mi	metre	m
grain	gr	decimetre	dm
ounce	oz	centimetre	cm
pound	lb	millimetre	mm
teaspoon	tsp	cubic centimetre	cm^3
tablespoon	tbsp	kilogram	kg
fluid ounce	fl oz	hectogram	hg
cup	c	dekagram	dag
pint	pt	gram	g
quart	qt	decigram	dg
gallon	gal	centigram	cg
cubic inch	in^3	milligram	mg
cubic foot	ft^3	kilolitre	kl
cubic yard	yd^3	hectolitre	hl
square inch	in^2	dekalitre	dal
square foot	ft^2	litre	L
square yard	yd^2	centilitre	cl
square mile	mi^2	millilitre	ml
Fahrenheit	F	dekastere	das
barrel	bbl	square kilometre	km^2
fluid dram	fl dr	hectare	ha
board foot	bd ft	are	a
rod	rd	centare	ca
dram	dr	tonne	t
bushel	bu	Celsius	C

Metric Tables

MEASURING SYSTEMS

ENGLISH   METRIC

LENGTH

12 inches = 1 foot	1 kilometre = 1000 metres
36 inches = 1 yard	1 hectometre = 100 metres
3 feet = 1 yard	1 dekametre = 10 metres
5,280 feet = 1 mile	1 metre = 1 metre
16.5 feet = 1 rod	1 decimetre = 0.1 metre
320 rods = 1 mile	1 centimetre = 0.01 metre
6 feet = 1 fathom	1 millimetre = 0.001 metre

WEIGHT

27.34 grains = 1 dram	1 tonne = 1,000,000 grams
438 grains = 1 ounce	1 kilogram = 1000 grams
16 drams = 1 ounce	1 hectogram = 100 grams
16 ounces = 1 pound	1 dekagram = 10 grams
2000 pounds = 1 short ton	1 gram = 1 gram
2240 pounds = 1 long ton	1 decigram = 0.1 gram
25 pounds = 1 quarter	1 centigram = 0.01 gram
4 quarters = 1 cwt	1 milligram = 0.001 gram

VOLUME

8 ounces = 1 cup	1 hectolitre = 100 litres
16 ounces = 1 pint	1 dekalitre = 10 litres
32 ounces = 1 quart	1 litre = 1 litre
2 cups = 1 pint	1 decilitre = 0.1 litre
2 pints = 1 quart	1 centilitre = 0.01 litre
4 quarts = 1 gallon	1 millilitre = 0.001 litre
8 pints = 1 gallon	1000 millilitre = 1 litre

AREA

144 sq. inches = 1 sq. foot	100 sq. millimetres = 1 sq. centimetre
9 sq. feet = 1 sq. yard	100 sq. centimetres = 1 sq. decimetre
43,560 sq. ft. = 160 sq. rods	100 sq. decimetres = 1 sq. metre
160 sq. rods = 1 acre	10,000 sq. metres = 1 hectare
640 acres = 1 sq. mile	

TEMPERATURE

FAHRENHEIT		CELSIUS
32 degrees F	Water freezes	0 degree C
68 degrees F	Reasonable room temperature	20 degrees C
98.6 degrees F	Normal body temperature	37 degrees C
173 degrees F	Alcohol boils	78.34 degrees C
212 degrees F	Water boils	100 degrees C

USEFUL CONVERSIONS

WHEN YOU KNOW:	MULTIPLY BY:	TO FIND:

TORQUE		
Pound - inch Pound - foot	0.11298 1.3558	newton-metres (N-m) newton-metres

LIGHT		
Foot candles	1.0764	lumens/metres^2 (lm/m^2)

FUEL PERFORMANCE		
Miles/gallon	0.4251	kilometres/litre (km/L)

SPEED		
Miles/hour	1.6093	kilometres/hr (km/h)

FORCE		
kilogram ounce pound	9.807 0.278 4.448	newtons (n) newtons newtons

POWER		
Horsepower	0.746	kilowatts (kw)

PRESSURE OR STRESS		
Inches of water Pounds/sq. in.	0.2491 6.895	kilopascals (kPa) kilopascals

ENERGY OR WORK		
BTU Foot - pound Kilowatt-hour	1055.0 1.3558 3600000.0	joules (J) joules joules (J = one W/s)

Metric Tables

CONVERSION TABLE
METRIC TO ENGLISH

WHEN YOU KNOW ⬇	MULTIPLY BY: * = Exact		TO FIND ⬇
	VERY ACCURATE	APPROXIMATE	
LENGTH			
millimetres	0.0393701	0.04	inches
centimetres	0.3937008	0.4	inches
metres	3.280840	3.3	feet
metres	1.093613	1.1	yards
kilometres	0.621371	0.6	miles
WEIGHT			
grains	0.00228571	0.0023	ounces
grams	0.03527396	0.035	ounces
kilograms	2.204623	2.2	pounds
tonnes	1.1023113	1.1	short tons
VOLUME			
millilitres		0.2	teaspoons
millilitres	0.06667	0.067	tablespoons
millilitres	0.03381402	0.03	fluid ounces
litres	61.02374	61.024	cubic inches
litres	2.113376	2.1	pints
litres	1.056688	1.06	quarts
litres	0.26417205	0.26	gallons
litres	0.03531467	0.035	cubic feet
cubic metres	61023.74	61023.7	cubic inches
cubic metres	35.31467	35.0	cubic feet
cubic metres	1.3079506	1.3	cubic yards
cubic metres	264.17205	264.0	gallons
AREA			
square centimetres	0.1550003	0.16	square inches
square centimetres	0.00107639	0.001	square feet
square metres	10.76391	10.8	square feet
square metres	1.195990	1.2	square yards
square kilometres		0.4	square miles
hectares	2.471054	2.5	acres
TEMPERATURE			
Celsius	*9/5 (then add 32)		Fahrenheit

CONVERSION TABLE
ENGLISH TO METRIC

WHEN YOU KNOW ⬇	MULTIPLY BY: * = Exact		TO FIND ⬇
	VERY ACCURATE	APPROXIMATE	
LENGTH			
inches	* 25.4		millimetres
inches	* 2.54		centimetres
feet	* 0.3048		metres
feet	* 30.48		centimetres
yards	* 0.9144	0.9	metres
miles	* 1.609344	1.6	kilometres
WEIGHT			
grains	15.43236	15.4	grams
ounces	* 28.349523125	28.0	grams
ounces	* 0.028349523125	.028	kilograms
pounds	* 0.45359237	0.45	kilograms
short ton	* 0.90718474	0.9	tonnes
VOLUME			
teaspoons		5.0	millilitres
tablespoons		15.0	millilitres
fluid ounces	29.57353	30.0	millilitres
cups		0.24	litres
pints	* 0.473176473	0.47	litres
quarts	* 0.946352946	0.95	litres
gallons	* 3.785411784	3.8	litres
cubic inches	* 0.016387064	0.02	litres
cubic feet	* 0.028316846592	0.03	cubic metres
cubic yards	* 0.764554857984	0.76	cubic metres
AREA			
square inches	* 6.4516	6.5	square centimetres
square feet	* 0.09290304	0.09	square metres
square yards	* 0.83612736	0.8	square metres
square miles		2.6	square kilometres
acres	* 0.40468564224	0.4	hectares
TEMPERATURE			
Fahrenheit	* 5/9 (after subtracting 32)		Celsius

Metric Tables

DIMENSIONAL AND TEMPERATURE CONVERSION CHART

INCHES	DECIMALS	MILLI-METRES	INCHES TO MILLIMETRES Inches	INCHES TO MILLIMETRES m.ms.	MILLIMETRES TO INCHES m.ms.	MILLIMETRES TO INCHES Inches	°F	°C	°C	°F
1/64	.015625	.3969	.0001	.00254	0.001	.000039	-20	-28.9	-30	-22
1/32	.03125	.7937	.0002	.00508	0.002	.000079	-15	-26.1	-28	-18.4
3/64	.046875	1.1906	.0003	.00762	0.003	.000118	-10	-23.3	-26	-14.8
1/16	.0625	1.5875	.0004	.01016	0.004	.000157	-5	-20.6	-24	-11.2
5/64	.078125	1.9844	.0005	.01270	0.005	.000197	0	-17.8	-22	-7.6
3/32	.09375	2.3812	.0006	.01524	0.006	.000236	1	-17.2	-20	-4
7/64	.109375	2.7781	.0007	.01778	0.007	.000276	2	-16.7	-18	-0.4
1/8	.125	3.1750	.0008	.02032	0.008	.000315	3	-16.1	-16	3.2
9/64	.140625	3.5719	.0009	.02286	0.009	.000354	4	-15.6	-14	6.8
5/32	.15625	3.9687	.001	.0254	0.01	.00039	5	-15.0	-12	10.4
11/64	.171875	4.3656	.002	.0508	0.02	.00079	10	-12.2	-10	14
3/16	.1875	4.7625	.003	.0762	0.03	.00118	15	-9.4	-8	17.6
13/64	.203125	5.1594	.004	.1016	0.04	.00157	20	-6.7	-6	21.2
7/32	.21875	5.5562	.005	.1270	0.05	.00197	25	-3.9	-4	24.8
15/64	.234375	5.9531	.006	.1524	0.06	.00236	30	-1.1	-2	28.4
1/4	.25	6.3500	.007	.1778	0.07	.00276	35	1.7	0	32
17/64	.265625	6.7469	.008	.2032	0.08	.00315	40	4.4	2	35.6
9/32	.28125	7.1437	.009	.2286	0.09	.00354	45	7.2	4	39.2
19/64	.296875	7.5406	.01	.254	0.1	.00394	50	10.0	6	42.8
5/16	.3125	7.9375	.02	.508	0.2	.00787	55	12.8	8	46.4
21/64	.328125	8.3344	.03	.762	0.3	.01181	60	15.6	10	50
11/32	.34375	8.7312	.04	1.016	0.4	.01575	65	18.3	12	53.6
23/64	.359375	9.1281	.05	1.270	0.5	.01969	70	21.1	14	57.2
3/8	.375	9.5250	.06	1.524	0.6	.02362	75	23.9	16	60.8
25/64	.390625	9.9219	.07	1.778	0.7	.02756	80	26.7	18	64.4
13/32	.40625	10.3187	.08	2.032	0.8	.03150	85	29.4	20	68
27/64	.421875	10.7156	.09	2.286	0.9	.03543	90	32.2	22	71.6
7/16	.4375	11.1125	.1	2.54	1	.03937	95	35.0	24	75.2
29/64	.453125	11.5094	.2	5.08	2	.07874	100	37.8	26	78.8
15/32	.46875	11.9062	.3	7.62	3	.11811	105	40.6	28	82.4
31/64	.484375	12.3031	.4	10.16	4	.15748	110	43.3	30	86
1/2	.5	12.7000	.5	12.70	5	.19685	115	46.1	32	89.6
33/64	.515625	13.0969	.6	15.24	6	.23622	120	48.9	34	93.2
17/32	.53125	13.4937	.7	17.78	7	.27559	125	51.7	36	96.8
35/64	.546875	13.8906	.8	20.32	8	.31496	130	54.4	38	100.4
9/16	.5625	14.2875	.9	22.86	9	.35433	135	57.2	40	104
37/64	.578125	14.6844	1	25.4	10	.39370	140	60.0	42	107.6
19/32	.59375	15.0812	2	50.8	11	.43307	145	62.8	44	112.2
39/64	.609375	15.4781	3	76.2	12	.47244	150	65.6	46	114.8
5/8	.625	15.8750	4	101.6	13	.51181	155	68.3	48	118.4
41/64	.640625	16.2719	5	127.0	14	.55118	160	71.1	50	122
21/32	.65625	16.6687	6	152.4	15	.59055	165	73.9	52	125.6
43/64	.671875	17.0656	7	177.8	16	.62992	170	76.7	54	129.2
11/16	.6875	17.4625	8	203.2	17	.66929	175	79.4	56	132.8
45/64	.703125	17.8594	9	228.6	18	.70866	180	82.2	58	136.4
23/32	.71875	18.2562	10	254.0	19	.74803	185	85.0	60	140
47/64	.734375	18.6531	11	279.4	20	.78740	190	87.8	62	143.6
3/4	.75	19.0500	12	304.8	21	.82677	195	90.6	64	147.2
49/64	.765625	19.4469	13	330.2	22	.86614	200	93.3	66	150.8
25/32	.78125	19.8437	14	355.6	23	.90551	205	96.1	68	154.4
51/64	.796875	20.2406	15	381.0	24	.94488	210	98.9	70	158
13/16	.8125	20.6375	16	406.4	25	.98425	212	100.0	75	167
53/64	.828125	21.0344	17	431.8	26	1.02362	215	101.7	80	176
27/32	.84375	21.4312	18	457.2	27	1.06299	220	104.4	85	185
55/64	.859375	21.8281	19	482.6	28	1.10236	225	107.2	90	194
7/8	.875	22.2250	20	508.0	29	1.14173	230	110.0	95	203
57/64	.890625	22.6219	21	533.4	30	1.18110	235	112.8	100	212
29/32	.90625	23.0187	22	558.8	31	1.22047	240	115.6	105	221
59/64	.921875	23.4156	23	584.2	32	1.25984	245	118.3	110	230
15/16	.9375	23.8125	24	609.6	33	1.29921	250	121.1	115	239
61/64	.953125	24.2094	25	635.0	34	1.33858	255	123.9	120	248
31/32	.96875	24.6062	26	660.4	35	1.37795	260	126.6	125	257
63/64	.984375	25.0031	27	690.6	36	1.41732	265	129.4	130	266

CAPACITY CONVERSION U.S. GALLONS TO LITRES

Gallons	0	1	2	3	4	5
	Litres	Litres	Litres	Litres	Litres	Litres
0	00.0000	3.7853	7.5707	11.3560	15.1413	18.9267
10	37.8533	41.6387	45.4240	49.2098	52.9947	56.7800
20	75.7066	79.4920	83.2773	87.0626	90.8480	94.6333
30	113.5600	117.3453	121.1306	124.9160	128.7013	132.4866
40	151.4133	155.1986	158.9840	162.7693	166.5546	170.3400

Auto Mechanics Fundamentals

MILLIMETRE CONVERSION CHART

mm. / Ins.	15 = .5905	30 = 1.1811	45 = 1.7716	60 = 2 3622	75 = 2.9527	90 = 3.5433	105 = 4.1338	120 = 4.7244
.25 = .0098	15.25 = .6004	30.25 = 1.1909	45.25 = 1.7815	60.25 = 2.3720	75.25 = 2.9626	90.25 = 3.5531	105.25 = 4.1437	120.25 = 4.7342
.50 = .0197	15.50 = .6102	30.50 = 1.2008	45.50 = 1.7913	60.50 = 2.3819	75.50 = 2.9724	90.50 = 3.5630	105.50 = 4.1535	120.50 = 4.7441
.75 = .0295	15.75 = .6201	30.75 = 1.2106	45.75 = 1.8012	60.75 = 2.3917	75.75 = 2.9823	90.75 = 3.5728	105.75 = 4.1634	120.75 = 4.7539
1 = .0394	16 = .6299	31 = 1.2205	46 = 1.8110	61 = 2.4016	76 = 2.9921	91 = 3.5827	106 = 4.1732	121 = 4.7638
1.25 = .0492	16.25 = .6398	31.25 = 1.2303	46.25 = 1.8209	61.25 = 2.4114	76.25 = 3.0020	91.25 = 3.5925	106.25 = 4.1831	121.25 = 4.7736
1.50 = .0591	16.50 = .6496	31.50 = 1.2402	46.50 = 1.8307	61.50 = 2.4213	76.50 = 3.0118	91.50 = 3.6024	106.50 = 4.1929	121.50 = 4.7885
1.75 = .0689	16.75 = .6594	31.75 = 1.2500	46.75 = 1.8405	61.75 = 2.4311	76.75 = 3.0216	91.75 = 3.6122	106.75 = 4.2027	121.75 = 4.7933
2 = .0787	17 = .6693	32 = 1.2598	47 = 1.8504	62 = 2.4409	77 = 3.0315	92 = 3.6220	107 = 4.2126	122 = 4.8031
2.25 = .0886	17.25 = .6791	32.25 = 1.2697	47.25 = 1.8602	62.25 = 2.4508	77.25 = 3.0413	92.25 = 3.6319	107.25 = 4.2224	122.25 = 4.8130
2.50 = .0984	17.50 = .6890	32.50 = 1.2795	47.50 = 1.8701	62.50 = 2.4606	77.50 = 3.0512	92.50 = 3.6417	107.50 = 4.2323	122.50 = 4.8228
2.75 = .1083	17.75 = .6988	32.75 = 1.2894	47.75 = 1.8799	62.75 = 2.4705	77.75 = 3.0610	92.75 = 3.6516	107.75 = 4.2421	122.75 = 4.8327
3 = .1181	18 = .7087	33 = 1.2992	48 = 1.8898	63 = 2.4803	78 = 3.0709	93 = 3.6614	108 = 4.2520	123 = 4.8425
3.25 = .1280	18.25 = .7185	33.25 = 1.3091	48.25 = 1.8996	63.25 = 2.4901	78.25 = 3.0807	93.25 = 3.6713	108.25 = 4.2618	123.25 = 4.8524
3.50 = .1378	18.50 = .7283	33.50 = 1.3189	48.50 = 1.9094	63.50 = 2.5000	78.50 = 3.0905	93.50 = 3.6811	108.50 = 4.2716	123.50 = 4.8622
3.75 = .1476	18.75 = .7382	33.75 = 1.3287	48.75 = 1.9193	63.75 = 2.5098	78.75 = 3.1004	93.75 = 3.6909	108.75 = 4.2815	123.75 = 4.8720
4 = .1575	19 = .7480	34 = 1.3386	49 = 1.9291	64 = 2.5197	79 = 3.1102	94 = 3.7008	109 = 4.2913	124 = 4.8819
4.25 = .1673	19.25 = .7579	34.25 = 1.3484	49.25 = 1.9390	64.25 = 2.5295	79.25 = 3.1201	94.25 = 3.7106	109.25 = 4.3012	124.25 = 4.8917
4.50 = .1772	19.50 = .7677	34.50 = 1.3583	49.50 = 1.9488	64.50 = 2.5394	79.50 = 3.1299	94.50 = 3.7205	109.50 = 4.3110	124.50 = 4.9016
4.75 = .1870	19.75 = .7776	34.75 = 1.3681	49.75 = 1.9587	64.75 = 2.5492	79.75 = 3.1398	94.75 = 3.7303	109.75 = 4.3209	124.75 = 4.9114
5 = .1968	20 = .7874	35 = 1.3779	50 = 1.9685	65 = 2.5590	80 = 3.1496	95 = 3.7401	110 = 4.3307	125 = 4.9212
5.25 = .2067	20.25 = .7972	35.25 = 1.3878	50.25 = 1.9783	65.25 = 2.5689	80.25 = 3.1594	95.25 = 3.7500	110.25 = 4.3405	125.25 = 4.9311
5.50 = .2165	20.50 = .8071	35.50 = 1.3976	50.50 = 1.9882	65.50 = 2.5787	80.50 = 3.1693	95.50 = 3.7598	110.50 = 4.3504	125.50 = 4.9409
5.75 = .2264	20.75 = .8169	35.75 = 1.4075	50.75 = 1.9980	65.75 = 2.5886	80.75 = 3.1791	95.75 = 3.7697	110.75 = 4.3602	125.75 = 4.9508
6 = .2362	21 = .8268	36 = 1.4173	51 = 2.0079	66 = 2.5984	81 = 3.1890	96 = 3.7795	111 = 4.3701	126 = 4.9606
6.25 = .2461	21.25 = .8366	36.25 = 1.4272	51.25 = 2.0177	66.25 = 2.6083	81.25 = 3.1988	96.25 = 3.7894	111.25 = 4.3799	126.25 = 4.9705
6.50 = .2559	21.50 = .8465	36.50 = 1.4370	51.50 = 2.0276	66.50 = 2.6181	81.50 = 3.2087	96.50 = 3.7992	111.50 = 4.3898	126.50 = 4.9803
6.75 = .2657	21.75 = .8563	36.75 = 1.4468	51.75 = 2.0374	66.75 = 2.6279	81.75 = 3.2185	96.75 = 3.8090	111.75 = 4.3996	126.75 = 4.9901
7 = .2756	22 = .8661	37 = 1.4567	52 = 2.0472	67 = 2.6378	82 = 3.2283	97 = 3.8189	112 = 4.4094	127 = 5.0000
7.25 = .2854	22.25 = .8760	37.25 = 1 4665	52.25 = 2.0571	67.25 = 2.6476	82.25 = 3.2382	97.25 = 3.8287	112.25 = 4.4193	
7.50 = .2953	22.50 = .8858	37.50 = 1.4764	52.50 = 2.0669	67.50 = 2.6575	82.50 = 3.2480	97.50 = 3.8386	112.50 = 4.4291	
7.75 = .3051	22.75 = .8957	37.75 = 1.4862	52.75 = 2.0768	67.75 = 2.6673	82.75 = 3.2579	97.75 = 3.8484	112.75 = 4.4390	
8 = .3150	23 = .9055	38 = 1.4961	53 = 2.0866	68 = 2.6772	83 = 3.2677	98 = 3.8583	113 = 4.4488	
8.25 = .3248	23.25 = .9153	38.25 = 1.5059	53.25 = 2.0965	68.25 = 2.6870	83.25 = 3.2776	98.25 = 3.8681	113.25 = 4.4587	
8.50 = .3346	23.50 = 9252	38.50 = 1.5157	53.50 = 2.1063	68.50 = 2.6968	83.50 = 3.2874	98.50 = 3.8779	113.50 = 4.4685	
8.75 = .3445	23.75 = .9350	38.75 = 1.5256	53.75 = 2.1161	68.75 = 2.7067	83.75 = 3.2972	98.75 = 3.8878	113.75 = 4.4783	
9 = .3543	24 = .9449	39 = 1.5354	54 = 2.1260	69 = 2.7165	84 = 3.3071	99 = 3.8976	114 = 4.4882	
9.25 = .3642	24.25 = .9547	39.25 = 1.5453	54.25 = 2.1358	69.25 = 2.7264	84.25 = 3.3169	99.25 = 3.9075	114.25 = 4.4980	
9.50 = .3740	24.50 = .9646	39.50 = 1.5551	54.50 = 2.1457	69.50 = 2.7362	84.50 = 3.3268	99.50 = 3.9173	114.50 = 4.5079	
9.75 = .3839	24.75 = .9744	39.75 = 1.5650	54.75 = 2.1555	69.75 = 2.7461	84.75 = 3.3366	99.75 = 3.9272	114.75 = 4.5177	
10 = .3937	25 = .9842	40 = 1.5748	55 = 2.1653	70 = 2.7559	85 = 3.3464	100 = 3.9370	115 = 4.5275	
10.25 = .4035	25.25 = .9941	40.25 = 1.5846	55.25 = 2.1752	70.25 = 2.7657	85.25 = 3.3563	100.25 = 3.9468	115.25 = 4.5374	
10.50 = .4134	25.50 = 1.0039	40.50 = 1.5945	55.50 = 2.1850	70.50 = 2.7756	85.50 = 3.3661	100.50 = 3.9567	115.50 = 4.5472	
10.75 = .4232	25.75 = 1.0138	40.75 = 1.6043	55.75 = 2.1949	70.75 = 2.7854	85.75 = 3.3760	100.75 = 3.9665	115.75 = 4.5571	
11 = .4331	26 = 1.0236	41 = 1.6142	56 = 2.2047	71 = 2.7953	86 = 3.3858	101 = 3.9764	116 = 4.5669	
11.25 = .4429	26.25 = 1.0335	41.25 = 1.6240	56.25 = 2.2146	71.25 = 2.8051	86.25 = 3.3957	101.25 = 3.9862	116.25 = 4.5768	
11.50 = .4528	26.50 = 1.0433	41.50 = 1.6339	56.50 = 2.2244	71.50 = 2.8150	86.50 = 3.4055	101.50 = 3.9961	116.50 = 4.5866	
11.75 = .4626	26.75 = 1.0531	41.75 = 1.6437	56.75 = 2.2342	71.75 = 2.8248	86.75 = 3.4153	101.75 = 4.0059	116.75 = 4.5964	
12 = .4724	27 = 1.0630	42 = 1.6535	57 = 2.2441	72 = 2.8346	87 = 3.4252	102 = 4.0157	117 = 4.6063	
12.25 = .4823	27.25 = 1.0728	42.25 = 1.6634	57.25 = 2.2539	72.25 = 2.8445	87.25 = 3.4350	102.25 = 4.0256	117.25 = 4.6161	
12.50 = .4921	27.50 = 1.0827	42.50 = 1.6732	57.50 = 2.2638	72.50 = 2.8543	87.50 = 3.4449	102.50 = 4.0354	117.50 = 4.6260	
12.75 = .5020	27.75 = 1.0925	42.75 = 1.6831	57.75 = 2.2736	72.75 = 2.8642	87.75 = 3.4547	102.75 = 4.0453	117.75 = 4.6358	
13 = .5118	28 = 1.1024	43 = 1.6929	58 = 2.2835	73 = 2.8740	88 = 3.4646	103 = 4.0551	118 = 4.6457	
13.25 = .5217	28.25 = 1.1122	43.25 = 1.7028	58.25 = 2.2933	73.25 = 2.8839	88.25 = 3.4744	103.25 = 4.0650	118.25 = 4.6555	
13.50 = .5315	28.50 = 1.1220	43.50 = 1.7126	58.50 = 2.3031	73.50 = 2.8937	88.50 = 3.4842	103.50 = 4.0748	118.50 = 4.6653	
13.75 = .5413	28.75 = 1.1319	43.75 = 1.7224	58.75 = 2.3130	73.75 = 2.9035	88.75 = 3.4941	103.75 = 4.0846	118.75 = 4.6752	
14 = .5512	29 = 1.1417	44 = 1.7323	59 = 2.3228	74 = 2.9134	89 = 3.5039	104 = 4.0945	119 = 4.6850	
14.25 = .5610	29.25 = 1.1516	44.25 = 1.7421	59.25 = 2.3327	74.25 = 2.9232	89.25 = 3.5138	104.25 = 4.1043	119.25 = 4.6949	
14.50 = .5709	29.50 = 1.1614	44.50 = 1.7520	59.50 = 2.3425	74.50 = 2.9331	89.50 = 3.5236	104.50 = 4.1142	119.50 = 4.7047	
14.75 = .5807	29.75 = 1.1713	44.75 = 1.7618	59.75 = 2.3524	74.74 = 2.9429	89.75 = 3.5335	104.75 = 4.1240	119.75 = 4.7146	

DICTIONARY OF AUTOMOTIVE TERMS

AAA: American Automobile Association.

ABDC: After Bottom Dead Center.

ABSOLUTE ZERO: A state in which no heat is present. Believed to be −459.7°F or −273.16°C.

AC: Alternating current.

ACCELERATOR: Floor pedal used to control, through linkage, throttle valve in carburetor.

ACCELERATOR PUMP: Small pump, located in carburetor, that sprays additional gasoline into air stream during acceleration.

ACCUMULATOR (Air Conditioning): Receiver-dehydrator combination.

ACCUMULATOR PISTON (Automatic Transmission): Unit designed to assist the servo to apply brake bank quickly, yet smoothly.

ACETYLENE: Gas commonly used in welding or cutting operations.

ACKERMAN PRINCIPLE: Bending outer ends of steering arms slightly inward so that when car is making a turn, inside wheel will turn more sharply than outer wheel. This principle produces toe-out on turns.

ADDITIVE: Solution, powder, etc., added to gasoline, oil, grease, etc., in an endeavor to improve characteristics of original product.

ADVANCE (Ignition timing): To set ignition timing so a spark occurs earlier or more degrees before TDC.

AEA: Automotive Electric Association.

AERA: Automotive Engine Rebuilders Association.

AFBMA: Antifriction Bearing Manufacturers Association.

AHRA: American Hot Rod Association.

AIR: Air Injection Reactor system of reducing objectionable exhaust emissions.

AIR BLEED: An orifice or small passageway designed to allow a specific amount of air to enter a moving column of liquid (such as fuel).

AIR CLEANER: Device used to remove dust, abrasive, etc., from air being drawn into an engine, compressor, power brake, etc.

AIR CONDITIONING: Controlling the temperature, movement, cleanliness, and humidity of air.

AIR COOLED: An object cooled by passing a stream of air over its surface.

AIR DAM: A device placed beneath front bumper to reduce amount of air turbulence and drag under car.

AIR FILTER: A device through which air is drawn to remove dust, dirt, etc.

AIR FOIL: Device, similar to a stubby wing, mounted onto a racing car or dragster to provide high speed stability. The air foil is mounted in a horizontal position.

AIR-FUEL RATIO: Ratio (by weight or by volume) between air and gasoline that makes up engine fuel mixture.

AIR GAP (Regulator): Distance between contact armature and iron core that when magnetized, draws armature down.

AIR GAP (Spark Plugs): Distance between center and side electrodes.

AIR HORN (Carburetor): Top portion of air passageway through carburetor.

AIR HORN (Accessory): Warning horn operated by compressed air.

AIR INJECTION REACTION: An emission control system used to lower levels of carbon monoxide and hydrocarbon emissions. Accomplished by injecting a stream of air into exhaust stream near exhaust valve.

AIR POLLUTION: Contamination of earth's atmosphere by various natural and manufactured pollutants such as smoke, gases, dust, etc.

AIR SPRING: Container and plunger separated by air under pressure. When container and plunger attempt to squeeze together, air compresses and produces a spring effect. Air spring has been used on some suspension systems.

ALIGN: To bring various parts of unit into correct positions in respect to each other or to a predetermined location.

ALLOY: Mixture of two or more materials.

ALNICO MAGNET: Magnet using (Al) aluminum, (Ni) nickel, and (Co) cobalt in its construction.

ALPHA NUMERIC (Tire): Tire size designation using letters to indicate load carrying capacity. Example: GR 78-15. The letter G = load/size relationship. R = radial construction. 78 = height to width ratio. 15 = rim diameter in inches.

ALTERNATOR: Device similar to generator but which produces AC current. The AC must be rectified before reaching the car's electrical system.

ALTERNATING CURRENT (AC): Electric current that first flows one way in circuit and then other. Type used in homes.

AMA: Automobile Manufacturers Association.

AMBIENT TEMPERATURE: Temperature of air surrounding an object.

AMC: American Motors Corporation.

AMMETER: Instrument used to measure rate of current flow in amperes.

AMPERE: Unit of measurement used in expressing rate of current flow in a circuit.

AMPERE HOUR CAPACITY: Measurement of storage battery ability to deliver specified current over specified length of time.

ANEROID: A device, such as a barometer bellows, that neither contains nor uses a liquid.

ANEROID BAROMETER: A device to measure atmospheric pressure. It utilizes an aneroid capsule (bellows) that expands and contracts with differences in pressure.

ANGLE OF APPROACH: The steepest angle that a vehicle can drive up on from a level surface without dragging the front end of vehicle.

ANGLE OF DEPARTURE: The steepest angle that a vehicle can descend and drive off onto a level surface without dragging rear of vehicle.

ANNEAL: To remove hardness from metal. Heat steel to a red color, then allow it to cool slowly. Unlike steel, copper is annealed by heating, and then plunging it immediately into cold water.

ANODE: In an electrical circuit—the positive pole.

ANTIBACKFIRE VALVE: Valve used in air injection reaction (exhaust emission control) system to prevent backfiring during period immediately following sudden deceleration.

ANTIFREEZE: Chemical added to cooling system to prevent coolant from freezing in cold weather.

ANTIFRICTION BEARING: Bearing containing rollers or balls plus an inner and outer race. Bearing is designed to roll, thus minimizing friction.

ANTIKNOCK (Fuel): Indicates various substances, such as tetraethyl lead, that can be added to gasoline to improve its resistance to knocking (spark knock, preignition, or detonation).

ANTIPERCOLATOR: Device for venting vapors from main discharge tube, or well, of a carburetor.

API: American Petroleum Institute.

APRA: Automotive Parts Rebuilders Association.

APPRENTICE PROGRAM: Educational program designed to teach a trade through on-the-job training and study.

ARC OR ELECTRIC WELDING: Welding by using electric current to melt both metal to be welded and welding rod or electrode that is being added.

ARCING: Electricity leaping the gap between two electrodes.

ARMATURE (Relay, regulator, horn, etc.): The movable part of the unit.

ARMATURE (Starter or generator): The portion that revolves between the pole shoes, made up of wire windings on an iron core.

ASBESTOS: Heat resistant and nonburning fibrous mineral widely used for brake shoes, clutch linings, etc. Do not inhale asbestos fibers or dust. Believed to cause cancer.

ASLE: American Society of Lubrication Engineers.

ASME: American Society of Mechanical Engineers.

ASSE: American Society of Safety Engineers.

ASPECT RATIO (Tire): Ratio between

height and width of a tire.

ASTM: American Society of Testing Materials.

ASYMMETRIC TIRE TREAD: Tire tread with a non-symmetrical (uneven) pattern. Designed to reduce tire vibration and noise.

ATA: American Trucking Association.

ATDC: After Top Dead Center.

ATMOSPHERE: Layer of gases (referred to as air) surrounding earth.

ATMOSPHERIC PRESSURE: Pressure exerted by atmosphere on all things exposed to it. Around 14.7 pounds per square inch or 101 kPa at sea level.

ATOM: Tiny particle of matter made up of electrons, protons, and neutrons. Atoms or combinations of atoms make up molecules. The electrons orbit around the center or nucleus made up of the protons and neutrons.

ATOMIZE: To break a liquid into tiny droplets.

AUTOMATIC CHOKE: A carburetor choke device that automatically positions itself in accordance with carburetor needs.

AUTOMATIC LEVELING CONTROL: Pressure system which maintains proper body height with changes in load.

AUTOMATIC TRANSMISSION: A transmission that shifts itself. Shift range and points are determined by road speed, quadrant position, engine loading, altitude, etc.

AWL (Tire): Sharp pointed steel tool used to probe cuts, nail holes, etc., in tires.

AXIAL: Direction parallel to shaft or bearing hole.

AXLE (Full-floating): Axle used to drive rear wheels. It does not hold them on nor support them.

AXLE (Semi or one-quarter floating): Axle used to drive wheels, hold them on, and support them.

AXLE (Three-quarter floating): Axle used to drive rear wheels as well as hold them on. It does not support them.

AXLE END GEARS: Two gears, one per axle, that are splined to the inner ends of drive axles. They mesh with and are driven by "spider" gears.

AXLE HOUSING: Enclosure for axles and differential. It is partially filled with differential fluid (oil).

AXLE RATIO: Relationship or ratio between the number of times the propeller shaft must revolve to turn the axle drive shafts one turn.

BACKFIRE (Intake system): Burning of fuel mixture in intake manifold. May be caused by faulty timing, crossed plug wires, leaky intake valve, etc.

BACKFIRE (Exhaust system): Passage of unburned fuel mixture into exhaust system where it is ignited and causes an explosion (backfire).

BACKLASH: Amount of "play" between two parts. In case of gears, it refers to how much one gear can be moved back and forth without moving gear into which it is meshed.

BACK PRESSURE: Refers to resistance to flow of exhaust gases through exhaust system.

BACKUP LIGHTS: White lights attached to the rear of a vehicle. Lights are turned on whenever transmission is placed in reverse. Provides illumination for backing at night.

BAFFLE: Obstruction used to slow down or divert the flow of gases, liquids, sound, etc.

BALANCE (Tire): See Static Balance and Dynamic Balance.

BALK RING: Ring attached to balk gear hub in overdrive unit. It lets gear rotate while ring is stationary.

BALL AND TRUNION: Type of universal joint using needle bearing mounted balls which swivel inside sockets.

BALL BEARING: (Antifriction): Bearing consisting of an inner and outer hardened steel race separated by a series of hardened steel balls.

BALL JOINT: Flexible joint utilizing ball and socket type of construction. Used in steering linkage setups, steering knuckle pivot supports, etc.

BALL JOINT ROCKER ARMS: Rocker arms that instead of being mounted on shaft, are mounted upon ball-shaped device on end of stud.

BALL JOINT STEERING KNUCKLE: Steering knuckle that pivots on ball joints instead of on a kingpin.

BALLAST RESISTOR: Resistor constructed of special type wire, properties of which tend to increase or decrease voltage in direct proportion to heat of wire.

BAROMETRIC PRESSURE: Atmospheric pressure as determined by a barometer.

BASE CIRCLE: As applied to camshaft — lowest spot on cam. Area of cam directly opposite lobe.

BATTERY: Electrochemical device for producing electricity.

BATTERY CAPACITY: Rating of current output of battery. Determined by plate size, number of plates, and amount of acid in electrolyte.

BATTERY CHARGING: Process of renewing battery by passing electric current through battery in reverse direction.

BATTERY — MAINTENANCE-FREE: A battery so designed as to not need any additional water during its normal service life.

BATTERY RATING: Standardized measurement of battery's ability to deliver electrical energy under specified conditions.

BATTERY RESERVE CAPACITY: Measurement (in minutes) of battery's ability to supply electrical energy to the electrical system in event generating system is inoperative.

BATTERY RESERVE CAPACITY RATING: The measure of number of minutes a full charged battery at 80°F (26.7°C) can be discharged at 25 amperes and still maintain a minimum voltage of 1.75 volts per cell.

BATTERY SHEDDING: Grids loosing active materials that fall off and settle in bottom of battery case.

BATTERY STATE OF CHARGE: Electrical energy available from a given battery in relation to that which would be normally available if battery were fully charged.

BATTERY VOLTAGE: Determined by the number of cells. Each cell has 2.1V. Three cells will produce a 6V battery and six cells a 12V battery.

BBDC: Before Bottom Dead Center.

BCI: Battery Council International.

BDC: Bottom Dead Center.

BEAD (Tire): Steel wire reinforced portion of tire that engages the wheel rim.

BEARING: Area of unit in which contacting surface of a revolving part rests.

BEARING CLEARANCE: Amount of space left between shaft and bearing surface. This space is for lubricating oil to enter.

BELL HOUSING (Clutch housing): Metal covering around flywheel and clutch, or torque converter assembly.

BELTED BIAS: Tire plies crisscrossed; belts beneath tread area.

BENDIX TYPE STARTER DRIVE: A self-engaging starter drive gear. Gear moves into engagement when starter starts spinning and automatically disengages when starter stops.

BEVEL GEAR: Gear in which teeth are cut in a cone shape, as found in axle end gears.

BEVEL SPUR GEAR: Gear in which teeth are cut in a cone shape. Teeth are aligned with cone centerline, as found in some differential gears.

BEZEL: Crimped edge of metal that secures glass face to an instrument.

BHP: Brake horsepower. Measurement of actual power produced by engine.

BIAS PLY: Tire plies crisscross; belts not used under tread area.

BLEEDING: Removing air, pressure, fluid, etc., from a closed system, as in air conditioning.

BLEEDING THE BRAKES: Refers to removal of air from hydraulic system. Bleeder screws are loosened at each wheel cylinder, (one at a time) and brake fluid is forced from master cylinder through lines until all air is expelled.

BLOCK: Part of engine containing cylinders.

BLOW-BY: Refers to escape of exhaust gases past piston rings.

BLOWER: Supercharger.

BLUEPRINTING (Engine): Dismantling engine and reassembling it to EXACT specifications.

BMEP: Brake Mean Effective Pressure.

BODY PUTTY: Material designed to smooth on dented body areas. Upon hardening, putty is dressed down and area painted.

BOILING POINT: Exact temperature at which a liquid begins to boil.

BONDED BRAKE LINING: Brake lining that is attached to brake shoe by adhesive.

BOOSTER: Device incorporated in car system (such as brakes and steering), to increase pressure output or decrease amount of effort required to operate or both.

BOOT: British term for trunk.

BORE: May refer to cylinder itself or to diameter of the cylinder.

BORE DIAMETER: Diameter of cylinders.

BORING: Renewing cylinders by cutting them out to a specified size. Boring bar is used to make cut.

BORING BAR (Cylinder): Machine used to cut engine cylinders to specific size. As used in garages, to cut worn cylinders to a new diameter.

BOSS: A rib or enlarged area designed to strengthen a certain portion or area of an object.

BOTTLED GAS: LPG (Liquefied Petroleum Gas) gas compressed into strong metal tanks. When confined in tank under pressure, gas is in liquid form.

BOUND ELECTRONS: Electrons in inner orbits around nucleus of atom. They are difficult to move out of orbit.

BOURDON TUBE: Circular, hollow piece of metal used in some instruments. Pressure on hollow section causes it to attempt to straighten. Free end then moves needle on gauge face.

BOXED FRAME: A frame in which two channel shaped rails are welded together (open side to open side) forming a box shape providing great strength.

BOXED ROD: Connecting rod in which I-beam section has been stiffened by welding plates on each side of the rod.

BRAKE ANCHOR: Steel stud upon which one end of brake shoes is either attached to or rests against. Anchor is firmly affixed to backing plate.

BRAKE ANTI-ROLL DEVICE: Unit installed in brake system to hold brake line pressure when car is stopped on upgrade. When car is stopped on upgrade and brake pedal released, anti-roll device will keep brakes applied until either clutch is released or, as on some models, accelerator is depressed.

BRAKE BACKING PLATE: Rigid steel plate upon which brake shoes are attached. Braking force applied to shoes is absorbed by backing plate.

BRAKE BAND: Band, faced with brake lining, that encircles a brake drum. Used on several parking brake installations.

BRAKE BLEEDING: See Bleeding the Brakes.

BRAKE CYLINDER: See Wheel Cylinder.

BRAKE – DISC TYPE: Braking system that instead of using conventional brake drum with internal brake shoes, uses steel disc with caliper type lining application. When brakes are applied, section of lining on each side of spinning disc is forced against disc thus imparting braking force. This type of brake is very resistant to brake fade.

BRAKE DRUM: Cast iron or aluminum housing, bolted to wheel, that rotates around brake shoes. When shoes are expanded, they rub against machined inner surface of brake drum and exert braking effect upon wheel.

BRAKE DRUM LATHE: Machine to refinish inside of a brake drum.

BRAKE FADE: Reduction in braking force due to loss of friction between brake shoes and drum. Caused by heat buildup.

BRAKE FEEL: Discernible, to driver, relationship between the amount of brake pedal pressure and the actual braking force being exerted. Special device is incorporated in power brake installations to give driver this feel.

BRAKE FLUID: Special fluid used in hydraulic brake systems. Never use anything else in place of regular fluid.

BRAKE FLUSHING: Cleaning brake system by flushing with alcohol or brake fluid. Done to remove water, dirt, or any other contaminant. Flushing fluid is placed in master cylinder and forced through lines and wheel cylinders where it exits at cylinder bleed screws.

BRAKE HORSEPOWER (bhp): Measurement of actual usable horsepower delivered at crankshaft. Commonly computed using an engine on a chassis dynamometer.

BRAKE HOSE: Flexible hose which connects brake lines to wheel cylinders. It allows suspension movement without damage.

BRAKE LINE: Steel tubing which carries brake fluid from master cylinder to wheel cylinders.

BRAKE LINING: Friction material fastened to brake shoes. Brake lining is pressed against rotating brake drum thus stopping car.

BRAKE – PARKING or EMERGENCY: Brake used to hold car in position while parked. One type applies rear brake shoes by mechanical means and other type applies brake band to brake drum installed in drive train.

BRAKE – POWER: Conventional hydraulic brake system that utilizes either engine vacuum or hydraulic pressure to operate a power piston. Power piston applies pressure directly to master cylinder piston. This reduces amount of pedal pressure driver must exert to stop car.

BRAKE SHOE GRINDER: Grinder used to grind brake shoe lining so it will be square to and concentric with brake drum.

BRAKE SHOE HEEL: End of brake shoe adjacent to anchor bolt or pin.

BRAKE SHOE TOE: Free end of shoe, not attached to or resting against an anchor pin.

BRAKE SHOES: Part of brake system, located at wheels, upon which brake lining is attached. When wheel cylinders are actuated by hydraulic pressure, they force brake shoes apart and bring lining into contact with drum.

BRAKES – POWER BOOSTER (Hydraulic): Brake booster employing hydraulic pressure from the power steering system to apply force to master cylinder.

BRAZE: To join two pieces of metal together by heating edges to be joined and then melting drops of brass or bronze on area. Unlike welding, this operation is similar to soldering, only a higher melting point material is used.

BREAK-IN: Period of operation between installation of new or rebuilt parts and time in which parts are worn to the correct fit. Driving at reduced and varying speed for a specified mileage to permit parts to wear to the correct fit.

BREAK-OVER ANGLE: Included angle that a vehicle can cross over without dragging underneath center section. Break-over angle is determined by vehicle ground clearance and wheelbase.

BREAKER (Tire): Rubber or fabric (or both) strip placed under tread to provide additional protection for main tire carcass.

BREAKER ARM: Movable arm upon which one of breaker points is affixed.

BREAKER POINTS (Ignition): Pair of movable points that are opened and closed to break and make the primary circuit.

BREATHER PIPE: Pipe opening into interior of engine. Used to assist ventilation. Pipe usually extends downward to a point just below engine so passing air stream will form a partial vacuum thus assisting in venting engine.

BROACH: Bringing metal surface to desired shape by forcing multiple-edged cutting tool across surface.

BRONZE: An alloy basically consisting of tin and copper.

BRUSH: Pieces of carbon, or copper, that rub against the commutator on generator and starter motor.

B&S GAUGE (Brown and Sharpe): Standard measure of wire diameter.

BTDC: Before Top Dead Center.

BTU (British thermal unit): Measurement of the amount of heat required to raise the temperature of one pound of water, one degree Fahrenheit.

BUDC: Before Upper Dead Center. Same as BTDC.

BURNISH: To bring a surface to a high shine by rubbing with hard, smooth object.

BUSHING: Bearing for shaft, spring shackle, piston pin, etc., of one piece construction which may be removed from part.

BUTANE: Petroleum gas that is liquid, when under pressure. Often used as engine fuel in trucks.

BUTTERFLY VALVE: Valve in carburetor that is so named due to its resemblance to insect of same name.

BYPASS: To move around or detour regular route or circuit taken by air, fluid, electricity, etc.

BY-PASS FILTER: Oil filter that constantly filters' PORTION of oil flowing through engine.

BY-PASS VALVE: Valve that can open and allow fluid to pass through in other than its normal channel.

CAFE: Corporate Average Fuel Economy.

CALIBRATE: As applied to test instruments—adjusting dial needle to correct zero or load setting.

CALIPER (Brake): Disc brake component which forms cylinder and houses piston and brake pads (linings). It produces clamping action on rotating disc to stop car.

CALIPERS (Inside and Outside): Adjustable measuring tool placed around or within an object and adjusted until it just contacts. It is then withdrawn and distance measured between contacting points.

CALORIE (Gram): A unit of heat. Amount of heat required to raise the temperature of one gram of water 1 deg. centigrade.

CALORIFIC VALUE: Measurement of the heating value of fuel.

CALORIMETER: Measuring instrument used to determine amount of heat produced when a substance is burned; also friction and chemical change heat production.

CAM: Offset portion of shaft that will, when shaft turns, impart motion to another part such as valve lifters.

CAM ANGLE or DWELL (Ignition): Number of degrees breaker cam rotates from time breaker points close until they open again.

CAM GROUND: Piston ground slightly egg-shaped. When heated, it becomes round.

CAMBER: Tipping top wheel centerline outward produces positive camber. Tipping wheel centerline inward at top produces negative camber. When camber is positive, tops of tires are further apart than bottom.

CAMSHAFT: Shaft with cam lobes (bumps) used to operate valves.

CAMSHAFT GEAR: Gear that is used to drive camshaft.

CANDLE POWER: Measurement of light producing ability of light bulb.

CAP: Cleaner Air Package System of reducing amount of unburned hydrocarbons in automobile exhaust.

CAPACITANCE: Property of condenser that permits it to receive and retain an electrical charge.

CAPACITOR: See Condenser.

CARB: California Air Resources Board.

CARBON: Used to describe hard, or soft, black deposits found in combustion chamber, on plugs, under rings, on and under valve heads, etc.

CARBONIZE: Building up of carbon on objects such as spark plugs, pistons, heads, etc.

CARBON MONOXIDE: Deadly, colorless, odorless, and tasteless gas found in engine exhaust. Formed by incomplete burning of hydrocarbons.

CARBON PILE: Refers to amperage or voltage regulator utilizing a stack of carbon discs in its construction.

CARBURETOR: Device used to mix gasoline and air in correct proportions.

CARBURETOR ADAPTER: Adapter used to fit or place one type of carburetor on an intake manifold that may not be originally designed for it. Also used to adapt four-barrel carbs to two-barrel manifolds.

CARBURETOR CIRCUITS: Series of passageways and units designed to perform a specific function—idle circuit, full power circuit, etc.

CARBURETOR ICING: Formation of ice on throttle plate or valve. As fuel nozzles feed fuel into air horn, it turns to a vapor. This robs heat from air and when weather conditions are just right (fairly cold and quite humid), ice may form.

CARBURIZING FLAME: Welding torch flame in which there is an excess of acetylene.

CARDAN JOINT: Type of universal joint.

CARRIER BEARINGS: Bearings upon which differential case is mounted.

CASE-HARDENED: Piece of steel that has had outer surface hardened while inner portion remains relatively soft.

CASTER: Tipping top of kingpin either forward or toward the rear of car. When tipped forward, it is termed negative caster. When tipped toward rear, it is termed positive caster.

CASTING: Pouring metal into a mold to form an object.

CASTLE or CASTELLATED NUT: Nut having series of slots cut into one end, into which cotter pin may be passed to secure nut.

CATALYTIC CONVERTER: Device used in exhaust system to reduce harmful emissions. Catalyst in converter may be coated with palladium, platinum, and rhodium. Catalyst may be of oxidizing and/or reducing design.

CATHODE: In electric circuit—the negative pole.

CCS: Controlled Combustion System of reducing unburned hydrocarbon emission from engine exhaust.

CEC: Combination Emission Control.

CELL (Battery): Individual (separate) compartments in battery which contain positive and negative plates suspended in electrolyte. Six-volt battery has three cells, twelve-volt battery six cells.

CELL CONNECTOR: Lead strap or connection between battery cell groups.

CENTERLINE: Imaginary line drawn lengthwise through center of an object.

CENTER LINK: Also called relay rod or connecting link, it transfers motion from pitman arm to tie rods.

CENTER OF GRAVITY: Point in object, if through which an imaginary pivot line were drawn, would leave object in balance. In car, the closer the weight to the ground, the lower the center of gravity.

CENTER STEERING LINKAGE: Steering system utilizing two tie rods connected to steering arms and to central idler arm. Idler arm is operated by drag link that connects idler arm to pitman arm.

CENTIGRADE: Thermometer on which boiling point of water is 100 deg. and freezing point is 0 deg.

CENTRIFUGAL ADVANCE (Distributor): Unit designed to advance and retard ignition timing through action of centrifugal force.

CENTRIFUGAL CLUTCH: Clutch that utilizes centrifugal force to expand a friction device on driving shaft until it is locked to a drum on driven shaft.

CENTRIFUGAL FORCE: Force which tends to keep moving objects traveling in straight line. When moving car is forced to make a turn, centrifugal force attempts to keep it moving in straight line. If car is turning at too high a speed, centrifugal force will be greater than frictional force between tires and road and the car will slide off the road.

CERAMIC FILTER: Filtering device utilizing porous ceramic as filtering agent.

CETANE NUMBER: Measurement of diesel fuel performance characteristics.

CFM: Cubic feet per minute. A measure of air flow.

CHAMFER: To bevel (or a bevel on) edge of an object.

CHANGE OF STATE: Condition in which substance changes from a solid to a liquid, a liquid to a gas, a liquid to a solid, or a gas to a liquid.

CHARCOAL CANISTER: Emission control device containing activated charcoal granules. Used to store gasoline vapors from tank and carburetor. When engine is started, stored vapors are drawn into cylinders and burned.

CHARGE (Air Conditioning): A given or specified (by weight) amount of refrigerant.

CHARGE (Battery): Passing electric current through battery to restore it to active (charged) state.

CHARGE RATE: Electrical rate of flow, in amperes, passing through the battery during charging.

CHARGING (Air Conditioning): Inserting the specified charge (amount) of refrigerant into the air conditioning system.

CHASE: To repair damaged threads.

CHASSIS: Generally, chassis refers to frame, engine, front and rear axles, springs, steering system and gas tank. In short, everything but body and fenders.

CHASSIS DYNAMOMETER: See Dynamometer.

CHECK VALVE: Valve that opens to permit passage of fluid or air in one direction and closes to prevent passage in opposite direction.

CHILLED IRON: Cast iron possessing hardened outer skin.

CHOKE: Butterfly valve located in carburetor used to enrichen mixture for starting engine when cold.

CHOKE STOVE: Heating compartment in or on exhaust manifold from which hot air is drawn to automatic choke device.

CID: Cubic Inch Displacement.

CIRCUIT (Electrical): Source of electricity (battery), resistance unit (headlight, etc.) and wires that form path for flow of electricity from source through unit and back to source.

CIRCUIT BREAKER (Lighting System): Protective device that will make and break flow of current when current draw becomes excessive. Unlike fuse, it does not blow out but vibrates on and off thus giving driver some light to stop by.

CLEARANCE: Given amount of space between two parts—between piston and cylinder, bearing and journal, etc.

CLOCKWISE: Rotation to right as that of clock hands.

CLOSED COOLING SYSTEM: Type of system which uses an overflow tank.

CLOSED LOOP FUEL SYSTEM: A fuel system in which air-fuel ratio is constantly adjusted in relationship to hydrocarbon content of exhaust. An oxygen sensor in exhaust, working through an electronic control unit, alters either carburetor jet size or fuel injection system pulse width.

CLUSTER or COUNTER GEAR: Cluster of gears that are all cut on one long gear blank. Cluster gears ride in bottom of transmission. Cluster provides a connection between transmission input shaft and output shaft.

CLUTCH: Device used to connect or disconnect flow of power from one unit to another.

CLUTCH DIAPHRAGM SPRING: Round dish-shaped piece of flat spring steel. Used to force pressure plate against clutch disc in some clutches.

CLUTCH DISC: Part of clutch assembly splined to transmission clutch or input shaft. Faced with friction material. When clutch is engaged, disc is squeezed between flywheel and clutch pressure plate.

CLUTCH EXPLOSION: Clutches have literally flown apart (exploded) when subjected to high rpm. Scatter shield is used on competition cars to protect driver and spectators from flying parts in event clutch explodes.

CLUTCH HOUSING or BELL HOUSING: Cast iron or aluminum housing that surrounds flywheel and clutch mechanism.

CLUTCH LINKAGE: Mechanism which transfers movement from clutch pedal to throw-out fork.

CLUTCH PEDAL FREE TRAVEL: Specified distance clutch pedal may be depressed before throw-out bearing actually contacts clutch release fingers.

CLUTCH PILOT BEARING: Small bronze bushing, or in some cases ball bearing, placed in end of crankshaft or in center of flywheel depending on car, used to support outboard end of transmission input shaft.

CLUTCH PRESSURE PLATE: Part of a clutch assembly that through spring pressure, squeezes clutch disc against flywheel thereby transmitting driving force through the assembly. To disengage clutch, pressure plate is drawn away from flywheel via linkage.

CLUTCH SEMI-CENTRIFUGAL RELEASE FINGERS: Clutch release fingers that have a weight attached to them so that at high rpm release fingers place additional pressure on clutch pressure plate.

CLUTCH THROW-OUT FORK: Device or fork that straddles throw-out bearing and used to force throw-out bearing against clutch release fingers.

CO: Symbol for carbon monoxide.

COIL (Ignition): Unit used to step up battery voltage to point necessary to fire spark plugs.

COIL CORE: Multilayered mass of iron around which coil windings are wrapped. Some designs place core outside of windings.

COIL SPRING: Section of spring steel rod

wound in spiral pattern or shape. Widely used in both front and rear suspension systems.

COLD: Little or no perceptible heat.

COLD CRANKING RATING (Battery): Measurement of cranking amperes that a battery can deliver over a period of 30 seconds at 0°F (−17.8°C) and still maintain a minimum cell voltage of 1.2 volts.

COLD START INJECTOR: Fuel injector which sprays additional fuel for cold engine starting.

COLLAPSED (Piston): Piston whose skirt diameter has been reduced due to heat and forces imposed upon it during service in engine.

COMBUSTION: Process involved during burning.

COMBUSTION CHAMBER: Area above piston with piston on TDC. Head of piston, cylinder, and head form the chamber.

COMBUSTION CHAMBER VOLUME: Volume of combustion chamber (space above piston with piston on TDC) measured in cc (cubic centimetres).

COMMUTATOR: Series of copper bars connected to armature windings. Bars are insulated from each other and from armature. Brushes (as in generator or starter) rub against whirling commutator.

COMPENSATING PORT: Small hole in brake master cylinder to permit fluid to return to reservoir.

COMPENSATOR VALVE (Automatic Transmission): Valve designed to increase pressure on brake band during heavy acceleration.

COMPOUND: Two or more ingredients mixed together.

COMPRESSION: Applying pressure to a spring, or any springy substance, thus causing it to reduce its length in direction of compressing force. Applying pressure to gas, thus causing reduction in volume.

COMPRESSION CHECK: Testing compression in all cylinders at cranking speed. All plugs are removed, compression gauge placed in one plug hole, throttle cracked wide open and engine cranked until gauge no longer climbs. Compression check is a fine way in which to determine condition of valves, rings and cylinders.

COMPRESSION GAUGE: Gauge used to test compression in engine cylinders.

COMPRESSION RATIO: Relationship between cylinder volume (clearance volume) when piston is on TDC and cylinder volume when piston is on BDC.

COMPRESSION RINGS: Top piston rings, generally two, designed to seal between piston and cylinder to prevent escape of gas from combustion chamber.

COMPRESSION STROKE: Portion of piston's movement devoted to compressing the fuel mixture trapped in engine's cylinder.

COMPRESSOR (Air Conditioning): Device using a series of pistons to raise pressure of refrigerant in system. Also causes refrigerant to flow through system.

COMPRESSOR PROTECTION SWITCH (Air Conditioning): A heat and/or pressure sensitive switch to protect compressor from damage caused by loss of oil and overheating.

COMPUTERIZED IGNITION: Ignition system using sensors which feed electrical information to computer. Computer then controls ignition system and sometimes other functions (carburetor, fuel injection, transmission) for maximum efficiency.

CONCENTRIC: Two or more circles so placed as to share common center.

CONDENSE: Turning vapor back into liquid.

CONDENSER (Ignition): Unit installed between breaker points and coil to prevent arcing at breaker points. Condenser has ability to absorb and retain surges of electricity.

CONDENSER (Refrigeration): Unit in air conditioning system that cools hot compressed refrigerant and turns it from vapor into liquid.

CONDENSATION: Moisture, from air, deposited on a cool surface.

CONDUCTION: Transfer of heat from one object to another by having objects in physical contact.

CONDUCTOR: Material forming path for flow of current.

CONE CLUTCH: Clutch utilizing cone-shaped member that is forced into a cone-shaped depression in flywheel, or other driving unit, thus locking two together. Although no longer used on cars, cone clutch finds some applications in small riding tractors, heavy power mowers, etc.

CONNECTING ROD: Connecting link between piston and crankshaft.

CONNECTING ROD BEARINGS: Inserts which fit into connecting rod and ride on crankshaft journals.

CONNECTING ROD CAP: Lower removable part of rod which holds lower bearing insert.

CONSTANT DRIVE OVERDRIVE: An overdrive unit that, when engaged, is constantly connected to drive wheels and will not permit freewheeling (coasting).

CONSTANT MESH GEARS: Gears that are always in mesh with each other

CONSTANT VELOCITY UNIVERSAL JOINT: Universal joint so designed as to effect smooth transfer of torque from driven shaft to driving shaft without any fluctuations in speed of driven shaft.

CONTACT POINTS also called BREAKER POINTS: Two removable points or areas that when pressed together, complete circuit. These points are usually made of tungsten, platinum or silver.

CONTINUOUS FUEL INJECTION: A fuel injection system in which injectors are always open and as such, feed fuel constantly. Amount of fuel delivered can be determined by an airflow sensor.

CONTRACTION (Thermal): Reduction in size of object when cooled.

CONTROL RACK: Toothed rod inside mechanical injection pump which rotates pump plunger to control quantity of injected fuel.

CONVECTION: Transfer of heat from one object to another when hotter object heats surrounding air and air in turn heats other object.

COOLANT: Liquid in cooling system.

COOLING SYSTEM: System, air or water, designed to remove excess heat from engine.

CORE: When referring to casting—sand unit placed inside mold so that when metal is poured, core will leave a hollow shape.

CORONA (Electrical): Luminous discharge of electricity visible near surface of an electrical conductor under high voltage.

CORRODE: Removal of surface material from object by chemical action.

COUNTERBALANCE: Weight attached to some moving part so part will be in balance.

COUNTERBORE: Enlarging hole to certain depth.

COUNTERCLOCKWISE: Rotation to the left as opposed to that of clock hands.

COUNTERSHAFT: Intermediate shaft that receives motion from one shaft and transfers it to another. It may be fixed (gears turn on it) or it may be free to revolve.

COUNTERSINK: To make a counterbore so that head of a screw may set flush, or below the surface.

COUPLING: Connecting device used between two objects so motion of one will be imparted to other.

COUPLING POINT: This refers to point at which both pump and turbine in torque converter are traveling at same speed. The drive is almost direct at this point.

COWL: Part of car body between engine firewall and front of dash panel.

CRANKCASE: Part of engine that surrounds crankshaft. Not to be confused with the pan which is a thin steel cover that is bolted to crankcase.

CRANKCASE DILUTION: Accumulation of unburned gasoline in crankcase. Excessively rich fuel mixture or poor combustion will allow some of gasoline to pass down between pistons and cylinder walls.

CRANKCASE VENTILATION: Process of drawing clean air through interior of engine to remove blow-by gases and other fumes.

CRANKING MOTOR: Starter. Device to revolve engine crankshaft to start engine. Works through a gear engaging another gear on flywheel.

CRANKSHAFT: Shaft running length of engine. Portions of shaft are offset to form throws to which connecting rods are attached. Crankshaft is supported by main bearings.

CRANKSHAFT GEAR: Gear mounted on front of crankshaft. Used to drive camshaft gear.

CRANKSHAFT THROW: Offset part of crankshaft where connecting rods fasten.

CROSS AND ROLLER: Type of universal joint using a center cross (spider) mounted in needle bearings.

CROSS SHAFT (Steering): Shaft in steering gearbox that engages steering shaft worm. Cross shaft is splined to pitman arm.

CRUDE OIL: Petroleum in its raw or unrefined state. It forms the basis of gasoline, engine oil, diesel oil, kerosene, etc.

CUBES: Cubic inches, or cubic inch displacement of an engine.

CU. IN. (C.I.): Cubic inch.

CUNO FILTER: Filter made up of a series of fine discs or plates pressed together in a manner that leaves very minute space between discs. Liquid is forced through these openings to produce straining action.

CURRENT: Movement of free electrons through conductor.

CUTOUT (Regulator): Device to connect or disconnect generator from battery circuit. When generator is charging, cutout makes circuit. When generator stops, cutout breaks circuit. Also referred to as cutout relay, and circuit breaker.

CYCLE: Reoccuring period during which series of events take place in definite order.

CYLINDER: Hole, or holes, in cylinder block that contain pistons.

CYLINDER BLOCK: See Block.

CYLINDER BORE: See Bore.

CYLINDER HEAD: Metal section bolted on top of block. Used to cover tops of cylinders. In many cases cylinder head contains the valves. Also forms part of combustion chamber.

CYLINDER HONE: Tool that uses an abrasive to smooth out and bring to exact measurements such as engine cylinders, wheel cylinders, bushings, etc.

CYLINDER LINER: See Cylinder Sleeve.

CYLINDER SLEEVE: Replaceable cylinder. It is made of a pipe-like section that is either pressed or pushed into the block.

CYLINDER STROKE: See Stroke.

DAMPER: A unit or device designed to remove or reduce vibration, oscillation, etc., of a moving part, fluid, air, etc.

DASHBOARD: Part of body containing driving instruments, switches, etc.

DASHPOT: Unit utilizing cylinder and piston, or cylinder and diaphragm, with small vent hole, to retard or slow down movement of some part.

DC (Electrical): Direct Current.

DC (Piston Position): Dead Center. Piston at extreme top or bottom of its stroke.

DEAD AXLE: Axle that does not rotate but merely forms base upon which to attach wheels.

DEAD CENTER (Engine): Point at which piston reaches its uppermost or downmost position in cylinder. Rod crank journal would be at 12 o'clock UDC or 6 o'clock LDC.

DECELERATION: The process of slowing down in rotational speed, forward speed, etc.

DECELERATION VALVE: It feeds air into intake manifold to prevent backfiring during deceleration.

DECIBEL: A unit of measurement used to indicate a sound level or to indicate the difference in specific sound levels.

DEFLECTION RATE (Springs): Measurement of force, in lbs., required to compress leaf spring a distance of one inch.

DEGLAZER: Abrasive tool used to remove glaze from cylinder walls so a new set of rings will seat.

DEGREE (Circle): 1/360 part of a circle.

DEGREE WHEEL: Wheel-like unit attached to engine crankshaft. Used to time valves to a high degree of accuracy.

DEHYDRATE: To dry out. Remove moisture.

DEMAGNETIZE: Removing residual magnetism from an object.

DEPOLARIZE: Removal of residual magnetism thereby destroying or removing the magnetic poles.

DESICCANT: Material, such as silica-gel, placed within a container to absorb and retain moisture.

DETENT BALL AND SPRING: Spring loaded ball that snaps into a groove or notch to hold some sliding object in position.

DETERGENT: Chemical added to engine oil to improve its characteristics (sludge control, nonfoaming, etc.).

DETONATION: Fuel charge firing or burning too violently, almost exploding.

DIAGNOSIS: Process of analyzing certain symptoms, readings, etc., in order to determine underlying reason for trouble at hand.

DIAL GAUGE OR INDICATOR: Often used precision micrometer type instrument that indicates exact reading via needle moving across dial face.

DIAPHRAGM: Flexible cloth-rubber sheet stretched across an area thereby separating two different compartments.

DICHLORODIFLUOROMETHANE: Refrigerant-12 used in air conditioning system.

DIE (Forming): One of a matched pair of hardened steel blocks that are used to form metal into a desired shape.

DIE (Thread): Tool for cutting threads.

DIE CASTING: Formation of an object by forcing molten metal, plastic, etc., into a die.

DIESEL ENGINE: Internal combustion engine that uses diesel oil for fuel. True diesel does not use an ignition system but injects diesel oil into cylinders. Piston compresses air so tightly that air is hot enough to ignite diesel fuel without spark.

DIESEL FUEL GRADE: Classification of diesel fuel operating characteristics, 1-D is for cold weather and 2-D is for normal conditions.

DIESEL INJECTION PUMP: Mechanically operated fuel pump which develops high pressure to force fuel out of injectors and into combustion chambers.

DIESELING: Condition in which engine continues to run after ignition key is turned off. Also called "running on."

DIFFERENTIAL: Unit that drives both rear axles at same time but allows them to turn at different speeds when negotiating turns.

DIFFERENTIAL CASE (Carrier): Steel unit to which the ring gear is attached. Case drives spider gears and forms an inner bearing surface for axle end gears.

DIFFERENTIAL WINDING: A secondary winding in an electrical device that is wound in a reverse manner as related to the primary (main) windings.

DIMMER SWITCH: Foot or hand operated switch that operates headlight low and high beams.

DIODE: Unit having ability to pass electric current readily in one direction but resisting current flow in the other.

DIPSTICK: Metal rod that passes into oil sump. Used to determine quantity of oil in engine.

DIRECT CURRENT (DC): Electric current that flows steadily in one direction only.

DIRECT DRIVE: Such as high gear when crankshaft and drive shaft revolve at same speed.

DIRECT FUEL INJECTION: Fuel is sprayed into combustion chamber.

DIRECTIONAL STABILITY (Steering): Ability of car to move forward in straight line with minimum of driver control.

DISCHARGE (Battery): Drawing electric current from battery.

DISCHARGE PRESSURE (Air Conditioning): Pressure of refrigerant as it leaves compressor.

DISCHARGE SIDE (Air Conditioning): The high pressure section of the air conditioning system extending from the compressor to the expansion valve.

DISC WHEEL: Wheel constructed of stamped steel.

DISPLACEMENT: Total volume of air displaced by piston traveling from BDC to TDC.

DISTILLATION: Heating a liquid and then catching and condensing the vapors given off by heating process.

DISTRIBUTION TUBES (Cooling System): Tubes used in engine cooling area to guide and direct flow of coolant to vital areas.

DISTRIBUTOR (Ignition): Unit designed to make and break the ignition primary circuit and to distribute resultant high voltage to proper cylinder at correct time.

DISTRIBUTOR CAP (Ignition): Insulated cap containing central terminal with series (one per cylinder) of terminals that are evenly spaced in circular pattern around central terminal. Secondary voltage travels to central terminal where it is then channeled to one of outer terminals by the rotor.

DIVERTER VALVE: A device used in the air injection system to divert air away from the injection nozzles during periods of deceleration. Prevents "backfiring."

DOHC: Refers to an engine with double (two) overhead camshaft.

DOT: Department of Transportation.

DOUBLE FLARE: End of tubing, especially brake tubing, has a flare so made that flare area utilizes two wall thicknesses. This makes a much stronger joint and from safety standpoint, it is a must.

DOWEL PIN: Steel pin, passed through or partly through, two parts to provide proper alignment.

DOWNDRAFT CARBURETOR: A carburetor in which air passes downward through carburetor into intake manifold.

DOWNSHIFT: Shifting to lower gear.

DRAG LINK: A steel rod connecting pitman arm to one of steering knuckles. On some installations drag link connects pitman arm to a center idler arm.

DRAW (Electrical): Amount of electrical current required to operate electrical device.

DRAW (Forming): To form (such as wire) by pulling wire stock through series of hardened dies.

DRAW (Temper): Process of removing hardness from a piece of metal.

DRAW-FILING: Filing by passing file, at right angles, up and down the length of work.

DRIER (Receiver-Drier): Tank, containing desiccant, inserted in air conditioning system to absorb and retain moisture.

DRILL: Tool used to bore holes.

DRILL PRESS: Nonportable machine used for drilling.

DRIVE-FIT: Fit between two parts when they must be literally driven together.

DRIVELINE: Propeller shaft, universal joints, etc., connecting transmission output shaft to axle pinion gear shaft.

DRIVE OR PROPELLER SHAFT SAFETY STRAP: A metal strap or straps, surrounding drive shaft to prevent shaft from falling to ground in event of a universal joint or shaft failure.

DRIVE SHAFT: Shaft connecting transmission output shaft to differential pinion shaft.

DRIVE TRAIN: All parts that generate power (engine) and transmit it to road wheels (transmission, clutch, drive shaft, differential, drive axles).

DRIVING LIGHTS: Auxiliary headlights, often very bright, that can be used to increase amount of illumination provided by regular headlights.

DROP CENTER RIM: Center section of rim being lower than two outer edges. This allows bead of tire to be pushed into low area on one side while the other side is pulled over and off the flange.

DROP FORGED: Part that has been formed by heating steel blank red hot and pounding it into shape with a powerful drop hammer.

DROPPED AXLE: Front axle altered so as to lower the frame of car. Consists of bending axle downward at outer ends. (Solid front axle.)

DRY CELL or DRY BATTERY: Battery (like flashlight battery) that uses no liquid electrolyte.

DRY CHARGED BATTERY: Battery with plates charged but lacking electrolyte. When ready to be placed in service, electrolyte is added.

DRY FRICTION: Resistance to movement between two unlubricated surfaces.

DRY SLEEVE: Cylinder sleeve application in which sleeve is supported in block metal over its entire length. Coolant does not touch sleeve itself.

DRY SUMP: Instead of letting oil throw-off drain into a regular oil pan sump, system collects and pumps this oil to a remote (separate) container or sump.

DRY WEIGHT: Weight of vehicle without fluid (oil, fuel, water) in various units.

DUAL BRAKES: Tandem or dual master cylinder to provide separate brake system for both front and rear of car.

DUAL BREAKER POINTS (Ignition): Distributor using two sets of breaker points to increase cam angle so that at high engine speeds, sufficient spark will be produced to fire plugs.

DUALS: Two sets of exhaust pipes and mufflers—one for each bank of cylinders.

DWELL: See Cam Angle.

DYNAMIC BALANCE: When centerline of weight mass of a revolving object is in same plane as centerline of object, that object would be in dynamic balance. For example, weight mass of the tire must be in the same plane as centerline of wheel.

DYNAMO: Another word for generator.

DYNAMOMETER: Machine used to measure engine horsepower output. Engine dynamometer measures horsepower at crankshaft and chassis dynamometer measures horsepower output at wheels.

EARTH (Electrical): British term for ground.

EARTH WIRE: British term for ground wire.

ECCENTRIC (Off Center): Two circles, one within the other, neither sharing the same center. A protrusion on a shaft that rubs against or is connected to another part.

ECONOMIZER VALVE: Fuel flow control device within carburetor.

EEC: Evaporative Emission Control.

EGR: Exhaust Gas Recirculation.

ELECTRIC ASSIST CHOKE: A choke utilizing an electric heating unit to speed up its opening time.

ELECTRIC FUEL PUMP: Fuel pump operated by electricity and electric motor. Normally mounted in or near fuel tank.

ELECTROCHEMICAL: Chemical (battery) production of electricity.

ELECTRODE (Spark Plug): Center rod passing through insulator forms one electrode. The rod welded to shell forms another. They are referred to as center and side electrodes.

ELECTRODE (Welding): Metal rod used in arc welding.

ELECTROLYTE: Sulphuric acid and water solution in battery.

ELECTROMAGNET: Magnet produced by placing coil of wire around steel or iron bar.

When current flows through coil, bar becomes magnetized and will remain so as long as current continues to flow.

ELECTROMAGNETIC: Magnetic (generator) production of electricity.

ELECTRON: Negatively charged particle that makes up part of the atom.

ELECTRON THEORY: Accepted theory that electricity is flow of electrons from one area to another.

ELECTRONIC: Refers to electrical circuits or units employing transistors, magnetic amplifiers, computers, etc.

ELECTRONIC FUEL INJECTION: An electric solenoid type injector, engine sensors, computer, etc., used to control fuel spray into engine.

ELECTRONIC IGNITION: Ignition system with no conventional breaker points. Primary circuit is broken by magnetic pickup and electronic control unit.

ELECTROPLATE: Process of depositing gold, silver, chrome, nickel, etc., upon an object by placing object in special solution and then passing an electric current through solution. Object forms one terminal, special electrode the other. Direct current is used.

ELEMENT (Battery): Group of plates. Three elements for a six volt and six elements for the twelve volt battery. The elements are connected in series.

ELLIOT TYPE AXLE: Solid bar front axle on which ends span or straddle steering knuckle.

EMF: Electromotive force. (Voltage.)

EMISSIONS: By-products of automotive engine combustion that are discharged into atmosphere. Major pollutants are oxides of nitrogen, carbon monoxide, hydrocarbons, and various particulates. Term also includes vapor (hydrocarbon) loss from fuel tank and carburetor.

END PLAY: Amount of axial (lengthwise) movement between two parts.

ENERGY (Physics): Capacity for doing work.

ENGINE ADAPTER: Unit that allows a different engine to be installed in a car—and still bolt up to original transmission.

ENGINE (Auto): Device that converts heat energy into useful mechanical motion.

ENGINE DISPLACEMENT (Size): Volume of space through which head of piston moves in full length of its stroke—multiplied by number of cylinders in engine. Result is given in cubic inches.

ENGINE MOUNTS: Pads made of metal and rubber which hold engine to frame.

EP LUBRICANT (Extreme Pressure): Lubricant compounded to withstand very heavy loads imposed on gear teeth.

EPA: Environmental Protection Agency. This is a Federal agency.

ESC: Electronic Spark Control.

ETHYL GASOLINE: Gasoline to which Ethyl fluid has been added to improve gasoline's resistance to knocking. Slows down burning rate thereby creating a smooth pressure curve that will allow the gasoline to be used in high compression engines.

ETHYLENE GLYCOL: Chemical solution added to cooling system to protect against freezing.

EVAPORATION: Process of a liquid turning into a vapor.

EVAPORATION CONTROL SYSTEM: Emission control system designed to prevent gasoline vapors from escaping into at-

mosphere from tank and carburetor.

EVAPORATOR: Unit in air conditioning system used to transform refrigerant from a liquid to a gas. It is at this point that cooling takes place.

EXCITE: To pass an electric current through a unit such as field coils in generator.

EXHAUST CUTOUT: Y-shaped device placed in exhaust pipe ahead of muffler. Driver may channel exhaust through muffler or out other leg of the Y where exhaust passes out without going through the muffler.

EXHAUST GAS ANALYZER: Instrument used to check exhaust gases to determine combustion efficiency.

EXHAUST GAS RECIRCULATION: Admitting a controlled amount of exhaust gas into intake manifold during certain periods of engine operation. This lowers combustion flame temperature, thus reducing level of nitrogen oxides emission.

EXHAUST MANIFOLD: Connecting pipes between exhaust ports and exhaust pipe.

EXHAUST PIPE: Pipe connecting exhaust manifold to muffler.

EXHAUST SENSOR: A device placed in exhaust stream to measure oxygen content. It can, through an electronic control unit, be used to alter air-fuel ratios, engine timing, etc.

EXHAUST STROKE: Portion of piston's movement devoted to expelling burned gases from cylinder.

EXHAUST SYSTEM: Parts which carry engine exhaust to rear of car—exhaust manifold, pipes, muffler, and catalytic converter.

EXHAUST VALVE (Engine): Valve through which burned fuel charge passes on its way from cylinder to exhaust manifold.

EXPANSION TANK (Cooling System): A tank, connected to cooling system, into which water can enter or leave as needed during coolant heating (expansion) or cooling (contraction).

EXPANSION VALVE (Air Conditioning): Device used to reduce pressure and meter flow of refrigerant into evaporator.

°F: Temperature measurement in degrees Fahrenheit.

FAHRENHEIT: Thermometer on which boiling point of water is 212 deg. and freezing point is 32 deg. above zero.

FAN: A device designed to create a moving stream of air. Generally employed for cooling purposes.

FARAD: Unit of capacitance; capacitance of condenser retaining one coulomb of charge with one volt difference of potential.

FEELER GAUGE: Thin strip of hardened steel, ground to an exact thickness, used to check clearances between parts.

FENDER SKIRT: Plate designed to cover portion of rear fender wheel opening.

FERROUS METAL: Metal containing iron or steel.

F-HEAD ENGINE: Engine having one valve in the head and the other in the block.

FIBERGLASS: Mixture of glass fibers and resin that when cured (hardened) produces a very light and strong material. Used to build boats, car bodies, repair damaged areas, etc.

FIELD: Area covered or filled with a magnetic force.

FIELD COIL: Insulated wire wrapped around an iron or steel core. When current flows through wire, strong magnetic force field is built up.

FIELD FRAME: That portion of an electrical generator or motor upon which field coil is wound.

FILAMENT: Fine wire inside light bulb that heats to incandescence when current passes through it. The filament produces the light.

FILLET: Rounding joint between two parts connected at an angle.

FILTER: Device designed to remove foreign substances from air, oil, gasoline, water, etc.

FINAL DRIVE RATIO: Overall gear reduction (includes transmission, overdrive, auxiliary transmission, etc., gear ratio as well as axle ratio) at front or rear wheels.

FINISHING STONE (Hone): Fine stone used for final finishing during honing.

FIRE WALL: Metal partition between driver's compartment and engine compartment.

FIRING ORDER: Order in which cylinders must be fired—1, 5, 3, 6, 2, 4, etc.

FIT: Contact area between two parts.

FLARING TOOL: Tool used to form flare connections on tubing.

FLASH POINT: The point in the temperature range at which a given oil will ignite and flash into flame.

FLAT HEAD: Engine with all the valves in block.

FLAT SPOT: Refers to a spot experienced during an acceleration period where the engine seems to "fall on its face" for a second or so and will then begin to pull again.

FLOAT: Unit in carburetor bowl that floats on top of fuel. It controls inlet needle valve to produce proper fuel level in bowl, can be of hollow metal, plastic, or cork.

FLOAT BOWL: The part of the carburetor that acts as a reservoir for gasoline and in which the float is placed.

FLOAT CIRCUIT: That portion of the carburetor devoted to maintaining a constant level of fuel in carburetor. Consists of float bowl, float, inlet valve, etc.

FLOAT LEVEL: Height of fuel in carburetor float bowl. Also refers to specific float setting that will produce correct fuel level.

FLOODING: Condition where fuel mixture is overly rich or an excessive amount has reached cylinders. Starting will be difficult and sometimes impossible until condition is corrected.

FLOW METER: Sensing device which measures flow of air or liquid.

FLUID COUPLING: Unit that transfers engine torque to transmission input shaft through use of two vaned units (called a torus) operating very close together in a bath of oil.

FLUTE: Groove in cutting tool that forms a passageway for exit of chips removed during the cutting process.

FLUX (Magnetic): Lines of magnetic force moving through magnetic field.

FLUX (Soldering, Brazing): Ingredient placed on metal being soldered or brazed, to remove and prevent formation of surface oxidation which would make soldering or brazing difficult.

FLYWHEEL: Relatively large wheel that is attached to crankshaft to smooth out firing impulses. It provides inertia to keep crankshaft turning smoothly during periods when no power is being applied.

It also forms a base for starter ring gear

and in many instances, for clutch assembly.

FLYWHEEL RING GEAR: Gear on outer circumference of flywheel. Starter drive gear engages ring gear and cranks engine.

FOG LIGHTS: Amber or clear lamps specially designed to provide better visibility in fog. Are usually mounted as close to road as is feasible.

FOOT POUND: Measurement of work involved in lifting one pound one foot.

FOOT POUND (Tightening): One pound pull one foot from center of an object.

FORCE: Pressure (pull, push, etc.) acting upon body that tends to change state of motion, or rest, of the body.

FORCE-FIT: Same as drive-fit.

FORGE: To force piece of hot metal into desired shape by hammering.

FOUR BANGER, SIX BANGER, ETC.: Four cylinder, six cylinder engine, etc.

FOUR-ON-THE-FLOOR: Four-speed manual transmission with floor mounted shift.

FOUR-STROKE CYCLE ENGINE: Engine requiring two complete revolutions of crankshaft to fire each piston once.

FOUR-WHEEL DRIVE: Vehicle, such as Jeep, in which front wheels, as well as rear, may be driven.

FRAME: Portion of automobile upon which body rests and to which engine and springs are attached. Generally constructed of steel channels.

FRAME (Conventional): Strong, steel members run from front to rear of body.

FRAME (Integral): Car body serves as portion or all of frame.

FRAME RAILS: Structural sections of the car frame. Often specifically used to refer to two outside longitudinal sections.

FREE ELECTRONS: Electrons in outer orbits around nucleus of atom. They can be moved out of orbit comparatively easy.

FREEWHEEL: Usually refers to action of car on downgrade when overdrive overrunning clutch is slipping with resultant loss of engine braking. This condition will only occur after overdrive unit is engaged but before balk ring has activated planetary gearset.

FREEZING: When two parts that are rubbing together heat up and force lubricant out of area, they will gall and finally freeze or stick together.

FREON-12: Gas used as cooling medium in air conditioning and refrigeration systems.

FREQUENCY: The rate of change in direction, oscillation, cycles, etc., in a given time span.

FRICTION: Resistance to movement between any two objects when placed in contact with each other. Friction is not constant but depends on type of surface, pressure holding two objects together, etc.

FRICTION BEARING: Bearing made of babbitt, bronze, etc. There are no moving parts and shaft that rests in bearing merely rubs against friction material in bearing.

FTC: Federal Trade Commission.

FUEL: Combustible substance that is burned within (internal) or without (external) an engine so as to impart motion to pistons, vanes, etc.

FUEL ACCUMULATOR: Spring loaded diaphragm device which dampens fuel pressure pulsations, muffles noise, and helps maintain residual pressure with engine off.

FUEL BOWL: Storage area in carburetor for

extra fuel.

FUEL DISTRIBUTOR: Device which meters fuel to injectors at correct rate of flow for engine conditions.

FUEL FILTER: A device that removes dirt, rust particles, and in some cases, water from fuel before it moves into carburetor or fuel injection system.

FUEL GAUGE: A device to indicate the approximate amount of fuel in tank.

FUEL INJECTION: Fuel system that uses no carburetor but sprays fuel either directly into cylinders or into intake manifold just ahead of cylinders.

FUEL LINE: That portion of the fuel system, consisting of tubing and hose, that carries fuel from tank to carburetor or injection system.

FUEL MIXTURE: Mixture of gasoline and air. An average mixture, by weight, would contain 16 parts of air to one part of gasoline.

FUEL PULSATION: Fuel pressure variations due to fuel pump action.

FUEL PUMP: Vacuum device, operated either mechanically or electrically, that is used to draw gasoline from tank and force it into carburetor.

FUEL TANK: A large tank of steel or plastic, used to store a supply of fuel aboard vehicle.

FULCRUM: Support on which a lever pivots in raising an object.

FULL-FLOATING AXLE: Rear drive axle that does not hold wheel on nor does it hold wheel in line or support any weight. It merely drives wheel. Used primarily on trucks.

FULL-FLOW OIL FILTER: Oil filter that filters ALL of oil passing through engine—before it reaches the bearings.

FULL HOUSE: Engine that is fully modified and equipped for all-out performance.

FULL PRESSURE SYSTEM: Type of oiling or lubrication system using an oil pump to draw oil out of a sump and force it through passages in engine.

FULL-TIME FOUR-WHEEL DRIVE: Setup in which all four wheels are driven—all the time—off road or on. Addition of a third differential, located at transfer case, permits front and rear wheels to operate at different speeds.

FULL-TIME TRANSFER CASE: Four-wheel drive transfer case that drives all four wheels all the time. Two-wheel drive is not possible. Such systems permit four-wheel drive on dry, hard surfaced roads by incorporating a differential in transfer case unit.

FUSE: Protective device that will break flow of current when current draw exceeds capacity of fuse.

FUSIBLE LINK: A special wire inserted into a circuit to provide protection in event of overloading, shorts, etc. Overloads will melt wire and break circuit. Unlike a regular fuse, fusible link will permit overloading for a short time before melting.

FUSION: Two metals reaching the melting point and flowing or welding themselves together.

GAL: Gallon.

GALVANOMETER: Instrument used to measure pressure, amount of, and direction of an electric current.

GAS: A nonsolid material. It can be compressed. When heated, it will expand and when cooled, it will contract. (Such as air.)

GAS BURNER or GASSER. Competition car with engine set up to operate on standard pump gasoline instead of an alcohol, nitro, etc., mixture.

GASKET: Material placed between two parts to insure proper sealing.

GASOHOL: Automotive engine fuel made up of around 90 percent gasoline and 10 percent ethanol alcohol.

GASOLINE: Hydrocarbon fuel used in the internal combustion engine.

GASSING: Small hydrogen bubbles rising to top of battery electrolyte during battery charging.

GAWR: See Gross Axle Weight Rating.

GEAR: Circular object, usually flat edged or cone-shaped, upon which a series of teeth have been cut. These are meshed with teeth of another gear and when one turns, it also drives the other.

GEAR RATIO: Relationship between number of turns made by driving gear to complete one full turn of driven gear. If driving gear turns four times to turn driven gear once, gear ratio would be 4 to 1.

GENERATOR: Electromagnetic device for producing electricity.

GENERATOR REGULATOR: See Regulator.

GLASS: Term used for the material "fiberglass."

GLASS PACK MUFFLER: Straight through (no baffles) muffler utilizing fiberglass packing around perforated pipe to deaden exhaust sound.

GLAZE: Highly smooth, glassy finish on cylinder walls.

GLAZE BREAKER or DEGLAZER: Abrasive tool used to remove glaze from cylinder walls prior to installation of new piston rings.

GLOW PLUG: A heating device placed in a diesel engine precombustion chamber to facilitate cold engine starting. When engine is cold, an electric current is passed through plug causing it to glow red hot. This helps ignite compressed fuel.

GMC: General Motors Corporation.

GOVERNOR: Device designed to automatically control speed or position of some part.

GPM: Gallons Per Minute.

GRADIENT: Angle of hill. A 20 percent gradient would be a hill that would rise two feet for every ten forward feet of travel. This is determined by rise as a percentage of forward travel.

GRID: Lead screen or plate to which battery plate active material is affixed.

GRIND: To remove metal from an object by means of revolving abrasive wheel, disc or belt.

GROSS AXLE WEIGHT RATING: Total load carrying capacity of a given axle (front or back) setup. Weight rating can be expressed as rating at springs (total load on springs) or at ground (total load measured where tire meets ground). Weight at ground rating includes weight of tires, wheels, axle, and springs.

GROUND (Battery): Terminal of battery connected to metal framework of car. In this country, NEGATIVE terminal is grounded.

GROWLER: Instrument used in testing starter and generator armature.

GUDGEON PIN: British term for piston or wrist pin.

GUM (Fuel system): Oxidized portions of fuel that form deposits in fuel system or engine parts.

GUSSET: A metal piece, usually of flat plate, used to strengthen a joint between two parts such as frame rails. Usually welded or riveted into place.

GUT: To strip the interior of car. May also refer to removing internal baffles from muffler.

GVW: Gross Vehicle Weight. Total weight of vehicle including vehicle passengers, load, etc. Used as indicator of how heavy vehicle can be loaded (GVW minus vehicle curb weight = payload).

GVWR: Gross Vehicle Weight Rating. See GVW.

HALF-MOON KEY: Driving key serving same purpose as regular key but it is shaped somewhat like a half circle.

HALOGEN BULB: Light bulb in which tungsten filament is surrounded by a halogen gas such as iodine, bromine, etc. Bulb glass is quartz to withstand intense heat.

HAND BRAKE: Hand operated brake which prevents vehicle movement while parked by applying rear wheel brakes or transmission brake.

HARMONIC BALANCER: See Vibration Damper.

HC: Symbol for hydrocarbon.

HEADLIGHTS: Main driving lights used on front of vehicle.

HEAD PRESSURE: See Discharge Pressure.

HEAT CROSSOVER (V-Type Engine): Passage from one exhaust manifold to, over, and under carburetor and on to other manifold. Crossover provides heat to carburetor during engine warmup.

HEAT ENGINE: Engine operated by heat energy released from burning fuel.

HEAT EXCHANGER: Device, such as radiator, either used to cool or heat by transferring heat from one object to another.

HEAT RANGE (Spark Plugs): Refers to operating temperature of given style plug. Plugs are made to operate at different temperatures depending upon thickness and length of porcelain insulator as measured from sealing ring down to tip.

HEAT RISER: Area, surrounding portion of the intake manifold, through which exhaust gases can pass to heat fuel mixture during warmup.

HEAT SINK: Device used to prevent overheating of electrical device by absorbing heat and transferring it to atmosphere.

HEAT STOVE: Sheet metal housing around a portion of exhaust manifold. An intake pipe from housing provides hot air to carburetor air cleaner when needed. Can also mean a small shrouded depression in exhaust manifold from which hot air may be drawn to automatic choke housing.

HEAT TREATMENT (Metal): Application of controlled heat to metal object in order to alter its characteristics (toughness, hardness, etc.).

HEEL (Brake): End of brake shoe which rests against anchor pin.

HEEL (Gear Tooth): Wide end of tapered gear tooth such as found in differential gears.

Hg: Abbreviation for the word MERCURY. Vacuum is measured in inches of mercury.

HELICAL: Spiraling shape such as that made by a coil spring.

HELICAL GEAR: Gear that has teeth cut at an angle to center line of gear.

HEMI: Engine using hemispherical-shaped (half of globe) combustion chambers.

HEMISPHERICAL COMBUSTION CHAMBER: A round, dome-shaped combustion chamber that is considered by many to be one of the finest shapes ever developed. Hemispherical-shape lends itself to use of large valves for improved breathing and suffers somewhat less heat loss than other shapes.

HERRINGBONE GEARS: Two helical gears operating together and so placed that angle of the teeth form a "V" shape.

HIGH COMPRESSION HEADS: Cylinder head with smaller combustion chamber area thereby raising compression. Head can be custom built or can be a stock head milled (cut) down.

HIGH-RISE MANIFOLD: Intake manifold designed to mount carburetor or carburetors, considerably higher above engine than is done in standard manifold, done to improve angle at which fuel is delivered.

HIGH TENSION: High voltage from ignition coil. May also indicate secondary wire from the coil to distributor and wires from distributor to plugs.

HONE: To remove metal with fine grit abrasive stone to precise tolerances.

HOOD PINS: Pins designed to hold hood closed.

HOPPING UP: Increasing engine performance through various modifications.

HORIZONTAL-OPPOSED ENGINE: Engine possessing two banks of cylinders that are placed flat or 180 deg. apart.

HORSEPOWER: Measurement of engine's ability to perform work. One horsepower is defined as ability to lift 33,000 pounds one foot in one minute. To find horsepower, total rate of work in foot pounds accomplished is divided by 33,000. If a machine was lifting 100 pounds 660 feet per minute, its total rate of work would be 66,000 foot pounds.

Dividing this by 33,000 foot pounds (1 horsepower) you find that the machine is rated as 2 horsepower (hp).

HORSEPOWER (Brake): See Brake Horsepower.

HORSEPOWER (Frictional): Amount of horsepower lost to engine friction.

HORSEPOWER (Gross): Maximum horsepower developed by engine without a fan, air cleaner, alternator, exhaust system, etc.

HORSEPOWER (Net): Maximum horsepower developed by engine equipped with fan, air conditioning, air cleaner, exhaust system, and all other systems and items normally present when engine is installed in car.

HORSEPOWER – WEIGHT FACTOR: Relationship between total weight of car and horsepower available. By dividing weight by horsepower, number of pounds to be moved by one horsepower is determined. This factor has a great effect on acceleration, gas mileage and all around performance.

HOSE CLAMPS: Devices used to secure hoses to their fittings.

HOSES: Flexible rubber tubes for carrying water, oil, air, and other fluids.

HOTCHKISS DRIVE: Method of connecting transmission output shaft to differential pinion by using open drive shafts. Driving force of rear wheels is transmitted to frame through rear springs or through link arms connecting rear axle housing to frame.

HOT SPOT: Localized area in which temperature is considerably higher than surrounding area.

HOT WIRE: Wiring around key switch so as to start car without key.

Wire connected to battery or to some part of electrical system in which a direct connection to battery is present. A current-carrying wire.

Hp: Horsepower.

HUB (Wheel): Unit to which wheel is bolted.

HYATT ROLLER BEARING (Antifriction): Similar to conventional roller bearing except that rollers are hollow and are split in a spiral fashion from end to end.

HYDRAULIC: Refers to fluids in motion. Hydraulics is science of fluid in motion.

HYDRAULIC BRAKES: Brakes operated by hydraulic pressure. Master cylinder provides operating pressure transmitted via steel tubing to wheel cylinders or pistons that in turn apply brake shoes to brake drums and/or discs.

HYDRAULIC LIFTER: Valve lifter that utilizes hydraulic pressure from engine's oiling system to keep it in constant contact with both camshaft and valve stem. They automatically adjust to any variation in valve stem length.

HYDRAULICS: The science of liquid in motion.

HYDROCARBON: A mixture of hydrogen and carbon.

HYDROCARBON — UNBURNED: Hydrocarbons that were not burned during the normal engine combustion process. Unburned hydrocarbons make up about 0.1 percent of engine exhaust emission.

HYDROCARBONS: Combination of hydrogen and carbon atoms. All petroleum based fuels (gasoline, kerosene, etc.) consist of hydrocarbons.

HYDROMETER: Float device for determining specific gravity of electrolyte in a battery. This will determine the state of charge.

HYDROPNEUMATIC SUSPENSION: Suspension system using both a liquid (oil) and compressed air for springing.

HYGROSCOPIC: Ability to absorb moisture from air.

HYPOID GEARING: System of gearing wherein pinion gear meshes with ring gear below center line of ring gear. This allows a somewhat lower drive line thus reducing hump in the floor of car. For this reason hypoid gearing is used in differential on many cars.

ICEI: Internal Combustion Engine Institute.

ICING: Formation of ice (under certain atmospheric conditions) on throttle plate, air horn walls, etc., caused by lowering of fuel mixture temperature as it passes through air horn.

ID: Inside diameter.

IDLE: Indicates engine operating at its normal slow speed with throttle closed.

IDLE VALVE or IDLE NEEDLE: Needle used to control amount of fuel mixture reaching cylinders during idling. It, or they, may be adjusted by turning the exposed heads.

IDLER ARM: Steering system part that supports one end of center link.

IDLER GEAR: A gear, between two other gears, that is driven by one and drives other. This permits both driving and driven gear to rotate in same direction with no change in gear ratio.

IGNITION: Lighting or igniting fuel charge by means of a spark (gas engine) or by heat of compression (diesel engine).

IGNITION SWITCH: Key operated switch in driver compartment for connecting and disconnecting power to ignition and electrical system.

IGNITION SYSTEM: Portion of car electrical system, designed to produce a spark within cylinders to ignite fuel charge. Consists basically of battery, key switch, resistor, coil, distributor, points, condenser, spark plugs and necessary wiring.

IGNITION TIMING: Refers to relationship between exact time a plug is fired and position of piston in degrees of crankshaft rotation.

I-HEAD ENGINE: Engine having both valves in the head.

IHP: Indicated Horsepower.

IMEP: Indicated Mean Effective Pressure.

IMI: Ignition Manufacturer's Institute.

IMPACT WRENCH: An air or electrical driven wrench that tightens or loosens nuts, cap screws, etc., with series of sharp, rapid blows.

IMPELLER: Wheel-like device upon which fins are attached. It is whirled to pump water, move and slightly compress air, etc.

IN.: Inch.

INCLUDED ANGLE (Steering): Angle formed by center lines drawn through steering axis (kingpin inclination) and center of wheel (camber angle) as viewed from front of car. Combines both steering axis and camber angles.

INDEPENDENT SUSPENSION: A suspension system that allows each wheel to move up and down without undue influence on other wheels.

INDICATED HORSEPOWER (ihp): Measure of power developed by burning fuel within cylinders.

INDIRECT FUEL INJECTION: Fuel is sprayed into intake manifold.

INDUCTION: Imparting of electricity into one object, not connected, to another by the influence of magnetic fields.

INERTIA: Force which tends to keep stationary object from being moved, and tends to keep moving objects in motion.

INERTIA SWITCH: An electrical switch designed to be operated by a sudden movement, such as that caused by a collision.

INHIBITOR: Substance added to oil, water, gas, etc., to prevent action such as foaming, rusting, etc.

INJECTOR: Refers to valve mechanism (used in fuel injection system) that squirts or injects measured amount of gasoline into intake manifold in vicinity of intake valve. In diesel engine, fuel is injected directly into combustion chamber.

INJECTOR TIMING (Diesel): Relationship between instant of fuel injection in any one cylinder, to position of piston in degrees of crankshaft rotation.

IN-LINE ENGINE: Engine in which all cylinders are arranged in straight row.

INPUT SHAFT: Shaft delivering power into mechanism. Shaft from clutch into transmission is transmission input shaft.

INSERT BEARING: Removable, precision made bearing which insures specified clearance between bearing and shaft.

INSULATION: Material used to reduce transfer of noise (sound insulation), heat (heat insulation), electricity (electrical insulation).

INSULATOR (Electrical): Material that will not (readily) conduct electricity.

INTAKE MANIFOLD: Connecting tubes between base of carburetor and port openings to intake valves.

INTAKE STROKE: Portion of piston's movement devoted to drawing fuel mixture into engine cylinder.

INTAKE VALVE (Engine): Valve through which fuel mixture is admitted to cylinder.

INTEGRAL: Part of. (The cam lobe is an integral part of camshaft.)

INTERMEDIATE GEAR: Any gear in auto transmission between 1st and high.

INTERMITTENT: Not constant but occurring at intervals.

INTERMITTENT FUEL INJECTION: Fuel system in which injectors are only open for short periods and remain closed rest of the time. Amount of fuel delivered is controlled by how long injector is held open.

INTERNAL COMBUSTION ENGINE: Engine that burns fuel within itself as means of developing power.

INTERNAL GEAR: A gear with teeth cut on an inward facing surface. Example: Outer gear in a planetary gearset. Teeth face inward towards center.

ION: Electrically charged atom or molecule produced by electrical field, high temperature, etc.

IONIZE (Air): To convert wholly or partly, into ions. This causes air to become a conductor of electricity.

JACKSHAFT: A shaft used between two other shafts.

JET: Small hole or orifice used to control flow of gasoline in various parts of carburetor.

JOULE: Metre-kilogram-second (mks) unit of energy or work equal to a force of 1 newton applied through a distance of 1 metre. Joule is the equivalent of 0.737324 foot-pounds.

JOURNAL: Part of shaft prepared to accept a bearing. (Connecting rod, main bearing.)

KEY: Parallel-sided piece inserted into groove cut part way into each of two parts, which prevents slippage between two parts.

KEYWAY: Slot cut in shaft, pulley hub, wheel hub, etc. Square key is placed in slot and engages a similar keyway in mating piece. Key prevents slippage between two parts.

KICKDOWN SWITCH: Electrical switch that will cause transmission, or overdrive unit, to shift down to lower gear. Often used to secure fast acceleration.

KILL SWITCH: Special switch designed to shut off ignition in case of emergency.

KILOMETRE: Metric measurement equivalent to 5/8 of mile.

KINGPIN: Hardened steel pin that is passed through the steering knuckle and axle end. The steering knuckle pivots about the kingpin.

KINGPIN or STEERING AXIS INCLINATION: Tipping the tops of the kingpins inward towards each other. This places the centerline of steering axis nearer centerline of tire-road contact area.

KNOCKING (Bearing): Noise created by part movement in a loose or worn bearing.

KNOCKING (Fuel): condition, accompanied by audible noise, that occurs when gasoline in cylinders burns too quickly. Also referred to as detonation.

KNUCKLE: A part utilizing a hinge pin (kingpin, swivel pin) that allows one part to swivel around another part. An example is a steering knuckle.

KNURL: To roughen surface of piece of metal by pressing series of cross-hatched lines into the surface and thereby raising area between these lines.

LACQUER (Paint): Fast drying automotive body paint.

LAMINATED: Something made up of many layers.

LAND: Metal separating a series of grooves.

LANDS (Ring): Piston metal between ring grooves.

LAP: One complete trip around race track or route laid out for racing.

LAP or LAPPING: To fit two surfaces together by coating them with abrasive and then rubbing them together.

LATENT HEAT: Amount of heat (Btu's) beyond boiling or melting point, required to change liquid to a gas, or a solid to a liquid.

LATENT HEAT OF EVAPORATION: Amount of heat (Btu's) required to change a liquid to a vapor state without elevating vapor temperature above that of the liquid.

LB: Pound.

LEAD BURNING: Connecting two pieces of lead by melting edges together.

LEADED GASOLINE: Gasoline containing tetraethyl lead, an antiknock additive. It must not be used in vehicles with catalytic converters.

LEAF SPRING: Suspension spring made up of several pieces of flat spring steel. Varying numbers of leaves (individual pieces) are used depending on intended use. One car uses single leaf in each rear spring.

LEAN MIXTURE (Fuel): A fuel mixture with an excessive amount of air in relation to fuel.

LETTER DRILLS: Series of drills in which each drill size is designated by letter of alphabet—A, B, C, etc.

LEVER: A rigid bar or shaft pivoting about a fixed fulcrum (shaft, pin, etc.). It is used to increase force or to transmit or change motion.

LEVERAGE: Increasing force by utilizing one or more levers.

L-HEAD ENGINE: Engine having both valves in block and on same side of cylinder.

LIGHTENED VALVES: Valves in which all possible metal has been ground away to reduce weight. This will allow higher rpm without valve float.

LIMITED-SLIP DIFFERENTIAL: Differential unit designed to provide superior traction by transferring driving torque, when one wheel is spinning, to wheel that is not slipping.

LINKAGE: Movable bars or links connecting one unit to another.

LIQUID LINE (Air Conditioning): High-pressure liquid refrigerant line between receiver-dehydrator and expansion valve.

LIQUID TRACTION: Special liquid applied to tires of drag racers to provide superior traction.

LIQUID-VAPOR SEPARATOR: Tank which prevents liquid fuel from entering vapor line.

LIQUID WITHDRAWAL (LPG): Drawing LPG from bottom of tank to insure delivery of liquid LPG. Withdrawal from top of tank will deliver LPG in the gaseous state.

LITRE: Metric measurement of capacity—equivalent to 2.11 pints. Five litres equals 1.32 gallon.

LIVE AXLE: Axle upon which wheels are

firmly affixed. Axle drives the wheels.

LIVE WIRE: See Hot Wire.

LOAD RANGE (Tire): Letter system (A, B, C, etc.) used to indicate specific tire load and inflation limit.

LOG MANIFOLD: Special intake manifold generally designed to accept four or more carburetors. Each side has bases for carburetors set on a pipe-like log area.

LONG and SHORT ARM SUSPENSION: Suspension system utilizing upper and lower control arm. Upper arm is shorter than lower. This is done so as to allow wheel to deflect in a vertical direction with a minimum change in camber.

LONGITUDINAL LEAF SPRING: Leaf spring mounted so it is parallel to length of car.

LOUVER: Ventilation slots such as sometimes found in hood of automobile.

LOW BRAKE PEDAL: Condition where brake pedal approaches too close to floorboard before actuating the brakes.

LOW LEAD FUEL: Gasoline containing not much more than 0.5 grams of tetraethyl lead per gallon.

LOW PIVOT SWING AXLE: Rear axle setup that attaches differential housing to frame via a pivot mount. Conventional type of housing and axle extend from differential to one wheel. The other side of differential is connected to other driving wheel by a housing and axle that is pivoted at a point in line with differential to frame pivot point.

LOW PRESSURE LINE (Air Conditioning): Low pressure refrigerant line between evaporator outlet and compressor.

LPG: Liquefied petroleum gas.

LUBRICANT: Any material, usually of a petroleum nature such as grease, oil, etc., that is placed between two moving parts in an effort to reduce friction.

LUBRICATION: Reducing friction between two parts by coating them with oil, grease, etc.

LUG (Engine): To cause engine to labor by failing to shift to a lower gear when necessary.

MACPHERSON STRUT: Front end suspension system in which wheel assembly is attached to a long, telescopic strut. Strut permits wheels to pivot and move up and down. Strut also acts as a shock absorber.

MAG: Magneto.

MAGNAFLUX: Special chemical process used to check parts for cracks.

MAGNET (Permanent): Piece of magnetized steel that will attract all ferrous material. Permanent magnet does not need electricity to function and will retain its magnetism over a period of years.

MAGNETIC CLUTCH (Air Conditioning): Electromagnetic clutch that engages or disengages air conditioning compressor pulley.

MAGNETIC FIELD: Area encompassed by magnetic lines of force surrounding either a bar magnet or electromagnet.

MAGNETO: Engine driven unit that generates high voltage to fire spark plugs. It needs no outside source of power such as battery.

MAGS or MAG WHEEL: Lightweight, sporty wheels made of magnesium. Term mag is often applied to aluminum, and aluminum and steel combination wheels.

MAIN BEARINGS (Engine): Bearings supporting crankshaft in cylinder block.

MAIN BEARING SUPPORTS: Steel plate installed over main bearing caps to increase their strength for racing purposes.

MAIN DISCHARGE TUBE: Carburetor fuel passage from bowl to air horn.

MANDREL: Round shaft used to mount stone, cutter, saw, etc.

MANIFOLD: Pipe or number of pipes connecting series of holes or outlets to common opening. See Exhaust and Intake Manifold.

MANIFOLD HEAT CONTROL VALVE: Valve placed in exhaust manifold, or in exhaust pipe, that deflects certain amount of hot gas around base of carburetor to aid in warmup.

MANOMETER: Instrument to measure pressure (vacuum).

MANUAL CONTROL VALVE (Transmission): Hand (linkage) operated valve which controls oil flow and transmission gear selection.

MASTER CYLINDER: Part of hydraulic brake system in which pressure is generated.

MASTER ROD (Radial Engine): Primary or main connecting rod to which other connecting rods are attached.

MATTER: Substance making up physical things occupying space, having weight, and perceptible to the senses.

MECHANICAL BRAKES: Service brakes that are actuated by mechanical linkage connecting brakes to brake pedal.

MECHANICAL EFFICIENCY: Engine's rating as to how much potential horsepower is wasted through friction within moving parts of engine.

MECHANICAL FUEL INJECTION: A mechanically driven pump forces fuel into engine.

MECHANICAL FUEL PUMP: Engine mounted pump operated by eccentric device.

MEGOHM: 1,000,000 ohms.

MEMA: Motor and Equipment Manufacturers' Association.

MEP: Mean Effective Pressure. Pressure of burning fuel (average) on power stroke subtracted by average pressure on other three strokes. Pressure is in pounds per square inch or kilopascals.

MESH: To engage teeth of one gear with those of another.

METAL FATIGUE: Crystallizing of metal due to vibration, twisting, bending, etc. Unit will eventually break. Bending a piece of wire back and forth to break it is a good example of metal fatigue.

METERING ROD: Movable rod used to vary opening area through carburetor jet.

METERING VALVE (Brakes): Valve in brake line that limits fluid pressure to disc brakes. This assures that the rear (drum) brakes apply at about the same time as front (disc) brakes.

METRIC SIZE: Units made to metric system measurements.

METRIC SYSTEM: A decimal system of measurement based on metre (area, length, volume), litre (capacity), and gram (weight and mass).

MICRO: When the word "micro" precedes measurement units, such as watt, ampere, etc., it means one-millionth of that unit.

MICROFARAD: 1/1,000,000 farad.

MICROMETER (Inside and Outside): Precision measuring tool that will give readings accurate to within fraction of one thousandth of an inch.

MIKE: Either refers to micrometer or to using micrometer to measure an object.

MILL: Often used to refer to engine.

To remove metal through use of rotating toothed cutter.

MILLIMETRE: Metric measurement equivalent to .039370 of an inch.

MILLING MACHINE: Machine that uses variety of rotating cutter wheels to cut splines, gears, keyways, etc.

MISFIRE: Fuel charge in one or more engine cylinders which fails to fire or ignite at proper time.

MODULATOR (Transmission): Pressure control or adjusting valve used in hydraulic system of automatic transmission.

MOLD: Hollow unit into which molten metal is poured to form a casting.

MOLECULE: Smallest portion that matter may be divided into and still retain all properties of original matter.

MONOBLOCK: All cylinders cast as one unit.

MOTOR: Electrically driven power unit (electric motor). Term is often incorrectly applied to internal combustion engine.

MOTOR (Generator): Attaching generator to battery in such a way it revolves like an electric motor.

MPH: Miles per hour.

MUFFLER (Exhaust): Unit through which exhaust gases are passed to quiet sounds of running engine.

MUFFLER (Air Conditioning): Device which reduces pumping noise and vibration in system.

MULTIPLE DISC CLUTCH: Clutch utilizing several clutch discs in its construction.

MULTI-VISCOSITY OILS: Oils meeting SAE requirements for both low temperature requirements of light oil and high temperature requirements of heavy oil. Example: (SAE 10W-30).

MUTUAL INDUCTION: Creating voltage in one coil by altering current in another nearby coil.

MVMA: Motor Vehicle Manufacturers Association.

NADA: National Automobile Dealers' Association.

NASCAR: Letters denoting National Association for Stock Car Auto Racing.

NBFU: National Board of Fire Underwriters.

NC THREADS: National Coarse thread sizes.

NEEDLE BEARING (Antifriction): Roller type bearing in which rollers have very narrow diameter in relation to their length.

NEEDLE VALVE: Valve with long, thin, tapered point that operates in small hole or jet. Hole size is changed by moving needle valve in or out.

NF THREADS: National Fine thread sizes.

NEGATIVE TERMINAL: Terminal (such as on battery) from which current flows on its path to positive terminal.

NEUTRON: Neutral charge particle forming part of an atom.

NEWTON'S LAW: For every action there is an equal, an opposite reaction.

NHRA: National Hot Rod Association.

NHTSA: National Highway Traffic Safety Administration.

NITROGEN OXIDES: In combustion process, nitrogen from air combines with oxygen to form nitrogen oxides.

NLGI: National Lubricating Grease Institute.

NONFERROUS METALS: All metals containing no iron — except in very minute quantities.

NON-SERVICEABLE: A part or device whose design and construction does not permit rebuilding. Can also be used to indicate a part of device that is no longer fit for use.

NORTH POLE (Magnet): Magnetic pole from which lines of force emanate; travel is from north to south pole.

NOx: See Oxides of Nitrogen.

NOZZLE: Opening through which fuel mixture is directed into carburetor air stream.

NSC: National Safety Council.

NUMBER DRILLS: Series of drills in which each size is designated by number (0-80).

OCTANE RATING: Rating that indicates a specific gasoline's ability to resist detonation.

OD: Outside diameter.

ODOMETER: Device used to measure and register number of miles traveled by car.

OEM: Original Equipment Manufacturer.

OFF-ROAD VEHICLE: Vehicle designed to operate in rough country (hills, sand, mud, etc.) without benefit of regular roads.

OHM: Unit of measurement used to indicate amount of resistance to flow of electricity in a given circuit.

OHMMETER: Instrument used to measure amount of resistance in given unit or circuit. (In ohms.)

OHM'S LAW: Formula for calculating electrical values in a circuit.

OIL BATH AIR CLEANER: Air cleaner that utilizes a pool of oil to insure removal of impurities from air entering carburetor.

OIL BURNER: Engine that consumes an excessive quantity of oil.

OIL CLASSIFICATION — CA, CB, CC, CD: Classifications for oil designed for use in diesel engines. Many automotive diesel engines require oil marked with classification SF/DC, SF/CC. Follow manufacturers recommendations.

OIL CLASSIFICATION — SA: (Utility Gasoline and Diesel Engine Service.) Oil for applications under light load, moderate speed, highly favorable service. Contains few or no additives.

OIL CLASSIFICATION — SC: (Minimum Duty Gasoline Engine Service.) For mild operating conditions. Contains some additives.

OIL CLASSIFICATION — SC: (1964 Gasoline Engine Service.) For service such as that experienced by engines built from 1964–1967. Contains additives to retard low temperature deposits, rust, wear, corrosion, etc.

OIL CLASSIFICATION — SD: (1968 Gasoline Engine Warranty Maintenance Service.) For service such as needed for 1968 through 1970 light truck and car engines. Contains more additives than SC oil.

OIL CLASSIFICATION — SE: (1972 Gasoline Engine Warranty Maintenance.) Oil for 1972 through 1979 light truck and car engines. Contains more additives than SD oil.

OIL CLASSIFICATION — SF: (1980 Gasoline Engine Warranty Service.) Oil recommended for 1980 and later car and light truck engines. Provides excellent protection against wear, heat, deposits, etc. Can be used where SE, SD, or SC are recommended.

OIL — COMBINATION SPLASH and PRESSURE SYSTEM: Engine oiling system that uses both pressure and splash oiling to accomplish proper lubrication.

OIL CONTROL RING (Piston): A piston ring designed to prevent excessive oil consumption by scraping excess oil from cylinder and returning it to oil pan sump. Usually lower (furthest down in cylinder) ring or rings.

OIL COOLER: Device used to remove excess heat from engine and/or transmission oil. Can be air or water cooled design.

OIL DIPSTICK: See Dipstick.

OIL FILTER: Device used to strain oil in engine thus removing abrasive particles.

OIL — FULL PRESSURE SYSTEM: Engine oiling system that forces oil, under pressure, to moving parts of engine.

OIL GALLERY: Pipe or drilled passageway in engine used to carry engine oil from one area to another.

OIL GAUGE: A dash mounted device that indicates engine oil pressure in pounds per square inch (psi) or kilopascals (kPa). Can be of either electrical or Bourdon tube design.

OIL PAN: See Pan.

OIL PICKUP: Connects to oil pump and extends into bottom of oil pan. Oil is drawn through pickup into pump.

OIL PUMP: Device used to force oil, under pressure, to various parts of the engine. It is driven by gear on camshaft.

OIL PUMPING: Condition wherein an excessive quantity of oil passes piston rings and is consumed in combustion chamber.

OIL RING: Normally bottom piston ring which scrapes excess oil off cylinder wall.

OIL SEAL: Device used to prevent oil leakage past certain area.

OIL SLINGER: Device attached to revolving shaft so any oil passing that point will be thrown outward where it will return to point of origin.

OIL — SPLASH SYSTEM: Engine oiling system that depends on connecting rods to dip into oil troughs and splash oil to all moving parts.

OIL STRAINER (Engine): A fine wire mesh screen through which oil entering oil pump is drawn. It will remove larger particles of dirt or other abrasives.

OIL SUMP: That portion of oil pan that holds supply of engine oil.

ONE-WAY CLUTCH: It locks shaft in one direction and allows rotation in other direction.

OPEN CIRCUIT: Circuit in which a wire is broken or disconnected.

OPEN CIRCUIT VOLTAGE (Battery): Cell voltage when battery has no completed circuit across posts and is not receiving or delivering energy.

ORIFICE: A small hole or restricted opening used to control flow of gasoline, air, oil, etc.

OSCILLATING ACTION: Swinging action such as that in pendulum of a clock.

OSCILLOSCOPE: Testing unit which projects visual reproduction of the ignition system spark action onto screen of cathode-ray tube.

OTTO CYCLE: Four-stroke cycle consisting of intake, compression, firing, and exhaust strokes.

OUTPUT SHAFT: Shaft delivering power from within mechanism. Shaft leaving transmission, attached to propeller shaft, is transmission output shaft.

OVERDRIVE: Unit utilizing planetary gearset so actuated as to turn drive shaft about one-third faster than transmission output shaft.

OVERDRIVE STAGES: Locked-out; direct, freewheeling; and overdrive.

OVERHEAD CAMSHAFT: Camshaft mounted above the head, driven by long timing chain or belt.

OVERHEAD VALVES: Valves located in head.

OVERRUNNING CLUTCH: Clutch mechanism that will drive in one direction only. If driving torque is removed or reversed, clutch slips.

OVERRUNNING CLUTCH STARTER DRIVE: Starter drive that is mechanically engaged. When engine starts, overrunning clutch operates until drive is mechanically disengaged.

OVERSQUARE ENGINE: Engine in which bore diameter is larger than length of stroke.

OVERSTEER: Tendency for car, when negotiating a corner, to turn more sharply than driver intends.

OXIDES OF NITROGEN (NOx): Undesirable exhaust emission, especially prevalent when combustion chamber flame temperatures are high.

OXIDIZE (Metal): Action where surface of object is combined with oxygen in air to produce rust, scale, etc.

OXIDIZING FLAME: Welding torch flame in which an excess of oxygen exists. Free or unburned oxygen tends to burn molten metal.

OXYGEN: Gas, used in welding, made up of colorless, tasteless, odorless, gaseous element oxygen found in atmosphere.

PAN: Thin stamped cover bolted to the bottom of crankcase. It forms a sump for engine oil and keeps dirt, etc., from entering engine.

PANCAKE ENGINE: Engine in which cylinders are on a horizontal plane. This reduces overall height and enables them to be used in spots where vertical height is restricted.

PAPER AIR CLEANER: Air cleaner that makes use of special paper through which air to carburetor is drawn.

PARABOLIC REFLECTOR: A light reflector (concave mirror) that emits parallel light rays. Bulb filament must be located at focal point of parabola.

PARALLEL CIRCUIT: Electrical circuit with two or more resistance units so wired as to permit current to flow through both units at same time. Unlike series circuit, current in parallel circuit does not have to pass through one unit to reach the other.

PARALLELOGRAM STEERING LINKAGE: Steering system utilizing two short tie rods connected to steering arms and to a long center link. The link is supported on one end on an idler arm and the other end is attached directly to pitman arm. Arrangement forms a parallelogram shape.

PARKING BRAKE: Hand operated brake which prevents vehicle movement while parked by locking rear wheels, or transmission output shaft.

PARKING LIGHTS: Small lights on both front and rear of vehicle. Usually red or amber color in rear and amber in front. Used so that vehicle will be more visible during dark hours. Lights are turned on whenever headlight switch is operated.

PARTICULATES (Lead): Tiny particles of lead found in engine exhaust emissions when leaded fuel is used.

PART-TIME TRANSFER CASE: Four-wheel drive transfer case that permits either four-wheel or two-wheel drive.

PASCAL'S LAW: "When pressure is exerted on confined liquid, it is transmitted undiminished."

PAWL: Stud or pin that can be moved or pivoted into engagement with teeth cut on another part—such as parking pawl on automatic transmission that can be slid into contact with teeth on another part to lock rear wheels.

PAYLOAD: Amount of weight that may be carried by vehicle. Computed by subtracting vehicle curb weight from GVW.

PCV (Positive Crankcase Ventilation): System which prevents crankcase vapors from being discharged directly into atmosphere.

PEEN: To flatten out end of a rivet, etc., by pounding with round end of a hammer.

PENETRATING OIL: Special oil used to free rusted parts so they can be removed.

PERIPHERY: Outside edge or circumference.

PERMANENT MAGNET: Magnet capable of retaining its magnetic properties over very long period of time.

PETROL: Gasoline.

PETROLEUM: Raw material from which gasoline, kerosene, lube oils, etc., are made. Consists of hydrogen and carbon.

PHILLIPS HEAD SCREW: Screw having a fairly deep cross slot instead of single slot as used in conventional screws.

PHOSPHOR-BRONZE: Bearing material composed of tin, lead, and copper.

PHOTOCHEMICAL: Relates to branch of chemistry where radiant energy (sunlight) produces various chemical changes.

PHOTOCHEMICAL SMOG: Fog-like condition produced by sunlight acting upon hydrocarbon and carbon monoxide exhaust emissions in atmosphere.

PICKUP COIL: Device in electronic type distributor which senses engine speed (distributor rotation) and sends electrical pulses to control unit.

PIEZOELECTRIC IGNITION: System of ignition that employs use of small section of ceramic-like material. When this material is compressed, even a very tiny amount, it emits a high voltage that will fire plugs. This system does not need a coil, points, or condenser.

PILOT SHAFT: Dummy shaft that is placed in a mechanism as a means of aligning parts. It is then removed and regular shaft installed.

PINGING: Metallic rattling sound produced by the engine during heavy acceleration when ignition timing is too far advanced for grade of fuel being burned.

PINION CARRIER: Part of rear axle assembly that supports and contains pinion gear shaft.

PINION (Gear): Small gear either driven by or driving a larger gear.

PIPES: Exhaust system pipes.

PISTON: Round plug, open at one end, that slides up and down in cylinder. It is attached to connecting rod and when fuel charge is fired, will transfer force of explosion to connecting rod then to crankshaft.

PISTON BOSS: Built-up area around piston pin hole.

PISTON COLLAPSE: Reduction in diameter of piston skirt caused by heat and constant impact stresses.

PISTON DISPLACEMENT: Amount (volume) of air displaced by piston when moved through full length of its stroke.

PISTON EXPANSION: Increase in diameter of piston due to normal piston heating.

PISTON HEAD: Portion of piston above top ring.

PISTON LANDS: Portion of piston between ring grooves.

PISTON PIN or WRIST PIN: Steel pin that is passed through piston. Used as base upon which to fasten upper end of connecting rod. It is round and is usually hollow.

PISTON RING: Split ring installed in a groove in piston. Ring contacts sides of ring groove and also rubs against cylinder wall thus sealing space between piston and wall.

PISTON RING (Compression): Ring designed to seal burning fuel charge above piston. Generally there are two compression rings per piston and they are located in two top ring grooves.

PISTON RING (Oil Control): Piston ring designed to scrape oil from cylinder wall. Ring is of such design as to allow oil to pass through ring and then through holes or slots in groove. In this way oil is returned to pan. There are many shapes and special designs used on oil control rings.

PISTON RING END GAP: Distance left between ends of the ring when installed in cylinder.

PISTON RING EXPANDER: See Ring Expander.

PISTON RING GROOVE: Slots or grooves cut in piston head to receive piston rings.

PISTON RING SIDE CLEARANCE: Space between sides of ring and ring lands.

PISTON SKIRT: Portion of piston below rings. (Some engines have an oil ring in skirt area.)

PISTON SKIRT EXPANDER: Spring device placed inside piston skirt to produce an outward pressure which increases diameter of skirt.

PISTON SKIRT EXPANDING: Enlarging diameter of piston skirt by inserting an expander, by knurling outer skirt surface, or by peening inside of piston.

PITMAN ARM: Short lever arm splined to steering gear cross shaft. Pitman arm transmits steering force from cross shaft to steering linkage system.

PITS: Area at a race track for fueling, tire changing, making mechanical repairs, etc.

PIT STOP: A stop at the pits by racer, for fuel, tires, repairs, etc.

PIVOT: Pin or shaft about which a part moves.

PLANET CARRIER: Part of a planetary gearset upon which planet gears are affixed. Planet gears are free to turn on hardened pins set into carrier.

PLANET GEARS: Gears in planetary gearset that are in mesh with both ring and sun gear. Referred to as planet gears in that they orbit or move around central or sun gear.

PLANETARY GEARSET: Gearing unit consisting of ring gear with internal teeth, sun or central pinion gear with external teeth, and series of planet gears that are meshed with both the ring and the sun gear.

PLATES (Battery): Thin sections of lead peroxide or porous lead. There are two kinds of plates—positive and negative. The plates are arranged in groups, in an alternate fashion, called elements. They are completely submerged in the electrolyte.

PLATINUM: Precious metal sometimes used in the construction of breaker points. It conducts well and is highly resistant to burning.

PLAY: Movement between two parts.

PLEXIGLAS: Trade name for an acrylic plastic, made by the Rhom and Haas Co.

PLIES (Tire): Layers of rubber impregnated fabric that make up carcass or body of tire.

PLUG GAPPING: Adjusting side electrode on spark plug to provide proper air gap between it and the center electrode.

PLY RATING (Tires): Indication of tire strength (load carrying capacity). Does not necessarily indicate actual number of plies. Two-ply four-ply rating tire would have load capacity of a four-ply tire of same size but would have only two actual plies.

P-METRIC (Tire): Tire size designation based on international standards. Example: P 155/80R13. P = passenger car use. 155 = section width in millimetres. 80 = height to width ratio. R = radial construction. 13 = wheel rim diameter in inches.

POLARITY (Battery Terminals): Indicates if the battery terminal (either one) is positive or negative (plus or minus) (+ or −).

POLARITY (Generator): Indicates if pole shoes are so magnetized as to make current flow in a direction compatible with direction of flow as set by battery.

POLARITY (Magnet): Indicates if end of a magnet is north or south pole (N or S).

POLARIZING (Generator): Process of sending quick surge of current through field windings of generator in direction that will cause pole shoes to assume correct polarity. This will insure that the generator will cause current to flow in same direction as normal.

POLE (Magnet): One end, either north or south, of a magnet.

POLE SHOES: Metal pieces about which field coil windings are placed. When current passes through windings, pole shoes become powerful magnets. Example: pole shoes in a generator or starter motor.

PONY CAR: Small, sporty car along the lines of the Mustang, Firebird, Camaro, etc.

POPPET: A spring-loaded ball engaging one or more indentations. Used to hold one object in position in relation to another.

POPPET VALVE: Valve used to open and close valve port entrances to engine cylinders.

PORCELAIN (Spark Plug): Material used to insulate center electrode of spark plug. It is hard and resistant to damage by heat.

POROSITY: Small air or gas pockets, or voids, in metal.

PORT: Openings in engine cylinder head for intake and exhaust flow during engine operation; opened and closed by valves.

To smooth out, align, and somewhat enlarge intake passageway to the valves.

POSITIVE TERMINAL: Terminal (such as on battery), to which current flows.

POST (Battery): Round, tapered lead posts protruding above top of battery to which battery cables are attached.

POTENTIAL: An indication of amount of available energy.

POTENTIOMETER: Variable resistor with three connections. One connection (called wiper) slides along resistive unit. Can be used as a voltage divider.

POUR POINT: Lowest temperature at which

fluid will flow under specified conditions.

POWER: Time rate at which energy is converted into work.

POWER BOOSTER (Brakes): Engine vacuum or power steering fluid operated device on fire wall which increases brake pedal force on master cylinder during stops.

POWER PLANT (Auto): The vehicle engine.

POWER STEERING: Steering system utilizing hydraulic pressure to increase the driver's turning effort. Pressure is utilized either in gearbox itself or in hydraulic cylinder attached to steering linkage.

POWER STEERING PUMP: Belt driven pump which produces pressure for power steering system.

POWER or FIRING STROKE: Portion of piston's movement devoted to transmitting power of burning fuel mixture to crankshaft.

PPM (Parts-Per-Million): Term used in determining extent of pollution existing in given sample of air.

PRACTICAL EFFICIENCY: Amount of horsepower delivered to drive wheels.

PRECISION INSERT BEARING: Very accurately made replaceable type of bearing. It consists of an upper and lower shell. The shells are made of steel to which a friction type bearing material has been bonded. Connecting rod and main bearings are generally of precison insert type.

PREHEATING: Application of some heat prior to later application of more heat. Cast iron is preheated to avoid cracking when welding process is started. A coil (ignition) is preheated prior to testing.

PREHEATING (Metal): Process of raising temperature of metal to specific level before starting subsequent operations such as welding, brazing, etc.

PREIGNITION: Fuel charge being ignited before proper time.

PRELOADING: Adjusting antifriction bearing so it is under mild pressure. This prevents bearing looseness under a driving stress.

PRESS-FIT: Condition of fit (contact) between two parts that requires pressure to force parts together. Also referred to as drive or force fit.

PRESSURE BLEEDER: Device that forces brake fluid, under pressure, into master cylinder so that by opening bleeder screws at wheel cylinders, all air will be removed from brake system.

PRESSURE CAP: Special cap for radiator. It holds a predetermined amount of pressure on water in cooling system. This enables water to run hotter without boiling.

PRESSURE DIFFERENTIAL SWITCH: Hydraulic switch in brake system that operates brake warning light in dashboard.

PRESSURE RELIEF VALVE: Valve designed to open at specific pressure. This will prevent pressures in system from exceeding certain limits.

PRIMARY CIRCUIT (Ignition System): Low voltage (6 or 12 volt) part of ignition system.

PRIMARY, FORWARD, or LEADING BRAKE SHOE: Brake shoe installed facing front of car. It will be a self-energizing shoe.

PRIMARY WINDING (Coil): Low voltage (6 or 12 volt) winding in ignition coil. The primary winding is heavy wire; secondary winding uses fine wire.

PRIMARY WIRES: Wiring which serves low voltage part of ignition system. Wiring from

battery to switch, resistor, coil, distributor points.

PRINTED CIRCUIT: Electrical circuit made by connecting units with electrically conductive lines printed on a panel. This eliminates actual wire and task of connecting it.

PROGRESSIVE LINKAGE: Carburetor linkage designed to open throttle valves of multiple carburetors. It opens one to start and when certain opening point is reached, it will start to open others.

PRONY BRAKE: Device utilizing friction brake to measure horsepower output of engine.

PROPANE (LPG): Petroleum product, similar to and often mixed with butane, useful as engine fuel. May be referred to as LP-Gas.

PROPELLER SHAFT: Shaft connecting transmission output shaft to differential pinion shaft.

PROPORTIONING VALVE (Brakes): Valve in brake line which keeps rear wheels from locking up during rapid stops.

PROTON: Positive charge particle, part of atom.

PSI: Pounds per square inch.

PTO: Power take off. A spot or place on transmission or transfer case from which an operating shaft from another unit (such as a winch) can be driven. Usually consists of a removable plate that exposes a drive gear.

PULL IT DOWN (Engine): Term often used in reference to dismantling and overhauling an engine.

PULSATION DAMPER: Device to smooth out fuel pulsations or surges from pump to carburetor.

PULSE AIR INJECTION: Emission control system which feeds air into exhaust gases by using pressure pulsations of exhaust system.

PULSE WIDTH: Often used to describe length of time a fuel injector is held open. Pulse being electric current applied to the injector winding and width being length of time current is allowed to flow. The wider the pulse, the more fuel delivered.

PUMP: A device designed to cause movement of water, fuel, air, etc., from one area to another.

PUMPING THE GAS PEDAL: Forcing accelerator up and down in an endeavor to provide extra gasoline to cylinders. This is often cause of flooding.

PURGE: Removing impurities from system. See Bleeding.

PUSH ROD: Rod that connects valve lifter to rocker arm. Used on valve-in-head installations.

PYLON: Marker for controlling traffic.

QUADRANT (Gearshift): A gear position indicator often using a shift lever actuated pointer. Can be marked PRND21 (3-speed), PRND321 (4-speed), etc.

QUADRA-TRAC: See Full Time Four-Wheel Drive.

QUENCHED (Flame): Flame front in combustion chamber being extinguished as it contacts colder cylinder walls. This sharply elevates hydrocarbon emissions.

QUENCHING: Dipping heated object into water, oil, or other substance, to quickly reduce temperature.

QUICKSILVER: Metal mercury. Often used in thermometers.

RACE (Bearing): Inner or outer ring that provides a contact surface for balls or rollers in bearing.

RACE CAMSHAFT: Camshaft, other than stock, designed to improve performance by altering cam profile. Provides increased lift, faster opening and closing, earlier opening and later closing, etc. Race camshafts are available as semi-race or street grind, three-fourths race or full race. Grinds in between these general categories are also available.

RACING SLICK: Type of tire used in "drag racing" as well as some "stock car" applications. Tread surface of tire is completely smooth, for maximum rubber contact with track surface.

RACK AND PINION GEARBOX (Steering): Steering gear utilizing pinion gear on end of steering shaft. Pinion engages long rack (bar with teeth along one edge). Rack is connected to steering arms via rods.

RADIAL (Direction): Line at right angles (perpendicular) to shaft, cylinder, bearing, etc., center line.

RADIAL COMPRESSOR: A small air conditioning compressor using reciprocating pistons working at right angles to shaft and spaced around shaft in radial fashion.

RADIAL ENGINE: Engine possessing various numbers of cylinders so arranged that they form circle around crankshaft centerline.

RADIAL TIRE: Plies parallel and at right angle to tread, belts under tread area.

RADIATION: Transfer of heat from one object to another when hotter object sends out invisible rays or waves that upon striking colder object, cause it to vibrate and thus heat.

RADIATOR (Engine Cooling): A device used to remove heat from engine coolant. It consists of a series of finned passageways. As coolant moves through passages, heat is conducted to fins where it transfers to a stream of air forced through fins.

RADIATOR CAP: Pressure cap that fits on radiator neck. It keeps coolant from boiling.

RADIUS: Distance (in a straight line) from center of a circle or circular motion, to a point on edge (circumference).

RADIUS RODS: Rods attached to axle and pivoted on frame. Used to keep axle at right angles to frame and yet permit an up and down motion.

RAIL: Dragster built around a relatively long pipe frame. Often the only body panels used are around the driver's cockpit area.

RAM AIR: Air "scooped" up by an opening due to vehicle forward motion.

RAM INDUCTION: Using forward momentum of car to scoop air and force it into carburetor via a suitable passageway.

RAM INTAKE MANIFOLD: Intake manifold that has very long passageways that at certain speeds aid entrance of fuel mixture into cylinders.

RATED HORSEPOWER (Engine): Indication of horsepower load that may safely be placed upon engine for prolonged periods of time. This would be somewhat less than the engine maximum horsepower.

RATIO: Fixed relationship between things in number, quantity, or degree. For example, if fuel mixture contains one part of gas for fifteen parts of air, ratio would be 15 to 1.

REACTOR: See Stator.

REAM: To enlarge or smooth hole by using round cutting tool with fluted edges.

REAR AXLE (Banjo Type): Rear axle housing from which differential unit may be removed while housing remains in place on car. Housing is solid from side to side.

REAR AXLE HOUSING (Split Type): Rear axle housing made up of several pieces and bolted together. Housing must be split apart to remove differential.

RECEIVER-DRIER: See Drier.

RECIPROCATING ACTION: Back-and-forth movement such as action of pistons.

RECIRCULATING BALL WORM AND NUT: Very popular type of steering gear. It utilizes series of ball bearings that feed through and around and back through grooves in worm and nut.

RECTIFIER: Device used to change AC (alternating current) into DC (direct current).

RED LINE: Top recommended engine rpm. If a tachometer is used, it will have a mark (Red line) indicating maximum rpm.

REDUCING FLAME: Welding flame in which there is an excess of acetylene.

REDUCTION (Gear): A gear that increases torque by reducing rpm of a driven shaft in relation to that of driving shaft.

REFRIGERANT: Liquid used in refrigeration systems to remove heat from evaporator coils and carry it to condenser.

REFRIGERANT-12: Name applied to refrigerant generally used in automotive air conditioning systems.

REFRIGERANT OIL: Special oil which lubricates air conditioning compressor.

REGULATOR (Electrical): Device used to control generator voltage and current output.

REGULATOR (Gas or Liquid): Device to reduce and control pressure.

RELATIVE HUMIDITY: Actual amount of moisture in a given sample of air compared to total amount that sample could hold (at same temperature).

RELAY: Magnetically operated switch used to make and break flow of current in circuit. Also called "cutout, and circuit breaker."

RELIEVE: Removing, by grinding, small lip of metal between valve seat area and cylinder—and removing any other metal deemed necessary to improve flow of fuel mixture into cylinder. Porting is generally done at same time.

RELUCTOR: A component in electronic ignition system distributor. It is affixed to the distributor shaft and triggers magnetic pickup. This, in turn, triggers control unit which breaks coil primary circuit causing coil to "fire."

RESIDUAL MAGNETISM: Magnetism remaining in an object after removal of any magnetic field influence.

RESISTANCE (Electrical): Measure of conductor's ability to retard flow of electricity.

RESISTOR: Device placed in circuit to lower voltage. It will also decrease flow of current.

RESISTOR SPARK PLUG: Spark plug containing resistor designed to shorten both capacitive and inductive phases of spark. This will suppress radio interference and lengthen electrode life.

RESONATOR: Small muffler-like device that is placed into exhaust system near end of tail pipe. Used to provide additional silencing of exhaust.

RETARD (Ignition Timing): To set the ignition timing so that spark occurs later or less degrees before TDC.

REVERSE-ELLIOT TYPE AXLE: Solid bar front axle on which steering knuckles span or straddle axle ends.

REVERSE FLUSH: Cleaning cooling system be pumping a powerful cleaning agent through system in a direction opposite to that of normal flow.

REVERSE IDLER GEAR: Gear used in transmission to produce a reverse rotation of transmission output shaft.

RHEOSTAT: A variable type resistor used to control current flow.

RICARDO PRINCIPLE: Arrangement in which portion of combustion chamber came in very close contact with piston head. Other portion, off to one side, contained more space. As the piston neared TDC on compression stroke, fuel mixture was squeezed tightly between piston and head thus causing mixture to squirt outward into larger area in very turbulent manner. This produced a superior mixture and allowed compression ratios to be raised without detonation.

RICH MIXTURE (Fuel): A fuel mixture with an excessive amount of fuel in relation to air.

RIDING THE CLUTCH: Riding the clutch refers to driver resting a foot on clutch pedal while car is being driven.

RIM (Tire): The outer portion of a wheel upon which tire is mounted.

RING (Chrome): Ring on which the outer edge has a thin layer of chrome plate.

RING (Pinned): Steel pin, set into piston, is placed in space between ends of ring. Ring is thus kept from moving around in groove.

RING GAP: Distance between ends of piston ring when installed in cylinder.

RING EXPANDER: Spring device placed under rings to hold them snugly against cylinder wall.

RING GEAR: Large gear attached to differential carrier or to outer gear in planetary gear setup.

RING GROOVES: Grooves cut into piston to accept rings.

RING JOB: Reconditioning cylinders and installing new rings.

RING RIDGE: Portion of cylinder above top limit of ring travel. In a worn cylinder, this area is of smaller diameter than remainder of cylinder and will leave ledge or ridge that must be removed.

RIVET: Metal pin used to hold two objects together. One end of the pin has head and other end must be set or peened over.

RMA: Rubber Manufacturer's Association.

ROAD FEEL: Feeling imparted to steering wheel by wheels of car in motion. This feeling can be very important in sensing and predetermining vehicle steering response.

ROCKER ARM: Arm used to direct upward motion of push rod into a downward or opening motion of valve stem. Used in overhead valve installations.

ROCKER ARM SHAFT: Shaft upon which rocker arms are mounted.

ROCKER PANEL: Section of car body between front and rear fenders and beneath doors.

ROCKWELL HARDNESS: Measurement of the degree of hardness of given substance.

ROD: Refers to a car, driving a car hard, or to a connecting rod.

ROD CAP: Lower removable half of connecting rod big end.

RODDING THE RADIATOR: Top and sometimes the bottom tank of the radiator is removed. The core is then cleaned by passing a cleaning rod down through tubes. This is done when radiators are quite clogged with rust, scale, and various mineral deposits.

ROLL BAR: Heavy steel bar that goes from one side of frame, up and around in back of the driver, and back down to the other side of frame. It is used to protect driver in the event that the car rolls over.

ROLLER BEARING: Bearing utilizing a series of straight, cupped, or tapered rollers engaging an inner and outer ring or race.

ROLLER CLUTCH: Clutch, utilizing series of rollers placed in ramps, that will provide drive power in one direction but will slip or freewheel in the other direction.

ROLLER TAPPETS or LIFTERS: Valve lifters that have roller placed on end contacting camshaft. This is done to reduce friction between lobe and lifter. They are generally used when special camshafts and high tension valve springs have been installed.

ROLLING RADIUS: Distance from road surface to center of wheel with vehicle moving under normal load. Rolling radius is dependent on tire size.

ROLLOVER VALVE: Valve in fuel delivery line to prevent escape of raw fuel during an accident in which car is upside down.

ROOM TEMPERATURE: An enclosed space air temperature of around 68-72°F (20.1-22.2°C).

ROTARY ENGINE: Piston engine in which the crankshaft is fixed (stationary) and in which cylinders rotate around crankshaft.

ROTARY ENGINE (Wankel): Internal combustion engine which is not of a reciprocating (piston) engine design. Central rotor turns in one direction only and yet effectively produces required intake, compression, firing, and exhaust strokes.

ROTARY FLOW (Torque Converter): Movement of oil as it is carried around by pump and turbine. Rotary motion is not caused by oil passing through pump, to turbine, to stator, etc., as is case with vortex flow. Rotary flow is at right angles to center line of converter whereas vortex flow is parallel (more or less depending on ratio between speeds of pump and turbine).

ROTARY MOTION: Continual motion in circular direction such as performed by crankshaft.

ROTOR (Distributor): Cap-like unit placed on end of distributor shaft. It is in constant contact with distributor cap central terminal and as it turns, it will conduct secondary voltage to one of the outer terminals.

ROUGHING STONE (Hone): Coarse stone used for quick removal of material during honing.

RPM: Revolutions per minute.

RUNNING-FIT: Fit in which sufficient clearance has been provided to enable parts to turn freely and to receive lubrication.

RUNNING ON: See Dieseling.

RUNOUT: Refers to a rotating object, surface of which is not revolving in a true circle or plane. Runout can be measured in a radial (at right angles to centerline of object) direction or in a lateral (lengthwise to centerline) direction.

SAE: Society of Automotive Engineers.

SAE or RATED HORSEPOWER: A simple formula of long standing is used to determine what is commonly referred to as the SAE or Rated Horsepower. The formula is:

$$\frac{\text{Bore Diameter}^2 \times \text{Number of Cylinders}}{2.5}$$

This formula is used primarily for licensing purposes and is not too accurate a means of determining actual brake horsepower.

SAFETY FACTOR: Providing strength beyond that needed, as an extra margin of insurance against part failure.

SAFETY HUBS: Device installed on the rear axle to prevent wheels from leaving car in event of a broken axle.

SAFETY RIM: Rim having two safety ridges, one on each lip, to prevent tire beads from entering drop center area in event of a blowout. This feature keeps tire on rim.

SAFETY VALVE: Valve designed to open and relieve pressure within a container when container pressure exceeds predetermined level.

SAND BLAST: Cleaning by the use of sand propelled at high speeds in an air blast.

SAYBOLT VISCOMETER: Instrument used to determine fluidity or viscosity (resistance to flow) of an oil.

SCALE (Cooling System): Accumulation of rust and minerals within cooling system.

SCATTER SHIELD: Steel or nylon guard placed around bell or clutch housing to protect driver and spectator from flying parts in event of part failure at high rpm. Such a shield is often placed around transmissions and differential units.

SCAVENGING: Referring to a cleaning or blowing out action in reference to the exhaust gas.

SCHRADER VALVE: Valve, similar to spring loaded valve used in tire stem, used in car air conditioning system service valves.

SCORE: Scratch or groove on finished surface.

SCREW EXTRACTOR: Device used to remove broken bolts, screws, etc., from holes.

SCS: Speed Control Switch. (Speed sensitive spark advance control.)

SEAL: Device which prevents oil leakage around moving part.

SEALED BEAM HEADLIGHT: Headlight lamp in which lens, reflector, and filament are fused together to form single unit.

SEALED BEARING: Bearing that has been lubricated at factory and then sealed. It cannot be lubricated during service.

SEAT: Surface upon which another part rests or seats. Example: Valve seat is matched surface upon which valve face rests.

SEAT (Rings): Minor wearing of piston ring surface during initial use. Rings then fit or seat properly against the cylinder wall.

SECONDARY CIRCUIT (Ignition System): High voltage part of ignition system.

SECONDARY, REVERSE, or TRAILING BRAKE SHOE: Brake shoe that is installed facing rear of car.

SECONDARY WIRES: High voltage wire from coil to distributor central tower and from outer towers to spark plugs.

SECTION MODULUS: Relative structural strength measurement of member (such as frame rail) that is determined by cross-sectional area and member shape.

SECTION WIDTH (Tire): Overall width minus height of any lettering or pattern extending outward from sidewalls.

SEDIMENT: Accumulation of matter which settles to bottom of a liquid.

SEIZE: See Freezing.

SELF-ENERGIZING: Brake shoe (sometimes both shoes) that when applied develops wedging action that actually assists or boosts braking force applied by wheel cylinder.

SELF-INDUCTION (Electromagnetic): Creation of voltage in a circuit by varying current in circuit.

SEMA: Specialty Equipment Manufacturer's Association.

SEMI-ELLIPTICAL SPRING: Spring, such as commonly used on truck rear axles, consisting of one main leaf and number of progressively shorter leaf springs.

SEMI-FLOATING AXLE: Type of axle commonly used in modern car. Outer end turns wheel and supports weight of car; inner end which is splined, "floats" in differential gear.

SEPARATORS (Battery): Wood, rubber, or plastic sheets inserted between positive and negative plates to prevent contact.

SERIES CIRCUIT: Circuit with two or more resistance units so wired that current must pass through one unit before reaching other.

SERIES-PARALLEL CIRCUIT: Circuit of three or more resistance units in which a series and a parallel circuit are combined.

SERVICEABLE: A part or unit whose design and construction permit disassembly for purposes of rebuilding. Can also be used to indicate a part or unit whose condition is such that it can still be used.

SERVICE MANAGER: Person in charge of overall shop or garage operation.

SERVICE VALVES: Valves in air conditioning system which allow system to be charged (filled), evacuated (emptied), and tested with pressure gauges.

SERVO (Transmission): Oil operated device used to push or pull another part—such as tightening the transmission brake bands.

SERVO ACTION: Brakes so constructed as to have one end of primary shoe bearing against end of secondary shoe. When brakes are applied, primary shoe attempts to move in the direction of the rotating drum and in so doing applies force to the secondary shoe. This action, called servo action, makes less brake pedal pressure necessary and is widely used in brake construction.

SHACKLE: Device used to attach ends of a leaf spring to frame.

SHAVE: Removal of some chrome or decorative part.

SHAVE (Engine): Removal of metal from contact surface of cylinder head or block.

SHIFT FORKS: Devices that straddle slots cut in sliding gears. Fork is used to move gear back and forth on shaft.

SHIFT MECHANISM: Device for changing transmission gears range.

SHIFT POINT: Point, either in engine rpm or road speed, at which transmission should be shifted to next gear.

SHIFT RAILS: Sliding rods upon which shift forks are attached. Used for shifting the transmission (manual).

SHIFT RANGE (4-wheel drive): Used to refer to two-speed transfer case gear position. Case can be shifted into HIGH RANGE (no gear reduction) or LOW RANGE (around two to one reduction).

SHIM: A thin piece of brass, steel, etc., inserted between two parts so as to adjust distance between them. Sometimes used to adjust bearing clearance.

SHIMMY: Front wheels shaking from side to side.

SHOCK ABSORBER: Oil filled device used to control spring oscillation in suspension system.

SHORT BLOCK: Engine block complete

Dictionary of Automotive Terms

with crankshaft and piston assemblies.

SHROUD: Metal enclosure around fan, engine, etc., to guide and facilitate flow of air.

SHORT or SHORT CIRCUIT: Refers to some "hot" portion of the electrical system that has become grounded. (Wire touching a ground and providing a completed circuit to the battery.)

SHRINK-FIT: Fit between two parts which is so tight, outer or encircling piece must be expanded by heating so it will fit over inner piece. In cooling, outer part shrinks and grasps inner part securely.

SHUNT: An alternate or by-pass portion of an electrical circuit.

SHUNT WINDING: Wire coil forming an alternate or bypass circuit through which current may flow.

SIDE-DRAFT CARBURETOR: Carburetor in which air passes though carburetor into intake manifold in a horizontal plane.

SIDEWALL: Part of tire between tread and bead, usually has size and rating information.

SIGHT GLASS: Clear glass window in air conditioning line which lets mechanic check refrigerant for air bubbles (low refrigerant) and moisture (pink color).

SILENCER: Muffler.

SILVER SOLDER: Similar to brazing except that special silver solder metal is used.

SINGLE-BARREL, DOUBLE-BARREL, and FOUR-BARREL CARBURETORS: Number of throttle openings or barrels from the carburetor to the intake manifold.

SINTERED BRONZE: Tiny particles of bronze pressed tightly together so that they form a solid piece. The piece is highly porous and is often used for filtering purposes.

SIPE: Small slits in tire tread designed to increase traction. Also called kerfs.

SKID PLATE: Stout metal plate or plates attached to underside of vehicle to protect oil pan, transmission, fuel tank, etc., from damage caused by "grounding out" on rocks, curbs, and road surface.

SKIVING: Cutting away a portion of tire tread to correct out-of-round problem.

SLANT ENGINE: In-line engine in which cylinder block has been tilted from vertical plane.

SLEEVE (Cylinder): See Cylinder Sleeve.

SLIDING-FIT: See Running-Fit.

SLIDING GEAR: Transmission gear splined to the shaft. It may be moved back and forth for shifting purposes.

SLIP ANGLE: Difference in actual path taken by a car making a turn and path it would have taken if it had followed exactly as wheels were pointed.

SLIP JOINT: Joint that will transfer driving torque from one shaft to another while allowing longitudinal movement between two shafts.

SLINGSHOT: Form of dragster using rather long thin frame with a very light front axle and wheel assembly.

SLUDGE: Black, mushy deposits throughout interior of the engine. Caused from mixture of dust, oil, and water being whipped together by moving parts.

SMOG: Fog made darker and heavier by chemical fumes and smoke.

SNAP RING: Split ring snapped into a groove in a shaft or in a groove in a hole. It is used to hold bearings, thrust washers, gears, etc., in place.

SNUBBER: Device used to limit travel of some part.

SODIUM VALVE: Valve in which stem has been partially filled with metallic sodium to speed up transfer of heat from valve head, to stem and then to guide and block.

SOHC: Engine with single overhead camshaft.

SOLDERING: Joining two pieces of metal together with lead-tin mixture. Both pieces of metal must be heated to insure proper adhesion of melted solder.

SOLENOID: Electrically operated magnetic device used to operate some unit. Movable iron core is placed inside of coil. When current flows through coil, core will attempt to center itself in coil. In so doing, core will exert considerable force on anything it is connected to.

SOLID AXLE: Single beam runs between both wheels. May be used on either front or rear of car.

SOLID STATE: An electrical device, such as a regulator, that has no moving parts. Such units use transistors, diodes, resistors, etc., to perform all electrical functions.

SOLVENT: Liquid used to dissolve or thin other material. Examples: Alcohol thins shellac; gasoline dissolves grease.

SPARK: Bridging or jumping of a gap between two electrodes by current of electricity.

SPARK ADVANCE: Causing spark plug to fire earlier by altering position of distributor breaker points in relation to distributor shaft.

SPARK ARRESTOR: Device used to prevent sparks (burning particles of carbon) from being discharged from exhaust pipe. Usually used on off-road equipment to prevent forest fires.

SPARK GAP: Space between center and side electrode tips on a spark plug.

SPARK KNOCK: See Preignition.

SPARK PLUG: Device containing two electrodes across which electricity jumps to produce a spark to fire fuel charge.

SPECIALIZATION: When a mechanic concentrates in one particular area of auto repair—brakes, tune-up, transmission, engines.

SPECIFIC GRAVITY: Relative weight of a given volume of specific material as compared to weight of an equal volume of water.

SPEED: Time rate of motion without regard to direction. Forward speed (mph or km/h) of a vehicle, rotational speed (rpm) of an engine, etc.

SPEEDOMETER: Instrument used to determine forward speed of an auto in miles per hour or kilometres per hour.

SPIDER GEARS: Small gears mounted on shaft pinned to differential case. They mesh with, and drive, the axle end gears.

SPINDLE (Wheel): Machined shaft upon which inside races of front wheel bearings rest. Spindle is an integral part of steering knuckle.

SPIRAL BEVEL GEAR: Ring and pinion setup widely used in automobile differentials. Teeth of both ring and pinion are tapered and are cut on a spiral so that they are at an angle to center line of pinion shaft.

SPLINE: Metal (land) remaining between two grooves. Used to connect parts.

SPLINED JOINT: Joint between two parts in which each part has a series of splines cut along contact area. The splines on each part

slide into grooves between splines on other part.

SPLIT MANIFOLD: Exhaust manifold that has a baffle placed near its center. An exhaust pipe leads out of each half.

SPONGY PEDAL: When there is air in brake lines, or shoes that are not properly centered in drums, brake pedal will have a springy or spongy feeling when brakes are applied. Pedal normally will feel hard when applied.

SPOOL BALANCE VALVE (Automatic Transmission): Hydraulic valve that balances incoming oil pressure against spring control pressure to produce a steady pressure to some control unit.

SPOOL VALVE: Hydraulic control valve shaped somewhat like spool upon which thread is wound.

SPORTS CAR: Term commonly used to describe a relatively small, low slung, car with a high performance engine.

SPOT WELD: Fastening parts together by fusing, at various spots. Heavy surge of electricity is passed through the parts held in firm contact by electrodes.

SPRAG CLUTCH: Clutch that will allow rotation in one direction but that will lock up and prevent any movement in the other direction.

SPRING (Main Leaf): Long leaf on which ends are turned to form an "eye" to receive shackle.

SPRING BOOSTER: Device used to "beef" up sagged springs or to increase the load capacity of standard springs.

SPRING CAPACITY AT GROUND: Total vehicle weight (sprung and unsprung) that will be carried by spring bent or deflected to its maximum normal loaded position.

SPRING CAPACITY AT PAD: Total vehicle sprung weight that will be carried by spring bent or deflected to its normal fully loaded position.

SPRING LOADED: Device held in place, or under pressure from a spring or springs.

SPRING STEEL: Heat treated steel having the ability to stand a great amount of deflection and yet return to its original shape or position.

SPRING WINDUP: Curved shape assumed by rear leaf springs during acceleration or braking.

SPROCKET: Toothed wheel used to drive chain or cogged belt.

SPRUNG WEIGHT: Weight of all parts of car that are supported by suspension system.

SPUR GEAR: Gear on which teeth are cut parallel to shaft.

SPURT or SQUIRT HOLE: Small hole in connecting rod big end that indexes (aligns) with oil hole in crank journal. When holes index, oil spurts out to lubricate cylinder walls.

SQUARE ENGINE: Engine in which bore diameter and stroke are of equal dimensions.

SQ. FT.: Square Foot.

SQ. IN.: Square Inch.

STABILIZER BAR: Transverse mounted spring steel bar that controls and minimizes body lean or tipping on corners.

STALL: To stop rotation or operation.

STAMPING: Sheet metal part formed by pressing between metal dies.

STARTER (Engine): Electric motor which uses a geardrive to crank (spin) engine for starting.

STARTER PINION GEAR: Small gear on

end of starter shaft that engages and turns large flywheel ring gear.

STARTER SOLENOID: Large electric relay that makes and breaks the electrical connection between the battery and starting motor.

STARTING SYSTEM: Parts (starter motor, gear drive, switch, solenoid, wires, battery, etc.) involved in system used to crank car for starting.

STATIC BALANCE: When a tire, flywheel, crankshaft, etc., has an absolutely even distribution of weight mass around axis of rotation, it will be in static balance. For example, if front wheel is jacked up and tire, regardless of where it is placed, always slowly turns and stops with the same spot down, it would not be in static balance. If, however, wheel remains in any position in which it is placed, it would be in static balance. (Bearings must be free, no brake drag, etc.)

STATIC ELECTRICITY: Electricity generated by friction between two objects. It will remain in one object until discharged.

STATIC PRESSURE (Brakes): Certain amount of pressure that always exists in brake lines—even with brake pedal released. Static pressure is maintained by a check valve.

STATIC RADIUS: Distance from road surface to center of wheel with vehicle normally loaded, at rest.

STATIC SUPPRESSION: Removal or minimizing of unwanted electromagnetic waves that cause radio static interference (hissing, crackling, etc.).

STATOR: Small hub, upon which series of vanes are affixed in radial position, that is so placed that oil leaving torque converter turbine strikes stator vanes and is redirected into pump at an angle conducive to high efficiency. Stator makes torque multiplication possible. Torque multiplication is highest at stall when the engine speed is at its highest and the turbine is standing still.

STEEL PACK MUFFLER: Straight-through (no baffled) muffler utilizing metal shavings surrounding a perforated pipe. Quiets exhaust sound.

STEERING ARMS: Arms, either bolted to, or forged as an integral part of steering knuckles. They transmit steering force from tie rods to knuckles, thus causing wheels to pivot.

STEERING AXIS INCLINATION: See Kingpin Inclination.

STEERING GEAR: Gears, mounted on lower end of steering column, used to multiply driver turning force.

STEERING GEOMETRY: Term sometimes used to describe various angles assumed by components making up front wheel turning arrangement, camber, caster, toe-in, etc.

Also used to describe related angles assumed by front wheels when car is negotiating a curve.

STEERING KNUCKLE: Inner portion of spindle affixed to and pivoting on either a kingpin or on upper and lower ball joints.

STEERING KNUCKLE ANGLE: Angle formed between steering axis and centerline of spindle. This angle is sometimes referred to as Included Angle.

STEERING LINKAGE: Various arms, rods, etc., connecting steering gear to front wheels.

STEERING SYSTEM: All parts (steering wheel, shaft, gears, linkage, etc.) used in transferring motion of steering wheel to front wheels.

STETHOSCOPE: Device (such as used by doctors) to detect and locate abnormal engine noises. Very handy tool for troubleshooter.

STICK SHIFT: Transmission that is shifted manually through use of various forms of linkage. Often refers to upright gearshift stick that protrudes through floor.

Either floor or steering column mounted manual shift device for transmission.

STOCK CAR: Car as built by factory.

STOICHIOMETRIC FUEL MIXTURE: A fuel mixture in which proportions of air and fuel are such as to permit complete burning. The ideal mixture for any given engine and set of conditions.

STOPLIGHT: Warning lights, red in color, attached to rear of vehicle. Stoplights come on whenever brake pedal is depressed.

STORAGE BATTERY: Another term for car battery. See Battery.

STOVEBOLT: Generally refers to Chevrolet (GMC) 6-cylinder, in-line, valve-in-head (push rod operated) engine.

STREET ROD: Slightly modified rod that will give good day-to-day performance on the streets.

STRESS: To apply force to an object. Force or pressure an object is subjected to.

STRIPING TOOL: Tool used to apply paint in long narrow lines.

STROBOSCOPE: See Timing Light.

STROKE: Distance piston moves when traveling from TDC to BDC.

STROKED CRANKSHAFT: Crankshaft, either special new one or stock crank reworked, that has connecting rod throws offset so that length of stroke is increased.

STROKER: Engine using crankshaft that has been stroked.

STUD: Metal rod with threads on both ends.

STUD PULLER: Tool used to install or remove studs.

SUCTION: See Vacuum.

SUCTION LINE: See Low Pressure Line.

SUCTION THROTTLING VALVE: Valve placed between air conditioning evaporator and compressor which controls evaporator pressure to provide maximum cooling without icing evaporator core.

SULFATION: Formation of lead sulphate on battery plates.

SUMP: Part of oil pan that contains oil.

SUN GEAR: Center gear around which planet gears revolve.

SUPER CAR: Car with high horsepower engine that will provide fast acceleration and high speed.

SUPERCHARGER: Unit designed to force air, under pressure, into cylinders. Can be mounted between carburetor and cylinders or between carburetor and atmosphere.

SUPERHEAT SWITCH: See Compressor Protection Switch.

SURE-GRIP DIFFERENTIAL: High traction differential which causes both axles to rotate under power.

SWAY BAR: See Stabilizer Bar.

SWEATING: Joining two pieces of metal together by placing solder between them and then clamping them tightly together while heat, sufficient to melt the solder, is applied.

SWING AXLE: Independent rear suspension system in which each driving wheel can move up or down independently of other. Differential unit is bolted to frame and various forms of linkage are used upon which to mount wheels. Drive axles, utilizing one or more universal joints, connect differential to drive wheels.

SWITCH (Electric): A device to make (complete) or break (interrupt) flow of current through a circuit.

SYNCHROMESH TRANSMISSION: Transmission using device (synchromesh) that synchronizes speeds of gears that are being shifted together. This prevents "gear grinding." Some transmissions use synchromesh on all shifts, while others synchronize second and high gearshifts.

SYNCHRONIZE: To bring about a timing that will cause two or more events to occur simultaneously; plug firing when the piston is in correct position, speed of two shafts being the same, valve opening when piston is in correct position, etc.

TACHOMETER: Device used to indicate speed of engine in rpm.

TAILLIGHT: Lights, usually red or amber, attached to rear of vehicle. Lights operate in conjunction with headlights.

TAIL PIPE: Exhaust piping running from muffler to rear of car.

TANK GAUGE UNIT: Variable resistor device in fuel tank. It operates fuel gauge in dashboard.

TAP: To cut threads in a hole, or can be used to indicate fluted tool used to cut threads.

TAP AND DIE SET: Set of taps and dies for internal and external threading—usually covers a range of the most popular sizes.

TAPERED ROLLER BEARING (Antifriction): Bearing utilizing series of tapered, hardened steel rollers operating between an outer and inner hardened steel race.

TAPPET: Screw used to adjust clearance between valve stem and lifter or rocker arm.

TAPPET NOISE: Noise caused by lash or clearance between valve stem and rocker arm or between valve stem and valve lifter.

TCS: Transmission Controlled Spark.

TDC: Top Dead Center.

TEFLON: Plastic with excellent self-lubricating (slippery) bearing properties.

TEMPER: To effect a change in physical structure of piece of steel through use of heat and cold.

TEMPERATURE GAUGE: Dash mounted instrument to indicate temperature of engine coolant. May be operated electrically or by Bourdon tube.

TENSION: Pulling or stretching stress applied to an object.

TERMINAL: Connecting point in electric circuit. When referring to battery, it would indicate two battery posts.

T-HEAD ENGINE: Engine having intake valve on one side of cylinder and exhaust on other.

THERMAL EFFICIENCY: Percentage of heat developed in burning fuel charge that is actually used to develop power determines thermal efficiency. Efficiency will vary according to engine design, use, etc. If an engine utilizes great deal of heat to produce power, its thermal efficiency would be high.

THERMISTOR: Resistor that changes its resistance in relation to temperature fluctuations.

THERMOSTAT: Temperature sensitive device used in cooling system to control flow of coolant in relation to temperature.

THERMOSTATICALLY CONTROLLED AIR CLEANER (TAC): An emission control device used to control temperature of air entering air cleaner. Cleaner receives heated air during engine warmup.

THERMOSTATIC SWITCH: A switch that is actuated by temperature changes.

THIRD BRUSH (Generator): Generator in which a third, movable brush is used to control current output.

THREE-QUARTER RACE CAMSHAFT: Description of custom camshaft indicating type of lobe grinding which, in turn, dictates type of use. Other grinds are one-quarter race, full-race, street-grind, etc.

THREE-WAY CATALYTIC CONVERTER: Converter, sometimes called dual converter, that combines both an oxidizing and reducing catalyst. Controls NOx, CO, and HC emissions.

THROTTLE RETURN DASHPOT: Carburetor device which slows throttle closing and prevents stalling.

THROTTLE VALVE: Valve in carburetor. It is used to control amount of fuel mixture that reaches cylinders.

THROTTLE VALVE SENSOR AND THROTTLE POSITION SENSOR: Sensor which measures amount of throttle valve opening and provides information for fuel injection computer.

THROTTLE VALVE (Transmission): Valve in automatic transmission which controls oil flow to regulator plug.

THROW: Offset portion of crankshaft designed to accept connecting rod.

THROWING A ROD: When an engine has thrown a connecting rod from crankshaft, major damage is usually incurred.

THRUST: A pushing or shoving force exerted against one body by another.

THRUST BEARING: Bearing designed so as to resist side pressure.

THRUST SURFACE: That portion (surface) of a part that either receives or transmits a force from or to another part.

THRUST WASHER: Bronze or hardened steel washer placed between two moving parts. The washer prevents longitudinal movement and provides a bearing surface for thrust surfaces of parts.

TIE ROD: Rod, or rods, connecting steering arms together. When tie rod is moved, wheels pivot.

TIG: Gas tungsten arc welding (Tungsten Inert Gas).

TIMED FUEL INJECTION: Fuel injection is timed to occur when intake valve opens.

TIMING: The act of coordinating two or more separate events or actions in relation to each other. Example: Timing the firing of plug to piston position on compression stroke.

TIMING BELT: A flexible, toothed belt used to rotate camshaft.

TIMING CHAIN: Drive chain that operates camshaft by engaging sprockets on camshaft and crankshaft.

TIMING COVER: Cover over timing chain, belt, or gear mechanism. May contain front crankshaft oil seal.

TIMING GEARS: Both the gear attached to the camshaft and the gear on the crankshaft. They provide a means of driving the camshaft.

TIMING LIGHT: Stroboscopic unit that is connected to secondary circuit to produce flashes of light in unison with firing of specific spark plug. By directing these flashes of light on whirling timing marks, marks appear to stand still. By adjusting

distributor, timing marks may be properly aligned, thus setting timing.

TIMING MARKS (Ignition): Marks, usually located on vibration damper, used to synchronize ignition system so plugs will fire at precise time.

TIMING MARKS (Valves): One tooth on either the camshaft or crankshaft gear will be marked with an indentation or some other mark. Another mark will be found on other gear between two of teeth. Two gears must be meshed so that marked tooth meshes with marked spot on other gear.

TIMING SPROCKETS: Chain type sprockets on crankshaft and camshaft.

TINNING: Coating piece of metal with a very thin layer of solder.

TIRE BALANCE: In that tires turn at relatively high speeds, they must be carefully balanced both for static balance and for dynamic balance.

TIRE BEAD: Portion of tire that bears against rim flange. Bead has a number of turns of steel wire in it to provide great strength.

TIRE CASING: Main body of tire exclusive of tread.

TIRE INFLATION PRESSURE: Recommended maximum tire air pressure as given on tire sidewall.

TIRE PLIES: Layers of nylon, rayon, etc., cloth used to form casing. Many car tires are two ply with a four ply rating. Two ply indicates two layers of cloth or plies.

TIRE ROTATION: Moving front tires to rear and rear to front to equalize any wear irregularities.

TIRE SIDEWALL: Portion of tire between tread and bead.

TIRE SIZE: Given on tire sidewall as coded letter-number designation of size, section height, and diameter across bead.

TIRE TREAD: Part of tire that contacts road.

TOE-IN: Having front of wheels closer together than the back (front wheels). Difference in measurement across front of wheels and the back will give amount of toe-in.

TOE-OUT: Having front of wheels further apart than the back.

TOE-OUT ON TURNS: When car negotiates a curve, inner wheel turns more sharply and while wheels remain in this position, a condition of toe-out exists.

TOGGLE SWITCH: Switch actuated by flipping a small lever either up and down or from side to side.

TOLERANCE: Amount of variation permitted from an exact size or measurement. Actual amount from smallest acceptable dimension to largest acceptable dimension.

TOOTH HEEL (Differential Ring Gear): Wider outside end of tooth.

TOOTH TOE (Differential Ring Gear): Narrower inside end of tooth.

TOP OFF: Fill a container to full capacity.

TORQUE: Turning or twisting force such as force imparted on drive line by engine.

TORQUE BAR or ROD: An articulated bar between frame and drive axle housing designed to relieve leaf springs of axle torque (twisting) strain. Prevents axle windup and/or hop during heavy acceleration or braking. Also called Traction Bar.

TORQUE CONVERTER: Unit, quite similar to fluid coupling, that transfers engine torque to transmission input shaft. Unlike

fluid coupling, torque converter can multiply engine torque. This is accomplished by installing one or more stators between torus members. In torque converter, driving torus is referred to as "pump" and driven torus as "turbine."

TORQUE (Gross): Maximum engine torque developed by engine without fan, air cleaner, alternator, exhaust system, etc.

TORQUE (Net): Maximum torque developed by engine equipped with fan, air cleaner, exhaust system, and all other systems or units normally present when engine is installed in the vehicle.

TORQUE MULTIPLICATION (Automatic Transmission): Increasing engine torque through the use of a torque converter.

TORQUE TUBE DRIVE: Method of connecting transmission output shaft to differential pinion shaft by using an enclosed drive shaft. Drive shaft is enclosed in torque tube that is bolted to rear axle housing on one end and is pivoted through a ball joint to rear of transmission on other. Driving force of rear wheels is transferred to frame through torque tube.

TORQUE WRENCH: Wrench used to draw nuts, cap screws, etc., up to specified tension by measuring torque (turning force) being applied.

TORSIONAL VIBRATION: Twisting and untwisting action developed in shaft. It is caused either by intermittent applications of power or load.

TORSION BAR: Long spring steel rod attached in such a way that one end is anchored while other is free to twist. If an arm is attached at right angles to free end, any movement of arm will cause rod or bar to twist. Bar's resistance to twisting provides a spring action. Torsion bar replaces both coil and leaf springs in some suspension systems.

TORSION BAR SUSPENSION: Suspension system that makes use of torsion bars in place of leaf or coil spring.

TORUS: Fluid coupling rotating member. There are two—driving and driven torus.

TPC: Tire Performance Criteria.

TRACK: Distance between front wheels or distance between rear wheels. They are not always the same.

TRACTION BAR: Articulated bar or link attached to both frame and rear axle housing to prevent spring windup (with resultant wheel hop) during heavy acceleration or braking.

TRACTION DIFFERENTIAL: See Limited-Slip Differential.

TRACTION (Tire): Frictional force generated between tire and road. Necessary for braking, steering, and driving.

TRAMP: Hopping motion of front wheels.

TRANSAXLE: Drive setup in which transmission and differential are combined into a single unit.

TRANSDUCER: Vacuum regulator actuated or controlled electrically. A device that converts an input signal (electrical) into an output signal (diaphragm movement) of a different form.

TRANSFER CASE: Gearbox, driven by transmission, that will provide driving force to both front and rear propeller shafts on four-wheel drive vehicle.

TRANSFORMER: Electrical device used to increase or decrease voltage. Car ignition coil transforms voltage from 12 volts to upward of 30,000 volts.

TRANSISTOR: Electrical device made of semi-conducting material and using at least three electrical connections. Often used as a switching device.

TRANSISTOR IGNITION: Form of ignition system utilizing transistors and a special coil. Conventional distributor and point setup is used. With transistor unit, voltage remains constant, thus permitting high engine rpm without resultant engine "miss." Point life is greatly extended as transistor system passes a very small amount of current through points.

TRANSMISSION: Device that uses gearing or torque conversion to effect a change in ratio between engine rpm and driving wheel rpm. When engine rpm goes up in relation to wheel rpm, more torque but less speed is produced. Reduction in engine rpm in relation to wheel rpm produces a higher road speed but delivers less torque to driving wheels.

TRANSMISSION ADAPTER: A unit that allows a different make or year transmission to be bolted up to original engine.

TRANSMISSION (Automatic): Transmission that automatically effects gear changes to meet varying road and load conditions. Gear changing is done through series of oil operated clutches and bands.

TRANSMISSION BRAKE: A brake of either drum or disc design, working at transmission. Stops rotation of propeller shaft.

TRANSMISSION (Standard or Conventional): Transmission that must be shifted manually to effect a change in gearing.

TRANSVERSE LEAF SPRING: Leaf spring mounted so it is at right angles to length of car.

TRAPS: Area over which car is raced for timing purposes.

TREAD: Distance between two front or two rear wheels.

TREAD (Tire): Portion of tire which contacts roadway.

TREAD WIDTH (Tire): Distance between outside edges of tread as measured across tread surface.

TRIP ODOMETER: Auxiliary odometer that may be reset to zero at option of driver. Used for keeping track of mileage on trips up to one thousand miles.

TROUBLESHOOTING: Diagnosing engine, transmission, etc., problems by various tests and observations.

TRS: Transmission Regulated Spark.

TRUNNION: One of two pivots, bearings, etc., placed opposite to each other so as to permit a swiveling or tilting action of some part. Example: Universal joint trunnion (yoke bearings) that allow cross to swivel.

TUBE CUTTER: Tool used to cut tubing by passing a sharp wheel around and around tube.

TUBELESS (Tire): Tire constructed for use without inner tube, valve stem snaps into and seals in wheel rim.

TUNE-UP: Process of checking, repairing, and adjusting carburetor, spark plugs, points, belts, timing, etc., in order to obtain maximum performance from engine.

TURBINE: Wheel upon which series of angled vanes are affixed so moving column of air or liquid will impart a turning motion to wheel.

TURBINE ENGINE: Engine that utilizes burning gases to spin a turbine, or series of turbines, as a means of propelling the car.

TURBOCHARGER: Exhaust powered supercharger.

TURBULENCE: Violent, broken movement or agitation of a fluid or gas.

TURNING RADIUS: Diameter of circle transcribed by outer front wheel when making a full turn.

TV ROD: Throttle valve rod that extends from foot throttle linkage to throttle valve in automatic transmission.

TVS: Thermostatic Vacuum Switch.

TWIST DRILL: Metal cutting drill with spiral flutes (grooves) to permit exit of chips while cutting.

TWO-STROKE CYCLE ENGINE: Engine requiring one complete revolution of crankshaft to fire each piston once.

UAW: United Auto Workers.

UNDERCOATING: Soft deadening material sprayed on underside of car, under hood, trunk lid, etc.

UNDER-SQUARE ENGINE: Engine in which bore diameter is smaller than length of stroke.

UNDERSTEER: Tendency for car, when negotiating a corner, to turn less sharply than driver intends.

UNIT BODY: Car body in which body itself acts as frame.

UNIVERSAL JOINT: Flexible joint that will permit changes in driving angle between driving and driven shaft.

UNLEADED GASOLINE: Gasoline not containing tetraethyl lead. Must be used with vehicles equipped with a catalytic converter.

UNSPRUNG WEIGHT: All parts of car not supported by suspension system; wheels, tires, etc.

UPDRAFT CARBURETOR: Carburetor in which the air passes upward through the carburetor into the intake manifold.

UPSET: Widening of diameter through pounding.

UPSHIFT: Shifting to a higher gear.

UTQGS: Uniform Tire Quality Grading System.

VACUUM: Enclosed area in which air pressure is below that of surrounding atmospheric pressure.

VACUUM ADVANCE (Distributor): Unit designed to advance and retard ignition timing through action of engine vacuum working on a diaphragm.

VACUUM BOOSTER: Small diaphragm vacuum pump, generally in combination with fuel pump, that is used to bolster engine vacuum during acceleration so vacuum operated devices will continue to operate.

VACUUM GAUGE: Gauge used to determine amount of vacuum existing in a chamber.

VACUUM MODULATOR: Device which uses engine vacuum to control throttle valve in automatic transmission.

VACUUM MOTOR: A device, utilizing a vacuum operated diaphragm, which causes movement of some other unit.

VACUUM PUMP: Diaphragm type of pump used to produce vacuum.

VACUUM RUNOUT POINT: Point reached when vacuum brake power piston has built up all the braking force it is capable of with vacuum available.

VACUUM SWITCH (Electric): An electrical switch that is operated by vacuum.

VACUUM TANK: Tank in which vacuum exists. Generally used to provide vacuum to power brake installation in event engine vacuum cannot be obtained. Tank will supply several brake applications before vacuum is exhausted.

VALVE: Device used to either open or close an opening. There are many different types.

VALVE CLEARANCE (Engine): Space between end of valve stem and actuating mechanism (rocker arm, lifter, etc).

VALVE DURATION: Length of time, measured in degrees of engine crankshaft rotation, that valve remains open.

VALVE FACE: Outer lower edge of valve head. The face contacts the valve seat when the valve is closed.

VALVE FLOAT: Condition where valves in engine are forced back open before they have had a chance to seat. Brought about (usually) by extremely high rpm.

VALVE GRINDING: Renewing valve face area by grinding on special grinding machine.

VALVE GUIDE: Hole through which stem of poppet valve passes. It is designed to keep valve in proper alignment. Some guides are pressed into place and others are merely drilled in block or in head metal.

VALVE HEAD (Engine): Portion of valve above stem.

VALVE-IN-HEAD ENGINE: Engine in which both intake and exhaust valves are mounted in the cylinder head and are driven by push rods or by an overhead camshaft.

VALVE KEEPER or VALVE KEY or VALVE RETAINER: Small unit that snaps into a groove in end of valve stem. It is designed to secure valve spring, valve spring retaining washer, and valve stem together. Some are of a split design, some of a horseshoe shape, etc.

VALVE LASH: Valve tappet clearance or total clearance in the valve operating train with cam follower on camshaft base circle.

VALVE LIFT: Distance a valve moves from full closed to full open position.

VALVE LIFTER or CAM FOLLOWER: Unit that contacts end of valve stem and camshaft. Follower rides on camshaft and when cam lobes move it upward, it opens valve.

VALVE MARGIN: Width of edge of valve head between top of valve and edge of face. Too narrow a margin results in preignition and valve damage through overheating.

VALVE OIL SEAL: Neoprene rubber ring placed in groove in valve stem to prevent excess oil entering area between stem and guide. There are other types of these seals.

VALVE OVERLAP: Certain period in which both intake and exhaust valve are partially open. (Intake is starting to open while exhaust is not yet closed.)

VALVE PORT: Opening, through head or block, from intake or exhaust manifold to valve seat.

VALVE ROTATOR: Unit that is placed on end of valve stem so that when valve is opened and closed, the valve will rotate a small amount with each opening and closing. This gives longer valve life.

VALVE SEAT: Area onto which face of poppet seats when closed. Two common angles for this seat are forty-five and thirty degrees.

VALVE SEAT GRINDING: Renewing valve seat area by grinding with a stone mounted upon a special mandrel.

VALVE SEAT INSERT: Hardened steel valve seat may be removed and replaced.

Dictionary of Automotive Terms

VALVE SPRING: Coil spring used to keep valves closed.

VALVE STEM (Engine): Portion of valve below head. The stem rides in the guide.

VALVE TAPPET: Adjusting screw to obtain specified clearance at end of valve stem (tappet clearance). Screw may be in top of lifter, in rocker arm, or in the case of ball joint rocker arm, nut on mounting stud acts in place of a tappet screw.

VALVE TIMING: Adjusting position of camshaft to crankshaft so that valves will open and close at the proper time.

VALVE TRAIN: Various parts making up valve and its operating mechanism.

VALVE UMBRELLA: Washer-like unit that is placed over end of the valve stem to prevent the entry of excess oil between the stem and the guide. Used in valve-in-head installations.

VANE: Thin plate affixed to rotatable unit to either throw off air or liquid, or to receive thrust imparted by moving air or liquid striking the vane. In the first case it would be acting as a pump and in the second case as a turbine.

VAPOR: Gaseous state of a substance usually a liquid or solid. Example: Steam.

VAPORIZATION: Breaking gasoline into fine particles and mixing it with incoming air.

VAPOR LOCK: Boiling or vaporizing of the fuel in the lines from excess heat. Boiling will interfere with movement of the fuel and will in some cases, completely stop the flow.

VAPOR SEPARATOR: A device used on cars equipped with air conditioning to prevent vapor lock by feeding vapors back to the gas tank via a separate line.

VARIABLE PITCH STATOR: Stator that has vanes that may be adjusted to various angles depending on load conditions. Vane adjustment will increase or decrease efficiency of stator.

VARIABLE VENTURI: A carburetor venturi whose opening size can be varied to meet changing engine speed and loading needs.

VARNISH: Deposit on interior of engine caused by engine oil breaking down under prolonged heat and use. Certain portions of oil deposit themselves in hard coatings of varnish.

V-BELT: V shaped belt commonly used to spin alternator, water pump, power steering pump, and air conditioning compressor.

VELOCITY: Time rate of motion. Speed with which an object moves as measured in feet per second, miles per hour, etc.

VENTURI: That part of a tube, channel, pipe, etc., so tapered as to form a smaller or constricted area. Liquid, or a gas, moving through this constricted area will speed up and as it passes narrowest point, a partial vacuum will be formed. Taper facing flow of air is much steeper than taper facing away from flow of air. Venturi principle is used in carburetor.

VIBRATION DAMPER: Round weighted device attached to front of crankshaft to minimize torsional vibration.

VISCOSIMETER: Device used to determine viscosity of a given sample of oil. Oil is heated to specific temperature and then allowed to flow through set orifice. Length of time required for certain amount to flow determines oil's viscosity.

VISCOSITY: Measure of oil's ability to pour.

(Thick, thin.)

VISCOSITY INDEX: Measure of oil's ability to resist changes in viscosity when heated.

VOLATILE: A substance that evaporates (turns to vapor) easily. Example: Gasoline.

VOLATILITY: Property of gasoline, alcohol, etc., to evaporate quickly and at relatively low temperatures.

VOLT: Unit of electrical pressure or force that will move a current of one ampere through a resistance of one ohm.

VOLTAGE: Difference in electrical potential between one end of a circuit and the other. Also called EMF (electromotive force). Voltage causes current to flow.

VOLTAGE DROP: Lowering of voltage due to excess length of wire, undersize wire, etc.

VOLTAGE REGULATOR: See Regulator — Voltage.

VOLTMETER: Instrument used to measure voltage in given circuit. (In volts.)

VOLUME: Measurement, in cubic inches, cubic feet, etc., of amount of space within a certain object or area.

VOLUMETRIC EFFICIENCY: Comparison between actual volume of fuel mixture drawn in on intake stroke and what would be drawn in if cylinder were to be completely filled.

VORTEX: Mass of whirling liquid or gas.

VORTEX FLOW (Torque Converter): Whirling motion of oil as it moves around and around from pump, through turbine, through stator and back into pump and so on.

V-TYPE ENGINE: An engine in which cylinders are arranged in two separate banks (rows) and set at an angle (V-shape) to each other.

VULCANIZATION: Process of heating compounded rubber to alter its characteristics — making it tough, resilient, etc.

WANDERING (Steering): Condition in which front wheels tend to steer one way and then another.

WANKEL ENGINE: Rotary combustion engine that utilizes one or more three-sided rotors mounted on drive shaft operating in specially shaped chambers. Rotor turns constantly in one direction yet produces an intake, compression, firing, and exhaust stroke.

WATER DETECTOR: Sensor in diesel fuel system which warns driver of water contamination of fuel.

WATER JACKET: Area around cylinders and valves that is left hollow so that water may be admitted for cooling.

WATER PUMP: The pump, usually a centrifugal type, used to circulate coolant throughout cooling system.

WEDGE: Engine using wedge-shaped combustion chamber.

WEDGE COMBUSTION CHAMBER: Combustion chamber utilizing wedge shape. It is quite efficient and lends itself to mass production and as a result is widely used.

WEIGHT (Curb): Weight of vehicle (no passengers) with all systems (fuel, cooling, lubrication) filled.

WEIGHT (Shipping): Basic vehicle weight including all standard items but without fuel or coolant.

WEIGHT (Sprung): See Sprung Weight.

WEIGHT DISTRIBUTION: Percentage of total vehicle weight as carried by each axle (front and rear).

WELD: To join two pieces of metal together

by raising area to be joined to point hot enough for two sections to melt and flow together. Additional metal is usually added by melting small drops from end of metal rod while welding is in progress.

WET FRICTION: Resistance to movement between two lubricated surfaces.

WET SLEEVE: Cylinder sleeve application in which water in cooling system contacts a major portion of sleeve itself.

WHEEL ALIGNER: Device used to check camber, caster, toe-in, etc.

WHEEL ALIGNMENT: Refers to checking or adjusting various angles involved in proper placement or alignment of both front and rear wheels.

WHEEL BALANCER: Machine used to check wheel and tire assembly for static and dynamic balance.

WHEELBASE: Distance between center of front wheels and center of rear wheels.

WHEEL BEARING: Ball or roller bearings on which wheel hub rotates.

WHEEL BRAKE: A brake operating at wheel, either drum or disc design.

WHEEL CYLINDER: Part of hydraulic brake system that receives pressure from master cylinder and in turn applies brake shoes to drums.

WHEEL HOP: Hopping action of rear wheels during heavy acceleration.

WHEELIE BARS: Short arms attached to rear of a drag racer to prevent front end from rising too far off ground during heavy acceleration. Arms are usually of spring material and have small wheels attached to ends that contact ground.

WHEEL LUG or LUG BOLT: Bolts used to fasten wheel to hub.

WIDE TREADS, WIDE OVAL, etc: Wide tires. Tire height (bead to tread surface) is about 70 percent of tire width across outside of carcass.

WINCH: An electrically or mechanically driven drum that will wind in a length of cable. Used to remove vehicles from mud, ascend very steep slopes, pull logs, etc.

WINDSCREEN: British term for windshield.

WIRING DIAGRAM: Drawing showing various electrical units and wiring arrangement necessary for them to function properly.

WISHBONE: Radius rod setup used in many older Ford cars to keep axle square with frame.

WITNESS MARKS: Punch marks used to position or locate some part in its proper spot.

WOBBLE PLATE: A round, flat plate with a shaft passing through its center. Plate is affixed to shaft at an angle to shaft centerline. When shaft turns, plate will rotate but will also wobble from side to side. Used on axial air conditioning compressor to operate pistons.

WORK: A force applied to a body causing body to move.

WORM GEAR: Coarse, spiral shaped gear cut on shaft. Used to engage with and drive another gear or portion of a gear. As used in steering gearbox, it often engages cross shaft via a roller or by a tapered pin.

WORM AND ROLLER: Type of steering gear utilizing a worm gear on steering shaft. A roller on one end of cross shaft engages worm.

WORM AND SECTOR: Type of steering gear utilizing worm gear engaging sector (a

portion of a gear) on cross shaft.
WORM AND TAPER PIN: Type of steering gear utilizing worm gear on steering shaft. End of cross shaft engages worm via taper pin.
WRIST PIN: See Piston Pin.

YIELD STRENGTH (Elastic Limit): Maximum force (in pounds per square inch) that can be sustained by given member and have that member return to its original position, length, shape, etc., when force or pressure is removed.

ZENER DIODE: A silicone diode that serves as a rectifier (allows electrical current flow in ONE direction only) until voltage being applied to diode attains a certain level (called Zener voltage) at which point diode becomes conductive.

ACKNOWLEDGMENTS

The production of a book of this nature would not be possible without the cooperation of the automotive industry. In preparing the manuscript for AUTO MECHANICS FUNDAMENTALS, the industry has been most cooperative. The authors acknowledge the cooperation of these companies with great appreciation:

Accurate Products, Inc.; AC Spark Plug Div. of General Motors Corp.; Aeroquip Corp.; Aimco; Air Lift Co.; Air Reduction; Albertson and Co.; Alemite Div. of Stewart-Warner; Alfa Romeo Cars, Allen Test Products; All-Lock Co., Inc.; Alondra, Inc.; Aluminum Co. of America; A.L.C. Co.; Amco Mfg. Corp.; American Brake Shoe Co.; American Bosch Arma Corp.; American Hammered Automotive Replacement Div.; American Iron and Steel Institute; American Manufacturers Assn.; American Motors Corp.; American Optical Co.; American Petroleum Institute; American-Standard; American Standards Assn., Inc.; Amerimac, Inc.; Ammco Tools, Inc.; Anti-Friction Bearing Manufacturers Assn., Inc.; AP Parts Corp.; Appleton Electric Co.; Armstrong Patents Co., Ltd.; Armstrong Tire & Rubber; Armstrong Tool Co.; Arnolt Corp.; Aro Corp.; Audi; Ausco Co.; Automotive Electric Assn.; Automotive Service Industry Assn.; Baldwin, J. A., Mfg. Co.; Band-it Company; Barbee Co., Inc.; Battery Council International; Beach Precision Parts Co.; Bear Mfg. Co.; Beckman Instruments, Inc.; Belden Mfg. Co.; Bendix Automotive Service Div. of Bendix Corp.; Benwil Industries; Bethlehem Steel Co.; BF Goodrich, Big Four Industries, Inc.; Binks Mfg. Co.; Black and Decker Mfg. Co.; Blackhawk Mfg. Co.; B & M Automotive Products; Bonney Forge and Tool Works; Borg & Beck; Bilstein Corp. of America; Borg Warner Corp.; Bosch, Robert, Corp.; Bowes Mfg., Inc.; Branick Mfg. Co., Inc.; Breeze Corp., Inc.; Bremen Bearing Co.; British-Leyland Motors, Inc.; British Motor Corp. — Hambro, Inc.; Brown and Sharpe, Indus. Prod. Div.; Cadillac Div. of General Motors Corp.; Buick Div. of General Motors Corp.; Bundy Tubing; Burke Co.; Carter Div. of ACF Industries, Inc.; Cedar Rapids Eng. Co.; Champion Pneumatic Machinery Co.; Champion Spark Plug Co.; Chevrolet Div. of General Motors Corp.; Chicago Rawhide Mfg. Co.; Chief Industries, Inc.; Chrysler Plymouth Div. of Chrysler Corp.; Citroen Cars Corp.; Clayton Manufacturing Co.; Cleveland Graphite; Bronze Div. of Clevite Corp.; Clevite Service Div. of Clevite Corp.; Cole-Hersee Co.; Colt Industries; Continental Air Tools; Continental Motors Corp.; Cooper Tire and Rubber Co.; Corbin Co.; Cornell, William Co.; Corning, Cox Instrument; CPI Engineering Services, Inc.; CRC Chemicals; Cummins Engine Co., Inc.; Dana Corp.; Datsun; Deere & Co.; Delco-Remy Div. of General Motors Corp.; Detroit Diesel Allison; Deutz Corp.; DeVilbiss Co.; Dodge Div. of Chrysler Corp.; Dole Valve Co.; Doug Nash Equipment; Dover Corp.; Dow Corning Corp.; Dual Drive, Inc.; Duff-Norton; Dunlop Tire Company; Dura-Bond Engine Parts Co.; Durke - Atwood Co.; Easco Tools; Eaton Corp.; Echlin Mfg. Co.; Edelmann, E., and Co.; E. I. du Pont de Nemours and Co.; EIS Automotive Corp.; Electrodyne; ESB Brands, Inc.; Ethyl Corp.; Eutectic Welding Alloys Corp.; Everco Industries, Inc.; Exxon Company USA; Fafnir Bearing Co.; FAG Bearing, Ltd.; Federal-Mogul Corp.; Fel-Pro, Inc.; Ferrari Cars; Fiat; Firestone Tire and Rubber Co.; Fiske Brothers Refining Co.; Fletch/Air Inc.; FMC Corp; Ford Div. of Ford Motor Co.; Fox Valley Instrument; Fram Corp.; Gates Rubber Co.; Gatke Corp.; General Electric; General Instrument Corp.; General Tire & Rubber Co.; G. H. Meiser & Co.; Girling Ltd.; GKN Automotive, Inc.; Globe Hoist Co.; GMC Truck and Coach Div. of General Motors Corp., Goodall Mfg. Co.; Goodrich Co.; Goodyear Tire and Rubber Co.; Gould Inc.; Graco, Inc.; Gray Co., Inc.; Graymills Corp.; Grey-Rock Div. of Raybestos-Manhattan, Inc.; Guaranteed Parts Co.; Guide Lamp Div. of General Motors; Gulf Oil Corp.; Gunite Foundries Div. of Kelsey-Hayes Co.; Gunk Chemical Div. of Radiator Specialty Co.; Halibrand Eng. Corp.; Hamilton Test Systems; Harrison Radiator Div. of General Motors; Hastings Mfg. Co.; Hayden, Inc.; H.E. Dreyer, Inc.; Hein-Werner Corp.; Heli-Coil Products; Helm, Inc.; H. K. Porter, Inc.; Holley Carburetor Div. of Colt Ind.; Homestead Industries, Inc.; Honda; Hub City Iron Co.; Huck Mfg. Co.; Hunter Eng. Co.; Hydramatic Div. of General Motors; Ideal Corp.; Ignition Manufacturers Inst.; Imperial

Eastman Corp.; Ingersoll-Rand; Inland Mfg. Co.; International Harvester Co.; International Mfg. Co.; Iskenderian Racing Cams; Jaguar Cars, Ltd.; Jeep Div. of American Motors Corp.; Johnson Bronze Co.; Johns-Manville; Kal-Equip. Co.; K-D Mfg. Co.; Kelly-Springfield Tire Co.; Kelsey-Hayes Co.; Kem Manufacturing, Inc.; Kent Moore Org.; Kester Solder Co.; Kleer-Flo Co.; K. O. Lee Co.; Koni America, Inc.; Kwik-Way Mfg. Co.; Land-Rover; Lear Siegler, Inc.; Leece-Neville Co.; Lenroc Co.; Libby-Owens-Ford Co.; Lincoln Electric Co.; Lincoln Eng. Co.; Lincoln-Mercury Div. of Ford Motor Co.; Lisle Corporation; Littlefuse, Inc.; Loctite Corporation; Lucas, Joseph, Ltd.; Lufkin Rule Co.; Mack Trucks, Inc.; MacMillan Petroleum Corp.; Magnaflux Corp.; Mansfield Tire & Rubber Co.; Maremont Corp.; Marquette Corp.; Martin Senour Paints; Marvell-Schebler Products Div. of Borg-Warner Corp.; Maserati; Master Pneumatic-Detroit Inc.; Mazda; McCartney Manufacturing Co., Inc.; McCord Corp.; McCreary Tire & Rubber Corp.; Meco, Inc.; Mercedes-Benz; Merit Industries, Inc.; Meyer Hydraulics; Midland-Ross Corp.; Mobil Oil Corp.; Monitor Manufacturing; Monroe Auto Equipment Co.; Moog Industries, Inc.; Morton-Norwich Products, Inc.; Motorcraft; Motorola Automotive Products, Inc.; Motor Wheel Corp.; Murray Corp.; Muskegon Piston Ring Co.; N.A.P.A.; Micro Test; National Board of Fire Underwriters; National Engines Co.; Nice Ball Bearing Co.; Nicholson File Co.; Nissan; Nugier, F. A., Co.; Oakite Products, Inc.; Oldsmobile Div. of General Motors Corp.; Omega Mfg. Co.; Owatonna Tool Co.; Packard Electric; P and G Mfg. Co.; Parker Fluid Connectors; Paxton Products; Pennsylvania Refining Co.; Perfect Circle Corp.; Permatex Co., Inc.; Peugeot Inc.; Phillips Temco, Inc.; Pontiac Div. of General Motors Corp.; Porsche; Porter, H. K., Inc.; Prestolite Co.; Proto Tool Co.; P. T. Brake Lining Co., Inc.; Purolator Products, Inc.; Pyroil Co.; Quaker State Corp.; Questor; Raybestos Div. of Raybestos-Manhattan, Inc.; Realmarket Associates; Rexnord; Rinck-McIlwaine, Inc.; Renault; Robertshaw Controls Co.; Rochester Div. of General Motors; Rockford Clutch Div. of Borg-Warner Corp.; Rockwell International; Rodac Corp.; Rootes Motors, Inc.; Rottler Boring Bar Co.; Rubber Manufacturers Assn.; Ruger Equipment Co.; Saab-Scania of America, Inc.; Saginaw Steering Gear; Salisbury Corp.; Schrader Div. of Scovill Mfg. Co., Inc.; Sealed Power Corp.; Semperit of America, Inc.; Shell Oil Co.; Sherwin-Williams Co.; Shim-A-Line Inc.; Sioux Tools Inc.; SKF Industries, Inc.; Skil; Slep Electronics; Snap-on Tools Corp.; Society of Automotive Eng., Inc.; Solex Ltd.; Sornberger Equip. Sales; South Bend Lathe, Inc.; Spicer; Standard Motor Products; Standard Oil Co. of Calif.; Standard-Thomson Corp.; Stant Mfg. Co., Inc.; Star Machine and Tool Co.; Starrett, L. S., Co.; Stemco Mfg. Co.; Stewart-Warner; Storm-Vulcan, Inc.; Straza Industries; Sturtevant, P. A., Co.; Subaru; Sun Electric Corp.; Sunnen Products Co.; Testing Systems, Inc.; Texaco, Inc.; The Aluminum Association; Thexton Mfg. Co., Inc.; Thompson Products Replacement Div. of Thompson-Ramo-Wooldridge, Inc.; Thor Power Tool Co.; 3-M Company; Timken Roller Bearing Co.; Torrington; Tomco Coupler; Toyota; Traction Master Co.; Trucut (Frank Wood and Co.); TRW, Inc.; Ultra-Violet Products, Inc.; Union Carbide Corp.; Uniroyal, Inc.; United Parts Div. of Echlin Mfg. Co.; UOP, Inc.; United Tool Processes Corp.; U.S. Chemicals; U.S. Cleaner Corp.; Utica-Herbrand Div. of Kelsey-Hayes Co.; Vaco Products Co.; Valvoline Oil Co.; Van Norman Machine Co.; Vellumoid Co.; Victor Mfg. And Gasket Co.; Volkswagen of America, Inc.; Volvo of America Corp.; Voss Inc.; Wagner Electric Corp.; Walbro, Walker Mfg. Co.; Warner Gear-Warner Motive; Weatherhead Co.; Weaver Mfg. Div. of Dura Corp.; Wessels Company; Westberg Mfg. Co.; Wheelabrator-Frye Inc.; Whitaker Cable Corp.; White Engine Co.; Williams, J. H., and Co.; Wilton Corp.; Wix Corp.; Woodhill Permatex; World Bestos Div. of the Firestone Tire and Rubber Co.; Wright-Austin Co.; Wudel Mfg. Co.; Young Radiator Co.

INDEX

A

Abbreviations, 570
Accumulator piston, 317, 318
Air cleaner
dry type, 155
oil bath, 155
oil-wetted polyurethane, 155
Air conditioning, 515
air flow, 532
Btu, 516
compressor, 524, 525
condensation temperatures, 517
condenser, 525, 527, 528
discharge and suction service
valves, 529, 530
evaporator, 521, 522
expansion tube, 521
expansion valve, 520, 521
latent heat, 516
magnetic clutch, 528, 529
muffler, 529
receiver-dehydrator, 520
sight glass, 520
specialist, careers, 564
transference of heat, 515
vaporization temperatures, 517
Air-cooled engines, 94, 95, 96
Air flow meter, 167
Air flow sensor, 172
Air injection system, 193
air injection tubes, 194
air pump, 193, 194
antibackfire valve, 194, 195
check valve, 193, 194
deceleration valve, 194, 195
distribution manifold, 193, 194
diverter valve, 193, 194, 195
Air spring, 374
Alcohol, 159
Alignment, front wheel, 405
Alternating current,
generator, 480, 489
Alternator, 489, 490, 493, 494, 495
Alternator, brushless, 496

Altitude compensation, 146, 147
Ambient air temperature cut-off
switch, 532
Ammeter, generator, 488
Antifriction bearing, 100
Antipercolator, 134
Apprentice program,
careers, 567
Armature, generator, 481
Armature loop, 498
Atoms, 465, 466
Automatic leveling control, 384
Automatic transmission, 307
accumulator piston, 317, 318
brake bands, 316
clutch, 318
compensator valve, 324
construction, 307
different types, 324, 327
fluid coupling, 307
gear pump, 320
hydraulic control circuits, 324
lubrication, 324
manual control valve, 320
oil cooling, 324
planetary gearsets, 314, 315
rotor pump, 319
servo, 316, 317
shifter valve, 320, 321, 322, 323
shifting, 324
sprag and roller one-way
clutches, 310
stator, 310
throttle valve, 322, 323
torque converter, 309, 310
vacuum modulator, 323, 324
vanes, 310
Axles,
front drive, four-wheel drive, 361
construction, 361, 363
operation, 363
front drive,
two-wheel drive, 361
rear, 349

solid, 376

B

Balance, tires, 399
Balk ring, 298
Ball and trunnion universal
joint, 340, 341
Ball joints, 378
Ballast resistor, 54
Battery, 53, 509, 510, 511
capacity, 477, 478
capacity rating, 476, 477
chemical action, 474, 475
discharge rate, 476
dry-charged, 478
electrical system, 472
electrolyte, 472, 473
negative plate, 473, 474
positive plate, 473
safety, 478
terminals, 476
voltage, 478
Bearing,
characteristics, 37
clearance, 104
construction, 100
Bearings, connecting rods, 37
Bendix Folo-Thru starter drive,
501, 502
Bendix self-engaging starter
drive, 501
Block, 10
engine, 23, 24
Bodies, 369
Body and fender specialist,
careers, 564
Bore, cylinder, 254, 255
Box end wrenches, 548
Brake,
bands,
automatic transmission, 316
check valve
and piston spring, 435, 436
disc, 449
double anchor, 447

drum, 445, 446
dual master cylinder, 436
emergency or parking, 451
fade, 446
flexible hose, 440, 441
fluid reservoir, 435
horsepower, 251, 252
hydraulic system, 442, 443
lights, 453
lines, 440
lining, 445
master cylinder, 434
mean effective pressure, 251
metering valve, 451
piston assembly, 435
power, 454, 455
pressure differential warning
switch, 440
proportioning valve, 451
quick take-up
master cylinder, 438, 439, 440
release, 436, 437
safety, 431
self-adjusting, 448, 449
servo action,
self-energizing, 446, 447
shoe arrangement, 446
shoe assembly, 444, 445
single anchor,
self-centering, 447
single-piston cylinder, 441
specialist, careers, 563
stepped cylinder, 441
wheel assembly, 444
wheel cylinder, 441, 442
Brakes, 431
Braking ratio, 449
Braking system, hydraulic
principles, 433
Breaker contact points,
ignition system, 57
Breakerless inductive discharge
ignition system, 75
Breaking up gasoline, 8, 9
British thermal unit, 516
Bronze-bushed shackle, 372
Brushes, generator, 481, 482
Brushless alternator, 496
Building an engine, 7
Bulbs, 506
By-pass filter system, 113

C

Caliper construction and
operation, disc brake, 450, 451
Calipers,
dial, 557
inside and outside, 557
Cam angle, 58

Camber, 406, 407
Cam ground piston, 26, 27
Camshaft, 15, 42
turning, 17
Capacity conversion, 575
Carbon monoxide, 193
Carburetion,
fuel systems, 119
rotary engine, 220
Carburetor, 128
acceleration pump circuit, 137
air horn, 128
automatic choke circuit, 138
choke stove, 139, 140
choke thermostatic coil, 139
choke vacuum piston, 139
circuits, 132, 133
downdraft, 148
dual, 148
float circuit, 142
four-barrel, 152, 153
fuel bowl, 128, 129
high speed
cruising circuit, 134
full power circuit, 134
icing, 145, 146
idle circuit, 133
low speed circuit, 134
offset choke valve, 139
secondary venturi, 129
sidedraft, 148
single barrel, 148
updraft, 148
variable venturi, 147, 148
venturi, 129
Carburetor circuits, 132, 133
high speed
cruising circuit, 134
full power circuit, 134
idle circuit, 133
low speed circuit, 134
Careers,
air conditioning specialist, 564
apprentice program, 567
armed forces, 567
availability of employment, 565
body and fender specialist, 564
brake specialist, 563
certification, 568
diagnostic technician, 562
electrical specialist, 563
front end specialist, 563
lubrication specialist, 562
mechanic, 561
parts specialist, 562, 563
salary, 565
school, 566
service manager, 564

shop supervisor, 564
specialization, 561, 562
supervisory positions, 564
trade school, 567
transmission specialist, 563
tune-up specialist, 562
working conditions, 564, 565
Caster, 405, 406
negative, 406
positive, 406
Catalytic converter, 198, 199
Center link, steering, 411
Centrifugal advance, timing, 66
Centrifugal type
supercharger, 157
Chassis dynamometer, 252
Check valve and piston spring,
brakes, 435, 436
Check valves, 122
Chisels, 538
Choke,
automatic circuit, 138, 139
control, 202
manual control, 141
offset valve, 139
stove, 139, 140
thermostatic coil, 139
vacuum piston, 139
Chrysler Sure-Grip
differential 352, 353, 354, 355
Circuit, breaker, 483, 484, 507
Circuits,
electrical, 469, 505
generator, 482, 483
parallel, 469
series, 469
series-parallel, 470
Cleaning tools, 545, 546
Closed cooling system, 91, 92
Closed loop system, 203
Clutch,
automatic transmission, 318
cooling, 266
definition, 257
diaphragm, 263
disc, 258
engine, 257
housing, 260
input shaft, 260
pedal free travel, 266
pedal linkage, 264, 265
pressure plate, 258, 259
release lever operating
mechanism, 259, 260
riding, 266, 267
roller, 310
self-adjusting, 265, 266
shaft, 260

sprag, 310
Coil,
 ignition, 55
 spring, 373
Cold start injector, 167, 168, 172
Combination box and open end
 wrenches, 549
Combination fuel and vacuum
 pump, 126
Combination splash and
 pressure lubrication system, 104
Combustion chamber, 11
 design, 226
 hemispherical, 227
 wedge shape, 227
Commutator, generator, 481
Commutator segments, 498
Compensator valve, 324
Compression ratio, 14, 218, 255
Compression rings, 30, 31
Compression stroke, 14, 218
Compressor,
 air conditioning, 524, 525
 discharge pressure switch, 530
Condensation,
 air conditioning, 517
Condenser, 59
 air conditioning, 525, 527, 528
 ignition, 59
Conduction, 515
Conductors, electrical, 468
Connecting rod, 10, 36
 bearing, 10, 37
 construction, 36, 37
Constant velocity universal
 joint, 345, 346
Construction,
 engine components, 23
Continuous injection,
 mechanical type, 168, 169
Convection, 515, 516
Conventional frame, 369, 370
Conversions,
 capacity, 575
 dimensional, 575
 English/Metric, 572, 574
 Metric/English, 573
 millimetre/inch, 576
 temperature, 575
Converter,
 catalytic, 198, 199
 multiple, 202
 three-way, dual bed, 200, 201
 torque, 309, 310
 two-way, 199, 200
Coolant flow, 85
Cooling,
 air conditioning, 515

classification, 229
 generator, 483
 rotary engine, 220, 221, 222
Cooling systems, 81
 air-cooled engines, 94, 95, 96
 care, 93, 94
 closed, 90, 91
 pressurized, 90, 91
 temperature gauge, 93
 water-cooled engines, 82
Crankcase, 11
Crankshaft, 10, 38
 flywheel, 42
 main bearings, 38
 throws, 38, 39
 timing gear or sprocket, 41, 42
 vibration, 39
 vibration damper, 39, 40
Crescent or adjustable
 wrenches, 550
Cross and roller
 universal joints, 339, 340
Current, 466, 467
Current regulator or
 limiter, 485, 486
Cutout relay, 483, 484
Cycle classification, 211
Cycle,
 four-stroke, 12
 two-stroke, 212
Cylinder, 10, 24
 arrangements, 229
 bore, 254, 255
 classification, 228
 head, 11, 47
 head removable, 11
 sleeves, 24

D

Design, engine components, 23
Detonation, 226
Diagnostic technician,
 careers, 562
Dial gauge or indicator, 557
Diaphragm clutch, 263
Dictionary of terms, 577
Dies, 545
 special, 545
Diesel,
 distributor type injection
 pump, 178
 fuel, 173
 fuel characteristics, 173
 fuel filter, 173
 fuel injection, 182
 injection pump, 173
 injection system, 173
 injector pump
 delivery valve, 177, 178

in-line injector pump, 174, 175
 water detector, 173
Dieseling, 190, 191
Differential, 350, 351, 352
 carrier and bearings, 352
 Chrysler Sure-Grip, 352, 353,
 gear ratio, 359
 hypoid gearing, 357
 lubrication, 360
 planetary gear, 360
 ring and pinion, 358
 spiral bevel gearing, 357
 special traction, 352
 spur bevel gearing, 357, 358
 swing axles, 359, 360
 transaxle, 360
Dimensional conversion, 575
Dimmer switch, 508
Diodes, 490, 492, 493
Dipstick, 115
Direct current generator, 480
Disc brake, 449
 caliper construction and
 operation, 450, 451
Distillation process, 100
Distributor cap, 62, 63
Distributor type
 injection pump, 178
Distributor type pump fuel
 injection system schematic, 173
Dividers, 557
Double anchor brake, 447
Double contact voltage
 regulator, 486
Downdraft carburetor, 148
Drills, 540, 541
 sharpening, 541
 using, 541
Drive axle,
 assemblies, 349
 axles, 349
 construction, 349
 housing, 349
Drive line, 339
 emergency brake, 453
 Hotchkiss drive, 342, 343
 propeller shafts, 339, 342
 slip joint, 341, 342
 torque tube drive, 343, 344
 universal joint, 339
Dry-charged battery, 478
Dry sleeve, 24
Dry type air cleaner, 155
Dual,
 carburetor, 148
 exhaust system, 204
 flow air injection system, 196
 master cylinder, 436

metering rod control, 136
points, distributor, 58
Dwell, 68, 72, 73
Dynamic balance, tires, 399, 400
Dynamometer,
  chassis, 252
  engine, 252

E

Eccentric shaft, 213
Efficiency,
  mechanical, 250
  practical, 250
  thermal, 250
  volumetric, 253, 254
Electrical,
  circuits, 505
  fundamentals, 509
  fuel shutoff, 179
  specialist, careers, 563
Electrical system,
  battery, 472
  fundamentals, 465
  generator, 478
Electrical test instruments, 558
Electrolyte,
  battery, 472, 473
  specific gravity, 475
Electromagnetic core, 480
Electron theory, 465
Electronic spark control ignition
  system, computer, 75, 76
Electronic spark timing control
  ignition system, 73
Emergency brake,
  brake shoe, 451
  drive line, 453
Emergency or parking brakes, 451
Emission control
  external engine controls, 185
  fuel system vapor controls, 185
  internal engine controls, 185
  rotary engine, 222
Engine,
  air-cooled, 94, 95, 96
  block, 23, 24
  building, 7
  classification, 211, 234
  clutches, 257
  cycle classification, 211
  definition, 7
  experimental, 232
  F-head, 222
  four-stroke cycle diesel, 230
  gas turbine, 230, 231, 232
  horizontal-opposed, 228, 229
  I-head, 223
  inclined type, 229
  in-line, 228

internal combustion gasoline, 7
  L-head, 222
  measurements, 249
  mounting, 232, 233
  parts identification, 211
  radial, 229
  size, 254
  slant type, 229
  T-head, 223
  tests, 249
  two-stroke cycle diesel, 230
  V-type, 228
  Wankel rotary piston, 213
  water-cooled, 82
Engine components, 23
  camshaft, 42
  connecting rods, 36
  crankshaft, 38
  cylinder head, 47
  engine block, 23, 24
  gaskets and seals, 48
  oil pan, 47, 48
  piston pins, 35
  piston rings, 29
  pistons, 25
  timing gear cover, 48
  valves, 42, 43
Engine dynamometer, 252
Engine oil service classification,
  100, 101
English abbreviations, 570
English/Metric conversions,
  572, 574
Evaporation control system, 186
Evaporator, air conditioning, 521
Evaporator temperature control,
  522, 523, 524
Exhaust gas recirculation
  valve, 191
  back pressure modulated, 192
  vacuum modulated, ported, 191
Exhaust manifolds, 205
Exhaust passages, 12
Exhaust pipe, 204
Exhaust pipe connection, 206
Exhaust, rotary engine, 220
Exhaust stroke, 14, 15, 218
Exhaust systems, 185, 203, 204
  dual, 204
  hangers, 206, 207
  single, 204
Expander devices,
  piston ring, 32, 33
Expansion tube, air
  conditioning, 521
Expansion valve, air
  conditioning, 520, 521
Experimental engines, 232

External engine controls, 185

F

Fan switch, 531, 532
Fast idle, 140, 141
Feedback solenoid controlled
  metering rod, 136
Feeler gauges, 557
F-head engine, 222
Files, 539
  cut and shape, 539
  using, 540
Filter,
  by-pass system, 113
  fuel, 173
  full-flow system, 112
  oil, 112
  operation, 112
Firing order, 229
Firing stroke, 14
First gear, transmission, 272
Five-speed transmission, 278
Flexible brake hose, 440, 441
Float circuit, carburetor, 142
Flooding, 140
Flow meter potentiometer, 167
Fluid coupling, 307, 308, 309
  efficiency, 309
Flywheel, 10, 19, 257
  crankshaft, 42
  magneto, 78, 79
  ring gear, 499, 501
Ford Dura Spark II system, 73
Ford Dura Spark III,
  distributor, 74, 75
Four-barrel, carburetor, 152, 153
Four-speed transmission, 277, 278
Four-stroke cycle engine, 12, 211
Four-stroke cycle
  diesel engine, 230
Four-wheel drive,
  front drive axles, 361
  construction, 361, 363
  operation, 363
  transfer case, 278
Frames, 369
  conventional, 369, 370
  integral, 369
Friction, 99
  bearing, 100
  reduction, 100
Frictional horsepower, 253
Front drive axles,
  four-wheel drive, 361
  construction, 361, 363
  operation, 363
  two-wheel drive, 361
Front end specialist, careers, 563
Front end suspension systems, 376

Front hub lubrication, 395
Front wheel alignment, 405
Front wheel hubs, 394
Fuel,
 accumulator, 169
 classification, 229, 230
 diesel, 173
 distributor, 169, 171
 filters, 124, 173
 intake, 12
 lines, 127
 preparing, 8
 pulsation, 124
 pulsation damper, 125
 pump, 169
Fuel injection, 163
 air flow meter, 167
 continuous, 164
 diesel, 182
 direct, 163
 electronic, 163, 164
 flow meter potentiometer, 167
 gasoline, 182
 indirect, 163
 intermittent electronic injection
 system, air flow meter type, 167
 intermittent electronic injection
 system, digital closed loop
 type, 165, 166
 intermittent, non-timed, 164
 intermittent, timed, 164
 mechanical, 163
 stoichiometric air-fuel
 mixture, 167
Fuel pump, 123
 efficiency measurements, 123
 electric, 125, 126
 mechanical, 121
 serviceable and
 nonserviceable, 126
Fuel systems,
 vapor controls, 185
 carburetion, 119
 fuel injection, 163
Full-flow fuel system, 112
Full pressure lubrication
 system, 104
Full-time transfer case,
 construction, 279
 operation, 280
Fully transistorized switching
 unit, 57
Fuses, 507, 511

G

Gaskets, 48
Gasohol, 159
Gasoline,
 breaking up, 8, 9
 definition, 8
 fuel injection, 182
 internal combustion engine, 7
 pickup pipe, 120
 tank, 120
 tank gauge unit, 121
Gas turbine engine, 230, 231
Gauges, 509
 feeler, 557
 dial or indicator, 557
Gear oil pump, 106
Gear pump, 320
Gear ratio, differential, 359
Gear ratios, transmission, 270
Gears,
 timing marks, 18
 transmission, 271
Gearbox,
 steering, 412
 worm and roller, 415
General Motors High Energy
 Ignition System, 73
Generator, 511
 alternating current, 481, 489
 ammeter, 488
 armature, 481
 brushes, 481, 482
 circuits, 482, 483
 commutator, 481
 cooling, 483
 direct current, 480
 electrical system, 478
 indicator light, 488, 489
 lubrication, 483
 polarity, 487, 488
 pole shoes, 481
 regulator, 483, 511
Glow plugs, 181, 182
Governors, 148, 320
Gross horsepower ratings, 252

H

Hacksaws, 543
 special, 543
 using, 543
Hammers, 538
Harmonic balancer, 40
Headlamp switch, 506, 507
Headlights, 506, 511
Heat control valves, 205, 206
Heat dam, 31
Heat transfer, 82
Heat transference, air
 conditioning, 515
High gear, transmission, 272,
 273, 276
High pressure relief valve, 531
High speed,
 cruising circuit, carburetor, 134

full power by-pass jet, 136
full power circuit,
 carburetor 134
Horizontal-opposed engine, 228
Horns, 505
Horsepower,
 brake, 251, 252
 definition, 249
 formula, 249, 250
 frictional, 253
 indicated, 250, 251
 potential, 250
 ratings, gross and net, 252, 253
Hose clamps, 87, 88
Hoses, 87
Hotchkiss drive, 342, 343
Housing, axle,
 banjo type, 349
 split type, 349
Hubs, 393, 394, 395
 front wheel, 394
 rear, 395
Hydraulic,
 brake fluid, 433, 434
 braking system, 433
 control circuits, automatic
 transmission, 324
 jack, 432, 433
 system, brakes, 442, 443
 valve lifters, 110, 112
Hydrometer, 475
Hypoid gearing, differential, 357

I

Icing, carburetor, 145, 146
Identification, parts, 10
Idle compensator, carburetor, 142
Idle speed up control, air
 conditioning, 143, 144
Idler arm, steering, 411
Ignition,
 primary circuit, 53, 59
 secondary circuit, 53, 60
 switch, 54
Ignition system, 53
 American Motors Breakerless
 Inductive Discharge, 75
 Chrysler, 75
 coil, 55
 condenser, 59
 Electronic spark timing
 control, 73
 Electronic spark control,
 computer, 75, 76
 General Motors High Energy, 73
 primary circuit, 53, 59
 secondary circuit, 53, 60
 spark plug, 60
I-head engine, 223

Impact wrenches, 542
Inclined type engine, 229
Independent front wheel
  suspension, 377
Indicated horsepower, 250, 251
Indicated mean effective
  pressure, 251
Individually suspended rear
  wheels, 383
Inflation, tires, 400
Injector pulse width, 164
Injector pump delivery valve, 177
In-line engine, 228
In-line injector pump, 174, 175
  metering control, 175
Insert bearing, 37
Insulators, electrical, 469
Intake,
  manifolds, 153, 154
  peripheral port, 220
  side port, 220
  stroke, 13, 218
  valve, 12
Integral frame, 369
Intermediate housing, 213, 214
Intermittent electronic injection
  system,
  air flow meter type, 167
  digital closed loop type, 165,
Internal combustion gasoline
  engine, 7
Internal engine controls, 185
Internal gear, 294

J

Jack, hydraulic, 432, 433
Jets, carburetor, 129, 130
Job opportunities, 561

K

Kingpin, 407, 408

L

Left-hand rule, 479, 480
Leveling control,
  automatic, 384
  manual, 387
Leveling or height control
  valve, 386
Leveling system, electric
  compressor, 387
L-head engine, 222
Lights, 505
  brakes, 453
  generator indicator, 488, 489
Lines of force, magnetism, 471
Linkage, steering, 410, 411
Linkage train, 411
Linkage type power steering, 424
Liquefied petroleum gas, 158, 159
Liquid check valve, 190

Liquid-vapor separator, 190
Load range, tires, 397
Low gear, transmission, 272, 274
Lubrication,
  automatic transmission, 324
  differential, 360
  front hubs, 395
  generator, 483
  suspension system, 383, 384
Lubrication system, 99
  combination splash and
    pressure, 104, 105
  full pressure, 104
  splash, 104

M

Magnetic clutch, air
  conditioning, 528, 529
Magnetism, 471
Magneto, 77, 78
Main bearing, crankshaft, 10, 38
Manifold,
  design, 153
  heat control valve, 144
  intake, 153, 154
  water heated, 144, 145
Manual control valve, 320
Manual leveling control, 387
Manual transmissions, 269
Master cylinder,
  braking system, 434
  dual, 436
  quick take-up, 438, 439, 440
  reservoir fluid level, 436
Matter, 465
Mean effective pressure, 251
Measuring systems, 571
Measuring tools, 552, 554
Mechanic, careers, 561
Mechanical efficiency, 250
  formula, 250
Mechanical fuel pump, 121
Metering rod control, 135
Metering valve, 178
  brake, 451
Metric abbreviations, 570
Metric conversions, 570, 571,
  572, 573, 574, 575, 576
Metric/English conversions, 573
Metric tables, 570
Micrometer, 554, 555
  metric, 556
  reading, 555, 556
Millimetre/inch conversion, 576
Molecule, 465
Mounting, engine, 232, 233
Muffler,
  air conditioning, 529
  exhaust, 204, 205

Multi-grade oils, 102, 103
Multiple converters, 202

N

Negative caster, 406
Net horsepower ratings, 252
Neutral, transmission, 274
Newton's Law, 311

O

Offset choke valve, 139
Ohm's Law, 470
Oil,
  changing, 103
  cooling, 115
    automatic transmission, 324
  filters, 112
  galleries and lines, 108, 109
  lubrication, 101, 102
  pickup, 105
  pressure gauges, 115
  pump, 105, 106, 107
  seals, 114, 115
  service classification, 100, 101
  viscosity, 102
Oil bath air cleaner, 155
Oil control, piston rings, 30, 31
Oil pan, 47, 48
Oil pump, 105, 106, 107
  automatic transmission, 319, 320
Oil-wetted polyurethane air
  cleaner, 155
Open end wrenches, 549
Overdrive,
  constant drive, 301
  construction, 294
  controls, 297
  direct drive mode, 301, 302
  direct, freewheeling stage, 300
  drive stages, 300
  internal gear, 294
  locked out stage, 296, 300
  operation, 294
  overdrive mode, 302
  overdrive stage, 300
  planetary gearset, 294
  planetary pinion carrier, 294
  roller clutch, 296, 297
  sun gear, 294
  transmission, 293
Overflow tank, 86
Overhead camshaft, 227, 228
Overhead valve adjustment, 224
Overrunning clutch,
  mechanically engaged, 502, 503

P

Parallel circuit, 469
Partial skirt piston, 27, 28
Parking brakes, 451
Parts identification, 10, 211, 234

Index

Parts specialist, careers, 562, 563
Pascal's Law, 432
PCV control valve, 185, 186
Part-time transfer case, 278, 279
Permanent magnet sensor, 71
Pickup coil, 70
Pins, piston, 35
Pipe wrenches, 550
Pistons, 10, 25
  accumulator, 317, 318
  assembly, brakes, 435
  cam ground, 26, 27
  head construction, 28
  head shape, 28
  lengthen, 11
  materials, 25
  partial skirt, 27, 28
  split skirt, 26
  stroke, 254, 255
  temperature, 28
  T-slot, 26
Piston pin, 11, 35
  boss, 28
  installation, 35
Piston rings, 29
  compression, 30, 31
  expander devices, 32, 33
  gap, 29, 30
  oil control, 30, 31, 32
  special coatings, 34
  types, 30, 31, 32
  wear-in, 33, 34
Pitman arm, steering, 411
Planetary gear differential, 360
Planetary gearset, 294, 295,
  296,, 314, 315
Planetary pinion carrier, 294
Pliers, 546
Plunger oil pump, 107
Ply rating, tires, 397
Polarity, generator, 487, 488
Pole shoes, generator, 481
Positive caster, 406
Positive crankcase ventilation,
  114, 185
Positive type valve rotator, 46
Potential horsepower, 250
Power booster,
  power brakes, 455
Power brakes,
  bellows type booster, 458
  diaphragm booster, 458
  hydraulic power booster, 458
  piston type booster, 458
  power booster, 455
  vacuum and atmospheric
  suspended booster, 455
  vacuum operated, 454

vacuum reservoir, 460
Power steering, 417
  in-line unit, 417, 421, 422
  linkage type, 424, 425
  offset gear, 420, 421
  pumps, 425, 426
  self-contained unit, 417
  types, 417
  units, manually operated, 426
Power stroke, 14, 218
Practical efficiency, 250
Precision thin wall casting, 24
Preignition, 62, 226
Pressure differential warning
  switch, brakes, 440
Pressure relief valve, 108
Pressurized cooling system, 90
Primary circuit,
  coil windings, 55
  ignition, 53
  ignition system, 59
Propeller shaft, 339, 342
Proportioning valve, brakes, 451
Pullers, 551
Pull rod, 122
Pulse air injection system, 196
  air check valves, 196, 197
Pump,
  charging cycle, 178
  combination fuel and
  vacuum, 126
  diesel injection, 173
  discharge cycle, 178
  distributor type injection, 178
  electrical fuel shutoff, 179
  fuel, 123
  fuel return circuit, 178, 179
  in-line injector, 174, 175
  mechanical fuel, 121
  oil, 105, 106, 107
  rotor, 319
  power steering, 425, 426
  transfer, 178
  vane oil, 319
  water, 82, 83
Punches, 538, 539

Q

Quick-change wheels, special
  hubs, 394, 395
Quick take-up master cylinder,
  brakes, 438, 439, 440
Quadra-Trac transfer case, 281

R

Rack and pinion
  steering gear, 415
Radial engine, 229
Radiation, 516
Radiator, 85, 86

Ram induction, 154, 155
Reamers, 542
Rear axle, 349
  Chrysler Sure-Grip, 352, 353
  differential, 350
  gear ratio, 359
  housing, 349
  hypoid gearing, 357
  lubrication, 360
  ring and pinion, 358
  special traction differential, 352
  spiral bevel gearing, 357
  spur bevel, 357, 358
  swing, 359, 360
Rear hubs, 395
Rear suspension, 380, 382, 383
Receiver-dehydrator, air
  conditioning, 520
Reed valve, 212
Refrigerant-12, 517
Refrigerant oil, 529
Refrigeration,
  principles, 515
  system, 518
Regulator,
  generator, 483, 511
  single unit, 495
  voltage, transistor, 495, 496
  voltage, transistorized, 495
Relays, 505, 506, 511
Release type valve rotator, 46
Removable cylinder head, 11
Resistance, electrical, 467, 468
Resistor, 54, 55
Resistor spark plug, 62
Resonators, 205
Reverse, transmission, 273, 276
Ribbed belt, 83, 84
Ring and pinion, differential, 358
Rings, piston, 29
Road feel, steering, 417
Rocker arm and link, 122, 123
Rods,
  connecting, 36
  push, 223, 224
Roller lifters, 46
Rollover check valve, 190
Rootes type supercharger, 156
Rotary engine,
  assembled, 214, 216
  carburetion, 220
  classification, 213
  compression ratio, 218, 219
  construction, 213
  cooling, 220, 221, 222
  emission control, 222
  exhaust, 220
  four-stroke cycle, 217, 218

operation, 216
Wankel, 213
Rotary files, 540
Rotary oil pump, 107
Rotary piston engine, 213
Rotary valve, 212
Rotary valve action, 424
left turn, 423
right turn, 423
straight ahead, 422
Rotation, tires, 401, 402
Rotor, 63, 64, 213, 214
apex seals, 219
housing, 213
pump, 319
side seals, 219
Rubber-bushed shackle, 372
Run-on, 190, 191
Runout, tires, 399

S

Safety,
battery, 478
brakes, 431, 440, 443, 444,
453, 460
carburetors, 141, 142
clutch, 267
engine, 233, 234
fan, 87
fire, 127
gasoline, 8
gasoline tank, 120
radiator, 93
refrigerant, 517, 518
steering system, 426
suspension system, 379, 380, 383
tires, 400
tools, 538, 539, 541, 542 546, 548
voltage, 53
wheels, 394, 395
Screwdrivers, 546, 547, 548
Seals, 48
oil, 114, 115
Secondary circuit, ignition, 53, 60
Secondary venturi, carburetor, 129
Second gear,
transmission, 272, 274
Select drive transfer case, 281, 283
Self-adjusting brakes, 448, 449
Self-adjusting clutch, 265, 266
Self-engaging starter drive,
Bendix type, 501
Semielliptical leaf spring, 370, 371
Series circuit, 469
Series-parallel circuit, 470
Service manager, careers, 564
Servo, 316, 317
Servo action, self-energizing
brakes, 446, 447

Shackle,
bronze-bushed, 372
rubber-bushed, 372
threaded, 372
Shifter valve, 320, 321, 322, 323
Shift mechanism, 276
Shock absorber,
construction and operation, 375
control action, 374
Shocks, 387
Shop supervisor, careers, 564
Sidedraft carburetor, 148
Sight glass,
air conditioning, 520
Single anchor, self-centering
brake, 447
Single barrel carburetor, 148
Single exhaust system, 204
Single leaf spring, 372
Single-piston cylinder,
brakes, 441
Single unit regulator, 495
Slant type engine, 229
Sleeves,
cylinder, 24
securing, 25
wet and dry, 24
Slip angles, steering, 409, 410
Slip joint, drive line, 341, 342
Snap ring, 35
Socket,
attachments, 550
handles, 549, 550
wrenches, 549
Solenoid, starter, 503
Spark plug, 60
auxiliary gap, 62
heat range, 61, 62
insulators, 61
preignition, 62
projected core nose, 62
shells, 61
Special coatings, piston rings, 34
Special traction differential, 352
Spiral bevel gearing,
differential, 357
Splash lubrication system, 104
Split ring, 309
Split skirt piston, 26
Sprag and roller one-way
clutches, 310
Spring, 369, 370
air, 374
coil, 373
oscillation, 374
semielliptical leaf, 370, 371
single leaf, 372
torsion bar, 373, 374

Sprung weight, 383
Spur bevel gearing,
differential, 357, 358
Stabilizer bar, 383
Starter, 511
actuating switch, 505
electrical circuits, 499
motor, 498, 499
pinion gear, 501
solenoid, 503
system, 496, 497
Stator, 310
variable pitch, 312, 313
Steel strut, 26
Steering,
arms, 410
axis inclination, 407, 408
camber, 406, 407
gearbox, 412
gearbox, manual or
standard, 413, 414, 415
gear reduction, 417
geometry, 410
knuckle angle, 408
linkage, 410, 411
power, 417
rack and pinion, 415
road feel, 417
shaft universal joints, 415
slip angles, 409, 410
system, 405, 410
toe-in, 408, 409
toe-out, 409
Stepped cylinder, brakes, 441
Stoichiometric air-fuel
mixture, 167
Stroke,
compression, 14, 218
exhaust, 14, 15, 218
firing, 14
intake, 13, 218
piston, 254, 255
power, 14, 218
Strut, steel, 26
Sump, 105
Sun gear, 294
Supercharger, 155, 156
centrifugal type, 157
rootes type, 156
vane type, 157
Superheat switch, 530
Suspension,
front end, 376
independent front wheel, 377
lubrication, 383, 384
rear, 380, 382, 383
system, 369
torsion bar, front, 380

Swing axles, differential, 359, 360
Switch,
 ambient air temperature
 cut-off, 532
 compressor discharge
 pressure, 530, 531
 dimmer, 508
 fan, 531, 532
 head lamp, 506, 507
 superheat, 530
 wide open throttle, 532
Synchronizing mechanism, 273
Systems,
 carburetion, 119
 cooling, 81
 exhaust, 185
 fuel injection, 163
 ignition, 53
 lubrication, 99
 starter, 496, 497
 steering, 405
 suspension, 369

T

Tables, metric, 570
Taps, 544, 545
Temperature conversions, 575
Temperature gauge, cooling
 system, 93
Terms, Dictionary of, 577
Test gauges, electrical, 468
Tests, engine, 249
T-head engine, 223
Thermal efficiency, 250
 formula, 250
Thermostat,
 bellows, 89
 cooling system, 88
 pellet, 89
Thermostatically controlled air
 cleaner construction and
 operation, 197, 198
Threaded shackle, 372
Three-phase AC, 490
Three-speed synchromesh
 transmission, 274
Three-speed transmission, 277, 280
Three-way, dual bed
 converter, 200, 201
Throttle positioners, 203
Throttle return dashpot, 142
Throttle valve, 130, 131, 322
Throttle valve sensor, 168
Thrust bearing, 38
Tie rods, steering, 411, 412
Timing 64, 65
 gear cover, 48
 gear or sprocket,
 crankshaft, 41, 42

marks, 18
 valves, 17, 18, 46, 47
Tires, 393, 395, 396, 397
 balance, 399
 construction, 395, 396, 397
 dynamic balance, 399, 400
 inflation, 400
 load range, 397
 ply rating, 397
 rotation, 401, 402
 runout, 399
 size, 398
 tubeless, 398
Toe-in, 408, 409
Toe-out, 409
Tools,
 electrical test instruments, 558
 identification, 537
 special purpose, 552
 types, 537, 538
 use, 537, 543, 544
Torque, 253
 converter, 309, 310
 multiplication, 310, 311
 multiplication curve, 314
 multiplication through
 gears, 270
 tube drive, 343, 344
 wrenches, 551
Torsion bar
 front suspension, 380
Torsion bar spring, 373, 374
Torus, 308
Transaxle,
 construction, 360, 361
 differential, 360
 operation, 361
Transfer case, 269
 four-wheel drive, 278
 full-time, construction, 279
 full-time, operation, 280
 part-time, construction, 278
 part-time, operation, 278, 279
 Quadra-Trac, 281
 select drive, 281, 283
Transfer pump, 178
Transistor, 69
 operation, 69
 voltage regulator, 495, 496
Transistor ignition,
 breaker ignition, 69
 contact controlled, 69
 electronic, 69
 systems, 72, 73
Transistorized voltage
 regulator, 495
Transmission,
 automatic, 307

construction, 271, 272
 first or low gear, 272
 five-speed, 278
 four-speed, 277, 278
 gear ratio, 270, 271
 gears, 271
 high gear, 272, 273, 276
 low gear, 274
 manual, 269, 274
 operation, 271, 272
 overdrives, 293
 reverse, 273, 276
 second gear, 272, 274
 specialist, careers, 563
 three-speed synchromesh, 274
T-slot piston, 26
Tubeless tires, 398
Tune-up specialist, 562
Turbocharger, 157
Two-stroke cycle engine, 212
Two-stroke cycle
 diesel engine, 230
Two-way converter,
 monolith type, 200
 pellet type, 199
Two-wheel drive, front drive
 axles, 361

U

Universal joint, 339
 ball and trunnion, 340, 341
 constant velocity, 345, 346
 cross and roller, 339, 340
 steering shaft, 415
 types, 339, 340
 yokes, 345
Unsprung weight, 383
Updraft carburetor, 148

V

Vacuum advance,
 diaphragm, 66, 67, 68
 mechanism, 66
 timing, 66
Vacuum controlled metering
 rod, 135, 136
Vacuum modulator, 323, 324
Vacuum pump, 12, 13
Valves, 12, 42, 43
 air check, 196, 197
 antibackfire, 194, 195
 check, 122, 193, 194
 compensator, 324
 deceleration, 194, 195
 discharge and suction service,
 air conditioning, 529, 530
 diverter, 193, 194, 195
 exhaust gas recirculation, 191
 guide, 12, 44
 heat control, 205, 206

high pressure relief, 531
leveling or height control, 386
lifter, 15
lifters, hydraulic, 44, 45
lifters, mechanical, 44
liquid check, 190
location, classification, 222
manifold heat control, 144
manual control, 320
offset choke, 139
opening and closing, 15
PCV control, 185, 186
ports, 12
reed, 212
rollover check, 190
rotary, 212
seats, 43, 44
shifter, 320, 321, 322, 323
springs, 44
timing, 17, 18, 46, 47
train, 15, 223, 224
throttle, 130, 131, 322, 323
Vane oil pump, 107, 319
Vane type supercharger, 157
Vanes, 310
Vaporization temperatures, air
 conditioning, 517
Vapor lock, 126, 127

Variable pitch stator, 312, 313
Variable venturi, carburetor, 147
Venturi, carburetor, 129
Vibration damper, crankshaft, 39
Viscosity,
 compensating valve, 179
 index, 102
 multi-grade, 102, 103
 oil, 102
Vise, 543, 544
Voltage, 467
Voltage drop, 469
Voltage regulator, 484, 485
 double contact, 486
 transistor, solid state, 495, 496
 transistorized, 495
Volumetric efficiency, 253, 254
Vortex flow, 313
V-type engine, 228

W

Wankel engine, 213, 214, 216,
 218, 220, 222
Wankel rotary piston
 engine, 213
Warm-up regulator, 172
Water-cooled engines, 82
Water detector, 173
Water heated manifold, 144

Water jacket, 82
Water nozzle, 84, 85
Water pump, 82, 83
Wear-in, piston rings, 33, 34
Weight,
 sprung, 383
 unsprung, 383
Wet sleeve, 24
Wheel, 393
 alignment, 405
 brake assembly, 444
 cylinder, brakes, 441, 442
 hubs, 350
 quick-change,
 special hubs, 394, 395
Wide open throttle switch, 532
Worm and roller gearbox, 415
Wrenches, 550, 551
 box end, 548
 combination box and open
 end, 549
 crescent or adjustable, 550
 impact, 542
 open end, 549
 pipe, 550
 socket, 549
 torque, 551
Wrist pin, 11